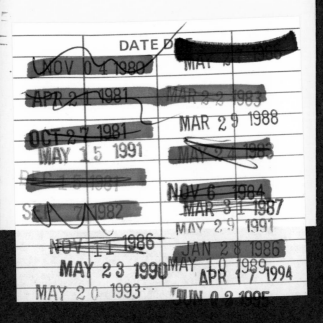

BIG STORY

Westview Special Studies in Communication

Big Story:
How the American Press and Television
Reported and Interpreted the Crisis
of Tet 1968 in Vietnam and Washington

Peter Braestrup

Using Tet as a case history in depth of the portrayal of the war in
Vietnam, Peter Braestrup--who covered the war himself for both the
New York *Times* and the Washington *Post*--has compiled a remarkable
document that reflects the analysis of millions of words published
in newspapers and news magazines and broadcast over radio and television; the examination of thousands of feet of TV film; and interviews with scores of participants in Vietnam. Reportage by leading
journalists appears in the work, and their reports and commentaries
are matched, not against official claims or a critic's polemics,
but against the facts and resources available to news organizations
at the time the original accounts were written. This is a landmark
work--the first dispassionate analysis of the role of the U.S. press
in the Vietnam war, and the most extensive study ever made of print
and electronic news coverage of a major event.

Peter Braestrup joined the Washington *Post* in 1968 as Saigon bureau
chief. He previously covered Algeria, Paris, and Southeast Asia
for the New York *Times* and was a member of the *Times*'s Washington
bureau. He is now editor of publications for the Woodrow Wilson
Center for International Scholars at the Smithsonian.

BIG
STORY

How the American Press and Television Reported and Interpreted the Crisis of Tet 1968 in Vietnam and Washington

Peter Braestrup

With an Introduction by
Leonard R. Sussman, Director of the Study,
and a Public Opinion Analysis by
Burns W. Roper

Volume 2

Published in Cooperation with Freedom House

Westview Press
Boulder, Colorado

Westview Special Studies in Communication

Published 1977 in the United States of America by

    Westview Press, Inc.
    1898 Flatiron Court
    Boulder, Colorado 80301
    Frederick A. Praeger, Publisher and Editorial Director

Library of Congress Cataloging in Publication Data

Braestrup, Peter
  Big story.

  Includes indexes.
  1. Tet Offensive, 1968. 2. Vietnamese Conflict, 1961-1975--Journalists. 3. Press--United States. 4. Television broadcasting of news. I. Roper, Burns W., joint author. II. Title.
DS557.8.T4B7   959.704'342   75-30560
ISBN 0-89158-012-3

Printed and bound in the United States of America.

Contents

APPENDIXES

TABLES

STORY INDEXES

PICTURE INDEXES

Appendixes

PROGRESS REPORT—ADDRESS BY GEN. WILLIAM C. WESTMORELAND, COMMANDER, U.S. MILITARY ASSISTANCE COMMAND, VIETNAM, NATIONAL PRESS CLUB, WASHINGTON, D.C., NOVEMBER 21, 1967

I would like to give you today a short progress report on some aspects of the war in Vietnam, because we in Vietnam are keenly aware of the genuine concern being expressed at home about the complex situation in that country.

The war in Vietnam eludes any precise numerical system of measurement or any easy portrayal of progress on battle maps. The war is unique and complicated in origin, in diversity of form, and in its diffusion throughout Vietnam. It is a war which probably could not have occurred in this pattern in any other country in these times. But, if we had not met it squarely, it well could have been the precedent for countless future wars of a similar nature.

But we have confronted this challenge. We have found it to be like no other war we have fought before. There are no moving front lines--just a changing picture of small actions scattered over the country. Only a few of these actions are reported in detail. Even the trained observer is drawn to the unusual and the spectacular, and finds his attention shifting to another action before the significance or impact of the first can be analyzed.

I have been observing the war in South Vietnam at close hand for almost four years. During the first one and one-half years we were confined generally to an advisory role. In the past two and one-half years I have seen the progressive commitment of U.S. troops in support of the Vietnamese. I am absolutely certain that whereas in 1965 the enemy was winning, today he is certainly losing. There are indications that the Vietcong and even Hanoi know this.

However, the enemy may be operating from the delusion that political pressure here combined with the tactical defeat of a major unit might force the United States to "throw in the towel." If he does *not* believe this, there is very little logic to be found in his continuing the war in its present pattern.

Let me review with you the enemy's situation and our own, and let me offer my estimate of our relative positions.

Since 1925, when Ho Chi Minh arrived in Canton, China, he has actively sought to gain control of the area known as Indo-China. In 1930, the Indo-China Communist Party was created with Ho Chi Minh as its chief. However, since that time, the cause and methods have been similar to those of other Asian communist parties.

Ho Chi Minh's party came to power amid the chaotic conditions at the end of World War II. Although the present government of North Vietnam has taken a façade of democracy, it has remained under tight control of the same small, determined group of communists who served Ho Chi Minh in the Communist Party of the 1930s.

By 1954 it appeared to them that they had overcome the last major obstacle to the original goal. A million people had been displaced from the North, and although they were fleeing communism, they created a burden on the new government of South Vietnam. For the next few years, the communists believed that South Vietnam would succumb politically. These hopes were dashed by the vigor of the noncommunist government and by U.S. assistance.

In 1957 they reverted to terror, both indiscriminate and selective, with the assassination of teachers and local leaders. This terror rate went up every year. Despite that, it did not succeed. So, to guerrilla terror was added the military buildup of Vietcong main force units from 1959. Even this was not enough.

In 1963 and 1964 there started the military invasion from the North, when the first North Vietnamese regiments entered the South. This almost succeeded. By early 1965, the Vietnamese government found its resolution exhausted by a decade of struggle, and its last resources committed. It was at that point that the intervention of our armed forces restored a future to the long-suffering people of South Vietnam, who grasped the opportunity.

As you know, in the midst of war the South Vietnamese have in the past year held free elections, and have turned out a larger percentage of the vote than we normally do in this country. The Vietcong have tried desperately to stop these elections by terror and intimidation. But the Vietnamese voted despite the Vietcong efforts. This mass disregard of Vietcong initiatives killed the myth that the Vietcong or the National Liberation Front speak for the people.

It is significant that the enemy has not won a major battle in more than a year. In general, he can fight his

large forces only at the edges of his sanctuaries, as we
have seen recently at Con Thien and along the DMZ, at Dak
To opposite the Laotian border, at Song Be and Loc Ninh
near the Cambodian border. His Vietcong military units
can no longer fill their ranks from the South, but must
depend increasingly on replacements from North Vietnam.
His guerrilla force is declining at a steady rate. Morale problems are developing within his ranks.

Despite this, our enemy seeks to prolong the war, occasionally sallying forth from his sanctuaries, and attempting by his countersweep operations to regain control of
the population and to rebuild his guerrilla forces. Of
essential importance is his desire to force us politically
to stop, unconditionally, the bombing of his support base
and his lines of communication. He appears to believe
that he can defeat the Vietnamese forces, over 600,000
strong and getting stronger, reinforced by over 50,000
troops from free-world allies, and our commitment now approaching 500,000 men.

Our common plan with the Vietnamese has involved four
distinct phases. In Phase I we came to the aid of South
Vietnam, prevented its collapse under the massive communist thrust, built up our bases, and began to deploy
our forces. In Phase I we planned and did the following:

> Built ports, airfields, and supply and maintenance
> areas.
>
> Set up a 10,000-mile-long supply pipe line.
>
> Constructed an extensive communication system.
>
> Brought in 400,000 men and several thousand aircraft.
>
> Deployed troops throughout South Vietnam.
>
> Learned to work alongside the Vietnamese Army while
> encouraging development of a representative govern-
> ment.
>
> Equipped and revitalized the Vietnamese armed forces,
> whose morale was low.
>
> Expanded the armed forces of South Vietnam in quanti-
> tative terms.
>
> Defended South Vietnam against defeat and against
> being cut in half.
>
> Learned to cope with guerrilla tactics.
>
> Set up an intelligence system for this new type of
> war.
>
> Limited inflation.

Developed our own confidence that we could operate
successfully in the environment of Southeast Asia.

We did all this by the middle of 1966.   It was a tribute
to U.S. organization, technology, and concerted diplomatic
and military professionalism by many people.   At that
point, during the summer of 1966, we moved into the second
phase of our plan.   In Phase II we continued the pattern
and did the following:

Drove the enemy divisions back to sanctuary or into
hiding.

Trained, expanded, and improved the quality of the
Vietnamese armed forces.

Assisted free-world forces of the Pacific area to
join the battle against communist aggression.

Entered enemy base areas and destroyed his supplies.

Raised enemy losses beyond his input capability.

Helped train the Vietnamese Army as a territorial
security force.

Encouraged combined U.S./Vietnamese operations.

Continued to help the Vietnamese armed forces in
professional development.

Completed free elections with South Vietnam.

Saw an elected civilian government installed.

Stabilized prices--opening roads and canals.

Encouraged enemy defection and resettlement.

Discovered and thwarted the enemy's battle plans
before they could be executed.

Unified the U.S. pacification assistance effort for
better management of widespread resources.

We will complete this second phase by the end of this
year.   Before leaving my discussion of this phase, there
is one other management aspect worthy of mention.   Our
rapid buildup 10,000 miles away in an undeveloped nation
lacking in logistics support facilities has created many
problems.   Some units brought to Vietnam equipment that
has not been needed.   Some supplies were shipped automatically based on experience in other wars and have not
been consumed in the quantities expected.   At the same
time, our magnificent fighting men have received what they
needed to do their job.   Now, at the end of this second
phase, we have been able to intensify logistical management and turn our attention to eliminating any excess
items which may have developed.   MACV has instituted an

efficiency and economy program to which I have given the thrifty-sounding name of Project MACONOMY.

With 1968, a new phase is now starting. We have reached an important point when the end begins to come into view. What is this third phase we are about to enter?

In Phase III, in 1968, we intend to do the following:

Help the Vietnamese armed forces to continue improving their effectiveness.

Decrease our advisors in training centers and other places where the professional competence of Vietnamese officers makes this possible.

Increase our advisory effort with the younger brothers of the Vietnamese Army: the Regional Forces and Popular Forces.

Use U.S. and free-world forces to destroy North Vietnamese forays while we assist the Vietnamese to reorganize for territorial security.

Provide the new military equipment to revitalize the Vietnamese Army, and prepare it to take an ever-increasing share of the war.

Continue pressure on the North to prevent rebuilding and to make infiltration more costly.

Turn a major share of front-line DMZ defense over to the Vietnamese Army.

Increase U.S. support in the rich and populated Delta.

Help the government of Vietnam single out and destroy the communist shadow government.

Continue to isolate the guerrilla from the people.

Help the new Vietnamese government to respond to popular aspirations, and to reduce and eliminate corruption.

Help the Vietnamese strengthen their police forces to enhance law and order.

Open more roads and canals.

Continue to improve the Vietnamese economy and standard of living.

Now for Phase IV--the final phase. That period will see the conclusion of our plan to weaken the enemy and strengthen our friends until *we* become progressively superfluous. The object will be to show the world that guerrilla warfare and invasion do not pay as a new means of communist aggression.

I see Phase IV happening as follows:

Infiltration will slow.

The communist infrastructure will be cut up and near collapse.

The Vietnamese government will prove its stability, and the Vietnamese Army will show that it can handle Vietcong.

The Regional Forces and Popular Forces will reach a higher level of professional performance.

U.S. units can begin to phase down as the Vietnamese Army is modernized and develops its capacity to the fullest.

The military physical assets, bases and ports, will be progressively turned over to the Vietnamese.

The Vietnamese will take charge of the final mopping up of the Vietcong (which will probably last several years). The United States, at the same time, will continue the developmental help envisaged by the President for the community of Southeast Asia.

You may ask how long Phase III will take, before we reach the final phase. We have already entered parts of Phase III. Looking back on Phases I and II, we can conclude that we have come a long way.

I see progress as I travel all over Vietnam.

I see it in the attitudes of the Vietnamese.

I see it in the open roads and canals.

I see it in the new crops and the new purchasing power of the farmer.

I see it in the increased willingness of the Vietnamese Army to fight North Vietnamese units and in the victories they are winning.

Parenthetically, I might say that the U.S. press tends to report U.S. actions; so you may not be as aware as I am of the victories won by South Vietnamese forces.

The enemy has many problems:

He is losing control of the scattered population under his influence.

He is losing credibility with the population he still controls.

He is alienating the people by his increased demands and taxes where he can impose them.

He sees the strength of his forces steadily declining.

He can no longer recruit in the South to any meaningful extent; he must plug the gap with North Vietnamese.

His monsoon offensives have been failures.

He was dealt a mortal blow by the installation of a freely elected representative government.

And he failed in his desperate effort to take the world's headlines from the inauguration by a military victory.

Lastly, the Vietnamese Army is on the road to becoming a competent force. Korean troops in Vietnam provide a good example for the Vietnamese. Fifteen years ago the Koreans themselves had problems now ascribed to the Vietnamese. The Koreans surmounted these problems, and so can and will the Vietnamese.

The Vietnamese armed forces have accomplihsed much in a short time. Here are a few examples:

Career management for officers, particularly infantry officers, has been instituted.

Sound promotion procedures have been put into effect.

Discipline and conduct is being stressed.

Increased emphasis is being devoted to small-unit tactics and leadership.

The promotion of enlisted men to the commissioned ranks is now commonplace (2,200 in 1966).

Officer candidates must now take basic training and prove that they have the leadership potential to be officers.

An Inspector General for the Vietnamese armed forces has been appointed and is now active in detailed inspections.

Corrupt and inefficient officials are being gradually eliminated.

The military school system has been revitalized.

The Military Academy has gone to a four-year curriculum.

A school for battalion commanders has been established.

A ten-month National Defense College has been organized for selected senior officers.

The same personnel management programs which have been installed successfully in the Vietnamese Army are being expanded to the Regional Forces and Popular Forces.

We are making progress. We know you want an honorable and early transition to the fourth and last phase.

So do your sons and so do I.

It lies within our grasp--the enemy's hopes are bankrupt. With your support we will give you a success that will impact not only on South Vietnam, but on every emerging nation in the world.

APPENDIX II

PRESS REGULATIONS AT DA NANG, 1967

(For some time in 1967, newsmen arriving in Da Nang received this "poop sheet." It sounded more restrictive than conditions actually were. Nobody had to be escorted, or inform the Marines where he was going to find a story. No one carried a gas mask or two canteens. But the information sheet hints at the highly developed creature comforts available [in quiet times, at least] to newsmen at Da Nang and other smaller press camps at Nha Trang [on the beach], Pleiku, and Can Tho, each with its attendant PIO corps.)

1. The Press Center is located on the west bank of the Da Nang River, near downtown Da Nang. It consists of small motel, press room (with telephones and typewriters), restaurant, and bar.

2. There are approximately 20 transient beds, in addition to long-term leased rooms held by major networks, wire services, and magazines. If the Press Center is filled, a nearby BOQ room will be arranged for you.

3. Before going on operations with field units, correspondents are required to possess the following minimum equipment:

    (a) Two canteens, with carrying belt; and field clothing, including boots. (These items should be purchased in Saigon.)

    (b) Steel helmet, "flak" vest, and gas mask (these will be issued to you on signature receipt by the Escort Section, CIB).

4. Services provided by Press Center:

    (a) Dormitory Rooms, including maid service, laundry (approx. 24 hours) and shoe (boot) shining service, for 300 piastres a day.

11

(b)   Interview appointments, arrangements for field trips, query responses, telephones for filing stories and typewriters for press use, aircraft reservation service, and ground transportation to news sites and air ports (correspondents obtain their own transportation within the city of Da Nang on personal business, such as PX trips, etc.). Commercial film-developing service is available in Da Nang city.

(c)   Restaurant service from 0630 to 2330. From 2230 until 2330 only sandwiches are available. Meals range from about 45 piastres for breakfast (two eggs, bacon, toast) to about 225 piastres for New York cut steak. Coffee and tea are free.

(d)   Bar service until midnight.

5.   Procedures for using the Press Center:

(a)   Upon arrival at Da Nang Air Base, call Da Nang 6259 or Parchment 286 and ask for transportation to the Press Center.

(b)   At the Press Center:

(1)   Check in with the Escort Station . . . present your MACV Accreditation Card, and tell the Escort Officer where you would like to go, or what type stories you are after.

(2)   Next check in with the manager's office to get your room and bed assignments. Because of the shortage of beds, it is necessary that you occupy the bed assigned.

(c)   Departing the Press Center:

(1)   Ask the Escort Section to arrange transportation to the place you wish to go.

(2)   Check out with the manager's office.

(3)   If you are remaining in the I Corps area and will return to the Press Center, you may retain your room by paying the daily rate.

CIVILIAN CASUALTIES FROM VC TERRORISM, JOINT U.S. PUBLIC AFFAIRS OFFICE, SAIGON, DECEMBER 28, 1967

(The following JUSPAO report was accompanied by a detailed list, province by province, of Vietcong terrorist activity.)

In 180 reported Vietcong incidents of terrorism, the following were confirmed casualties during the week ending December 23, 1967:

	SMPD[1]	I Corps	II Corps	III Corps	IV Corps	Total
Killed	22	16	10	17	12	77

Including:
14 RD workers
2 village council members
1 civil servant
1 hamlet official
1 hamlet chief
2 inter-family chiefs

	SMPD	I Corps	II Corps	III Corps	IV Corps	Total
Wounded	57	65	12	12	29	175

Including:
2 RD Workers
6 Hoi Chanh
9 national police
2 civil servants

	SMPD	I Corps	II Corps	III Corps	IV Corps	Total
Abducted	0	64	39	6	24	133

Including:
1 hamlet chief
2 RD workers

To date since January 1, 1967, there have been 3,950 civilians killed, 7,760 wounded, and 5,349 abducted. Since June 1, 1967, there have been 3,948 reported incidents of VC terrorism.

ARVN military casualties as reported by the GVN for the week ending December 23, 1967: KIA: 234; WIA:629; MIA:26.

---

[1] Saigon Metropolitan Police Directorate.

STATEMENT BY ROBERT S. MCNAMARA, SECRETARY OF DEFENSE, BEFORE THE SENATE ARMED SERVICES COMMITTEE ON THE FY 1969-73 DEFENSE PROGRAM AND 1969 DEFENSE BUDGET, JANUARY 22, 1968 (EXCERPTS CONCERNING VIETNAM)

. . . Southeast Asia remains for the United States a test of the viability of our collective defense policy. Here in close proximity to Red China lie a number of small, noncommunist states, each of which in its own way is striving to maintain its freedom and independence. The confusion and discord within the communist camp is well illustrated in this region. The U.S.S.R. is nominally joined with the Peking regime in supporting Hanoi's operations against South Vietnam, but each of the major communist powers is seeking to prevent the other from gaining dominance in Hanoi, while North Vietnam itself probably wishes to fall under the dominance of neither. It is thus possible that Moscow, Peking, and Hanoi all disagree as to what the future shape of Southeast Asia should be, yet these disagreements have allowed Hanoi-- while pursuing its drive to conquer the South--to play the Soviet Union off against China for material as- sistance. Thus, while polycentrism within the communist world is generally a welcome development, there will be cases, as in Vietnam, where it may intensify our problems rather than easing them.

The Soviet leadership may now believe that North Vietnam will be an outpost for their more pragmatic form of Marxism, to serve as a buffer hemming in the doctrinaire zealots of Peking. If this is their calculation, they are playing a dangerous game. A communist victory in South Vietnam would erode the position of all the non- communist states in Southeast Asia, and the chief beneficiary would be China--not the Soviet Union. Such a victory would be seen as a triumph for the Chinese militancy and as a vindication of her position in the ideological dispute with the Soviet Union. And, in contrast to North Korea, which borders both, Southeast Asia is separated from the Soviet Union by the great land

mass of China. It is, therefore, unlikely that the
Soviets could long maintain a special position in that
area in defiance of China.

But our real concern is not over which of the two rivals
emerges dominant. Our concern is that no great power
dominate the area. As I have so often told this committee, the United States has no desire to compete with
either the Soviet Union or Red China for hegemony in
Southeast Asia, or to achieve any special position there.
This is not to say that we are indifferent to what
transpires on the other side of the Pacific Ocean.   Whether we like it or not, we are a Pacific Ocean state.   Our
west coast borders on the Pacific and our 50th state lies
halfway across that ocean.   Moreover, we have important
historical ties and treaty commitments to many of the
nations in the western Pacific: So, we have a vital
strategic interest in that area, an interest that we
cannot ignore.

In this connection, I want to clear up one misunderstanding
that has gained some currency in the press during the last
few months. It has been alleged by some commentators that
the Administration, last fall, changed its rationale for
our military involvement in Southeast Asia--that we are
now emphasizing the importance of Southeast Asia to our
own security, whereas earlier we had said that we entered
the conflict to honor the commitments of four Presidents,
to protect the freedom and independence of the people of
South Vietnam, and to ensure their right to decide their
own destiny.

The fact is that all of these reasons have been involved
all along; no one is exclusively determining, as we have
repeatedly tried to make clear. The important point is
that all of the reasons we have given for our involvement
in the Southeast Asian conflict are directly derived from
a single basic policy, which is collective security. We
are fighting there for the right of nations to live in
freedom and independence, unmolested by their neighbors
and free of fear of domination or attack by any of the
great powers. It is from this right, as I have so often
stated, that our own security derives, and it is precisely
the objective of our collective defense policy in all
parts of the world. Not to honor our commitments in
South Vietnam would thus cast doubt on our determination
to honor our commitments elsewhere in the world.

I believe that over the long run a truly independent
Southeast Asia would best serve the interests of all the
nations involved. It would remove one more source of
strife between the outside world and the communist camp,

and within the latter as well. Moreover, it would create
the kind of environment required for the rapid development
of the region's basically rich natural resources, to the
benefit of all.

This vision of a peaceful and more prosperous order in
Southeast Asia is shared by our friends and allies in
the western Pacific. I am sure that you have noticed an
increased appreciation among the leaders of Asian and
Pacific nations for the contribution which our efforts in
Southeast Asia are making to their own freedom and independence. Of the seven nations actively participating
in the struggle with their own military forces (South
Vietnam, Australia, New Zealand, Thailand, the Republic
of Korea, the Philippines, and the United States), all
but one have agreed in the last 12 months to increase
their force contributions in South Vietnam. And, all of
these leaders--and those of many other noncommunist
nations--are firm in their support for our goals and
objectives in Southeast Asia. I think there can be no
doubt but that this trend is directly related to our
determination to fulfill our obligations in that area and
to a rising confidence among Asian leaders that we will
persist in that determination.

The Statement of Principles enunciated at the Manila
Conference of October 1966 continues to guide our efforts
in Southeast Asia. These principles include the following
four points: (1) Aggression must not succeed in South
Vietnam; (2) we must break the bonds of poverty, illiteracy, and disease throughout Asia and the Pacific area;
(3) we must strengthen economic, social, and cultural
cooperation within the region; (4) we must seek reconcilia-
tion and peace throughout Asia.

The seven participating nations agreed that the South
Vietnamese people shall not be conquered by aggressive
force and shall enjoy the inherent right to choose their
own way of life and their own form of government and that
this commitment shall be backed by military force and other
efforts as necessary. But at the same time, the seven
nations also proclaimed their readiness to pursue any and
all avenues which might lead to a secure and just peace,
either through discussion and negotiation or through
reciprocal action on both sides to reduce the level of
violence. They made it clear that their sole demand on
the leaders of North Vietnam is that they abandon their
aggression. More specifically, the Manila Declaration
stated that:

> Allied forces are in the Republic of Vietnam because
> that country is the object of aggression and its
> government requested support in the resistance of its

people to aggression. They shall be withdrawn,
after close consultation, as the other side withdraws its forces to the North, ceases infiltration,
and the level of violence thus subsides. Those
forces will be withdrawn as soon as possible and
not later than six months after the above conditions
have been fulfilled.

These are still our policies. As you well know, the U.S.
government has continued to explore every possible means
of achieving a just settlement of the Vietnam conflict.

These efforts have thus far yielded no positive results,
but our search for peace continues.

The importance of our efforts in Vietnam to the ultimate
achievement of economic development, area cooperation, and
political independence in Southeast Asia and the southwest
Pacific is accepted not only by the seven nations actively
involved in the conflict, but by leaders of other Asian
countries as well. Prime Ministers Sato of Japan and Lee
of Singapore are among those who have recently spoken out
in unequivocal fashion on the need for the allied shield
in Vietnam to permit orderly Asian development. The
Suharto regime in Indonesia, though remaining unaligned,
is painfully aware of the sources of danger. Wholesale
North Vietnamese violation of Laotian territory has been
officially denounced by Prime Minister Souvanna Phouma.
Burma and Cambodia also recognize the threats of Chinese
Communist pressures. This is not to imply that these
nations will revamp their present foreign policies, but it
does suggest that even those least willing to appear
aligned with the United States are increasingly disturbed
about Red Chinese or North Vietnamese designs.

The turmoil in Vietnam has tended to obscure the substantial progress being achieved elsewhere in the area. The
time being purchased in Vietnam at such heavy cost is being
put to good use by the noncommunist Asian states, and
there is a growing appreciation of the need for collective
action to meet common problems. Although the conflict
slowed the Mekong Development Project, it and other
regional efforts, such as the Asian Development Bank and
the Asia and Pacific Council, are moving forward.

The most significant regional development during the past
year was the formation in August of the Association of
Southeast Asian Nations, comprising Singapore, Indonesia,
Thailand, Malaysia, and the Philippines. The Association
is starting modestly with annual Foreign Ministers'
meetings and proposed economic, social, and technical
programs.

Thus, there is a growing web of cooperation among the
area's noncommunist nations, comprising both functional
efforts focused on common practical problems and broader
ties with more ambitious goals. We can hope that such
evolving mechanisms will eventually provide the region
the collective political, economic, and military strength
necessary to guarantee that its destiny will be determined
by these nations themselves.

Our role in this process will be particularly important.
First, we must see the Vietnam conflict through to a
conclusion that permits the growth and maturing of
regional cooperation. We will, of course, maintain our
SEATO, ANZUS, and other commitments in the area. We
should also continue our carefully structured assistance
to countries in the area. Beyond this, American policy
toward Southeast Asia and the southwest Pacific area must
blend concern and restraint as we help the East Asian
nations to build among themselves the true security that
flows from economic and social progress. We must lend
support and assistance, where requested, yet remain
constantly aware that these countries are both equipped
and entitled to lead themselves, and that it is in our
interest that they do so.

Clouding this picture are intra-regional political
frictions that could frustrate Asian security cooperation.
Nevertheless, some elements are relatively clear. We
shall encourage a prominent Australian-New Zealand role
and continuing Australian efforts to consult the countries
of the region about arrangements that will compensate
for the British withdrawal. We shall encourage Japan to
increase its contributions to the area commensurate with
its own economic and security interests. We intend to
avoid unilateral action that forces the pace or the
nature of the evolving regional economic organizations.

Outright overt aggression by large conventional forces
is unlikely in the region. Internal conflicts, fostered
by socio-economic stagnation, communal disputes, or
externally supported, communist-nurtured subversion are
the more plausible threats.

Let me now briefly touch on the special situations in
Thailand and Laos in view of their relationship to the
Vietnam conflict.

Both of these nations are themselves threatened by
externally supported insurgencies. They are also threatened by the debilitating economic, social, and political
conditions common to much of the area. During the past
year the Thai government assumed a leading role in
regional cooperation. It was instrumental in the creation

of the Association of Southeast Asian Nations and was a
prime mover in fostering closer political consultation
and action among neighboring nations. At the same time
it stepped up its assistance to free-world forces in
Vietnam. An additional 10,000 Thai troops will be sent
to South Vietnam, and, as you know, we are using Thai
bases for air operations against North Vietnam. The
Thais' own counterinsurgency effort against the guerrillas
in the northeastern provinces improved measurably during
1967. This effort, which consists of combined military/
civilian/police operations, is designed not only to quell
the externally supported insurgency but also to eradicate
the factors which facilitate its growth--such as poverty,
illiteracy, and long years of minimal contact with the
area by the central government.

Internal conflict is greater in Laos than in Thailand
primarily because external involvement there is greater.
The North Vietnamese Army continues to infiltrate south
through Laos, and North Vietnamese troops reinforce the
Pathet Lao against the Royal Lao government. North Vietnam is also providing substantial military assistance to
the insurgents. But, for a number of reasons, including
continued international support for the 1962 Geneva
Accords, our economic and military assistance to the
government, and Laos' own growing political stability,
Prime Minister Souvanna Phouma has been able to maintain
a partially successful defense against North Vietnamese
aggression. We intend to continue to support his efforts
while at the same time respecting the neutrality of his
government. . . .

SOUTHEAST ASIA OPERATIONS

Last year and the year before, I discussed in considerable
detail our military objectives in Southeast Asia and the
concept of operations developed to achieve them. However,
it might be worth pointing out once again that we are
dealing here with an immensely complicated problem,
involving not only our immediate and longer range military
and foreign policy objectives, but also local political,
economic, and social considerations as well. While the
military task in Vietnam is beginning to assume some
aspects of a conventional limited war against overt
external aggression, our overall Vietnam task remains that
of making it possible for the South Vietnamese to cope
with and suppress an insurgency which is externally
directed and supported; to rectify the social ills on
which that insurgency battens; to reestablish law and
order; to revive and sustain the economy; and to create
a viable, independent political structure. This total

effort is thus one in which the people of South Vietnam
must play the primary role. We and the other free-world
nations who have come to South Vietnam's assistance can
only help. No matter how great be the resources we commit to the struggle, we cannot provide the South Vietnamese
with the will to survive as an independent nation; with a
sense of national purpose transcending the claims of family, friendship, or regional origin; or with the ability and
self-discipline a people must have to govern themselves.
These qualities and attributes are essential contributions
to the struggle only the people of South Vietnam themselves
can supply.

Our objectives in Vietnam are quite different and far more
limited than they were, for example, in World War II. We
do not seek North Vietnam's capitulation or even the surrender of her regular Army units engaged in the conflict
in the South; we would be content to have them return home.
Neither do we seek the surrender of the Vietcong forces;
we would be content to see them lay down their arms and
take their place as peaceful citizens of South Vietnam, or
move to the North if they so desire. But we do insist
that North Vietnam cease its effort to dictate the shape
of South Vietnam's future by terrorism, subversion, and
force of arms.

In pursuing these goals, we have tried to adapt our
military response to the limited character of our objectives, using limited means in a limited geographic area
to achieve them. We have no desire to widen the conflict.
We are convinced that the issue must ultimately be resolved
in the South, and we have no wish to incur the risk that
the fighting might escalate, perhaps directly involving
other nuclear powers. The danger of such a development
to the entire world is readily apparent.

While we have been making general progress towards our
objectives over the last two and one-half years, progress
has been uneven. With regard to large-scale military
actions, I can tell you again what I said last year. Our
forces have won every major battle in which they have been
engaged since their commitment in South Vietnam. I
believe it has been conclusively demonstrated that the communist main force units are simply no match for our forces
in such engagements. Moreover, because of our great firepower and mobility, we are able to come to the aid of the
South Vietnamese and other friendly forces whenever they
encounter sizable enemy concentrations.

Indeed, during the last year the free-world forces have
severely mauled most of the communist main force units in
the coastal areas (excluding the IV Corps, where no regular
North Vietnam units and few U.S. units are engaged). Many

strategic lines of communication have been recovered from
enemy control and allied forces now conduct military
operations in sectors of the country which previously had
been inviolate communist sanctuaries for two decades.
Total communist battle losses are running much higher than
in 1966, the enemy's "in-country" recruitment appears to
be markedly declining, and the population base from which
he can draw support is shrinking.

These successes, however, have created new problems. As
you no doubt know, the communists have now concentrated
a large portion of their main force units in the highlands
along the northern and western borders of South Vietnam,
where their lines of communication are shorter and, to the
extent that they lie outside the borders of South Vietnam,
more secure from ground attack. (Later, I will discuss
some of the new tactics and techniques which have been
developed to help cope with these new problems.)

While many of the communist main force units in the highlands continue to absorb heavy casualties, they are still
effective in the field. By continuing heavy inputs of
manpower from the North and shifting strategy and tactics,
the communists apparently hope to offset the advantages
gained by the allies through the introduction of U.S.
combat troops. Operating close to their sanctuaries in
North Vietnam and Laos, the communists hope to regain
the initiative in deciding when and where to fight, thus
conserving their forces, prolonging the conflict, and
forcing us to deploy our troops in response to their
thrusts.

Although the combat efficiency of the communist main force
units in the coastal areas appears to have been reduced,
they still constitute a formidable threat, particularly
in the crucial pacification effort. Through defensive
maneuver operations, unit dispersal, and other tactics,
these units have managed to survive and continue offensive
operations in and on the fringes of the populated areas.
In some areas, these attacks have slowed our efforts to
consolidate our gains; in other parts of the coastal
provinces, the increasingly aggressive behavior of surviving main force units has reversed previously favorable
trends and caused some deterioration in local security
situations.

In the Delta, the combat effectiveness of many of the
Vietcong main force battalions has also been reduced as
a result of continuing combat attrition, difficulty in
recruiting local manpower, and the transfer of key cadre
to units outside the Delta. However, none of these Delta
units has been completely destroyed. Furthermore, partly

to conserve their forces, the communists are increasingly resorting to hit-and-run attacks with mortars and recoilless rifles not followed up by sustained ground action.

Countrywide, the evidence appears overwhelming that, beginning in 1966, communist local and guerrilla forces have sustained substantial attrition. As a result there has been a drop in combat efficiency and morale among many such units, though the guerrilla situation varies radically from area to area. In the northern I Corps, for example, where guerrillas are backed up by strong main force units, the guerrilla elements remain an important threat. They also seem to have maintained their effectiveness in the Delta, where allied pressure has been the lightest. Elsewhere in the country these forces appear considerably less effective than in 1965. I should caution, however, that the communists are well aware of the deterioration of their guerrilla forces and they are making great efforts to increase their effectiveness through consolidation and new tactics, and the augmentation of guerrilla efforts with main force specialists, such as sapper units.

In the second major area--pacification--progress continues to be slow and uneven, with gains in some areas and setbacks in others. Although the pacification program registered definite net progress in 1967, achievements fell short of the goals.

As I pointed out last year, the military problem in pacification operations is to eliminate the Vietcong guerrilla forces district by district, and village by village. For the most part, guerrilla forces are local groups whose mission is harassment, sabotage, control, and intimidation of the local population, as well as the provision of intelligence, terrain guidance, supplies, and recruits for main force units. Only when these local guerrilla forces are permanently dispersed or harried into the ground can the full range of revolutionary development measures be undertaken on a permanent basis.

Pacification is a very slow and painstaking process. Even after an area has been essentially "cleared" of main force elements, a free-world military presence must be maintained to cope with residual guerrilla units. In fact, we have found that it is very difficult to clear, completely and permanently, any area in which the guerrillas were once well established. Even where we have been conducting clear-and-secure operations for several years, guerrilla hit-and-run attacks still occur. It was for this reason that we decided last year to increase substantially the amount of military resources devoted to the pacification

effort. To this end, about one-half of the regular South
Vietnam Army has been assigned to this mission (one
obviously best performed by Vietnamese), and we are now
engaged in building up and retraining the Regional and
Popular Forces who are most directly involved in providing
the local security that permits pacification efforts to
proceed. We also intend to continue to build up the
national police, whose task is to ferret out the hidden
Vietcong infrastructure, and the Revolutionary Development
cadres, whose task is to help the villages and hamlets
restore local government, construct community facilities,
and improve agricultural practices.

In the final analysis, the ultimate success of our entire
effort in South Vietnam will turn on the ability of the
government to reestablish its authority over its territory
so that peaceful reconstruction can be undertaken.

Perhaps the best single measure of pacification is the
extent to which the population has been brought under
government control and protection. To provide a more
valid standard of measurement, we have developed a device
called the Hamlet Evaluation System. This new reporting
system, which went into effect early in 1967, indicates
that about 67 percent of the people of South Vietnam live
under allied military protection and some form of continuing GVN administration.

For a number of reasons, the pace of the pacification
program in 1967 was relatively slow. The security problem
has already been touched on. Village and hamlet elections
last spring and national elections in September and October
preoccupied the GVN authorities and diverted security
forces from purely pacification objectives. Although this
diversion of effort contributed importantly to long-term
nation-building objectives, it has slowed the momentum
of the pacification program. Furthermore, even under
optimum conditions, pacification progress is not going to
be rapid, since pacification involves nothing less than
the restructuring of Vietnamese society.

Moreover, Vietcong counteraction to the pacification
program intensified appreciably during 1967 in a manner
that constitutes an indirect tribute to the program's
concepts but inhibited its rate of progress. In addition
to continuing their direct attacks on pacification teams
in the secure hamlets, the Vietcong stepped up their attacks against district towns and provincial capitals.
While the Vietcong have been unable to hold any of these
urban centers, the attacks have heightened the feeling of
insecurity in those areas. The overall impact of the
Vietcong attack on the pacification effort is reflected in

the Hamlet Evaluation System reports for 1967, which
indicate that there was improvement in 35 districts but
some deterioration in 29. By and large, the gains occurred in areas near large cities where allied forces were
concentrated, and the losses occurred in the more remote
areas where allied forces operate in a more dispersed
pattern.

In a related effort, we believe progress is beginning to
be made in ferreting out the hidden Vietcong infrastructure.
Despite some overall management problems, the Vietnamese
military and security services, including the national
police, are now mounting an increased number of attacks
on their infrastructure at the local level with encouraging
results. The tempo of this activity can be expected to
increase significantly in 1968.

Similarly, the Revolutionary Development cadres program
is moving forward despite a number of difficulties. Almost all teams have now completed their work in their
initial hamlet assignments and have moved on to their
second assignments. Losses from Vietcong attacks and other
causes were high in 1967, but they have been more than offset by the output of new cadres from the training center
(which is now meeting its monthly quota), and steps have
been taken to improve the discipline, morale, leadership,
and overall quality of recruits.

With regard to the economy, the principal problems have
been to keep the inevitable rise in prices under control
and to revive agricultural production. Although the
general price level continued to rise during 1967 as the
result of the continued influx of U.S. troops and our
large construction program, the rise has been kept to
manageable proportions. We, ourselves, have taken drastic
action to limit our expenditures in South Vietnam. To
reduce the personal spending of our troops in South
Vietnam, we have made full use of the new authorization
to pay 10 percent interest on the savings deposits of
military personnel serving in Southeast Asia. We are
also sending our military personnel to other countries
for rest and relaxation. Finally, to offset the in-
flationary impact of our presence in South Vietnam, we
are providing a substantial amount of economic assistance,
particularly in the form of imports. As a result of
these efforts, the increase in the overall price level was
held to under 35 percent during 1967, far less, for example, than the Korean price level rose in the second
year of that war.

Because most of the combat operations are conducted in
rural areas, and because of the diversion of indigenous
manpower to wartime tasks, agricultural production and

distribution have suffered greatly. Deliveries of
domestic rice to Saigon (which is the main distribution
point for the rice-deficit region to the north) have
declined sharply since 1963. But we hope the decline
has bottomed out, and we are attempting to increase production and deliveries in 1968. The rice producers are
now using increasing amounts of fertilizer and some simple
farm machinery, as well as some new more productive
varieties of rice, all of which should help to increase
yields both per hectare and per hour of labor. In addition, vegetable and poultry production have been rising
steadily, and we are meeting some of our own needs from
local sources. All in all, I believe we have seen the
worst of the agricultural decline and the future looks
much more promising.

However, much more needs to be done by the government of
South Vietnam. Incomes of government employees, both
military and civilian, have not kept up with the rising
price level and will have to be raised if corruption is
to be reduced and efficiency increased. Rural income
will also have to be raised to promote pacification and
reduce migration to urban areas. In contrast, incomes
in other private sectors of the economy have been increasing faster than the price level and should be re-
strained. This will require new tax legislation and a
restraint on nonessential government spending. Finally,
restrictions on the movement of goods throughout the
country must be eliminated.

In the political arena as well, there has been encouraging
progress. Step by step, and notwithstanding the Vietcong
attacks and the great skepticism expressed both within and
without South Vietnam, the people of that country have
moved to constitutional government. A Constituent Assembly
has been elected, a new constitution written and a new
national government elected and installed. Although
the political structure is still very fragile, the first
essential steps in the evolution of a viable South Vietnamese state have been taken. Furthermore, over half of
the entire adult population of South Vietnam (including
those adults working or serving with the Vietcong) participated in the electoral process through which these new institutions were brought into being. Political evolution,
moveover, has not been confined to the national arena.
Some of the hamlet and village councils recently established by popular election represent a structure that over
the long run could outweigh in importance the more widely
publicized advances in the national government. But at
all levels of government, continued progress toward stability and responsiveness requires a determined attack on

basic social ills, including the problem of corruption.
The fate of the government rests on its success in sur-
mounting obstacles to the prompt development and introduction of the economic and political programs that will
gain and retain wide popular support.

The air campaign against North Vietnam has included attacks on industrial facilities, fixed military targets,
and the transportation system.

Attacks against major industrial facilities through 1967
have destroyed or put out of operation a large portion
of the rather limited modern industrial base. About 70
percent of the North's electric-generating capacity is
currently out of operation, and the bulk of its fixed
petroleum storage capacity has been destroyed. However,
imported diesel generators are probably producing sufficient electricity for essential services and, by dis-
persing their petroleum supplies, the North Vietnamese
have been able to meet their minimum petroleum needs.
Most, if not all, of the industrial output lost has been
replaced by imports from the Soviet Union and China.

Military and economic assistance from other communist
countries, chiefly the Soviet Union, has been steadily
increasing. In 1965, North Vietnam received in aid a
total of $420 million ($270 million military and $150
million economic); in 1966, $730 million ($455 million
military and $275 million economic); and preliminary
estimates indicate that total aid for 1967 may have
reached $1 billion ($660 million military and $340
economic). Soviet military aid since 1965 has been concentrated on air defense materiel--SAMs, AAA guns and
ammo, radars, and fighter aircraft.

Soviet economic assistance has included trucks, railroad
equipment, barges, machinery, petroleum, fertilizer, and
food. China has provided help in the construction of
light industry, maintenance of the transportation system,
and improvements in the communications and irrigation
systems, plus some 30,000 to 50,000 support troops for
use in North Vietnam for repair and AAA defense.

Damage inflicted by our air attacks on fixed military
targets has led to the abandonment of barracks and
supply and ammunition depots and has caused a dispersal
of supplies and equipment. However, North Vietnam's air-
defense system continues to function effectively despite
increased attacks on airfields, SAM sites, and AAA positions. The supply of SAM missiles and antiaircraft
ammunition appears adequate, notwithstanding our heavy
attacks, and we see no indication of any permanent drop
in their expenditure rates.

Our intensified air campaign against the transportation
system seriously disrupted normal operations and has
increased the cost and difficulties of maintaining traffic
flows. Losses of transportation equipment have increased,
but inventories have been maintained by imports from communist countries. The heavy damage inflicted on key
railroad and highway bridges in the Hanoi-Haiphong areas
during 1967 has been largely offset by the construction
of numerous by-passes and the more extensive use of inland
waterways.

While our overall loss rate over North Vietnam has been
decreasing steadily, from 3.4 aircraft per thousand sorties
in 1965 to 2.1 in 1966 and to 1.9 in 1967, losses over the
Hanoi-Haiphong areas have been relatively high.

The systematic air campaign against fixed economic and
military target systems leaves few strategically important
targets unstruck. Other than manpower, North Vietnam
provides few direct resources to the war effort, which is
sustained primarily by the large imports from the communist
countries. The agrarian nature of the economy precludes
an economic collapse as a result of the bombing. Moreover,
while we can make it more costly in time and manpower, it
is difficult to conceive of any interdiction campaign
that would pinch off the flow of military supplies to the
South as long as combat requirements remain at anything
like the current low levels.

THE COMMUNIST FORCES IN SOUTH VIETNAM

Last year I described in some detail the complexities involved in estimating the communist "order of battle" in
South Vietnam. Since that time, MACV has been restudying
the entire problem and has now evolved a new format which
we believe more clearly depicts the significant trends
in the strength and character of the communist fighting
forces. We have never been satisfied with the estimates
of the communist political cadres (i.e., the Vietcong
infrastructure) or the so-called Self-Defense and Secret
Self-Defense forces. These are very vague categories
which do not lend themselves to any kind of reasonably
precise measurement. Even more important, they are not
fighting forces and, therefore, didn't really belong in
the order-of-battle estimates. Accordingly, the new
order-of-battle estimates now include only three categories of fighting forces: combat, administrative
services, and guerrillas. The first category includes
the combat and combat-support units; the second, the rear-
area technical services; and the third, the full-time
irregular but organized units.

The estimates of enemy strength are subject to frequent
change, and it is difficult to spell out at any one time
the detailed changes in enemy force structures; however,
it seems quite certain that total enemy strength did
decline during 1967. Most of the decline took place
among the irregular forces. The strength of enemy regular
combat forces has been maintained at a relatively constant
level of about 110,000-115,000 during the past year. The
participation of the NVA increased from about 9,000 men in
June 1965 to between 50,000-55,000 at the end of 1967.
In addition, some 10,000 NVA troops have been placed in
Vietcong combat units to help them maintain their strength
at about 60,000-65,000 troops. The number of administrative support troops who back up the combat regulars is
at least 35,000-40,000. The number of guerrillas has
been declining during the past year and is estimated at
between 70,000-90,000.

It is estimated that, during all of 1967, the communists
lost about 165,000 effectives; about 88,000 killed in
action, 30,000 dead or disabled from wounds, 6,000 prisoners of war, almost 18,000 defectors to the government
of South Vietnam, and about 25,000 disabled by disease,
deserted (other than to GVN), etc. These estimates,
however, must be used with a great deal of caution. We
know the number of communist prisoners of war and defectors. But the estimates of the number killed in action
are based on a body count which includes many judgment
factors, and the number dead or disabled from wounds is a
computed figure representing 35 percent of the body
count. The number disabled by disease, etc., is simply
a guess, since we have no solid basis for calculating
this figure. In any event, communist losses in 1967
were extremely heavy and were at least 50 percent
higher than in 1966.

These losses are replaced by recruitment within South
Vietnam and infiltration from the north. The Vietcong
have had considerable difficulty in meeting recruitment
goals. Although we can make only rough estimates of
actual recruitment, we believe that it has declined from
a level of about 7,000-8,000 men a month during 1966 to
something on the order of 3,000-5,000 men a month by
the end of 1967. The balance of the manpower drain must
be filled by infiltration. Infiltration from the North
averaged about 7,000 men a month during the first half
of 1967. It will be several months before we have final
estimates for the second half of 1967, but preliminary
indications are that it has been continuing at about
the same rate.

A recent appraisal of the manpower situation in North
Vietnam shows that North Vietnamese manpower reserves
are adequate to meet current demands and that Hanoi could
support a military mobilization effort higher than present
levels. North Vietnam's present force level of 480,000
represents only about three percent of the population.
More than half its male population of 2.8 million between
the ages of 17 and 35 are believed to be fit for military
service. But Hanoi apparently satisfies its military
force level requirements at the present time simply by
drafting all or almost all of the estimated 120,000
physically fit men who reach the draft age every year.

As to the future, our estimates are, of course, very
uncertain. We believe that any net increase in communist
strength during 1968 will have to come from North Vietnam;
the local supply of Vietcong manpower is growing more
limited with each succeeding year. We have reason to
believe that new North Vietnamese divisions have moved
South. (As I pointed out last year, North Vietnam has
not infiltrated into the South any very large part of its
active Army. The limiting factor is not the total size
of the North Vietnamese Army but rather the number of men
that they are capable of training and infiltrating into
South Vietnam, particularly the number of essential cadre
available.) These divisions have not yet been reflected
in the order of battle. Thus the combat strength of the
NVA in the South may increase sharply in the next few
months, and we have provided for this development in our
own plans.

THE SOUTH VIETNAMESE ARMED FORCES

At the end of 1967, the government of South Vietnam had
a total of about three quarters of a million men under
arms--about 341,000 in the regular forces (Army, Navy,
Marine Corps, Air Force), 150,000 each in the Regional
and Popular Forces, 42,000 Civilian Irregular Defense
Group (CIDG) forces, and 70,000 national police.

The regular Army now stands at about 301,000 compared with
284,000 in December 1966. Last year I noted that a major
effort would be made in 1967 to bring the "present-for-
duty" strength of the Army maneuver battalions up to an
acceptable level. This has been substantially accomplished
with the increase of about 17,000 men in Army strength.

The strength of the Regional and Popular Forces will be
substantially increased. In addition, as I noted earlier,
these forces will be retrained and provided better equipment since they play a major role in the pacification

effort. Similarly, the government will continue its effort to increase the size of the national police force,
the expansion of which has consistently fallen behind
schedule. Although recruitment for this force has lagged
and certain units are still not properly assigned, the
government hopes to increase the strength to about 98,000
by June 1969, compared with about 58,000 at end 1966.
A further small increase will also be made in the CIDG,
and many of these units will be moved from the coastal
provinces into the highlands where they are now most
needed.

To meet these increased manpower goals and to replace
losses (i.e., casualties and desertions), a partial
mobilization has been decreed by the government, and the
details of the new measure are now being debated in the
legislature. It is our hope that the draft will be expanded and intensified, since we feel very strongly that
the recently announced increase in our deployments should
be matched by an increase in the South Vietnamese forces.

In this connection, I should point out that the performance
of the South Vietnamese forces improved in 1967. Many
of their units have achieved major victories, particularly
those operating with our own forces. Desertions are down
sharply from the first half of 1966.

OTHER FREE-WORLD FORCES IN SOUTH VIETNAM

Excluding U.S. forces, there are now a total of about
60,000 other free-world military personnel in-country.
South Korea, with a strength of 48,800 has furnished two
divisions and one brigade--a total of 22 infantry-type
battalions. Australia, with a present strength of 6,600
has furnished three infantry battalions, a squadron of
eight attack bombers, and a guided missile destroyer.
New Zealand has increased its strength to about 500 and
the Philippines have furnished a reinforced construction
battalion of about 2,000 men. Thailand now has one maneuver battalion in South Vietnam with about 2,400 men. This
force will grow to 12,000 men by June 1969. All of these
nations, except the Philippines, have increased their
force commitments since last year.

U.S. FORCES IN SOUTHEAST ASIA

Last year we budgeted for a total of about 470,000 men in
South Vietnam by June 1968, but last summer General Westmoreland requested and the President agreed to provide
additional forces. Thus, by December 31, 1967, we had
about 485,000 men there, and this number will grow to a
total of 525,000. (Total allied forces in South Vietnam
increased from 690,000 in June 1965 to 1,298,000 in

December 1967 and are scheduled to grow to about 1,400,000 by June 1968.)   The U.S. ground forces in December 1967 included 102 maneuver battalions (79 Army, 23 Marine Corps).   The ground forces are now supported by about 3,100 helicopters, and this number will continue to grow.

In June 1965, before the major buildup of U.S. forces in Vietnam began, both the consumption and production of ground ammunition were running at relatively low levels, as is normal in peacetime.   Since then, both consumption and production have increased manyfold.   During the early months of the force buildup, when consumption outpaced production, ammunition requirements were met by drawing down war reserve stocks which, of course, is just what our planning envisioned.   Actually, the amount drawn down was small in relation to our total stocks.   (All ground ammunition figures relate to the 40 major items accounting for about 85 percent of the tonnage used in Vietnam.)

During the past year, ammunition production has nearly tripled--from 39,000 tons in December 1966 to 113,000 tons in December 1967--and since June has equaled or exceeded consumption.   Actual consumption of the 40 major items in 1967 was a little over one million tons (compared with last year's estimate of 900,000 tons).   Production will continue to increase during the next few months and should level off at about 130,000 tons per month by December 1968, well above the projected consumption rate.   The excess of production over consumption will be used to replace the reserve stocks drawn down earlier and will also serve as a safety factor in case consumption exceeds the planned levels.   Our reserve production capacity, which will still be large, serves as a second safety factor to meet an even larger consumption requirement.   The FY 1969 Budget includes about $2.8 billion for ground ammunition.

We now have a total of about 1,000 fighter/attack aircraft based in South Vietnam, Thailand, and aboard carriers offshore.   We are now flying a total of about 28,000 to 30,000 attack sorties per month.   In addition, the B-52 force in 1967 flew a total of more than 800 sorties per month.   Total air ordnance consumption was running about 83,000 tons per month in the last few months of 1967. (Air ordnance data refer to the 53 major items which account for about 95 percent of the tonnage used in Southeast Asia.)   Production at the close of 1967 was running at about 100,000 tons per month.

As of that date, the worldwide inventory considerably exceeded the June 1965 figure.   This is more than we believe is needed with a "hot" production base.   Accordingly, we now plan to reduce these inventories somewhat, resuming the buildup to our "cold base" objective after hostilities are terminated. This will allow us to shut down the lines gradually, thereby avoiding unwanted surplus and cushioning the impact on the economy.

Large quantities of air-delivered munitions will continue to be needed, and a total of about $3.5 billion is included in our FY 1969 request for these items for all the Services.

No major change is planned in the "offshore" naval forces, except for the battleship *New Jersey*, which will deploy to the South China Sea. The river patrol force will be further increased from about 159 vessels in December 1967 to about 250 by December of this year.

During the past year, we have battle-tested the first mobile "Riverine" force in the Mekong Delta. This force of three battalions has been stationed on two naval barracks ships (plus a barracks barge) and at a nearby land base (two battalions afloat and one ashore). We now plan to increase the size of this force.

Other additional deployments to Southeast Asia will require only a very small increase in the number of U.S. military personnel in Thailand, to a total of about 48,000. No significant increase will be needed at our bases in the western Pacific (Ryukyus, the Philippines, Taiwan, Japan, and Guam), where we have about 120,000 military personnel.

I noted earlier that our success in pushing the communist main force units back into the highlands along the borders of South Vietnam has created new problems. Operating in such close proximity to the borders, our forces do not have much room for maneuver in attempting to cut off communist units from their lines of communication. Consequently, we have had to develop new means for interdicting the flow of men and supplies to these units, e.g., the barrier system just south of the DMZ.

NEWS CONFERENCE, AMBASSADOR ROBERT KOMER, SAIGON, JANUARY 24, 1968

General Winant K. Sidle: It's a pleasure this morning to have Ambassador Komer back again. This morning, as you know, he's going to give a sort of wrap-up of pacification during '67 and a little bit on the future. We will have a handout with the statistics involved, which is bound to reach here before we're through. It is not here yet due to the traffic, but I'm sure it will make it. Without further ado, Ambassador Komer.

Ambassador Komer: Thank you, Si. What I want to do this morning as part of our series of year-enders is to try and sum up how we did in pacification in 1967. Pacification isn't a very sexy subject, but everybody agrees that it's pretty doggoned important to what's happening in Vietnam. So I'd like to talk a little bit about what pacification is, who pacifies, why is pacification going better in '67, what did we accomplish, what's the outlook for '68, before throwing myself open for questions.

First of all, what is pacification? It's by its very nature a pretty slow and undramatic process of extending security, providing assistance to the people in the countryside, showing that the GVN cares for the people, taking care of refugees and the like. It's really a very complex set of interlocking programs. First of all, as I say, the key is adequate local security for the people. This is primarily a military function. It's a function, as you know, of the ARVN, of the RF, of the PF. There's just no point in trying to build roads or train teachers or provide fertilizer if the countryside is insecure, because you just can't do it. So until the VC/NVA main forces have been driven away, until you've got a situation where you can bring in the pacification units, you really can't move on pacification in Vietnam. This is a lesson that we learned the hard way.

33

The 59-man RD teams in black pajamas that everyone has
seen and heard about are the leading edge of pacification, if you will. But we've learned from experience
that you've got to think about it in much larger terms,
because the RD cadre make up only about 10 percent, I`
think, of the total manpower involved in pacification.
Nor can about 700 RD teams of one kind or another take
care of 12,700 hamlets--it just can't be done.

So you've got to think of a much larger picture--of attacking the VC infrastructure, of the Chieu Hoi program
(inducing the enemy to rally), of PSYOPS, of refugee care,
of opening roads and waterways, of restoring law and
order (a police function), reviving local government
(an administrative job), expanding the rural economy,
and a lot of other things as well.

The pattern of pacification outfits that the GVN has is
almost kaleidoscopic. We not only have the RD teams,
we have the APTs [Armed Propaganda teams], the Census
Grievance cadre, the special police, the regular police,
the police field force, the culture drama team, the VIS
(Vietnamese Information Service cadre), the Revolutionary
Development People's Groups, the Chieu Hoi workers, and
tens of thousands of technical service cadre from the
various GVN civil ministries--like the Agricultural Land
Service, and the land reform people and the like.

Who pacifies? Pacification is 99 percent Vietnamese
business. The United States just provides advice. We're
also the bankers. Too often people forget this. Our big
military task in cooperation with ARVN is to try and get
the Vietcong and NVA main forces off the pacifiers' backs,
push them out to the frontiers, and contain them there.
This is indispensable to pacification. But this is done
largely with U.S. forces. General Westmoreland is chief
military advisor to the ARVN--but he also commands
500,000 U.S. troops. I have only about 3,900 pacification advisors, 2,700 of them military, and about 1,200
civilians. The reason why the military are a larger
component is that most of the advisors down at district
level are soldiers. We have advisors in about 222 of
the 242-odd districts in all 44 provinces and in the IV
Corps, of course. Three-quarters of our advisors are
outside of Saigon, which isn't a bad record when you
think about it. In addition, we've got about 400 civilians from other free-world nations who are helping us
out.

Now, let's look at our banking function. We provide a
very substantial portion of the resources that the GVN
employs in pacification. We're up in 1967 to over $350

million dollars of dollar input, and we expect to go up
to well over $500 million in 1968. But the GVN contribu-
tion, partly from our counterpart, is pretty substantial
too. The other interesting thing about this chart is the
way funds have gone up.

The next thing to bear in mind about pacification is that
the current program, the one we're calling the RD program,
is only about two years old. It really began at the
Honolulu Conference in February 1966, when President Thieu
and Prime Minister Ky agreed with President Johnson that
there ought to be a new thrust in pacification as a
result of the fact that we had finally stemmed the erosion
in the main force war. But at that time we hadn't even
started the Vung Tau school; the first class was just getting underway--the first class of RD teams at Vung Tau
didn't even graduate until May 1966.

And we had some fairly unrealistic goals. With the wisdom
of hindsight, we can admit that now. The plan was to
pacify about 1,800 hamlets in 1966 and we fell pretty far
short--as a matter of fact, by the end of the calendar year
we met only about a quarter of that goal.

The next big landmark was the Manila Conference in October
1966. The big thing about it from the standpoint of
pacification was that it was there that the government of
Vietnam committed itself to put an increasing proportion
of its regular security forces into the pacification business, to provide the essential sustained local security.
We also laid plans to expand other resources too.

As a result, the '67 program was much better planned than
the '66--in fact, it was the first really planned pacification effort since the Strategic Hamlet Program in 1962.
Now, it got started late, as many of you who were here
recall--didn't get going until after Tet, which came late
in '67. The targets were cut back to about 1,100 hamlets
in the '67 program. But we selected 26 priority provinces,
and tried to concentrate our effort in 1967 much more than
we had in '66.

Why did pacification go better in '67 than in the previous
year? I don't kid myself that it was all because of the
pacifiers. Unquestionably there is a direct relationship
between military success against the enemy main and local
forces and pacification success. Unless our large units
can get the enemy's large units off the backs of the
population and drive them back into the jungle and mountain
areas toward the frontiers, pacification has great difficulty in getting off the ground. So the first ingredient
in our better performance in '67 was the increased performance of the American/ARVN/ROK/etc. forces. It widened

opportunities for pacification of a sort that simply hadn't existed in this country before.

Better organization, on both the GVN and U.S. sides, was another reason why things went better. I think by 1967 the Ministry of Revolutionary Development was generally agreed to be one of the best functioning ministries in the Vietnamese government. Other ministries also per-formed better. We just *knew* more about pacification by the time '67 came around, because we'd had a learning period, and we'd taken our knocks in '66.

And we pumped a lot more assets into pacification in order to capitalize on the opportunities. This chart goes all the way back to 1965, but you can see (just as you saw on the previous chart) how we've been putting more re-sources in.   The previous chart was money; this is man-power. Back at end-1965, about 350,000; by the end of '66, up to about 442,000; end of '67 we were up to 513,000. Now, one can slice these figures different ways--this is just one way of looking at them--but no matter how you do it, the trend has been substantially upward. In fact, I think 1967 was the first year in which we had even marginally adequate resources, especially on the security side, to do the job that we set ourselves. This sustained local security effort became top priority in '67--I think that's one reason why pacification went better. We got the assignment of 54 ARVN battalions in direct support of RD, as they call it. You add to those 218-odd RF companies and about 738 PF platoons, all of which were put together in another new wrinkle--the RD campaign area. We selected 39 priority areas and sought to concentrate all of these resources--the RD teams, PF, RF, ARVN--under a single commander in what we called an RD campaign area. This "oil spot" technique was very successful, as I think the figures will show. Let me turn to the figures, then.

What did we accomplish in '67? I think it was a year of forward movement on the pacification front, even though it was somewhat less productive than we had hoped. We gave more high-level attention to pacification than in any previous year; we invested more manpower and resources in it; and I think the results showed.

Now, it's pretty hard to measure pacification results. It's easy enough to go out to one or two or three hamlets and, if they look good, to say pacification is doing well. It's equally easy to go out to a couple of hamlets and, if pacification is doing poorly, well, that's easy enough to see, too. But you've got 12,700 hamlets in this country that we've identified so far, and no doubt there are some others, too. So you've got to look at the

assessing the program

averages. Similarly, when you're looking at the performance of the local security forces, it's easy enough
to find an indifferent PF platoon, or one that breaks and
runs when the outpost is attacked, but you've got 4,500
PF platoons in the RVNAF right now. You've got to take
the averages--it's whether they're improving on the
average or not which is significant, not whether in any
individual case they are doing better or doing worse. So
when you're dealing with the hamlet-by-hamlet business
called pacification, with a hamlet war involving all sorts
of small outfits like PF platoons, RD teams, RF companies,
and the like, you've got to use figures.

Let me try to show you, based on the system that we've
developed, after a considerable period (this Hamlet
Evaluation System) what the trends look like. Because I
think that the HES is probably the best pacification
measure that we've been able to devise. We keep trying
to improve it, but it's so much better than anything we
had before that it gives a fairly reasonable picture.

First, in terms of hamlets. We only added about 640
hamlets to the secure (A, B, or C)--relatively secure
category--in 1967. That's a pretty modest increase. As
you can see, the increase was rather more substantial
in IV Corps, but of course there are more *hamlets* in IV
Corps--about 5,000 of them--than any place else in the
country. There was also an improvement in the number
that were raised to the contested level. There was a
decline in the number of VC. The reason why these figures
don't add up is because in the course of the 11 months
that we've been using the HES (it's really only 11 months
because our first reports were in at the end of January
last year) we added some 873 hamlets to the base. We just
kept finding more hamlets, or hamlets divided, or there
were other changes in the picture. I hope in '68 we will
have less variation in the base; that this gradually gets
worked out. As a result, you can't look at these and
say that "How did you get 600 and 500 out of a reduction
of 341?" I'll say in defense of these figures that most
of the add-ons--most of the new hamlets we found--turned
out quite logically to be either VC or contested. We
knew where the hamlets were that we were in, but we didn't
know about a lot of the VC hamlets. So the biggest
increases were in the VC and contested categories, which
suggests that these figures are rather more valid than
less.

It's even better if you look at population trends than if
you look at hamlets. As I've said many times, hamlets
vary so widely in size that it isn't worthwhile to compare
apples and grapefruit. Hamlets of 50 people occur in this

country, and I think there are a couple of hamlets that
have as many as 20,000 people. So you've got to look at
population rather than hamlets if you want to get a picture of the trends in security. The population picture
looks rather more hopeful. About 1.3 million more people
came into urban areas--this includes urban areas, of
course--or into hamlets that were upgraded to the secure
category (there was a reduction once again because of an
increase in the base in the contested and VC areas). Now
the year-end reports (which we've just gotten in and
which I'm giving to you now) on the 12,722 hamlets show
that about 67 percent of the total population--some 11.5
million people out of the 17.2 million that we're carrying
as the total population of South Vietnam--are now living
either in the secure cities and towns or under reasonably
good security conditions in the country. This is about
a 5 percent increase in the course of the 11 months--4.8
percent to be precise.

Now, I'm not going to try and kid you. This didn't all
come because we gained more hamlets. This increase is
partly a movement of population to the cities where there
are better jobs and more security. It's partly a refugee
movement, especially here in I Corps. So there is a
significant number of refugees in here, too. The increase
in secure population is composed of many factors, not
just of the expansion of the pacification area, although
we think that was reasonably good too, as you saw from
the earlier chart.

Another big plus in 1967--and one that I'm trying to focus
on much more in 1968--is the start of economic revival in
the countryside. I was down in An Giang just yesterday--
and in the Delta--and it's amazing how much of a difference
there is down there in the course of a year. Of course,
An Giang itself is not a particularly good indicator; but
flying over you can see lots of tractors, you can see a
lot more rice, you can see a lot more roads open. This
is very significant to pacification. I think economic
revival of the countryside--giving the farmer more for
his paddy, giving him consumer goods that he can buy with
the piastres he earns--is going to be one of the most
significant inputs to the pacification process that has
occurred to date.

As you know, we've opened just about all of the roads and
waterways that we set ourselves as goals in 1967. Route 1
is open from Saigon all the way up to the DMZ. We've
kept Route 4 open with very few breaks of more than four
hours in duration throughout 1967. Everywhere in the
Delta we see the signs of prosperity, and in some of the

central lowland provinces, too. A lot more pumps, a lot
more outboard motors, 75 Tri-Lambretta buses showing up
in an isolated area like Ba Tri District in Kien Hoa.

The rice harvest is up in 1967. The preliminary estimates
suggest that it might be 8 or 10 percent higher, particularly in the Delta, than it was in '66. There are a lot
more Hondas out in the hamlets. We've discovered that
whereas this country imported about 500 new tractors in
'66, it imported about 800 new tractors in '67--I saw some
of them the other day. Then it expects to import, based
on the estimated licensing--about 1,300 tractors in 1968.
Now you don't start buying tractors with your piastres unless you expect you're going to be able to use them, because for the average farmer that's a big investment.

The work of the RD teams improved during '67. [General
Nguyen Duc] Thang's energy, [and] improvement in the Vung
Tau training, strengthened the program considerably.
We're much more pleased with it than we were in 1966. The
number of black pajama teams went up from about 420 to
about 555, and each team had an average strength greater
than '66, although the attrition is still too high as far
as I'm concerned. We're going to do something about that
in 1968, if Thang and I have our way. The Montagnard (the
so called Truong-Son cadre) teams increased from about 84
to 108. And we had about 40 of these new civil/military
teams, based on a PF platoon, that we experimented with
up in Binh Dinh.

Now, how close did we come to our '67 hamlet goal? The
goal was cut, you remember, to 1,100 hamlets. We did
quite well in these 1,100. The HES already grades over
900 of these hamlets as being in the A, B, C category.

This is just a vast improvement. We didn't meet the
goals, but it's a mighty big improvement over what we did
in 1966, when we only met about a quarter of the 1,800
hamlet goal.

There were gains in other programs as well. You're
familiar with the Chieu Hoi rate. For the year as a whole,
it was about 34 percent higher than '66. Unfortunately,
most of this was in the big Tet surge at the beginning of
'67 and the trend has been rather substantially downward.

The refugee effort, which I've discussed with you before,
was a great deal more systematic and impressive in 1967.

Census grievance caught on as a means of finding out the
aspirations and the complaints of the people--and we've
got about 7,000 of those.

Police strength went up from 60,000 to about 73,000. Our intelligence was significantly better in the countryside. And in Saigon, we had some quite substantial successes in rolling up various terrorist cells.

Well, I could go on citing facts and figures but that's not the point of the exercise. The main thing I want to show is that, by such indicators as we have, the trend has been upward.

One more very interesting thing, which I think is a very useful indicator--self-help projects which are run by the RD Ministry out in the country. We had only about 2,000 of them with popular participation in '65. It went up to about 5,700 in '66, and we had 11,500 self-help projects out in the hamlets in 1967. We've checked the contributions that go into them; and the contributions both in kind and in cash went up to 365 million p's in '67 from only 130 million p's in '66. Now I offer this one to you because it does suggest, and only suggest, an increasing degree of commitment on the part of the people in the hamlets to the self-help process.

Enough for 1967. What's the outlook for '68. Let me say briefly I don't see how we can fail to do somewhat better in '68 than we've done in '67. Why? The '68 plans are built on our '67 experience. We made a special effort with the government of Vietnam and the ARVN to develop the 1968 plans before the end of the year; and we succeeded in almost every case. The Central RD Council has been revived by President Thieu in order to provide a coordinating machinery at the top of the GVN to pull together the efforts of all the ministries that contribute to pacification.

We also have a lot more resources in '68 than we did in '67. We're going to upgrade the RF and PF. They should be expanded by more than 40,000 in 1968 to provide continued local security, if the manpower is available. There should be increased military pressure on the local guerrillas. We expect a continued substantial increase in the strength of the national police. Another very important thing is that an attack on the Vietcong infrastructure-- the political infrastructure, a critical element in the enemy line-up--is being geared up by the government of Vietnam under the leadership of the Minister of Interior. This is a highly specialized, largely police-type operation, but there should be the beginning of a substantial payoff on that in 1968.

I certainly expect to see a great deal more economic revival in the countryside. As you know, the GVN is hoping

for and counting on and making a resource input to get
about a 20 percent increase in the rice crop in 1968.
There should be more farm machinery. So I see the agricultural revival curve going up much more substantially
because of increased security and increased inputs.

Now there'll still be serious problems. We begin '68 in
a better position than we ever had before, but we've
still got the problem of bureaucratic inefficiency.
There are still leadership difficulties that will degrade
performance. There's still a requirement for tackling
corruption in the countryside. We've got to cut down
more on the RD team attrition. There's a crying need for
better province and district chiefs, which the GVN itself
has recognized.

So where do we stand? I'm not going to say that we've
won the pacification war by any means yet. Even if these
figures look good, we still have a long way to go. There
are about 2.9 million people in the hamlets who are still
under VC control, and there are another 2.8 million who
are still living in the contested hamlets where the government and the VC are fighting over them. But the trend is
significantly upward. And I would say that, just as the
government did better in '66 than it did in '65, just as
it did somewhat better in '67 than it did in '66, with
the added input of resources and the increasing emphasis
being placed on pacification, it's hard to see why we
won't do still better in 1968.

Now the '68 plans worked out by the GVN call for about
1,480 hamlets, so from 1,100 we've gone back up to 1,480,
a reflection of our increased resources. The bulk of
them will be in III and IV Corps and, as a matter of fact,
we expect to raise this goal by the middle of the year
if it turns out that we're living up to it.

What'll happen if we just do as well as last year? Not
better, just as well. If we bring another 1.3 million
people under the sway of the government of Vietnam, it
will among other things cut the VC's population base by
another 25 percent, say out of both the contested and VC
categories. The VC already have severe recruiting problems (the pacification war is largely a war against the
VC, not the NVA, although they get involved). So this
will create even more recruiting problems for the Vietcong, who, as you know, are already declining in strength.
The new replacements coming in to replace enemy losses
are more and more NVA. This is becoming more and more a
North Vietnamese Army war. Well, if we can further attrite
the population base of the Vietcong, it'll accelerate the
process of degrading the VC. So while I don't see miracles

in the offing (I still don't see them, boundless optimist
though I am), I don't think you can call pacification any
longer "stalled" or "a failure" or "faltering." At the
least, I think we're up from a crawl to a walk. Next
year maybe we'll get up to a trot. Before I get too carried away, let me stop there and invite any questions
that you might have.

Q.: Have you prepared any breakdown for the number of
people who were removed from VC control without moving
them from their villages--in other words, who were genu-
inely pacified on the spot as opposed to those who came,
as you say, under the sway of the GVN. . . .

A.: No, but it would be easy enough to do that by deduct-
ing the number of refugees. We can look into that. . . .
No, we do not. A large portion of these are refugees.
It's very simple to answer your question. You just take
the number of refugees who came in in 1967--they obviously
came in from either contested or VC-controlled areas--we
don't have the breakdown between the two--that gives you
the input of that category.

Q.: Bob, you said that the GVN listed 900 more hamlets
in the A, B, C category this past year. . . ,

A.: We did, they didn't. We checked up on them.

Q.: Mr. Komer, you mentioned General Thang's energy as an
important factor in the successes this year. What's going
to happen to him? Is he still working with you?

A.: Well, all I can say on that matter is, yes, he is.
I just had a conference with him on Monday and I'm having
another one with him tomorrow at 3 in the afternoon--he's
back at his office in the JGS.

Q.: Was he away from his office?

A.: He was away on leave.

Q.: Could you comment on his decision at one time to leave
the Army and public work?

A.: I think that commenting on another man's presumed
decision is dangerous business. I suggest you put that
question to General Thang.

A.: You mentioned the function of the U.S. in clearing
out or destroying the large main force units so that the
GVN could then take over in a more secure environment and
continue on with pacification. How does this process. . . .
how does it seem that this process has worked in such
provinces as Hau Nghia and Gia Dinh, where U.S. forces
which had been there had moved into more isolated areas?

A.: Well, you found in Hau Nghia in particular, I was
surprised at this, that as a result of the operations--I
don't happen to have the figures handy--but that the increase in secure population in Gia Dinh and the number
of hamlets went up quite substantially. Do you happen
to have those, Bob? . . . It was also the case in Hau
Nghia. Now, there's a lot of activity in both and there
may have been some regression--I don't have the breakdown as to whether the curve upward was greatest in the
first 10 months of the year and back down in the last
two--but the improvement in both was substantial. What I
suggest is why don't you give us a buzz and we'll be happy
to give you the figures--precise figures--for both Hau
Nghia and Gia Dinh.

Q.: I know this has little to do with pacification, but
you mentioned the increase in rice production in '67.
Will that, do you think, lead to a diminution of rice
imports in '68 or will it remain at the level of about
700,000 tons?

A.: It's very hard to tell because there has been a substantial increase in urbanization, and there is also at
least 2.5 percent population increase in South Vietnam.
Therefore, even though the rice crop goes up, it may not
reduce this year (with this modest increase) the amount
of imported rice that has to be brought in. But certainly
it will stop the trend of steady increase in imports which
has occurred over the last four years. So we are sure--
reasonably certain--that we're not going to have to . . .
that the GVN isn't going to have to import any more rice.
We think, depending on how the crop goes in the Delta--and
it's still a little too early to be definitive 'cause you
have to wait usually till about early February--there's a
possibility that imports might go down. For next year I'll
be bold and make a prediction--they'll definitely go down.

Q.: Bob, since rice production is an indication of pacification, how much of the increase in the rice crop last
year do you attribute to the fact that there were no floods
or to increased rice land in production?

A.: The economic people can give you a pretty good
estimate of the amount of rice that was lost by that flood,
which was in the upper Delta provinces--Chau Doc, An Giang,
Kien Phong, etc. It was not too great in terms of overall
production, so the bulk of this increase is not just because there was no flood this year. I would say of the
increase maybe from a third to a half was because of better weather conditions. But the rest was because of increased productivity and increased security. Not much
more rice land, Barry.

A.: Ambassador, would you be willing to comment on the
new supply system that was initiated in October, whereby
all AID commodities are handled through GVN channels
once they come into the country. Has this been a success, or. . . .

A.: I can't speak about AID commodities, I can only
speak about the pacification supplies. This was a
deliberate policy of ours to build up a warehouse system
under the control of the Ministry of Revolutionary
Development which would serve both the RD program and all
other programs in the countryside with a much more ef-
ficient logistics system. Yes, I think it's proving to
be a considerable success. As you know, we have some
people in each of these warehouses to assist them in
accounting procedures, and I'm reasonably satisfied that
the logistic effort is considerably better this year
than it was before. I notice Mr. Lathram, who set up
the system, has sneaked out. He could answer the
question rather better than I. It has worked out quite
well and we're pleased with it.

General Sidle: Any further questions, gentlemen? Thank
you very much, Mr. Ambassador.

APPENDIX VI

NEWS RELEASE, OFFICE OF INFORMATION, U.S. MILITARY ASSISTANCE
COMMAND, VIETNAM, APO SAN FRANCISCO 96222, JANUARY 31, 1968

With little concern for civilian life and at heavy cost
to his own forces, the enemy pushed attacks throughout
South Vietnam during the last 24 hours, aimed primarily
at province capitals and other heavily populated areas.
Airfields and military headquarters were also attacked
in an effort to harass U.S., free-world, and RVNAF forces,
and to divert attention from the northern part of the
country. During the last 48 hours, preliminary reports
list 1,788 enemy killed in action. Friendly casualties
have been extremely light.

* * *

III CORPS TACTICAL ZONE

In Bien Hoa province at Long Binh this morning at 0255,
II Field Force V Headquarters and Long Binh complex under
rocket and mortar attack. At 0315 Bien Hoa Airfield and
III Corps Headquarters received sporadic mortar fire. At
0430, II Field Force V received light mortar attack. At
1030 receiving light scattered mortar and sniper fire.
Contact broke at unknown time. Friendly casualties: 1
KIA, 12 WIA. Enemy: 23 KIA, 3 detainees. Twelve machine
guns and 10 AK-47 captured. Buildings and vehicular damage
light.

In Hau Nghia province vicinity Cu Chi at 0315 25th Infantry
Division base camp received light mortar fire. In Binh
Duong province, town of Ben Cat under mortar and ground
attack at unreported time. 1st Infantry Division reacting.

In Bien Hoa province vicinity of Bien Hoa at 0555 enemy
conducting heavy ground attack from east end of runway at
Bien Hoa through III Corps compound toward Highway One.

In Bien Hoa province vicinity Long Binh at 0635 this
morning POW camp under ground attack from north, east, and
west.

Capital Military District BOQ under attack between 0300 and 0330 this morning. It was reported that the following installations were under attack: American Embassy, Presidential Palace, Splendid BOQ, Vietnamese heavy Headquarters, and Tan Son Nhut Airfield. All under mortar and small-arms attack. At 0400 the following additional places reported under attack: Saigon main motor pool, New Prince Hotel, BOQ Number 1, BOQ Number 3, Town house BEQ.

Reaction forces from Capital Military District were sent to BOQ, Number 3 and ran into heavy resistance suffering estimated 7 U.S. KIA, 13 WIA. Building secured at 0815. No one inside reported injured.

A large enemy force was reported near [Phu Tho] Race Track on north side of Saigon. A reaction force engaged the enemy at 0915. Fighting very intense. No report of casualties.

TSN Air Base: The base came under mortar and small-arms attack at 0330 at the east end of the field. At 0420 the west perimeter of the base was reported overrun. Two light helicopter fire teams were deployed over the base along with C-47 flare ship. Over 100 VC were reported to be on base. At 0730 it was reported that the main gate at Tan Son Nhut, the northeast storage area, gates 5 and 10, and airmen's barracks were under attack. There was also close contact in the golf course area, and the extreme west was receiving mortar and B-40 rocket rounds.

At 0900 the southwest gate near runway under heavy attack with small arms and mortars. Enemy firing from nearby houses. Also heavy concentration of enemy in the northeast storage area. At 1000 it was reported that the defenders were holding the perimeter but had many wounded casualties at the southwest gate. At 1030, eight light fireteams were sent to the area for support. At 1100 fighting reported as very intense in the southwest area and northeast storage area.

Embassy: During the time-frame 0245 to 0928 the following events occurred: At about 0300, the American Embassy was reported under attack. Embassy Duty Officer called reporting explosions in embassy compound and ground attack outside of building. Duty Officer reported also mortar rounds inside compound. Embassy building was not entered by enemy forces as well as could be determined. Heavy contact was reported in compound and streets around embassy. Duty Officer reported at 0430 that the situation was critical. Numerous large explosions, rocket and mortar rounds in compound and near embassy. Relief force from 101st Airborne Division landed on the embassy and commenced

clearing building and compound. At 0928 embassy Duty
Officer reported compound cleared and all enemy killed.
Identified as being from the C-10 VC Sapper BN. Nineteen
enemy in civilian clothes entered embassy compound with
demolitions to destroy embassy. Enemy was supported from
hotel roof across the street from embassy with unknown
type fire support. Enemy did not gain access to embassy
building.

Preliminary casualty report: friendly: 6 KIA, 5 WIA; and
enemy: 19 KIA.

MAF: A cursory check of casualty figures for the period
1800, 30 January, to 1200, 31 January, shows the following
interim results: U.S. and free-world forces: 15 killed
and 140 wounded; RVNAF: 15 ARVN killed and 20 wounded.

Operation Scotland: East of Khe Sanh, yesterday at 0035
a company from the 26th Marine Regiment detected 10-15
enemy moving southeast from friendly position. Unit fired
10 rounds 60 mm. mortar. Results: friendly: none; enemy:
10 killed.

Operation Lancaster: In Quang Tri province, six kilometers
west of Camp Carroll, Sunday at 1300, a 3rd Marine Division
recon team found the following enemy arms cache: 150-200
rounds of 82 mm. mortar ammunition, 33 individual weapons
QI RPG rocket launchers, 1 82 mm. mortar tube. Numerous
gear was also found.

Operation Kentucky: In Quang Tri province 10 kilometers
north Con Thien, a U.S. regiment observed an enemy convoy
and fired artillery and requested tactical aircraft which
resulted in secondary explosion and a fire was started.
Nearby, in southern North Vietnam, four to five suspected
SAM sites were located. An aircraft strike was directed
onto the suspected SAM sites. Results: nine secondary
explosions, including a huge fireball.

In Quang Tri province, nine kilometers south-southeast of
Quang Tri city at 0410 this morning, a Marine position
came under mortar and ground attack. The enemy force was
repulsed. Area reported secure 0900. Result: 14 enemy
KIA, 2 detained. Friendly casualties were 9 WIA (USMC).

In Thua Thien province, 12 kilometers southeast of Hue
this morning at 0410 the Phu Bai Airfield received approximately 35 rounds of mixed 60 mm. mortar and 122 mm.
rocket rounds. No damage to airfield. Minor damage to
facilities. Result: friendly: 4 KIA, 14 WIA; enemy:
unknown.

In Quang Nam province, 19 kilometers west of Hoi An at
0110 this morning the 7th Marine Regiment command post

came under mortar attack. No casualties, negligible damage. At 0405, a 7th Marines company received harassing mortar fire. Results: no casualties and negligible damage.

In Quang Nam province, three kilometers southeast of Da Nang, at 0335 this morning, the USMC air facility at Marble Mountain was attacked with approximately 25 rounds of estimated 122 mm. rockets. The attack ended at 0346. Result: friendly: 1 USMC WIA. Material and aircraft damage was reported as moderate.

In Quang Nam province, 21 kilometers northwest of Da Nang, yesterday at 1800, 1st Marine Division recon team engaged approximately 25 enemy with small-arms and automatic-weapons fire. Artillery supported. Result: Marines: none; enemy: 11 KIA.

In Quang Nam province, four kilometers west of Da Nang, at 1640 hours, elements of the 1st Marine Division conducted ground sweep in the suspected areas from which the attack on the Da Nang Air Base was initiated. Result: 1,000 detained.

In Quang Nam province, 14 kilometers east of An Hoa at 2230 yesterday, 1st Marine Division reconnaissance team observed an unknown size enemy force carrying radio equipment and rockets. Tactical air strikes conducted with excellent target coverage. Result: friendly: none; enemy: 30 KIA.

Korean Marine force inserted as reaction force to enemy attack at Hoi An repulsed the enemy attack and killed 52 enemy. Nineteen suspects were detained. ROK casualties were light. Five Marines were wounded.

The results of the attack against the I Corps headquarters complex have been updated to 64 enemy killed and 80 suspects detained. Friendly casualties were light.

In Quang Nam province, three kilometers southeast of Da Nang from 0400 to 1731 yesterday, the 1st Marine Division Military Police Battalion and ARVN military forces conducted an area sweep operation east of the Da Nang Bridge. Result: enemy: 31 KIA, 1,748 detained; friendly: 2 Marines killed and 6 wounded. ARVN casualties were light.

Operation Wheeler/Wallowa Area, 14 kilometers northwest of Tam Ky at 0930 yesterday, cavalry elements engaged an estimated 200-300 enemy with organic weapons. Artillery supported. Time enemy broke contact unknown. Result: U.S.: none; enemy: 36 killed.

In Quang Tin province, 22 kilometers southeast of Tam Ky at 0410 this morning, Chu Lai Airfield came under mortar and rocket attack. Suspected rocket position was identified and counterfire was called with unknown results. Two Marines were killed and 5 wounded. Aircraft and material damage was reported as moderate.

In Quang Tin province, this morning at 0505 Tam Ky city received an unknown number of mortar rounds. No damage and no casualties were reported.

In Quang Ngai province, Quang Ngai city received a mortar and ground attack this morning at 0405. Gun and flare ships from Americal Division supported by fire. ARVN AC-47 aircraft also supported. Attack ceased prior to daybreak. Light contact reported. Results: friendly: no casualties; enemy: unknown.

IV CORPS TACTICAL ZONE

Casualties report for period from 31 January 0007 to 31 January 1330 hours: U.S.: 12 killed, 34 wounded. . . ; enemy: 197 killed, 47 detained.

In Dinh Tuong province: The provincial capital, My Tho, came under enemy mortar attack. Results: none reported.

The town of Can Be came under attack from enemy mortars. Results: 4 civilians wounded.

The town of Cai Lay came under enemy mortar attack. Results: none reported.

In Chau Doc province: The provincial capital, Chau Phu [under mortar and ground attack. Second Battalion, 15th Regiment (ARVN) Infantry sent] from Long Xuyen and [2nd Battalion, 16th Regiment] (ARVN) Infantry from Cam Lanh. . .

In Kien Hoa province: The provincial capital of Truc Giang [Ben Tre] came under enemy mortar attack. No results reported. . . .

The district capital of Ba Tri came under enemy mortar attack. No results reported.

The district capital of Binh Dai came under enemy mortar attack. No results reported.

In Vinh Long province: The Vinh Long Airfield came under mortar and ground attack by an estimated three enemy companies. Results: 7 U.S. KIA, 20 U.S. WIA, light damage to facilities and material; enemy: unknown.

In Sa Dec province: The provincial capital of Sa Dec came under enemy mortar attack and ground attack. No results reported.

In Phong Dinh province: The provincial capital of Can Tho came under enemy mortar and ground attack. Results:

friendly: 5 U.S. KIA, 19 U.S. WIA; ARVN unknown; enemy: 85 KIA, 33 detained, 13 individual weapons and 1 crew-served weapon captured.

In Vinh Binh province: In Tra Vinh, enemy attacked and blew up power plant. Results: 2 U.S. wounded; enemy unknown.

In Ba Xuyen province: The airfield at Soc Trang came under enemy mortar attack. Results: none reported.

In Kien Giang province: The provincial capital of Rach Gia came under enemy mortar and ground attack. Results: friendly: none; enemy: 25 killed, 8 detained, 2 75 mm. recoilless rifles and numerous individual weapons captured.

In Bac Lieu province: The provincial capital, Vinh Loi, came under enemy mortar attack and small-arms harassing fire. Results: friendly: none reported; enemy: 1 KIA, 6 detained, 3 individual weapons and 1 crew-served weapon captured.

In An Xuyen province: The provincial capital, Quang Long [Camau], came under enemy mortar and ground attack. Results: friendly: 40 (ARVN) WIA; enemy: 80 killed, 1 75 mm. recoilless rifle and 50 individual weapons captured.

I FIELD FORCE

Cumulative Casualty Figures from 1800 29 January to 1200 31 January: friendly: 157 KIA, 330 WIA   (breakdown: U.S., 50 KIA, 126 WIA; ROK, 7 WIA; ARVN, 93 KIA, 183 WIA; CIDG, 14 KIA, 14 WIA); enemy: 818 KIA, 160 detained, 254 individual weapons and 32 crew-served seized.

Qui Nhon: Yesterday at 1800 ROK Army elements secured the radio station. At 1840 CIDG [Civilian Irregular Defense Group] elements secured the railroad station. Today at 0145 sniper fire was being received in the outpost LINE. At 0325 the Army supply depot received three rounds mortar fire--light damage.

Kontum city: Received and repulsed 19 separate ground attacks between 1845 and 2330 yesterday at various installations. As of 2330 Kontum city area had received an estimated 400 rounds mixed caliber mortar fire.

This morning at 0230 Kontum Airfield and ARVN headquarters and Kontum sector headquarters all came under intense mortar fire. At 0445 the U.S. Special Forces Camp north of Kontum Airfield was attacked by an estimated 300 to 500 VC. Enemy force repelled at 0515 and contact broke at 0550. At 0700 Kontum city again came under intense mortar attack. Airfield received intense sniper fire. U.S. 4th Infantry Division presently moving one battalion to reinforce

defending force. One CIDG company also moving to reinforce. At first light TAC air engaged 600 to 700 enemy
three kilometers northeast of Kontum. Results: 130
enemy KIA by body count.

Ban Me Thuot: At 0215 today east airfield received a
mortar attack, followed by a ground attack. Contact
broke at 0240. At 0446 the MACV compound received a
ground attack by an unknown size enemy force employing
small arms and automatic weapons. Contact broke at 0450.

Nha Trang: At 0130 today Roberts Compound (MACV and
CORDS) received sniper fire. BOQ received ground attack.
Headquarters I Field Force Victor received sniper fire.
City reported quiet at 1030 with two CSF companies sweeping
to west of city.

Casualties: friendly: no change from that previously
reported; enemy: 103 KIA, 33 detained, 54 individual
weapons and 4 crew-served captured.

Pleiku: Pleiku city was reported quiet as of 2400 last
night, with elements of 22nd ARVN Ranger Battalion in
sporadic contact with unknown size enemy force outside
city. Cumulative results: friendly: 7 KIA, 22 WIA;
enemy: 104 KIA, 9 individual weapons and 2 crew-served
captured.

Phu Cat: This morning at 0445, the subsector headquarters
at Phu Cat received intense mortar attack followed by
ground attack. VC sappers penetrated compound at 0550.
Contact reported light at 0630. Results unknown.

Plei Djereng: Under rocket and mortar attack at 0350
this morning. No further information on this.

Phan Thiet: At 0315 this morning received mortar attack
followed by ground attack by estimated two enemy battalions.
Enemy penetrated outer defenses but was ejected from town.
Heaviest action vicinity MACV compound. Action reported
sporadic at 1020 with elements 1st Brigade, 101st U.S.
Airborne Division coordinating with ARVN units to block
enemy routes of withdrawal. City continues to receive
sporadic 60 mm. and 82 mm. and small-arms fire. U.S.
personnel report that VC within city observed changing to
civilian clothes. Initial results: friendly: 2 U.S.
WIA; enemy: unknown.

AIR NORTH

Air Force: Eight military storage structures and supplies
in a transshipment point were destroyed when F-4 Phantom
crews from the 366th Tactical Fighter Wing at Da Nang
struck the areas 3.2 kilometers (two miles) west of Dong

Hoi to 35.2 kilometers (22 miles) northwest of the coastal city. The pilots also reported silencing one AA gun and causing one secondary explosion and two sustained fires.

Five 20-foot sampans were destroyed and four more damaged by Phantom crews from the 8th TFW [Tactical Fighter Wing] hitting a concentration of water supply craft 35.2 kilometers (22 miles) northwest of Dong Hoi.

Two 50-foot barges were damaged by F-105 Thunderchief pilots from the 388th TFW on a strike 19.2 kilometers (12 miles) northwest of the same city. They also sank three boats and caused one secondary fire 17.6 kilometers (11 miles) west-southwest of there.

Twelve sustained fires and one secondary explosion were caused by F-105 pilots from the 388th Tactical Fighter Wing when they hit a military storage area 22.4 kilometers (14 miles) northwest of Dong Hoi.

Navy: Six trucks were destroyed in a 20-truck convoy 65.6 kilometers (41 miles) south-southeast of Vinh. A-6 Intruder pilots from the USS *Kitty Hawk* reported numerous fires were burning as they left the area.

Three trucks were destroyed by F-4 Phantom pilots when they attacked an eight-truck convoy heading south 72 kilometers (45 miles) south-southeast of Vinh.

Eleven more trucks were destroyed or damaged along Route 1-A between Vinh and Dong Hoi. The *Kitty Hawk* A-6 crews reported this traffic was also moving south when struck.

Marine Corps: Two secondary fires resulted from A-6 Intruder strikes on truck convoys 16 kilometers (10 miles) north of Gio Linh. Other Chu Lai-based Intruder crews reported four secondary explosions when they hit more truck convoys just north and south of Dong Hoi.

Artillery positions 11.2 kilometers (seven miles) north-northwest of Con Thien were hit by A-4 Skyhawks from Chu Lai.

Truck and river traffic 8 kilometers (five miles) south of Dong Hoi was struck by Da Nang-based Intruders.

Air Force pilots flew 27 missions over North Vietnam yesterday. Marine Corps pilots flew eight missions. Number of Navy missions is unavailable at this time.

APPENDIX VII

NEWS RELEASE, OFFICE OF INFORMATION, U.S. MILITARY ASSISTANCE
COMMAND, VIETNAM, APO SAN FRANCISCO 96222, FEBRUARY 1, 1968

Morning Release: Situation as of 1000 Hours, Saigon Time

I CORPS SUMMARY

In Quang Tri province: At 1500 hours, 31 January,
Quang Tri city was attacked by an estimated two NVA
battalions in the northeastern portion of the town.
Elements of the 1st Air Cav Division are in the center
of the town. The area is under control with sporadic
action continuing. Casualties undetermined.

In Thua Thien province: At 1300 yesterday, Hue city was
attacked by an estimated enemy company. U.S. Marine
companies were dispatched as a reaction force, getting
there at 1500. The enemy force holding a bridge and the
amphibious landing ramp southeast of Hue were attacked
by the Marines. The bridge and loading ramp are now
under friendly control. The 1st ARVN Division compound
in Hue received sporadic small-arms fire and automatic-
weapons fire. That portion of Hue north of the river in
the Imperial City is surrounded by enemy elements. However, no contact has been reported. Casualties are
undetermined.

Quang Nam province: Morning 31 January villages four and
seven miles west of Hoi An were attacked by an unknown
size enemy force. ARVN and ROK Marines were inserted
into the respective areas and encountered sporadic resistance. All MACV personnel reported ok in the Hoi An
area, and the city reported secure at 1200 yesterday.
At 2345 yesterday ARVN sources reported that the Duy Xuyen
district headquarters was occupied at approximately 1940
by an unknown size enemy force.

In Quang Tin province from 0500-1650, Tam Ky city was
reported under attack by an unknown size enemy force

attempting to overrun the area. All attacks repulsed by
ARVN and Americal Division personnel. Artillery and gun-
ships supported throughout. Area reports secure at 1650.
Results: friendly: KIA 27 ARVN, 57 WIA ARVN; enemy:
KIA 226, 65 detained. Weapons: IW 86, CS [crew-served]
14 captured.

Early 31 January Quang Ngai city attacked by unknown
sized enemy force. Late afternoon reported that city was
in a secure status with sporadic contact in isolated areas.
No casualties reported. As of 0425 this morning sporadic
contact continues. Accumulative casualties for I
Corps. . . . 1800, 29 January through 2400, 31 January:
friendly: 146 KIA (U.S. 74, 69 ARVN, 3 ROK), 580 wounded
(U.S. 357, 208 ARVN, 15 ROK); enemy: 1,653 KIA, 1,394
detained.

II CORPS SUMMARY

Kontum: Yesterday the Kontum Airfield received approximately 200 rounds of unknown caliber mortar fire. Field
now closed. MACV sector compound and Special Forces
compound also received mortar fire. As of 2400 hours,
sporadic small arms and mortar fire continued. Enemy
controls 50 percent of city; however, all friendly compounds and installations are controlled by friendly forces.
Results: U.S.: 7 KIA, 55 WIA; enemy: 210 KIA, 2 detained.

Pleiku: No contact reported at 2400 yesterday. Results
of yesterday's action: friendly: unknown; enemy: 104
KIA, 9 detained.

Darlac-Ban Me Thuot: 1620 hours estimated two to three
enemy battalions reported in the city. Contact is heavy.
MACV compound and 23 ARVN Division headquarters receiving
small-arms fire. At 0100 this morning, some probing of
the 47th ARVN region in the defensive perimeter continued.
Cumulative results: friendly: total: 42 KIA (2 U.S.
and 40 ARVN); enemy: 91 KIA and 28 detained.

Phan Thiet: At 2400 hours yesterday. No further contact
reported.

Ninh Hoa: All contact report as broken at 2400 yesterday.
Results: 1 WIA, unknown light damage to material and
facilities; enemy: 15 KIA and 3 detained.

Nha Trang: 2300 yesterday I Field Force headquarters and
Nha Trang Air Base and 5th Special Forces headquarters all
received mortar attacks. Also small-arms fire in vicinity
of the artillery headquarters. Results: friendly: 21
KIA (12 U.S., 7 ARVN, 2 CIDG [Civilian Irregular Defense
Group]), 56 wounded (10 U.S., 23 ARVN, 22 CIDG); enemy:
103 KIA, 33 detained, 54 individual weapons taken.

Tuy Hoa: At 2400 yesterday reported that all contact had
broken. Results: friendly: 14 KIA, 54 WIA (ARVN);
enemy: 76 KIA, 12 detained (weapons quantity captured
unknown).

Qui Nhon: At 2215, an ammo supply point was attacked by
unknown sized force with recoilless rifles and small arms.
Cumulative results are: friendly: 1 KIA (ARVN), 12 WIA
(6 U.S., 5 ARVN, 1 CIV); enemy: 50 KIA, 1 detained.

Cumulative casualty figures for II Corps from 1800, 29th
to 2400, on the 31st: friendly: 157 KIA (50 U.S. and
107 ARVN), 330 WIA (126 U.S. and 197 ARVN); enemy: 818
KIA, 160 detained, 250 individual weapons and 32 crew-
served weapons captured.

III CORPS SUMMARY

A battalion from the 25th Infantry Division exchanged fire
with unknown sized enemy unit four miles southeast of Gia
Ray in Hau Nghia province. Enemy broke contact at 1820.
No friendly casualties. Enemy KIA is 20.

In Bien Hoa province near Long Binh, 2203 yesterday, a
battalion of the 101st Airborne made contact with the
enemy. No tactical details were available. Friendly
casualties were 6 KIA and 14 medevac. Enemy lost 99 KIA.

Capital Military District: Tan Son Nhut: Yesterday from
1200 to 1500, a strong enemy force located on the west
side of the air base and in storage area on northeast side
of base. U.S. forces moved in to clear enemy strongpoints.
The Joint General Staff compound on east side of the air
base came under mortar attack at 1230 yesterday. The base
perimeter was generally secure with some reports of snipers
on the base at 1300. By 1545 the enemy was reported with-
drawing from its positions on the west perimeter of the
base. One mile east of the base there were heavy skir-
mishes as enemy forces attempted to withdraw to the village
northeast of the base. Two U.S. units in the southwest
area of the base forced the enemy to withdraw. By 2030
it was reported that all enemy had been cleared from the
southwest portion of the air base, with only sporadic
sniper fire being received. At 0705 this morning light
contact was reported continuing on the east perimeter of
Tan Son Nhut with an unknown sized enemy force.

Race Track area: There was initially heavy fighting around
the track yesterday. U.S. forces arrived (MPs) and drove
the enemy out of their positions, toward the PX warehouses
on Plantation Road. A platoon was dispatched to the PX
warehouse complex to reinforce. By 1800 that area was
secure and under control of U.S. forces.

Yesterday at the New Embassy Hotel in downtown Saigon an
enemy company established a strongpoint. [Vietnamese MPs
with] U.S. and ROK MPs took the hotel at 1730.

At the American ambassador's house, U.S. report small-arms
fire and a reaction force was dispatched. Two Claymore
mines were detonated near the house without causing any
damage.

At the southeast corner of the JGS compound in the
vicinity of BOQ 3, an estimated enemy company moved into
the surrounding houses yesterday morning. An MP unit first
attack and later a U.S. unit with two tanks and two APCs
moved into the area and secured it by 1800 hours. Results:
16 U.S. KIA; enemy: 2 KIA.

Cumulative casualties in III Corps from 1800 on 29 through
2400 on 31 January: friendly: 45 KIA U.S., 313 WIA,
ARVN figures not available at present; enemy: 1,290 KIA,
119 detained, 62 IW and 65 CS captured.

Cumulative figures of casualties in the Capital Zone from
1800 on 29 through 2400 on 31 January: friendly: 114 KIA
(U.S. 43, ARVN 71), WIA 304 (U.S. 91, ARVN 213); enemy:
639 KIA, 51 detained, 249 IW, 0 CS.

IV CORPS SUMMARY

Major contact in Dinh Tuong province was made at My Tho.
Firing continued in the city with concentrations of enemy
on the western edge of the city. The U.S. Advisory compound isolated from the ARVN headquarters, 7th Division.
Cumulative results: 1 U.S. KIA and 5 WIA.

In Kien Hoa province: The enemy is in and around the city
of Ben Tre with a major concentration in the soccer field.
Enemy forces are believed to be of regimental strength.
Cumulative results: friendly: 14 ARVN KIA, 23 WIA; enemy:
1 detained.

In Vinh Long province, the major contact is in and around
Vinh Long city and airfield. Cumulative results are 10 U.S.
KIA, 23 U.S. WIA; enemy: 30 KIA and 8 detainees.

In Vinh Binh province: In the town of Tra Vinh action has
quieted down from the previously reported heavy contact.
Light to moderate contact reported on the outskirts of
town. Results: friendly: unknown; enemy: 22 KIA and
12 weapons captured.

In An Xuyen province an attack of undetermined size was
made in the provincial capital of Ca Mau. Cumulative results: 16 ARVN KIA and 26 ARVN WIA; enemy: 200 KIA and 6
detained, 73 IW captured.

Soc Trang, in Ba Xuyen province: An estimated enemy battalion still reported in contact with ARVN Ranger and infantry

elements on the outskirts of town. Contact is diminishing. Cumulative results: 6 ARVN KIA, 22 ARVN WIA; enemy:
30 KIA and 15 IW captured.

Can Tho: Contact continues with friendly forces in control
of the city hunting down small bands of the enemy. Cumulative results are 5 U.S. KIA, 5 U.S. WIA, and 5 ARVN KIA,
17 ARVN WIA; enemy: 95 KIA and 33 detained, 62 IW.

Chau Doc province: Chau Phu city reports major enemy units
holding large portions of the city . . . contact reported
light. ARVN infantry elements engaged with the enemy on
the southeast edge of town.

Cumulative casualties for all action in IV Corps for same
dated periods: friendly: 73 KIA (20 U.S., 53 ARVN) 171
WIA (42 U.S. and 129 ARVN); enemy: 559 KIA, 138 detained.

AIR NORTH

Air Force: Forty-seven miles northwest of Dong Hoi
yesterday, seven railroad cars were destroyed by F-105s,
also three trucks 19 miles north of Mu Gia pass. Three
50-foot barges destroyed along the coast 24 miles southeast of Dong Hoi. An automatic-weapons site 116 miles
northwest of Hanoi was silenced by F-105s. Railroad
lines were cut 78 miles northwest of Hanoi, with nine
road cuts reported in the Panhandle.

Marine: [Attacked] trucks, got secondaries [explosions]
near Dong Hoi. . . .

Navy: Twenty-nine miles northwest of Vinh pilots cratered
approaches to a railroad bridge. Bridge damaged. A truck
convoy 43 miles northwest of Dong Hoi was damaged. A
highway bridge 34 miles north of Vinh was bombed and no
BDA [bomb damage account] is available.

AIR SOUTH

Air Force tactical fighter aircraft were airborne 402
times yesterday. Bombed and strafed troop concentrations
and base camps throughout the Republic. Supported Operation Scotland 184 times. There were 25 FAC [Forward Air
Control] missions flown in Operation Scotland. Eight air
rescue missions were flown in Scotland. There were 52
air strikes supporting other allied forces in other
search-and-destroy missions. Twenty-five of these supported MacArthur in the 4th Division and the 173rd in
Pleiku area. Air Force pilots and crews were airborne
122 times answering immediate air requests from allied
forces and free-world forces who were in immediate contact
with the enemy. In the Quang Ngai province 27 enemy were
credited to [Air Force] strike pilots. Republicwide,
Dragon ships [AC-47s] were airborne 30 times in support of
military installations under attack. They provided firepower and flare light.

In other actions, FAC were airborne 57 times in the Republic.

B-52 item: Hit bunkers, trench network, observation posts, and artillery positions 16 miles north of Khe Sanh in the Operation Scotland area yesterday afternoon. This morning, the big bombers struck enemy troop concentrations three miles southeast of Khe Sanh.

Evening Release

CASUALTY REPORT

1. The interim casualty figures for all action in the Republic for the period 1800, 29 January to 2400, 31 January are: enemy--4,959 killed and 1,862 detained; total allied--555 killed and 1,698 wounded: U.S.--232 killed and 929 wounded, ARVN--300 killed and 727 wounded, FWMAF--3 killed and 22 wounded.

MARINE AMPHIBIOUS FORCE

2. Operation Wheeler/Wallowa (Quang Tin province)--Four kilometers northwest of Tam Ky yesterday at 1155, a cavalry unit engaged an unknown size enemy force east of Route 1. Result: friendly: 1 KIA, 2 WIA (medevac); enemy: 57 KIA.

3. Operation Muscatine (Quang Ngai province)--Seventeen kilometers northeast of Quang Ngai city at 0940 yesterday, a company from the 198th Light Infantry Brigade engaged an estimated 150 enemy moving east. Artillery and gunships supported. Time enemy broke contact is unknown. Result: friendly: none; enemy: 44 killed.

Yesterday in Quang Ngai province, seven kilometers northeast of Quang Ngai city at 1300, a company from the 11th Light Infantry Brigade engaged an estimated 90-100 enemy carrying weapons and packs. Artillery and gunships supported. Time enemy broke contact is unknown. Result: friendly: none; enemy: 18 KIA.

4. In Thua Thien province, at Phu Bai at 0210, two enemy mortar rounds impacted in the Phu Bai ammunition dump. Material damage was reported as light.

5. Yesterday afternoon in Quang Nam province 14 kilometers east of An Hoa--an enemy force estimated at 400 sighted moving east on a trail with packs, weapons, rockets, and radio equipment. Artillery missions were fired and an AC-47 supported. One secondary explosion was observed. Cumulative results: friendly: none; enemy: 80 KIA.

I FIELD FORCE, VIETNAM

6. The situation in Kontum city is as follows; Kontum Airfield is under almost continuous small-arms fire and is closed. Highway 14 through the city is open. All key

compounds are in friendly hands. Estimated two-three
enemy battalions in the city, but only light and sporadic
contacts with enemy employing small-arms and automatic-
weapons fire and occasional mortar fire. Enemy forces
have been identified as elements of the 304 VC LF Battalion, 407 VC Sapper Battalion, K2 Battalion, and the
174th NVA Regiment.

7. At Ban Me Thuot: At 1240 an estimated NVA regiment
was observed approximately three kilometers south of
Ban Me Thuot. Forward air controller was on station,
tactical air strikes were flown in support. . . . ARVN
forces made contact as of 1320.

8. Qui Nhon: Small-arms attacks against the national
police station were repulsed. Some small-arms attacks
in western part of city. Two CIDG companies presently
sweeping western part of the city. One battalion ROK Army
securing northern part of the city. An element of the 41st
ARVN Infantry Regiment is in the city. Enemy forces are
identified as two-three platoons of D-10 VC Sapper Company.

9. In Tuyen Duc province at Da Lat this morning at 0100,
one VC company launched an attack from within the city
towards the southwestern portion of the city. Initial
attack was against a U.S. MP billet. Enemy employed unknown caliber mortar and small-arms fire followed by a
ground attack. Billet presently in VC hands. An additional two VC platoons are holding the market place in
the vicinity of the center of the city, and seizing Vietnamese civilians apparently as hostages. Another additional VC platoon is holding the center of the city
firing on targets of opportunity, Vietnamese civilians,
and military. A provisional company, being formed from
personnel stationed at the National Military Academy
(Da Lat) and RF units are being deployed as reaction
forces. U.S. gunships are in support of friendly forces.
Results: friendly (U.S.): 2 WIA (evac. unknown); enemy:
unknown.

II FIELD FORCE, VIETNAM

10. In Hau Nghia province at 0113 Cu Chi subsector received a mortar and ground attack. Sixty to 80 rounds
of 82 mm. mortar fire were received. The ground attack
by an unknown size enemy force reached the subsector
headquarters gate but was repulsed. The enemy broke
contact at 0410. Gunships and AC-47 Dragon ships supported. Results: friendly: 2 U.S. KIA, 1 PF WIA;
enemy: unknown.

11. Yesterday afternoon an attack on Ben Cat subsector
was reported. Rapid reaction force from U.S. 1st Infantry
Division was inserted with no contact reported. Enemy
broke contact at 0600. Result: friendly: 13 KIA (ARVN),

26 WIA (5 U.S., 21 ARVN); enemy: 42 KIA, 16 individual weapons captured, and 5 crew-served weapons captured.

12. At 0645 this morning, an enemy force estimated at 200 strong attacked the Can Tho radio station. At last report, the attack was continuing.

13. In Chau Phu, provincial capital of Chau Duc province, ARVN forces are conducting clearing operations in the city. It has been reported that enemy units are using civilians as shields in the fighting. The MACV compound, which received an enemy attack, was reached by ARVN elements early this morning. Results: friendly: 1 U.S. killed, 20 wounded (5 U.S. and 15 ARVN). In addition, 50 civilians have been injured. Enemy casualties are unknown.

14. In Ben Tre, it was reported at 1200 today that ARVN elements continue to engage elements of an estimated enemy regiment. The enemy are dug in on the south bank of the Ben Tre River. Results: ARVN: unknown; 150 civilians injured or killed (no breakout). One hundred fifty enemy have been killed.

AIR NORTH

15. The following Air North information is repeated from the MACV morning release:

U.S. pilots flew 58 missions over North Vietnam yesterday in generally overcast weather conditions. Air Force pilots flew 38, Marine Corps pilots 12, and Navy aviators 8.

Air Force: Seven railroad cars were destroyed by F-105 Thunderchief pilots from the 388th Tactical Fighter Wing 76 kilometers (47 miles) northwest of Dong Hoi yesterday.

Other 388th TFW Thunderchief pilots destroyed three trucks 30 kilometers (19 miles) north of Mu Gia Pass.

Three 50-foot barges were destroyed along the coast 38 kilometers (24 miles) southeast of Dong Hoi by Phantom crews from the 366th TFW.

An automatic weapons site 187 kilometers (116 miles) northwest of Hanoi was silenced by F-105 pilots from the 355th TFW. Other pilots reported cutting rail lines 125 kilometers (78 miles) north-northwest of Hanoi.

Nine road cuts were reported by Air Force pilots hitting lines of communication and storage areas in the Panhandle.

Marine Corps: A secondary explosion was touched off by A-6 Intruder crews from Da Nang and Chu Lai hitting truck traffic near Dong Hoi yesterday.

Marine F-8 Crusader and A-4 Skyhawk pilots struck enemy troop concentrations, artillery positions, and antiaircraft positions in and north of the DMZ.

Navy: A railroad and highway bridge 46.6 kilometers (29
miles) north-northwest of Vinh was damaged and the approaches cratered by A-4 Skyhawk pilots from the USS *Kitty
Hawk* yesterday.

A four-truck convoy 68.8 kilometers (43 miles) northwest
of Dong Hoi was damaged by A-6 Intruders.

A highway bridge 54.4 kilometers (34 miles) north of
Vinh was bombed by other Intruder crews but bomb damage
assessment was not available.

AIR SOUTH

16.   B-52 Missions: Air Force B-52 crews flew two missions in support of Operation Scotland this morning. Both
strikes were directed against ammunition storage areas
located 12 kilometers (eight miles) north-northwest of
Khe Sanh in Quang Tri province.

On the first mission, pilots reported 13 secondary explosions two to four times the size of a normal bomb burst.
No BDA was reported on the second.

Marine Corps: 1st Marine Air Wing pilots flew 85 tactical
sorties in South Vietnam yesterday. The pilots were
credited with killing 60 enemy and destroying or damaging
107 fortifications, nine bunkers, two gun positions, and
a sampan. They also touched off five secondary explosions
and three fires.

Helicopter crews flew 108 armed sorties throughout the
northern provinces.

PRESS BRIEFING, GEN. WILLIAM C. WESTMORELAND, SAIGON, FEBRUARY 1, 1968

It seems to me that the plan we have seen unfolded was drafted in Hanoi in September of last year. As I reconstruct the plan it was in three phases.

The first phase began the latter part of October and continued through the middle of January--involved both a military and a psychological campaign.

The psychological campaign had two major parts--first an international campaign designed to stop the air strikes in North Vietnam. The second was focused at the people of those countries providing troops to South Vietnam and to South Vietnam itself. This involved . . . starting a rumor that a coalition government was in the offing.

The military campaign during the first phase involved attacks in four places within South Vietnam designed to inflict casualties on RVN and U.S. and [free-world forces] to force us to deploy large numbers of troops to counter their offensives and hopefully to secure pieces of real estate that they could call their own.

These four [places] were: around Dak To as the first objective in domination of the Kontum province. . . .

The next area was in southern I Corps and northern II Corps, designed to secure population that had been lost in the past several months.

Third, along the Cambodian border . . . to force us to deploy large numbers of forces. . . .

Fourth, Binh Duong province--Highway 4. This campaign was designed to dominate Binh Duong and Highway 4. . . .

The second phase--we have seen unfold these past several days beginning with Tet. This phase was designed to infiltrate provincial areas, cities, and towns [and] destroy government installations and military headquarters--to shell airfields, etc.

This was a change in strategy by the enemy where he is using NVA forces to spearhead his terroristic attacks.

Phase three is yet to come. It will involve the largest number of troops committed to date. It will involve a major campaign in Thua Thien [province]. He has prepared for this campaign. He has built up a major logistics system in Laos to support this campaign. During the dry season in Laos he has been moving supplies in unprecedented numbers to support this campaign.

REVIEW OF THE SITUATION AS IT NOW STANDS

Since 1800 hours, 29 January, official beginning of the Tet truce, the enemy has lost 5,800 men killed. The GVN, U.S., and free-world forces have taken 2,500 detainees. As you know, they are detained and then screened for POWs . . . unusual characteristic of this number is that a high percentage [of detainees] are POWs.

Five hundred thirty friendly forces have been killed--of this number 200 are American.

I CORPS

The enemy infiltrated Quang Tri province. Most of the troops seem to have changed into civilian clothes. Three hundred enemy have been killed. The enemy has infiltrated here with a sizable force and now hold a sizable portion of [Quang Tri] city. The ARVN is attempting to clear the city of enemy units.

Da Nang is quiet but the enemy force is reported south of Da Nang this morning, and attempts are being made to establish contact.

There is some rocket fire near Hue-Phu Bai. . . . South of Da Nang at Hoi An there is considerable action to rout the enemy who have infiltrated that area.

The enemy has infiltrated the hospital at Quang Ngai. This is characteristic of the enemy--to infiltrate hospitals, churches, etc.

II CORPS

The enemy still holds a portion of the town of Kontum.

Pleiku now is quiet. There was . . . shelling and there has been considerable destruction as a result of this fighting.

An NVA regiment has infiltrated the environs of Ban Me Thuot.

Qui Nhon infiltrated by the enemy.

Nha Trang now clear and the enemy driven out. During the
withdrawal the enemy was interdicted and there was a running battle.

Some activity in Da Lat today along the roads leading to
the city, and some VC activity at the market place.

III CORPS

Major infiltration was in Saigon and Cholon. The enemy
is now in several pockets and in many cases is broken
down into small elements and continues to harass.

Bien Hoa was a major target in the III Corps area . . .
U.S. installations as well as the airfield. Here the
enemy suffered great casualties.

IV CORPS

Can Tho--some enemy elements . . . major infiltration into
Ben Tre, the capital of Kien Hoa, where the enemy holds a
part of this provincial capital.

My Tho--heavy fighting within the city and considerable
destruction. The enemy is being progressively driven out.

In summary . . . this second phase was a bold one, showing
callous disregard for human life. . . .

The enemy has paid dearly--has lost to date at least 5,800
men.

Q.: How long will he be able to keep up this tempo?

A.: Several more days.

There is evidence that he is about to run out of steam,
yet he does have some reserves yet to be committed. We
are aware of these. We are watching the situation carefully and I am confident that any further initiatives can
be blunted.

In respect now to the third phase which is yet to come,
the enemy has massed a number of troops into the Quang
Tri, Thua Thien area. Since the 17th of January I have
concentrated heavy air strikes into the area. Our pilots
and Forward Air Controllers have observed over 2,000
secondary explosions or fires. These massive air strikes
have no doubt hindered the enemy plans. But I still give
him the capability of striking in force in that area. If
he does attack, he will have to accept great risks because
of the preparations we have made and the firepower available to us.

Q.: Is there any evidence the enemy was counting on a
general uprising?

A.: He has classified this phase as one where a general

uprising will take place. It is interesting to note that the propaganda that has come from the NLF says that the Vietnamese troops were turning their guns against their allies.

Q.: Who do you think has made this plan?

A.: No doubt the plan was developed by a military staff and approved by the leadership in North Vietnam. I felt that there would be fireworks during the Tet period, and therefore had my troops in a state of alert. We foresaw the initiatives in the populated areas, and certain re-deployments were made in anticipation of it. . . .

Q.: Redeployments?

A.:   . . . We had a number of troops committed in the Bien Long, Phuoc Long, north Tay Ninh areas . . . when it ap-peared evident to me that the enemy was changing his strategy and was redeploying his force so as to disrupt the civilian population and to penetrate population areas.

Although I am frank to admit I did not know he would do it during the Tet period. I thought he would do it either before or after Tet. It appeared evident that he would take the initiative in the populated areas. Upon learning this, troops were withdrawn from the border areas and re-disposed in and around the populated areas in the III Corps.

Likewise, similar dispositions were made in the II Corps, but to a lesser degree because of the nature of the problem being different.

Q.: Is the enemy growing weaker?

A.: Many of the battalions have suffered in previous bat-tles. A defector said this campaign was an all-or-nothing campaign.

Q.: Will he now be washed up?

A.: It will take him many weeks to recover, weeks or months.

Q.: Do you expect a large ground assault at Khe Sanh by the enemy? What do you think is going to happen?

A.: It would be a bit awkward for me to answer that.

Q.: Is there any indication of a general popular uprising anywhere?

A.: I have received no information that the population has been receptive to this intrusion. It seems more to be an attitude of outrage.

Q.: Yesterday you said that the attacks were diversionary and not of military significance.

A.: I did not say they would have no military significance. Of course, phase one was diversionary for phase
two, and phase two was diversionary for phase three, so
implicit in his master plan was the principle of diversion.

Q.: Is there some chance he might not attack at Khe Sanh?

A.: I would give it very poor odds. They are pretty well
set up. I think they have built up to their plan level.

Q.: Don't you think these attacks will set back some of
the government programs like pacification? In the rural
areas?

A.: Yes, it will set back some of the programs without
question, but I think all of these losses are recoverable
in a short time.

Q.: Do you think the fourth phase is one of negotiation?

A.: I cannot forecast.

Q.: Had the United States ceased bombing North Vietnam
as of the beginning of the year?

A.: The enemy would be much stronger in posture.

Q.: Where does this "Go for Broke" aspect come in? Is
this not the next phase?

A.: Yes, which is his major effort as far as I can see it.

Q.: When do you think the next phase will take place?

A.: It could occur at any time.

Q.: What caused so much heavy damage in the populated
areas?

A.: House-to-house fighting.

APPENDIX IX

SECRETARY OF DEFENSE ROBERT S. MCNAMARA AND CHAIRMAN OF THE
JOINT CHIEFS GEN. EARLE G. WHEELER, INTERVIEW FOLLOWING
APPEARANCE BEFORE THE SENATE ARMED SERVICES COMMITTEE,
FEBRUARY 1, 1968

Q.: Mr. Secretary, there's a great deal of unrest over
the events of the past few days, particularly the events
in Vietnam. How can you explain the apparent lack of
preparedness out there for guerrilla attacks of this
nature?

Secretary McNamara: First, let me comment on what may be
the enemy's objectives in this current series of attacks
in South Vietnam. I think they may be two. He may be
trying to inflict on the South Vietnamese, the U.S., and
allied forces a severe military defeat. We believe we
are well prepared for that. We had intelligence information that gave us the basis for such preparation. Or,
alternatively, in the event that such an objective eludes
him, he may be seeking to achieve a substantial psychological or propaganda victory. I think it's particularly
with respect to the latter objective that he has launched
the series of suicidal attacks on the American Embassy,
airfields, province and district capitals, and other objectives around the country. General Wheeler talked to
General Westmoreland by telephone just an hour before we
came to this committee session. Perhaps he would like to
elaborate on that.

General Wheeler: General Westmoreland informed me that
he estimated the objectives of the enemy were essentially
as outlined by Secretary McNamara. He added that the
enemy had engaged in what he characterized as suicidal
efforts to gain objectives set for them, that their losses
have been extremely heavy. He estimates, or his commanders
estimate, that they [the enemy] have lost in the last
three days some 6,200 men killed. We, too, have suffered
some losses, but theirs have been ten times greater than
ours.

Q.:   What have ours been--600?

General Wheeler: A little over 500.   As of right now,
his report on losses of U.S. men killed is 193.   The
enemy effort has not been successful.   He has not forced
General Westmoreland to draw troops from the critical
Khe Sanh-DMZ area; he has not succeeded in overrunning
and holding a major Vietnamese city; he has not succeeded
in achieving a military success which in my judgment, or
General Westmoreland's is worth the cost to him.

Q.:   Would you say that this Vietcong guerrilla and terror
campaign is now under control by our forces?

General Wheeler: General Westmoreland figures that they
have the capability for keeping this up possibly for
another couple of days with diminishing activity.

Q.:   Can you tell me, sir, if we knew these attacks were
coming, why there were only three Marines on guard outside
the American Embassy?

General Wheeler: I'll have to correct what you said.   The
three Marines were on guard *inside* the American Embassy,
at least according to what I have heard.   The responsibility for the security outside the American Embassy is
that of the host country, that is, the South Vietnamese.
I do not know to what degree the security had been established outside the embassy.

Q.:   Do you think we should bolster our own defenses at
American installations there in light of this?

General Wheeler: I would say that the American defenses
of our installations proved to be quite satisfactory
under the circumstances.

Q.:   Could we ask Secretary McNamara if we are reassessing
our military commitment in South Vietnam because of these
incidents and the expected attack at Khe Sanh?

Secretary McNamara: No, we believe that the American
forces there at present are adequate and we think the
results during the past two or three days, the tremendous
disparity in losses of the enemy versus allied losses,
demonstrate that point.   I want to emphasize also the
point that General Wheeler made.   One of the enemy's
objectives was undoubtedly to drain away allied strength
from the Khe Sanh area preparatory to an attack in that
area.   That objective has not been successful.   I think
it simply demonstrates we are capable of meeting the
threat there while continuing to retain our forces elsewhere in the country.   I emphasize again that we believe
our present strength and the planned strength is adequate
for the purpose.

Q.: Mr. Secretary, can I ask you the inverse of that?
Do you think General Giap's strategy in sending three
divisions down from the North to the Khe Sanh area might
have been in the first place to divert our forces to the
northern province and thus weaken us in the populated
areas?

Secretary McNamara: I think that may have been one of
his objectives. This is sheer speculation, of course,
but it's an obvious speculative thought. If that had been
his objective, I don't think it's succeeded to date and
I don't believe it will succeed in the future.

Q.: General Wheeler, do you have any doubt that we can
repel the expected enemy assault at Khe Sanh?

General Wheeler: I have no doubt whatsoever. As a
matter of fact, in the last couple of days after receiving
reports from General Westmoreland, my colleagues and I
on the Joint Chiefs of Staff examined the situation
there, [and] General Westmoreland's plans to cope with it.
We concluded that the position can be held and should be
held.

Q.: Mr. Secretary, can I ask you a question about the
posture statement which you are discussing with the
Armed Services Committee? How is it that the Soviet Union
has managed to suddenly acquire 380 more ICBMs?

Secretary McNamara: The Soviet Union, as we predicted
last year, has been expanding its intercontinental bal-
listic force, and well they might, facing the very heavy
superiority we have in our own forces. The expansion
during the year was substantial, on the order of two or
three hundred missiles, as you implied. It leaves us
with a very substantial numerical superiority. In terms
of separately targetable warheads, both missile and
bomber-carried warheads, we have a superiority on the
order of four to one today. Now, having said that, I
want to emphasize that it is of only limited significance
because both we and the Soviet Union have sufficient
power to deter the other from the use of strategic nuclear
weapons in an offensive role, a large attack, and each
of us has power to survive such attack and retaliate
with unacceptable results.

I'm afraid we are going to have to leave.

Q.: Can we ask you one more question, Mr. Secretary,
about troop levels--whether you think 525,000 troops are
enough?

Secretary McNamara: I answered that.

Q.: How about Korea? Could we get one more?

Secretary McNamara: We'll be back.

Press: Thank you.

APPENDIX X

SECRETARY OF DEFENSE ROBERT S. MCNAMARA AND CHAIRMAN OF THE
JOINT CHIEFS GEN. EARLE G. WHEELER, INTERVIEW FOLLOWING
APPEARANCE BEFORE THE SENATE ARMED SERVICES COMMITTEE,
FEBRUARY 2, 1968

Q.: Mr. Secretary, having had a chance to get a little
longer view on what happened in South Vietnam, do you
agree that we have suffered a political and psychological
defeat in this offensive?

Secretary McNamara: No, I don't. I'll give you my
reasons in a moment, but let me ask General Wheeler to
comment first. He just talked to General Westmoreland
within the past three hours on the subject.

General Wheeler: I talked to General Westmoreland this
morning and asked him what the situation was throughout
the country. He reported to me that things remain quiet
along the DMZ and in the Khe Sanh area, that there are
enemy still in a portion of the city of Hue, which is
being dealt with, however, by a combination of American
and Vietnamese forces. The cities of Quang Tri and Nha
Trang, which had been under attack, are now clear.

In the II Corps area, the middle of the country, there
continues to be heavy fighting in the vicinity of the
city of Kontum. However, our forces and the Vietnamese
forces hold all of the installations and he is not worried about the outcome. In the vicinity of the city of
Pleiku, there has been a heavy contact between United
States forces and the enemy with sizable defeat inflicted
on the enemy. In the Saigon area, there continue to be
small forces of Vietcong operating from churches, schools,
pagodas, and factories. These elements are being rounded
up by Vietnamese forces.

In the IV Corps area, he stated that the situation had
improved substantially over the last 24 hours. The city
of My Tho, which had been under very heavy attack, is
now secure. He still continues to have some problems in
the Vinh Long area. There was a heavy fight in the very

south of the country, in the Ca Mau Peninsula, between
ARVN and Vietcong forces and the ARVN secured what he
described as a substantial victory.

He believes it is going to take several days finally to
clear up the situation and return the country to the pre-
Tet situation. He reported to me that he had been very
pleased with the performance of the Vietnamese forces.
They have responded quickly and actively to the enemy
threats. I regret to say that at the time he spoke to
me we had lost 249 American soldiers killed, some 555
Vietnamese forces killed, and he estimates that we have
inflicted over 9,500 casualties on the enemy.

Secretary McNamara: I think in answer to the question. . . .

Q.: 9,500 dead?

General Wheeler: Dead.

Secretary McNamara: In appraising the results of the
enemy attacks in South Vietnam, I think one should keep in
mind the enemy's probable objectives. I believe them to
be two. They hoped to inflict a severe military defeat
on the South Vietnamese, the United States, and allied
forces. I think the results to date indicate very clearly
they haven't accomplished that objective. General Westmoreland and General Wheeler and all of us believe they
cannot. And why should they be able to? We have substantial advantages in the numbers of men and in the firepower and mobility of our forces. The allied forces total
substantially in excess of one million men, the Vietcong
and North Vietnamese probably on the order of 250,000.
In our U.S. forces alone available in the area, we have
over 5,900 fixed-wing and rotary-wing aircraft, as an
illustration. Our firepower advantage is immense. Why
shouldn't we expect to achieve a military advantage? We
should expect it. We believe we have. We believe we
will continue to do so. So we think it quite unlikely
that he can achieve his first objective, which we believe to be the infliction of a severe military defeat
on the South Vietnamese and allied forces.

But I expect he had a fall-back objective. In the
event he was denied the first, as we think he will be
denied, his fall-back objective undoubtedly was to achieve
a psychological or propaganda victory. I think we can
deny him this as well, if we will realistically appraise
the results taking place. Recognizing that estimates of
killed in action can only be approximations, nonetheless
there is every reason to believe that he has suffered
far, far more heavily in these actions than have the
South Vietnamese and allied forces. Roughly in the ratio

of 9,500 to 800 South Vietnamese and allied forces killed
in action, and again those figures, as dramatic advantages
they portray for the South Vietnamese and U.S. and allied
forces, must be appraised in relation to the relative force
strengths. As I suggested, a quarter of a million for the
Vietcong and North Vietnamese and well in excess of a million for the allied forces.

Q.: Mr. Secretary, a ranking member of the House Armed
Services Committee said ultimately the blame for these
Saigon attacks will fall on your shoulders. Is there
any way this could have been averted?

Secretary McNamara: I think not. I think that the
military commanders in the field have stated on many occasions, General Wheeler did again this morning to the
Senate committee, our belief that the military field
commanders must assess the men and materiel necessary
to carry out a strong defense of the people of South
Vietnam. We think they are doing it.

Let me say, if there is any blame to be apportioned,
I'll accept mine. I don't think "blame," at the moment,
is the word to be used.

Q.: Was there an intelligence failure?

Secretary McNamara: Certainly not the latter. We had,
and as a matter of fact, we've been predicting--we had
information on, we have been predicting the possibility of
attacks just such as this. The statement that I distributed yesterday, which bears a preparation date of January
26, certainly pointed in this direction. But let me ask
General Wheeler to comment on each of these questions, if
he would.

General Wheeler: As to the question of whether there was
an intelligence failure, my answer to that is no. As
Secretary McNamara stated, our field commanders had information which appraised them the enemy was going to
undertake attacks of this kind over a wide area of South
Vietnam. Unfortunately, intelligence is seldom available
which leads one to anticipate the precise time, the precise
place, and the precise size of an attack. This would be
a commander's dream, to have information of that kind.
I feel that our information was accurate, it was timely,
and it was used by our commanders successfully to repulse
this heavy series of attacks. Moreover, gentlemen, I
would like to call your attention to one significant fact.
The Tet holiday to the Vietnamese is a combination of
Christmas, New Year's, and Easter. It is truly a holy
period. In their minds it would be sacrilegious to violate
this period by military action, and yet the Vietcong and

North Vietnamese obviously chose this period to initiate this series of attacks in order to gain the greatest possible advantage in launching their attacks against the Vietnamese and American forces. I think that this indicates the utter desperation tactics that they employed in mounting these attacks.

Secretary McNamara: We'll be back this afternoon.

Press. Thank you.

NEWS CONFERENCE, PRESIDENT LYNDON JOHNSON, THE WHITE HOUSE, FEBRUARY 2, 1968

The President: . . . We have known for several months, now, that the communists planned a massive winter-spring offensive. We have detailed information on Ho Chi Minh's order governing that offensive. Part of it is called a general uprising.

We know the object was to overthrow the constitutional government in Saigon and to create a situation in which we and the Vietnamese would be willing to accept the communist-dominated coalition government.

Another part of that offensive was planned as a massive attack across the frontiers of South Vietnam by North Vietnamese units. We have already seen the general uprising.

General Westmoreland's headquarters report the communists appear to have lost over 10,000 men killed and some 2,300 detained. The United States has lost 249 men killed. The Vietnamese, who had to carry the brunt of fighting in the cities, lost 553 killed as of my most recent report from the Westmoreland headquarters.

There were also a number of attacks on the United States airfields throughout the country. We have confirmed the loss of 15 fixed-wing aircraft, and 23 helicopters were destroyed. A good many more were damaged but will be returned to service.

This is a small proportion of our aircraft and helicopters available in that area. Secretary McNamara, General Westmoreland, and the Joint Chiefs of Staff do not think that our military operations will be materially affected.

The biggest fact is that the stated purposes of the general uprising have failed. Communist leaders counted on popular support in the cities for their effort. They found little or none. On the other hand, there have been

civilian casualties and disruption of public services.
Just before I came into this room, I read a long cable
from Ambassador Bunker which described the vigor with
which the Vietnamese government and our own people are
working together to deal with the problems of restoring
civilian services and order in all of the cities.

In the meanwhile, we may at this very moment be on the
eve of a major enemy offensive in the area of Khe Sanh
and generally around the Demilitarized Zone.

We have known for some time that this offensive was
planned by the enemy. Over recent weeks I have been in
close touch with General Westmoreland, and over recent
days in very close touch with all of our Joint Chiefs
of Staff to make sure that every single thing that
General Westmoreland believed that he needed at this
time was available to him, and that our Joint Chiefs
believe that his strategy was sound, his men were sure,
and they were amply supplied.

I am confident in the light of the information given to
me that our men and the South Vietnamese will be giving
a good account of themselves.

As all of you know, the situation is a fluid one. We
will keep the American people informed as these matters
develop.

Now, I will be glad to take any questions.

Q.: Mr. President, in your State of the Union Message,
you said we were exploring certain so-called offers from
Hanoi and as soon as you could you would report to the
people on that. Is there anything you can tell us today
about the status of possible peace negotiations with them?

The President: No. I would think that that statement
is about as good as I could make on that general subject.
That accurately describes what has been going on and what
is going on. But I do not have any success or results
to report on it.

Q.: Mr. President, does this present rampage in South
Vietnam give you any reason to change any assessment that
you have made previously about the situation in South
Vietnam?

The President: I am sure that we will make adjustments
to what we are doing there.

So far as changing our basic strategy, the answer would
be no. I think that there will be changes made here and
there as a result of experience that comes from efforts
such as they have made. Our best experts think that they
had two purposes in mind.

First was a military success. That has been a complete
failure. That is not to say that they have not disrupted
services. It is just like when we have a riot in a town
or when we have a very serious strike, or bridges go out,
or lights--power failures and things. They have disrupted
services. A few bandits can do that in any city in the
land.

Obviously, they have in the Vietcong hundreds and thousands,
so it is nothing unexpected to anticipate that they will
try in cooperation with their friends from the North to
coordinate their activities.

The ferocity and violence, the deception and the lack of
concern for the basic elements that appeal to human
beings--they may have shocked a lot of people in that
respect.

But the ability to do what they have done has been anticipated, prepared for, and met.

Now, so much for the military movements. This is not just
a civilian judgment. This is the judgment of the military
men in the field for whatever that judgment is worth to
us back here as experts--Monday morning quarterbacks.

That is the judgment of the best military advice I have
here. I met with them yesterday at lunch at some length.
I had Gen. [Matthew B.] Ridgway come down and spend some
time with me and talked to him.

I have spent a good deal of time talking to Gen. [Maxwell
D.] Taylor. I had all of the Joint Chiefs of Staff in
yesterday. We explored and discussed what had happened,
what was happening, what might happen, and so forth.

I have talked to the Pentagon this morning, very early,
and have been in touch with Secretary McNamara before
his testimony.

Their general conclusion is that as a military movement
it has been a failure.

Now, their second objective, obviously from the--what you
can see from not only Vietnam but from other communist
capitals--even from some of our unknowing people here at
home--is a psychological victory.

We have to realize that in moments of tenseness and trial--
as we will have today and as we have had in the past
days--that there will be a great effort to exploit that
and let that substitute for military victory they have not
achieved.

I do not believe when the American people know the facts,
when the world knows the facts, and when the results are

laid out for them to examine, I do not believe that they will achieve a psychological victory.

I do not want to be interpreted as unduly optimistic at all. I would rather wait and let the facts speak for themselves because there are many things that one far removed from the scene cannot anticipate.

In all of the battles, there are many disappointments for the commanders and even the commanders in chief.

So I think that at this very critical stage I would much prefer to be played low key than to give any false assurances. I can only say this: that based on the best military advice that I have, I feel confident that the men will give a good accounting of themselves. . . .

Q.: Sir, I was going to shift from that question in view of what you just said to another question.

The President: Go ahead.

Q.: Have you any news on the crew of the *Pueblo*?

The President: We understand from neutral nations and from reports from North Korea that the men are being treated well; that those who have suffered wounds are receiving treatment; that the body of the man who died is being held.

We have received those reports and examined them. That is about the extent of the information we have on it.

Q.: Did you say "men" or "man," sir, who died?

The President: Man.

Q.: Mr. President, are you confident that we can get back both the ship and the crew?

The President: No, I am not. I don't want to hold out any hopes on information that I have that is not justified. All I can say is that these things take time.

The most comparable incident, I am told by the military people, to this one was the RB-47 that went down in 1960 and it took some seven months of negotiations to get our pilots back.

We are exploring every diplomatic means that is available to us. We have our best military men reviewing all that happened and, as I said in my statement to you and to the country some time ago, we are taking such precautionary steps as we may think the military situation justifies.

Q.: Clark Clifford's testimony before the Armed Services Committee has raised some questions about the San Antonio formula.

The President: Only in the press, not with anyone in the Administration. Mr. Clifford said what I have said, what Mr. Rusk has said, what everybody has said, so far as the San Antonio formula is concerned. The country should know once and for all this morning that Mr. Clifford said just what I said at San Antonio.

Q.: Mr. President, is it possible that these developments in Vietnam that you had outlined, plus the imminence of this major offensive, could lead to deployment of additional American combat troops in Vietnam?

The President: I would not want to make predictions. Of course it is possible. The answer is yes. I wouldn't want your lead to say, though, "Johnson predicts possibility of troops" because that is not anticipated. We see no evidence of that.

Yesterday I saw that George [E. Christian, Special Assistant to the President] said that of course we would consider calling up specialists, or, of course we could consider some of these things. I must emphasize to you that lots of things would be considered, but so far as adding additional men, we have added the men that General Westmoreland has felt to be desirable and necessary.

There is nothing that has developed there that has caused him to change that estimate. We have something under 500,000. Our objective is 525,000. Most of the combat battalions already have been supplied. There is not anything in any of the developments that would justify the press in leaving the impression that any great new overall moves are going to be made that would involve substantial movements in that direction.

I would not want to foreclose any action in a matter like this. Anything can happen on a moment's notice. But we have constantly under advisement various things that we would want to anticipate. And after reviewing them now for several days, I have not seen the requirement or the necessity, nor have the Joint Chiefs, of making any additional requests to the Congress at this time involving additional authority.

It would be desirable, as it was last year, to have legislation a little more generous in one respect or two, or maybe more funds appropriated for military assistance that were reduced. We may have to get some adjustments in those fields, but there is nothing that is imminent at this moment.

Q.: Mr. President, how much if any, definite information do you have on the connection between the *Pueblo* incident and what is happening now in Vietnam?

The President: I do not have evidence that would say
that they are definitely, positively one and the same
here because I cannot prove that. Practically every
expert I have talked to on Korea and North Vietnam and
the communist operation--all of them, I think without
exception, believe there is a definite connection.

I would have you know, though, that that is based on
their opinion and not on hard evidence that I could
establish to CBS's satisfaction in a court of law.

Q.: Mr. President, in light of what has happened in
the last few days, or going back to the *Pueblo* incident,
do you have any reason to believe that in the last two
years there have been any genuine peace feelers put out
by the North Vietnamese or other Vietnamese communists,
or have they been phony, except when they were winning
in '64?

The President: We have tried to explore every suggestion
made by enemy and friend. I must say that in retrospect
I do not think we have overlooked anything, and I do not
think that we have found anything that would give an
impartial judge reason to be encouraged.

Q.: Sir, do you see anything in the developments this
week in these attacks in Vietnam that causes you to
think you need to reevaluate some of the assumptions
on which our policies, our strategy there has been based?
I am thinking in terms of the security ratings, amount
of population that is considered under government control?
Do you think the basic assumption is still valid?

The President: We do that every week. I see nothing
that would indicate that that shouldn't be done. We must
do it all the time to try to keep up, and to be sure we
have not made errors and mistakes. If you are saying,
have we felt that what happened could not happen, the
answer is no. As a matter of fact, . . . if you have seen
any of the intelligence reports, the information has
been very clear that two things would happen:

One is that there would be a general uprising, as I
stated.

Two, there would be a general invasion and attempt to
secure military victory, and that the objective would be
to get a military victory and a psychological victory.

That is one of the great problems the President has to
deal with. He is sitting there reading these information
reports while his own people, a good many of the best
intentioned, are supplying him with military strategy,
and the two do not fit in.

So you have to be tolerant and understand their best intentions while you are looking at the other fellow's hole
card. This is what General Westmoreland has been doing
while all of these Monday morning quarterbacks are pointing out to him that this is the way he should move, or
this is the way he should move.

This is a part of what happens when you look at history.
It may be that General Westmoreland makes some serious
mistakes or that I make some. We don't know. We are
just acting in light of the information we have. We
believe we have information about what they are trying
to do there. We have taken every precaution we know of.
But we don't want to give you assurance that it will all
be satisfactory. We see nothing that would require any
change of great consequence.

We will have to move men from this place to that one.
We will have to replace helicopters. Probably we had 100-
odd helicopters and planes seriously damaged and we will
have to replace them.

Secretary McNamara told me he could have that done very
shortly.

We will have to replace the 38 planes lost, but we have
approximately 5,900 planes there. We anticipate that
we will lose 25 or 30 every month just from normal crashes
and so forth.

Q.: Mr. President, do you believe, sir, their winter-
spring offensive and their call for an uprising and their
attempt to impose a coalition government is based on
their belief that they are taking military punishment
that they cannot sustain for a long time? In short, sir,
are we still winning the war?

The President: Well, I see nothing in the developments
that would indicate that the evaluation that I have had
of this situation throughout the month should be changed.

I do think that the second phase is imminent. What we
have expected is upon us. We have gone through the first
phase of it. We will have to see what happens in the
second phase. If it comes out as expected, I think I
can give you a better answer to your question when it is
over with.

I do not want to prophesy what is going to happen, although
we feel reasonably sure of our strength.

Q.: Mr. President, one of the problems people seem to be
having in making up their minds on the psychological
importance of this goes back to our reports that the Vietcong were really way down in morale, that they were a

shattered force. Now people ask: Well, how, then, can
they find the people who are so well-motivated to run
these suicide attacks in so many places in such good
coordination? Some people say: Well, that proves they
know they are licked and this is their dying gasp. And
some people say: Well, it proves that we underestimated
their morale. How do you feel, sir?

The President: I haven't read those reports about under-
estimating all their morale, and their being out of it,
and no more problems, and so forth. That hasn't been the
information the government has received.

We do think that we have made good progress there. We
are for that. We don't want to overplay it or play it
in high key. We just want to state it because we believe
it is true.

But no one in authority has ever felt--that I know anything about--that you could not have an uprising of this
kind, particularly when they have ordered it and predicted
it and we have been expecting it.

As I view history, I think that you have things of this
type replete throughout. You can expect it. I see it
even in domestic problems. The fact that people's morale
may be suffering and that they may be having great difficulty doesn't keep them from breaking glass windows and
shooting folks in a store or dashing into your home or
trying to assassinate somebody. That goes with it. That
is a part of the pattern.

Now whether they are doing this from a position of greater
strength or greater weakness--I would say neither. I
don't think that they are as weak as you picture them in
your straw man that you place up there--that the government has this feeling. I don't think we feel that way.

I think we know that a march on the Pentagon can disrupt
traffic and tie up things and cause problems here. I
think we can see what happened in Detroit. I think we
can see what happened in Saigon.

I think these are times when a few highly energetic and
courageous people could seize National Airport. But,
could they hold it? Does it endure? Is it a victory?
Do they pay more than it is worth and so on and so forth?
Those are the things you have to evaluate.

Now, I am no great strategist and tactician. I know that
you are not. But let us assume that the best figures we
can have are from our responsible military commanders.
They say 10,000 died and we lost 249 and the South Vietnamese lost 500. Now that doesn't look like a communist

victory. I can count. It looks like somebody has paid a
very dear price for the temporary encouragement that
some of our enemies had.

We have approximately 5,900 planes and have lost 38
completely destroyed. We lost 100-odd that were damaged
and have to be repaired. Maybe Secretary McNamara will
fly in 150 shortly.

Now, is that a great enemy victory?

In Peking today they say that we are in panic. You have
to judge that for yourself. In other communist capitals
today they say that we have definitely exhibited a lack of
power and that we do not have any military strength. You
will have to judge that for yourself.

But General Westmoreland--evaluating this for us and the
Joint Chiefs of Staff reviewing it for me--tell me that
in their judgment it has not been a military success.

I am measuring my words. I don't want to overstate the
thing. We do not believe that we should help them in
making it a psychological success.

We are presenting these reports daily to the Armed Services
Committee of the Senate, where the Secretary of Defense
is testifying and will be through a large part of next
week.

There will be moments of encouragement and discouragement.
And as things go on ahead, we can't estimate them, but
they will be given to the committees who have jurisdiction.

Since the Armed Services Committees help draft our people
and raise our armies and provide the equipment and so
forth, the Secretary is appearing there morning and afternoon. He will be giving periodic reports that will be
much more in detail and will supplement what I have said
to you.

Q.: Mr. President, do you still support talks between the
South Vietnamese and the NLF?

The President: I have not changed the viewpoint that I
expressed when I quoted the statement of President Thieu
of South Vietnam in my interview with the correspondents.

Q.: Mr. President, in your judgment, did the interview
Premier Kosygin gave to *Life*'s editors reflect any
deterioration in our relations with Russia since the
Glassboro talks?

The President: I don't care to weigh and speculate on
the developments in the Soviet Union. We just tabled
last week a nonproliferation agreement with them. We have
other plans for exchanges of thoughts on various subjects.

We would always like to improve our relations with the Soviet Union and with all nations where we can do that consistently.

Q.: Mr. President, some people interested in civil rights, including Martin Luther King, are planning a massive march on Washington this spring. There is some talk that they would like to stop the wheels of government.

Are you planning to try to talk them out of this? Would you assess that for us?

The President: I don't know what their plans are. I am not sure that they have developed them yet.

Of course, I would be hopeful that our energies, our talents, and our concerns could be directed in a more productive and a more effective manner.

I would hope that some of these people who are leaders of the causes could recognize that the Congress is having hearings every day on subjects of vital importance to their cause.

By coming there and following constitutional methods, presenting their evidence to the Congress and persuading the Congress, it would be more helpful than just trying to stop the functioning of the government who is also trying very much to help their cause to eliminate discrimination, get more jobs, and improve housing. Whatever time and attention the government has to give to these things is taken away from things that they could be doing to help them.

So we will do all we can to work with all groups in this country to see that their views are heard, considered, and acted upon with promptness and understanding.

Q.: Mr. President, the *Pueblo* appears to have put a certain strain on relations between Washington and Seoul. Some political figures in South Korea are saying that the United States appears more interested in getting back the 83 men than in doing something about North Korean incursions into South Korea.

The President: I don't know which political figures you refer to. I can't comment on that.

We are in very close touch with the President of that country. I think he understands how we feel.

I would be less than frank if I didn't tell you I was deeply concerned about 83 Americans, as I am sure the President of Korea is.

I am also deeply concerned about the situation in South Korea and the obligations we have there. We are going to be equal to that obligation. We are going to be true to our commitment.

We have some 50,000 men there. We are going to see that not only are they adequately informed and supplied, but that all of our plans take into consideration the recommendations of that government that we have found to be not only a friendly government but an effective one--and one of our best allies.

I have great respect for the President of South Korea and his judgments. They are being received, considered, and acted upon every day.

I see nothing in any of these developments to justify a concern on the part of South Korea or America that there is a strain in our relations. I think that is largely talk and speculation and so-called reports.

Q.: Are we now trying to arrange talks with North Korea at Panmunjom or has there been a meeting since yesterday there?

The President: Yes, there has been a meeting between representatives of North Korea and the United States. We hope there will be additional meetings.

These meetings have not produced any satisfactory results as far as the United States is concerned.

I know nothing that I should add to that statement. And I don't plan to.

Merriman Smith, United Press International: Thank you, Mr. President.

The Washington *Post,*
February 2, 1968

RED RAIDS ON CITIES ARE SIGN OF WEAKNESS, NOT STRENGTH

By Joseph Alsop

We are already engulfed in another spate of warnings that all is hopeless in Vietnam, because of the attack on the U.S. Embassy and the other VC efforts in Saigon and other cities.

In reality, however, this flurry of VC activities in urban centers will almost certainly prove to have just the opposite meaning in the end. The nearest parallel is probably the fruitless Japanese use of Kamikaze pilots in the Second World War's final phase.

Beginning at the beginning with Hanoi's basic doctrine, the war has always been supposed to culminate in a "general uprising," engulfing towns as well as countryside in South Vietnam. In prudent preparation for this "general uprising," the enemy's high command long ago began to accumulate hidden assets, in the form of men and weapons, within or on the fringes of the various urban centers where their writ has never run.

Everyone has known that such hidden assets existed. Occasionally, this or that bit of the VC network in Saigon or some other town has been discovered and removed. Most of the network has always remained in place, largely inactive and therefore difficult to locate, but ready for use on the word of command from Hanoi.

That word was evidently given some weeks or months ago. The numerous attacks in Saigon, in Hue, in Da Nang and at other points were obviously long planned and most carefully coordinated. The execution, in most cases, was quite admirable, showing very careful coordination as well as great daring.

There are still serious trouble spots waiting to be cleared up. Important elements of VC strength in the countryside have been committed to give striking power to the people of the urban network.

But in the upshot all these immense assets are just about sure to have been wastefully expended, without producing anything dimly resembling the general uprising Hanoi has always dreamed of. It is as though a college boy who had been saving up for a new sports car, suddenly put all his savings into a useless rattletrap. The question is, why?

Quite certainly, therefore, the decision was consciously taken to settle for the rattletrap instead of the longed-for sports car. Equally certainly, there were two aims behind this decision. One was the obvious propagandistic aim--to weaken American and South Vietnamese resolution by causing people to write and talk the kind of guff that one is currently hearing here.

The other aim was military. Everything indicates that the big show in Vietnam this winter is to be the battle at Khe Sanh. The North Vietnamese preparations strongly suggest, by their mere unprecedented scale, that this battle is intended to be climactic. And it will obviously help the enemy at Khe Sanh if there is acute worry about security throughout the rest of Vietnam.

But from all this, a single, central point rather emerges. What has happened in the cities, what is happening at Khe Sanh, cannot possibly be made to fit into Hanoi's familiar and classic blueprint for "protracted war."

The sudden expenditure of the hidden urban assets, like the preparations at Khe Sanh, in truth make no sense at all unless the Hanoi leaders are instead basing all their current hopes on a short, convulsive, final or semifinal effort. Their adoption of the system of win-lose-or-draw is the only rational reading of the facts, including the fact that many recent captured documents show the Hanoi leaders promising their troops in the field peace-by-coalition "in 1968."

That means, on the one hand, that the stakes at Khe Sanh are almost unbearably high. But that means, on the other hand, that the Hanoi war-planners have been driven to conclude that "protracted war" is not a safe strategy to adopt.

This should surprise no one. Quite aside from the heavy pressure of the bombing of the North, countless captured documents reveal that "fear of protracted war" is the central "weakness"--the word is regularly used--of the North Vietnamese troops and VC cadres and troops in South Vietnam.

There is considerable evidence, indeed, that at some time last summer the Hanoi leaders seriously contemplated retreat into the patient strategy of classicial "protracted

war," only to rebound into the patient strategy of a
climactic effort. And the chances are that the reason
for the rebound was the effect on the troops and cadres
in the South of the calls from Hanoi for "protracted
war . . . up to 20 years."

God knows, none can predict exactly what Hanoi will do if
the preparations at Khe Sanh fail, DV [*Deo volente*], to
produce the result that Hanoi hopes for. But it is certainly idiotic to go on talking about a war "with no end
in sight," as so many do in this country, when the other
side so obviously thinks (or fears) that a rather early
end is in sight.

APPENDIX XIII

PRESS BRIEFING, BRIG. GEN. JOHN CHAISSON, USMC, SAIGON, FEBRUARY 3, 1968

Brig. Gen Winant Sidle: In order to try to prevent so many phone calls from you tonight, I've arranged for a double-barrel briefing for you all. We'll have Brig. Gen. Chaisson lead off. John is the director of the combat operations center at MACV and he's going to give you an update on the entire situation--less Saigon. The second speaker will be [Army] Col. Bill Schroeder . . . and he'll give you an update on Saigon. Both will be available after they have given their little presentations to answer questions. . . .

General Chaisson: It's been a week of surprises. I think the VC surprised us with their attacks and I must confess I'm surprised to find myself up here this afternoon. We have been faced this past week with a real battle. There is no sense in ducking it; there is no sense in hiding it. When you look at figures that are in the magnitude of 1,000 friendly killed in less than five days of fighting, and something of the magnitude of 12,000 of the enemy killed in the same period, you're talking about real fighting. And when you spread it across the map from the DMZ down to the tip of IV Corps, when you're working on that type of battlefield, it increases the difficulty of the battle.

I'd say that, from the enemy side, at least looking at it from how I look at it as the operations officer over at MACV, I've got to give them credit for having engineered and planned a very successful offensive in its initial phases. It was surprisingly well coordinated, it was surprisingly intensive, and I think, in conducting it, [the enemy] showed a surprising amount of audacity because he had put an awful lot of his goods up on the table in this battle. Now it's up to us to see what we can do about cleaning the table.

Looking at the situation as it stands right now on the
whole battlefield, from north to south: In the north,
the I Corps area, the most intensive fighting going on
right now is still in the Hue area. There are still at
least two enemy companies in the Citadel area of Hue,
in the north part of the town (as you know, the Perfume
River splits it there and the Citadel is in the north).
The Citadel encompasses the . . . airstrip, and the 1st
ARVN Division headquarters. There are still a couple of
enemy companies at least in the western part of the
Citadel. There are heavy ARVN forces in the town, working
them over--both ARVN airborne and elements of the 3rd and
2nd ARVN Regiments. The Marine forces have been pretty
much working south of the river; they have been blocking
there--the area south of the river is not in contention.
There was one report I got just before I came over here,
and I don't have enough details to go into it in any
detail, but the Marines got up to the jail there (that's
right on the edge of the river, the north side) and they
found the jail was empty. There were some 2,000 to 3,000
prisoners who had been in the jail. The facts of the release or anything else I don't know. Obviously it took
place while the VC had the town.

But this fighting is going on. There is no estimation of
how long it's going to take to get them out of there, but
I'm convinced, with the forces we have in Hue right now,
that it is just a matter of time and, I would feel, that
within the next day or so we'll have Hue cleared.

To the north of Hue, Quang Tri is now clear. Quang Tri
city is now clear. And the operation that was taking
place up north of the Cua Viet River right here south of
the eastern extremity of the DMZ--there's been a Marine
battalion operating in there for the past few days (an
operation called Saline). They have just terminated this
sweep through the area--from the Cua Viet up--and just
before I came back I saw some figures: there were 30
Marines killed in this operation and about 155 NVA killed
in that sweep along the beach from the Cua Viet up to the
DMZ. In the two northern provinces, however, . . . [there
is still] the enemy along the DMZ extending from Khe Sanh
right up across by the Rock Pile through the center part
over to Cam Lo and then right to the coast.

The enemy does have a very significant force in this
[DMZ] area. I would say, without any exaggeration, the
largest concentration he's ever put together in one area
in the country. Now he hasn't sprung this one yet. How
it is going to be synchronized with this battle of the
country that's been going on all week we haven't quite put
together. Synchronization seems quite obvious. Synchro-

nization would have many advantages from his standpoint.
But as to this point right now, . . . [there is] this
rather sharp but large contact which took place yesterday
morning near Cam Lo, virtually the center anchor on the
DMZ line. I think you'll recall one of the press releases
I brought out here. There was a Marine platoon in position there and this was hit by a fairly heavy force--it
could be a battalion-size force. There was a reaction
company available. They had some mounted there; they
moved in and they caught them and it was about 111 of the
enemy that was killed. They picked up quite a haul of
weapons, some 20 crew-served weapons and 20 or 50 individual weapons; about seven friendly killed. We had a
feeling when that first hit the board yesterday morning
that this might be the initiation of the attack, because
that area has a certain amount of attraction for the enemy
if he's going to attack Khe Sanh, since it does lie
astride our position out toward the west.

We are watching the northern area very carefully. We're
putting high priority on it with regard to our tactical
air strikes and our B-52 air strikes, and we will continue to do so, I am certain, until such time as we get
the situation--shall I say--better adjusted in the rest
of the country and then I think we'll maybe be making
more moves in that area.

Now, moving down, below Hoa Vang Pass, down into Quang
Nam, in the southern part of I Corps, there hasn't been a
great deal of activity except for the attacks that have
taken place on Da Nang this week, and the attacks on
Duy Xuyen south of Da Nang; and the operations of the ROK
forces in the area north of Hoi An, as you know, is just
directly south of Da Nang. The Da Nang attack, including
two rocket attacks on the airfield, efforts to get into
the city, to get at the MACV compound, which is right
near the Da Nang bridge there--these have all been so
far successfully repulsed.

This morning there was the second rocket attack (again, I
believe that is in today's press release)--some 40 rounds
commencing at 0315 this morning, about 25 minutes, some
40 rounds of 122. We got away very lightly on this one.
There was only one plane destroyed; personnel casualties
were extremely light (four, I believe, wounded, the last
report that I saw) and the field was completely operational
at sunup this morning. However, this does highlight the
fact that the enemy does have the capability of putting
rockets into the Da Nang area on that vast open area to
the south and west of Da Nang, although we have extensive
patrolling out in that area; with his new medium-range
rocket and his range of 11-12 kilometers you get into such

a geometric proportion when you try to put the thickening
in after that range that it's virtually impossible to pre-
clude it. The answer is selective screening and real
rapid reaction. In that regard, this morning's attack
had one significant feature and that is the weather was
overcast. We couldn't put the gunships on the rocket
position but the artillery was able to take it under attack almost immediately upon the first rockets opening
up, and they did have one large secondary explosion in
the vicinity. The patrols had not been over the area
when I left to come down here. I had not received a
report of what the patrols had found in the area.

In the southern two provinces of I Corps, in Quang Tin
and Quang Ngai, there has been very little activity in
the past 24 hours.

Moving down into II Corps, I'd say that the most significant fighting that is going on, number one, is still
around Kontum. At Kontum, fighting has been heavy. There
are still some enemy forces in portions of the city--they
managed to lodge a couple of attacks last evening. The
city is reported as quiet this afternoon at 1500. This
could be the time of day rather than the status of the
forces in the town. We do have a sufficient force in
there, I believe, to keep these dramatic happenings from
occurring, but there's still going to be some fighting
around Kontum. I'd say, of all the cities that have been
hit in II Corps, this is the one right now that's more
nearly in the balance, although I don't really believe
it's really in the balance.

The other attacks on Pleiku [and elsewhere] . . . up
near Dak To . . . these seem to be, as of this afternoon,
well under control. Possible exception is Da Lat, in
that we do not have any significant forces in Da Lat.
We have a lot smaller outfit there, but so far there has
been no major surge by the enemy. There have been varying
reports of the size of the enemy force in there, and
we're in the process of doing something about the situation in Da Lat to prevent anything further from happening.
The pattern of the attacks in II Corps is a little different from I Corps and a little different--as I go on
down to II Corps--in that, generally speaking, the enemy
threw into the attacks on these cities a far more considerable portion of what we know of his order of battle
than what he did in the north. For example, [as] I
pointed out in the north, he did not commit his main forces
that he had along the DMZ with his attacks. In II Corps,
except for those that are residing in and out of Cambodia,
he pretty much delivered with most of the known elements
of his order of battle and as a result of this, I think,

he made a rather broad canvas with regard to his attacks
on II Corps. As I say, as of tonight, only Kontum seems
to be a troublesome spot.

Down in III Corps (I'm going to avoid talking about the
Saigon area because Colonel Schroeder is going to get into
that in some detail . . .), outside of the Saigon area,
there has been reasonably light activity. Cu Chi has
had a couple of attacks by mortar and by patrol. All
around Phuoc Long there [have] been a few indications
that something is stirring. There have been two contacts out there by separate elements of the 1st Division.
Both of them have been reasonably small affairs, but it
would indicate that there would be some enemy force in that
area, and that's one of the areas that we're watching.
Except for that, if you include in the Saigon area generally, if you think of Long Dinh and Bien Hoa, then there has
been very little.

Yesterday there was some activity down in Ba Ria in Phuoc
Tuy province. I was told by an officer that they killed
some sniper firing in Ba Ria, but there is no significant
enemy force in and around the city--at least no visual
one. Xuan Loc did get attacked this morning; it was attacked from both the east and the west. It looked like
a fairly sizable attack; the contact was still going on
sporadically there at noontime, and I'm sorry but I don't
have any real good feel for that situation. My reports
haven't been coming in too fast from that one, but there
is one attack on the Xuan Loc area--that was a new one
today.

Bien Hoa and Long Binh would be very attractive targets
for the enemy and he must have felt that way also, because, as you have been following it, he made two efforts
on consecutive nights against both of these and was able
to get indirect fire on them and was able to penetrate
at least portions of both areas. Last night it was quiet
out there. We have a very good force in the area and we're
sweeping the area and we hope that that situation is under
control.

Now, moving down into the Delta. The Delta has probably
had the most widespread coverage. Nearly every one of
the province capitals have been hit in some form. A
couple of them--well, at Ben Tre and Vinh Long, and early
this morning in My Tho--the situation was looking sort of
fifty-fifty. At Ben Tre yesterday, [it] was not looking
good. We did deploy some U.S. forces down into Ben
Tre . . . , and these forces have been working with the
ARVN 9th Division in Ben Tre and My Tho . . . and my reports are that of all the cities in the Delta right now,

as of this afternoon, there was no major enemy that has
the significant force in the city.

The last tough one was at Ben Tre and the last report from
there was 1,200 of the enemy has left the city. We do
have a fairly good size U.S. force down in Ben Tre working
with the ARVN. He did go to considerable effort down
there, however, and, as I say, his coverage was somewhat
like II Corps--very good and extensive.

Now, what we have seen in looking ahead for the future.
We do give the enemy credit for possibly recycling an attack of this nature because it is our opinion that he has
used extensively his local forces and his main forces.
And he still has a fairly good grip, except in II Corps,
on some of his NVA forces, and it is not beneath the
realm of possibility or his capability to recycle attacks
in some of these areas. However, if he goes at anything
like the same targets that he went at the last time--to
wit, the populated areas and the major installations--we
most certainly are in fair position and my only other observation would be that just as this one has been a very
costly venture, I unequivocally would state that any efforts on his part to make these major onslaughts against
our installations and against the city is going to be
very costly. I can't say that it is not going to be
either damaging or costly to our side, but it is going to
be extremely costly to him.

I have always contended in the two years that I've been
out here that the most difficult thing to do was to get
at this fellow. Well, now this week my problem has been
solved: He certainly has exposed himself to most of our
firepower capability, although I must confess that in the
environment in which you are operating there have been
certain definite limitations on how we do go at them.
But I have been impressed, I might say, by the size of
his casualty figures. I'm handling these at MACV; I'm
trying just as hard as I can to make sure that there is
no error creeping into them and whatever integrity you want
to attribute to me, I can tell you that those are the
figures that are coming in from the battle commanders and
those are very broad and large figures. If these figures
pan out to be exactly correct--with whatever develops
after the heat of the battle is over--I'd say that the
enemy had suffered an extremely great loss this week. But
as I said at the outset, it has not been without great cost
on our part, because it has been a tough battle and that
tough battle is still going on. That's about all I have.

APPENDIX XIV

NBC TELEVISION-RADIO, "MEET THE PRESS," FEBRUARY 4, 1968

MODERATOR: Lawrence E. Spivak

GUESTS: Dean Rusk, Secretary of State
            Robert S. McNamara, Secretary of Defense

PANEL: Warren Rogers, *Look*
            Max Frankel, New York *Times*
            Peter Lisagor, Chicago *Daily News*
            Elie Abel, NBC News

Spivak: This is Lawrence Spivak inviting you to a special
edition of "Meet the Press". . . . Our guests today . . .
are the President's two chief Cabinet officers, the Secretary of State, Dean Rusk, and the Secretary of Defense,
Robert S. McNamara.

The interview originally announced for today with Governor
John Connally of Texas has been postponed because of the
importance of recent developments in the Far East. We will
have the first questions for our guests from Elie Abel of
NBC News.

Abel: Secretary Rusk, there is a report this morning from
Seoul that the North Koreans have agreed to release the
body of one dead American and the wounded crew members of
the *Pueblo*. Can you confirm this?

Rusk: No, I cannot confirm that. We met with them a little more than 12 hours ago. We met with them on the second
and the fourth, Korean time, and I have no information that
indicates they are prepared to do so, or even to give us
the names of the injured and the dead.

Abel: Mr. Secretary, about a week ago you were talking
rather urgently about the need to get these men and the
ship back. You spoke of the seizure of the *Pueblo* as an
act of war. What has happened between now and then to
cause the Administration to moderate its tone here?

95

Rusk: There has been no moderation in that sense. President Johnson has made it clear that we would prefer to get
these men back through diplomatic process. We are using a
variety of means. First, diplomatic contacts through capitals; secondly, the Military Armistice Commission machinery
at Panmunjom and Korea; and, third, the United Nations
Security Council. The fact that we are now meeting at
Panmunjom has caused the Security Council to wait for a bit
to see what happens at Panmunjom. The only satisfactory
answer is the prompt release of the ship and the crew. I
cannot report to you this morning that this is occurring,
and therefore we shall have to continue with it.

Abel: But you hope to continue on the diplomatic route
yet for some time?

Rusk: Well, I don't want to put a time factor on it. The
important thing is that we get the ship and the crew back
immediately, and we shall press that very hard indeed, and
report as soon as we see a blue sky ahead on that point.

Abel: Secretary McNamara, it is three years this week
since we started bombing North Vietnam. It was also in '65
that we started the big buildup on the ground. What
happened this week? How do you relate the ability of the
Vietcong to stage as major an offensive as this one was to
the efforts we have been making these past three years?

McNamara: Three years ago, or more exactly two-and-a-half
years ago, in July of 1965, President Johnson made the
decision, announced to our people the decision, to move
significant numbers of combat troops into South Vietnam.
At that time the North Vietnamese and their associates,
the Vietcong, were on the verge of cutting the country in
half and of destroying the South Vietnamese Army. We said
so at the time, and I think hindsight has proven that a
correct appraisal. What has happened since that time of
course is that they have suffered severe losses; they have
failed in their objective to destroy the government of
South Vietnam, they have failed in their objective to take
control of the country. They have continued to fight.

Just four days ago I remember reading in our press that I
had presented a gloomy, pessimistic picture of activities
in South Vietnam. I do not think it was gloomy or pessimistic; it was realistic. It said [that] while they
had suffered severe penalties, they continued to have the
strength to carry out the attacks which we have seen in
the last two or three days.

Abel: Mr. Secretary, are you telling us the fact that the
Vietcong after all these years were able to, temporarily
at least, grab control of some 20-odd provincial capitals
and the city of Saigon, are you telling us that this has
no military meaning at all?

McNamara: No, certainly not. I think South Vietnam is such a complex situation one must always look at the pluses and the minuses, and I do not mean to say there have not been any minuses for the South Vietnamese in the last several days; I think there have been. But there have been many, many pluses. The North Vietnamese and the Vietcong have not accomplished either one of their major objectives, either to ignite a general uprising or to force a diversion of the troops which the South Vietnamese and the United States have moved into the northern areas of South Vietnam, anticipating a major Vietcong and North Vietnamese offensive in that area. And beyond that, the North Vietnamese have suffered very heavy penalties in terms of losses of weapons and losses of men in the past several days. They have of course dealt a very heavy blow to many of the cities of South Vietnam.

Spivak: Thank you, gentlemen. . . . (Interruption for commercial.)

Spivak: Resuming our interview. . . . We will continue the questions now with Mr. Rogers.

Rogers: Secretary Rusk, in 1957 the prime minister of North Korea boasted that by the early seventies he was going to have all of South Korea under communist domination. Now, we have the *Pueblo* incident. What is behind the *Pueblo* incident? Is it a grand design, the beginning of a Vietnam-type operation, a guerrilla operation to take over all of Korea?

Rusk: There have been two parts to the present crisis in Korea. One has been the rapidly increasing infiltration of the North Koreans into South Korea, including the dispatch of a group of about 30 highly trained officers for the purpose of assassinating the President of South Korea and the American ambassador. Those were promptly dispatched. But that infiltration has gone up 10 times in 1967 over 1966, from about 50 incidents to about 570 incidents.

Now, if these people in North Korea think that they are going to take over South Korea by force they could not make a worse mistake. The South Koreans and Korea's allies are going to insure that that cannot happen.

Now, the seizure of the *Pueblo* may or may not be a part of that general effort. We are not quite clear why the North Koreans should undertake this action, which is almost literally without precedent, which is contrary to all of the general accepted rules of international law and practice. It may be that they wanted to create some sense of insecurity in South Korea because of South Korea's assistance to Vietnam. It may be that these fellows up there in Pyongyang actually believe that somehow they can intimidate the South Koreans and make a political impact on South Korea. This is not going to happen. South Korea has been thriving in the last few years, moving from strength to strength, not only politically, but economically and militarily.

I cannot read what is in the minds of these people about seizing the *Pueblo*. I do know what the answer must be, and that is the prompt release of the ship and the crew.

Rogers: Well, we are told that the North Koreans have gone underground with a lot of their heavy industry, etcetera; they have put in a lot of new ground-to-air missiles, and that sort of thing. Is it possible that they are prepared to undertake a military adventure, with the understanding, of course, that we are committed heavily in Southeast Asia and may not be able to resist the thing?

Rusk: Well, Secretary McNamara can talk about the extent to which we are overcommitted. As a matter of fact, we have the wherewithal to do what is required in Korea without drawing down on our forces in Vietnam.

Rogers: I was talking about the other side's intentions. Do you think that they are possibly harboring this possibility?

Rusk: Gen. [Charles Hartwell] Bonesteel, our commander in Korea, said the other day that we do not have indicators showing that they intend to put on a mass offensive against South Korea. Now you will recall that, when the 16 nations who had troops in Korea reviewed the situation after the peace in 1953, they made a very firm declaration that this sort of thing is not going to happen again.

I have no doubt whatever that if North Korea entertains any such hopes they are fruitless, and they would be well advised to abandon any such hopes because it just is not going to happen. It is not going to happen.

Frankel: Secretary McNamara, does the Navy know for sure that the *Pueblo* at no time entered North Korean waters?

McNamara: No. I think we cannot say beyond a shadow of a doubt [that] at no time during its voyage it entered North Korean waters. We can say this--I think it bears on the answer: First, the commander [of the *Pueblo*] had the strictest of instructions to stay in international waters. We believe he did. Second, at the time of seizure we are quite positive it was in international waters. Thirdly, there was a period of radio silence appropriate to its mission from the period of roughly January 10 to January 21, and it is in that period that

we lack knowledge, and we will not be able to obtain
knowledge of that until the crew and the commander are
released.

Frankel: Since the North Koreans seem to want to salvage
some piece of face here, and since our primary objective
is to get the ship and the crew back, why couldn't we say,
more or less, well, we think they were in the right,
there is a possibility, we do not know until we talk to
them, that they did something wrong, or that they shouldn't
have, or that they violated their orders. In that case, if
that turns out to be true, we're sorry. Now, let's cancel
this whole incident. Why don't we speak in that tone?

McNamara: The diplomatic track is a question for Secretary
Rusk to address, let me suggest to you, Mr. Frankel.

Rusk: Well, I think we can say on that we cannot be one
thousand percent sure until we get our officers and crew
back and we have a chance to interrogate them and look at
the log of the ship. This was a ship peculiarly qualified
to navigate with accuracy. Now, it would not disturb us
to let everybody know that, when we get them back, if we
discover that they were at any point within a 12-mile
limit, for example, as claimed by North Korea, despite
the fact that we recognize only a three-mile limit, that
we will make those facts available. We will make them
available.

But we cannot do that on the basis of the testimony that
we get from men who are being held prisoner, or from
spliced tapes of broadcasts that they are alleged to have
made. We have got to have access to hard information.
And I would add that we have not a single scrap of information from any source whatever that this vessel was inside
the 12-mile limit at any time during its voyage.

Frankel: Secretary McNamara, did this raise havoc with
our whole intelligence operation? That is, the equipment
that may have fallen into enemy hands?

McNamara: No. We are not certain how much equipment or
classified information did fall into enemy hands. The
orders of the commander and crew were to destroy the equipment in the event of boarding as occurred. We know from
the messages that we received that they went far to that
end. Exactly how much they destroyed and how much was
undestroyed we don't know. We do know that our worldwide
communications were not compromised. Within the hour
after the event we had changed the foundation of those
communications.

Frankel: Thank you.

Lisagor: Secretary Rusk, President Johnson said last
Friday that the Vietcong did not achieve their objective
of a general uprising in the South.   What does that say
to you, that they did not or have not yet achieved a
general uprising?

Rusk: You know, I think it's possible, Mr. Lisagor,
that these people living within totalitarian practices of
thought and expression may actually have believed that if
they came into town, came into the provincial capitals, that
there would be a popular uprising.   Now that has not
occurred.

Today, for example, the National Assembly out there has
passed a very strong resolution on solidarity with the
government.   One of the important Presidential candidates
in opposition to the present President, Dr. Suu, issued
a similar statement.   The labor groups have issued statements of solidarity.   We have not seen evidences around
the countryside of what the Vietcong might call a popular
uprising.

Now, we have known for some months that they were going to
launch a winter-spring offensive, as they call it, which
they anticipated would trigger off such a popular uprising.
Now, I have no doubt that there are some people in South
Vietnam who are grumpy, as there are a few people here
who are grumpy, because somehow it was not possible to
give them complete protection against what has happened
in the last few days.

But, on the other hand, we find widespread sense of outrage and reaction against this campaign of terror put on
by the Vietcong.   So I would say that there is very little
prospect or evidence of that popular uprising that they
were talking about when they launched the offensive.

Lisagor: Secretary Rusk, at the time of the Bay of Pigs
in 1961, the Cuban rebels thought that when they landed
there, there would be a popular uprising against Castro.
At that time we did not say that the people in Cuba were
in favor of Castro because there was no popular uprising.
My question is, might it not be that the South Vietnamese
people are just simply apathetic about this whole war?

Rusk: Oh, I think that there are those in some of the
villages who are villagers, as are people all over the
world who pay little attention to what is going on at the
center of political power.   They are not basically
politically motivated.   They want to know what is going
to happen to the crops, whether their babies are going
to be born in good health, whether they can be protected
against outside marauders of any sort.   But I have been
very much impressed with the fact   that all of the

principal groups in South Vietnam--the Buddhists, the
Catholics, Montagnards, the two sects that occupy the
southwest part of the country, the million refugees from
North Vietnam that came down 10 years ago--these groups,
although they differ among themselves on various aspects,
seem to be united on the fact that they do not want what
Hanoi is trying to impose upon them, or what the Vietcong
is offering them. We just have not seen it in any grass-
roots movement flowing through the country in this connection.

Lisagor: But, Mr. Secretary, in order to have infiltrated
as many men and as much equipment as they did into cities
like Saigon, didn't they have to have a large measure of
acquiescence if not actual collusion from the people in
those cities?

Rusk: I would not say a large measure. You see, during
the Tet period the entire population of Vietnam is on
the move. People are going back to their places of birth,
they are rejoining their families, there is a lot of traffic on the roads. The suicide group that attacked the
American Embassy apparently came in in a truckload of
flowers according to some of the reports I have seen.

Now, that kind of infiltration in civilian clothes, on
motor scooters, on buses, that kind of infiltration can
occur. What is important is that they did not succeed,
and were not permitted to succeed.

Spivak: Secretary McNamara, may I ask you a question?
According to the latest press reports the communists
lost about 15,000 men killed against only 350 for the
United States. Now there are many people [who] are
skeptical of those tremendous odds. How do our military
men have time, in an emergency like that, to count the
dead? How do they obtain these figures?

McNamara: They make the best estimate possible. And,
by the way, let me correct one of your figures. The
latest reports of Americans killed total 415. But in any
event, the estimates of enemy dead are based on battlefield reports. They carry the error that you would expect from battlefield conditions; but they are a reasonable approximation of the price the enemy is paying for
his current operations. To some degree they may be
overstated, but we know there are many understatements
as well. Those reports do not include the dead from
artillery and air action, for example. We know the enemy
seeks to remove the dead from the battlefield. So
they're a reasonable approximation of the price the enemy
is paying, corroborated in part by the actual count of

enemy weapons captured, some 3,800. And we know normally there's a ratio of three or four to one between weapons captured and men killed on the battlefield.

Spivak: Mr. Secretary, one more question. The President described the recent attack against South Vietnam as a complete failure as a military movement. That's not the impression any of us get from the press reports. Would you describe that as a complete failure?

McNamara: Well, I think the President pointed out that this was but the first act of a three-act play. And we can't forecast the second and third scenes at the present time. Furthermore, there are pluses and minuses that we should watch, as I mentioned a moment ago. It's quite clear that the military objective of the attack has not been achieved. It was to divert U.S. troops and South Vietnamese troops from the probable offensive action of the Vietcong and North Vietnamese around Khe Sanh; and secondarily it was to penetrate and hold one or more district or provincial capitals. In that sense the military objective has not been achieved, because the troops have not been diverted, and the district and provincial capitals have not been held. The political objective of an uprising which Mr. Lisagor referred to has not been achieved.

And let me say, since he mentioned the Bay of Pigs, that I have never said publicly, and I want to say today, that when President Kennedy assumed full responsibility for that action he didn't say what he might have said, that every single one of his advisors, me included, recommended it. So I was responsible for that.

In any event, they did not achieve their political objective. Nor have they fully achieved their psychological objective, although I think there have been pluses and minuses psychologically. There's no question but what the people of the cities and towns of South Vietnam have been dealt a heavy blow. They must have been surprised, they must have been impressed by the weight of the attack. But at the same time we know that they have been revolted by the violence and the brutality of the attack. And the Vietcong are going to leave those cities and towns with less support than when they entered them.

Abel: Secretary Rusk, to return just for one moment to the *Pueblo*, you were saying a few minutes ago that if, after recovering the ship and crew, we were to discover that it had in fact been inside territorial waters, we would make those facts known. Are you prepared to go one step farther and to say now, or to have Secretary McNamara say now, that if there was such an infraction the men would be disciplined?

Rusk: Well, if there were such an infraction--and we have not the slightest evidence that there was such an infraction--presumably those men would have to--at least the skipper--would have to face the fact that there was a violation of very stringent orders in this respect; and I leave that question to Secretary McNamara.

But let me point out something that is quite important here. Warships on the high seas, according to the 1958 Conventions on the Law of the Sea, warships on the high seas have complete immunity from the jurisdiction of any state other than the flag state. Now, let's assume just for a moment that what is obviously not true from the testimony from all sides, including the North Vietnamese side, that this ship was picked up in territorial waters or in waters claimed by North Korea to be territorial waters. Even there, under the Convention of the Law of the Sea, 1958, Article 23 makes it quite clear that if any warship comes into territorial waters the coastal state can require it to leave; it does not obtain a right to seize it. Now in 1965 and 1966 there were three incidents in which a Soviet war vessel came into American territorial waters, within our three-mile limit. We didn't seize those vessels. We simply required them to depart. That is the civilized practice among nations in dealing with such questions because warships have a sovereign immunity attached to them, you see. Under no theory of the case can the action taken by North Korea be justified.

Abel: Secretary McNamara, would you care to follow up on this point about disciplining the skipper if in fact we discover he was in territorial waters?

McNamara: We would always discipline a commander if he violated his instructions consciously or through negligence. We have no evidence that he did here. I certainly wouldn't want to predict any action we would take following his return.

Rogers: Secretary McNamara, on the question of enemy dead in this latest offensive, upward of 15,000, how can you tell if a dead person was a Vietcong?

McNamara: In some cases they wear Vietcong uniforms; in other cases they have Vietcong weapons in their hands. Roughly a third or a fourth of them had Vietcong weapons in their hands. In other cases they carry Vietcong documents and identification on them. I don't think we should imply that the 15,000 dead are all from the main force units of the Vietcong or the North Vietnamese regular army units that have been infiltrated into South Vietnam. Undoubtedly some of the dead represent guerrillas, porters, logistical personnel.

Rogers: Well now, since the South Vietnamese forces were primarily engaged in this action, your figures, I guess, come primarily from the South Vietnamese; and in a short space of time do you have any way to check up on this, to make sure that the figures aren't inflated?

McNamara: Let me first emphasize a point you implied by your question. It is true the South Vietnamese forces were primarily engaged in this action. They're the ones who are bearing the brunt of the fighting; and of course they're also bearing the heaviest casualties. I mentioned a moment ago that there have been 415 Americans killed, but there have been 904 South Vietnamese killed.

Now, to specifically answer your question--how in the midst of battle do we in the United States know of the accuracy of these figures--and of course the answer is we don't. They're the best possible estimates. They come to us not from the South Vietamese, but from the American advisors who are accompanying the South Vietnamese units.

Rogers: Even if those figures are correct down to almost the fractions that we get--you know, you get figures like 13,722--even if those are correct, how can a small country like North Vietnam continue to suffer these heavy losses and still be able to, as you said a moment ago, fight and, apparently in some cases, improve their fighting.

McNamara: The population of North Vietnam is about 17 million. I think it's quite clear they have a manpower supply that will continue to support losses of the kind they're absorbing. Whether they can support them psychologically and politically is another question.

Rogers: Isn't there something Orwellian about it, that the more we kill, the stronger they get?

McNamara: I don't think it's fair to say that they're getting stronger. It's the balance of force that's important here. And it's very clear that they're not as strong today as they were three-and-a-half years ago. Three-and-a-half years ago the South Vietnamese forces were on the verge of defeat; the North Vietnamese and Vietcong forces were on the verge of victory. That is not true today. The balance has definitely moved toward the South Vietnamese. I think, however, that you are putting undue emphasis on the military aspects of this war. This is a complicated situation. There isn't a simply military solution to it. It's a political-economic-military problem. Each of these facets intertwined. And we should not only examine the military operations when we're talking about relative balance of progress.

Spivak: I must interrupt briefly here. . . . (Interruption for commercial.)

Spivak: . . . We will continue the questioning now with Mr. Frankel.

Frankel: Secretary Rusk, the Administration has naturally enough been stressing the things that they think the Vietcong did not achieve in this week of attacks--didn't cause an uprising which you say may have been one of their goals; didn't seize cities for any permanent period. But yet we've also been given to understand that the real name of this game out there is who can provide safety for whom. And haven't they in a very serious way humiliated our ability in major cities all up and down this country to provide the South Vietnamese population that is listed as clearly in our control with a degree of assurance and safety that South Vietnamese forces and American forces together could give them?

Rusk: There's almost no way to prevent the other side from making a try. There is a way to prevent them from having a success. I said earlier that I though that there would be a number of South Vietnamese who would take a very grumpy view over the inability of the government to protect them against some of the things that have happened in the last three or four days. But the net effect of the transaction is to make it clear that the Vietcong are not able to come into these provincial capitals and seize provincial capitals and hold them; that they're not able to announce the formation of a new committee, of a coalition, sort of federation and have it pick up any support in the country. That they're not able to undermine the solidarity of those who are supporting the government. No, I think there's a psychological factor here that we won't be able to assess until a week or two after the event. And I might say also that we know there's going to be some hard fighting ahead; we're not over this period at all.

As a matter of fact, the major fighting up in the northern part of South Vietnam has not yet occurred. So there [are] some hard battles ahead.

Frankel: Are we sure, by the way, sir, that that whole buildup in the North was not intended as a diversion from what has already taken place?

Rusk: Well, it has not succeeded in drawing forces away from other missions. After all, the other side has to take into account the fact that something in the order of 15,000 of their people have been killed and another 4,000 or 5,000 have been taken prisoner. We can see some of the

pains on our own side, but imagine yourself at the general
headquarters of the Vietcong-North Vietnamese forces and
see how they would be toting up the situation at the
present time.

In the III and IV Corps areas they've committed practically every unit they had. There have been some up in II and
I Corps that have not been committed in the situation. Now
they've had disastrous losses. Undoubtedly there is going
to be some sag in morale due to what has happened in the
last three or four days, but this could be followed by a
sharp increase in morale when it is discovered that even
this kind of an effort has produced no result for the
other side.

Frankel: What does this tell us, in terms of American
impatience with this war, about what we could really
negotiate and leave out there? Is it really still possible to say that, unless every Vietcong were to be turned
in, and if they were to turn their weapons cache in, that
we could leave that country in six months and that the
South Vietnamese government is capable of extending its
writ if it can't control Saigon?

Rusk: Well, if the North Vietnamese forces go home, if
the violence in the South subsides, the countries with
troops in South Vietnam have indicated they could take
their forces out in a period of about six months' time.

Frankel: But these attacks were not organized by the
North Vietnamese, were they, sir?

Rusk: Well, of course they were. There were North
Vietnamese regiments involved in these attacks. Let's
not be under a misapprehension, Mr. Frankel, that these
military actions are not under the control of Hanoi.

Frankel: No, I'm not questioning the control of the
organization; but weren't they largely Vietcong forces?

Rusk: Well, the Vietcong forces in III and IV Corps made
the principal, made up the principal numbers of those
conducting the attack, but there were North Vietnamese
elements involved there, and in the II Corps there were
significant numbers of North Vietnamese. The concentration of North Vietnamese forces around the Khe Sanh area
did not take part in these operations, but this is a
North Vietnamese-Vietcong operation which cannot be sorted
out and separated out as between one and the other. This
was a joint enterprise.

Lisagor: Secretary McNamara, a great many people, myself
included, have been puzzled by why, in view of the advance
intelligence we had about the enemy actions in Vietnam,
they were able to achieve such tactical surprise? They

apparently directed their attacks against areas supposed-
ly defended by South Vietnamese Army units. Was that correct? And what happened to those South Vietnamese Army
units?

McNamara: We did have advance intelligence of the winter-
spring campaign offensive that the North Vietnamese were
planning. We know that it includes a major attack in the
northern part of South Vietnam. We believed it also included planned attacks on the cities and towns, particularly the district headquarters and province capitals in
the 44 provinces. We didn't know the date on which these
guerrilla attacks would take place, and we didn't know
the specific targets.

I doubt very much that intelligence would ever provide
that much detail. I think it's perfectly clear that the
South Vietnamese had sufficient intelligence to maintain
their forces in a state of alert such that they were able
to inflict these very heavy penalties on the Vietcong and
North Vietnamese. But I would be the last to tell you
that we had perfect intelligence. We certainly did not.

Lisagor: Mr. Secretary, the White House itself said that
we knew to the day, to be precise and quote them, that
these attacks would occur.

McNamara: We knew that they were scheduling very large
attacks in the north part of South Vietnam for the Tet
or post-Tet period. We certainly didn't know to the hour,
the day, the attack planned on the American Embassy, for
example, or some other structure. And it's absolutely
impossible to obtain that kind of knowledge. We'll never
have an intelligence system that will provide it to us.

Lisagor: Would the Vietcong have been less able to stage
these attacks, especially in the Highlands area, if we
had not diverted the 15,000 troops to the Khe Sanh area?

McNamara: No, I think that it's very clear that the
Vietcong would have had essentially the same capability.
The diversion of troops from other areas in South Viet-
nam--which wasn't great, by the way--the buildup in the
Khe Sanh area has come largely from the total increase
in our forces in South Vietnam over the past three or
four months. But in any event I think the result would
have been essentially the same.

Lisagor: Secretary McNamara, you said in your posture
statement before the Congress this week that the main
force units of the enemy are not capable of winning major
battles against U.S. forces. The President said last
Friday that a full-scale battle is now imminent at Khe
Sanh, and I think you suggested that earlier on this

program. Why are they trying this kind of tactic? Why
are they throwing themselves into a major battle against
what should be our long suit?

McNamara: Well, this is sheer speculation on my part.
I can only suggest to you that they hope to inflict a
severe defeat upon us, a defeat of the kind they inflicted
on the French at Dienbienphu. We believe we're prepared
with such forces and such strategy and tactics and equipment and supplies to prevent that.

Spivak: Secretary Rusk, may I ask you a question?

Rusk: Yes.

Spivak: The President the other day asked this question--
he said, what would the North Vietnamese be doing if we
stopped the bombing and let them alone? Now, there is
some confusion about what we want them to do. What is it
we want them to do today if we stop the bombing?

Rusk: Well, many, many months ago the President said
almost anything as a step towards peace. Now, I think
it is important to understand the political significance
of the events of the last three or four days in South
Vietnam. President Johnson said some weeks ago that we
are exploring the difference between the statement of
their foreign minister about entering into discussions
and his own San Antonio formula.

Now we have been in the process of exploring the problems
that arise when you put those two statements side by side.
Hanoi knows that. They know that these explorations are
going on, because they were a party to them. Secondly,
we have exercised some restraint in our bombing in North
Vietnam during this period of exploration, particularly
in the immediate vicinity of Hanoi and Haiphong. Again,
Hanoi knows this. They also knew that the Tet cease-fire
period was coming up.

Spivak: Have we stopped the bombing there?

Rusk: No, we have not had a pause in the traditionally
accepted sense, but we have limited the bombing at certain
points in order to make it somewhat easier to carry forward
these explorations so that particularly difficult incidents
would not interrupt them. We have not gone into a pause
as that word is generally understood.

But they've also known that the Tet cease-fire was coming
up. And they've known from earlier years that we've been
interested in converting something like a Tet cease-fire
into a more productive dialogue, into some opportunity to
move toward peace.

Now, in the face of all these elements, they participated in laying on this major offensive. Now, I think it would be foolish not to draw a political conclusion from this that they are not seriously interested at the present time in talking about peaceful settlement. Or in exploring the problems connected with the San Antonio formula. I remind those who don't recall that formula that it was that we would stop the bombing when it would lead promptly to productive discussions. And we assumed that they would not take advantage of this cessation of bombing while such discussions were going on.

Now, it's hard to imagine a more reasonable proposal by any nation involved in an armed conflict than that. And I think we have to assume that these recent offensives in the South are an answer, in addition to their public denunciation of the San Antonio formula.

Abel: Are you saying, Mr. Secretary, that we interpret this offensive as their rejection of the diplomatic overtures that have been made?

Rusk: Well, they have rejected the San Antonio formula publicly, simply on the political level. And I think it would be foolish for us not to take into account what they're doing on the ground when we try to analyze what their political position is. You remember the old saying that what you do speaks so loud I can't hear what you say. Now we can't be indifferent to these actions on the ground and think that these have no consequences from a political point of view. So they know where we live. Everything that we've said, our 14 points, 28 proposals to which we've said yes and to which they've said no, the San Antonio formula, all these things remain there on the table for anyone who is interested in moving toward peace. They're all there. But they know where we live and we'd be glad to hear from them sometime at their convenience when they decide that they want to move toward peace.

Abel: I'm assuming, sir, that the San Antonio formula stands as our longer-term position here.

Rusk: That is correct.

Abel: Aren't we leaving out of account, however, a thought that is embodied in these many captured documents that have been thrown around so much in the discussion here, namely that they did speak of a general uprising and of inflicting humiliating defeats upon us, of capturing province capitals, but all of this was somehow keyed to imminent negotiations, to strengthening their position beforehand. Isn't that right?

Rusk: Well, I would suppose if that is true--and I can't confirm that that is true in terms of what I know about the attitude of the other side--but to the extent that is true, then I would suppose that they would be further off from negotiations than before, because they now have to count 20,000 killed and captured in the last few days.

Rogers: Secretary McNamara, you're approaching the end of a long and distinguished career as Secretary of Defense, and during that time I don't think I've ever heard you make quite the statement you made a moment ago in which you said that you were--pleaded that you had made a mistake in your Bay of Pigs recommendation. Can you think of any other cases where you also failed?

McNamara: I can think of far more than the time would permit me to list, and I don't propose to start trying. But I do want to emphasize what I said a moment ago, and it's very much on my conscience that I recommended that we undertake the Bay of Pigs, and it was a serious error; and it was an error for which President Kennedy assumed full responsibility, and that was a gallant deed, but I want the American people to know that it wasn't by any means a decision that was not supported by others in the government. It was recommended to him unanimously by all of his advisors.

Rogers: Let me prod you on another case and get back to Vietnam. It seems to me to go really to Mr. Lisagor's point a moment ago, that the fact that this thing was able to succeed as much as it did may, it seems to me, indicate a failure at least of our pacification program. If the people were coming over they would have told us.

McNamara: No, I don't think so, any more than we could expect to stop uprisings in our cities in this country. These guerrilla-type actions can be initiated by a few, and the many can't stop them. The many can prevent them from succeeding, but the many cannot stop them from starting. And I think that's exactly what's happened in South Vietnam today.

Frankel: Secretary McNamara, let me take advantage of your valedictory mood. Looking back over this long conflict, and especially in this rather agonized week in Vietnam, if we had to do it all over again would you make any major changes in our approach?

McNamara: This is not an appropriate time for me to be talking of changes, with hindsight. There's no question but what five or ten or twenty years from now the historians will find actions that might have been done differently; I'm sure they will. As a matter of fact, my wife pointed out to me the other day four lines from T. S. Eliot that answer your question. Eliot said: "We shall not cease from exploration. And the end of all our exploring will be to arrive where we started and know the place for the first time." Now that applies to Vietnam. I'm learning more and more about Vietnam every day. There's no question I see better today than I did three years ago or five years ago what might have been done there. On balance, I feel much the way the Asian leaders do. I think the action that this government has followed, the policies it's followed, the objectives it's had in Vietnam are wise. I don't by any means suggest that we haven't made mistakes over the many, many years that we've been pursuing those objectives.

Frankel: You seem to suggest that we really didn't, that none of us appreciated what we were really getting into.

McNamara: I don't think any of us predicted seven years ago or fifteen years ago the deployment of 500,000 men in Vietnam; I know I didn't.

Rusk: But I think, Mr. Frankel, if I may interrupt here, part of this is that we have tried at every stage to bring this matter to a peaceful conclusion. Now in retrospect, was it a mistake or not to go to the Laos conference in 1962? There President Kennedy and I thought that we ought to try to remove that little country from the conflict in Southeast Asia. Had we succeeded, that would have been a major step toward peace in Southeast Asia. On the other hand we got no performance on that agreement. The North Vietnamese troops stayed there. They continued to use it for infiltration. Now, some of our mistakes, if you like, have been through an effort to bring it to a peaceful conclusion without an enlargement of the conflict. And that is something that I think this country will always be inclined to do because our major purpose is peace in these situations.

Lisagor: Secretary Rusk, I'd like to quote a statement from Secretary McNamara and then ask you a question about it. In his posture report he said that we cannot provide South Vietnam with the will to survive as an independent nation, or with a sense of national purpose. I'd like to ask you whether you're satisfied that they're developing this will and sense in view of the fact that they've not yet declared a state of mobilization, they still don't draft 18- and 19-year olds for their army.

Rusk: Well, I've seen many countries in a state of crisis in my lifetime and it' s always easy to find one or another weak spot in a particular performance. But I must say what impresses me is the dogged determination of all of these major elements in South Vietnam not to accept what

Hanoi is trying to impose upon them by force. Now of course there are difficulties. If you listened to the expression of difficulties among the Allies during World War II you would have wondered how we ever won the war. There were enormous difficulties in the Korean struggle. No one minimizes those. But there has been, despite 20 years of conflict in Vietnam, there has been apparent a determination not to accept what Hanoi is trying to impose upon them by force. That doesn't mean they act with complete solidarity on every question. And I think they are going ahead with their manpower program. I think surely it is fair to give the legislature a chance to look at these mobilization decrees. After all, we claim we're interested in a democratic government out there. So the legislature is now looking at those measures; just as we would expect our Congress to look at similar measures in this country. So we can't have it both ways. We can't expect from them the efficiency of a totalitarian society and the relaxation of a democratic society.

McNamara: Since you quoted me, may I interrupt one moment to say that the South Vietnamese would be the first to endorse what I said. This is their war, and the reason it's their war is that it's not primarily a military war. It's a political war. And what they're trying to do is create a state and they can do it, not we. Only they can do it; and that's basically what I said, and what I believe.

Rusk: May I just illustrate this point again, Mr. Lisagor, because we are in situations where whatever you do there is bound to be some criticism. The South Vietnamese could have prevented much of this infiltration had they organized themselves as a totalitarian society. This kind of infiltration and this kind of exercise could not have been carried on in North Vietnam because every hamlet, every precinct, every home has got a watchdog in it.

Now if the South Vietnamese had organized themselves to prevent, in line with some of the present criticism, prevent what happened, then they would have their ears boxed most roundly by people in this country for being so totalitarian about it. In other words, you can't win if the determination is to criticize whatever happens.

Lisagor: But the point, Mr. Secretary, is that South Korea is not totalitarian and yet I understand that 85 percent of those who had infiltrated into South Korea from the North recently were informed about by the South Korean citizens.

Rusk: Yes; we're talking about hundreds there and not tens of thousands as we're talking about with Vietnam.

Spivak: Secretary McNamara, may I ask you a question on the *Pueblo*? There are many Americans [who] are very greatly disturbed that a ship as important as the *Pueblo* could be captured so easily. Why wasn't it better protected?

McNamara: I think it's a good question, and the answer is threefold. First, to have protected it would have been a provocative act. Secondly, it would have compromised the mission. This ship went undetected by the North Koreans for 10 to 12 days; during that period of time it carried out its mission. Not only would it have been subject to capture during that period had it been detected, but also their reaction, a reaction that it was sent there to determine, would have been quite different. And, finally, the protection itself always runs the risk of leading to military escalation.

There is, of course, beyond that the fact that is very important that Secretary Rusk mentioned; we are operating on the high seas in an entirely legal fashion. Neither the Soviets or we protect ships of this kind. Nor do we protect aircraft of similar kinds. You will remember that we lost an RB-47 shot down by the Soviets on a mission similar to this in 1960. It was unprotected. Neither then nor now do we protect it for reasons I've outlined.

Spivak: Well now, Mr. Secretary, I understand that it took two hours to tow the *Pueblo* into the port of Wonsan. Why did we fail to rescue the ship during that time?

McNamara: There were three or four reasons why reaction forces were not sent. First, it was necessary to find out what happened. It takes time. In the case of the *Liberty* in the Mediterranean in June as an example, I thought the *Liberty* had been attacked by Soviet forces. Thank goodness our carrier commanders did not launch immediately against the Soviet forces that were operating in the Med at the time. I then thought it had been attacked by Egyptian forces. Who else could have done it? Thank goodness we didn't launch against the Egyptians; we took time to find out that it was the Israelis.

Now the same kind of a problem exists with respect to the *Pueblo*. Secondly, we don't maintain contingency plans to prevent the hijacking of each individual American ship operating on the high seas. Thirdly, any reaction force that would have moved into the area would have moved into the air-control sectors of the North Korean air defenses manned by about 500 aircraft. And almost surely any reaction force that we could have mounted or could have been expected to mount would have faced a bloody battle at the time. And, finally, I think it's quite clear with hindsight that no reaction force could have saved those men.

Rusk: I would like to add, if I may on that, that the Soviets have about 18 of these ships scattered around the world: some of them off our own coasts, some of them in the Sea of Japan, one of them off Guam.   I would hope very much they would not attempt to put aircap and pro- tection around these vessels when they come into our general vicinity.

Spivak: Well, Secretary McNamara, am I to conclude from what you have just said that the same thing can happen to other American ships?

McNamara: Yes, I think so.   I think it can happen to our ships, it can happen to British ships, it can happen to Japanese ships, it can happen to Russian ships.

Spivak: Gentlemen, we have less than four minutes.

Abel: I don't know which of you ought to get this ques- tion, but it has to do with the fact that the 1965 ground buildup and the beginning of the bombing was triggered, you will recall, by similar terror attacks at Pleiku and Qui Nhon, similar to what we have now seen in some 20-odd cities of Vietnam.   What is our answer going to be this time?   Do we send more men?

McNamara: The commanders haven't asked for more men; they feel they have adequate strength to meet the situation now and as far into the future as they project.   I don't want to foreclose the possibility of requests in the future, but we have received none to date.

While I'm on that, let me simply say we're prepared to send more men if more are required.   We've sent three carriers into the Korean waters, plus substantial reinforcements to our air power there, all out of active forces, without in any way reducing the forces in Western Europe or Southeast Asia.   We can send additional aircraft or additional ground forces from our active forces, should that prove necessary.

Rogers: Secretary Rusk, Roger Hilsman, who used to work for you, says that we either have to change our goal now in Vietnam--which is to prevent the spread of communism to the South--or invade North Vietnam.   What is your re- action to that?

Rusk: Well, it's been some three years now since I've had the benefit of Mr. Roger Hilsman's advice; I don't expect to take it seriously now.

Frankel: Secretary McNamara, we've--the sum total of what you and Mr. Rusk say is that while they were hitting us in the guts of our cities in South Vietnam we were in fact restraining ourselves on their biggest cities in North Vietnam.   Are we going to retaliate?

McNamara: I don't want to anticipate future decisions of military operations.

Lisagor: Secretary Rusk, to clarify our terms now for halting the bombing, you've said just a little while ago almost anything now; Mr. Clifford says normal activity. Whatever happened to the concept of reciprocity and mutual de-escalation that was talked about in the past?

Rusk: Yes. President Johnson stated at San Antonio that we assume that the other side will not take advantage, military advantage, of a cessation of the bombing while discussions are going forward. Now, that is something which can be explored privately. Such explorations were in process. It would not be, I think, advisable for me to get into details because it may be that we'll reach a point where that process can be picked up again. But these are matters which can only get somewhere if there is some interest on the other side in a peaceful settlement of this situation; and thus far we don't see much evidence of that.

Lisagor: But since we are somewhat confused about the terms, is the enemy perfectly clear about them, Mr. Secretary?

Rusk: I would think that Hanoi is more clear than you are, Mr. Lisagor.

Abel: Mr. Secretary, do you find it at all odd or contradictory that in the same week in which we lost a nuclear armed bomber in Greenland we appealed to the Russians of all people to help spring our men from Korea?

Rusk: No, I wouldn't connect these two in any way. This was an unfortunate accident there, but it had no political significance; it was an operational accident. We called upon the Russians and other governments because they have effective contact with the North Koreans and also because they have a very important stake in these elementary principles of international law with respect to open seas.

Spivak: I'm sorry to interrupt, Mr. Secretary, but our time is up. Thank you Secretary Rusk and Secretary McNamara for being with us today on "Meet the Press."

APPENDIX XV

The Washington *Post,*
February 6, 1968

A THIRD OF MY THO DESTROYED IN DELTA BATTLE

By Lee Lescaze

My Tho, South Vietnam, Feb. 5--A third of My Tho is
destroyed. Perhaps 50 percent of this prosperous Mekong
Delta city's people have lost their homes.

No one is sure how many civilians have been killed. About
300 are known dead, some killed by allied bombing, others
by the Vietcong or after being caught in a cross fire.
More than 1,000 wounded have been treated in the provincial
hospital.

Rue Pasteur on the west side of the city is a dusty line
between piles of broken brick and a few standing walls.
Twenty-one beat and burned-out buses stand where they
were parked last Tuesday night, before three Vietcong
battalions, operating from a command post in the bus station, opened the battle for My Tho at 3 a.m., Wednesday.

The Vietcong began infiltrating My Tho on January 29, according to American officials trying to reconstruct the
battle. They arrived in small groups by bus, motor
scooter, sampan, and foot. People now say they noticed
numbers of men entering the city with heavy parcels and
without the wives or children of family groups traveling
for the Tet holidays.

Police officials said many of these men went straight to
a barbershop and came out minutes later without their
parcels. The barber was not questioned because no one
wanted to embarrass him, one account has it.

In the first hours Vietcong patrols were in almost every
part of the city. U.S. civilians, none of whom was injured
during the battle, watched from windows and rooftops.

Those that fired, such as deputy senior province advisor
Peter Brownbeck of Arlington, Virginia, were quickly pinned
down by Vietcong automatic weapons.

"Ive seen a lot of scrawny, little Vietcong prisoners and corpses," one American said, "but that night the Vietcong outside my window looked seven feet tall."

The 33rd Vietnamese Rangers blunted part of the Vietcong offensive at their headquarters on the edge of town. Although the Rangers had fired off a lot of ammunition the night before to celebrate Tet, and had about 300 of their 580 men away on holiday leave, they made a brave and successful stand.

Rangers dropped hand grenades from the second floor of their headquarters at Vietcong who had penetrated three lines of barbed wire surrounding the building. After clouding the courtyard with smoke grenades, the Rangers counterattacked and routed the enemy. Of the 360 Vietcong bodies reported in My Tho, 102 were killed in the clash.

The 1st Battalion of the Vietnamese 11th Regiment, which was guarding the 7th Division headquarters and My Tho, was also down to less than 200 men when the Vietcong attacked. The Tet holiday appears to have worked both ways, however. A number of Vietnamese armored personnel carriers, which usually patrol Highway Four around the city, were in My Tho the morning of the attack.

The armored units and the infantry battalion kept the Vietcong away from division headquarters, the provincial headquarters for Dinh Tuong province, and other key buildings. By the afternoon of the 31st, about 12 hours after the fighting started, the Vietcong occupied the north and west sections of the city, but were no longer active in other areas.

Brig. Gen. Nguyen Viet Thanh, commander of the 7th Division, considered calling for air strikes and infantry battalions from the U.S. 9th Infantry Division camp three miles west. For the moment, he decided the battle of My Tho was going to be a Vietnamese show.

The next day, however, General Thanh changed his mind, and jets and helicopter gunships began to blast the city. Two battalions of U.S. infantry from Dong Tam arrived 24 hours later.

Most Americans believe the bombing was necessary to save other sections of the city and the lives of the thousands of people who had left their homes to camp in the streets and park on the southeast corner of the city.

The area bombed was one of the poorer sections of My Tho --and one of the most crowded. Bombs and artillery shells touched off numerous secondary explosions as they hit Vietcong ammunition storage areas, and parts of the area are blackened by fire.

As for the casualties, all Vietnamese doctors and nurses
were away for Tet and many have been unable to get back
to My Tho. U.S. and Filipino medical teams handled most
of the emergency patients but couldn't get at many needed
medical supplies that had been locked up.

My Tho still smells of death. Most of the bodies--Viet-
cong and friendly--have been removed from the streets, but
some remain. In the wreckage of their homes, people are
looking for things to save.

There is little emotion and less noise: For a crowded
area in Vietnam it is almost impossibly quiet.

In recent months My Tho knew that the Vietcong were coming
closer to the city but it has been years since My Tho was
attacked by Vietcong troops.

The city has grown rapidly to about 80,000 people because
of the war in the countryside and because of its prosperity.
It is the first important city south of Saigon and supplies
much of the capital's food from its rice and vegetable
fields.

Vegetable farming was pushed by American advisors and it
was a great success here. Now Highway Four, which must
carry the produce to Saigon, is closed--cut in 48 places
in Dinh Tuong province both north and west of My Tho with
main bridges out and one bridge on the outskirts of this
city still in Vietcong hands today. No vegetables can be
shipped and many will rot.

Before the coordinated Vietcong attacks against 31 of
Vietnam's 44 province capitals plus Saigon and other major
cities last week, the road from Saigon to My Tho was one
of the most secure in Vietnam. No one knows how long it
will be closed.

The Vietcong have been driven out of My Tho but they are
staying close to the city. Mortar rounds landed last
might and there was a small probe against the power stations.

Initially, Vietnamese officials have responded quickly
to the problems of reconstruction. Seven committees have
been established and the 5,000 to 7,000 homeless are being
taken care of in schools and churches. The majority of
the estimated 40,000 whose homes were destroyed have been
taken in by family and friends.

"The attack made the official community realize this isn't
a play war," one official said. It is too early to tell
what the people of My Tho are thinking, most observers
agree. Their respect for the power of the Vietcong has
been increased, it is generally acknowledged, but they are
also angry that the attack came during the Tet holiday.

One result of their anger has been a new willingness to give information to the South Vietnamese Army and the Americans. "They're going out of their way to tell us things now they never would have volunteered before," an American said.

APPENDIX XVI

The New York *Times,*
February 8, 1968

SURVIVORS HUNT DEAD OF BEN TRE, TURNED TO RUBBLE IN ALLIED RAIDS

By Bernard Weinraub

Ben Tre, South Vietnam, Feb. 7--On this warm, languid day in Ben Tre, children picked through the smoldering rubble in the marketplace, American soldiers patrolled shattered streets, South Vietnamese troops scoured empty blocks for bodies, and Mrs. Dieu Thi Sam sat stunned in the bombed wreckage of her home and wept.

She pointed to the sky. "The first bomb landed on the next house," she said in Vietnamese. "I ran down the street and began to cry. My house exploded. I keep crying. I cannot stop."

In this provincial capital in the Mekong Delta, 30 miles south of Saigon, nearly 1,000 South Vietnamese are believed to be dead after one of the bitterest battles of the week's Vietcong offensive.

"STILL DIGGING THEM OUT"

"We're still not too sure of the casualties," said one American officer in the steamy military compound facing the Ben Tre Canal. "We figure 1,000 dead and 1,500 wounded. We're still digging them out."

Four hamlets thought to be controlled by the Vietcong have been razed by allied bombing and artillery attacks and fire from armed helicopters. Near the canal, still fringed with pines and mango trees, is an area of the town where a zigzag row of bricks is the only remnant of two-story and three-story houses.

"The VC had people all over this town," said Maj. Phillip Cannella, the operations officer for the Military Assistance Command in Ben Tre. "Christ, they were everywhere."

As the capital of Kien Hoa province, this town of 50,000 has long been a stronghold of the Vietcong. Among South Vietnamese, Ben Tre is sometimes considered a Vietcong rest and recreation area where guerrillas prepare for moves throughout the Delta and Saigon.

REGIMENT SWEEPS IN

The Vietcong attacks on Ben Tre began last Wednesday shortly after 1 a.m. Firing recoilless rifles, 82 mm. mortars, and rockets, a reinforced Vietcong regiment of 2,500 men swept into the capital from the south and east, hitting the Ben Tre airstrip and moving swiftly toward a four-block square in the heart of town, the headquarters of the government provincial chief and the American and South Vietnamese military forces.

"They had apparently infiltrated into most of the town," an American officer said today. "They were probably living with the people. It was Tet and there were plenty of strangers in town."

Because of Tet--the Lunar New Year--the protection of Ben Tre was limited. The two South Vietnamese battalions guarding the perimeter had a total of only 500 men, half the normal number. The other soldiers were on a holiday.

The 40-man United States military compound, under heavy ground attack, called for support. Five patrol boats with .50 caliber machine guns steamed south along the canal, opening fire on the Vietcong, who were staging their heaviest ground attacks at the South Vietnamese military headquarters.

"In those first 24 hours," an American military official said, "We can credit those Navy PBRs with keeping them off. If it weren't for them, we wouldn't be here." PBRs are river patrol boats.

For nearly 40 hours, American officers say, the Vietcong contolled the town except for the four blocks near the canal.

By Thursday afternoon, bombing raids and fire by helicopter gunships and artillery were ordered for sections of the town. "We were calling artillery and gunships just yards away from our own positions," one officer said.

TWO COMPANIES LAND

As stucco and brick and straw homes collapsed under the bombing, two companies of the United States 9th Infantry Division landed in the center of the city and were immediately attacked.

Within the square and at a nearby bridge, the American troops and the Vietcong fought bitterly through the night.

Two more 9th Division companies were brought in by helicopter.

By dawn Friday, the fighting subsided. The Vietcong lost as many as 400 men, according to officers here. The number of Americans who died remains unclear, but may be 20 to 30 men.

At the 350-bed hospital, the maimed and wounded filled the beds and floors and aisles.

The market place is rubble and near the gutted homes near-by women in shawls sit in the noon heat and mourn with loud groans.

APPENDIX XVII

BACKGROUND PRESS BRIEFING,
GEN. CREIGHTON W. ABRAMS, USA, SAIGON, FEBRUARY 8, 1968

What I'd like to do to start this, I--some of it may be repetitive of what you've already heard--in that case I apologize. What I want to do--I went up to the Highlands on the 3rd and went down to the Delta on the 4th and talked to division commanders and advisors and the corps commander and his advisor, and on the 5th I went to the 5th and 25th Divisions and talked to those division commanders and advisors and on the 6th I went to the 18th and 22nd and 23rd ARVN Divisions and talked to those three commanders and advisors. All of this to have a more informed picture of what was going on and a better appreciation of what the enemy was doing, and along with it the shape that ARVN was in and how they were performing.

Now, to begin with up in the Highlands, early in January, the 4th U.S. Division came into the possession of a plan for the attack of Pleiku. This was a very comprehensive plan to include a civil affairs--what we would call a civil affairs annex--or the establishment of government and its operation--the organization of people--such things as utilities, food, and so on. As the days went along they gathered other intelligence which confirmed to them that the Vietcong were going, in fact, to execute this plan. Some of the moves that they made--were positionings to be executed. Now, remember this is a plan that applied only to Pleiku. So, on the 26th [Maj.] Gen. [Charles P.] Stone [4th U.S. Division commander] assembled all the commanders in the Pleiku area--a lot of them, of course, are not under his command--like the hospital commander and the airfield commander, Camp Holloway airfield, and so on--but he got them all together, including the advisors to the province districts and to the corps commander, and briefed them all thoroughly on this plan and the corroborating intelligence he had, and told them what he was going to do, and provided them with, in some cases, assets to improve their own defensive posture--and then

cleared up things like how to get gun ships and reaction
forces and that sort of thing. And then, of course, on
the night of 29-30 Pleiku and Kontum cities and Ban Me
Thuot were all attacked. As it appeared then on the 3rd,
these three attacks all took pretty much the same form.
It began with an infiltration of guerrillas and political
leadership. Some of these infiltrated in civilian clothes,
some in I Corps in uniforms, and some in ARVN uniforms.
Of course, on that night, the night of the 29th, firecrackers were going off--and in Kontum city the political
leadership took up temporary residence in the vacant bunker
not far from the province chief's house. Now they were
later all killed in there, and the Vietnamese were able
to identify them. The job of the bands of infiltrators
was to overpower the local security--simultaneously the
Vietcong main force would enter the town, followed by an
NVA regiment--in the case of Kontum city, the 24th NVA,
and at Pleiku 95 Bravo, and Ban Me Thuot the 33rd NVA
Regiment. Now, as the fighting went on, two battalions
of the 24th did get into Kontum city and were later
driven out. The 3rd Battalion of the 24th attempted in
daylight to come in. In fact, the 6th Battalion, the 4th,
and the 5th were the ones that got in. The 6th later
attempted to get in, in the daylight, but they were intercepted. In Pleiku, 95 Bravo has not yet made it. General
Stone thinks that some of his units intercepted elements
of 95 Bravo and so now--the H-15 Battalion, which is a
main force battalion in Pleiku, on the 2nd they were supposed to come into Pleiku, that night of the 1st and 2nd,
and come in with an NVA battalion--two of them. The H-15
got to the rendezvous point and was not joined by the
other battalion, so he waited and requested instructions.
I'm now really talking--he was taken prisoner in the end,
and this is what he said. But finally, about 9:30 in the
morning, he was ordered by his fire headquarters to go
anyway, and so he started off for Pleiku city--a beautiful
day--not a cloud in the sky--and he came out of the jungle
and across some open rice paddies there--a good time of
year in the Highlands--the rice paddies are dry--and . . .
vegetation. And he had to cross a highway with his battalion, and the ARVN had about 28 APCs and nine tanks
there. Now, after this fight was over, we swept the
battlefield--and they had the battalion commander captured
and six others, and, between the papers they had on them
and interrogation, they arrived at an inventory of the
battalion before--when it came into the attack; and the
ARVN report that they're able to account for the entire
battalion in that attack, except for one mortar and eight
rifles. All the radios, personnel, and the rest, they
think they have got.

Now, in Ban Me Thuot. . . . The 33rd [NVA] Regiment did get in Ban Me Thuot, elements on different occasions--they got in the city four times and were thrown out four times and they. . . . I'll come back to that.

Now, a little bit about . . . the Delta. The 7th ARVN Division, Gen. [Nguyen Viet] Thanh, he was there as CG in My Tho on--as you know, the attack in the III and IV Corps zone came one day, actually about 24 hours, after the attack in II Corps, and so that was the night 30-31 January. It really began in My Tho with four battalions, three of which came into the city--one stayed on the outskirts--and, also, a sapper company came in the city. The 263rd Vietcong Battalion, they had during the course of the fighting captured their written battle plan, and their objective was to capture and overrun the headquarters of the 7th Division, and, if possible, to take General Thanh alive. Now, the fighting raged there in My Tho and finally the combination of the ARVN and elements of the [U.S.] Mobile Riverine force got the city clear. . . . [Also] in the 7th ARVN area of responsibility, Kien Hoa province, Ben Tre, the capital, and very heavy fighting in that city. There were two ARVN battalions in there, and later reinforced by a two-company force from the U.S. 9th Division, and together these forces cleared out Ben Tre.

Interesting sidelight on the province chief there, Lieutenant Colonel Thieu, province chief of Kien Hoa, he was there in Ben Tre that night, and his family were at their home in Saigon, and sometime in the early morning hours of the 31st his family was murdered in their home--he knew about this in the afternoon, so he quit. But Colonel Thieu, according to [Maj.] Gen. [George S.] Eckhardt, has been a real leader, and a magnificent performer down there--held the people together--has been a leader to the RF and PF forces and the ARVNs that are there in the city now. . . .

Now, we're in the 9th Division--Gen. [Lam Quang] Thi --now, at 2 [a.m.], General Thi was in his TOC--Tactical Operations Center there--division headquarters, and word came to him that there were Vietcong in his house, which is not far away from the headquarters itself, so he sent a platoon over there who killed several Vietcong in his house and captured one. Their mission was to capture General Thi and his family and make him call over to the headquarters, and have his deputy and chief of staff come over for instructions, and then, with those in hand, and their families, they would give them a choice of joining the movement or of losing their families.

He had some fighting in Sa Dec, but it was cleared up fairly easily. Vinh Binh they were able to clear the first day. There was another problem--there were three Vietcong battalions who got into Vinh Long, and it took two or three days to shove them out, and even after that there was hard fighting outside the city.

Then down in 21st Division, when I was there on the 4th, [Maj.] Gen. [Nguyen Van] Minh was up in charge of the battle at Can Tho, which is in his area of responsibility. He was there with his division when this thing all started and he had a lot of outbreaks in his area of responsibility which he reshuffled his force and reacted to very well.

I might say about all these three divisions--they had men who were on leave for Tet, so that the 7th Division, its average battle strength per battalion is about 200; in the 9th Division, it is about 300, and what we like to see in these battalions is 450. They frequently fight with less, but our goal is 450 in the field, present and operating, and in the 21st Division it was about 250. The--according to General Eckhardt's headquarters up to the 4th, the fighting down there has killed 2,345 and captured 289 and a total of 184 ARVN killed and 615 wounded. This was as of the 4th, and I'd say about 800 on the 4th. They also had 135 detainees. . . . None missing. They broke loose 55 weapons and they captured 913, which included 128 crew-served.

. . . [Replying to a question.] I was going to run through this, that's why I went back and picked it up in this particular case. As I go through. . . . Now, I have not--this is the 1st and 2nd, so--1st and 2nd ARVN Division. One of the characteristics of this whole thing that was different to them in the Delta is that, [from] the plans they captured, and the interrogation of prisoners that they had interrogated by that time, none of these units had plans for withdrawal. As you know, ordinarily, especially in their written plans, they had a rally point and routes [for] withdrawals, and so they felt that the mission was to stay in the capital. And at that time, on the 4th, 13 of the 16 province capitals had been attacked. I think they all, except An Giang, have now been attacked. The IV Corps advisor estimates that the enemy strengh that made these attacks was about--altogether--all over the Delta-- was about 10,800. On the 4th, every Vietcong battalion that we carry in the Delta had been identified in combat except one.

Q.: How many?

A.: I believe it's 20.

Q.: Any new units?

A.: There was evidence of one--a--it's a pretty tenuous
sort of thing, but in My Tho there was a battalion which
they took prisoners out of--some of them said it was the
261 Bravo and some the 265. And they thought it was apparently made up of companies from other battalions that
we do carry. So this is a--I don't know the real answer
to this right now. It does not appear to be a battalion
that was built from the ground up--it looks like it was
put together from pieces of others.

Q.: [Did the Vietcong take any towns?]

A.: No, the heavy attacks which were both by fire and
by ground--the heavy ones were Vinh Long, Vinh Binh,
My Tho, Can Tho and in--of the 13 [province capitals]
everyone of them received an attack by fire, and everyone
received a small ground attack. But in most cases,
these capitals were not really penetrated--except for the
ones that I've mentioned. By any real force. Can Tho
was--Vinh Long, Vinh Binh and Chao Phu, Chao Duc province.
Ben Tre was, yes. And--what? No, there hasn't been much
go-on in Go Cong. I don't know whether anybody got into
the capital or not, but there hasn't been an awful lot of
fighting in Go Cong at all.

Q.: [Did any ARVN return to duty?]

A.: Yes, as a matter of fact, it was a sort of encouraging
thing, but on the 4th, when I was at the 7th Division, they
had 250 that came back on the 3rd, and already 100 on the
4th. So this was true on their other divisions, but they
did have men coming back from leave. Same thing is true
in the 18th, the 25th, and 5th. Now, a little bit about
the 5th Division? General Thuan's division. In January,
I think in about the middle of January, the 101st [U.S.]
Division captured a document which told--which was an attack by the Dong Ngai regiment on Phu Cuong, the capital
of Binh Duong [province], and this was a document--con-
fined itself totally to the Dong Ngai regiment--and
they, the 5th [ARVN] Division knew this. Later, they
picked up a defector from the 273rd Regiment and he told
them that the 273rd was to attack Phu Cuong. The objective there was the province capital, the Phu Loi U.S.
Base, division headquarters of the 5th ARVN, and the
compound of the 1st [ARVN] Armored Cavalry Regiment--you
know they call these regiments--they're really squadrons--
as far as numbers are concerned--and the 1st Armored
Cavalry is the one that supports the 5th ARVN Division.

The attack came on the morning of the 31st--it must have
been the same pattern as the others--on Phu Cuong, and
about 4:30 in the morning they got into Phu Cuong--right
up to the province headquarters and the province

operations center--that day the 5th Division counterattacked with two battalions-- . . . a divisional recondo
[company] and elements of the 1st Cavalry, and they had
cleared Phu Cuong by nightfall. The advisors--the division
commander himself--were very proud of this effort. By
his own statement, this is the first [offensive] . . .
that a unit of the 5th Division have participated in since
1965.

Q.: [Was this really an offensive?]

A.: Well, let's put it this way. I think you're right--
technically it is a counteroffensive, but what they're
bragging about is they moved out after the enemy and gave
it to them, and, as you probably know, this division,
especially the 9th Regiment, has fought some very fine
defensive action--here and during the calendar year 1967.

Now, this division reacted well, they, too, their bat-
talions were about 150 operational strength, and General
Thuan told me that on the 31st Radio Hanoi announced that
General Thuan and Col. [Ly Tong] Ba had been killed. Colonel
Ba is the province chief of Phu Cuong.

Q.: [Was the ARVN strength only 150 men per battalion?]

A.: The figure I'm giving you is what they had at the
time this battle was started and, as I said before, our
objective was as advisors of these.

. . . .

Q.: Battalion   strength before Tet holiday?

A.: I would say 400. This is a real horseback figure.

Q.: [Is 450 the regular ARVN battalion strength?]

A.: It is below 70 percent--450, as I say, is *our objective* and, on the average, across the board, these battalions were below the strength that we desired to have
them. On contrast, I went over to the 5th Ranger Group
on the afternoon of the 30th and talked to the advisor
over there, and most of these battalions were all over
600 at the present. The group commander had ruled that
there had been no Tet leave--5th Ranger Group--[stationed
in Gia Dinh province outside Saigon].

Q.: The Marines? Airborne?

A.: I don't know. Yes, they do seem to be up to strength,
I agree with you. The airborne is a mixed bag. They've
got--I know they've got some [recruits] lately--but some
of their battalions have been in some very heavy fighting
over the last month--and their strength is somewhat down.

Q.:   . . . .

A.:   Well, the--we really haven't discussed New Year's
resolutions very much. The situation out in the 25th
Division-- . . . they knew that an attack was coming--they
didn't know where it would hit--they didn't have specifics
like there were in some other cases. . . . Overall the
25th Division, I think, reacted quite well. They--well,
they beat off the attack on their own headquarters; they
were attacked in Hau Nghia and in Long An and were able
to handle each of these.

Q.:   Their battalion strength?

A.:   It was also about 250--average. Little bit about the
18th ARVN--[at] Xuan Loc--his responsibility included Bien
Hoa Long, Phuoc Tuy. His battalions averaged about 200.
When I was there on the 5th, his strength was then averaging
about 275 though, he had begun to get some of his people
back. They had been alerted for attack coming on the night
of 30-31 January. Largely through a directive General
Weyand put out to all of his units and the advisors.
Gen. [Do Ke] Giai accepted this and increased his security
measures. Ba Ria was attacked about 5 o'clock in the
morning. The province chief requested reinforcements at
7 and they had a battalion in there at 9:35. General Giai
sent an ARVN battalion of his to Ba Ria--about a 25-minute
chopper distance--and what he did was pick up a battalion
that was located in strong points along Route 1 for its
security--and that's the kind that went down there. This
is the morning of the 31st.

Q.:   [What was defending Ba Ria?]

A.:   RF and there was also a battalion of the 18th there
at the time. I really don't have a feel for it. I just
don't know. . . .

Q.:   What was the damage done to Vietcong units? Do you
know?

A.:   No, I can't [say] off hand. I just, I asked them
[the ARVN] for that because--and what they did was take
the [enemy] units that they had thus far identified in
the course of the battle and they took the strength . . .
credited [to] them . . . at that time and added them up
and I got the figures and I got some feel for what the
enemy casualties were. What degree of attrition to come
out of this? Your question is an interesting one.

Q.:   What was the ARVN strength?

A.:   . . . Well, maybe 515 strong. But 450--it's supposed to be 70 percent. So you have to do the arithmetic
backwards and get the answer.

Q.:   . . . .

A.:   Huh? 700. OK.

Q.:   [Did ARVN grant leave to everyone?]

A.:   No, I believe that they had authority to grant up to
50 percent and so, no, except for some battalions and
the airborne, the strength of the ARVN [battalion] before
this began, while it averaged about 400, which is 50
percent below our objective--and, remember, all the time,
I'm talking operational stuff--the difference between 450
and 700 is--450 is what you take in the helicopters when
you go out to fight. That's what that is. And the
difference between 450 and 700 is not only those that they
just don't have, but also those that have to stay behind at
the base camp and that sort of thing.

Q.:   So the regular operating strength was 450?

A.:   That's right. 450. That's right. . . .

Q.:   . . . .

A.:   . . . Another new thing in the 18th Division area of
operation--the outfit that attacked Xuan Loc was what we
call the 84th group--it's a service group that makes up
the--handles the logistics and administrative support of
Vietcong units in the Xuan Loc, Phuoc Tuy, Bien Hoa area.
In the 22nd [23rd] Division, Col. [Dao Quang] An--and . . .
this is a top division, and his responsibilities are
Lam Dong, Darlac, Binh Thuan, and Tuyen Duc. He also had
a Ranger battalion. . . . They had a captured document
about the 20th of January. While it was not a plan, it
nevertheless discussed preparations for an attack on Ban
Me Thuot on 28 January and through Tet. Based on this,
Colonel **An** decided there would be no Tet leave in his
division. When this thing started, the operational
strength at Ben   Tuy--he has two battalions--there were
500.

Q.:   . . . .

A.:   He's a division commander. . . . Excuse me, I'm
talking about the 23rd and not the 22nd. But the 22nd
Division . . . the same thing. They captured this document on [January] 22nd. Now, he [Colonel An] had in
the days immediately preceding Tet, he had chose[n] two
battalions on a road-opening operation along [Highway]
21 and to move a convoy--actually there [were] 100 trucks
--of rice and fish and food into Ban Me Thuot. That was
in there when they started. On the night--around the day
before it started, he deployed one of his battalions to
the south of Ban Me Thuot and one north. He had patrols
out as far as 10 kilometers.

Now, the way that thing started there at 2200 on the 29th,
a group that they estimate to be about 100 individuals,
including the political cadre, got in the police station
and killed the six policemen there and set up a temporary
CP there in the police station and Colonel An learned
this about 2200 on the 29th. He used, he had his cavalry
units there in Ban Me Thuot--the RF and a recon. company.
They succeeded in getting the people out that got in
there that night--they captured some of the political
cadre. A very interesting thing here--Colonel An describes at least a couple of these men, the same way
[another officer] describes them that afternoon, and these
two officers hadn't even talked to each other. And,
Colonel An said that these are real cadre--they have
never answered a question, they only smile. At that
time he didn't know whether they were North Vietnamese or
South Vietnamese--they hadn't even given their name,
rank, and serial number. He thinks they're important
and obviously strong men.

As I mentioned before, they got into Ban Me Thuot four
times and incidentally--and he kicked them out four times
--but incidentally, the first major contact of enemy units
was with the battalion which he had put to the south of
Ban Me Thuot--he'd been fortunate, and put them along
the route which they [the enemy] had elected to come in
on. It was the heart of the 33rd NVA.

Colonel An told me that initially in this fighting in
Ban Me Thuot his men took casualties because of their
lack of experience in city fighting, but he quickly began
reorganizing them into teams, and with the help of the
American advisors, most of whom had some experience at
this, they became very effective. He told me that the
hardest decision that he had to make was to use artillery
fire and air in populated areas. He delayed doing this
for three-and-a-half days, then he did. Colonel Barber
[his U.S. advisor] is tremendously impressed with this
officer's performance.

That battle was hot for nine days and nights and they are
impressed there. . . . It was planned by the enemy to
maintain the pressure 24 hours a day to try to tire them
out and that sort of thing. Even after they get them
cleared out of town, they--there would be another enemy
attack developed on the other side of town--out in one of
the hamlets, and Colonel An kept at this for nine days with
only snatches of sleep he could get from time to time,
and, according to Barber, he does not believe that An
made a tactical mistake in all that time. He also feels
that the only reason that they have Ban Me Thuot today is
because of Colonel An's decision that there would be no

Tet leave, and his decision to deploy his battalions outside the city.

Q.:   . . . .

A.:   . . . I will say this . . . that the relationship
between Colonel Barber and Colonel An is as good a relationship between commanders that there is.   An's a
well trained man--he's a Leavenworth graduate and fluent
in English and he--I'm only trying to convey the impression that An does not have to be led around by the hand
in everything. He is a capable officer.

Q.:   What was Colonel An's strength?

A.:   Five hundred. *His* battalions were in operational
strength of 500.

Q.:   . . . .

A.:   . . . My impression is that RD areas were safe--were
not objectives in this particular phase of the battle.
It is my impression that RD areas were not one of the objectives.

. . . .

A.:   Well, the enemy in both II Corps and III Corps have
the capability of recycling these offensive efforts. Now,
I don't mean by that that if he elects to do that--that it
would be done in the same way that this was. Obviously
that would--he wouldn't do that, because a lot of the
advantages that he enjoys in this type of thing have now
disappeared. But he has the capability in II Corps and III
Corps of making a further offensive effort.

Q.:   . . . .

A.:   IV Corps--he has the capability to continue harass-
ments and small attacks, but he, I don't believe he has the
capability to recycle anywhere near the scale he has put
on so far. I Corps he's got it--they, well, he's got a
lot of force in I Corps that has not been committed at all.

Q.:   . . . .

A.:   Lang Vei has been overrun--and there was a reaction
operation conducted over the last 24 hours which got [the]
major portion of the U.S. advisory group out, and we feel
that there are a few--may well be gone to Laos. For
that reason, we're going to be very tricky talking about
that.

Q.:   Do you know any tanks?

A.:   Well, we've got an aerial photograph of one of these
tanks, and it looks like its a PT-76, which is a, has a

very fine gun on it--76 mm.--but it's an amphibious tank
--you should be able to knock it out with a .50 caliber
machine gun and the--and it has one machine gun--a 76
mm. machine gun--crew of three, 15.4 tons. I can say
this--we have an aerial photograph of one that was knocked
out up there and that was a PT-76.

Q.: An old tank?

A.: Oh, this is an old model tank. Yeah. Well, let me
say--I was going to add--the Marines have a--I forgot
the number--but they've got a hell of a lot of 106 recoilless stuff there. . . .

. . . .

Q.: Is Lang Vei critical?

A.: It is not critical to, I wouldn't say--to the defense
of Khe Sanh--it's critical to us in the sense that we want
to be able to control the borders.

. . . .

Q.: Did you think you could hold Lang Vei?

A.: The--we thought that we could hang on to it--covered
by the artillery of Khe Sanh--we've put a tremendous
amount of air around it. The strike bombing was all
registered, and also it [was] recently rebuilt . . . so
that [it] had excellent positions, bunkers.

Q.: What caused its loss?

A.: I would expect it was numbers.

. . . .

Q.: . . . .

A.: I know that [Lt.] Gen. [Robert] Cushman has to--put a
lot of effort in improving the strength of all those
positions around Khe Sanh and I know that he's been up
there himself several times, as has Gen. [Rathvon McC.]
Tompkins [commander of the 3rd Marine Division]. . . .

Q.: How many Americans at Lang Vei?

A.: Lang Vei? I think 20. About 20.

Q.: What happened there?

A.: Well, Lang Vei, I think that it would be just speculation for me to get into that now because we've got to get
read out from these men on what transpired there. And
that's going on at the moment--then we'll know a little
better.

. . . .

A.: Well, we have to look at it from the--we've got to
secure Da Nang . . . Hue, Quang Tri, and Khe Sanh is one
of the parts of that. And you maneuver your forces--we've
got a combination of fixed and mobile forces up there and
that's the way we play it.

Q.: . . . .

A.: No, helicopter--combination. Well, you say primarily
a helicopter operation--well, nobody walked into Khe Sanh.

Q.: . . . Lang Vei?

A.: Seven hundred to 800 metres. That's about right.
Kind of an irregular-shaped thing.

Q.: How many tanks?

A.: I don't know the answer to that, do you? I think it
was five.

. . . .

A.: Any more intelligence?

A.: The best number that we had in this area was nine, and
we can only assume that there are more.

Q.: Will they use them against Khe Sanh?

A.: I don't really know, but I know that he wants to take
Khe Sanh.

Q.: How can you tell?

A.: I say that because of the amount of force that he's
deployed around it.

Q.: How can you be sure?

A.: Well, it--at least it's my opinion--it's what I feel
he's going to do.

Q.: Is it possible to do that?

A.: No, we were not able to do it, as a matter of fact--as
far as this technique is concerned, we didn't fight with
either.

Let me just finish off one--I wanted to tell you--maybe I
have said already that [the General] of the 22nd Division
[decided] there would be no Tet [holiday]; he also had wind
of this thing, and so his battalions--his lowest PFD
[present for duty] was 250, and his best was 500. And
they looked great. Then on the--he's well tied in with
the MSS [Military Security Service] up there in Qui Nhon
--and on the 29th they told him there are a lot of unusual
meetings [of Vietcong] going on in Qui Nhon, so they

captured six people at one of these meetings and they had
a tape recorder with two prepared tapes, and it developed
that they were going to seize the radio station, and these
tapes were to broadcast over the radio station, and he
tells me that what the tapes said was that there are not--
seizure of several province capitals in South Vietnam by
the peace government--the government of the people, and it
called upon all people to rally round the peace government,
encouraged a general uprising in support of it, reported
that the ARVN had joined with the uprising and that the
ARVN were fighting the United States. . . .

Q.:   . . . .

A.:   I don't know. As of the moment there are still Vietcong in the Cholon area and they--estimates vary there from
500 to 800. Part of this, apparently, is a Vietcong battalion that's lived in Saigon for years. They, I don't
have a unit identification on it--210 I guess I've heard.
No--C-10 is not from outside, no, I don't have one. Now,
. . . it's the winter-spring campaign and it has three
phases. The first and second phase are the general offensive phase and the military phase during which time you
--began on December 5--you attack the--the enemy attacks
the basic military installations--district towns, and at
the same time prepares the people for the third phase.
And the third phase is the political phase which involves
a general uprising of the people, the seizure of government
centers of control, province capitals, and this phase is
supposed to be completed by the 10th of February. Another
interesting thing that happened up there in--especially
in Phu My district--the Vietcong got people together to
try to get them to march on district towns with--supplied
them with placards and so on. This began 10 days before
Tet. The two things that they concentrated on was a
seven-day truce and let the soldiers go home to their
families during Tet. They--I've been impressed in going
around listening to these various people talk about the
depth of the enemy planning--detail of it and the orches-
tration of military efforts--political and psychological
efforts.

. . . .

. . . It doesn't appear to me that they have--it appears
to me that they have achieved very little. Now, obviously
they didn't count on achieving everything, but my feeling
would be that they have fallen far short of what they
would have considered minimum acceptable achievements for
this period. Now, I must say that this is going to
require a tremendous effort now to capitalize on what I

believe is an opportunity--tremendous effort by both the
government of South Vietnam and its armed forces, and the
aid and assistance that we can give them in support, and
this means the restoration of law and order and getting
the things--getting the highways open and things moving,
and establish a--reestablish an air of normalcy to a
population--take care of those that have lost so much,
and . . . attack and damage his remaining units as much
as we possibly can.

Q.: [Was] Lang Vei softening up before Khe Sanh? . . .

A.: We think about this question quite a lot--but what I
really believe is that, first of all, they will make
their effort in the DMZ-Khe Sanh area when they are convinced in their own judgment that their preparations are
complete, they have things where they want them, and what
they want, and that it is enough to assure them in their
judgment of success. The--I don't think that they'll do
anything like, for instance, the H-15 Battalion that
sallied forth at Pleiku--they really--it's not a very good
thing for them to do. Looking at it from their side--it's
quite unprofessional, they lack reconnaissance, they. . . .
Now, we have been, I must say, expecting it--and it would
appear logical that it should go while our attention is
focused on all these other things--one would think that--
it would appear that. I think the real answer is that
they'll kick that off, as I say, when they feel they are
thoroughly prepared by their techniques.

Q.: . . . .

A.: I think that it's all part of the same big piece. I
think that they planned big on this. And now, and these
things that have gone on from the Delta to Quang Tri, and
the things that are bound to come in the DMZ-Camp Carroll,
Rock Pile, Ca Lu, Khe Sanh area, are all part of a great
plan, and in that sense it is a coordinated thing. Now,
when you get to details and timing--myself, I find it
very difficult to understand why this thing went in II
Corps one day before it went in III and IV Corps--first
of all why it had to--if that's what makes the difference
--or why the planned it that way--it would have seemed to
me it would have been more effective had they led them all
off the same night.

. . . .

Q.: . . . .

A.: I'm told that the group that overran the armored
training center and the artillery command compound were
all officers and men from the North Vietnamese armored

training center and they were going to take the tanks and
the APCs and the armored training center and the artillery
and the artillery command compound, and this was to be an
armored attack task force operating in Saigon. They--now,
this information comes from a major and one other officer
of the Armored Training Center who were captured by these
people, and then the [South Vietnamese] Marines counterat-
tacked--the major and the other officer came back into
Vietnamese hands.

Q.:   These are ARVN?

A.:   The South Vietnamese major and another officer--I've
forgotten whether he's a lieutenant or a captain--and that's
where this comes from. I'm always reluctant to latch on
to these things too tightly--always when a lot of fighting
and the battle's going, and so on--imagination just gets
into it. So you have to--but then also you can make a
case--you know the fighting that broke out around BOQ
No. 3--in the early morning of the 31st-- Now, actually,
President Thieu's residence--his home--is not far. In
fact, what started that apparently were the MPs who were
stationed at the BOQ No. 3--and they saw these fellows
moving and they took them under fire, and then they got
into the buildings around there and. . . . So one could
say that that was part of it. Now [Lt.] Gen. [Frederick]
Weyand told me the other day, and again you can't say--I
don't know, but--over in the ARVN III Corps Operation
Center they've got a direct line to a pagoda--there are
direct telephone lines to a pagoda there in the city--why
they have it I don't know--but, anyway, they do--and during
the course of this thing, why, it rang and the Chief of
Staff out there picked it up, and the fellow on the other
end said that he was a man of four-star rank and he wanted
to be connected immediately with President Thieu, and . . .
he insisted on this, and finally hung up, and they dispatched a group over there right away to surround the
pagoda and all that sort of thing--search it out--and they
found nothing. But maybe that's another war story.

Q.:   . . . .

A.:   Now, this is out in Bien Hoa. Well, they tried hard to
take it. But they did want apparently to take the facilities intact, and this sort of fits into the same thing--
Now--they wanted to be able to use it--that's what it
appears like. . . . Now, that--up at Ban Me Thuot they
always have the capability of shelling the ammunition
dump and the POL [petroleum, oil, and lubricants] storage
area up there. They shelled the town, they shelled the
compound, the shelled the airfield, I guess they shelled
the airfield every night; they never shelled the ammunition

dump or the POL--yet--so, and this fits with the artillery
attacking the artillery positions up there so they could
take over the guns. This happened at Ban Me Thuot too--
I don't know if I mentioned that before, but the force
that attacked the artillery compound up there were the
NVA artillery. . . . And the executive officer of the
supporting artillery regiment was killed. He came in with
the assault waves of the Vietcong supporting artillery
regiment. He came in with the first wave--assault wave,
and that was a mixture of infantrymen and artillerymen.
And the obvious reason for that was to take the artillery
and then use it as part of their force and they had the
crews and that sort of thing there to do it.

. . . ./ . . . . . .

Q.: . . . .

A.: Well, I don't--let me say this about it. Here in
III Corps, the 5th and 9th Vietcong Divisions are located
out there in the fringes of the provinces surrounding
Gia Dinh--Bien Hoa, Bien Duong and Hau Nghia, Tay Ninh,
and as far as the best information we have, they have not
withdrawn. Now the 7th NVA Division is somewhat behind
them in Quan Loc--Route 13 corridor--back in Binh Long.
The 1st NVA Division is around Dak To--and there's also
95 Bravo Regiment up there in the Pleiku-Kontum area.
We don't feel [they] have been committed in these attacks
--or if they have they were intercepted way out, and we
just don't have a good feel for what kind of shape they're
in. In the coastal plain of II Corps it looks like . . .
those forces--for instance, the 3rd NVA Division--they
fought in the early part of December and suffered quite
a bit of casualties. But no element of the 3rd NVA
Division participated in this phase three, and I can only
conclude that they just were not in shape to. The 95th
Regiment in the coastal plain did participate in this so-
called third phase with two of its battalions; one of
them has not been committed and so there exists a substantial strength uncommitted in the Highlands in the
form of the 1st NVA Division.

Up in I Corps you've got . . . the 341st Regiment and the
2nd NVA Division in the Quang Nam area, and then you've
got still some force left in the Base Area 101 near Quang
Tri, although it's hard to estimate how--that went very
badly for them up there at Quang Tri--I haven't been up
there, but apparently they did take very bad losses. Oh,
Rattan, Skipper Rattan [Col. Donald V. Rattan, commanding
a 1st Cavalry Division brigade]--well, Skipper Rattan
was over there . . . in Base Area 101, and Gen. [George]
Forsythe went over to see him and said you'd better come

over and help us at Quang Tri--there's a whole--they're
massing at the gates, and Skipper Rattan said, my mission
is over here in Base Area 101, and, of course, I told him,
"Skipper, you haven't got any enemy over there--they're
all up around Quang Tri and, if you want to kill enemy,
that's where you got to go." Well, it hit Rattan in the
weak spot--he just turned around and went over to Quang
Tri and apparently had a field day over there.

Q.: Did they want Tan Son Nhut?

A.: No, well, you could have all of those things. What
I'm really--my impression of all this is--see, what this
started out with is, do you really believe that they meant
to take a place like Saigon and hold it? And my impression at the moment is that they did plan big. Now,
whether they believe they--that all of this, or a major
portion of it, would in fact come true--is another thing,
but they--if it did, they had placed all of the tickets
in it to take advantage of it. And in other words, they
were prepared for any degree--they were prepared to
capitalize on any degrees of success which this effort
managed to produce. Now, I would not, on the other hand,
say that they were convinced that all of this could happen.
But they were willing to give it a try and they had prepared themselves.

Q.: The man who identified himself as a four-star of-
ficer--NVA?

A.: No, he [could be] a minister or--he said he was a
man of four-star position--no, it's not by all means the
Chief of Staff of II Corps--by all means, say that it was
a general--it was a man of this position. [Talking around
by several.] No, no. He said "could he have been," and
I said, "That's right, or he could have been somebody from
Hanoi."

Q.: . . . .

A.: The only specific I know of is that, counting Xuan
Loc, they arrested six or seven city officials who were
harboring Vietcong in their homes--Xuan Loc. Yeah, now,
what they were I don't know--whether they were the sanita-
tion men or just what--but they were members of the city
government.

Q.: . . . .

A.: Xuan Loc, yeah. And, also, General Giai told me that
a similar thing happened in Ba Ria. I don't know the
numbers.

Q.: . . . .

A.: Yes. Well, I--now, let me take that back. I cannot
vouch for every province. I just don't know. . . .

APPENDIX XVIII

RATIONALE FOR THE DEFENSE OF KHE SANH—STATEMENTS BY GENERALS EARLE G. WHEELER, USA, AND LEONARD F. CHAPMAN, JR., USMC

(In the following statement, which he made on NBC-TV's "Huntley-Brinkley Report," February 5, 1968, Gen. Earle Wheeler gave only part of the rationale later detailed by General Westmoreland. Wheeler did not use the word "infiltration," but did, unwisely, suggest that holding Khe Sanh would prevent the foe from going into South Vietnam. In fact, the enemy already had almost a division in Hue, and had hit Quang Tri city with a regiment or more:)

Khe Sanh is a very important tactical and strategic locality. It is the western anchor of our defense line along the Demilitarized Zone in South Vietnam. Secondly, the North Vietnamese themselves recognize the significance of this terrain because, as you will recall, last year they attempted, at a great price, to seize this same terrain. It is psychologically important because, if lost, it would permit North Vietnamese troops to advance deep into South Vietnamese territory, come very close to the heavily populated coastal regions, and thereby exacerbate the fears of the South Vietnamese that the North Vietnamese will be able to take over the two northern provinces of South Vietnam, a long-time objective of theirs.

Some days ago the President asked me to have the Joint Chiefs of Staff review the situation at Khe Sanh and provide him with our advice. We did so after having consulted with General Westmoreland and obtaining the views of the Commander in Chief of the Pacific. . . . We confirmed that General Westmoreland's assessment of the situation was correct and that Khe Sanh can be and should be defended.

(Wheeler also told newsmen: "We do not plan to sustain a Dienbienphu."

Gen. Leonard F. Chapman, Jr., the Marine Corps commandant, in an unreported speech to the Marine Officers' Wives Club

*in Bethesda, Maryland, on February 7, 1968, used the
"infiltration" cliché. However, he also reflected Westmoreland's feeling that holding Khe Sanh was a good way
to hurt the enemy, who had to mass to attack the base and
thus presented a target for U.S. B-52 strikes. It was
one of the few explicit discussions of what came to be
known as the "tethered goat" theory, namely, that one
mission of the 5,000-man Marine garrison at Khe Sanh was
to serve as "bait" to draw in the NVA for pounding--far
from populated areas--by the B-52s. Chapman, whose son
was in the garrison, told the wives:)*

Why are we at Khe Sanh? . . . We're there because Khe
Sanh is a key terrain feature that must be held. It's
astride the infiltration route from North to South. It
retards infiltration and major penetration. It's an
excellent location from which to inflict casualties on
the enemy.

*(Wheeler was interviewed again about Khe Sanh on February
14, on Capitol Hill, following his appearance before a
House defense appropriations subcommittee. His remarks
included a whiff of the "tethered goat" theory:)*

Wheeler: You will have won the opportunity to inflict a
very serious defeat upon the North Vietnamese Regular
Army; you will have protected the two northern provinces
of South Vietnam from invasion by the enemy; and I would
suggest that you will have won a psychological victory
as well, because you will have reassured the people in
the northern portion of South Vietnam that they can be
secure from invasion by the North Vietnamese.

Q.: What about the speculation that the United States
may be falling into a trap by allowing the North Vietnamese to choose the site and conditions of battle?

Wheeler: Well, I'm afraid I can't quote for the radio and
TV the words of General Abrams at the time of the Battle
of Bastogne. But you remember, paraphrasing it carefully, he said those fellows have got us surrounded again,
poor guys.

Q.: There is a lot of speculation up here on the Hill
that ultimately we may have to use nuclear weapons. What
can you say on that subject?

Wheeler: I do not think that nuclear weapons will be
required to defend Khe Sanh.

APPENDIX XIX

Associated Press
February 12, 1968

LIFE IN THE V RING

By John T. Wheeler

KHE SANH, Vietnam (AP)--The first shell-burst caught the Marines outside the bunkers filling sandbags. More exploding rockets sent showers of hot fragments zinging. The Americans dove for cover.

"Corpsman! Corpsman!"

The shout came from off to the right.

"We've got wounded here."

"Corpsman! Corpsman!" The shouts now came from the distance. You could see the men dragging a bleeding buddy toward cover.

Inside the bunkers the Marines hugged their legs and bowed their heads, unconsciously trying to make themselves as small as possible. The tempo of the shelling increased and the small opening to the bunker seemed in their minds to grow to the size of a barn door. The 5,000 sandbags around and over the bunker seemed wafer thin.

Although it could increase their chances of survival only minutely, men shifted their positions to get closer to the ground.

Some measured the angle to the doorway and tried to wiggle a bit more behind those next to them.

There were no prayers uttered aloud. Two men growled a stream of profanity at the North Vietnamese gunners who might snuff out their lives at any moment.

Near misses rocked the bunker and sent dirt cascading down everyone's neck.

Outside the random explosions sent thousands of pounds of shrapnel tearing into sandbags and battering already damaged mess halls and tent areas long ago destroyed and abandoned for a life of fear and filth underground.

142

This is the life in the "V ring," a sharpshooter's term for the inner part of the bull's-eye. At Khe Sanh the V ring for the North Vietnamese gunners neatly covers the bunkers of Bravo Company, 3rd Reconnaissance Battalion. In three weeks, more than half the company had been killed or wounded. It was recon's bad luck to live in an area bordered by an ammunition dump, a flight-line loading area, and the 26th Marine Regiment's command post.

Shrapnel and shell holes cover the area. The incoming rounds could hardly be noticed once the barrage stopped, such is the desolation.

And then the shells did stop. Silent men turned their faces from one to the other. Several men scrambled out of the bunker to see if more dead or wounded men from their unit were outside. Medics scurried through the area, crouching low.

Inside one bunker a Marine returned to his paperback book, a tale of Wild West adventure. Another man whose hand had stopped in the midst of strumming a guitar resumed playing. Two men in a card game began flipping the soggy pasteboards again.

The shelling wasn't worth discussing. It was too commonplace, and none from Bravo Company had been hit this time. Like jungle rot, snipers, and rats, artillery fire was something to be hated and accepted at the same time.

But the shellfire had taken its toll. Minutes before the barrage opened, Army Sp4c. William Hankinson had drifted off from the other members of his communications team assigned to this Marine base.

When the first shell hit, he dived into a Marine bunker. After the explosions stopped, he talked with the Marines awhile before starting back to his bunker.

A white-faced Leatherneck joined the group.

"You look kind of sick," a Marine buddy said. "What happened?"

"The whole Army bunker got wiped out," he replied. "Jesus, what a mess."

Hankinson started to run toward the smashed bunker where his friends' shattered bodies lay. Marines caught and blocked him. Then with a tenderness not at all out of place for hardened fighting men, they began to console the Army specialist, a man most had never spoken to before that day.

One dud mortar round was half-buried in the runway of the airstrip. Planes carrying priority supplies had to be waved off until the round could be removed.

Two demolition experts raced from shelter with fire axes and chopped it out of the aluminum-sheet runway. Neither would give his name. Both had told their families they were safely out of the war zone.

"An awful lot of Marines are big liars on that point," one said.

The men of No. 2 gun, Charlie Battery, didn't think of cover when the shelling began. After what they had been through when the main ammunition dump 200 yards away exploded during an earlier barrage, "This is coasting," one gunner said.

And alone of the Marines at Khe Sanh, the artillery could fire back at the enemy. No 2 gun, commanded by Cpl. Anthony Albo, kept pouring out 105 mm. rounds even though a shell splinter had started a fire in the gun's ready ammo bunker.

At Charlie Med, the main casualty clearing station, wounded were coming in. Some were on stretchers, some hobbled by themselves, some were hauled in across the shoulder of a comrade.

One prayed, a few cried, some were unconscious. Many showed shock on their faces.

In between shellings, Lance Cpl. Richard Noyes, 19, of Cincinnati, Ohio, roughhoused on the dirt floor of his bunker with a friend. Noyes lives with five buddies in the center of the V ring. The war was pushed far into the background for a moment as ripples of laughter broke from the tangled, wrestling forms.

Then the first shell of a new barrage hit.

Both men recoiled as if a scorpion had been dropped between them. Even though they were underground in a bunker, everyone put on helmets. Across the front of his "brain pot," Noyes long ago had written in ink, "God walks with me."

A blank stare in the eyes of some is not uncommon at Khe Sanh, where the communists have fired up to 1,500 rounds of rockets, artillery, and mortar shells in a single day.

It is called the 1,000-yard stare. It can be the sign of the beginning of combat fatigue.

For Noyes and thousands of others at this surrounded combat base, the anguish is bottled up within tolerable limits.

Noyes had had luck, lots of it. A rocket once drove through the bunker's sandbags and exploded, killing 4 and wounding 14 of the 20 men inside. Noyes was slightly wounded.

It was Noyes's second Purple Heart. One more and he automatically would be sent out of Vietnam under Marine regulations. Noyes doesn't want the third medal.

Despite heavy casualties, the survivors of the recon company are frightened but uncowed. When the call for stretcher-bearers comes, the young Marines unhesitatingly begin wriggling through the opening in their bunker to help.

At night the men in Noyes's bunker sit and talk, sing, play cards, almost anything to keep from being alone with their thoughts. During a night when more than 1,000 rounds hit Khe Sanh, Noyes turned to a buddy and said: "Man, it'll be really decent to go home and never hear words like incoming shells, mortars, rifles, and all that stuff. And the first guy who asks me how it feels to kill, I'll . . . ." A pause. Then: "You know, my brother wants me to go duck hunting when I get home. Man, I don't want to even see a slingshot when I get out of here."

Lt. C. J. Slack of Carlsbad, California, said: "When I get back to California, I'm going to open a bar especially for the survivors of Khe Sanh. And any time it gets two deep at that bar, I'll know someone is lying."

Noyes smokes heavily and his hands never seem to be entirely still. Looking at the side of a cigarette pack, Noyes said with a wry smile, "Caution, Khe Sanh may be hazardous to your health. Oh, man, yeah."

Still later, he called out, "Okay, we're going to sing now. Anyone who can't sing has to hum. Because I said so. Okay, let's hear it."

Lance Cpl. Richard Morris, 24, of North Hollywood, California, began playing a guitar. Two favorites that night were "Five Hundred Miles" and "Where Have All the Flowers Gone?"

A hard emphasis accompanied the verse that went: "Where have all the soldiers gone? To the graveyard every one. When will they ever learn? When will they ever learn?"

Finally the two small naked light bulbs were turned out and the Marines struggled toward sleep.

APPENDIX XX

The Los Angeles *Times*
February 16, 1968
LANDING AT KHE SANH AN AGONIZING ORDEAL

By William Tuohy

KHE SANH, Vietnam--In a switch on the Cunard Line slogan, a correspondent friend once remarked of the problems of covering the Vietnam War: "Getting there is half the agony."

Nowhere does the dictum hold truer than the trip to Khe Sanh, the harried Marine base in the high valley in the northwesternmost corner of South Vietnam.

You begin at Da Nang, the big U.S. base 105 air miles to the southeast.   The first day that we tried--arising dull and early before dawn--we spent the day at the grubby military passenger terminal.   It was saved from a total news washout by the young Marine--perhaps deranged, perhaps eminently sane--who tried to depart Vietnam by hijacking a Pan American airliner at gunpoint.   A story --but not the Khe Sanh story.

The next day we arose again, this time with special clearance to ride ammo or fuel cargo flights.   A plane was available.   And shortly before noon we were making our descent through a gooey sky into Khe Sanh.   Suddenly the word crackled over the radio that a Marine transport had been shot down and was in flames, closing the air field.

The third day, another long wait.   An Air Force plane was hit, and field again closed.   You lie down on the tarmac and try to concentrate on a paperback, attempting to avoid thinking about airplanes taking hits on the final approach to Khe Sanh.   Another uneasy flight through the soup.

This time we broke through the overcast with the 4,000-foot strip dead ahead.

After three days we are in Khe Sanh.   The only trouble is that enemy gunners have opened up with mortar fire, trying to knock out the taxiing plane.

Now, everyone leaps off the transport--just before the
cargo is "speed off-loaded." We run for the dubious
comfort of some skimpy-looking bunkers at the edge of
the parking apron. In front of me, Murray Fromsom of
CBS, darting like an expert broken-field runner, is hit
by the powerful prop blasts of the turbojets and knocked
flat, banging badly both knees.

For the next 10 minutes, while the plane turns around,
we huddle in the bunker. Then it departs, and we move
to a second trench near the airstrip.

"There comes another mortar magnet," yells a Marine, "keep
your head down."

As the big Air Force C-130 comes in, we duck into the
trench. Two rounds hit nearby. We stay under cover until
the plane unloads and takes off.

Khe Sanh, of course, is not fun city. And getting out of
Khe Sanh is worse than getting in.

You wait for an incoming plane--if there is an incoming
plane--in a bunker by the airstrip. As we wait--a half-
dozen Marines on a mission to Da Nang--several rocket and
mortar rounds land nearby.

"How much incoming will this bunker stop?" an Air Force
man asks a Marine lieutenant.

"Fragments," he replies airily. "A direct hit would blow
it all away."

Another hit. This one closer.

A Marine pops his head inside the bunker and says to no
one in particular, "That one got a jeep and a fork-lift
truck."

"Now I know how a clay pigeon must feel," a waiting
corporal remarks. "This air strip is in the center of
the bull's-eye."

You wonder about transferring to a better built bunker--but
that would take you farther away from the strip and require
a longer dash for the plane. We now have an inkling of
what these Marines face day after day after day. It's the
waiting that gets you, they say. True.

A controller sticks his head into the bunker and says,
"There's a plane unloading at the end of the strip--he
doesn't want to get hit on the parking apron. You can
try to run for it if you want."

We decided to run--a headlong dash over the red earth
pitted every dozen feet or so with the telltale mortar
craters.

Desperately out of breath from the dash and the weight of helmet, flak jacket, camera, and pack, I tell myself this is not the way.

We wait for the 105 mm. ammunition to be rolled off the cargo plane. Then we toss our gear aboard the rear ramp and scramble aboard--belly down on the aluminum decking to make a smaller target for enemy gunners.

We gesture at the loadmaster to get under way--but at that moment a truck rolls up with two Marines carrying a sea bag and a footlocker. It takes perhaps 30 seconds more for them to haul the stuff aboard. For us, hours.

Finally they are aboard, but the loadmaster fiddles for moments with the rear ramp. It won't close properly. More hours.

At last the plane begins to roll toward the runway. We are all up-tight, waiting for mortar or machine-gun fire.

Then the welcome sound of the engines running up to full power and the swift acceleration down the strip. Wheels up. Bellies still exposed. Then the blessed cocoon of the clouds.

Lying flat on the deck of the climbing cargo plane, the sight of the protective cloud cover was better than that of a pretty stewardess bringing you a belt of scotch on a jetliner. Much better.

APPENDIX XXI

Time, **February 16, 1968**

KHE SANH: READY TO FIGHT

By Don Sider

*(Time correspondent Don Sider spent several days at Khe
Sanh last week ducking incoming shells and observing the
unique quality of life in the besieged Marine base. His
report:)*

A chill, gray mist hangs over the jungled hills around Khe
Sanh and drifts down onto the base's metal runway. The
morning mist often lasts into the afternoon, the bright
sun of recent weeks is lost in monsoonal overcast, and
the air is raw and wet with winter. The camp seems to
have settled into a dull, lethargic pace to match the
dull, damp weather that envelops it. In a mood of resig-
nation, Marines go about their life-or-death work, digging
into the red clay, filling sandbags, bolstering the bunkers
they know are their one protection against the real rain:
the whining rockets and the mortars that come with no
warning--just the awful cracking sound as they explode.

The dash for cover is part of every man's routine. "It's
a *modus vivendi*," says Protestant Chaplain Ray Stubbe, 29.
"The men run for shelter, but they don't cringe when they
get there." Except for an occasional case of what the
corpsmen call "acute environmental reaction" (shell shock),
the Marines at Khe Sanh are taking their ordeal with
considerable composure: Only their unwelcome bunkermates
--the rats--become frantic under fire. When the "incoming"
starts, the rats race for the bunkers and wildly run up
to the ceilings made of runway matting and logs. One
sergeant has killed 34 rats, establishing a base record.

Khe Sanh grows steadily shabbier. More and more "hardbacks"
(metal-roofed shacks) are tumbled by the incoming; day by
day the protective sandbags and runway matting rise higher
on bunkers. Even so, the bunkers cannot withstand direct
hits. A rocket or mortar round will collapse a bunker and
likely kill its occupants. The Seabees are finishing strong
underground bunkers for the control-tower crew of Khe Sanh's

airstrip and the evacuation hospital, rushing to complete
the work before the threatened battle erupts. Meanwhile,
the doctors must make do in cramped quarters: The operating room is an empty metal box used to ship military
goods, and measuring only eight feet by six feet by six
feet.

The top Marine at Khe Sanh is Col. David E. Lownds, 47,
the mustachioed commander of the 26th Marine Regiment,
who oversees the defense of the base from an underground
bunker left over by its original French occupants. Sitting
in a faded lawn chair, he seldom rests, night or day. He
keeps constant watch over the nerve center, a labyrinth
of whitewashed rooms lit by bare bulbs and bustling with
staff officers and enlisted aides. Is he worried about
the huge enemy concentration surrounding him? "Hell, no,"
says Lownds. "I've got Marines. My confidence isn't
shaken a bit." He fully recognizes his stand-and-fight
mission: "My job is to stay here. My job is to hold. I
don't plan on reinforcements."

Several large U.S. combat units are ready at nearby bases
for just such a necessity, but the fact is that there is
neither space nor cover for them at Khe Sanh. Its buildup
completed, Khe Sanh is waiting to fight. Last week, to
cover their attack on nearby Lang Vei, the North Vietnamese hit Khe Sanh with a massive barrage of up to 1,500
rounds of 60 mm. and 82 mm. mortars and 122 mm. rockets--
50 percent more than Con Thien ever received in a single
day at the peak of its shelling last year. Fortunately,
the Reds' aim was bad: They scored no direct hits and
caused no serious wounds or deaths.

Not all the metal was incoming. Even under that pounding,
Khe Sanh's artillerymen fired back 3,000 rounds. Fighter-
bombers rake the surrounding hills on a seemingly nonstop
basis, while B-52 strikes lay a carpet of bombs on suspected enemy positions, four to six times a day. This
outpouring of U.S. air power may have delayed the communist attack on Khe Sanh, though some officers wonder
about the effectiveness of bombing against dug-in artillery and troops and trucks moving under triple-canopy
jungle.

Nonetheless, air power is what keeps the entire effort
at Khe Sanh afloat. Because there is no really passable
road in the area, and the North Vietnamese control the
ground, the mammoth supply needs must be flown in by
helicopters and C-123 and C-130 transport planes. Because of the danger of incoming fire, supply planes now
unload in as little as three minutes. Cargoes are shoved
down their rear loading ramps while the transports taxi
slowly toward take-off. Airdrop systems are planned in

case heavy fighting or poor weather prevents any landings at all.

Most Marines at Khe Sanh feel more than ready for the battle they know they are there for, but they are becoming impatient. The waiting is wearying and frustrating, as day by day they undergo incoming, see friends wounded and killed (total casualties equal 10 percent of the base's men), and remain unable to fight back. "I wish they'd come and get it over with," said Pfc. Larry Jenkins, 18. Despite their perilous position, Jenkins and his comrades at Khe Sanh are spoiling for a fight.

APPENDIX XXII

MEMORANDUM TO NEWSMEN FROM AMBASSADOR ROBERT KOMER,
SAIGON, FEBRUARY 24, 1968

FOR BACKGROUND USE ONLY

N.B.   Many of the figures given below are best estimates,
which are continually being updated. For example, number
of Tet evacuees includes unscreened, early figures--later
information suggests that many of them have now returned
to their homes. Similarly, estimates on strengths of
local security forces were as of mid-February. We believe
they are higher as of today.

I.   Status of Recovery Effort

    A.   Post-Tet evacuees as of 23 February: around
       471,000 (best combination U.S./GVN figures).
    B.   Houses destroyed during Tet offensive as of 23
       February: about 63,700.
    C.   Cities and district towns assaulted or mortared:
       102.
    D.   Civilian casualties: about 4,300 KIA, 17,800 WIA.
    E.   GVN relief funds as of 22 February: allocated by
       Central Committee to provinces--$VN 147 million;
       private donations--$VN 44 million in Saigon, more
       than $VN 220 million countryside.
    F.   Movement of U.S.-funded commodities, 1-22 February:

bulgur	293 MT
rice	25,789 MT
dried milk	85 MT
beans	140 MT
cooking oil	98 MT
blankets	13 MT

    G.   Thirty countries/organizations have pledged aid.
       Contributions received or en route from 17.
    H.   Price levels are dropping back: Food prices were
       80-100 percent above pre-Tet levels by 5-8 February.

Presently food prices only about 17 percent above pre-Tet levels. Nonfood prices have fallen back to pre-Tet levels.

II. Pacification Status

    A. Considerable setback, but varies widely from province to province. For example, U.S. province senior advisors assess serious current impact on pacification in 13 provinces, moderate effect in 16 provinces, and only slight effect in 15 provinces.

    B. Adverse effects are largely after-effect of VC/NVA attack on cities; enemy avoided relatively secure hamlets during attack; perhaps 50 hamlets damaged in violent fighting between 30 January and 23 February.

    C. However, partial vacuum developed in countryside as GVN/FW forces protect cities and LOCs [lines of communication] or pursue enemy units. Enemy still oriented on cities, disruption of LOCs, or self-preservation.

    D. Only 18 of 51 ARVN battalions in direct support of pacification (i.e., stationed in RD campaign areas) withdrawn to protect cities or pursue VC/NVA units.

    E. RF/PF generally remain in pre-Tet positions, although even more statically employed than normally. Perhaps 100 outposts (mostly squad size) have been overrun or abandoned. Only about 50 out of 900 RF companies redeployed from territorial security role. Less than 20 PF platoons are known to have been redeployed, but information is still incomplete. RF company present for duty strength generally 80 percent or better; PF platoon strength running 85 percent or better.

    F. Half (278 by latest count) of 555 RD cadre teams are in hamlets. Two hundred forty-five were withdrawn to province/district towns to provide security, to protect teams, or perform social welfare work. Seventy-nine RD cadre KIA, 111 WIA, 845 MIA based on preliminary figures.

    G. Eighty-six out of 108 Truong Son (Montagnard) cadre teams in hamlets. Twenty-two were withdrawn. Fourteen TS cadre KIA, 39 WIA, none MIA.

    H. Police strength on-the-job was 90 percent of pre-Tet level by 12 February. Higher now. Only 10 Police Field Force companies were withdrawn from rural areas into cities. Four hundred forty-seven police KIA, 758 WIA, and 157 MIA between 30 January-23 February.

I. In interpreting above figures, must bear in mind
that substantial numbers of ARVN, RF/PF, RD,
police personnel granted Tet leave and have not
yet returned to units because of disruption of
transportation, fear, or other causes.

APPENDIX XXIII

GEN. WILLIAM C. WESTMORELAND, INTERVIEW BY WES GALLAGHER,
ASSOCIATED PRESS GENERAL MANAGER, FEBRUARY 25, 1968

SAIGON (AP)--Gen. William C. Westmoreland expressed doubt
Sunday that North Vietnam could stand a long war. But he
said communist forces could strike again and more U.S.
troops probably will be required in the war.

The four-star commander of U.S. forces in Vietnam compared
the recent communist Lunar New Year offensive to the Battle of the Bulge in World War II, the last major German
drive in that conflict.

Westmoreland said:

"I liken the recent Tet offensive by the leadership in
Hanoi to the Battle of the Bulge in World War II. By
committing a large share of his communist forces to a
major offensive, he achieved some tactical surprise. This
offensive has required us to react and to modify our plans
in order to take advantage of the opportunity to inflict
heavy casualties upon him.

"Although the enemy has achieved some temporary psychological advantage, he suffered a military defeat."

Westmoreland, after a two-hour informal interview, answered
in detail in writing 17 questions submitted to him by the
Associated Press covering many phases of the war. He made
these points among others:

1. In answer to a question whether his basic strategy was
changed by the Vietcong offensive, Westmoreland explained
his shifting of forces to the cities and then said: "Basically, I see no requirement to change our strategy.
Friendly forces still must find, fix, fight, and destroy
the enemy, and concurrently provide the necessary security
for the population.

2. "However, one fact is clear as a result of the challenge posed by the recent Tet offensive: The time has come
for debating to end, for everyone to close ranks, roll up
their sleeves, and get on with the job."

2. "The enemy did achieve tactical surprise. . . . The
tactic of infiltration into the population centers was
used to a far greater degree than anticipated. . . . Without question, the capability of the enemy to employ this
tactic was underestimated."

3. American forces are temporarily on the defensive, but
have killed more than 40,000 of the enemy and are resuming
the offensive as rapidly as possible.

4. "The enemy's general offensive does seem to be a go-
for-broke effort."

5. Westmoreland still envisions that the South Vietnamese
Army can be developed to carry a greater share of the war.
In the interim, however, "additional U.S. forces may be
required."

6. In answer to the question whether the willingness of
the Vietcong to sacrifice 10 men for one didn't mean a
long war, Westmoreland explained his view of the effect
of losses on North Vietnam and added: "In sum, I do not
believe Hanoi can hold up under a long war. The present
enemy offensive attitude may indicate that Hanoi realizes
this also."

The questions and answers:

Q.: Your strategy in Vietnam has generally been described
as having the South Vietnamese forces supply security for
the cities and pacification program, while U.S. forces
strike at the North Vietnamese and the main bodies of Vietcong. In view of the fact that you have had to use American troops to help clear at least 10 major cities because
the ARVN Armed Forces of Vietnam were unable to complete the
job themselves, where does this leave your basic strategy?

A.: At the time U.S. troops were deployed to South Vietnam, and particularly after the Honolulu conference in
early 1966, it was conceptually agreed that the Vietnamese
forces would concentrate on providing security to the
populated areas, while the U.S. forces would provide a
shield behind which pacification could be carried out.

U.S. forces would, in general, confront the North Vietnamese Army and Vietcong main force units, since their
firepower and mobility made them more effective than the
Vietnamese troops.

However, as the situation evolved, the division of responsibility was not so clear-cut. We found it expedient and
desirable to have some of our forces work with the Vietnamese forces in the populated areas, and the Vietnamese
wanted to participate with the U.S. forces in taking the
war to the enemy's main force units. Shortly before the

recent offensive by the enemy at Tet, many American troops were pulled back closer to the populated areas, based on intelligence that an attack was pending. These troops did not initially deploy in the cities, but some did so subsequently to support the Vietnamese Army.

I do not visualize that the temporary success by the enemy in penetrating the cities will bring about a change in strategy, since the enemy did not enter the cities in military formation but infiltrated by road and by water and as a part of the migration of people during the Tet period, when traditionally families and close friends get together and celebrate.

During the follow-on phase of the offensive, there were efforts by the enemy to move into cities in military formation, but, with few exceptions, these efforts were repulsed. Basically, I see no requirement to change our strategy. Friendly forces still must find, fix, fight, and destroy the enemy, and concurrently provide the necessary security to the population.

However, one fact is clear as the result of the challenge posed by the recent Tet offensive: The time has come for the debating to end, for everyone to close ranks, roll up their sleeves, and get on with the job.

Q.: If the Vietcong didn't achieve a surprise in their offensive, how do you account for their assaulting about 35 population centers? Did the allies underestimate the Vietcong capability?

A.: The enemy did achieve tactical surprise in the timing and character of his offensive, although the Vietnamese and Americans had intelligence that there was to be an offensive. The tactic of infiltration into the population centers was used to a far greater degree than anticipated and was generally successful, since controls imposed along the highways by the police were inadequate to detect the major infiltration and to stop it. Without question, the capability of the enemy to employ this tactic was underestimated. Certainly, it was by me, and I believe likewise by the Vietnamese. The enemy will probably try this tactic again and we must give him credit for having this potential.

Q.: Doesn't the ease with which the Vietcong infiltrated the cities, starting the battles within them, indicate they have a lot more sympathizers than we were led to believe?

A.: It does not necessarily follow that the Vietcong have more sympathizers than we believed. It only takes a few collaborators to aid infiltrators entering into a populated area, particularly if these infiltrators are well trained and disciplined.

The use of public roads and civilian disguise made it very difficult to detect the infiltrators. Many were riding public buses and bicycles in civilian clothes.

What I am saying is, that in most cases, the Vietcong infiltrated into cities by by-passing the civilian population, mingling with them only incidentally as they moved, largely disguised, along public highways.

There is no doubt that some people saw this movement by the enemy but remained silent through fear, apathy, or because they were sympathizers.

Q.: In 1967, you were largely on the offensive in such large operations as Junction City. Hasn't the Vietcong attack put you on the defensive as far as tactics are concerned?

A.: In 1967, we did conduct a number of large operations to clear Vietcong base areas near the cities and to disrupt jungle areas that had served as his hide-outs during years past.

The recent Vietcong attacks have necessitated a redeployment of many of our troops, not only to help defend the population centers but also to take advantage of the opportunity to inflict heavy casualties on the enemy, which has been accomplished, incidentally, with unprecedented success. It would make little sense not to take advantage of an opportunity to attack an enemy who had surfaced himself, as opposed to searching for him in his jungle hide-outs.

In a very real sense, when he moved out of his jungle camps he made himself more vulnerable and gave us an opportunity to hurt him severely. That is why over 40,000 of the enemy have been killed in less than one month, which is over 40 percent of all the enemy killed in 1967.

His attack put us temporarily on the defensive, but he has run into a buzz saw. We are maintaining pressure on him wherever we find him and are resuming the offensive as rapidly as possible.

Q.: The Vietcong offensive has been described as a go-for-broke attack. Do you feel that they can mount another attack similar to the one just mounted?

A.: The enemy's general offensive does seem to be a go-for-broke effort. The second wave was feeble compared to the first if, in fact, it was intended as a second wave.

Although the enemy maintains the capability of mounting another series of ground attacks, they would have to be more limited in scope than was the first. I say this because it is doubtful that he will be able to equal the intensity of the first wave unless and until he can pull back, regroup, fill his ranks, and make the necessary complicated and thorough preparations.

Our continuing pressure on the enemy is designed to impede any regrouping efforts.

Finally, a strong follow-on attack would not have the essential advantage of surprise that occurred at Tet.

Q.: In view of the attacks on the cities plus the threat of attack in Khe Sanh, can present U.S. troop strength do the job? In this it is recalled that you said in Washington that you thought in two years there would be a stable Vietnamese Army to allow at least some token withdrawal of U.S. troops.

A.: The recent VC-NVA attacks and their disregard for the lives of the civilian population have indeed taxed the flexibility and mobility of our forces. At the same time, the attacks have offered us an excellent opportunity to exploit [the enemy's] losses and capitalize on his defeats. To take advantage of this opportunity requires acceptance of a calculated risk with respect to our ability to maintain the present level of security.

With additional troops we could more effectively deny the enemy his objectives, capitalize on his recent defeats to a greater degree both in time and place, and clearly demonstrate to Hanoi our firm determination to prevent him from taking over any part of South Vietnam.

I still envision that, as the Vietnamese Army completes its modernization and develops its potential capability, it will be able to carry a greater share of the war, and, to that extent, the level of our commitment can be reduced.

In the interim, however, additional U.S. forces will probably be required.

I should add that one very beneficial by-product of the Tet offensive was the excellent overall performance by the ARVN. Their morale and fighting spirit were undoubtedly enhanced by their successes, a fact which augurs well for the future.

Q.: Do you still expect the communists to make a main effort at Khe Sanh or could this buildup be a feint?

A.: It is conceivable that the enemy's buildup around Khe Sanh is a feint. But I do not believe that this was

his intention, and I have no reason to believe at this
time that his plans have changed. He can attack at any
time if he is prepared to accept the casualties that would
be inflicted upon him.

Of course, there is always another possibility--that our
heavy air attacks may force him to modify his plans.

Q.: The Vietcong has been steadily able to escalate its
weaponry with larger rockets and mortars and large in-
filtrations, particularly in the Khe Sanh area. Isn't
this indicative of a failure of the bombing program
against the North?

A.: No reasonable person ever expected the bombing
campaign to stop infiltration of personnel and the movement of supplies to the South. The fact that the enemy
has been able to move troops and supplies does not indicate that the bombing against the North has been a failure.

One has to judge the bombing program based on the problems
that it has created for the communist regime in Hanoi and
its present posture in the South compared to what would
have happened had there been no interdiction of his lines
of communication.

The bombing program has forced the enemy to organize a
large and expensive air-defense system which has required
the diversion of large numbers of men, many of whom are
skilled technicians. It has required him to divert a
very considerable portion of his available manpower and
effort to keeping his transportation system operative.

It has slowed the movement of men and equipment to the
South and has degraded the amount of weapons, ammunition,
and supplies that would otherwise have arrived in the
South.

It has not stopped the flow of men, materiel, and supplies, but it certainly has reduced the level that would
have been possible otherwise. The fact that the enemy
has waged a concerted international propaganda campaign
to stop the bombing suggests that the campaign is hurting
him.

Q.: There have been statements from time to time that the
Vietcong morale has been deteriorating. In view of the
fact that the VC in the last offensive have been willing
to sacrifice themselves in suicide attacks, particularly
in Hue, doesn't this indicate their morale is still high
and the highest it has ever been?

A.: We have had thousands of reports over the past year
that the morale of the Vietcong was deteriorating. These
came from hundreds of captured documents and thousands of

interrogations of prisoners of war and defectors. One reason that the enemy launched his recent large-scale offensive was that he was seriously concerned about this deterioration in morale.

The fact that the defection rate almost doubled between 1966 and 1967 we know was a matter of concern to Hanoi.

When the enemy planned his Tet offensive, extraordinary steps were taken to propagandize the leaders and troops within the Vietcong and North Vietnam Army ranks.

Many were told that the people in the cities would welcome them and that a general uprising would take place. They were told that the ARVN troops had low morale, possessed poor fighting qualities, and would join their ranks to support the uprising.

The enemy, in effect, created a "home by Christmas" atmosphere which, coupled with a high state of discipline and intensified indoctrination, assisted in assuring a morale level suitable for the attacks.

However, there is little evidence of VC willingness to sacrifice themselves in suicidal attacks. Many fought halfheartedly, a number surrendered, and in several cases small units gave themselves up.

No prisoner has stated that he thought of the attacks as suicidal. Rather, some thought that it was merely a matter of occupying the cities.

As for Hue, the troops involved were North Vietnamese Army, not VC. Further, they are not now attacking but defending.

Frankly, I would very much doubt that the morale of the enemy units which have been badly beaten during the last few weeks is very high. Moreover, the artificial morale boost provided by VC promises is subject to rapid reversal as the military campaign fails.

Q.: In view of the fact that the Vietminh, in seven years of war against the French, lost half a million men killed and the Vietcong have been willing on occasion to spend 10 lives to kill one, doesn't this indicate a long war?

A.: It is well known that the communists have little regard for human life, either military or innocent civilian. There is ample evidence that the leadership in Hanoi and the Vietcong in the South [do] not hesitate to sacrifice thousands of men in order to achieve political ends. There is no evidence that this policy will change.

However, the greater their casualties, the greater the price, the longer it will take North Vietnam to recover

from the war and the greater the disillusionment among the
rank and file of the enemy in the South as in the North.

We know that the Vietcong in the South have encountered
recruiting problems throughout the past year. This situation has necessitated sending more men from the North to
fill up the depleted ranks of the Vietcong. The tremendous
losses during the recent offensive will have to be replaced.
This is going to impose an even greater drain on the resources available to the enemy.

No doubt he realizes that it takes people to build a
nation, and if the leaders and the young men are progressively destroyed, the future of the nation is in doubt.

In sum, I do not believe Hanoi can hold up under a long
war. The present enemy offensive attitude may indicate
that Hanoi realizes this, also.

Q.: Three years ago, the main problem for American forces
was getting intelligence on the Vietcong, where they were
hiding among the population. It was said then that if
the population provided this information, the war could be
shortened immeasurably. What is happening today with the
intelligence from the South Vietnamese?

A.: The amount of voluntary reporting of intelligence by
ordinary citizens was gradually increasing prior to the
recent offensive. As it becomes evident that the enemy's
military offensive has failed, intelligence from the
people will increase. This trend is already evident.

Q.: What is your view of the performance of the South
Vietnamese Army, since it was expected that it hold the
cities? It is understood that the Vietnamese in a number
of places were able to hold their compounds but unable to
drive the Vietcong out without the help of the American
forces.

A.: In general, the South Vietnamese Army performed well,
indeed. As an example, all 11 of the Vietnamese division
commanders were at their posts at the time of the attack
and commanded their units effectively.

As I've already pointed out, the cities were attacked from
within by the enemy who had infiltrated into them under
the cover of crowds and the noise of Tet firecrackers.

Few cities of Vietnam are organized as fortresses. However,
certain key installations within the cities are protected
by fortifications. Therefore, these compounds were, in
most cases, able to hold out, but reinforcements in many
cases had to be brought in from outside to drive the enemy
out of the cities. These reinforcements were both Vietnamese and Americans.

I should add that U.S. and free-world forces also per-
formed with characteristic heroism and effectiveness.

Q.: There is great disbelief in the United States in the
body count of Vietcong casualties. Since many of the
Vietcong fight in civilian clothes, how can civilian dead
be distinguished from Vietcong? If the ratio of wounded
to killed is the same as it is in most wars, the body count
would indicate tremendous casualty figures for the Vietcong, who would certainly need large hospital facilities
to care for them. What is your view of the body count?

A.: I believe that one of the great distortions of the
war has been the allegation that casualties inflicted on
the enemy are padded. I can say categorically that such
is not the case.

I have given my personal attention to this matter and have
had a number of checks made on the accuracy of our system.
I am confident that the officially reported enemy killed-
in-action figures are conservative and that any inaccuracies
are more than offset by enemy deaths that we do not know
about.

Let me explain. We have set up accounting procedures that
are designed to come up with the most honest and accurate
count possible of enemy killed in action. Certainly, there
are cases of duplication and where noncombatants have been
reported as enemy casualties. This latter is particularly
true of porters pressed into service who, in some cases,
could be innocent civilians.

However, we seldom know the number of KIAs resulting from
B-52, tactical air, and artillery strikes. We never know
how many dead the enemy is able to remove from the battlefield. We never know how many die from their wounds,
and this is certain to be a substantial number.

Finally, we are continually finding mass graves of enemy
dead. I am convinced that these unknowns more than offset
the relatively small inaccuracies of our accounting system.

Q.: The Vietminh were very successful in their war in
recruiting sympathizers to their side by going into the
cities, infiltrating the population, and then having the
French bomb the cities in order to get at the enemy, so
the French would bear the blame. In view of the widespread destruction these days, is not the same thing
happening now?

A.: Certainly the communist planners in Hanoi drew on
their success in earlier wars in planning the recent widespread offensive.

When the Vietcong and the North Vietnamese units infiltrated the cities, they attempted to knock out military
headquarters, police stations, and seize the communication facilities. Also, they attempted to seize churches,
pagodas, schools, hospitals, and public buildings and
utilize them as headquarters, supply points, and combat
areas.

Regrettably, this did bring about destruction of some
of these buildings as the battle was waged against the
enemy, although there were a number of cases where the
South Vietnamese were successful in dislodging the enemy
without major destruction.

There are few indications that the enemy has gained a
psychological advantage by this tactic and that sympathizers have been recruited to his side. On the contrary,
the people in the cities are largely indignant at the
Vietcong for violating the sanctity of the Tet period and
for their tactics which brought about damage to the cities.

But two points stand out to both the Vietnamese and their
allies. First, a large portion of the destruction, particularly the fires, was caused directly by the VC themselves,
firing mortars and recoilless rifles in the cities.
Second, none of the destruction would have occurred had
the VC not undertaken to attack the cities.

Q.: Has not the Vietcong offensive, which forced concentration of men, set back the pacification program many
months, if not years? And it has been said that pacification is the heart of the effort. For example, the Mission
--even last year before the offensive--announced that
Vietnamese pacification officials, civilians and officers
and those sympathetic to the government, were being killed
at a rate of 10 a day in 1967, which was twice the amount
of the 1966 rate.

A.: It is too early to assess the impact the recent offensive by the enemy has had on the pacification program.
However, it is reasonable to assume that in many areas
the program has been set back. On the other hand, in some
areas we know it was untouched.

In the areas where there was a setback, certainly it will
take months in some instances to restore the effort to its
former level, although the exact time involved depends on
a number of imponderables.

Although it was not emphasized countrywide during the Tet
attacks, the methods of the enemy do involve killing government officials and leadership that is sympathetic toward
the government. The rate in 1967 was greater than in 1966,

but it is impossible at this point in time to forecast the rate in 1968.

Q.: The history of wars generally indicates that they do not come to an end until the enemy has lost the will to fight, and the first indications of this have always been that crack troop units surrendered intact. Have any hard-core Vietcong units surrendered, or do you see any indication of this coming in the near future?

A.: It is true that one evidence of the deterioration of an army is the surrendering of entire units. This has not yet occurred to any significant degree in this war. The enemy does not yet have sufficient pressure upon him to bring about this phenomenon, and I cannot predict if and when it will occur. It is entirely possible that the high rates of individual defections which occur from time to time may have essentially the same effect.

Q.: Limited war obviously poses many heavy burdens on the military. To mention a few, the inability to invade enemy home strongholds, or strike supply bases in Laos or Cambodia and to try to preserve Vietnamese cities. Isn't "limited war" a contradiction in terms which makes victory in a conventional sense impossible?

A.: This is indeed a limited war with limited objectives fought with limited means. Since our objective is to save the people of South Vietnam from communist domination and to permit them to develop a government of their own choosing, and since our policy does not involve conquest of North Vietnam or expansion of the war into other parts of Southeast Asia, our effort has been limited.

On the other hand, the enemy's objective is to conquer the South and to impose his will and form of government on the people of the South. The enemy has not used the same ground rules that we have and has ignored the neutrality of Laos and Cambodia.

Southeastern Laos has been used for several years as a major line of communications for the movement of men, weapons, ammunition, and supplies. It has become a de facto part of North Vietnam, since it is entirely controlled by Hanoi.

The eastern border areas of Cambodia adjacent to South Vietnam are characterized by jungle-covered, unpopulated terrain. The border is ill defined and in some areas it is under dispute. The North Vietnamese have taken advantage of this situation and have used the border areas of Cambodia for purposes of infiltration, supply, and troop rehabilitation and training.

Even in the populated areas of Cambodia adjacent to South Vietnam, a smuggling operation of major proportions has been conducted to supply the Vietcong forces with arms, ammunition, and medical supplies. The ethnic Vietnamese living in Cambodia along the border areas have been utilized by the Vietcong in this logistic enterprise.

As in South Vietnam, the enemy's tactics have been covert, and through well-developed techniques and a high state of discipline could well have eluded the attention of Cambodian central government officials.

A limited war places certain limitations on the military and is a factor that makes it difficult to project the defeat of the enemy. Aside from these factors, however, a guerrilla war in the pattern of Mao Tse-tung's doctrine, in which guerrillas as well as conventionally armed large forces must be defeated, makes victory in a classic sense illusive.

Our military efforts, therefore, must be focused at raising the cost of aggression by the enemy to the point where, as a matter of prudence, he will reconcile his objectives with the realistic long-range cost.

I liken the recent Tet truce offensive by the leadership in Hanoi to the Battle of the Bulge in World War II. By committing a large share of his forces in a major offensive, he achieved some tactical surprise. This offensive has required us to react and to modify our plans in order to take advantage of the opportunity to inflict heavy casualties upon him.

Although the enemy has achieved some temporary psychological advantage, he suffered a military defeat. He has paid a big price for what he has gained.

The enemy has recently changed his strategy and now apparently wants "to go for broke." The price that he has paid and will continue to pay should, in time, cause him to make another assessment.

In any case, his ability to pursue a protracted war has been reduced by the losses that he has recently suffered.

APPENDIX XXIV

The Washington *Post*
February 25, 1968

GIAP OFFENSIVE AIMS AT WAR'S END BY MIDYEAR

By Douglas Pike

(A U.S. Information Agency officer and author of Vietcong, *Pike prepared this analysis in a personal capacity. It is not an official U.S. government assessment or policy statement.)*

The Lunar New Year offensive launched by the communists against 36 major South Vietnamese population centers in the early hours of January 31 bears the unmistakable stamp of North Vietnamese Defense Minister Vo Nguyen Giap. Any assessment of the objectives, magnitude, and subsequent developments of the campaign must attend closely to the mind and personality of this master tactician, victor of the Vietminh war against the French and supreme strategist of the present one.

General Giap is one of the best tactical commanders of the 20th century, expert at seizing the local initiative and master of the surprise diversion. He is meticulous in his planning, imaginative and bold in executing his military strikes. Only Giap, among all North or South Vietnamese Communists, could have supervised the elaborate synchronization not only of the Tet offensive but of the broader winter-spring campaign of which it is part. For this audacious strike--and audacity is what carried it as far as it did go--must not be viewed as something isolated nor unique, but rather as the intensified continuation of something under way at least since August 1967.

The backdrop against which General Giap planned and acted was both temporal and internally political. He was working against time, trying to cope with what he knows is in the long run a strategically hopeless situation in which American firepower eats deeper into his reserves of men and arms. And he faced, in the world of Politburo politics in Hanoi, increased pressure from younger members who see "his preoccupation with military victory as a

167

forlorn attempt to restage the Vietminh war under vastly
changed conditions, because a generation of military
technology has outdated many of the military techniques
that were successful against the French."

DISSENSION IN HANOI

The broad view of the war, as Giap sees it, and as he outlined it in an important series of articles published in
Hanoi last September, goes something like this:

The American military buildup in South Vietnam, beginning
in mid-1965, resulted in two American military offensives
in the dry seasons of 1965 and 1966. Both offensives
failed, Giap believes, and resulted in a condition of
stalemate which offered him unprecedented opportunities
if only they could be properly seized. Dissension was
rising in the United States, he held, and pessimism was
spreading in the American ranks in Vietnam. Foreign support for the communist cause was growing abroad, in terms
of increased hostility to American military activities in
Vietnam.

But, at the same time, a sort of mirror-image condition
was developing in Hanoi. The stalemate which General
Giap thought he saw was, of course, a stalemate in both
directions. Dissension in the Politburo developed over
the lack of progress and particularly over the "no-win"
policy for which General Giap held the chief responsibility.

A sense of impotency developed as American planes continued to pound away at the North Vietnamese transportation
and communication centers, curtailing the flow of food,
consumer goods, and people throughout the country as well
as military material in from China and out to South Vietnam.

From the communist capitals, especially from Peking (where
the Chinese Communists appear to consider that the Vietcong are doing virtually everything wrong), but also
from the U.S.S.R., came muted but stronger criticism of
the manner and means by which General Giap was conducting
the war.

In Hanoi, especially among younger Politburo members,
General Giap was in trouble. It was not serious trouble,
for there is nothing definite to suggest that the dissension or dissatisfaction was at the level of a schism. But
the stalemate condition which General Giap had proclaimed
did have the effect of putting him--as well as Ho Chi Minh
and Pham Van Dong, the other two of the big three in Hanoi
--on the defensive, and forced General Giap to act more
precipitately in commitment than he prefers, being by
nature a cautious man reluctant to act while loose ends
remain.

Three Phases

Throughout the Vietminh war and during the present war, General Giap has pursued what he calls his Three-Phase Strategy, namely: resistance, general offensive, and general uprising. The Vietminh war is today divided by Hanoi historians into these stages, and the three also have been used in explaining the course of events of the present war.

In the summer of 1967, General Giap decided that for political and personal reasons, if not for military ones, the moment had arrived when he must order the start of the general offensive and, subsequently, the general uprising phases in the South. He and his staff began work on what internally was called the winter-spring campaign. The broad characteristics of the campaign have been:

- An intensification of what General Giap calls Coordinated Fighting Methods, manifested at Dak To in Kontum province, Con Tien in Quang Ngai province, and Loc Ninh in Binh Long province, all three in the mountainous interior of South Vietnam along the Cambodian and Laotian borders

- An intensification of what he calls Independent Fighting Methods, that is, revolutionary guerrilla war, aimed at the cities, airfields, military headquarters, and allied military logistic, transportation, and communication networks

These were the military aspects. Also part of the winter-spring campaign was a stepped-up program of terrorism, especially against the government of Vietnam's pacification program, which largely had been ignored before this. And, by increased organizational and motivational work by political cadres employing the three long-standing communist programs or techniques known as:

- *Dan van*, or motivating and harnessing the energies of those South Vietnamese people controlled by the communists

- *Dich van*, or nonmilitary activities by the communists in areas controlled by the government of South Vietnam--specifically, in this case, social organization work by covert cadres to form the people of the towns and cities into mass movements that would engage in public disorders and, eventually, the general uprising, thus supporting the military assault

- *Binh van*, or proselyting efforts among members of the Vietnamese armed forces and civil services

DECISION BY MIDYEAR

General Giap's campaign had three phases following the
initial planning, training, and indoctrinational work,
which began in July of last year. The first phase came
in October, November, and December, the second is taking
place in the first three months of 1968, and phase three
is scheduled for April, May, and June. The scenario therefore calls for an end to the war by mid-1968.

This is not to say Giap anticipated peace arriving by midyear, rather that a decisive point of no return would be
passed. Then, inexorably and irreversibly, the war would
begin to work itself out to final victory, much like the
situation in Europe in late 1944 when the fate of Germany
was sealed and the final victory, no longer in doubt,
became simply a matter of time, although months of hard
fighting lay ahead.

Seen lying along the route to this goal are the destruction of at least a portion of American military capability
in South Vietnam, disintegration of the Vietnamese armed
forces as a military organization, seizure of the governmental centers in South Vietnam down to and including the
district or county level, establishment of a broad-based
coalition government, although not one which would include
present power-holders in Saigon, and unification of North
and South Vietnam.

The final objective is the goal which General Giap and
fellow members of his Politburo have been pursuing cease-
lessly and relentlessly since 1954.

The Coordinated Fighting Methods attacks in Dak To, Loc
Ninh and Con Tien in the early winter, resulted in heavy
North Vietnamese casualties and were, for General Giap's
purposes, inconclusive.

They served to increase the grumblings by the younger
elements in the Politburo, joined perhaps by certain of
the "professional" generals in Hanoi, the line commanders,
who argued that they had lost a sizable number of good
men in these mountain battles to no very good purpose in
a campaign large enough to extract a real price but too
small to be decisive.

Nevertheless, the campaign ground on and the plans went
forward for the general offensive, which was to deal a
major or, it was hoped, catastrophic blow at the enemy--in
actuality the South Vietnamese rather than the Americans.

PEACE OVERTURES

Meanwhile, the diplomats and propagandists in Hanoi were
busy developing a peace overture campaign, which was a

fabric woven of many threads.

Peace or "talks" overtures--the difference between the two being lost as the word "peace" spread around the world-- served propaganda ends, possibly could achieve a cessation of air strikes into North Vietnam, helped reduce the grumbling in the Politburo, and, above all, formed the right hook which together with the left jab was to assure victory.

Thus, in the broadest terms, the grand strategy of Hanoi, which goes beyond General Giap's military contributions, is a two-salient thrust, one salient being military and the other being diplomatic-negotiational.

The military salient has two prongs. Employing independent fighting methods, a maximum strike is being mounted in South Vietnam and focuses on the cities. It is billed as the general uprising and portrayed to the rank and file as Armageddon. General Giap used at least 50 percent of his main strike forces, estimated at 118,000 total, al- though he employed Southern Vietcong soldiers rather than Northern troops wherever possible. The Tet offensive, heart of the general offensive, concentrated on airfields and air-support activities, military headquarters, civilian governmental complexes, materiel and logistic centers, as well, of course, as the 36 largest towns and cities of the country.

General Giap hopes the general offensive will have these results: the Americans will crack, militarily and psycho- logically; a significant portion of what he regards as the real American strength--aircraft, communication, and transportation techniques and well-coordinated command centers--will be destroyed; the Vietnamese armed forces will disintegrate; and the population will rise up in massive support of the communists (if not enthusiastically, at least because it appears to be the wise individual thing to do).

Employing concentrating fighting methods, the other prong of the salient, comes the Dienbienphu gambit, probably at Khe Sanh. The essence of the military salient is a play for time--take and hold is the order, so that time will run out, especially for the Americans.

POLITICAL ATTACK

The diplomatic-negotiational salient is the political at- tack. Its first prong is the negotiational ploy, offering a political "settlement" of the war. Beginning in December of last year, Hanoi began its overtures directed at talking the Americans out of South Vietnam under the worst pos- sible circumstances to them.

The second prong is aimed at the establishment of a coalition government in South Vietnam, a coalition government as that term is used peculiarly by the communists. The vehicle for this is a series of specially designed interim communist front organizations in South Vietnam, most important of which is the Alliance of National Peace Forces in Saigon. These sprang up in South Vietnam beginning in early February of this year. They are supposed to help establish a new ruling group in South Vietnam that excludes the present members of the government of Vietnam.

Implicit in this double-pronged salient strategy is a difference of opinion among members of the North Vietnamese Politburo. Giap continues to see the route to victory as military--the way to win, he argues, is militarily, on the ground, in South Vietnam, not at the conference table and not as the result of the American Presidential elections. This view, from all evidence, is shared by Ho Chi Minh and Pham Van Dong, who is Ho's most likely successor.

Le Duan, the fourth leading figure in the Politburo, probably supports the big three, but with some reservations. Truong Chinh, the fifth man, plays a role which, if it is important, is unclear.

The younger members of the Politburo, while subscribing to the two-salient approach, argue for greater emphasis on the diplomatic-negotiational salient, regarding the military salient as valuable chiefly as a means of closing the ring.

Essentially this fighting-negotiating method was the pattern during the 1954 Indo-China Conference in Geneva, and, in Korea, during the period prior to and during the armistice talks that ended Korean hostilities.

MYTH OF UPRISING

The Tet offensive, within this context, quickly became many things to many men. Assessment of the degree of failure must be built on an assessment of the enemy's intentions.

If intentions in the offensive were limited, then the failure was a limited one; if more ambitious, then the failure was a major one. And if the enemy intention was a knockout punch then, quite obviously, the failure was monumental. In short, intentions are a continuum.

The Tet offensive was wrapped in the great Vietnamese Communist social myth of the general uprising (the same myth, in an agrarian setting, as French sociologist Georges Sorel's idea of the general strike, the day when all the workers of the world simultaneously strike, bringing society to a standstill and allowing the workers to take over). Like all social myths, that of the general uprising essentially is something existing in men's minds, not in the finite world. What counts is not truth but what is believed to be true.

In communist public statements, the events of early February generally were termed "the offensive campaign and uprising campaign." Internal documents called it a "general offensive to culminate in the general uprising." During indoctrination sessions for the rank and file, in previous months, it was most frequently billed as a general uprising; and the political cadres mingling with the population during the offensive almost universally said or implied it was the general uprising.

An indication of what the offensive meant to the rank-and-file communists can be found in a tabulation of prisoner interrogation reports.

With respect to the basic purpose of the assignment given individuals, a sample shows 40 percent were told this was to be the general uprising; 33 percent were told simply they were to take part in an attack of unspecified dimensions (overwhelmingly, this is what those who attacked Saigon in individual actions, such as the attack on the U.S. Embassy, were told); 26 percent were told they were to seize and hold the cities (chiefly the explanation in central Vietnam area); about 20 percent were told the purpose of the attack was "to drive out the American"; and about 15 percent were given to understand that the military attack would culminate in establishment of a coalition government. (Some prisoners gave more than one explanation.)

An oblique indication of the direction in which the leadership believed the offensive would move lies in the fact that large numbers of the rank and file, especially in central Vietnam, did not have any specific withdrawal plans. Some 47 percent of the prisoners said they did not receive withdrawal plans as part of their individual assignment; 31 percent did have some such plan; and 22 percent either were given no instructions (although their officers may have received them) or were told that subsequent actions would depend on developments.

These troops may have been regarded by the leadership as expendable, but the pattern is quite unlike previous communist military behavior in the war and most certainly will hurt future communist leadership credibility.

BATTLE ORDER

One of the best indications of the leadership's calculation can be found in the battle order of the Presidium of

the Central Committee of the National Liberation Front.
The heart of this order was these specific instructions
to the troops:

- Wipe out a good deal of the enemy's potential, defeat
  the U.S. and satellite troops, cause disintegration
  of the puppet army

- Overthrow the lackey government at all echelons,
  drastically punish all high-level traitors and all
  tyrants

- Establish a People's Revolutionary Government at all
  levels, strive to defend this government, and reso-
  lutely smash all enemy counteroffensive attempts

- Implement all policies set down by the National
  Liberation Front

The major anticipated results of the Tet offensive and the
winter-spring campaign appear to be threefold. First,
that the Vietnamese armed forces would disintegrate as a co-
herent military organization, that is, reach a condition
in which individual military units might remain intact
but in which the system would be in disarray, fragmented,
and chaotic--its officers receiving no orders since higher
headquarters would have been overrun, its troops disori-
ented and demoralized. The pattern of the attacks, it is
clear from documents, consisted of strikes at the ARVN
(Army of the Republic of Vietnam) chain of command rather
than at the decimation of large numbers of troops. The
documents and prisoner reports also indicate the leadership counted heavily on the soldiers of the Vietnamese
armed forces not only not fighting, but joining the communists en masse. The creation of the paper organization,
the Patriotic Armed Forces, was for the purpose of quickly
employing the services of vast numbers of defecting ARVN
soldiers.

Second, the calculation of General Giap was that a great
deal of public support would be forthcoming. This is the
political dimension of the Tet offensive.

It is a safe estimate that for every five communist
soldiers in the offensive there was one political cadre in
action. During individual city operations, political
cadres moved from house to house or among the early morning
crowds, mingling with the people, explaining the general
uprising, and soliciting support. Many carried with them
lists of names of persons ostensibly willing to take part
in public demonstrations.

PEACE THEME

A common theme used by these cadres was that the National Liberation Front stood for democracy, social welfare, neutralism. Peace was a recurrent theme, directed especially toward Buddhist women. Commando units striking at specific targets in the cities had satellite political cadres circling four or five blocks away, the installation under attack [*sic*], keeping people out of the fire fight and soliciting support. A special "coalition" flag was flown.

Typical of this political activity was a "people's court" held at the intersection of Minh Mang and Suvanmanh streets in Cholon. A cadre on a soap box told an assembled crowd that standing next to him was a woman whose son was a government security agent. He asked the crowd what "justice" should be meted out. The crowd shouted: "Don't execute her." So the cadre replied that she would be let off with a warning to call her son back from the government ranks.

Then the cadre went on to explain the general uprising. A clique of other political cadres in the crowd applauded throughout the speech, urging those next to them to do likewise. No one of these incidents in itself may be significant. What is important is that the communists expended a great deal of effort and allocated considerable resources, especially manpower, in creating them.

NO AID FROM PEOPLE

Although almost all of the rank-and-file communists were told to expect support from the population, either specific assistance or the general uprising, 90 percent of the prisoners said they received no aid from the general population and only 2 percent said they received unsolicited assistance. Six percent of the reports did not touch on this matter.

The third expectation by General Giap was that a strong punitive blow could be delivered against the Americans. Again, the pattern of the offensive suggests that he sought not to decimate large numbers of Americans--this being futile in a manpower sense, like trying to bail the ocean dry--but to cripple the American air-strike ability, and to disrupt the American military and civilian network that ties central command centers with field headquarters through an elaborate communication network. In short, the target was the American ability to assess and respond quickly to attack.

Beyond this lies the domain of the unknowable: how much General Giap was the victim of overly optimistic reports

from his commanders in the South and to what degree
Politburo politics caused him to override his better
judgment. Only historians, far into the future, will be
able to answer these questions with certainty.

FUTURE PROSPECTS

At this writing the prospects for the remainder of the
winter-spring offensive, in a very tentative way, appear
to be these:

1. Communist assertion of victory and the semblance of
    continuity, the "all is going according to plan"
    approach. Doctrinally, increased emphasis can be
    expected on the protracted-conflict theme.

2. Continued public reference to a negotiated settlement
    but actually, for the short run, a tapering off of
    negotiational overtures.

3. An effort to maintain the appearance of high-tempo
    military activity--especially political work and
    military pressure on the urban centers--while the
    obviously necessary regrouping, resupplying, and
    retraining missions are pursued. Military activity
    by North Vietnamese troops can be expected, especially
    at Khe Sanh, although this need not involve a full
    closing of the battle of Khe Sanh.

4. Possible introduction of new, more sophisticated
    weapons by the communists. Possibly there may be
    Hanoi requests for more foreign assistance from
    communist nations.

APPENDIX XXV

The New York *Times,*
February 25, 1968

U.S. ADMITS BLOW TO PACIFICATION

By Bernard Weinraub

SAIGON, South Vietnam, Feb. 24--The United States Mission conceded today for the first time that the allied effort to pacify the countryside had suffered a "considerable setback" as a result of the Vietcong offensive.

"There has been a loss of momentum, there has been some withdrawal (of security troops) from the countryside, there has been a significant psychological setback both on the part of pacification people themselves and the local population," said a high official of the Mission.

The pacification effort, which seeks to win the allegiance of South Vietnam's peasants, has been regarded here as having the same importance as the military drive.

TEAMS TERMED SHAKEN

The comments today, unusually blunt for a high-level official, were made at a formal news conference. The official asked that he not be identified.

While the impact of the enemy offensive has varied from province to province, the official said that there was "little doubt" that local security forces as well as government pacification teams had been shaken by the attacks, which began in earnest three and a half weeks ago during the Lunar New Year celebrations.

"Unquestionably there's been a considerable setback," the official said. "The real question now is who will fill the vacuum in the countryside."

"It depends on how fast the South Vietnamese government moves in and how aggressive and how fast the enemy will be," the official went on. "We hope the government can show the population things are returning to normal."

The provinces that suffered most, the official said, were in the Mekong Delta, and in the northern I Corps area.

"We will have to do more pacification work in hamlets previously considered pacified," he observed.   "There's been a loss of momentum--no blinking at that."

PLANS TO BE REEXAMINED

The official said that there would be "a major reexamination" of the 1968 pacification plan and that it would be "significantly modified." He also disclosed that the enemy offensive began at about the same time that the 1968 pacification program was scheduled to begin.

"The hardest thing to measure is the psychological impact on the pacifiers and the rural population in looking at the vacuum that's developing in significant parts of the countryside," he said.   "You have to consider that the Vietcong suffered some very heavy losses, too.

"Our side is weaker," he went on, "but I ask myself--is the enemy weaker or stronger than he was on January 28? I would answer that he is considerably weaker."

During the Lunar New Year offensive, the United States command said that nearly 28,000 enemy troops were killed --a figure considered extravagant by many observers here. United States dead, from January 28 to last Saturday, amounted to 1,359.

SHOWCASE PROGRAM HIT

In assessing the impact of the Vietcong attack, official reports from American provincial advisors indicated that the offensive had a "serious impact" on 13 provinces, "moderate effect" in 16 provinces, and "slight effect" in 15 provinces.

In some provinces, the official said, such as the northern province of Binh Dinh, the showcase of the program, the enemy's impact was considerable on some districts that were considered pacified.   The disruption of pacification in the province began weeks before the Lunar New Year offensive.

One of the major problems, the official said, was the vacuum created by the withdrawal of thousands of South Vietnamese troops from the countryside to protect the cities. A total of 18 battalions--about 8,000 men--were moved into the cities.   These battalions were part of a total of 51 battalions committed to direct support of the pacification program.

In addition, about half of the 555 pacification teams in hamlets were withdrawn to larger provincial or district towns, where they are providing security.

EARLY RETURN PLANNED

The teams are groups of young men and women who move into hamlets for a six-month period. They train the local residents, build farms and dispensaries, and provide a link, usually for the first time, between the villagers and the South Vietnamese government.

The official said he hoped that by March 1 most of the pacification teams would return to the countryside. "This pullback has not been as great as some of us thought in the dark days of early February," he said.

During the Lunar New Year offensive, the casualties among the 555 pacification teams, a total force of about 29,000 men and women, were 79 killed, 111 wounded, and 845 missing.

The official said the pacification program was not a target in the Lunar New Year offensive. "The enemy did not try to take over the countryside," he said. "What they sought was to take over the cities, quite deliberately, quite logically.

"If the enemy (now) chooses pacification as a main target, we'll have problems, real problems," he said.

APPENDIX XXVI

CBS TELEVISION, "WHO, WHAT,WHEN, WHERE, WHY: REPORT FROM VIETNAM BY WALTER CRONKITE," FEBRUARY 27, 1968

Cronkite: These ruins are in Saigon, capital and largest city of South Vietnam. They were left here by an act of war, Vietnamese against Vietnamese. Hundreds died here. Here in these ruins can be seen physical evidence of the Vietcong's Tet offensive, but far less tangible is what those ruins mean, and like everything else in this burned and blasted and weary land, they mean success or setback, victory or defeat, depending upon whom you talk to.

President Nguyen Van Thieu: I believe it gives to the VC, it shows first to the VC that the--the Vietnamese people from whom they hoped to have a general uprising, and to welcome the VC in the cities, this is a very bad test for them.

Nguyen Xuan Oanh (critic of government): I think the people have realized now that there [are] no secure areas. Your own home in the heart of the city is not secure. I am stunned myself when I see that the Vietcong can come to your door and open the door and just kill you instantly, without any warning, and without any protection from the government.

Cronkite: There are doubts about the measure of success or setback, but even more, there are doubts about the exact measure of the disaster itself. All that is known with certainty is that on the first two nights of the Tet Lunar New Year, the Vietcong and North Vietnamese Regular Forces, violating the truce agreed on for that holiday, struck across the entire length of South Vietnam, hitting the largest 35 cities, towns, and provincial capitals. How many died and how much damage was done, however, are still but approximations, despite the official figures.

The very preciseness of the figures brings them under suspicion. Anyone who has wandered through these ruins knows that an exact count is impossible. Why, just a short while ago a little old man came and told us that two VC were buried in a hastily dug grave up at the end of the block. Had they been counted? And what about these ruins? Have they gone through all of them for buried civilians and soldiers? And what about those 14 VC we found in the courtyard behind the post office at Hue? Had they been counted and tabulated? They certainly hadn't been buried.

We came to Vietnam to try to determine what all this means to the future of the war here. We talked to officials, top officials, civilian and military, Vietnamese and American. We toured damaged areas like this, and refugee centers. We paid a visit to the Battle at Hue, and to the men manning the northernmost provinces, where the next big communist offensive is expected. All of this is the subject of our report.

(Announcement.)

Announcer: Tonight, "Report from Vietnam by Walter Cronkite."

Cronkite: How could the Vietnamese communists have mounted this offensive with such complete surprise? After all, the cities were supposed to be secure, except for the occasional, unpreventable attack of terrorism. As a matter of fact, a whole measure of the success of this war has been that we were pushing out from the secure cities, pacifying the countryside around them in an increasingly widening ring. Now all that seemed to be knocked into a cocked hat. How could it happen? Well, let's take a look.

Well, for one thing, there was the enemy's timing, the Tet Lunar holiday. For Asiatics, it's Christmas, New Year's, and Fourth of July all rolled into one, with a little touch of Memorial Day, too. And just like Americans, they all take to the roads to go visit their family and friends. This is a normal day's traffic in Saigon. Imagine it two or three times this big for the Tet holiday. The job of stopping each of these cars, searching them, and checking the people for their papers, why, it staggers the imagination. It staggered the ability of the Vietnamese police to handle, too.

While some residents of Saigon certainly had to be privy to the communist plans, there didn't have to be a lot of them, as some people have charged. Just a few Vietcong sympathizers in whose homes arms could be stored, arms smuggled into town one by one, or even piece by piece. And then on the night of Tet the soldiers, Vietcong and

North Vietnamese, slipped into town one by one, rendez-
voused at the arms caches, and the offensive was on.

Intelligence people, American and Vietnamese, agree on
the same story. They figured the enemy might launch
a big attack on Saigon or another South Vietnamese city,
but they admit they grossly underestimated the enemy's
ability to plan, to provision, to coordinate, to launch
such a widespread full-scale attack as this. There are
some odd stories about this intelligence failure. High
American sources, for instance, say that they warned the
Vietnamese, but they let their troops go on Tet leave
anyway, until some units were down to just 10 percent of
normal strength. Some American newsmen say they tried to
reach the Vietnamese General Staff headquarters, and only
a sergeant was on duty. There are even stories, believed
by many Vietnamese intellectuals, that Chief of Police
Loan and Vice President Ky warned President Thieu, but
Thieu thought it was some sort of a trick, perhaps a coup,
and ignored the warnings. Thieu himself was at his
country home at My Tho outside of town; took him six hours
to get back after the attack, and, in the meantime, Vice
President Ky signed the first defensive orders, and many
Vietnamese intellectuals thought that indeed Ky had
engineered a coup. There was even a suspicion that some
of the police on checkpoint duty on the highways outside
of town accepted bribes instead of identity papers, all
in the spirit of Tet, and that many communists got in that
way.

But with all of this planning, what did the North Vietnamese and the Vietcong hope to accomplish? We talked to
a long-time expert on the Vietcong, who translated many
of the captured documents and interrogated prisoners,
Douglas Pike, about that.

Pike: Well, I think that General Giap, who I see as the
master architect of the whole thing, was trying to do three
things. I think he was trying to cause the disintegration
of ARVN, the Vietnamese armed forces, as an organized
military system. I think he was trying to cause an uprising of people in the cities--civilians--in a kind of
spontaneous outburst of support for the Vietcong, and I
think he was trying to throw a monkey wrench into the--
what he considers the well-oiled American military
machine here. It seems to me, all the evidence, trying
to put things together after this, this battle, that those
were his major calculations.

Cronkite: If the communists' intention was to take and
seize the cities, they came closer here at Hue than

anywhere else, and now, three weeks after the offensive began, the firing still goes on, here on the new side of the city, and across the Perfume River to the old side, the Citadel.

Probably a week before this offensive began, the army of North Vietnam, with Vietcong support, began moving into the mountains south of here, one day's march away. And then the day before the offensive began, January 30th to 31st, they began that march toward the city. Meanwhile, another regiment of the NVA were moving in from the north, into the city, the old Citadel, from the north, and they swept quickly through it, too, except for a small corner in the northeast of the Citadel held by the South Vietnamese Army headquarters.

It was a tough fight. It was house-to-house, door-to-door, room-to-room. They found they couldn't get into the doors and the windows; the North Vietnamese Army held them too tightly and had booby-trapped them as well. They had to blast their way in with plastic charges placed against the sides of the houses. It was such a tough fight that although the American Army hoped not to use heavy weapons and air strikes against this old city, they finally had to bring them in to begin to win the battle.

The destruction here was almost total. There is scarcely an inhabitable building in the city of Hue. Whatever price the communists paid for this offensive, the price to the allied cause was high, for if our intention is to restore normalcy, peace, serenity to this country, the destruction of those qualities in this, the most historical and probably serene of all South Vietnam's cities, is obviously a setback. Now, a job no one dreamed we were going to have to undertake. It is now the rebuilding of an entire city, and the lives of the people in it.

What did the communists hope to achieve by this attack on the cities? As to their ultimate objectives, their maximum goal, prisoner interrogations and captured documents seem to leave no doubt. They hoped, at the best, to bring down the Saigon government and win the war, presumably either by forcing a defeated enemy to the peace table, or by actually capturing his capital. To achieve that knockout victory, the 60,000 or so troops they committed to the battle had two prime targets. First, to seize as much real estate as possible, such as the Presidential Palace, the U.S. Embassy, military headquarters, provincial capitals; and second, to kidnap or assassinate members of the thinning ranks of Vietnamese leadership. But they had shorter-range objectives, about which they could be far more certain of success.

They expected the allies to pull their troops off the pacification campaign in the countryside and bring them in for the defense of the cities. They expected the Americans, too, to commit some of their reserves at least to the defense of the cities, rather than hold them for the big battles expected at the Demilitarized Zone. They expected to create maximum economic confusion and disruption, and to create new hordes of refugees, among which the seeds of discontent against the government could be sown. They expected by destroying the myth of the security of the cities to widen the credibility gap that exists here, too, between what the people are told and what they see about them. And the experts do not agree on the objectives or on the amount of success the communists had in achieving them.

Ellsworth Bunker: They have, certainly, disrupted the pacification effort for the time being, for how long I don't know. We haven't yet the full reports on the situation. They have interrupted--interdicted lines of communication, which are now being opened up again. What other effect they may have had, I don't know, on the population.

Nguyen Xuan Oanh: The war damages, I think, have been tremendous. I have talked to quite a few Vietnamese here who have been in Vietnam during the struggle for independence, during the partition of the country, and they all say, they all concur in the opinion that nothing has been so serious. I think that it will take perhaps weeks, if not much, much more, for the people to realize that we are going back to normal. Production is disturbed. You will have the problem of shortage of jobs in the future. The refugee problem is tremendous. The re-habilitation of the--sort of the damaged areas is a tremendous job, and I think that this is of all the things [sic] which the Vietcong attempt to achieve by this attack.

Cronkite: In that sense, they were successful, then?

Nguyen Xuan Oanh: In that sense, I think they have been very successful.

(Announcement.)

Cronkite: The government's first big test in the wake of the Tet offensive was the speed with which it could pick up the shattered pieces of its pacification program, and, translated into priorities, that meant how quickly could it get the troops that had been pulled into the cities for their defense back into the countryside? The American military leadership, believing this a matter of great urgency, watched carefully, with some trepidation, the government's performance. Would it permit the troops brought into the cities to simply hunker down there indefinitely, or would it move with dispatch to get them back on the offensive out in the country?

Well, these are pacification troops, the black-pajamaed men of the government's so-called Revolutionary Development teams, but they are not back in the countryside, bringing it and keeping it under government control. They are standing guard in the city--this one happens to be Qui Nhon--because the South Vietnamese feel the cities still are far from secure. This is the nature of the setback, what's left of a typical hamlet once believed secure, but abandoned as the pacification forces rushed to the cities. This District used to be a model of pacification. Now, again, most of it is at the mercy of the enemy. Correspondent Robert Schakne talked to Capt. Donald Jones, Deputy Pacification Advisor for the District.

Schakne: Tuy Phuoc District used to be considered just about one of the most pacified areas in Vietnam. It isn't any more, is it?

Jones: No. It used to be considered the bowl of pacification for South Vietnam. It was the area where the Revolutionary Development Program first began. It was a test phase for the pacification in South Vietnam. Now I cannot say that any longer. If it's not contested, the District is certainly challenged by main force units.

Schakne: Well, in effect is there any pacification program left in Tuy Phuoc District at this point?

Jones: No. For most of the District, pacification does not exist. This is a war.

Schakne: There were places we used to be able to go to in Tuy Phuoc--in fact, where we filmed, like Tin Giang and Go Boi and Vinh Quang. Could we go back there today?

Jones: We couldn't go to Vinh Quang. We might be able to get to Tin Giang. I wouldn't want to try it unless we have some local security. Go Boi--we can get to the south part of Go Boi. We can go straight out the road here to Go Boi. We can't cross the bridge.

Schakne: I walked unarmed with just one major casualty through Go Boi in December. Could I do it today?

Jones: No, you could not. You could not walk through Go Boi today.

Schakne: Are you discouraged?

Jones: Yes.

Cronkite: Pacification is not the only casualty of the
Tet offensive.   These are refugees, most pathetic of all
the victims of the attacks on the cities.   Just yesterday
the U.S. command in Saigon estimated their number at
470,000, new human flotsam, living in unbelievable squalor,
huddled in schools and sheds and shanties.   Before Tet
there were 800,000 officially listed as refugees.   One
of the South Vietnamese government's greatest failures had
been to provide them with decent food and shelter and a
role in the economic life.

The government could salvage a measure of victory from
defeat by moving with decision and dispatch to ease the
plight of the new homeless, but there are few signs that
it has the capacity or will to do so.   And there may be
more refugees to come, for the battle for the cities
probably is not over.   Here in Saigon, three weeks after
the first wave of the attack was beaten back, there are
still small but ferocious battles, on the city's perimeter,
and even within the city's limits.   At the big air base
and U.S. military headquarters, on the edge of town, there
are still occasional mortar and rocket attacks.   There
are reports that elements of three North Vietnamese
divisions, perhaps 15,000 men, are within a day's march
of the city.   The helicopters fill the air during the
day in the constant hunt for them, and at night air-drop
flares light the city as the search goes on.   And this is
but phase two of a master Vietcong plan called the winter-
spring offensive.

Part one was the fall campaign against the allied positions
astride the Vietcong supply routes through the Central
Highlands.   The attacks on Dak To and Loc Ninh were part
of that campaign, and they failed.   If they had succeeded,
the Vietcong would have opened up a supply route to bring
in even more troops for the attack against the cities
along the coast.

Those attacks, against 35 cities from Quang Tri in the far
north to the Delta in the far south, were phase two, which,
at least in their initial military phase, also have failed
--failed, that is, to seize the cities, although they
have brought them to near paralysis.   Now it's believed
the enemy is ready to move on to phase three of the winter-
spring offensive with the hope that he can recoup there
what he lost in the first two phases.

Phase three is to be the attack along the Demilitarized
Zone.   He has massed perhaps 40,000 men along here, and
is expected to kick off at any moment a wide-scale

offensive believed intended to overrun Vietnam's two
most northernmost provinces, and perhaps thus to bring
the Saigon government in defeat to the conference table.
He may move against any of those positions, but perhaps
the most dramatic and significant battle may develop at
Khe Sanh.

Khe Sanh was designed to be a small border stronghold to
block enemy infiltration, and to provide forward air
observation.   Now surrounded and by-passed, it no longer
serves that function, but for reasons of U.S. pride as
much as U.S. tactics, Khe Sanh has been built up into a
major bastion, where 5,500 Marines are isolated, and not
far from which 20,000 more reserves are tied down, far
from the now unprotected coastal plains.

From the North Vietnamese point of view, Khe Sanh is an
ideal target for rocket and mortar attacks from the surrounding hills while they decide the time to attack, or
whether to attack.   But in an interview with CBS News
correspondent Jack Laurence, the Marine general in charge
was confident his men can outlast the enemy at Khe Sanh
and elsewhere.

Laurence: How long do you feel that he can continue this
increased tempo of the fighting?

Lt. Gen. R. E. Cushman, Jr.:   Well, I can't really give a
finite answer, but it would seem to me it would be in
terms of a matter of months--four, five, how long I
wouldn't know exactly.   He always has the capability, of
course, of suddenly stopping this tremendous sacrifice of
personnel, and going back into the guerrilla type of war.
So it's hard to prophesy.   But if he continues this all-
out attack day and night, exposing himself to our firepower, I just don't think he can keep it up for longer
than a matter of months.

Cronkite: Whatever the battle for Khe Sanh and the DMZ
means, whatever all of this means, there is one meaning
to the Vietcong's winter-spring offensive that is in-
escapable.   The nature of the Vietnamese War has changed.
It no longer is a series of small engagements fought for
local areas against small bands of communists.   It no
longer is to be fought primarily in the sparsely occupied
countryside.   It is now more along the classic Western
fashion of war, large armies locked in combat, moving
toward a decision on the battlefield.

Some final, personal observations will be the concluding
portion of this report.

(Announcement.)

Cronkite: Tonight, back in more familiar surroundings in
New York, we'd like to sum up our findings in Vietnam,
an analysis that must be speculative, personal, subjective.
Who won and who lost in the great Tet offensive against
the cities? I'm not sure. The Vietcong did not win by a
knockout, but neither did we. The referees of history may
make it a draw. Another stand-off may be coming in the big
battles expected south of the Demilitarized Zone. Khe Sanh
could well fall, with a terrible loss in American lives,
prestige, and morale, and this is a tragedy of our stub-
bornness there; but the bastion no longer is a key to the
rest of the northern regions, and it is doubtful that the
American forces can be defeated across the breadth of the
DMZ with any substantial loss of ground. Another stand-off.
On the political front, past performance gives no confidence that the Vietnamese government can cope with its
problems, now compounded by the attack on the cities. It
may not fall, it may hold on, but it probably won't show
the dynamic qualities demanded of this young nation.
Another stand-off.

We have been too often disappointed by the optimism of
the American leaders. both in Vietnam and Washington, to
have faith any longer in the silver linings they find in
the darkest clouds. They may be right, that Hanoi's
winter-spring offensive has been forced by the communist
realization that they could not win the longer war of
attrition, and that the communists hope that any success
in the offensive will improve their position for eventual
negotiations. It would improve their position, and it
would also require our realization, that we should have
had all along, that any negotiations must be that--negotia-
tions, not the dictation of peace terms. For it seems
now more certain than ever that the bloody experience of
Vietnam is to end in a stalemate. This summer's almost
certain stand-off will either end in real give-and-take
negotiations or terrible escalation; and for every means
we have to escalate, the enemy can match us, and that applies to invasion of the North, the use of nuclear weapons,
or the mere commitment of 100-, or 200-, or 300,000 more
American troops to the battle. And with each escalation,
the world comes closer to the brink of cosmic disaster.

To say that we are closer to victory today is to believe,
in the face of the evidence, the optimists who have been
wrong in the past. To suggest we are on the edge of
defeat is to yield to unreasonable pessimism. To say
that we are mired in stalemate seems the only realistic,
yet unsatisfactory, conclusion. On the off chance that
military and political analysts are right, in the next
few months we must test the enemy's intentions, in case

this is indeed his last gasp before negotiations. But it is increasingly clear to this reporter that the only rational way out then will be to negotiate, not as victors, but as an honorable people who lived up to their pledge to defend democracy, and did the best they could.

This is Walter Cronkite. Good night.

APPENDIX XXVII

The New York *Times*
March 3, 1968

PACIFICATION TEAMS RETURNING TO HAMLETS ABANDONED AFTER
VIETCONG DRIVE

By Charles Mohr

SAIGON, South Vietnam, Mar. 2--South Vietnamese rural
pacification teams are beginning to return to hamlets
that had been abandoned for a month to take up again the
flagging program to win the allegiance of rural families.

Qualified South Vietnamese sources said today that the
administrative chiefs of the nation's 44 provinces had
been ordered to resume pacification efforts.

After the Vietcong Lunar New Year offensive, which began
January 30, most of the more than 400 Revolutionary
Development, or pacification, teams were withdrawn into
towns and cities for guard duty and relief work.

Many of the 54 regular South Vietnamese Army battalions
assigned to protect pacification teams were also withdrawn.

In effect, the South Vietnamese government temporarily
abandoned its own countryside. To some observers, this
was the most disturbing result of the Vietcong offensive,
and basically more important than the destruction in the
cities.

The orders to return to the countryside by March 1, which
were issued in mid-February, have not yet been fully
implemented, informed sources said.

In Quang Tri and Quang Tin provinces, in the northern part
of South Vietnam, all the pacification teams have returned
to the hamlets in which they had been working before the
offensive, the sources asserted.

In the more populous northern provinces of Quang Nam and
Quang Ngai, about 30 percent of the teams are back, but
the number is expected to rise soon.

In Thua Thien province, which surrounds the badly damaged
city of Hue, the devastation has been so great and the

enemy threat remains so critical that little progress
has evidently been made in resuming pacification efforts,
the sources said.

As many as 8 percent of the pacification teams have
returned to rural duty in the Central Highlands and
central coast, they said. In the provinces surrounding
Saigon, the figure was put at 70 percent.

MANY BACK IN DELTA

In the heavily populated Mekong Delta region south of
Saigon, two provinces reported that 100 percent of the
teams were back at work. The figure was put at 80 percent
in a number of other provinces.

However, relatively little has been done in such provinces
as Phong Dinh, Kien Giang and Kien Phong, the sources said.

Each pacification team is supposed to contain 59 armed,
trained men, but many teams are understrength.

South Vietnamese sources were quick to say that they were
worried that Army security battalions were returning too
slowly.

In the Mekong Delta area, there had been 15 army battalions
--about 6,000 soldiers--assigned to protect pacification
teams before the offensive.

Six of the battalions were left in place after the attacks,
but the nine others were withdrawn to urban areas. A
month later, they were still there.

"This is extremely dangerous," one official said. "The
teams are returning to their hamlets, but, without the
security battalions, they are in the most exposed and
dangerous position in which they have ever worked."

One United States expert said that the progress described
by the South Vietnamese in the northern and central
provinces was apparently correct. But he expressed doubt
that as many as 70 or 80 percent of the pacification
teams had gone back to work around Saigon or in the Delta.

It is still unclear how the pacification teams will be
received by the rural population after a month in which the
people were presumably helpless to resist small but armed
"agitation and propaganda" teams of the Vietcong.

A basic part of the pacification concept was to convince
the rural people that the government would never abandon
them.

But one South Vietnamese official said that he was more
and more convinced that the offensive had in at least some

cases hardened public opinion against the Vietcong and had made the people blame the guerrillas for their suffering.

"Some teams say they find the people more receptive than before," he said.

BACKGROUND BRIEFING, GEN. WILLIAM C. WESTMORELAND, SAIGON,
MARCH 6, 1968

Ladies and gentlemen, I thought that since the dust had
settled on the battlefield and the smoke had almost
cleared in the field of combat--although combat con-
tinues--it might be helpful if I discuss the general situation with you.

I would like, as I go into my discussion, to consider
this background, nonattributable. And then I will entertain questions, and, during the course of the questions,
I will answer the questions as a senior military official,
unless I specify to the contrary.

I find this little blackboard helpful in saving words,
describing the situation. I'm sure you recognize it as
an outline of South Vietnam, divided between the three and
four active zones. The dots being the major cities--Cam-
bodia, Laos, North Vietnam, and Thailand.

As I reconstruct the enemy's strategy--which I think was
planned following the death of Nguyen Chi Thanh, who was
killed or died back in July, last year, 1967--the leadership in Hanoi decided to change their strategy and, instead of pursuing a war of attrition, they decided to
make a major military-psychological attack.

I believe that they had concluded that time was not on
their side in the pursuit of a war of attrition, of a
protracted war.

It's interesting that, having made this decision as I
reconstruct the situation, that their propaganda continued
to talk about a protracted war, wherein they would wear us
down not only physically but also wear down the will of the
people who support our efforts.

I believe that this campaign was conceived in two phases.
The first phase started near the end of October and continued into November. As you recall, on the first of

November, the government--the new government--was in-
augurated, President Thieu installed. There were a
number of dignitaries in town from the free-world countries at the time, and by initiating his first phase at
that time, he captured the headlines--or hoped to capture the headlines from the political progress that was
manifest by the inauguration of the new government. But
at the same time he had in mind certain military objectives.

You'll recall the battle of Dak To, which, in my opinion,
was designed to take over Kontum province. He had suf-
ficient strength there, according to his plans, to do so.
You'll recall the battles around Loc Ninh, Song Be, and Bu
Dop, and these were designed to control Phuoc Long, Binh
Long, and the northern part of Tay Ninh, War Zone C.

This would set the stage for preparations for the second
phase.

During the interim he concentrated on RF/PF outposts and
attempted to recruit in the countryside to fill up his
depleted ranks, and his ranks had indeed been depleted
over the period of the previous years, and he was having
very serious recruiting problems.

During this period of time he initiated a major campaign
along the coastline of the southern I Corps, namely, in
Quang Ngai province and Quang Tin province.

This was designed to hopefully divert forces, as I reconstruct the situation, from the DMZ area; in other words,
force a concentration of forces in this particular area
(indicating) in southern I Corps, and distract our attention from his buildup, which was already starting up
in the DMZ area.

His phase two was started at Tet, and which was supposed
to be coordinated, and which was not in that the VC and
the North Vietnamese forces in the II Corps area jumped
off one day ahead of those in the III Corps. This was a
major undertaking, as history has reported. It involved
the infiltration of the cities for the purpose of creating
a public uprising. He had prepared his plans very well
in that regard to include his propaganda themes. It
included the assassination or kidnaping of senior ARVN
officials, and he had hoped that he could intimidate a
number of the military commanders to defect their entire
units.

He used to infiltrate the cities, in the main, local
forces; some main forces, however, were utilized, and some
North Vietnamese troops; approximately 30 percent, we feel,
of the initial force were North Vietnamese. However, the

percentage of North Vietnamese was far greater in I Corps and II Corps than in III and IV Corps.

His main force units he held back in order to follow up his expected successes in his first wave. It was interesting to note that he concentrated on radio stations, communications centers, police and ARVN headquarters. He avoided the destruction, in the main, of bridges and utilities because he expected to use those.

He pretty much left U.S. troops alone in connection with his initial assault, because he wanted to give credibility to his propaganda campaign that the Americans were not too unhappy about this because they were interested in a coalition government, and he made considersble capital on this propaganda campaign.

Of course, his psychological war campaign, warfare campaign, that started well before phase one and continued until phase two started, played the theme of coalition government. This had quite an impact on the defection rate, the Chieu Hoi rate, because, if there was going to be a coalition government, why should an individual join the government forces? He should stride the fence and wait for developments.

And, of course, another element of this psychological war campaign, which was focused at American public opinion, was to stop the bombing. And, of course, he attracted a number of unwitting citizens to this particular propaganda theme who publicly supported it, and if the bombing had been stopped it would have facilitated his campaign. Of course, there were also in the propaganda arena at that time, you'll remember--announcements were made that if the bombing were stopped, it was not a question of whether Hanoi might talk, but that Hanoi would talk.

Now, in the Highlands, there was a special purpose to the attacks at Kontum city, Pleiku, and Ban Me Thuot. There was a special purpose to that attack across the DMZ, the overrunning of Khe Sanh, the seizure of Quang Tri and Hue.

And as I reconstruct the situation, this particular campaign was an important part of the phase two, and directly associated with the effort to creat a public uprising in the cities.

By seizing the cities in the Highlands, in addition to the public uprising, taking over the government control apparatus, the enemy would have brought about a de facto partition of the country. He holds A Shau--this is pretty much wilderness, no man's land here. If he had taken Khe Sanh, Quang Tri, Hue, and had been able to hold it, and if he had been able to take over Kontum, Pleiku, and Ban Me Thuot, which he desperately tried to do, he would have brought about a partition of the country.

The result would have been a situation that existed in Laos in 1954. And regardless of the success of his public uprisings, in other parts of the country, he would have established for himself a very strong political and psychological position.

As I look back over the situation, I say again that I believe that the campaign in I Corps North--northern I Corps--was planned as a part of the second phase, which started at Tet.

This was pre-empted by our air strikes, which were massive and which started in the middle of January, and the enemy in that area has not been able to get himself squared away since, to the point he could muster the control in order to launch an attack that he thought had a reasonable chance of success.

Now, let me talk a moment about the situation that has evolved, and the results of this major campaign.

First, starting in northern I Corps, which we refer to now as I Corps North. The enemy did seize Hue and it took some time to dislodge him. Those of you who have visited Hue fully understand why, because the Citadel is a formidable fortification.

The enemy placed in Hue a considerable number of troops, perhaps the equivalent of a division. He had the benefit of very poor weather, (unintelligible) weather, which made it very difficult to use air power or to use even--fly helicopters. He was successful in seizing Hue, and concurrently he attempted to seize Quang Tri but was very, very badly defeated at Quang Tri. Concurrently, he expected to overrun Khe Sanh.

And that would have put our troops in Quang Tri and Thua Thien province in almost an untenable position.

Now I'm sure most of you realize that these two northern provinces have been under MR-4 located at Vinh for some time. We've had any number of prisoners tell us that Tri Ten Military District, which consists of Quang Tri and Thua Thien provinces, are a part of the Southern District of North Vietnam, which is known as the North Vietnamese Military District Four. That is why they've ignored the Demilitarized Zone, because they consider that these two provinces are a part of North Vietnam.

And they frequently refer to Hue as the gateway to South Vietnam. We received a prisoner the other day who referred to this city, Hue, as the gateway to South Vietnam.

In anticipation of this offensive action which we did foresee and accordingly made certain logistic preparations in the area, and certain troops were deployed from other areas to reinforce, I had to think of the command and control arrangements in I Corps North, Quang Tri-Thua Thien, which became--which was destined to become, in effect, a war zone. And we do indeed have there a different type of war going on than we have in the rest of the country, although there are, needless to say, some common characteristics.

One of the major problems there was logistics, and although we had been anticipating his contingency for well over a year and had taken certain, made certain preparations, it was necessary to finalize those preparations. The period of the year was certainly not optimum. The particular area is under the command of the Commanding General of the III Marine Amphibious Force, General Cushman, a man for whom I have a very high regard as a Marine and as a soldier and as a man. However, as we reinforced up there and as we proceeded to make logistic preparations which concerned considerable engineer effort, the complexity and the expanse of control became greater than the III Marine Amphibious Force headquarters could control because they were designed to control two Marine divisions, nothing more. In addition, of course, as you know, he serves as senior advisor to General Lam.

Concerning the logistic preparations, we had not only Marine troops to control but we had to--I had to develop a rather large Army logistic operation. The Air Force had to expand their logistic operations and, of course, the Navy, that provides a major share of the logistics for the Marines. The naval support activity reports to the naval component commander, but the Navy was very much involved.

So this whole activity became a joint undertaking. I had my choice of three courses of action. I could delegate to General Cushman joint authority, which would not have been fair to him because he could not--he would have devoted too much of his energy to this undertaking as opposed to commanding his own troops.

I could have made the decisions from here and sent up by telephone calls and cables and so forth made the appropriate decisions. I ruled this out because this is not an effective way of making timely decisions.

I could have gone up myself but with all the activities here in Saigon and my association with the Ambassador and the whole scope of my responsibilities this did not seem to be practical.

So I sent up my deputy, General Abrams, my alter ego, to
make the appropriate decisions involving all the services
concerned with the logistic buildup and the deployment
of troops that had been programmed, and we established a
MACV forward headquarters so that General Abrams would
have a staff to deal with.

And in accordance with my general guidance, and we were
on the telephone from time to time, and frequently exchanged visits, General Abrams gave the necessary instructions to the Marines, the Air Force, the Navy, and
to the Army elements that were moving in in order to get
ourselves established, so that we could deploy and support troops of the magnitude that I felt would be needed.

Now, on about the 10th of this month in accordance with
my plan, and this you have not heard about . . . before
for obvious reasons, the MACV forward headquarters will
be redesignated as Provisional Corps Vietnam with the
short title of PROV Corps. It will be commanded by
Lieutenant General Rosson, who was--at one time was my
chief-of-staff. He activated Task Force Oregon, which
became subsequently the Americal Division. He had been
commanding I Field Force V at Nha Trang for some period
of time. He worked for General Cushman when he commanded
the Americal Division. He is junior to General Cushman
and is a very well qualified soldier and commander. He
will take care of this Provisional Corps; his staff will
be a joint staff, mainly Army and Marine but with a few
Naval and Air Force officers.

PROV Corps V, a provisional corps, PROV Corps, will be
under the command of General Cushman, who commands the
III Marine Amphibious Force, who has the overall responsibility as my representative for all U.S. troops,
ground troops in the I Corps tactical zone. General
Cushman will be serving, tactically speaking, and
organizationally speaking, at the field army level. This
is indeed a unique arrangement, but almost everything in
Vietnam is unique.

And I've attempted to organize and tailor this command not
to any doctrine, not to any experience in past wars, but
to the situation we face here on the ground, which has no
historical precedent.

Now, let me diagram this to be sure you understand it.
(Pointing to map on blackboard.)

This is III MAF and this is General Cushman. He will
have under him (marking on board) PROV Corps commanded by
General Rosson, and under General Rosson will be the
tactical ground maneuver elements in the area--the 3rd

Marine Division, the 1st Cavalry Division, and any other
ground tactical units that I choose to send up to that war
zone in order to confront the North Vietnamese Army invasion.

Also, under General Cushman will be the 1st Marine
Division, and the Americal Division. The Americal Division. He will be serving at the field army level with a
tactical corps under his command and two divisions under
his command or other elements. This unit here (indicating
on blackboard) will command north of the Hai Van Pass,
control all tactical elements, a matter of command control
and management, and he will command directly the 1st Marine
and the Americal Divisions, which are of course, as you
well know, south of the Hai Van Pass.

Now, he can adjust this as he sees fit. He can transfer
units to General Rosson's command or he can pull units
from General Rosson's command and assign them, or put
them under the operation of his control, of these two
division level elements, and as you well know he's the
counterpart to the CG I Corps, who is General Lam. Now,
the ARVN 1st Infantry Division is also north of the Hai
Van Pass, and General Rosson will be working very, very
closely in day-to-day association with General Truong,
who commands the ARVN 1st Division, who, incidentally,
did a magnificent job during the past several weeks.

It is my plan to activate this arrangement and publicly
announce it on or about the 10th; it may be later. But
I wanted you to know about it now.

Now, since we have a Marine division here, and we have
an Army division here, and we have some Marines here and
some Army troops actually just south of Hue (marking on
board), you can see this is indeed a joint Army-Marine
command, with more Army troops than Marines, or more Army
units than Marines, therefore General Rosson commands,
but General Cushman has on his staff Brigadier General
Flannigan who is deputy chief of staff for operations.

And General Cushman's III MAF staff has been augmented
by a number of Army officers, so that his staff, although
it will still be designated as the III Marine Amphibious
Force, Marine Corps staff, it has been augmented by Army
officers. General Rosson's staff will be--will comprise
mostly Army but will be augmented by a number of Marines,
with a seeding of Air Force and Navy.

Now, by virtue of this arrangement, it has become necessary to better integrate our tactical air effort. This
will be done under Gen. [William F.] Momyer [USAF], who is

my deputy commander for Air Operations, and General Momyer
will be integrating the entire tactical air effort that
will be supporting General Cushman, General Rosson, and
other elements of this corps as he does in the other field
force areas.

He will integrate his total air effort--Air Force, Marine--
but the Marines will still be given close support by their
own flyers. However, the system that has been developed
which provides for integration to a better degree and a
more effective degree than in the past, . . . will provide
for Air Force planes to support Marines if it is expedient
to do so. By the same token, Marine planes can support
Army ground troops if they can get there quicker. In other
words, if it's tactically expedient for them to do so. So
we have full flexibility in connection with our tactical
air support.

Now I might pause for a moment and see if there are any
questions as to this, and maybe I could clarify it.

Q.: General, on that chart you have there, with Generals
Cushman and Rosson, could you fill in General Abrams?

A.: Oh, yes. You see, I sent General Abrams up here to
establish MACV forward. (Marking on blackboard.) He
went up there as my alter ego in order to sort out the
joint aspects of the logistics, the construction, the deployments, to make decisions which could not be delegated
to a field commander, but had to be made either by me or
by my alter ego. And, to assist him in doing that, I gave
him a staff to assist him. It's a long way between here
and Hue, as you well know. So he needed a staff. Now,
there was a second purpose for that, and that was--I did
this in order to start building this corps headquarters,
so while serving General Abrams in carrying out this
function I delegated to him, he was building this corps
headquarters and the headquarters is almost built, and I
hope that by the 10th it will be the--it will be fully
constituted, well shaken down, so that it can become immediately operational.

And then General Abrams comes back here to Saigon--be-
cause I need him, because I look to him to assist the
ARVN, the Vietnamese Armed Forces, and his--the primary
function that I delegate to him routinely is to work with
the Vietnamese Armed Forces, and help them in every way he
can.

Q.: In other words, General Abrams' move was just a
temporary move--

A,: Oh, it was an expediency, just an expediency. It was
a managerial expediency, a managerial expediency, but

served another purpose, and that is to get established
this corps headquarters, and it had been my plan all the
time to redesignate it as a corps headquarters once it
was established and when I thought the time was ripe.

Q.:   Is "V" for "Five"?

A.:   Pardon me?

Q.:   Is "V" for "Five"?

A.:   No, it's for Vietnam, Vietnam.   Provisional Corps,
Vietnam.

Q.:   You have created another corps, however provisional?

A.:   It is provisional, correct.   I created a tactical
corps.   It is provisional at this time, because I don't
have the authority to do anything else.   But I do have
the authority to create provisional organizations, which
I've done on a number of occasions.   Usually it's an
interim measure before they are institutionalized.   And
say, authorized as a bookkeeping proposition where you
could requisition for officers, et cetera.

In other words, I've taken these officers out of my hide,
and I must say that we're beginning to feel the pinch at
this headquarters, so I've asked for additional authorization of staff officers to man us.

Q.:   General, does that mean General Cushman's quarters
is a higher echelon than the other corps--

A.:   Yes.   He is serving at the field army level and that
he'll be commanding a corps.   He'll have subordination in
the corps.

Q.:   Is that to say there's a possibility of putting Field
Force I and Field Force II at the same level?

A.:   No, no.   Let me--let me go back.   When I designed
this military organization, which is unique . . . and
unprecedented but tailored to the situation, I chose the
words "field force" and I created the term field force.
I knew that under these field force headquarters, which
would be a counterpart to the Vietnamese corps, I knew
that they would have divisions under them.   This was our
plan.   I do not choose to call them corps, for several
reasons.   One was it would have been awkward to have a
set of Vietnamese territorial corps and a set of U.S.
corps.   It would have been very confusing.   So I created
the name field force, because it is a unique arrangement
where he is senior advisor to his counterpart, the Vietnamese, and he has other responsibilities other than those
normally vested in a tactical corps.   But he has those
responsibilities also.

As an example, he has the CORDS responsibility. Now, also I call them field forces because I anticipated they might--that the day might come when I might want to organize a corps and subordinate it to one of the field forces, and I did not want to get involved in a lot of awkward terminology, so I created the word field force because under a field force you could put a division, you can put a brigade, you can put a corps.

Now, it would be conceivable that a corps could be organized and put under I Field Force or II Field Force. This is not contemplated at this time, but it could be done and I had this in mind for any of the corps depending on what the tactical requirements or the managerial requirements; in other words, concerned with span and control.

So, there's no plan to do this, Bill, but it is conceivable, yes, and we'll have the flexibility.

Q.:   I was wondering, we got into this, what you'd probably call this problem of integrating the air, in Korea--

A.:   Yes. Yes.

Q.:   --and I guess everybody knows the arguments and irritations--the delay for one thing--

A.:   Yes.

Q.:   --and so on, that is this going to cause any delay up there?

A.:   There is not. I do not foresee any problems whatsoever in this. As a matter of fact, it's going to give us--it's going to give more flexibility to support the Marines, more flexibility to support the Army troops; it will be by far a better arrangement.

Q.:   Is it going to be handled--I believe in Korea there was a common tactical control center that all requests for strikes had to go through--

A.:   Well, well--I tell you this is a very complex thing. There are all types of strikes. There are preplanned strikes. The preplanned strikes will be processed through a control center where they'll be [assigned]. On the immediates, immediates can be--will be available to the Marines at any time. On diverts, the diverts can come from the Air Force, they can come from the--from the Marines. In other words, if we got a plane heading toward North Vietnam and the Marines need a strike and they don't happen to have an airplane in the air, that plane can be diverted. It gives us far more flexibility. And its no major change; the Marines' air-ground team will still obtain.

They will, in the main, in general, the Marines will be supported by their own pilots, but . . . in an emergency or under unusual circumstances, the system is so flexible you can bring in Air Force.

By the same token you could bring in Marines to support the 1st Cavalry. After all, they're up there, too. In other words, it's again a managerial arrangement and one designed to provide for flexibility.

Q.: What will General Truong's relationship be?

A.: General Truong? General Truong will be under the command of General Lam, but General Lam will no doubt ask him to work in close coordination with General Rosson.

Q.: General Lam still has the political power?

A.: Correct. Now, I am glad you brought that up, because I neglected to mention this.

In I Corps, General Cushman still has the CORDS responsibility on the U.S. side, as General Lam has the RD and the administrative responsibility. In other words, General Rosson has a tactical command. Now, in addition, General Cushman has the log--the logistics are pretty well squared away now. Division of labor has been worked out, and all the services are involved in this logistic complex, but General Cushman now has the job of insuring coordination of this. Now, fortunately, General Cushman has got a deputy whose former assignment was the G-4 with the U.S. Marine Corps. He's an expert logistician, and he will be spending most of his time on logistics to insure coordination of all of the logistic elements, Army logistics for the Army, Marine and Navy supporting the Marines' troops, et cetera.

Q.: With the battle going on in northern I Corps, General Rosson would be in command?

Spokesman: Right.

Q.: General, I wonder if you could go--

A.: Let me say--

Q.: Yes.

A.: --in passing, can you imagine the difficulty that General Cushman would have without having a control agency to fight the battle? He couldn't do it at Da Nang, and with all the other responsibilities he has, his span of control would be completely out of reach.

Q.: If a battle is going on around Da Nang, say, instead of the DMZ, General Rosson would be in charge?

A.: No. General Rosson has the responsibility only for the tactical units north of Hue, north of Hai Van Pass.

Q.: If the main battle is below that line, General Cushman is in charge?

A.: Well, General Cushman is in command, but General Rosson is subordinate to him for the battles in Quang Tri-Thua Thien. Now if the battle is in Quang Nam, General Robertson, who commands the 1st Marine Division, reports to him and fights that battle. If the battle is in Quang Ngai, General Koster commands the Americal Division.

Q.: Can you tell us--some of us have been to Khe Sanh, and we're a little disturbed by the state of the entrenchments. I wonder if you could tell us a little bit more about the planning that led to the establishment of the garrison in Khe Sanh. I went there once, I think two days after you did in September '66, and a captain said you had your eye on it then, a Special Forces camp. And I'd like to get a little background on how the decision was made to go in there in such strength when it had been sort of weakly held, and, secondly, why wasn't it built up a little more physically--maybe this is just personal reaction to "incoming"--and a little more background on why the enemy sort of hasn't gone in there, given the terrain, and so on.

A.: Well, I'll be happy to address this briefly because I'm going to have to meet the Ambassador in about 45 minutes and that's a lot of material to cover, but we'll address it briefly.

Khe Sanh, of course, has been an outpost for some time. It is an important outpost. If it wasn't an important outpost, certainly we wouldn't have reinforced it. But it became evident that the enemy had designs on it. The extent of the reinforcement was determined by General Cushman, who had the responsibility working with his division commander. There was one battalion there and this was reinforced over a period of time to its present level.

Once the troops moved in, they proceeded to dig in. Now, how fast they dug in, of course, is the responsibility of the local commander. The transportation of materials in there has been a problem. It is fundamental military doctrine that one digs in when one fortifies, and I've--I know that it has been the intention of General Cushman and General Tompkins to dig in and they are dug in.

They didn't have mechanical equipment to do it with, no. The enemy's reinforcement with several divisions. Of course, we did receive some prisoners that gave us indications of this reinforcement, but we didn't know--these reinforcements could have gone to the Highlands or they could have gone to Saigon, or they could have gone anywhere. It was not my desire nor the responsible commander on the scene's desire to reinforce that area until we had judged the enemy's intentions. And then to reinforce it with what we considered the minimum essential force.

And this was done on a very timely basis. Now, the enemy's plans have been set back. He intended a Tet offensive in my opinion to overrun the place, and by virtue of his massing he exposed himself to multiple air strikes in the area and 2,000 secondary explosions; many, of course [of] the B-52 strikes have been at night under zero-zero conditions--

Q.: 200 or 2,000?

A.: Two thousand secondary explosions and, of course, this was not the total, I'm sure, because of the weather conditions when the bombs were dropped. I think the enemy has had great difficulty getting himself set for this--for this final assault, and I'm not suggesting he won't try it. I'm sure he realizes the risks involved. He has diverted a number of troops to an investiture of the area and of course he's exposed himself accordingly.

The area is important; he has a motorable road that goes in from Laos; were we not at Khe Sanh, he could move wheeled artillery, tanks, rockets; make a logistic base on that plateau, and Quang Tri province would be--in my opinion can be ultimately untenable. As far as Quang Tri province is concerned, . . . the defenses there of Khe Sanh is important.

Now, I'd like to just cover a few other things so we'll have time for questions.

Now, as I review the enemy's campaign I think his intelligence was faulty in two respects. He had been led to believe that he could create a public uprising and failed--failed miserably. He had been led to believe that the morale and fighting spirit of the Vietnamese armed forces was low, and that they could be defeated or persuaded to defect. The fact is the Vietnamese fought extremely well. There are very few exceptions to this statement.

The enemy as of midnight last night has lost over 50,000 people. And I consider this a reasonably valid figure. There have been questions asked, "Well, how in the world can you tell if it's 50,113?" And that happens to be the figure. Well, if you're going to deal in statistics you have to deal in definitive numbers. You have to have a

disciplined system that comes in with numbers, and these
numbers are added up.

Now, Im not trying to suggest by any means that there were
not supporters in that group. I'm sure there were and,
as you well appreciate, there were a number of very young
men, maybe 15 to 20 percent teenagers, scraped up, given
arms, and pushed into battle. There were a number of
these.

As a matter of interest, these enemy casualties amount to
87 percent of the total enemy killed in 1966 and 56 percent
of the total enemy killed, according to our records, in
1967. The number of weapons that were captured were
large--16,609 individual weapons, 6,255 crew-served
[weapons] in as of midnight last night.

These weapons amount to 88 percent of the total weapons
captured in '66; and 53 percent of the total weapons captured in 1967.

Now, as we look to the future, it appears to me that the
contest is one of rebuilding forces . . . "the battle of
the rebuild." And needless to say the enemy has a
formidable task to recruit and to rebuild his forces.
There's evidence he's attempting to round up all the manpower he can by persuasion or at the point of a gun in
the countryside. I've no doubt he will continue to move
to the South numbers of North Vietnamese troops.

It was noted during the campaign [that] some of the North
Vietnamese are young and not well trained because of the
haste of preparing troops for this major campaign.

As far as the ARVN is concerned, they're working hard to
recover their losses. Vietnamese ground forces suffered
almost 10,000 casualties, but so far they have been able
to provide over 14,000 replacements. These figures that
have been gathered by my staff for me . . . show the
losses suffered by the divisions and the number of replacements that they've received. You'll note the 1st
Division suffered very heavy losses, because they bore
the brunt of the battle in Hue. But they have been able
to provide over 2,000 replacements for them.

Now, this manpower is being provided by a number of sources.
The men in the reserves were recalled. And men--graduated
men from their training centers early. They were giving
them a 13-week training program. Now they're giving them
a 9-week training program, and some of these have had,
even had less than that, during the last several weeks
when manpower was important and they cleared the training
centers to fill up the units. Their labor units that

were established about a year ago primarily for deserters have been given amnesty and returned to duty, and as a matter of fact some of the military jails have been emptied in order to provide the manpower.

As far as the RF/PF are concerned, my figures, or I would say our reports from the field, which are not conclusive, are that most of the RF companies are intact and on their posts. And they have in general fought very well. But 66 percent of the popular forces are at their posts. Some are still in provincial towns and cities. Some of the posts were overrun and members killed or captured. About 60 percent of the RD cadre are reportedly at their posts.

The training centers are now beginning to operate again. Of the nine National Training Centers, seven of them have resumed training. The Dong Da training center which is near Hue-Phu Bai has been severely damaged, in other words the facilities have been damaged in the fighting to the point where some reconstruction is in order before they can start training recruits again.

And the Rangers--the unit training center at Truong Hoa, north of here, which is ready to go as soon as a Ranger battalion can be made available.

Seventeen of the 24 ARVN schools have resumed full or part-time training. Those schools that have not resumed training are the administration-finance school; the C&GS [Command and General Staff] Collge, the intelligence school, the logistics school, the National Defense College, and the cold-war college and the quartermaster school.

Four of the 10 division training centers have resumed operations.

Popular forces--eight of the 37 popular force training centers have resumed training and more are being activated every day.

Air Force and Marine centers have resumed normal training, as well as the three Navy training centers. And the CIDG [Civilian Irregular Defense Group] training centers, five of those are conducting normal training.

According to our present count, [there are] 623,000 refugees who have been created by the Tet aggression; 72,000 homes destroyed. Ten cities received major damage through battles that ensued. These are: Hue, Kontum, Pleiku, Ban Me Thuot, My Tho, Can Tho, Ben Tre, Vinh Long, Chou Doc, and Saigon.

In some way the best analogy that comes to my mind from
history, as I reviewed the events of the last several
weeks, is that of the Battle of the Bulge, which was
initiated by the Germans on 16 December 1944. The
Germans achieved surprise at that time; to counter their
successes required major redeployment of U.S. forces and
reactions. Many of you were there. So was I. I know
"Beaver" was there. It was about seven weeks later before
things were back to normal. We're on our sixth week now
and things are getting back to normal in this country. It
will take some time to recover from the damage inflicted.
But I'm very heartened about the progress that's being
made.

Now, with that general summary, I will entertain questions.
I will answer these as senior military spokesman unless I
specify to the contrary.

Q.: General, I wonder if you could go back to the statements I think that were made earlier that the enemy still
has--because he did not commit so many of his main force
and NVA units--what is his capability now? We keep
thinking about a third wave and a second wave.

A.: I don't believe the enemy has any great capability
to resume a major offensive action in the near future.
He's been hurt, he's been hurt badly. Obviously, from the
losses that I just announced to you. He's tired. His
logistic efforts were adequate to support his campaigns
thus far, but there is evidence he is developing logistic
problems.

He will continue, in my opinion, to try to spoil the
countryside, having failed to take over the cities--not
to be unexpected--will concentrate on the RD, RF/PF outposts, or to secure control in the countryside, interdict
lines of communication, and to accumulate manpower to fill
his depleted ranks. He will continue stand-off rocket
and mortar fire against the populated areas for the purpose
of hopefully keeping the troops in and around the populated
areas; keeping the people nervous, suggesting that he is
stronger than he really is.

Now, having said all this, I do give him a capability in
I Corps--I Corps North--where he has large forces near Hue;
and, in my opinion, Hue is his next objective. I think this
will be his next big battleground.

Voice: Another try at Hue?

A.: Yeah. And I don't rule out an attack against Khe Sanh,
but my impression is he has greater interest in Hue than in
Khe Sanh at the present time.

Q.:   He may do both?

A.:   He may do both. Now, he has also some interest in
Quang Tri. And he has forces up there to a point where
he could attack, but of course the risks will be great.

I don't think he--I don't believe his plans visualized that
we would be able to deploy troops and develop the forces
that have been possible. We have capability for further
reinforcement if required.

Q.:   Immediately after the Tet offensive you gave very
slim chances on the enemy's not attacking Khe Sanh. . . .
(Inaudible.) What do you think of changing that opinion?

A.:   Well, of course, my objective was that he not attack
it. What I think I said was, I think that it was his
plan, his intention, to attack, and it was, in my opinion.
The fact that he hasn't attacked it is because of our
counteractions, our pre-emptive actions through the use
of our firepower, and that's the only reason, in my
opinion, he hasn't attacked. As I said before, I don't
rule out an attack in the future.

Q.:   How do you explain, despite all these pre-emptive
measures that you've taken in the area, that the enemy
still managed to trench right up to the outer wire?

A.:   He has dug some trenches toward the base, and he's
had a number of enemy killed in those trenches too. He
will continue, in my opinion, to entrench. I don't
think--he hasn't given up his objective. I think his
leadership is driving him hard to accomplish his objectives, but the weather is now--well, let us put it this
way: The bad weather is, has been, in his favor, except
we have been able to run strikes without the benefit of
visual conditions, but as the weather improves--and we
have had better days during the past week than we've had
in the previous month--we can get visual strikes in and
he will become far more vulnerable than he's been.

Q.:   Irrespective of a military assessment of the Tet
offensive, it was recognized by everybody that there was
a psychological and political setback; there's a great
deal of feeling that we have to in some way change the
psychological and political setback that resulted from
the Tet offensive through military action. Can you
address yourself to that problem?

A.:   I think it was basic to this campaign, was a
psychological objective, and I agree with you that he has
achieved success in that regard, but now that the dust
has settled I think that success is not as great as it
was apparent two weeks ago.

The Vietnamese are ready, willing, and able to go on the offensive. They're reconstituting their forces, their strength is being built up as I indicated a month ago and they--they're mad.

They're capable of going on the offensive and in my opinion will.

Q.: General, the relocation of significant numbers of American troops up to the northern provinces and the certain weakening in other parts of the country, what do you see are the long-run results if the situation continues?

A.: We haven't materially weakened other parts of the country. I've had to redeploy troops from other areas, but not at the expense of incurring any major risks in other areas.

Q.: Well, significant numbers of troops have left the Central Highlands and you have the 1st Air Cav. up north now. Doesn't this sort of create a vacuum for the 4th Division still there?

A.: I think we're in good solid shape in the Highlands.

A.: Come again?

Q.: How many enemy troops would you estimate are around Hue?

A.: Around Hue?

Q.: Yes.

A.: I would say better than a division. Better than a division.

A.: Pardon me, again now?

Q.: Where did you get info about the enemy around Khe Sanh and Hue?

A.: Oh, from prisoners, yes.

Q.: (Inaudible.)

A.: Yes. Or, from prisoners, we've identified units that were around in the DMZ area; they are now around Hue.

Q.: When you say around the DMZ area, do you mean around Khe Sanh?

A.: No, both.

Q.: (Inaudible.)

A.: Come again?

Q.: This division plus that's around Hue, is this all North Vietnamese?

A.: Mostly, yes. There are some local units, but mostly NVA.

Q.: General, are we in a position to go on the offensive now in the northern part of I Corps?

A.: I can't answer that on the public record.

Q.: Can you answer off the record? Do you have the capability to go on the offensive?

A.: We're on the verge of going on the offensive. Off the record, yes.

Q.: In the event fighting develops in Hue, then Rosson would not command that fighting. In other words, he commands forces north?

A.: No. No. That's in his area, Quang Tri-Thua Thien. He could--Rosson--commands all U.S. troops in Quang Tri-Thua Thien. Both provinces? Yes.

Q.: Of the 50,000, can you give us a comparison of allied losses in that period?

A.: Yes.

A.: Yes. Yes. We lost approximately 2,000 Americans and 4,000 Vietnamese.

Q.: KIA?

A.: Yeah.

Q.: You're figuring now from the 29th of January to the present for the 50,000?

A.: Yes. 1800 hours on the 29th to midnight last night.

Q.: Can you deduct the 50,000 from the enemy's pre-Tet strength?

A.: No. No. No, we've--I think--and our calculations are that he scraped up a lot of manpower at the last moment, a lot of young people, and swelled his ranks with untrained types.

Q.: Were those the people primarily that you killed?

A.: Our best estimate, 10 to 15 percent were in the teen-age category, but, frankly, this is really an estimate. We'll have better data on that in due time.

Q.: Fifteen to 20 percent?

A.: I thought I said 10 to 15.

Q.: 15 to 20?

A.: Fifteen to 20? All right, I'll stand by 15 to 20. (Laughter.) I mean--frankly, it's a guesstimate, really.

My J-2--I talked with him this morning--I guess he did say, I think that was probably right. I think as I recall, he--his best estimate was 15 to 20. My first comment was what he advises me.

Q.: Any guesses on the net loss out of the 50,000?

A.: Well, we're studying that now. Our best estimate is about 30,000. About 30,000 net loss. That's our best estimate for the moment.

Q.: Do you have any breakdown, General, on the Hue casualties, the Hue area--

A.: Enemy casualties in the Hue area? Gee, I'd have to-- I'd have to research this. My recollection is at about 4,000.

Q.: Why now would the communists' interest be more at Hue than at Khe Sanh, after they've been driven out of there once?

A.: I think for political reasons, and according to prisoners--they refer to this as the gateway to South Vietnam. Political and psychological reasons.

Q.: On saying that Hue now has a higher priority, can we quote you by name?

A.: Well, let's say comparable.

Q.: Your statement about enemy objective being Hue--

A.: Let me say parenthetically that--I'm very sensitive on this area here from a security viewpoint. Extremely sensitive on it. And that's why--in other words, I don't want, through the medium of the press, to give the enemy any more intelligence on our strengths and weaknesses than we possibly can. I'm sure you understand my concern, and you've been, in general, very good about recognizing this, but, of course, sometimes it is difficult to judge as to what he knows and what he doesn't know. But I'm inclined to lean over backwards and not give him any more information than we have to.

As an example, if we're going to tell the enemy that the 1st Cavalry Division is short of POL [petroleum, oil, and lubricants] or had an X number of helicopters destroyed in a mortar raid, I'd like to--very much to know where the enemy's short POL and when. So, I'm really rather sensitive about the general security in that war zone. And that's why I've been rather delicate in handling your questions. You understand, I'm sure.

Q.: Will you clarify your quotation as to Hue attributable to you by name?

Q.: That was my question earlier.

A.: I'm sorry. I didn't understand that.

Q.: My question earlier was would it be possible to quote you by name as saying that--

A.: No, senior military spokesman.

Q.: General, what about the plan for the Provisional Corps? Did you say the U.S. command has this in mind or will we have to wait until you announce it?

A.: I'm going to announce it just as soon as I can. There are a couple of developments that have to occur before I want to announce it.

Q.: We ran into the same situation with the Americal-- people who are not here--

A.: Yes. Yes. That's correct.

Q.: --and other people who aren't here--

A.: Yes. Right. I realize your--

Q.: (Inaudible.)

A.: Yeah. All right. In all fairness to your colleagues --I don't believe I can give this to you on the record today, but I will do so as soon as I can.

Q.: In other words everything you said about the Provisional Corps is off the record until you announce it?

A.: Well, I said background nonattribution.

Q.: Can we attribute this to sources--"it was learned today" basis?

A.: What do you advise on that?

Voice: No, sir, I don't think we should.

A.: Well, I'll tell you what I had in mind. I wanted to give you the rationale and the background so that when it was announced you would know why. Now, of course, these background sessions are not designed to bring forth news stories. They're designed to give you the rationale and the background.

Now, let me tell you this, Bill. I shall--I'll do every-- I will release this as soon as I practically can, but I cannot do it today.

Q.: Do you mean that you would regard it as a breach of confidence if we speculate on this? (Laughter.)

A.: I would say please hold it. Please hold it.

Voice: In effect, it's off the record.

A.: Let's put it this way: I will ask you to hold it for 48 hours, during which time there will be a public announcement on it. So I would say, to get down to simplest terms, I ask you to consider it off-the-record until you get an announcement.

Q.: Are the statistics attributable?

A.: Right.

Q.: Can you speak about American troop increases over the 525,000 troops?

A.: Well, I don't have the 525 yet.

Q.: Sir, one more question. I believe General Abrams, in a backgrounder yesterday, said that he didn't think that Giap was the commander of this more or less (un-intelligible) . . . the enemy's operations. Do you concur in that or--

A.: I just don't know.

Q.: How is the pipe line of replacements going?

A.: It's continuing to flow, and I'd say we're in adequate shape.

(Mixed voices.)

A.: Pardon me?

Q.: What is the time usually to--

A.: Well, we have the men in the replacement depots. It's just the physical matter of getting them in.

Q.: General, do you expect the enemy to match us buildup by buildup? In other words, what I'm driving at is that [is there] any level that we can arrive [at] in our combat troop strength where we will gain the advantage?

A.: I won't speculate on that.

I will do my best to put out a public release on the PROV Corps. I cannot do it today for reasons that I won't at-tempt to explain. But I will--if you will just hold that and consider it off the record until you get the release, and my explanation was designed to give you the background and the rationale.

Now, since there have been some stories suggesting that I do not have confidence in the Marines, I do have one--and this has been associated with speculation on Abrams going north and so forth which I've explained--I do have a statement for the record which will be passed out to you in writing, which will make my position known in this regard.

Have you got those?   Fine.   You'll pass them out as the gentlemen leave the room.

Well, I guess I better be on my way to see the Ambassador.

APPENDIX XXIX

Newsweek, March 11, 1968
THE TET OFFENSIVE: HOW THEY DID IT

It is now five full weeks since the communists launched
their audacious Lunar New Year offensive in South Vietnam and, in a single stroke, dramatically altered the
complexion of the war. At first glance, the attack
appeared to be a faultless military triumph. Impressive
it was. But recently, U.S. intelligence has compiled
stacks of captured documents and transcripts of prisoner
interrogations which suggest that the communists--for
all their success in battle--were still plagued by the
confusion that is characteristic of all military operations. Last week, *Newsweek* correspondents in Saigon
and Washington sifted through this material and cabled
their findings:

The roots of the Tet offensive go back to the spring of
1967. At that time, the leaders of North Vietnam,
alarmed at the devastating losses U.S. firepower was
inflicting on communist ranks in the South, seriously
began to reexamine their long-standing strategy of waging
a protracted war of attrition from rural base areas.
"If we keep fighting five more years," declared one
Hanoi official "all that will be left of Vietnam will be
a desert." And this view was borne out by a secret
delegation of communist military experts from North
Korea, China, and Cuba who visited the war theater and
reported back that the Vietcong and North Vietnamese
forces could not hold out many months longer against
the U.S. and its allies.

As a result, a group of Politburo members in North Vietnam, led by Marxist theoretician Truong Chinh, demanded
a change in plans. And in March or April the Central
Committee of the Lao Dong (communist) Party passed
"Resolution 13" calling for a new strategy to achieve
victory "in the shortest possible time." Exactly what
role Defense Minister Gen. Vo Nguyen Giap played in all

216

this is still a matter of speculation, but there is some
indication that Giap--until then a cautious exponent of
protracted warfare--was not enthusiastic about the stepped-
up timetable. Nonetheless, Giap felt obliged in the
interest of party unity to swallow his objections and,
in July, when Hanoi's commander in South Vietnam, Gen.
Nguyen Chi Thanh, died in a B-52 raid, Giap proceeded with
his plans for the Tet offensive.

THREE PHASES

Giap's master plan was code-named "TCK-TCN"--the abbrevia-
tion for the Vietnamese words *Tong Cong Kich-Tong Khoi
Nghia* (General Offensive-General Uprising). His strategy
envisioned a three-phase campaign beginning in the fall of
1967 with attacks along South Vietnam's borders aimed at
tying down large numbers of U.S. troops. That would be
followed by a coordinated general offensive against South
Vietnam's major cities. (In the event this initial offensive failed, Giap planned to pull his forces back and
encircle the cities.) In phase three, scheduled to
begin in the spring of 1968, political cadres would set
off a general uprising of the populace, which was expected to culminate in the formation of a communist-
dominated coalition government. Though Giap planned to
win a political victory over the Saigon regime by summer-
time, he apparently also planned to wage decisive battles
against the United States in the western highlands and
at the U.S. Marine outpost dug in at Khe Sanh.

In October, with preparations well under way, Giap, Party
Secretary Le Duan, and Foreign Minister Nguyen Duy Trinh
stopped off in Peking on their way to Moscow's 50th-
anniversary celebration of the Bolshevik Revolution. In
conversations with top Chinese leaders, Giap outlined
his new strategy. Though the Chinese were distressed
to discover that Hanoi had abandoned the Maoist concept
of protracted warfare, they agreed to help. To free as
many North Vietnamese troops as possible for combat
roles, they reportedly offered to send Hanoi some 100,000
additional Chinese logistic troops and truck drivers and
200,000 rail- and road-maintenance workers. (It remains
unclear, however, whether Hanoi accepted Peking's offer.)
The Chinese also promised to deliver two new types of
rockets--a lightweight 107-mm. model and a jumbo 240-mm.
version with a range of 18 miles. Later in Moscow, the
Russians pledged to speed up shipments of armor and other
weapons.

As Christmas approached, North Vietnam's Chief of Staff
Gen. Van Tien Dung sent his commanders new instructions
for the "winter-spring campaign." And at New Year's,

Foreign Minister Trinh made his now-famous remark that
peace talks would definitely start once the United States
stopped bombing North Vietnam. Trinh, of course, was well
aware of Giap's plans, and some U.S. officials now are
convinced that his "peace offer" was merely a device to
elicit a bombing halt during the critically important
days preceding the Tet attack.

THE WORD

By mid-January, the date for the start of the offensive
was set and Giap moved his headquarters to a command post
in the southern panhandle of North Vietnam, not far from
the beleaguered base at Khe Sanh. Awaiting the final word
to attack were approximately 240,000 communist troops,
at least 65,000 of whom were assigned to take part in the
first-wave assault on the cities. Finally, the word
came--a cryptic poem read over Radio Hanoi by none other
than President Ho Chi Minh. "This spring shines far
brighter than any before," Ho recited. "Happy news of
victories blooms across the land. South and North challenge each other to fight the U.S. aggressors. Forward!
Total victory will be ours."

In Saigon, at the end of January, the Mardi gras atmosphere
of the Tet celebration was at its peak when North Vietnamese
Maj. Gen. Tran Do entered his command post in a small farm-
house at Phu Tho Hoa, just outside the rambling capital
city. Selected by the Central Office for South Vietnam
(COSVN) to coordinate the offensive against Saigon, Tran
Do, a handsome, bull-necked man of 50, reported directly
by radio to a four-star general with the *nom de guerre*
of Tran Nam Trung and to Huynh Tan Phat, vice president
of the National Liberation Front. In turn, these two men,
stationed at the main COSVN headquarters near the Cambodian
border, kept their superiors in North Vietnam informed on
an hour-to-hour basis of the unfolding battle in Saigon.

RUNNERS

Communist communications inside Saigon were less sophisticated. Tran Do's commanders had to rely on runners, often
women and young boys, sneaking past government outposts.
The system lacked flexibility and, once the go signal was
given, there was little chance to reinforce one unit from
another. As a result, highly motivated political cadres
were charged with the duty of seeing to it that nothing
went amiss. They were to march with their units--and die
with them if necessary.

For tactical purposes, Tran Do divided the Saigon area into
five subsectors like the slices of an apple pie. The center
of the pie was the Presidential Palace; the crust included

parts of the teeming suburbs where secret guerrilla cells
were ready to provide guides, shelter, and food to the
troops. Weapons and ammunition were smuggled into Saigon
by sampan, inside empty Esso and Shell gasoline trucks and
in hollowed logs hauled all the way from the forest of
Zone D, and under truckloads of flowers and big watermelons,
the traditional fruit served at Tet feasts. Once inside
the capital, this massive arsenal was sorted out, placed
in coffins, and buried in local cemeteries or cached in
houses rented by the communists throughout the city.

So confident were the communists that they would sweep all
before them that, shortly before the offensive began, they
placed an order at a renowned Chinese restaurant in Cholon
for 400 meals to celebrate their victory. In addition,
the communists invited Vietnamese émigrés living in Paris
to return to Saigon in order to participate in a coalition
government. One intellectual who flew back to Saigon to
accept the invitation cabled a friend in Paris: "If
anyone asks you what I'm doing in Saigon, say I've come to
bury my mother."

DECEPTION

Of the 40,000 men under Tran Do's Saigon command, about
4,000 had infiltrated into the city disguised as peasants
or in the uniforms of South Vietnamese troops. As part
of his plan of deception, Tran Do had positioned his larger
units 30 miles away from Saigon in an effort to lure allied
troops away from the capital. Then, only 12 hours before
the attack, he ordered his regiments to converge on the
city in a forced march. Many of the North Vietnamese
units simply trooped through government-controlled villages and hamlets, gambling that they would not be reported
by local officials during the Tet holiday. Other units,
however, used more caution. The three regiments of
the Vietcong's 9th Division, which marched on the capital
through uninhabited forests, did not use cooking fires
for fear that they would be detected by U.S. aircraft
with infra-red cameras. Instead, the soldiers of the 9th
Division were each provided with three liters of cold
rice, one kilo of brown sugar, one can of sweet condensed
milk, and one can of dried fish.

Even when communist movements were reported, South Vietnamese Army headquarters did not take the threat seriously,
or refused to believe that Saigon was the target. In fact,
Tran Do's deception worked so well that, when the attack
began, the nearest mechanized U.S. unit was 38 miles away
from Saigon near the Hoc Mon bridge. According to Tran
Do's careful plans, the bridge was supposed to be blown up.
But inexplicably, his men failed to carry out their
important assignment.

That was only the first in a series of communist missions that went afoul. North of Tan Son Nhut airport, the Vietcong's 6th "Go Mon" Battalion was ordered to capture the South Vietnamese armor school and seize its tanks and armored personnel carriers. Half of the vehicles were to be used to support an attack against the airport itself, and half to spearhead an assault on Gen. William C. Westmoreland's headquarters and the South Vietnamese Joint General Staff. But when the communists arrived at the school they found that all of the vehicles had been moved out of Saigon two months before.

To capture such key objectives as the U.S. Embassy, Tran Do relied on the C-10 Sapper Battalion, a dedicated group of terrorists led by a man known as Brother Tam Ho. Dressed in South Vietnamese Army uniforms with red linings sewn into the cuffs of their pants for identification, one C-10 unit was assigned the task of seizing the Saigon radio station where it was then to play a tape-recorded message from Ho Chi Minh. Another unit was ordered to capture South Vietnam's Premier Nguyen Van Loc, take him to the station, and force him to broadcast a cease-fire order to all government troops. In the end, neither of these bold schemes succeeded.

PRISONERS

Yet another objective of Tran Do's plan was to free several thousand prisoners in the Chi Hoa Prison, arm them, and then turn them loose on the police. But the hard-pressed 6th Vietcong Battalion assigned this task was so busy occupying the Phu Tho Race Track and setting up a command post in the An Quang Pagoda that it never got around to attacking the prison. Later, when the battle for Saigon was at its height, the prisoners themselves tried to break out, but they were subdued.

Throughout the rest of South Vietnam, the story was much the same. With the exception of Hue, where strong North Vietnamese forces entrenched themselves in the easily defended redoubt of the Citadel, the communist plan was conceived as a lightning *coup d'état* in which the organs of state power would be knocked out of commission. For this task, enemy commanders cautiously fragmented their units into small, platoon-size groups and often held back their main forces in supporting roles. Thus it is not true, as some U.S. officials claim, that the communists "bet all their chips" during the first wave of the Tet offensive. On the contrary, captured post-action critiques prepared by communist military leaders complain that field commanders failed to use adequate forces to overwhelm South Vietnamese and U.S. battalions and take full advantage of mass and surprise.

SURPRISED

Nor was this the communists' only mistake. Enemy units were sent into pro-government villages and sections of cities in the mistaken belief that the U.S. and South Vietnamese would not risk the political consequences of calling in air strikes and artillery on friendly populations. When this happened, the communists were badly surprised. More important yet, in order to maintain strict security within their own ranks, communist commanders did not rehearse their troops with the usual sand-table models of their objectives. And many enemy soldiers were not even informed about the Tet offensive until a few hours before they went into combat. Finally, the communists' problems were further complicated by the deaths of some of their top leaders, including Gen. Tran Do himself.

But despite the fact that the communists did not achieve most of their objectives, their offensive was far from a failure. For one thing, it caught the U.S. and South Vietnamese by surprise and made a mockery of numerous allied claims that the enemy was too weak to stand up and fight. For another, it forced thousands of allied troops to withdraw to the defense of the cities and laid bare the South Vietnamese countryside to communist encroachments. Most important of all, by launching their Tet offensive, the communists seized the battlefield initiative from half a million U.S. troops and raised serious doubts in the minds of millions of Americans at home about the future course of the war. "Personally," said one U.S. intelligence expert, "I'm discouraged. I don't know what it will take to regain our previous position. We don't know how many Vietcong there are and how many there were before Tet. We don't know how many are infiltrating and where they are going or what they are going to do. But this much is clear: Giap did not let go with one blow, a *coup de grace*. There is more coming."

APPENDIX XXX

Time, **March 15, 1968**
AFTER "TET": MEASURING AND REPAIRING THE DAMAGE

In the first shock and confusion that followed the communists' countrywide Tet offensive six weeks ago, it was
difficult, dangerous, and, in remote areas, impossible
to assess accurately the damage done by the enemy. Now,
with roads, communications, and security gradually being
restored, a firmer measure can be taken--even though the
final, definitive picture may not emerge for some months
yet. For military and administrative purposes, South
Vietnam is divided into four corps areas that run from
north to south, plus the special capital zone of
Saigon and surrounding Gia Dinh province. Last week
Time sent a team of five correspondents from its Saigon
bureau, one to each of the corps areas and the capital
zone, to find out just how much havoc the communist attacks had wrought, and what the allies are doing to
repair it. Their reports:

I CORPS

Vietnam's northernmost corps, unwilling host to some
55,000 North Vietnamese invaders, is less a pacification
prospect than an open battlefield. It was there that the
24-day battle for Hue took place, the most determined of
the communists' 35 attacks on South Vietnamese cities.
Some 5,350 civilians were killed in all, including 4,100
in Hue; another 4,500 were seriously injured. The
existing refugee ranks of 250,000 were swelled by an
additional 107,000, some 90,000 of these from Hue alone--
out of the city's pre-Tet population of 130,000. Three-
fourths of the 12,000 houses destroyed and the 10,000
heavily damaged were in Hue; destruction was made easier,
of course, by the fact that in many parts of I Corps, as
elsewhere in Vietnam, houses are often primitive and
fragile structures.

Largely because of interdicted roads and waterways,
business and commerce throughout I Corps is down some

20 percent. Pre-Tet, the pacification program embraced fewer than 300 of the corps' 4,000 hamlets. Even so, two-thirds of the Revolutionary Development pacification teams had to abandon their assigned hamlets when the shooting started. Some 80 RD teams have since gone back to their hamlets.

The allies are making major efforts to improve security along the highways and waterways; two weeks ago the first truck convoy since Tet, bearing relief goods for Hue, moved up the vital Highway One from Da Nang to the stricken city. In the face of the massive communist threat throughout the corps, little else but mobile defense is being undertaken. Some 2,000 civilian volunteers are being armed in Hue, Da Nang, Quang Tri city, and other cities as "people's self-defense forces."

II CORPS

Despite the savage fighting in Kontum and Pleiku during Tet, the early evidence indicates that the large central part of Vietnam--the Highlands--may have escaped with less damage than any of the other corps areas.

The civilian dead in II Corps total 1,100, the wounded 4,000, the new refugees 103,000. Some 12,000 houses were destroyed and another 4,000 heavily damaged. The security of the corps road network is about the same as pre-Tet, but that is not saying much; even then, an armed convoy was needed to traverse all major roads. Sixty of the 252 RD teams assigned to hamlets are still out of position, unable to go back because security cannot be guaranteed them. One area abandoned: the coastal strip just north of Qui Nhon. "The '68 pacification program has been set back," admits Maj. Gen. William R. Peers, acting commander of Field Force I, "and we'll have to take another look." Nevertheless, as another U.S. official put it: "My heart went up into my throat when the Tet offensive came. But now it appears that we did not get hurt as badly as we first thought."

III CORPS

The overall situation in strategic III Corps, a 10,000-square-mile area ringing the capital zone of Saigon, remains guardedly favorable. There is firm evidence that if the government reacts promptly enough, it may be able to recoup practically all the losses sustained at Tet.

Before Tet, CORDS (Civil Operations and Revolutionary Development Support) estimated that 82 percent of the population of 5.3 million lived in secure hamlets, some 13 percent in contested hamlets, and only a scant 5 percent under hardcore Vietcong hegemony. "We're still

in a state of flux concerning recent losses or gains,"
says CORDS Deputy John P. Vann. "We're not sure what
resulted from drawing in over 6,000 RD cadre and some
of the regional and popular forces to province and
district towns." But the estimates are that communist
real estate and population gains will be small in III
Corps. Civilian casualties were also low: 188 dead,
some 1,000 wounded or missing. But 10,000 houses were
destroyed, and the area has 50,000 new refugees.

Fully 95 percent of the 5,000 RD workers are now back in
their hamlets, and local officials have moved quickly to
care for refugees and begin reconstruction of houses.
In Tay Ninh province, building materials and food supplies arrived as soon as the communists were routed
from Long My, and cash payments of $42 were made at
once to each homeless family. The communists made a
major effort to cut the corps' road system, mostly by
blowing up bridges, but all but one of the corps' major
roads have been kept open, with no break lasting longer
than 24 hours.

THE SAIGON CAPITAL ZONE

South Vietnam's capital now wears the air of "nervous
normalcy" to which more isolated province capitals have
grown accustomed. Most businesses have reopened, but
stocks are low. The western one-third of the Chinese
quarter of Cholon is still insecure at night, the work
of several hundred Vietcong who are still holed up
around the race track. Saigon lost, it is now estimated,
6,300 civilians during the fighting; another 11,000
were wounded.

A total of nearly 19,000 structures were destroyed in
the city itself, and more than 2,300 in Gia Dinh province.
All told, the capital district has 206,000 new refugees
living in 114 temporary quarters and camps. It will
probably take eight months to find adequate new housing
for them all. For once, the Saigonese have given the
government good marks--for its prompt aid to the
refugees. There has also been a noticeable decrease in
neutralism among the populace, which seems to be swinging
more toward anticommunism. The South Vietnamese Army
is getting an unprecedented average of 300 volunteers
a day from the Saigon area.

IV CORPS

The Tet blows left the Delta stunned--disoriented, inert,
and so traumatized that it could not even assess its own
wounds. But now there is a stirring in hot, flat, sun-
baked IV Corps, a probing of wounds, an application of
first aid, and even plans for recovery.

Estimates of damage and casualties in the Delta are spottier than elsewhere, because even pre-Tet the government's control was a sometime thing. Of the 5,274 hamlets in IV Corps, 2,000 were under Saigon's rule, 2,000 under that of the Vietcong, and the rest neither quite one nor the other. But 1,300 civilians are believed dead, 3,700 wounded. Before Tet, the Delta had 14,000 refugees; now there are 170,000, the product of 19,000 houses destroyed and 5,000 heavily damaged. Road traffic is a fifth or less of normal traffic.

Some provinces are an exception, says Fitzhugh Turner, chief of U.S. psychological warfare in the Delta, "but, in general, we're pinned down." The other half of the Delta's transport system, its waterways, are running at nearly 75 percent of normal traffic loads, however. There is little shortage of food in the rice-rich Delta, and thus little inflation. The attacks closed the Delta's schools, pulled most of the 10,000 pacification workers into the towns. There is no doubt that the Vietcong have added to their extensive Delta holdings, and will dig in.

The government has launched an ambitious program to put the Delta's new homeless back under their own roofs, but the actual rebuilding of houses is only just beginning. The schools will reopen within a month. CORDS officials are trying to organize commercial convoys--fleets of trucks guarded by military vehicles--over the enemy-interdicted roads. Some 70 percent of the RD workers have returned to their posts but, in some provinces, such as Kien Giang, Phong Dinh, and Kien Phong, there is no chance of a return. The Vietcong pressure is just too heavy.

*   *   *

When all the parts are added up, the dimensions of South Vietnam's losses since Tet become clear: 14,300 civilians dead, 24,000 wounded, 72,000 houses destroyed, 627,000 new refugees. Of the 35 cities hit, 10 suffered major damage: Kontum, Pleiku, Ban Me Thuot, My Tho, Ben Tre, Vinh Long, Chau Doc, Can Tho, Saigon, and Hue. CORDS officials estimate that 13 of the country's 44 provinces were so badly hit that pacification has been set back to where it stood at the beginning of 1967. In an additional 16 provinces, it will take three to six months to get the program working again. Only 60 percent of the Revolutionary Development workers have so far been reported at their posts. And, even when nearly all the pacification workers are back on the job, it will be a different kind of job for quite a while: rebuilding the ruins of Tet rather than nation-building for the future.

APPENDIX XXXI

Newsweek, March 18, 1968

THE DUSTY AGONY OF KHE SANH: "WHAT'S THERE TO PANIC ABOUT?
WE'RE HERE TO STAY"

By Merton Perry

War as the strategist sees it and war as it appears to
the foot soldier are vastly different things. Last week,
after a visit to the U.S. Marine base at Khe Sanh,
Newsweek's Merton Perry cabled the following report:

The North Vietnamese are busy all around Khe Sanh.
Borrowing from their own military history, they have
begun to dig trenches that zigzag up to within a hundred
yards of the Marine lines. So far, there are only a few
trenches--nothing like the intricate, spidery maze dug
by the Vietminh at Dienbienphu--but the Marines suspect
that the communists have also started to tunnel down
toward the base from the back slopes of the ridges that
surround the Khe Sanh plateau. "These people are moles,"
declared Capt. Jack Egger, 28, of Columbus, Ohio, commander of a Marine company on the camp's northern
perimeter.

No one knows just how many "moles" are actually outside--
or, worse yet, under--Khe Sanh. Higher headquarters
says there are two North Vietnamese Army divisions in
the immediate vicinity, but few of the enemy troops have
been seen from inside the camp. From beyond the
perimeter, an occasional sniper plinks away at the
Marines, and there have been five or six battalion-size
probes against the defenses. The greatest danger, however, comes from the daily barrage by NVA mortars, rockets,
and artillery pieces, some of them dug in under the jungle
canopy miles away from the base. The constant shelling
is not enough to destroy the camp, but it is enough to
make the men who live there wonder constantly about what
is coming next. And the wonder and the waiting inevitably
tauten the nerves of the 5,000 Marines who crouch inside
Khe Sanh.

Even though Marine morale is high, Khe Sanh is physically and emotionally a miserable place, a noisy, dusty, dangerous hell. The men who live there have a special gait known as the "Khe Sanh double step"--a crouching walk accompanied by a constant swiveling of the head. The point of the Khe Sanh double step is to make sure that there is always a hole within easy reach.

Red laterite dust clogs everything at Khe Sanh--your eyes, your ears, your throat. A jeep drives by and the red dust settles on you like talcum powder, making you gag and choke. The longer you stay in Khe Sanh, the redder you get. A Khe Sanh veteran has red hair, red hands and feet, and red clothes; when he blows his nose, his handkerchief is stained red.

Rats infest the camp. One Marine walked past me with an armload of huge traps. "If these don't work," he said, "we've got this"--he held up a bottle of rat poison--"and if that don't work, I got a .45 pistol, and as a last resort we use hand grenades on them."

NAPALM

Now that the weather is clearing, jet fighter-bombers roar overhead most of the day, plastering the ridges with napalm that burns off the scrub trees and elephant grass where the NVA are dug in. But somehow the enemy troops seem to survive, and during the day they can be seen moving through their trenches. For weeks, one North Vietnamese, armed with a .50-caliber machine gun and known to the Marines as "Luke the Gook," has been ripping off his deadly bursts at low-flying aircraft from a foxhole barely 100 yards outside the lines. No amount of napalm has been able to burn Luke out.

Several times a day, the ground trembles with B-52 strikes that hit within a mile or two of the camp. During the daylight hours, helicopters flutter in, kicking up massive new waves of the devil dust. Almost every one of them takes out wounded men. The attrition among the Marines is not as high now as in weeks past, but there is still a steady trickle of casualties. The men who remain behind live much like their enemies, the moles. Most hunker down in sandbagged bunkers connected by a trenchline that runs around the camp. Beyond the trench, concertina barbed wire lies in tangled coils, supplemented by a new type of German "razor" wire. The prickly strands are studded with explosive charges and Claymore mines--a deadly obstacle course through which the enemy will have to advance if he wants to get inside the camp.

COLD NIGHTS

Along the perimeter, the men sleep in shifts, napping
between watches. The nights are cold--when it is really
chill, the men say "the hawk is out"--and no one has
had a freshly cooked meal since the siege began on
January 21. The best meals available are C-rations; slimy
chunks of franks and beans or turkey loaf cooked over
heat pellets. They are not very good--and the coffee
fortified with ascorbic acid (for Vitamin C) is even
worse.

The 40 Seabees assigned to Khe Sanh are a little better
off than the Marines. Trained for engineering jobs, the
Seabees have worked longer and more skillfully on their
bunkers, and one of their dwellings, an elaborate fortification dubbed the Alamo Hilton, has timbers and sandbags
six-feet thick overhead. It is the safest place in Khe
Sanh, and not surprisingly has become the unofficial
press headquarters. The grateful journalists import
beer and whiskey for the Seabees, which does not sit
at all well with the Marines. "The Seabees have got more
beer than we have water," gripes a Leatherneck. The
Seabees are not embarrassed, however. Says one sailor:
"Before the siege began, Marines sat on their tails when
they should have been digging. They worked 9 to 4,
knocked off and went to their beer hall. Charlie [the
NVA] missed his golden opportunity--maybe many golden
opportunities--by not attacking right away. Perhaps now
the Marines are dug in well enough." And perhaps they
are not. Digging in is not the Marine way of war.

Most of the Marines are pretty tough customers, and so
far there have been only a few cases of men going around
the bend. During my visit, an NVA shell landed in a
foxhole, killing five Marines; the sole survivor was not
even scratched, but, after brooding all night, the young
Marine tried to make a desperate one-man assault out
through the perimeter. He had to be knocked down and
carried back. Another Marine was killed when he opened
a latrine door and set off a grenade that had been attached to it as a booby trap. "It was either a crazy
Marine who did it," explained a Marine noncom, "or the
gooks have got a tunnel in here."

BARBECUE

Despite their isolation the vast majority of the Marines
at Khe Sanh--from the lowliest, tiredest grunt on up to
Col. David Lownds, the camp's 47-year-old commander--re-
main totally confident. A major factor behind this
optimism is the awesome firepower of the U.S. forces.
I saw this demonstrated in a sector of the perimeter

defended by South Vietnamese Rangers. The American
advisor to the South Vietnamese, Capt. Walter Gunn, 31,
of Columbus, Georgia, ordered an air strike on the
enemy trenches. His radioman Pfc. John Burleson, 22, of
Chicago, called higher headquarters and announced:
"Captain Gunn wants a barbecue." A while later, when
the napalm splashed in on the NVA positions, Captain Gunn
remarked to no one in particular, "I don't care what they
say back in the States, I say God bless Dow Chemical."

So confident is Khe Sanh's garrison, in fact, that many
of its members would almost welcome an all-out enemy
assault. "I wish they would come in now," says Pfc.
Charles Hughes, 20, of Chattanooga. "We'll kick them
around a little, no question about that." The Marines
feel sure that the U.S. air and artillery attacks have
damaged the enemy. "You can still see them out there,"
says Gunnery Sgt. Freddie J. Morris, 36, of Thomaston,
Georgia. "But not like we used to. They've had the
hurt put on them some."

OPTIMIST

Colonel Lownds, a 20-year Marine veteran who has raised
an upswept British-style military mustache since taking
over the Khe Sanh command, answers questions with firm,
blunt optimism. Isn't it possible that the North Vietnamese could keep him pinned down with only a token
force, diverting major units to a big attack on important
northern cities, like Quang Tri, Hue, or Da Nang? "I
don't think so," he responds. "It's almost inconceivable
to me that we won't get hit." Could the Marines fight
their way out of Khe Sanh on the ground if they had to?
"I don't even think about that," replies Lownds. "My
mission is to stay here, damn it, and we're going to stay
here."

Lownds, in short, is certain that the North Vietnamese
will try to overrun Khe Sanh sooner or later. "It's only
a question of how much Giap is willing to lose," he says.
"I would hope it would cost him 40,000 or 50,000 men,
maybe more. What's there to panic about? We're here to
stay. That's our job, that's what we get paid for."

APPENDIX XXXII

The Washington *Post*
March 24, 1968

BUSY SPOTTER PILOT HELPS CLEAR ROAD TO KHE SANH

By Peter Braestrup

Da Nang, Mar. 23--Flying in an Air Force spotter plane over the Khe Sanh battlefield is like riding a roller coaster, only worse.

"Sorry," said the forward air controller Capt. John J. Jacobcik. "It's the only way to avoid getting hit by ground fire."

Piloting a little Cessna 0-2, Jacobcik, a 30-year-old Air Force Academy graduate, called in three jet air strikes this afternoon in three busy hours of snooping and swooping over the Khe Sanh area.

His targets were along the "Santa Fe Trail," the nickname for Highway Nine, the heavily bombed North Vietnamese truck route, which comes into Khe Sanh from Tchepone on the Ho Chi Minh Trail in Laos.

It was obvious today that, despite two months of heavy bombing, Highway Nine was open for business.

A broad, well traveled dirt road, it runs straight east over the border from Laos and winds slightly south between the Xepan River and the jumbled shell-battered ridge where the Marines defending Khe Sanh have outposts on Hill 881 South and Hill 861.

The road runs east past Lang Vei, the old Special Forces camp that the enemy overran in January. Two Soviet PT-76 amphibious tanks, knocked out by the American defenders, still stand on the slope below Lang Vei's smashed defenses and dugouts.

Jacobcik flew above the road, noting the fresh footpaths leading off into the jungle, the trenches used by the enemy to hide from air attacks, the by-passes built around each wrecked bridge and each big bomb crater.

Near the Xepan River he spotted fresh trails leading to a cluster of thatched huts, long abandoned by the local

230

Bru tribesmen. Two of the huts were freshly thatched.
Jacobcik figured it was probably an enemy storage area.

He radioed for fighter aircraft. Two F-4 jets circled
high as the forward air controller gave them instructions.

Then Jacobcik bore in on the target himself. From a wing
pod, he fired a 2.75-inch smoke rocket into the cluster
of huts to mark it for the jets. As the spotter plane
came out of the sky, several figures could be seen running
out of the houses. The North Vietnamese apparently knew
what was coming.

The F-4 jets swooped down and then climbed steeply. Their
napalm landed on target. The huts burned briskly under a
pall of black smoke.

Alerted by radio to the reported presence of three trucks
elsewhere on the highway, Jacobcik circled and dived for
a closer look. He found a battered Soviet-model truck
lying on its side, victim of an earlier air strike, but
nothing was moving on the ground.

Flying back and forth over the road, he operated the
controls with one hand while with the other he peered
through a binocular and snapped 35-mm. pictures through
a telescopic lens. Being short of qualified airmen, the
Air Force puts only one man in its spotter planes, and
his task is a difficult one.

Jacobcik called in another air strike, using bombs instead
of napalm on the area near the first target, hoping to
destroy underground ammunition or fuel caches. Again the
jets came in, smoke billowed from the ground and Jacobcik
spotted a secondary explosion.

Circling Highway Nine again, he saw a half-dozen bunker
entrances by the roadside. "I've been looking for those,"
he said. "That's where their repair crews hole up during
the daytime." Shortly thereafter, two F-4s from Cam Ranh
Bay flashed in at right angles to the highway and put
bombs right on both road and bunkers.

"That will disturb their afternoon nap," said Jacobcik.

Fuel was running low. Jacobcik headed east for home as
other 0-2s arrived to take over. Across the river in
Laos could be seen the flat tops of Coroc Mountain. The
cliff was dotted with cave entrances. It was here that
the enemy installed 152-mm. artillery to bombard Khe
Sanh less than 10 miles away.

The mountain had been heavily bombed, but no one claimed
to have knocked out the guns. Only infantrymen do that.

Back here at their Da Nang base, Jacobcik's fellow pilots voiced their respect for the enemy's ability to survive the thousands of bombs that have made a moonscape of the hills west and south of Khe Sanh.

Even the bomb craters are used as foxholes by the enemy. The roads are repaired the same night they are bombed. The enemy is moving trucks on Highway Nine almost all the way to Lang Vei and possibly beyond.

Marine sources believe that the bombing forces the enemy to keep shifting his mortars and rockets, slowing his efforts to hit specific targets.

After two months, the enemy's bombardment of Khe Sanh has been surprisingly imprecise and erratic.

Some Air Force pilots argue that the same kind of intensive surveillance and round-the-clock interdiction by air now used at Khe Sanh must be applied to the growing enemy road network elsewhere in South Vietnam.

As one of Jacobcik's colleagues noted, the North Vietnamese are building roads from northern Cambodia and Laos at a rapid rate.

Enemy truck traffic is no longer confined to the Khe Sanh area close to the Ho Chi Minh Trail. His trucks have been spotted west of Hue, the A Shau Valley, and around Kontum in the Central Highlands. He is speeding up the resupply of rocket and artillery shells for use against American bases and Vietnamese cities.

No longer must the enemy rely solely on human porters to supply his troops in the South.

At Khe Sanh, because of the concentration of U.S. air power, his movements are inhibited even at night. Elsewhere, this is not the case, and the American command has yet to devise an effective answer.

APPENDIX XXXIII

The Washington *Post*
March 24, 1968

THE LITTLE MARINE AND HIS NEW BOOTS

By John Randolph

KHE SANH--"It was the saddest thing of all--to have to cut
his new boots off," said Lt. Donald J. Magilligan, standing
on the bloodsoaked floor of the underground medical bunker
and shaking his head slowly.

The young and very tired Navy doctor had been telling the
story of 19-year-old Jonathan Spicer, a round-faced little
Marine whose death, even by the harsh standards of this
terrible place, was both heroic and pathetic. And when
Magilligan came to the part about those wonderful boots
that Spicer wore for such a short time, the tears welled
up in his eyes.

Private Spicer, the rarest kind of Marine--a conscientious
objector--died March 15 in the U.S. Naval Hospital at
Yokosuka, Japan, after a week-long struggle by Navy doctors to save his life, from shell fragments that ripped
open his heart, blinded his left eye, and covered his body
with other wounds while he was serving as a stretcher-
bearer at Khe Sanh.

AN UNOFFICIAL CONCESSION

Although "Marine" and "conscientious objector" are a
contradiction in terms, young Spicer, son of a Methodist
minister in Miami, had nevertheless been allowed to enlist
in the Corps. And though his stipulation that he not
have to take life was never officially conceded, the
Marines solved the problem informally by passing the word
not to make an issue of it.

When the shooting started, his outfit, the 1st Battalion,
26th Marines, simply loaned him to the Navy medics for
stretcher duty. In beleaguered Khe Sanh, that is a duty
almost as important as shooting--and even more dangerous.

"He was one of the bravest men in Khe Sanh," said Magilligan, who comes from Brooklyn. "It was always the wounded
first with him. And it wasn't only bravery under fire--he
would pull a sergeant off a helicopter if he accidentally

got on ahead of a wounded, or push an officer out of the way of a stretcher. That takes guts in the Marines when you're only a private.

"He was only a loan to us, of course, but he was one of us. We were trying to solve his problem by getting him transferred to the medical service. He really belonged here. I can tell you there were not a few tears shed when he died.

"And those boots--how he wanted those boots. You were here yourself. You remember how happy he was."

A WOUNDED LADY

Khe Sanh is a small place, full of chance meetings and coincidences, and I had been there when Spicer got his boots. It happened this way:

One noontime, an enemy mortar shell wounded a young woman free-lance correspondent--Jurate Kazickas, 24, of New York and Chicago, a long-haired, good-looking girl. Steel fragments caught her in the forearm, lower leg and--more painfully but not too seriously--the middle of the left side of the part she sits down with.

Jurate's arrival at the medical bunker in such a piquant plight created a sensation. However, Lt. James Finnegan, 29, from the faculty of the University of Philadelphia and the senior medical officer in Khe Sanh, chased away all eager volunteers and treated the lady himself. Her principal wound's unelegant location led to some earthy banter in the bunker--in which Jurate more than held her own.

Word of her wounding raced around Khe Sanh, and I got to the bunker just in time to talk to her for a moment. Then a four-man stretcher crew led by Spicer carried her at a run to a medical evacuation helicopter that had just touched down, rotors roaring for a fast take-off. Although the 150 feet from the bunkers to the pad are the deadliest patch of ground in all Khe Sanh, Charlie didn't shoot this time and the big bird soared away.

AN ODD SIZE

The stretcher crew dashed back and Spicer came clattering down the bunker steps. Suddenly he seemed to remember something. He reached behind a big metal tub used for bloody field dressings, torn uniforms, and field gear cut off wounded Marines and pulled out a pair of unusually small Army green jungle boots.

These boots are one of the finest pieces of tropical gear ever developed--a real smash hit in the Vietnam War--but they are devilishly hard to get in odd sizes. Spicer was grinning broadly. I glanced at his feet and saw why.

He was wearing the sleazy black high-topped sneakers issued to Vietnamese soldiers--obviously the only small-size
tropical boots that Spicer, a real half-pint, had been
able to get.

He held the new ones up in his hands, almost dancing with
pleasure, like a child with a Christmas toy. Then he saw
me watching and his grin vanished. After a short but
visible struggle, his conscience won out.

"I think these were an extra pair she had with her pack,"
he explained. "See--the laces aren't cut. They would be
if these were the ones Mr. Finnegan cut off her with the
surgical shears. She must have taken the others and forgot these."

Then he did the noble thing and asked me if I would take
them back to her when I left.

Now Jurate had probably had a hard time getting those
boots, since they were not only an off-size but there is
no legal way for correspondents to buy them; they require
much scrounging. But friendship is one thing--and suicide
is another.

Leaving Khe Sanh is the most dangerous moment of any visit
--a desperate sprint, often under fire, for an airplane or
helicopter that can hardly wait to take off. Since half-
a-dozen correspondents have been wounded on such dashes,
I had resolved to dump every last thing I had--cameras,
binoculars, portable typewriter, and pack--if it would
help me reach that aircraft in time. Jurate's boots had
no part in that program and I told Spicer so.

He was enormously relieved, and his Christmas morning grin
blossomed out again like a neon sign.

"Mr. Finnegan," he called out across the bunker," the correspondent here says he can't take the lady's boots back
to her. Is it all right if I keep them?"

"Sure," replied Finnegan with a smile. "Hope they fit."

In a moment the sneakers were off and Jurate's boots were
on--a perfect fit. Spicer laced them, using a fancy pattern, then walked around the bunker showing them off--
literally walking on his toes while everyone watched and
felt good about it. I got his name and made a few notes
so I could report to Jurate that her boots were in good
hands. Then I left.

About two hours later, they carried in an artilleryman
with both legs blown off. His heart stopped. The doctors
slashed him open and massaged it back to life. Then
Spicer and his stretcher crew raced him to another helicopter and started back to the bunker.

This time Charlie was quicker. A heavy shell came straight

into the center of that deadly pathway. Spicer, upright and running, had no protection. Survivors carried him, torn, unconscious, and literally dying, back down into the bunker.

With ruthless, desperate surgery, Magilligan, Finnegan, and their assistants managed to push death back again. When Spicer's own heart stopped, Magilligan slashed an opening and Finnegan massaged the heart back into motion. Then Magilligan cut away restraining tissue, partly lifted out the heart and Finnegan closed the fragment tear in the right ventricle with three silk stitches.

Multiple transfusions of whole blood followed, then treatment for the other wounds. Spicer was still gravely wounded, but he was breathing and alive. Then the man who had carried so many stretchers was himself carried back over that deadly walk to another helicopter--then to Dong Ha, Da Nang, Yokosuka.

Back in the bunker, the new boots lay in the big metal tub, already half covered with dirty waste and parts of uniforms cut off other wounded. By this time, they did not look so new. The bloodsoaked green nylon sides flopped down heavily and Spicer's fancy lacing was in ruins where Magilligan's surgical shears had slashed it from bottom to top.

That night, when the firing died down, a couple of corpsmen carried the tub outside and emptied it into a pit.

APPENDIX XXXIV

The New York *Times*
March 28, 1968

U.S. OFFICERS SAY AIR POWER MAKES KHE SANH A DISASTER FOR FOE

By Gene Roberts

Da Nang, South Vietnam, Mar. 27--A Marine colonel leans across his desk at a forward command post and tells his listener to mark his words well: Khe Sanh will never prove a disaster for the United States Marines, but American air power is making it one for the enemy.

Another colonel, this one in the Army, jabs a finger in the air and says it is not the 6,000 Marines at Khe Sanh who are trapped but the far larger enemy force that surrounds them--at the cost of becoming an easy target for American planes.

Still another colonel, a Marine, reads a letter from his wife and flushes with anger. His wife says some neighbors and stateside editorial writers cannot understand why the Marine Corps units hang on at Khe Sanh, getting pounded day after day by artillery, mortar, and rocket fire.

"Damn it," says the Colonel, "we are hardly getting pounded at all. For every round they drop in on us, we drop a whole plane-load of bombs on them."

AND FOE MOVES CLOSER

This is the way the conversation goes among senior officers in the northern battle zone. Each day the enemy moves closer to Khe Sanh with his intricate network of zigzag trenches, but each day fresh waves of American bombers and fighter-bombers fly in and send American optimism soaring anew.

The senior officers are now so convinced that the aerial bombardment is a major success that they have no plans for pulling the Marines out no matter how much the enemy might increase his shelling at Khe Sanh.

"By keeping those 6,000 Marines there, we're tying up two entire enemy divisions that are trying to overrun them,"

237

says a high-ranking American intelligence officer.   "If
we pulled out, then those divisions would go some place
else--say to Hue--and cause more problems.   This way
we've got them where we can hit them with our bombs."

80,000 TONS OF BOMBS

Just how intense has the bombing become?   And what is it
doing to the enemy?

"Since January 22," an Air Force spokesman says, "Air
Force, Navy, and Marine planes have hit him with 80,000
tons--160 million pounds--of ordnance around Khe Sanh.
We, plan to keep up the pace indefinitely."

And 80,000 tons, the spokesman continues, adds up to more
than the non-nuclear tonnage dropped on Japan throughout
World War II, more than was dropped on all of Europe
during 1942 and 1943 combined, and a fifth as much as
was dropped on all Korea in the three years of the war
there.

Most of the tonnage has fallen on a 10-square-mile area
around the Marine encampment, and the once lush jungle
valleys and hillsides are now a wasteland.   Trees have
been demolished and red-clay craters have replaced much
of the jungle vegetation.

"The destruction is almost unbelievable," says Maj. Billy
F. Nunley of Knoxville, Tennessee, an Air Force pilot who
makes frequent observation flights over the area.   "It
looks like the world caught smallpox and died."

Senior military officers who have seen the desolation find
it inconceivable that the enemy is not suffering greatly.
Front-line Marines at Khe Sanh report having seen enemy
soldiers hurled high into the air by the impact of bombs
weighing up to 2,000 pounds.

But except for these observations and for military reports
of well over a thousand secondary explosions, which indicate that the bombs have hit a gun emplacement, a
munitions cache, or a fuel dump, there is no real way
of measuring the damage caused by the bombing.

TUNNELS, CAVES, FOXHOLES

Most of the enemy operate from tunnels, caves, foxholes,
trenches, and bunkers.   And if the bombs score a hit they
bury the enemy soldiers in tons of earth and make it impossible to conduct a meaningful "body count" from the
air.

"But even though we can't see their bodies we know many
of them are dead," said a Marine officer.   "You couldn't

drop as much bombs and napalm as we have dropped without killing them by the hundreds."

A spokesman who reflects the views of Gen. William C. Westmoreland, commander of United States forces in Vietnam, says the high command is convinced that the enemy would already have attacked Khe Sanh had it not been for the American bombs.

"The attack was pre-empted," the spokesman said, adding that he believed that the bombers could pre-empt attack plans again and again.

But there are students of warfare in Vietnam--including military men attached to the Saigon embassies of friendly powers--who remain unconvinced. They point out that aerial bombardment failed to stop the Vietminh from conquering the French at Dienbienphu in 1954, and they add that it is obvious that the bombs have not stopped the enemy around Khe Sanh.

Two days ago, for example, a Marine patrol was turned back by heavy enemy machine-gun and mortar fire after traveling only 100 to 200 yards past the camp's barbed-wire perimeter. Last Saturday the enemy proved that many of his mortars, rockets, and artillery pieces were still intact by firing about 1,500 rounds at the Khe Sanh base.

"They are well dug in and they are masters of camouflage," says a former military officer who is now a diplomat. "You can be sure that many of them are surviving the bombs."

The same official argues, too, that the fact that the enemy has not yet attacked Khe Sanh does not necessarily mean that the attack has been pre-empted. It could mean, he says, that Gen. Vo Nguyen Giap, the North Vietnamese Defense Minister, is preparing for the attack slowly just as he did at Dienbienphu.

COMPARISON IS DISPUTED

Many senior American military officers counter that it is wrong to attempt to compare Dienbienphu and Khe Sanh, since the French at Dienbienphu had only limited air power. The officers cite one of the favorite books of their critics-- *Hell in a Very Small Place* by the late Bernard Fall--to make their point.

Mr. Fall said that during the 167-day siege of Dienbienphu in 1954, the French were able to mount 3,700 combat missions against the enemy. In French parlance, some senior officials say, a mission usually meant the same as an American sortie, that is, a single flight by a single plane.

In contrast, United States fighter-bombers flew 17,731 sorties against enemy positions near Khe Sanh in the 63 days between January 22 and March 24. In addition, B-52 bombers flew 334 missions, a mission including a minimum of three and a maximum of 12 planes.

What is more, the officers add, the average American fighter-bomber carries 2,000 to 2,700 pounds of ordnance, while the B-52s carry 27 tons. France's largest fighter-bombers carried only 500 pounds.

"Compared with what we are doing to the enemy, the French planes conducted only harassment raids," one Air Force officer said, adding that Mr. Fall concluded in his book that the outcome would have been different had even 100 American planes come to the aid of the French.

"You have to remember that if we have to, we could send many more planes against the enemy at Khe Sanh," another United States military official said. "We aren't hitting him with all we have by any means."

He added that Khe Sanh would ultimately become a major test of the ability of bombers to stop a major ground assault.

"We believe that, while we have not stopped all enemy activity around Khe Sanh, we have reduced his strength enough to prevent him from being able to wage a successful attack," he said.

APPENDIX XXXV

The New York *Times*
March 28, 1968
IN HUE, GRAVES DISCLOSE EXECUTIONS BY THE ENEMY

By Stewart Harris

The following dispatch is by Stewart Harris, a corre-
spondent of the Times *of London.*

HUE, South Vietnam--North Vietnam's army and the Vietcong
executed many South Vietnamese, some Americans, and a few
other foreigners during the fighting last month at Hue.

I am sure of this after spending several days in Hue in-
vestigating allegations of killings and torture. I am
not convinced about the torture, although men who saw
many bodies and seem balanced in their judgment are so
convinced.

Frank Jakes, an American official in charge of psychological operations, said that he could get no conclusive
evidence of torture, noting that no bodies had been
medically examined.

In the green valley of Nam Hoa, about 10 miles southwest
of Hue, I was with Warrant Officer Ostara, an Australian
advisor with the South Vietnamese Army, who has been here
for four years, speaks a little Vietnamese, and knows
the village of Nam Hoa very well.

TWO BODIES FOUND

We were standing on the sloping sides of a recently dug
hole. In the bottom were rush mats over sheets of plastic.
Mr. Ostara drew them back, revealing the bodies of two
Vietnamese with their arms tied behind their backs just
above the elbows. They had been shot through the back
of their heads.

The day before, 27 women from the village walked out three
miles carrying mattocks to dig for their missing husbands
and sons, having heard about this patch of disturbed earth
near the roadside. Mr. Ostara was with them as they
worked. They left the unrecognized bodies for others to
look at.

241

Driving back to the village, Mr. Ostara said that the enemy had come through on the way to Hue. They had taken 27 men. Some were leaders and some were younger, strong enough to be porters or even auxiliary soldiers.

Graves are still being discovered. On the previous afternoon, Mr. Jakes took me to Long Tho, about three miles west of Hue on the south side of the Huong River.

We came upon a woman wailing and throwing herself about between two coffins. In them were her two sons, who had been at high school and had gone with or been taken by the enemy on February 29. Their bodies were taken from a grave discovered two miles away the previous day.

Another family was gathered beside two more coffins. They wore the traditional white headbands for mourning. One body was that of a 20-year-old youth whose sister said that he had disappeared on February 15.

Another body was brought in, slung between two bamboo poles. Down the road, in a shattered house, was the body of the hamlet chief, the father of six little children.

Earlier that afternoon I had talked with Bob Kelly, the senior provincial advisor in Thua Thien, who has been in Vietnam for many years and speaks the language fluently.

"I have heard of no confirmed instances of torture," Mr. Kelly said. "Men were simply condemned by drumhead courts and executed as enemies of the people. These were the leaders, often quite small men. Others were executed when their usefulness ceased; or when they didn't cooperate they were shot for their trouble."

TORTURE IS DOUBTED

"Some of my staff were badly mutilated, but I am inclined to believe this was done after they were killed. Their hands were tied and they were shot behind the head. I helped to dig one body out, but I have been told by Vietnamese whom I respect that some people were buried alive."

Lt. Gregory Sharp, an American advisor with the South Vietnamese 21st Ranger Battalion, said that his men came across about 25 new graves in a cemetery five miles east of Hue on March 14.

From half a dozen of the graves, the heads were sticking up out of the sandy soil.

"They had been buried alive, I think," Lieutenant Sharp said. "There were sort of scratches in the sand in one place, as if someone had clawed his way out, but then he may have been playing possum. I don't really know."

At Quan Tan Gan, three Australian warrant officers saw seven men in one of three graves they had found. The seven, they said, had been shot one after the other, through the back of the head, hands tied.

INSPECTED SITES

Soon after arriving in Hue, I went in a jeep with three South Vietnamese officers to inspect sites where the bodies of executed men were said to have been found.

We went first to Gia Hoi High School in District 2, east of the Citadel. Here, 22 new graves had been found, each containing three to seven bodies. It is still a horrifying place. The officers told me that victims had been tied and, again, that most had been shot through the head. But some had been buried alive, they added.

Estimates of the number of people executed in the Hue area vary. The most conservative was given by the police chief, Doan Cong Lap, who said the figure was about 200. Other civilian casualty figures he gave were: killed 3,776; wounded, 1,909; captured or taken away, 1,041.

There are about 40,000 Roman Catholic Vietnamese in Hue. What happened to them? Information comes from several people who would be safer if they were anonymous.

CATHOLIC RESISTED FOE

About three-quarters of the Catholics in Hue live in Phu Cam, on the southern outskirts of the city. They resisted strongly when the enemy came in and some were executed. Four South Vietnamese priests were taken away and three foreign priests were killed.

Two French priests were given permission by the Vietcong to return to Phu Cam and help the sisters--and then were shot on the way back. But this might have been an error. Another French priest, a Benedictine, was executed, perhaps because he was chaplain to the Americans.

One thing is abundantly clear: The Vietcong and North Vietnamese put into practice, with their usual efficiency, the traditional communist policy of punishing by execution selected leaders who support their enemies, the government

of South Vietnam and its American allies. They also
executed American allies. They also executed American
civilian advisors.

In Hue, as elsewhere, they were unable, on the whole, to
capture and execute the more important officials, because
these men are careful to protect themselves in heavily
fortified compounds, defended by soldiers and the police.
In Hue, as elsewhere, the more defenseless people were the
victims--the village and hamlet chiefs, the teachers, and
the policemen.

According to the police chief, Doan Cong Lap, the government has 477 Vietcong and North Vietnamese soldiers in
custody.

"What about suspects?" he was asked. "What about officials
and civilians who should have supported the government
and either went over to the enemy or went into hiding
until they saw the government would win? How many of
these have you taken?"

After three visits to the police chief and one to the new
provincial chief, Colonel Than, the figure was given:
"Nearly 300."

They also said that none of these people had been executed
and that none had been brought to trial. Colonel Khoa,
the provincial chief until two weeks ago, had been given
temporary power to execute summarily any traitor holding
a senior position. Moreover, six weeks ago the South
Vietnamese promised to set up immediately a military
tribunal in Hue. Yet no one has been tried.

Colonel Khoa disappeared for several days, and then
reappeared with a tale about shooting, with his guards, 11
Vietcong. Yet his house must be one of very few in Hue
that is not damaged.

According to Chief Lap, the only men likely to be executed
are two who have been members of the Vietcong for a long
time and a third man whose name he could not remember.

PRESS LIST: CORRESPONDENTS ACCREDITED BY THE
U.S. MILITARY ASSISTANCE COMMAND, VIETNAM, APRIL 1, 1968

ABE, Hiroyoshi (Japan), *Manichi Shimbun* (Tokyo); ADAM,
Raymond (France), ORTF-TV (Paris); ADAMS, Edward T.
(U.S.A.), AP; AHMAD, Ishtiaq (India), ITV News (London);
AHN, Chyel-hoon (Korea), *Daihan Ilbo* (Seoul); AHN, Kyong-
Ho (Korea), Saehan Film Co. (Seoul); ALLEN, Anne (U.S.A.),
Overseas Weekly; ALLEN, George N. (U.S.A.), ABC News
(Ass't Bureau Chief); ALLOT, Emanuel (France), *Minute*
(Newspaper) (Paris); ALSOP, Joseph W. (U.S.A.), Washington
Post; AMINOFF, Cary A. (U.S.A.), CBS News; AN, Pham Xuan
(Vietnam), *Time-Life* News Service; ANDERSON, Virginia M.
(U.S.A.), Free Lance; ANH, Nguyen Ngoc (Vietnam), UPI;
ARAKAKI, Seikyo (Japan), Ryukyu *Shimpo* (Naha); ARMSTRONG,
O. K. (U.S.A.), *Readers Digest*; ARNDT, Detlev (Germany),
NBC News; ARNETT, Peter (New Zealand), AP.

BA, Phan-Van (Vietnam), CBS News; BA, Phung-Van (Vietnam),
NHK-TV; BAI, Soung-yung (Korea), Daihan News Film; BAKER,
Donald E. (U.S.A.), ABC News; BALSIGER, Peter (Switzerland),
Blick (Switzerland); BARBER, Charles H. (U.S.A.), Free
Lance; BAY, Le-Dinh (Vietnam), Vietnam Press; BEL, Gary L.
(U.S.A.), NBC News (Ass't Bureau Chief); BELDEN, James L.
(U.S.A.), Graphic Publications (Manila); BENNETTS, Richard
J. (Australia), Melbourne *Age*; BERNSTEIN, Kenneth M.
(U.S.A.), NBC News; BINGHAM, Samuel A. (U.S.A.), Empire
News Service; BINH, Roan (Vietnam), Vietnam Press; BINH,
Thai Don (Vietnam), *Time-Life* News Service; BIRCH, Michael
Y. (Australia), Australian Associated Press; BLEWETT,
Denis H. (Gr. Britain), London *Daily Express*; BLOCKER, Joel
L. (U.S.A.), *Newsweek* (Bureau Chief); BLOCKER, Karin B.
(France), *Newsweek*; BLOOM, Daniel H. (U.S.A.) CBS News
(Bureau Chief); BOHMAN, Kristina (Sweden), *Dagens Nyheter*
(Stockholm); BOLO, Felix P. (France), AFP: BOLO, Joyce R.
(U.S.A.), Washington *Post*; BONAVIA, David (Gr. Britain),
London *Times*; BONG, Bach-Huu (Vietnam), CBS News; Braestrup,
Peter (U.S.A.), Washington *Post* (Bureau Chief); Brannigan,
William A. (U.S.A.), ABC News; Brauer, Alex (France), CBS

News; BRIGGS, Charles W. (U.S.A.), *Contact* Magazine; BROOKS,
William B. (U.S.A.), *Free Pacific* Magazine; BROWNING, Robert
(Australia), Free Lance; BROWNLOW, Cecil A. (U.S.A.),
Aviation Week Magazine; BRYAN, Ann (U.S.A.), *Overseas Weekly*
BUCHARD, Robert (Switzerland), ORTF-TV (Paris); BUCKLEY,
Kevin P. (U.S.A.), *Newsweek*; BUCKLEY, Thomas F. S. (U.S.A.),
New York *Times* (Ass't Bureau Chief); BULAONG, Manuel Q.
(Philippines), *Philippine Daily Star* (Manila); BURKE,
Patrick J. (Ireland), National Catholic News Service; BURNS,
Michael K. (U.S.A.), Washington *Post*; BURROWS, Larry (Gr.
Britain), *Life* Magazine.

CAM, La Van (Vietnam), ABC News; CAN, Ha Thuc (Vietnam),
CBS News; CANTWELL, John L. (Australia), *Time-Life* News
Service; CAPPO, Jolynne (U.S.A.), Vietnam Press; CARROLL,
John S. (U.S.A.), Baltimore *Sun* (Bureau Chief); CASTLE,
Francis J., Jr. (U.S.A.), Okinawa *Morning Star*; CAT,
Nguyen Khiem (Vietnam), CBS News; CAU, Nguyen-Van (Vietnam),
UPI; CHA, Soo Yil (Korea), *News of Korea* (Seoul); CHAI, Iel
(Korea), *Meil Kyung Je Shinmun* (Seoul); CHANG, Albert
(U.S.A.), AP: CHANG, Joon-Wou (Korea), Dongyang Broadcasting
Co., Ltd.; CHANG, Pham Cong (Vietnam), CBS News; CHAUVEL,
Jean (France), *Le Figaro* (Paris); CHEATHAM, Thomas W.
(U.S.A.), UPI; CHINH, Trinh-Xuan (Vietnam), Vietnam Press;
CHO, Sung-Gack (Korea), *Joong-ang Ilbo* (Seoul); CHOI, Dong-
hi (Korea), *Korea Herald* (Seoul); CHOI, In Jip (Korea), ABC
News; CHOI, Kwang-Tae (Korea), Australian TV News; CHOI,
Tae Soon (Korea), Donghwa News Agency (Seoul); CHU, Yong-
Fan (Korea), *Korea Life* (Seoul); CHUN, Hee Ryung (Korea),
KBS-TV (Seoul); CHUNG, Byung-Mo (Korea), Okinawa *Morning
Star*; CHUNG, Haeng-Soo (Korea), *Kyonghyang Shinmun* (Seoul);
CHUNG, Nguyen-Huu (Vietnam), CBS News; COATES, John W.
(U.S.A.), NBC News; COFFEY, Raymond R. (U.S.A.), Chicago
Daily News (Bureau Chief); COI, Nguyen Dinh (Vietnam), NBC
News; COLLANDER, Lars (Sweden), Swedish Broadcasting
Corp. (Stockholm); CORPORA, Thomas (U.S.A.), UPI; CORRADI,
Egisto (Italy), *Corriere Della Sera* (Milan); COZART, Douglas
(U.S.A.), World Vision (Tokyo)(Bureau Chief); COZZI,
Angelo (Italy), *Corriere Della Sera* (Milan); CRANBOURNE,
Raymond (Australia), Empire News Service; CROYDON-FOWLER,
Robin (Gr. Britain), BBC; CUNG, Le Ngoc (Vietnam), AP;
CUNNINGHAM, Paul J. (U.S.A.), NBC News; CUONG, Pham-Gia
(Vietnam), CBS News; CUTTS, Robert L. (U.S.A.), Free Lance.

DAN, Pham Tan (Vietnam), CBS News; DAN, Vinh (Vietnam),
CBS News; DANG, Le-Quang (Vietnam), UPI; DANG, Nguyen Thuy
(Vietnam), *Time Life* News Service; DANG, Phan Bach
(Vietnam), NBC News; DANOIS, Jacques (Belgium), Radio
Luxembourg; D'ARAZIEN, Steven S. (U.S.A.), Collegiate
Press; Dau, Truong-Thi (Vietnam), German TV (Cologne);
DAVIS, Michael (U.S.A.), Baltimore *Afro-American*; DAVIS,
Neil Brian (Australia), Visnews, Ltd. (London); DAY, Bonner
H. (U.S.A.), *U.S. News & World Report*; DE, Hoang-Dinh

(Vietnam), CBS News; DE, Nguyen Xuan (Vietnam), ABC News;
DE ANDRADE, Luis Edgar (Brazil),*Manchete* Magazine (Brazil);
DECKARD, James F. (U.S.A.), ABC News; DEEPE, Beverly
(U.S.A.), *Christian Science Monitor*; DE JONG, Daniel S.
(U.S.A.), World Vision (Tokyo); DELL, Thomas (U.S.A.),
Free Lance; DEMARCO, Joseph (U.S.A.), Okinawa *Morning
Star*; DEMBART, Lee B. (U.S.A.), Queens College *Phoenix*;
DERBY, Daniel H. (U.S.A.), Washington College *Elm*
(Chestertown, Md.); DESYLVA, James C. (U.S.A.), ABC News;
DEVENISH, Ross (Gr. Britain), Rediffusion TV (London);
DEWEY, George (U.S.A.), World Wide Press (Burbank, Cal.);
DEWHURST, Brian (Australia), UPI; DICKERMAN, Sherwood
(U.S.A.), *Newsday*; DICKERSON, Dennis (Gr. Britain),
World Vision (Tokyo); DINH, Le Kim (Vietnam), UPI; DINH,
Le Phuc (Vietnam), NBC News; DINH, Nguyen Ai (Vietnam),
Kyodo News Service (Tokyo); DINH, Pham-Ngoc (Vietnam),
Reuters; DOAN, Huynh Van (Vietnam), NHK; DOE, Charles O.
(U.S.A.), Free Lance; DONG, Duong Thien (Vietnam), *U.S.
News & World Report*; DONGHI, Frank F. (U.S.A.), NBC News;
DONNELLY, John B. (U.S.A.), *Newsweek*; DRUMMEN, Jean C.
(Netherlands), Z.O.P. News Syndicate (Netherlands);
DUC, Nguyen Van (Vietnam), World Vision (Tokyo).

EDDY, Frank M. (Australia), ABC News; EEG-
HENRIKSEN, Jan (Norway), Free Lance; EGGLESTON, Charles R.
(U.S.A.), UPI; ELLENA, Nicholas R. (U.S.A.), Chico (Cal.)
Enterprise-Record; ELLISON, Robert J. (U.S.A.), Empire
News Service; ELPHICK, Robert E. (Gr. Britain), BBC;
EMERY, Fred (Gr. Britain), London *Times*; ESPER, George
(U.S.A.), AP; EVERLY, Joe R. (U.S.A.), Free Lance.

FAAS, Horst (Germany), AP; FALLON, John N. (U.S.A.), UPI;
FAN, Wei-tao (China), Continental Research Institute
(Hong Kong); FANE, Francis D. (U.S.A.), Mutual Broadcasting
System; FAVIER, Claude A. (France), CBS News; FINCHER,
Terence E. (Gr. Britain), London *Daily Express*; FITZGIBBON,
Alan L. (U.S.A.),*Medical Tribune* (New York); FITZSTEVENS,
John A. (U.S.A.), *Christian Children's Fund World News*;
FLACHMEYER, Hansjoerg (Germany), *Neue Revue* (Hamburg);
FLEMING, James S. (Canada), Rogers Broadcasting, Ltd.
(Toronto); FOISIE, Jack F. (U.S.A.), Los Angeles *Times*;
FOX, Thomas C. (U.S.A.), *National Catholic Reporter*;
FRANKLAND, F. Mark (Gr. Britain), London *Observer*;
FREPPEL, Denis A. (France), NBC News; FRIED, Joseph
(U.S.A.), N.Y. *Daily News*; Mutual Broadcasting System;
FROMSON, Murray (U.S.A.), CBS News; FUJITA, Hiroshi (Japan),
Kyodo News Service.

GALE, Kenneth A. (U.S.A.), ABC News; GIAC, Vi (Vietnam),
NBC News; GIANG, Ngo Anh (Vietnam), CBS News; GIBSON, Nathan
C. (U.S.A.), UPI; GLENNON, Thomas J. (U.S.A.), NBC News;
GLORVIGEN, Bjorn Erik (Norway), *NA* Magazine (Oslo); GOLD-
SMITH, Michael (Gr. Britain), AP; GORDON, John (U.S.A.),
Empire News; GORDON, Susanne W. (U.S.A.), Empire News;

GRALNICK, Jeffrey C. (U.S.A.), CBS News; GREEN, Martyn
K. E. (Gr. Britain), Free Lance; GREENSPON, Arthur R.
(U.S.A.), Free Lance; GREENWAY, Hugh (U.S.A.), *Time-Life*
News Service; GRIFFITHS, Philip (Gr. Britain), Magnum
Photos (Paris); GROUSSARD, Serge H. (France), *L'Aurore*
(Newspaper) (Paris); GRUBNAU, Lutz E. (Germany), NBC News;
GRUDINISKI, Ulrich (Germany), DPA (Hamburg).

HA, Ho-Thi-My (Vietnam), *Life* Magazine; HACKETT, Daniel
J. (Gr. Britain), BBC; HAI, Doan Van (Vietnam), CBS
News; HALL, Wilson D. (U.S.A.), NBC News; HAN, Hyohk Hoon
(Korea), *New Nation*; HANDY, Robert D. (U.S.A.), Free Lance;
HANGEN, Welles (U.S.A.), NBC News; HANH, Tran-Binh
(Vietnam), *Newsweek*; HARRIS, Richard G. (U.S.A.), ABC News;
HARRIS, Stewart (Australia), London *Times*; HATHAWAY, Paul
R. (U.S.A.), Washington *Star*; HEDMAN, Lars H. (U.S.A.),
Free Lance; HELLER, Ib (Denmark), UPI; HENDRICKS, Billy H.
(U.S.A.), Fort Worth *Star-Telegram*; HENKEL, Eloise E.
(U.S.A.), Free Lance; HERENDEEN, Dale S. (U.S.A.),
Christianity Today; HERR, Michael D. (U.S.A.), *Esquire*
Magazine; HESS, Peter (Switzerland), *Neue Zurcher Zeitung*
(Zurich); HEWETT, Herbert Glenn (U.S.A.), Free Lance;
HIEN, Do Thi Thuy (Vietnam), ABC News; HIRASHIKI, Yasutsume
(Japan), ABC News; HIROSE, Shozo (Japan), *Yomiuri Shimbun*
(Tokyo); HIRUNSI, Thonong (Thailand), CBS News; HOA, Le
Vinh (France), CBS News; HOAN, Pham Boi (Vietnam), CBS
News; HOANG, Dang Khac (Vietnam), NBC News); HOANG, Vu-Thuy
(Vietnam), Washington *Post*; HOFFMAN, Volker D. (Germany),
German TV-2; HOLLINGWORTH, Clare (Gr. Britain), *Daily
Telegraph* (London); HOLLOWAY, Joseph O. Jr. (U.S.A.),
AP; HONG, Dang-Thi-Le (Vietnam), Manila *Times*; HONG, Ingoon
(Korea), *Dong-A Ilbo* (Seoul); HONG, Kyung-Han (Korea),
Dong-A Ilbo (Seoul) (Bureau Chief); HONG, Sung Chan
(Korea), Australian TV News; HONG, Tran-Dinh (Lam) (Vietnam),
ABC News; HONORIN, Michael (France), ORTF-TV (Paris); HOOK,
Donald J. (Australia), Australian Broadcasting Commission;
HOSHINO, Kyoichi (Japan), NHK; HUAN, Dang-Van (Vietnam),
AP; HUGHES, John (U.S.A.), *Christian Science Monitor*;
HUMPHRIES, James F. (U.S.A.), Baptist Mission Press; HUYNH,
Vo (Vietnam), NBC News; HWANG, Ching Fung (China), Central
News Agency (Taiwan); HWANG, Chong-ik (Korea), *Chosun Ilbo*
(Seoul); HYDRAIOS, Steve (Canada), CBS News; HYMOFF, Edward
(U.S.A.), M.W. Lads Publishing Co.

I, Chen-hua (China), *Min Tsu Evening News* (Taipei); IKEBE,
Shigetoshi (Japan), *Asahi Shimbun* (Tokyo); ISAKSSON, Bo
(Sweden), Swedish Broadcasting Corp.

JAFFE, Sam A. (U.S.A.), ABC News; JESSEN, Alex F. (U.S.A.),
Free Lance; JOHNER, Claude (France), Free Lance; JOHNSON,
Thomas A. (U.S.A.), N.Y. *Times*; JOHNSON, Howard (Gr. Britain)

Daily Mirror (London); JOHNSTON, Frank B. (U.S.A.), UPI;
JONES, Harold Y. (U.S.A.), Free Lance; JORDAN, Philip
Jr. (U.S.A.), Free Lance.

KALB, Bernard (U.S.A.), CBS News; KALISCHER, Peter (U.S.A.),
CBS News; KANG, Won-Kyun (Korea), *Christian Times*
(Seoul); KANN, Peter R. (U.S.A.), *Wall Street Journal*;
KARSHAN, Howard A. (U.S.A.), CBS News; KATO, Tsugio (Japan),
Asahi Shimbun (Tokyo); KAWAMOTO, Kazutaka (Japan),
Kyodo News Service (Tokyo); KAY, Keith (U.S.A.), CBS News;
KAYLOR, Robert L. Jr. (U.S.A.), UPI; KAZICKAS, Jurate C.
(U.S.A.), Free Lance; KEATLEY, Robert (U.S.A.), *Wall Street
Journal*; KHA, Tran-Van (Vietnam), ABC News; KHIEM, Tran
(Vietnam), CBS News; KHOO, Terence (Singapore), ABC News;
KIM, Beong-gil (Korea), *Sedae* Magazine (Seoul); KIM, Chuong-
Up (Korea), *Hankook Ilbo* (Seoul); KIM, John W. (Korea),
Seoul *Shinmun* (Bureau Chief); KIM, Ki Sam (Korea), AP;
KIM, Sook-Kyu (Korea), Australian TV News; KIM, Tae-Ho
(Korea), *Korean Resident News*; KIM, Trinh Van (Vietnam),
ABC News; KIRK, Donald (U.S.A.), Washington *Star*; KIRK,
Susanne S. (U.S.A.), Washington *Star*; KLEVEN, Leslie S.
(U.S.A.), KBHB Radio (Sturgis, S.D.); KO, Byong Eun (Korea),
Yowon Magazine (Seoul); KRAMER, Barry (U.S.A.), AP; KRAMER,
Fred A. (U.S.A.), *Stars & Stripes*; KUMADA, Masahiro (Japan),
Sankei Shimbun.

LAMBERT, Frances H. (U.S.A.), Okinawa *Morning Star*; LAN,
Dang Tran (Vietnam), Reuters; LANGGUTH, Arthur J. (U.S.A.),
N.Y. *Times*; LARAMY, Ronald B. (Gr. Britain), Reuters;
LAURENT, Cecil Saint (France), *Combat Journal* (Paris);
LEBON, Andre (France), Gaumont Actualités; LEE, Albert
(U.S.A.), *Asian Industry* (Hong Kong); LEE, Bok-whan (Korea),
Myung Rang Magazine (Seoul); LEE, Chang-Min (Korea), *Asia*
Magazine (Hong Kong); LEE, Chang-one (Korea), KBS-TV
(Seoul); LEE, Duk (Korea), *Korea Report* (Seoul); LEE, Hao-
bum (Korea), Seoul *Shinmun*; LEE, James (Korea), Australian
TV News; LEE, Tae Hung (Korea), ABC News; LEINSTER, Colin
R. (Gr. Britain), *Life* Magazine (Ass't Bureau Chief);
LEME, Jose Camere (Portugal), *Diario Popular* (Lisbon);
LENGEL, John B. (U.S.A.), AP; LEROY, Catherine (France),
Free Lance; LESCAZE, Lee (U.S.A.), Washington *Post*; LESCAZE,
Rebecca (U.S.A.), Washington *Post*; LETT, Patrick A. (Gr.
Britain), ABC News; LEWIS, Lang (U.S.A.), *Army Times*;
LEYDEN, Peter (Australia), ABC News; LIEN, Do Xuan (Vietnam),
UPITN; LINH, Doan Van (Vietnam), German TV (Bureau Chief);
LIVINGSTON, James (U.S.A.), World Vision (Tokyo); LOC,
Germaine (Vietnam), NBC News; LOC, Pham (Vietnam), UPI;
LOC, Truong (Vietnam), Vietnam Press; LONG, Nguyen Thanh
(Vietnam), ABC News; LORIEUX, Claude (France), AFP;
LUMINELLO, Patrick A. (U.S.A.), *Stars & Stripes*; LYLAP,
Marie Helene (France), CBS News.

MACH, Nguyen-Van (Vietnam), UPI; MACLEISH, Roderick
(U.S.A.), Westinghouse Broadcasting Co. (London);
MACLENNAN, John W. (Gr. Britain), Reuters; MANGOLD,
Thomas C. (Gr. Britain), BBC; MARAVENTANO, Vanni (Italy),
La Nazione (Florence); MARRIOTT, Michael E. (Australia),
CBS News; MARRIOTT, Rikki E. M. (Australia), CBS News;
MARTIN, T. Craig (U.S.A.), Lerner Home Newspapers
(Chicago); MARTINEZ, Vincente G. (Philippines), *Philippine
Daily Star* (Manila); MASON, Herbert H. G. (Gr. Britain),
BBC; MASUOKA, Tadatoshi (Japan), *Mainichi Shimbun* (Tokyo);
MATHER, Ian J. (Gr. Britain), London *Daily Mail*; MAYR,
Heini (Austria), *Neue Revue* (Hamburg); MCARTHUR, George
(U.S.A.), AP (Ass't Bureau Chief); MERICK, Wendell (U.S.A.),
U.S. News & World Report; MERRON, Richard (U.S.A.), AP;
MILLIGAN, Ronald E. (U.S.A.), Westinghouse Broadcasting
Co. (London); MINH, Dang Van (Vietnam), ABC News; MINH,
Tran Dai (Vietnam), UPI; MINH, Truong Ve (Vietnam), Radio
Vietnam; MOCHIDA, Takeshi (Japan), Jiji Press Service
(Tokyo); MOHR, Charles H. (U.S.A.), N.Y. *Times*; MOORE,
Peyton M. (U.S.A.), Baptist Mission Press; MOORE, S. Gary
(U.S.A.), NBC News; MORITA, Koichiro (Japan), International
News Service (Tokyo); MORROW, Michael D. (U.S.A.),
Dartmouth Daily News (Hanover, N.H.); MOSER, Donald R.
(U.S.A.), *Life* Magazine (Bureau Chief); MUI, Dao-Duc (Viet-
nam), UPI; MUSGROVE, Helene A. (U.S.A.), Free Lance;
MYDANS, Carl M. (U.S.A.), *Life* Magazine.

NAM, Chau-Van (Vietnam), Pan-Asia Newspaper Alliance
(Tokyo); NAM, Nguyen Van (Vietnam), UPI; NANCE, John
(U.S.A.), AP; NASH, Max O. (Gr. Britain), AP; NEEDHAM,
Edgar H. (U.S.A.), ABC News; NEEDHAM, Gloria (U.S.A.),
Free Lance; NESCH, Udo (Germany), CBS News; NESSEN, Ronald
H. (U.S.A.), NBC News; Neuhauser, Peter (Austria), *Stern*
Magazine (Hamburg); Newson, Dennis O. (Gr. Britain),
London *Sun*; NGHIA, Hoang-Trong (Vietnam), NBC News; NGOC,
Dinh-Van (Vietnam), AP; NGOC, Pham-Thi (Vietnam), *Yowon*
Magazine (Seoul); NGUON, Tieu-Lan (Vietnam), *Asahi Shimbun*
(Tokyo); NGUYEN, Ba-Linh (Vietnam), *Chunichi Shimbun* (Tokyo);
NGUYEN, Ngoc-Hanh (Vietnam), Vietnam Television; NGUYEN,
Nguyen Trong (Vietnam), *Time-Life* News Service; NGUYEN,
Pham Hoang (Vietnam), Vietnam Television; NGUYEN, Xuan-
Thai (Vietnam), NBC News; NHA, Thai-Thuc (Vietnam), Alpha
Films; NHUT, Trang-Van (Vietnam), NHK; NISHIMURA, Toshio
(Japan), *Asahi Shimbun* (Tokyo); NIVOLON, François (France),
Le Figaro (Paris); NODINE, Gladys Mae (U.S.A.), Okinawa
Morning Star; NOGUCHI, Hakushi (Japan), Hokkaido *Shimbun*;
NORMAN, John B. (Gr. Britain), BBC; NORMAND, Jean-Louis
(France), ORTF-TV (Paris); NORTH, Donald G. (Canada),
ABC News; NORUM, Roger F. (U.S.A.), UPI (Audio); NOSSAL,
Frederick C. (Canada), Toronto *Telegram*.

OBERDORFER, Donald Jr. (U.S.A.), Knight Newspapers;
O'CONNER, Patrick (Ireland); National Catholic Welfare
News Service; OGAWA, Satoshi (Japan), *Sankei Shimbun*;
OGURA, Sadao (Japan), *Yomiuri Shimbun* (Tokyo); OHMAN,
Robert D. (U.S.A.), AP; OKUO, Koichi (Japan), *Asahi Shimbun*
(Tokyo); OKUYAMA, Tatsu (Japan), *Yomiuri Shimbun* (Tokyo);
OLIVER, Richard V. (U.S.A.), UPI.

PABEL, Hilmar (Germany), *Stern* Magazine (Hamburg); PALADINO,
Ralph (U.S.A.), Queens College *Phoenix*; PALMOS, Francis
J. (Australia), Free Lance; PARIS, Richard (Australia),
Reuters; PARK, Ansong (Korea), Orient Press (Seoul);
PARK, Chin-seo (Korea), Seoul *Shinmun*; PATEL, Suresh M.
(Gr. Britain), German TV; PEARSON, Andrew (U.S.A.), ABC
News; PELOU, François (France), AFP (Bureau Chief); PELOU,
Shirley (U.S.A.), AFP; PERRY, Merton (U.S.A.), *Newsweek*;
PETERSON, Roger (U.S.A.), ABC News; PHILBY, John D. (Gr.
Britain), Free Lance; PHUOC, Dang Van (Vietnam), AP;
PICARDO, Percival S. (Philippines), Free Lance; PICKERELL,
James H. (U.S.A.), Free Lance; PIERCE, Robert W. (U.S.A.),
World Vision (Tokyo) (Ass't Bureau Chief); PIGOTT, Bruce S.
(Australia), Reuters; PINWILL, William R. (Australia),
Australian Broadcasting Co.; PISOR, Robert L. (U.S.A.),
Detroit *News* (Bureau Chief); POTTER, Kent B. (U.S.A.),
UPI; POWELL, David L. (U.S.A.), Free Lance; PRAGER, Karsten
(Germany), *Time-Life* News Service; PRINGLE, James (Gr.
Britain), Reuters (Bureau Chief), PY, Gerard (France),
CBS News.

QUAN, Ly Trieu (Vietnam), United Newspapers Photos (Taiwan);
QUANG, Le Tuong (Vietnam), CBS News; QUINT, Bert (U.S.A.),
CBS News; QUOC, Truong-Kien (Vietnam), *Yomiuri Shimbun*
(Tokyo); QUYEN, Nguyen Ba (Vietnam), Westinghouse
Broadcasting Co. (London).

RACE, Jeffrey (U.S.A.), Free Lance; RADEMAEKERS, William
(U.S.A.), *Time-Life* News Service (Bureau Chief); RANDOLPH,
John (U.S.A.), Los Angeles *Times*; RAO, Nguyen Ngoc (Vietnam),
Washington *Post*; REED, David E. (U.S.A.), *Reader's Digest*;
RENARD, Michel (Belgium), Free Lance; RENTMEESTER, Co
(Netherlands), *Time-Life* News Service; RI, Duong-Van (Viet-
nam), CBS News; RESLER, Elizabeth A. (U.S.A.), Free Lance;
RIBEIRO, Jose H. (Brazil), *Revista Realidade* (Sao Paulo);
RIDDICK, John D. (U.S.A.), Tucson (Ariz.) *Daily Citizen*;
RIDGEWAY, James (U.S.A.), *Contact* Magazine (Bureau Chief);
RISHER, Eugene V. (U.S.A.), UPI (Bureau Chief); RO, Shi-
hong (Korea), *Korea Herald* (Seoul); ROBERTS, Michael D.
(U.S.A.), Cleveland *Plain Dealer*; ROBERTSON, Frank
(Australia), *Daily Telegraph* (London); ROBINSON, Carl D.
(U.S.A.), AP; RODBOON, Vallop (Thailand), CBS News; ROLFES,
Frederic K. (U.S.A.), Free Lance; RONK, Donald E. (U.S.A.),
Collegiate Press Service; ROSEN, Sidney M. (U.S.A.),

Free Lance; ROSENBAUM, Richard (U.S.A.), ABC News
(Bureau Chief); ROSENBAUM, Thea L. (Germany), DPA
(Hamburg); ROSS, Denis A. (Australia), UPITN; ROSS,
Phillip A. (U.S.A.), NBC News; ROSS, Ronald M. (Gr.
Britain), Minneapolis *Tribune*; ROSSBACH, George (U.S.A.),
Bild-Zeitung (Hamburg); ROWAN, Roy (U.S.A.), *Life*
Magazine; RUDD, Hughes D. (U.S.A.), CBS News; RUSSELL,
John R. (U.S.A.), NBC News.

SAGER, Peter (Switzerland), *Correspondence Politique
Suisse*; SAHASHI, Yoshihiko (Japan), *Chunichi Shimbun*
(Tokyo); SAITO, Sanji (Japan), NHK; SAKAI, Tatsuo (Japan),
Nihon Keizai Shimbun; SATO, Shigebumi (Japan), Jiji Press
Service (Tokyo); SAW, Charles R. S. (Australia), Sydney
Daily Mirror; SAWADA, Kyoichi (Japan), UPI; SCHARLAU,
Winfried (Germany), German-TV (Hamburg); SCHNEIDER, John
A. (U.S.A.), Free Lance; SCHOETTLER, Carl A. (U.S.A.),
Baltimore *Sun*; SCHOUTE, Hendrika G. (Netherlands), Free
Lance; SCHWEDEN, Heinrich (Germany), *Rheinische Post*
(Dusseldorf); SEMZAKI, Takayuki (Japan), *Mainichi Shimbun*
(Tokyo); SENNA, Osamu (Japan), *Asahi Shimbun* (Tokyo);
SHAKER, Kenneth R. (U.S.A.), M.W. Lads Publishing Co.;
SHAPLEN, Robert (U.S.A.), *The New Yorker* (Bureau Chief);
SHIMAMOTO, Keisaburo (Japan), Imperial Press (Tokyo);
SHIN, Yeung-Ho (Korea), Korean Broadcasting System;
SIDER, Don (U.S.A.), *Time* Magazine; SILAYAN, Victor P.
(Philippines), Interisland Broadcasting Corp. (Manila);
SIMONPIETRI, Christian (France), Gamma Photo Agency (Paris);
SIMONS, Carol L. (U.S.A.), CBS News; SIMONS, Lewis M.
(U.S.A.), AP; SING, Yi-Ping (China), *Ta Hua Evening News*
(Taipei); SJOBERG, Sven-Erik (Sweden), *Dagens Nyheter*
(Stockholm); SKAKKE, Jorgen (Denmark), Denmarks Radio
(Copenhagen); SLOAN, Howard A. (U.S.A.), Penman House
(Seattle); SMITH, Charles P.(Gr. Britain), London *Sunday
Times*; SMITH, Jan (U.S.A.), CBS News; SMITH, John E.
(U.S.A.), CBS News; SMITH, Keith V. (Australia), Australian
Associated Press; SNEAD, Charles W. (U.S.A.), UPI; SO, Kim
(Vietnam), UPI; SON, Tran-Van (Vietnam), NHK; SON, Trinh-
hong (Vietnam), Gaumont Actualités; SON, Vo Thanh (Vietnam),
CBS News; SONG, Hochang (Korea), *Dong-A Ilbo* (Seoul);
SONG, Young-Wan (Korea), *Chosun Ilbo* (Seoul); SORENSEN,
Carl (Denmark), CBS News; SOUTHERLAND, Daniel R. (U.S.A.),
UPI; SOUTHERLAND, Thankful (U.S.A.), UPI; STEINMAN, Ronald
(U.S.A.), NBC News (Bureau Chief); STEPHANUS, Paul S.
(U.S.A.), Free Lance; STOKES, Robert S. (U.S.A.), *Newsweek*;
STONE, Dana (U.S.A.), UPI; STONE, Louise S. (U.S.A.), UPI;
STRAUSS, Suzanne (France), Canadian Broadcasting Corp.; SUH,
Kwo-zong (Korea), *Daihan Ilbo* (Seoul); SULLY, Francois
(France), *Newsweek*; SUM, Ma (Vietnam), United Newspapers
Photos (Taipei); SUONG, Josephine Tu Ngoc (Vietnam), NBC
News; SUU, Tran Duc (Vietnam), Independent TV News (London);
SUU, Vo (Vietnam), NBC News; SUZUKI, Toshio (Japan),
Yomiuri Shimbun (Tokyo); SWANSON, Richard L. (U.S.A.), Black

Star Publishing Co.; SYVERTSEN, George (U.S.A.), CBS News; SYVERTSEN, Gustawa (U.S.A.), CBS News.

TAKANO, Hiroshi (Japan), NHK; TAKEUCHI, Sadao (Japan), FUJI TV (Tokyo); TANAKA, Itaru (Japan), NHK; TANG, Y. B. (Gr. Britain), ABC News; TATE, Donald C. (U.S.A.), Scripps-Howard (Washington, D.C.); TATE, Frances D. (U.S.A.), Scripps-Howard (Washington, D.C.); TERRY, Wallace (U.S.A.), *Time* Magazine; THAI, Vu Van (Vietnam), Visnews; THAN, Nguyen-Cong (Vietnam), Kyodo News Service (Tokyo); THANH, Nguyen Ngoc Hoang (Vietnam), *Bild Zeitung* (Hamburg); THEM, Tran Kiem (Vietnam), *Chien Thang*; THEODORE, William J. (U.S.A.), NBC News; THEVENIN, Francois M. (France), Free Lance; THIEN, Tran Huu (Vietnam), CBS News; THIEP, Nguyen Dang (Vietnam), ABC News; THOMPSON, John H. (U.S.A.), Chicago *Tribune*; THONG, To-Van (Vietnam), ABC News; THU, Nguyen-Thang (Vietnam), Baltimore *Sun*; THU, Nguyen Thien (Vietnam), Okinawa *Morning Star*; TIEN, Truong Kha (Vietnam), ABC News; TO, Tran Khac (Vietnam), Vietnam National Motion Picture Center; TO, Vo-Van (Vietnam), Mainichi Newspapers (Tokyo); TOI, Le Van (Vietnam, *Life* Magazine; TOKUOKA, Takao (Japan), *Mainichi Shimbun* (Tokyo); TOMODA, Seki (Japan), *Sankei Shimbun* (Tokyo); TONG, Giang Chan (Vietnam), *Time-Life* News Service; TRAN, Gia Thai (Vietnam), CBS News; TREASTER, Joe (U.S.A.), N.Y. *Times*; TRINH, Huynh Minh (Vietnam), AP; TROELSTRUP, Glenn C. (U.S.A.), *Time-Life* News Service; TRONG, Nguyen (Vietnam), Los Angeles *Times*; TRONG, Tran Huu (Vietnam), ABC News; TU, Bien Van (Vietnam), Visnews; TU, Duong The (Vietnam), Washington *Star*; TU, Nguyen-Dinh (Vietnam), *The New Yorker*; TUAN, Phan-Manh (Vietnam), Alpha Films; TUCKER, Donald (U.S.A.), ABC News; TUCKMAN, Robert (U.S.A.), AP (Bureau Chief); TUCKNER, Howard (U.S.A), NBC News; TUNG, Hoang Van (Vietnam), ABC News; TUNG, Truong-Thanh (Vietnam), UPI; TUOHY, Johanna I (Switzerland), Los Angeles *Times*; TUOHY, William K. (U.S.A.), Los Angeles *Times* (Bureau Chief); TUONG, Ho Van (Vietnam), UPITN; TY, Du-Ngoc (Vietnam), *Newsweek*.

VAN DER BYL, Andrew (Netherlands), Guideposts; VAN, Lim-Thanh (Vietnam), UPI; VAN GEEM, Isabelle (France), *Vietnam Nouveau*; VAN PEURSEM, Melvin J. (U.S.A.), World Vision (Tokyo); VERNON, John Oliver (Gr. Britain), BBC; VOLKERT, Kurt (U.S.A.), CBS News; VON ARNIM, Bernd (Germany), German TV-2; VON STOCKHAUSEN, Hans (Germany), German Radio & TV; VU, Nguyen (Vietnam), CBS News; VUONG, Nguyen Hung (Vietnam), *The New Yorker*.

WAGEN, Michael A. B. (Gr. Britain), BBC; WALLACE, Haya S. (U.S.A.), *U.S. News & World Report*; WALLACE, James N.

(U.S.A.), *U.S. News & World Report*; WALSH, John J.
(U.S.A.), UPI; WALSH, Lawrence A. (U.S.A.), CBS News;
WARD, Lawrence (U.S.A.), World Vision (Tokyo) (Ass't
Bureau Chief); WARREN, Douglas R. (U.S.A.), Free Lance;
WATSON, George H. Jr. (U.S.A.), ABC News; WEBB, Alvin
B. Jr. (U.S.A.), UPI; WEBB, Catherine M. (Gr. Britain),
UPI; WEBSTER, Donald H. (U.S.A.), CBS News (Ass't Bureau
Chief); WEINRAUB, Bernard (U.S.A.), N.Y. *Times*; WEISS,
Carl (Germany), German TV; WELDON, Harry L. (U.S.A.),
ABC News; WELTERS, Johann H. (Germany), German TV;
WHEELER, John (U.S.A.), AP; WHEELER, Nik J. (Gr. Britain),
Free Lance; WHISENANT, James L. (U.S.A.), ABC News
(Ass't Bureau Chief); WHITE, Edwin (U.S.A.), AP (Ass't
Bureau Chief); WHITE, Marvin E. Jr. (U.S.A.), NBC News;
WHITE, Sidney (U.S.A.), N.Y. *Times*; WILDAU, Robert P.
(U.S.A.), *Time-Life* News Service; WILKINSON, Raymond M.
(Gr. Britain), UPI; WILLIAMS, Marion L. (U.S.A.), *Twin
Cities Courier* (Minneapolis-St. Paul, Minn.); WILLS-EVE,
Anton P. (Gr. Britain), Reuters; WILSON, Derek J. (Gr.
Britain), AFP; WILSON, George C. (U.S.A.), Washington
Post; WINGO, Hal C. (U.S.A.), *Life* Magazine; WINTER,
Robert L. (U.S.A.), North Asia Press (Korea); WISE,
Donald A. (Gr. Britain), London *Daily Mirror*; WITTNER,
Dale E. (U.S.A.), *Life* Magazine; WOLEN, Seymour (U.S.A.),
CBS News; WOODRUFF, Lance R. (U.S.A.), National Council
of Churches News Service.

XUAN-MINH, Cong-tang Ton Nhu-Thi (Vietnam), Chicago *Daily
News*.

Y, Nguyen Van (Vietnam), NHK; YAMAMOTO, Kazuo (Japan),
Yomiuri Shimbun (Tokyo); YANG, Tae-jo (Korea), *Joong-Ang
Ilbo* (Seoul); YEN, Hoang-Xuan (Vietnam), Free Lance;
YOCUM, Lynn D. (U.S.A.), Sacramento *Report*; YOON, Tae
Ro (Korea), *New Nation*; YOSHIE, Masayoshi (Japan),
Asahi Shimbun (Tokyo); YOUNG, Perry D. (U.S.A.), UPI;
YU, Ji-hyung (Korea), *Chosun Ilbo* (Seoul); YU, Jin Seung
(Korea), Global Publishing Corp. (Boston); YU, Tae-wan
(Korea), *Hankook Ilbo* (Seoul); YUN, Pyong Uk (Korea),
Pusan *Ilbo*.

ZAUGG, Ernest L. (U.S.A.), Hometown Feature Service.

APPENDIX XXXVII

MILITARY CHRONOLOGY OF EVENTS AT KHE SANH

January 21   Khe Sanh Combat Base comes under heavy mortar, artillery, and rocket attack which destroys main ammunition dump. NVA battalion attacks and partially overruns Khe Sanh village before CAC (Combined Action Company) and RF companies drive off enemy. After second attack, Colonel Lownds withdraws defenders to confines of combat base.

January 22   COMUSMACV (Westmoreland) initiates Operation Niagara (B-52s) to provide massive air support for Khe Sanh.

           Lt. Col. Mitchell's 1/9 (1st Battalion, 9th Marine Regiment) arrives KSCB (Khe Sanh Combat Base) and takes up positions which encompass rock quarry southwest of combat base.

           E/2/26 (Company E, 2nd Battalion, 26th Marine Regiment) is relocated from Hill 558 to prominent ridgeline northeast of 861 as covering force for flank of 2/26; E/2/26 passes to operational control of 3rd Battalion. New position is called 861A.

January 23-28   Large number of tribesmen and families are evacuated from Khe Sanh area to avoid hostile fire.

Source: This chronology was compiled from material contained in Capt. Moyers S. Shore, USMC, *The Battle for Khe Sanh* (Washington, D.C.: Government Printing Office, 1969) and from entries in the 26th Marine Regiment Diary, Headquarters USMC, Washington, D.C.

January 27	37th ARVN Ranger Battalion (318 men) arrives KSCB and takes up positions in eastern sector of combat base.
January 30	Communists launch nationwide Tet offensive.
February 2-4	Two platoons ambushed from Lang Vei Special Forces camp and FOB (Special Forces base) #3.
February 5	NVA battalion attacks E/2/26 on Hill 861A in concert with heavy shelling of KSCB. Enemy gains foothold in northern sector of Company E perimeter but is driven out by savage counterattack; 109 NVA and 7 Marines KIA.
February 7	Special Forces camp at Lang Vei overrun by enemy battalion supported by PT-76 Soviet-built tanks; first use of NVA tanks in South Vietnam.
February 8	Some 3,000 indigenous personnel, both military and civilian, from Lang Vei move overland to Khe Sanh. After being searched and processed, several hundred refugees are air-evacuated.
	(Company) A/1/9 combat outpost 500 meters west of 1/9 perimeter hit and partially overrun by reinforced NVA battalion. During three-hour battle, reinforcements drive NVA from Marine position and with aid of supporting arms kill 150 North Vietnamese; Colonel Lownds decides to abandon outpost and units withdraw to 1/9 perimeter.
February 10	Marine C-130 (four-engine cargo plane) of VMGR (Marine Squadron)-152, hit by enemy fire during approach, crashes after landing at Khe Sanh and six are killed.
February 12	Enemy vehicle noises heard.
February-April	Paradrops, low-altitude extraction systems, and helicopters are primary means of resupplying 26th Marines due to bad weather and heavy enemy fire.

February 16	ARVN patrol gets contact, withdraws.
February 21	After heavy mortar and artillery barrage, NVA company probes 37th ARVN Ranger lines but withdraws after distant fire fight. It is estimated that 25-30 NVA were killed.
February 23	KSCB receives record number of incoming rounds for a single day--1,307.
	ARVN patrol finds estimated NVA battalion dug in.
	First appearance of enemy trench system south and southeast of KSCB.
	A/1/26 (Company A, 1st Battalion, 26th Marine Regiment) patrol seeking water near Hill 950 gets contact.
February 25	B/1/26 patrol ambushed south of KSCB; 23 Marines KIA.
February 27	CH-46 helicopter destroyed by mortar fire.
February 29–March 1	Estimated NVA regiment maneuvers to attack 37th ARVN Ranger positions but fail to reach defensive wire. B-52s hit within 1,800 meters. AO (Aerial Observer) reports NVA trenches parallel runway. 78 enemy KIA.
March 4	Small probe against ARVN.
March 6	USAF C-123 (twin-engined cargo plane) shot down east of runway; 43 USMC, 4 USAF, and 1 USN personnel killed.
	C-123 crashed/another damaged, burned March 17.
March 7	Large groups of refugees begin to filter into the combat base and are evacuated.
March 8	2 ARVN patrols attack enemy trenchline east of runway and kill 26 North Vietnamese.
March 12	ARVN "contact."
March 13	Probe against ARVN.

March 14	CH-46 helicopter downed.
March 15	American intelligence notes withdrawal of major NVA units from Khe Sanh area.[1]
March 15, 18	Light probe ARVN.
March 20	FOB #3 (Special Forces) patrol ambushed.
March 23	KSCB receives heaviest saturation of enemy rounds for the month of March--1,109. G-2: 325C Division at 5,000 meters of XD (map coordinates) 7040, two battalions of 29th NVA Regiment 325C Division near Hue, 8th Battalion/29th Regiment on Route 9 with 66th Regiment.
March 24	A/1/9 patrol kills 31 NVA west of 1/9 perimeter. Losses: 3 Marines. UH-1-E chopper lost.
March 25	1/9 Cav. Sqd. (1st Squadron/9th Cavalry Regiment), 1st ACD (Air Cavalry Division) begins reconnaissance in force operations east of Khe Sanh in preparation for Operation Pegasus.
March 26	B/1/9 kills 26 NVA from 325C Division.
March 28	CH-46 helicopter lost.
March 30	B/1/26 attacks enemy fortified position south of combat base and kills 115 NVA; 9 Marines are KIA.
	D/1/9 kills NVA on patrol XD 827416.
	Operation Scotland I terminates with 1,602 confirmed NVA and 205 Marines KIA; estimates place probable enemy dead between 10,000 and 15,000.
	In March: 718 enemy KIA, 65 friendly KIA, 286 WIA (evacuated).
	Task Force KILO launches diversionary attack along Gio Linh coastal plain to divert attention away from Ca Lu where

---

[1]320th Division never closer than 20 kilometers to Khe Sanh; 325C Division came in from west and north; 304th Division south of Highway Nine.

1st ACD, and 1st Marines are staging for Operation Pegasus.[2]

April 1   Operation Pegasus begins; 2/1 and 2/3 (1st Marines) attack west from Ca Lu along Route 9. Elements of 3rd Brigade, 1st ACD conduct helo assaults into LZ (Landing Zone) Mike and Cates. Joint engineer task force begins repair of Route 9 from Ca Lu to Khe Sanh.

April 3   2nd Brigade, 1st ACD assaults LZs Tom and Wharton.

April 4   1/5 Cav. Sqd. moves northwest from LZ Wharton and attacks enemy units near old French fort; 1st Battalion, 9th Marines moves southeast from rock quarry and assaults Hill 471.

April 5   1/9 repulses enemy counterattack on Hill 471 and kills 122 NVA.

           1st Brigade, 1st ACD departs Ca Lu and assaults LZ Snapper.

April 6   One company of 3rd ARVN Airborne Task Force airlifted to KSCB for the initial link-up with defenders.

           Elements of 2nd Brigade, 1st ACD relieve 1st Battalion, 9th Marines on Hill 471; 1/9 commences sweep to northwest toward Hill 689.

           1st Brigade, 1st ACD helilifted north of KSCB. 2/26 and 3/26 push north of combat base; Company G, 2/26 engages enemy force and kills 48 NVA.

April 8   2/7 Cav. Sqd. links up with 26th Marines and conducts official relief of combat base. 1/26 attacks to the west.

           3rd ARVN Airborne Task Force air assaults into LZ Snake west of Khe Sanh and kills 78 NVA.

---

[2]Only five days went by without close air support in March.

CORRESPONDENT VISITS TO AMERICAL DIVISION, 1968-1969
(DEPARTMENT OF THE ARMY, STAFF COMMUNICATIONS DIVISION)

Date	Visits	Press (Printed) Media	Visits	Broadcast Media
1968				
January	0	--	0	--
February	1	*Christian Science Monitor*	1	NBC
March	4	AP, London *Times*, AFP, Washington *Post*	1	NBC
April	1	*National Geographic*	1	NBC
May	1	AP	0	--
June	1	UPI	3	NBC, ABC, CBS
July	3	UPI	10	ABC, NBC, CBS, UPI Telenews
August	2	AP, UPI	2	UPI Telenews, ABC
September	5	AP, UPI, AFP, *Time-Life*	3	ABC, NBC, CBS
October	7	AFP, *U.S. News & World Report*	1	CBS
November	1	Washington *Post*	2	CBS
December	0	--	0	--
Total 1968	26		24	

1969

January	10	UPI, AFP, AP	20	CBS, ABC, NBC
February	4	Reuters, AP, UPI	5	NBC, CBS, ABC, BBC
March	2	AP, UPI	1	NBC
April	4	AP, UPI, Boston *Globe*	3	NBC, ABC
May	4	AP, UPI	0	--
June	4	UPI, AP, Reuters	5	NBC, CBS
July	2	New York *Times*	1	NBC
August	18	AP, UPI, Reuters, *Newsweek*, New York *Times*, *Time-Life*, Washington *Star*, Scripps Howard	8	CBS, ABC, NBC
September	0	--	1	NBC
October	5	AP, UPI, New York *Times*	2	CBS, NBC
November	25	AP, New York *Times*, *Newsweek*, Reuters, UPI, *Time-Life*, AFP	11	ABC, NBC, CBS
December	0	--	0	--
Total 1969	78		57	
Grand Total	104		81	

APPENDIX XXXIX

BACKGROUND MEMORANDUM, FREEDOM HOUSE NEWS MEDIA CONFERENCE, DECEMBER 11, 1969

FOR: Conference participants

FROM: Leonard R. Sussman

It is not news to this group that print and broadcast technology and economics are increasingly complex; social instability particularly in America more intensified; and the interplay between these forces demanding of more balance, perspective, and objectivity than the news media presently demonstrate.

More than two years ago Freedom House recognized the critical dilemma posed by the communications media and shared by other vital American institutions. We titled an opening statement of the problem ". . . *must free institutions be overthrown because of the very freedoms they sustain?*" We called then for the creation of our Public Affairs Institute, one of the prime programs of which would be the continuing analysis of the mass news media.

Its broad purpose was to represent the public interest both in striving for an objective press operating with social responsibility, and in warding off repressive efforts by government or private groups.

. . . .

Dr. Harry D. Gideonse, president of Freedom House, has invited you to this conference to share our concerns and aspirations, and elicit your advice in planning for the period immediately ahead. We have kept our options flexible. We hope this session on December 11 will productively examine a series of questions and enable us to set our course immediately thereafter.

The opening question is the general approach to the *influencing* of the media. Should we conceive of the media analysis program as basically *collaborative*, oriented in

major respects to privately persuasive techniques
through nonpublicized channels; or should we regard the
program as *adversarial*, based essentially upon generating
public pressure to induce correctives?

A second basic question is the approach to the *continuing
media analysis*. Should it be developed as a *creative
judgment* by one or several informed specialists; or a
structured sequence of interpretations flowing from the
objective facts and the treatment of them by the media?

The answers to the foregoing questions are intimately
related to the following possible elements of the continuing analysis:

1. Basic to any analysis of media performance must be
    some criteria for determining and working toward ob-
    jectivity and balance. This implies a realistic
    determination of relatively objective fact-situations.
    Who is to say what really happened, what was dis-
    torted, what was neglected? Is it sufficient to
    say, as Walter Cronkite stated on November 25 ("60
    Minutes," CBS-TV) that journalists trained to be
    objective can be counted on, by and large, to be
    objective? Do we need a panel of specialists drawn
    from the major fields--foreign affairs, urban,
    campus, and racial affairs, etc.--committed to year-
    round observation of assigned media? Would their
    monitoring of the media be enhanced by quarterly
    feedbacks to a central office of data elicited by
    questionnaires? These would provide depth responses
    to coverage, lack of coverage, or distortion of
    particular public issues or trends; they would not
    emphasize individual articles or broadcasts, or run-
    of-the-mill stories. Should the data from a fact-
    finding panel be:

    (a) turned over to a creative writer-analyst who
         would draw implications for publication; or

    (b) fed into a conference at which media people and
         specialists consider correctives (see 4[c]
         below)?

2. If one or more creative writer-analysts were to
    provide the analysis without bolstering by any
    other data and without media collaboration, what
    form would the critique take? Would it be a regular
    publication similar to the *Columbia Journalism
    Review* but published by and for laymen with con-
    centration on media handling of varied fact-situa-
    tions? What would be the natural channels of
    distribution for such a publication?

3. If we were still to depend essentially upon creative
    analysts without further data or media collaboration,
    could we persuade the broadcast media to provide a
    regular time segment for analysis of the print and
    broadcast media, produced independently by qualified
    specialists?

4. If we were to go the collaborative route would it be
    necessary to structure the presentation of data so
    that media people would recognize that the problem
    is sufficiently serious to require corrective action?
    The post-Agnew response of television generally
    justifies media performance, presumably to ward off
    government intimidation and potential censorship.
    Some "errors" are made, it is quickly agreed, but
    these are regarded as "only human." No fundamental
    problems have been generally admitted to exist.
    Before media people may agree to examine reasonable
    and detailed complaints, do they need carefully
    drawn bills of particulars?

    (a) Should there be some *content analysis* dealing
         with several key issues in foreign or domestic
         affairs? For example, the foreign press,
         particularly the British, have undertaken a con-
         siderable reevaluation during the past six
         months of the 1968 Tet offensive. Their
         findings are greatly at variance with the
         American public's understanding of the events
         in 1968 and probably today. If reliable
         Asianists and others agree with this sober re-
         interpretation, one may ask what went wrong
         with press coverage in 1968 and thereafter.
         This is important not only for historians but
         for newsmen covering critical stories everywhere.

         Examination of media content may reveal the
         virtual ignoring of foreseeable danger spots
         abroad. The number of U.S. correspondents
         throughout Asia and the Pacific, exclusive of
         Vietnam, is still appallingly low--yet much of
         the world's fate will be decided there during
         the next decade. Economics alone should not be
         the answer.

         Since competitive journalism apparently does not
         make the assignment profitable, perhaps the
         analysis can stimulate the creation of a news
         consortium financed by leading papers, wire
         services, and broadcast media to man some key
         news stations abroad.

(b) Should there be some *polling* to ascertain what the audience understands and/or retains after exposure to the media on particular issues? Could meaningful use be made of existing polling data so that expensive new polling might not be necessary? Would there be a value in polling a representative live audience after it is shown both raw TV news film and then commentary on a related subject? A correlation of such findings with the content analysis and the matching of both with the fact-situation provided by the panel of specialists could provide a revealing body of data for the media people to ponder.

(c) Bringing together the media people and the specialists with their data could be the next step in collaboration. All would have in advance the feedback from the questionnaires as well as the findings of the content analysis and the polling. The aim of the conference would be to develop correctives for faulted techniques, coverage omissions, or distortions. What would follow?

5. Assuming the effectiveness of the program up to this point, how could we then assure the adoption of the suggested changes by the media? Should the findings (the raw data) be publicized? If so, before or after the collaborative conferences? Should there be created something akin to the British Press Council to shame recalcitrant media people into correctives by having their peers publicize departures from objectivity or responsible news handling? Could the American Society of Newspaper Editors or the National Association of Broadcasters be persuaded to participate?

In brief, where is the "clout" behind the entire program--what would produce sufficient leverage to make the news analysis effort more than a theoretical pursuit?

Throughout our discussion on December 11, I hope we will keep before us the stark criterion of feasibility.

APPENDIX XL

Journalism Quarterly
Summer 1972
ROUGH JUSTICE ON A SAIGON STREET: A GATEKEEPER STUDY OF NBC'S
TET EXECUTION FILM

By George A. Bailey and Lawrence W. Lichty

*Step by step, person by person, decision by decision,
the authors record the story of the filming and
telecasting of General Loan's famed shot. The "organization" proved to be the gatekeeper:*

The Vietcong had announced a Tet truce but on January
29, 1968, and for the next few days, the VC and NVA
attacked nearly every city and many villages in South
Vietnam.1 Heavy fighting followed for several weeks
in Saigon and Hue. The first film reports of the attack
were seen on American television January 30.

On Wednesday, January 31, the "Huntley-Brinkley Report"
switched via satellite to Jack Perkins live in Tokyo.
Perkins announced that he would show unedited film of
fighting in and around the U.S. Embassy. The film had just
been developed and Perkins narrated the story partly from
information he was receiving at that time talking by telephone with Executive Producer Robert Northshield in New
York. In other reports the networks covered the war in the
cities along with reaction at home.

On Thursday, February 1, David Brinkley introduced John
Chancellor who narrated seven still photographs from the
wire service. Part of his narration follows:

> There was awful savagery. Here the Vietcong killed
> a South Vietnamese colonel and murdered his wife and
> six children. And this South Vietnamese officer came
> home during a lull in the fighting to find the bodies

1For a detailed analysis of Tet and its impact on American opinion
and policy, see Oberdorfer, *Tet!* Oberdorfer calls the Loan story
"one of the most powerful ever shown by television news." His section
entitled "The Flight of a Single Bullet," pp. 161-71, is based in part
on the manuscript for this article.

of his murdered children. There was awful retribu-
tion. Here the infamous chief of the South Vietnamese national police, General Loan, executed a
captured Vietcong officer. Rough justice on a Saigon
street as the charmed life of the city of Saigon
comes to a bloody end.[2]

The last picture was the now-famous photograph by Eddie
Adams of the Associated Press. That picture won the
Pulitzer Prize for spot news photography and many other
awards.

Broadcasting those stills, the Huntley-Brinkley newsmen
in New York did not yet know that an NBC film crew in
Saigon had color motion pictures of the Loan execution and
those pictures could be available for the next day's program. That next day, February 2, 1968, would be the most
sensational day of broadcast coverage in that sensational
week of the Tet offensive, and to many observers the turning point in American opinion and policy toward the Vietnam War.

REPORTING THE LOAN STORY

By Thursday morning, Saigon time, the fighting was fierce
all over the city. Particularly hard hit was Cholon, the
Chinese quarter of Saigon where the Vietcong had set up a
headquarters in the Buddhist An Quang Pagoda. An NBC
news crew and AP photographer Eddie Adams decided to share
a car into Cholon. (The AP and NBC bureaus were adjacent
on the fourth floor of the Eden building.) The NBC correspondent was Howard Tuckner, the cameramen were two
Vietnamese brothers, Vo Huynh and Vo Suu, and the sound man
was Le Phue Dinh. Huynh took an Arriflex to shoot silent
film. Suu carried an Auricon sound-on-film camera.

The Tuckner crew and Adams were standing in a street near
the Pagoda before noon. At the far end of the block they
saw several South Vietnamese Marines with a prisoner in
civilian clothes. The Marines walked up toward the newsmen
to present the prisoner to Brig. Gen. Nguyen Ngoc Loan,
who had taken charge of the Pagoda action. The cameramen
began filming, one Vo brother on each side of the street.
Huynh shot a close-up of a pistol being carried by an
ARVN Marine which had been taken from the prisoner, who
appeared to have been beaten. Tuckner later described
what happened:

---

[2]*Webster's Seventh New Collegiate Dictionary* defines "rough" as (2b)
"characterized by harshness, violence, or force" and (4b) "executed
hastily, tentatively, or imperfectly."

He [the captive] was not scared; he was proud. I
will never forget that look when he walked up the
street. General Loan took one look at him and knew
he was going to get no information out of him. Loan
had been through this with many prisoners. There was
not one word. Loan did not try to talk to him nor to
scare him. He did not wave his gun at his face or his
head. He did not put the gun to his temple. He just
blew his brains out.3

During that time Tuckner kept whispering into Suu's ear,
"Keep rolling, keep rolling." Eddie Adams was snapping
many photographs. Later Adams wrote that as Loan's hand
came up, so did his camera, and he just snapped by in-
stinct.4 The prisoner dropped to the street with blood
spurting out of his head. An ARVN Marine placed a small

3Unless otherwise noted, all quotations are from personal interviews
or correspondence as follows:

Howard Tuckner, ABC News--earlier NBC News--interviewed by Bailey and
Lichty, Madison, Wisconsin, June 26, 1969.

Robert Northshield, John Chancellor, and Jack Perkins, all NBC News,
interviewed by Bailey, Milwaukee, Wisconsin, Mar. 31, 1968.

Vo Suu, Vo Huynh, and Ron Steinman, all NBC News, interviewed by
Lichty, Saigon, Vietnam, July 1968.

Jack Reynolds, NBC News, and Roger Peterson, ABC News, interviewed by
Lichty, Tokyo, Japan, July 1968.

David Burrington and Jack Perkins, both NBC News, interviewed by
Lichty, New York, June 1969.

Bill Brannigan, ABC News, letter to Lichty, Jan. 1970.

Edward Adams, Associated Press, New York, reply to letter from
Lichty, Aug. 1970.

Harold Buell, executive newsphoto editor, Associated Press, letter
to Lichty, Sept. 2, 1970.

Ron Steinman, NBC News, London , letters to Lichty, Sept. 3, 1970 and
Aug. 10, 1971.

Jack Reynolds, NBC News, Hong Kong, letter to Lichty, Sept. 19, 1970.

Roger Peterson, ABC News, interviewed by Lichty, Washington, D.C.,
Nov. 6, 1970.

4Eddie Adams, "They Had Killed . . . Many of My Men," _Editor and
Publisher,_ Feb. 10, 1968, p. 9.

red Vietcong propaganda leaflet over the corpse's face.
Tuckner and Adams were the only Westerners in sight.
Tuckner feared that their film would be confiscated or
worse. He signaled Suu to quickly change film magazines
and hide the exposed footage. Tuckner stood silent as
Loan walked up to him and said:

> Many Americans have been killed these last few days
> and many of my best Vietnamese friends. Now do you
> understand? Buddha will understand.[5]

The NBC crew walked away and continued shooting scenes
around the Pagoda. The corpse was lifted off the pavement and thrown on a flatbed truck. The South Vietnamese
forces cleared the Pagoda of Vietcong and their hostages
as the Tuckner crew filmed the action. Later Tuckner took
time to write a "standupper" for the execution story, and
his crew filmed him as he read the standup summary to the
camera. Tuckner's summary was written to be shown after
the execution film. In that standupper he related what
Loan had said.

In the afternoon, Thursday, February 1, Tuckner and the
crew returned to NBC's Saigon bureau. Ron Steinman, the
bureau chief, debriefed each crew member individually.
Vo Suu was sure that he had recorded the shooting on the
film; Tuckner was not convinced. Steinman also talked
with Eddie Adams. Now it seemed that the film report would
best end with the execution and the "standupper" would be
anticlimactic. Tuckner wrote a simple substitute nar-
ration--with several variations to provide for the possibility that not all the film was good. This narration
was recorded on audio tape at the bureau. In this script
the story of the pagoda fighting is played first, before
the execution, in a reordering of actual events. Cameraman Suu wrote out captions for the film describing the
material shot by shot and various technical matters for
developing and editing.

Meanwhile in the next office, under the direction of
Horst Faas, AP developed, printed, and transmitted the
Adams photo to New York. At 8:16 a.m. Thursday morning,
New York time, it was sent out to newspapers around the
country--about 11 hours after the shooting. The NBC film
was still in Saigon undeveloped.

---

[5]Tuckner provided the quotation to the wire services that day and
it was printed in several slightly varying versions. The version
here is as remembered by Tuckner several months after the event.

During this period of the war, film was ordinarily sent
by plane to New York for developing and editing but alternatively could be received in San Francisco, Los
Angeles, or, less frequently, Seattle or Chicago for
editing and subsequent transmission via land lines if this
would make a deadline for one of the evening or morning
network programs. For faster transmission, the film could
be sent to Tokyo, developed and edited there, and sent via
Pacific satellite to New York for broadcast live or video-
taped. Each network had an arrangement with a Japanese
broadcasting company to use Tokyo studios to originate
the live and film transmissions.

Thursday the Tan Son Nhut Airport was closed to commercial
planes. The next flight out, a medevac taking wounded men
to Japan or the United States, would be Friday. During Tet
the military provided special cars or jeeps to carry news
film to the airport. NBC newsmen had prepared six film
stories for shipment. The undeveloped film and audio tape
was in cans with scripts and additional instructions. The
material was placed in the standard red burlap bags marked
"NBC" in big white and black letters. By one o'clock
Friday afternoon in Saigon--about 28 hours after the
shooting--the Loan film was still at the bureau.

Cable connections between Saigon and Tokyo were always poor.
During Tet they were worse. NBC usually had fairly good
TELEX connections between Saigon and New York. Steinman
sent a TELEX message to New York advising the availability
of the six film stories. New York would relay the information to Tokyo. Steinman did not want to overemphasize the
shock nature of the film since he was convinced that if it
was as Suu insisted, the impact would be obvious. Further,
he feared that the TELEX might be monitored and there was
still a chance that the film might be confiscated. The
following is part of his TELEX to NBC New York sent at 0537
GMT--1:37 p.m. Friday afternoon in Saigon; 12:37 a.m.
Friday morning in New York.

> THE FOLLOWING IS THE SHIPPING ADVISORY. FILM HAS NOT
> YET BEEN SHIPPED. WHEN SHIPPED WE WILL CONFIRM
> FASTEST AND BEST WAY POSSIBLE. HOPEFULLY THE TELEX
> WILL STILL BE WORKING. SHIPPED IN THREE SEPARATE BAGS
> ARE FILM NUMBERS 456, 457, 458, 459, 460, AND 461.
>
> FILM NUMBER 456 IS TUCKNER'S PAGODA FIGHTING. GOVERN-
> MENT TROOPS WENT INTO THE AN QUANG PAGODA, SEAT OF
> BUDDHIST MILITANCE, AND TRIED TO CLEAN OUT THE VIET-
> CONG WHO HAD TAKEN IT OVER. THIS STORY IS COMPETITIVE.
> CBS AND ABC WERE THERE BUT WE ARE THE ONLY ONES WHO
> HAVE FILM ON THE EXECUTION. TUCKNER HAS WRITTEN
> PRODUCTION NOTES AND SCRIPT TO GO WITH SUU AND HUYNH'S

720 SOF 360 SIL NORMAL. DINH WAS SOUNDMAN. NARRA-
TION ON FULL COAT AND AUDIO TAPE. ONE WILDTAPE.
CLOSER ON FILMROLL ONE AND TWO BUT READ TUCKNER'S
DETAILED NOTE FOR EXACT CLOSER WE PREFER AND THINK
SHOULD BE USED. THIS IS IMPORTANT BECAUSE WE ARE
DEALING WITH A DELICATE PROBLEM.[6] . . . . VIET-
CONG OPEN UP ON MARINES. THEN THE LOAN SEGMENT.
THIS IS ON SUU'S SOUNDROLL AND HE THINKS HE GOT
MOST OF IT. HIS CAPTIONS IN BRIEF READ AS FOLLOWS:
A VC OFFICER WAS CAPTURED. THE TROOPS BEAT HIM.
THEY BRING HIM TO LOAN WHO IS HEAD OF SOUTH VIET-
NAMESE NATIONAL POLICE. LOAN PULLS OUT HIS PISTOL.
FIRES AT THE HEAD OF THE VC, THE VC FALLS, ZOOM ON
HIS HEAD. BLOOD SPRAYING OUT. IF HE HAS IT ALL ITS
STARTLING STUFF. IF HE HAS PART OF IT IT'S STILL
MORE THAN ANYONE ELSE HAS. TUCKNER'S COPY COVERS IT
IN STRAIGHT NARRATIVE WITH SOME ALTERNATIVE COPY
JUST IN CASE SOME OF THE SHOTS MAY BE DIFFERENT OR
NOT ALL THERE. I SUGGEST YOU DEVELOP ALL OF THE
FOOTAGE.[7]

Just over two hours later New York sent Steinman's message
on to the Tokyo bureau. The five other stories were each
described as was the Loan story. That is, for each piece
Steinman gave technical data, crew names, synopsis, sug-
gestions for editing, and whether the other networks had
similar film. A total of more than 4,000 feet of film was
readied for shipment, a running time of nearly two hours.
From all that, less than eight minutes would finally be
broadcast on that day's "Huntley-Brinkley Report." This
ratio of 15 to one is typical for NBC (see Table 1).

NBC correspondent Ron Nessen had filed two of the other
stories. One was film of fighting at Hue, where the enemy
was holding much of the city, and the other was film of a
Da Nang napalm dump destroyed by rockets. Wilson Hall had
covered the heavy fighting in the streets of Cholon and
narrated a silent film story of aftermath in the provincial
capital of Ban Me Thout shot by soundman Arndt. The last

---

[6] Some technical jargon may need explanations: 720 and 360 are numbers
of feet of film. SOF means sound-on-film, that is, taping sound and
exposing film simultaneously on one strip of magnetic-coated film. A
wildtape is an audio tape of sounds not synchronized with particular
film footage.

[7] TELEX, NBC News Saigon to NBC New York, 0537 Greenwich Mean Time, Feb.
2, 1968. Provided by NBC. We are especially grateful for the cooperation of Robert Northshield in obtaining this correspondence and much
other material.

TABLE 1

News Film from Vietnam for the "Huntley-Brinkley Report"
of February 2, 1968

TITLE OF STORY	FILM EXPOSED		FILM BROADCAST	RATIO (Exposed/
	(Feet)	(Time)	(Time)	Broadcast)
Tuckner's Pagoda/Loan	1080	30:00	3:55	7.7 to 1
Hall's Cholon Fighting	590	16:24	——	——
Nessen's Hue Fighting	350	9:44	2:30	3.9 to 1
Arndt's Ban Me Thuot	930	25:50	1:25	20.7 to 1
Nessen's Da Nang	100	2:47	——	——
Westmoreland Briefing*	1100	30:34	——	——
TOTALS	4150	115:19	7:40	15.0 to 1

film was unnarrated footage of a news conference by General Westmoreland in which, according to the New York _Times_, he said the enemy's main effort still was to be an attack on the Marines at Khe Sanh.

At this time there was only one color film processing lab in Tokyo and it was used by the three networks. The film was processed in the order it arrived at the lab. During Tet NBC hired a grand prix motorcycle racer to speed the NBC film to the lab first.

EDITING AND BROADCASTING TO THE NETWORK

Robert Northshield, executive producer of the "Huntley-Brinkley Report," arrived at the New York office that Friday about 10 a.m. The night before he had broadcast the Adams stills. That morning he saw most of the major newspapers consensually validate his assessment of the stills. The New York _Times_ printed the moment-of-death picture on the front page and reprinted it with others on page twelve. The Washington _Post_ printed it across five columns of the front page. The Chicago _Tribune_ printed three Adams photos, but on the third page. The Los Angeles _Times_ filled three front-page columns. The New York _Daily News_ filled the bottom half of its front

---

*[The table is extremely revealing in that it clearly shows TV priorities. General Westmoreland's first briefing on the initial Tet attacks, which made page one in the New York _Times_ and the Washington _Post_, was ignored on film by NBC, and the more dramatic Loan film footage easily got the play--P.B.]

page. Several papers printed another photo nearby the
Loan shot. That photo showed an ARVN officer carrying the
body of one of his children murdered by the Vietcong. The
"Huntley-Brinkley Report" had broadcast that one also
Thursday evening.

Northshield read the overnight cables and learned that NBC
had color film of the Loan incident that might include the
moment of the execution. He then placed a phone call to
talk with those who could view the film.

At the Tokyo bureau were Jack Reynolds, news manager and
satellite producer, and several part-time editors used
regularly by the bureau. Also reinforcing the staff for
the Tet and *Pueblo* stories were Ray Weiss, sent from New
York to help coordinate the bureau; Fred Rheinstein, an
NBC staff director and editor; and correspondent David
Burrington, who had previously reported from Vietnam.
Correspondent Jack Perkins, producer Bill Wordam, camera-
man Grant Wolfkill and soundman Waku, just returned from
Korea, also took part in the discussion.

In the discussion, Northshield said that the TELEX from
Saigon mentioned a zoom to a close-up of the corpse's
bloody head and that would probably be in bad taste for
television. Wordam assured Northshield that the film was
"quite remarkable," and there was enough time "for the
director to cut away before the zoom at the end of the
film." He referred to the video director of the program
in New York. So the film was deliberately edited long so
that a final decision could be made in New York.

Another member of the NBC staff working on the film later
said he thought some of the close-up should have been
shown, for Americans were getting a "too sanitized" picture
of the war and they should have had "their noses rubbed
in" the violence and gore.

Northshield authorized use of the satellite to transmit
the film to the States. The bill would be about $3,000
for a 10-minute minimum. After a late lunch Northshield
called Tokyo again. The Loan film had been edited to
4:12 and was set for transport to the NHK studio along
with two of the other Saigon-oriented stories. Ron
Nessen's Hue report and Wilson Hall's narration of Ban
Me Thuot fighting and aftermath had been selected.

The "Huntley-Brinkley Report" was fed over the NBC network twice each day. The first show was live at 6:30
p.m. Eastern time. If it went well, then a video tape
was fed at 7 p.m. Changes could be made for the second
feed if necessary. Northshield recalled the Friday broadcasts:

The film came in over satellite between 6:20 and 6:30
p.m. before airtime and it was recorded routinely on
tape. I saw the pictures then and heard what was
said over the pictures. John Chancellor happened to
be in the studio that day. He saw it with me. We
were both stunned, because, the way it came in, the
general took the gun, shot him in the head, the man
fell down, and we held the picture while Loan re-
holstered the gun and walked through the frame. You
still see the corpse from whom blood is now gushing.
So it was too much for me. Now, here the interesting
point is that those men in Tokyo had been looking at
the rawest, roughest film anyone has ever seen. They
saw it differently than I did in an air-conditioned
control room in New York. It was too rough for me.
So I said to Chancellor, "I thought that was awful
rough." He could hardly speak. I said I was going
to trim it off a little. So when it went on the air
you saw less than what I have described. That is,
as soon as the man hits the ground we went to black.
It had already been established between me and the
director that we would go to black after the film,
which is unusual for our show. Usually we go right
to the Huntley-Brinkley slide. This time we went
to black for three seconds and then to the slide.

The "Huntley-Brinkley Report" typically used a title
slide (logo) between a film story and a commercial break.

The program that day presented Chet Huntley with Vietnam
news. He said that the Tet offensive was now five days
old and heaviest fighting was at Hue. He introduced the
Nessen film from there. After that, Huntley read some
copy about fighting in provincial cities and introduced
the Hall film from Ban Me Thuot. Then Huntley was framed
in the lower left of the screen with a map of Saigon at
his back. He read this introduction:

> A pall lay over Saigon where American and South Viet-
> namese forces struggled to eliminate stubborn
> pockets of Vietcong resistance. The Americans even
> battled the enemy near the Saigon home of General
> Westmoreland, the American commander. There was
> fighting in the Cholon section, where the city's
> Chinese live. But the conflict was sharpest at the
> An Quang Pagoda near the Saigon race track. Here
> via satellite is a report from NBC News correspondent
> Howard Tuckner on the battle for Saigon.

Tuckner's report as edited by the program's director in
New York for the first feed ran 3:55. The last 17 seconds

of the Tokyo-edited version were trimmed off, excluding
the zoom to a close-up of the victim's head. *The first
3:03 of the report was the clearing action at the Pagoda
which had actually taken place after the execution.** The
Loan sequence itself ran only 52 seconds. The following
is the narration Tuckner read over the first part of the
film. Taped sounds of gunfire, shouting, and other battle
sound were included:

> In this part of Saigon, government troops were ordered
> to get as much revenge as possible. The fighting was
> only one block from the An Quang Pagoda, a Buddhist
> church the Vietcong had been using as their head-
> quarters with the reported approval of the militant
> Buddhist monk Tri Quang. An hour earlier Vietcong
> flags had flown from these rooftops. Now snipers were
> up there and government troops were trying to locate
> their positions. Crack South Vietnamese Marines con-
> sidered all civilians potential enemies. No one was above
> suspicion. The Vietcong were working their way to the
> An Quang Pagoda and now the government troops had to
> clear the area no matter how high the risk. The Viet-
> cong were now firing from the roof of the Pagoda. For
> half an hour it was like this. The Vietcong fled
> through the back of the Buddhist church but many
> others were there. Some of these are undoubtedly
> Vietcong sympathizers; some are undoubtedly religious
> Buddhists who felt the temple was the safest place to
> be in times like these in Saigon. The bullets had
> wounded at least 20 of them. The government Marines
> knew that, the night before, here the Vietcong had
> held a meeting and that the Buddhists had cheered when
> they were told the Vietcong were in the city to
> liberate Saigon.

The execution sequence followed directly. Tuckner recorded
very little narration relative to that recorded above.
In the first scene the prisoner was marched down the street
toward NBC cameras while the ARVN Marines questioned the
captive. Tuckner said, "Government troops had captured the
commander of the Vietcong commando unit." During a medium
close-up of the prisoner Tuckner said, "He was roughed up
badly but refused to talk." The camera tilted down to show
a pistol carried by one of the Marines. Tuckner said, "A
South Vietnamese officer held the pistol taken from the
enemy officer." A camera angle from behind Loan, a wide-
angle view, showed the general drawing his own revolver

---

*[Emphasis added--P.B.]

and waving it to shoo away onlookers. Tuckner said,
"The chief of South Vietnam's national police force, Brig.
Gen. Nguyen Ngoc Loan, was waiting for him." That was the
last line of narration. Loan moved around to the side
of the captive and shot him directly in the side of the
head. The corpse dropped to the pavement while blood
spurted out his head. The time between the gun shot and
the end of the film broadcast was six seconds.

If the film had been broadcast in its complete Tokyo-
edited version, then the time allotted to showing the
bleeding corpse dropping and on the pavement would have
been 23 seconds.

The interval from the execution in Saigon to its broadcast
by NBC was 46 hours.

Robert Northshield viewed the first feed of the "Huntley-
Brinkley Report" that day and decided to trim another
two seconds from the film for the second feed at 7 p.m.

LATER BROADCASTS OF THE FILM

Some NBC affiliate stations video-taped segments of the
network newscasts for use in local news programs. There
was no practical way to determine how many local stations
replayed the Loan film that day. To our knowledge, the
film was broadcast nationally only two other times. The
first was a special edition of the "Frank McGee Report"
on March 10, 1968. That broadcast reviewed Tet and
introduced an upcoming series of such news summaries,
"Vietnam: The War This Week." The McGee broadcast included the following added narration:

> South Vietnam's national police chief had killed a
> man who had been captured carrying a pistol. This
> was taken as sufficient evidence that he was a Viet-
> cong officer, so the police chief put a bullet in
> his brain. He's still the chief of police.

Nineteen months later, on October 7, 1969, NBC broadcast
a special produced by Northshield, "From Here to the 70s."
It presented the Loan film without introduction or comment
spliced among many other pieces of news film from the
decade.

The Adams photograph has been reprinted in many newspapers,
magazines, books, posters, and broadcast on television all
over the world.[8] The award of the Pulitzer Prize in spring

---

[8]The NBC film was distributed to foreign news organizations. The BBC
chose to not show the film but televised the AP still. A frame-by-
frame analysis of the Loan film shows that the precise instant of the
gun shot is *not* on film. Just as Loan raised his arm to fire, someone

1969 stimulated another wave of reproduction of the Adams photograph. It is certainly one of the most widely circulated photographs in history.

One reason the NBC film of Loan was not circulated as widely as the Adams photograph was, of course, the differential natures of the print and cinematographic media. The motion film could not be presented in books or magazines.[9] Both ABC and CBS were to later refer to the Loan story on television newscasts and both displayed the AP photo.[10]

A Cybernetic Gatekeeping Model

The production of the Loan story by NBC News provides an opportunity to apply various gatekeeping models to the process of network journalism.

In early models--best described as linear--the news editor was the object of analysis. He made private, binary, irrevocable decisions allowing portions of the news content arriving at his desk further passage toward publication. Generally, he acted on one story at a time and usually only once. Case studies and experiments often ignored even the most popularized concepts of the organization man whose behavior is a function of his position in a bureaucracy.

---

stepped across the front of the camera lens. The view was blocked for seven frames (about 1/4 of a second). In motion, however, the film does appear to show the complete action of the shooting.

[9]An interesting example of this is Erik Barnouw, *The Image Empire: A History of Broadcasting in the United States from 1953* (New York: Oxford University Press, 1970). The Adams still is shown and it is noted that: "Some Congressmen considered television use of photo in bad taste." There is no mention of the NBC film.

[10]ABC did not have a correspondent at the scene but did have a film cameraman. That film was edited in Tokyo by bureau chief Roger Peterson. The film ran 1:55 and with voice-over narration by Peterson was sent via satellite. ABC did not have the moment of the gun shot on the film--only the walk leading up to it, and the bleeding corpse on the ground and then thrown on a truck. At the point in the film where the shot occurred ABC-TV in New York cut from the color motion picture film to the AP photo, and then back to the film. The ABC cameraman said he was afraid of General Loan and stopped filming.

CBS had no film of the shooting, although correspondent Don Webster and a film crew were nearby and filed a report of the Pagoda action.

Later studies introduced intervening variables which influenced gatekeeper behavior and noted the effect of peer groups, reference groups, formal training, informal socialization, and the like--concession that the journalist was a human being after all with social and psychological determinants of his actions.

A cybernetic model, such as suggested by Robinson,[11] takes the news organization as the object of analysis. The "Huntley-Brinkley Report" was the output of formal and informal organizational processes centered at NBC News, a complex communication-decision network populated by members of a trained and socialized subculture. Input included all the events within the surveillance of the organization's reporters, cameramen, bureau managers, and assistants, news and film editors.

Decisions by NBC personnel which may have appeared to be personal, individual acts were in fact governed by powerful norms. Being members of the journalistic subculture, NBC gatekeepers assessed the newsworthiness of the Loan story along traditional, identifiable standards. For example, on the exclusivity of the story, Northshield said, "We alone had the story . . . we were way ahead of the competition." This attention to the story as a scoop was reflected throughout the organization. Steinman had cabled, "CBS AND ABC WERE THERE BUT WE ARE THE ONLY ONES WHO HAVE FILM ON THE EXECUTION."

Another traditional standard of newsworthiness is a story's significance, often measured by the importance of persons involved. Northshield said:

> The one thing that matters on this program is the significance of the story. This was, in my view, a significant event. That the chief of the security police, at a time like this, in the view of certainly hundreds and eventually millions, chose to kill a man. I think the fact that this is significant is unarguable, without question.

Northshield's judgment conformed to traditional criteria.

The journalistic subculture crosses formal organizational boundaries to influence gatekeeping decisions. Consensual validation of the newsworthiness of the film was provided by the New York *Times*, which ran the picture

---

[11]Gertrude J. Robinson, "Foreign News Selection Is Non-Linear in Yugoslavia's Tanjug Agency," *Journalism Quarterly*, 47:340-51 (Summer 1970). Robinson also provides review of many of the major earlier gatekeeping studies.

twice.   Those editors functioned as a reference group for
NBC gatekeepers.

Informal communication-decision networks operated within
NBC to reduce the individuality of decision.   As one example of peer influence, John Chancellor happened to view
the film as it came into New York before airtime.   Northshield and Chancellor had great mutual respect.   They had
worked together on the "Today Show" and on a Chicago newspaper
years before.   The two had a short conversation about the
film before Northshield made his decision to edit it.
While that decision was formally the executive producer's
alone, the judgment of a highly respected peer worked
to reduce the individuality of Northshield's action.

More formal communication-decision networks also influenced individuals in the organization.   Involved in the
production of this story were such matters as the organizational decision more than three years earlier to maintain
a large Saigon bureau, the daily assignment made by the
bureau chief, and the interaction of the reporter-camera-
men-soundman--even before the event.   The film editor
might seem the classic gatekeeper, but this case does not
support that simplistic interpretation.   The Loan film
story was edited by a group.   *The organization was the
gatekeeper.*   When the story was transmitted to New York
little time remained to change it before going on the air.
It was possible to shorten the film, and shorten it still
more for a second feed.   The range of possibilities in New
York were small--go or no go.   Yet, this should not be
perceived as a simple "gate."   New York had participated
in the decision-making many times.   The power of the
executive producer is great.   This complex matter cannot
be fully discussed here, but reporters, editors, producers,
others know which stories are most likely to be broadcast.
Each "gatekeeper" has to estimate how the program's executive producer--and even his superiors--will receive the
story.   A cybernetic organization functions with consideration to its environment--in this case the audience.   The
one standard news judgment overtly applied throughout the
production of the Loan story was that of taste.[12]

The film included full-color shots of spurting blood and
a close-up of the dead man's face.   NBC edited the film
according to its estimate of the taste standards of the
audience.   Feedback on the audience's reaction would come
only later.   But the cybernetic organization functions

---

[12]Gans notes that much of the decision-making in TV news is on matters
of taste.   Herbert J. Gans, "How Well *Does* TV Present the News?" *The
New York Times Magazine,* Jan. 11, 1970, p. 31.

with the help of memory--knowledge of past reactions from
its audience. This conception of audience thus influences
gatekeeping decisions.

What then of the possible influence of an individual
journalist's political or moral value system on his
decision-making in the Loan case? Much has been written
arguing that the professional journalist is one who controls his prejudices aiming at a goal of objectivity.
Correspondent Tuckner recorded his narration to play with
the film. That narration was sparse, not much more than
an identification of the principals in the film and the
setting. The narration ended before the execution was
actually seen. Later, off the air, Tuckner freely revealed
his strong personal point of view on General Loan:

> It was the responsibility of the network to broadcast
> that film. The film showed, at a time when all eyes
> were on Saigon, that although the United States went
> over there ostensibly to keep South Vietnam free from
> communism, and the communists were accused of
> atrocities, that a leading figure of the Saigon gov-
> ernment killed a man in the street without a trial.

No similar comment or interpretation had been offered by
Tuckner or the anchormen on the program.

AUDIENCE REACTION

According to audience research services, about 20 million
people might have seen the execution film on NBC that
night. Viewers from 31 different states sent 90 letters
to NBC about the Loan film story.

NBC was accused of bad taste in 56 of the letters. The
next most often mentioned criticism was that children
might have seen the film, and more than a third of the
letters were from parents of young children who had seen
the film.

A questionnaire sent the letter-writers in April 1968
was returned by 69 respondents. Those who wrote were
more likely to be politically active--as judged by
membership in organizations, the signing or circulation
of petitions, campaigning for political candidates, and
other measurements. Of the respondents 61 percent said
that the Vietnam War was a mistake--the same figure for
the United States reported by Gallup in May 1968.

The analysis of the NBC gatekeeping decisions in preparing this film indicates most discussion was about
taste in editing the film. An analysis of letters written
to NBC, and questionnaires returned by the letter-writers,
shows that viewers objected most often to the film as
being in bad taste.

Interestingly, few persons referred to the Vietnam War
in their letters or in responding to the questionnaire.
Only four said that the film showed a "true picture" of
the war but no one questioned the truthfulness of the
NBC film.

APPENDIX XLI

Freedom at Issue
September - October **1973**

THE NEWS MEDIA AND THE GOVERNMENT: CLASH OF CONCENTRATED POWER

For longer than six years Freedom House has been troubled by the changing perception of the news media in American society. A major evaluation of press performance has been under way at Freedom House for several years. There has recently been particular concern over the deteriorating relationship between the media and government at all levels.

Freedom House consequently convened a News Media/Government Consultation at the University of Maryland, College Park, June 26-27 [1973]. Leading newsmen and present and past government officials took part.

The call to the consultation posed the question whether "the press" and/or "the government" has each in its own way hardened its adversarial position; whether there is now a closing of ranks on both sides, producing a de facto war of the worlds (press vs. government).

The meeting was asked to define the real areas of press/ government conflict, setting forth the operative Constitutional rules, and recommending specific common sense procedures by which to maximize the flow of information to the public without destructive confrontations.

Participants included newspaper publishers, editors, reporters, and a columnist; radio and television management and editorial personnel; the deputy assistant secretary of defense for public affairs; the chief counsel of the Senate Subcommittee on Constitutional Rights; and the former adversaries in the Pentagon Papers-New York *Times* case, former U.S. Attorney Whitney North Seymour, Jr., and Professor Alexander M. Bickel of Yale Law School.

The two days of discussion and preparation of papers resulted in the subsequent drafting of a single statement and guidelines entitled "The News Media and the Government: the Clash of Concentrated Power." We publish here the full text and list of participants.   —Editor

PARTICIPANTS

William Attwood, president and publisher, *Newsday*

George Backer, author, former publisher, New York *Post*

Lawrence M. Baskir, chief counsel and staff director, Subcommittee on Constitutional Rights, United States Senate

William Beecher, Deputy Assistant Secretary of Defense

Alexander M. Bickel, professor, Yale Law School

Erwin D. Canham, editor-in-chief, *Christian Science Monitor*

Leo Cherne, executive director, Research Institute of America

Roscoe Drummond, syndicated Washington columnist

Harry D. Gideonse, chancellor, New School for Social Research

Allan Jackson, CBS Radio News

John Lynch, Washington bureau chief, ABC-TV News

Thomas B. Ross, Washington bureau chief, Chicago *Sun-Times*

Whitney North Seymour, Jr., former federal attorney, Southern District of New York

Leonard R. Sussman, executive director, Freedom House

Philip van Slyck, public affairs consultant

Wallace Westfeldt, executive producer, NBC-TV News

Relations between the news media and the executive branch of the federal government are deplorable,[1] though in many instances able officials and conscientious journalists still fulfill their respective responsibilities admirably. Yet the general situation is harmful to the public interest and should be rectified.

The danger is that there is too much power in government, and too much in the institutionalized press, too much power insufficiently diffused, indeed all too concentrated,

---

[1] By Wallace Westfeldt: "I think this characterization is much over-drawn. The condition that exists between the press and the government may be uncomfortable at times for those people who inhabit those institutions. But the result of this condition has been more information to the people about how their government operates and certainly this is not deplorable."

both in government and in too few national press institutions, print and electronic. The accommodation works well
only when there is forbearance and continence on both
sides.

But these qualities have not prevailed. Instead, both
government and news media have exacerbated their normal
adversarial relationship so that each has suffered losses
of credibility in the estimate of the public. Still
graver breakdowns may ensue, if popular trust and confidence in both institutions continue to erode.

How did we get into this plight? Over recent decades
government has grown immensely, the bureaucracy has
become unwieldy, the structures of information offices
and of news reporting have mushroomed; electronic news
has made instant impact, vividly and emotionally conveyed;
the atmosphere of wars, hot and cold, has intensified
the classification and withholding and even manipulation
of information on grounds of national security; particularly traumatic have been the controversies over the
American involvement in Indo-China, the tragedies and
abuses of Watergate, the growing bitterness and misunderstanding in the Presidential relationship with the press
in the past decade, the immense buildup of power and
isolation in the White House offices, the dreadful
pyramiding of costs for running for office and some of
the lamentable techniques now used to gain votes, the
growth of mistrust toward most institutions. All these
and many other factors have contributed to the corrosive
conflict between government and press.

What can be done about it? Let us note that while relations between the news media and the executive branch
of government have become increasingly strained, little
such stress exists between the press and the legislative
branch. Does this not suggest that a genuine diffusion
of power through the executive branch and the Cabinet
offices, with attendant decentralization of news sources,
might lead to a better, freer, more open relationship?

We urge that both government and media reexamine their
responsibilities to the citizen public. The executive
branch should greatly diminish the classification of
information and cease efforts to manage the news, should
cooperate in greater access of news people to those in
government who are substantively informed about the significant news of the day.

The media need always act with integrity and a sense of
responsibility toward the national welfare, which tran-
scends the interest of a particular officeholder, or of

a particular news enterprise, or a particular section of
the country.

The longstanding adversary relationship between press
and government has often been very healthy. It can be
again, just as soon as an attitude of mutual respect is
deserved and restored.

A GENERAL GUIDE FOR GOVERNMENT OFFICIALS

We believe government should forthrightly provide information about its activities, except in the narrow area of
legitimate national security.[2] National security is hard
to define. It means different things to different people.
We believe this phrase has been overused, frequently mis-
used, and therefore must be used with care. We recognize
that genuine national security must include certain information relating to this country's military strength
and diplomatic processes. For instance, we believe that
national security requires protection of information dealing with such things as the precise details of certain
current military deployments, cryptographic material,
and the technology of advanced weaponry.

As to the diplomatic process, we recognize there may
be instances in which the details of negotiating positions
should for a time remain confidential, if the parties to
the negotiations so insist and if the United States government is convinced that such confidentiality is essential
to success.

Because of the vagueness of the phrase "national security"
and its susceptibility to abuse, we believe that the
government has the obligation to define through public
debate what specifically must be kept secret, under what
circumstances and conditions.

We recognize also that as a part of the system of checks
and balances, a diligent and skeptical Congress and press
must do everything possible to make the government fulfill this obligation.

Beyond the area of national security, we believe that
the federal government, as well as state and local governments, are obligated to provide the freest flow of information. This flow must be consistent with the protection
of the privacy of private citizens; of individual rights
in such things as due process in criminal investigations,
matters relating to personal taxes or family welfare; and

_____
[2]By Wallace Westfeldt: "I have serious reservations about the
phrase 'national security.' I believe 'national defense' is a more
appropriate one."

in such fields as Securities and Exchange Commission restrictions created to protect the public in the market
place. We believe the proper guideline is demonstrable
proof that the information at issue would interfere with
the rights of the individual or hamper the administration
of justice or breach the privacy of certain nonsecurity
information, such as advance crop data which in the
national interest should be withheld until released in
appropriately fair fashion.

Government also has the obligation to protect the privacy
of its own negotiating and decision-making process. Just
as the judicial conferences of the Supreme Court are held
in privacy--and not only to protect individuals appearing
before the Court--so decision-makers in the executive
branch are entitled to privacy in seeking advice of staff
and weighing alternative policies. The limits of protection may be difficult to set. Often it is a matter of
timing--protecting privacy until decisions are made or
negotiations completed. While the executive officer's
privacy should be of limited duration, the staff is
entitled to more than temporary protection.

A GENERAL GUIDE FOR THE NEWS MEDIA

The effective performance of journalism sometimes requires
it to be an adversary to other centers of power. It is
vital, however, that the adversary relationship not be
antagonistic. It is equally important that government
understand that the adversary function of journalism is
in the long-term best interests of effective government.
In that spirit responsible journalists should undertake
more critical and investigative reporting.

The journalist has the right and obligation to penetrate
the decision-making process but not to publish information
which would clearly endanger national security or public
safety. Civil disorders which have characterized the
recently turbulent period call for self-restraint by
the news media and, only in grave emergencies, the re-
striction of the press by government (as with speech and
assemblage).[3]

---

[3] By Lawrence Baskir, joined by Erwin D. Canham, Thomas B. Ross, and
Wallace Westfeldt: "I do not believe there properly are any restrictions on the right to publish, even information which clearly en-
dangers public safety. A newsman might be admonished to use discre-
tion in critical cases, but the implication that he has no 'right' to
publish is one on which I vigorously dissent. Similarly, I disagree
that the government's ability to restrict assemblage in emergencies
is a measure of its power to restrict the press. Should there be
emergencies great enough to raise the question of press control, they
are so extreme (and hypothetical) as not to justify even mentioning."

The press properly asserts but does not necessarily fulfill the public's right to know. The public therefore has
the right to know how the press operates, its limitations
and weaknesses. The daily press report, at best, is a
rough first draft of history. Because it is sometimes
misled, because it is sometimes obtuse or careless, the
information it provides may in the long run prove to be
incomplete or erroneous. When in error, it should apply
correctives as rapidlly as possible. But press and
public alike should recognize and accommodate to the fal-
libility inherent in a medium called upon to report increasingly complex and widespread issues and events under
stringent deadlines.

The Constitutional freedom of the press includes the
right of all news media to inform, but they must not
resist legitimate inquiries by the public into their
performance.

We urge that the press be sensitive to the complaint of
any segment of the community which feels it has insuf-
ficient access to the media.

Responsible journalism provides a balance so that adequate
play is given to all sides of controversial news.

Opinion and advocacy journalism should be clearly, visibly
identified as such.

All journalism schools would do well to include a basic
course in law, particularly as it pertains to the rights
of the individual. There should also be an obligation
assumed by public legal agencies--from criminal prosecutors to regulatory authorities at state and federal
levels--to make their facilities available to brief
journalists and journalism students on government processes. In the Southern District of New York, the U.S. Attorney's office invited journalists to observe the complete
judicial process, restricting only the reporting of particular cases. This experiment may well serve as a model.

A GENERAL GUIDE FOR GOVERNMENT AND THE NEWS MEDIA IN
DIRECTING THEIR RELATIONSHIP IN JUDICIAL AND OTHER PROCESSES

1.   The successful free-press/fair-trial guidelines and
     conferences which have been adopted in several states
     should be extended throughout the nation, with the
     fullest possible participation by representatives of
     news media, bench, and bar. Constructive dialogues
     on other subjects of mutual concern and interest
     should be encouraged and facilitated among the
     participants.

2.   (a) The news media should continue to be free at
     their own discretion--and risk--to publish any

information which comes into their possession concerning judicial proceedings, including grand jury testimony.

It should be understand that in the grand jury system in many jurisdictions, including the federal, the witness is free to reveal what happens in a grand jury room; sessions are held in secret primarily to protect the witness. Publishing information concerning grand jury proceedings should be carefully weighed against the possibility that publication may place the witness in jeopardy, may impede the administration of justice, and may unfairly injure third persons.

In this or other matters, journalists are not free to engage in criminal conduct, or to aid or abet others in criminal conduct, in order to obtain such information, and are fully answerable for any such violation of law on their part.

(b) Confidential news sources should be protected. Investigative reporting is today seriously endangered. We support implementation of standards to be followed by courts in passing on motions to quash subpoenas generally in keeping with the principles referred to in the opinions of Justices Powell and Stewart concurring and dissenting in the *Caldwell* case.[4] We recognize there has been a breakdown, at times, in the tacit relationship between press and prosecutors which had existed, without statutes, at the federal and most state levels.

The mutual respect of the press and prosecutors ought to be reestablished so that reporters may fulfill their legal, moral, and public obligation to confide in prosecutors when necessary in the public interest, and prosecutors may inquire into press sources when they feel it is absolutely essential. This

---

[4]Justice Powell declared: "If the newsman is called upon to give information bearing only a remote and tenuous relationship to the subject of the investigation, or if he has some other reason to believe that his testimony implicates confidential source relationships without a legitimate need of law enforcement, he will have access to the court in a motion to quash and an appropriate protective order may be entered." Justice Stewart wrote: "When a reporter is asked to appear before a grand jury and reveal confidences, I would hold that the government must (1) show that there is probable violation of law; (2) demonstrate that the information sought cannot be obtained by alternative means less destructive of First Amendment rights, and (3) demonstrate a compelling and overriding interest in the information."

relationship cannot be restored by legislation, but only by mutual trust.

3. No "Official Secrets Acts" should be adopted which would permit government officials to control press publication of documents through a document classification procedure. A sensible revision of the Espionage Act to clarify its scope and applicability is long overdue.

4. The government should not force news media to rely on formal litigation under the Freedom of Information Act to obtain access to information in the possession of government agencies.

5. National and local press councils should be carefully observed to discover whether they do indeed help restore and maintain public confidence in the fairness and objectivity of the press. At a time when the press faces a credibility crisis, the councils might enable the public to scrutinize the news media, provide for the airing of legitimate grievances, and open a useful dialogue between the press and the public. But press councils could become counterproductive if they lack the time, knowledge, or balance properly to fulfill their self-assigned mission. In taking positions on the "fairness" of press coverage of an issue, any council also risks becoming ensnared in the controversy over the issue itself.

6. In light of the loss of remedy for injured persons resulting from the strict limitation on the right to sue for libel, consideration should be given to creating a new statutory right of redress under which a person who believes he has been aggrieved because of a false news account may demand publication of a retraction, upon a showing of grounds therefor. In the event no retraction is published, he may then recover compensatory damages if he can prove in a court of law that the original news account was false.

7. The American people should have the right to the free flow of news in the broadcast media, unregulated by government. With the increasing diversity of radio stations, television channels, and cable TV technology, the original rationale for governmental regulation is passing. We hope the day will soon arrive when the Fairness Doctrine and other regulatory procedures may be eliminated.

A. SPECIFIC GUIDELINES FOR GOVERNMENT OFFICIALS

1. Upon request, a government official should be willing candidly to discuss the substance of information which comes into his possession during the course of his official duties, unless he is convinced that public disclosure will harm the public interest. A government official ought not refuse to make disclosure of information in his possession in order to protect personal or political interests.

2. In the event that a government official believes that disclosure of information will harm the public interest, he should inform any journalist requesting such information of the fact of its existence and the general reasons for his decision not to make disclosure.

3. A government official should not resort to the device of "leaking" information to a journalist or providing the information "off the record" unless there is good and sufficient reason why he cannot openly make disclosure of such information and he advises the journalist of his reason for doing so indirectly.

4. A government official should not release false information or make false representations as to the existence or nonexistence of requested information.

5. A government official should, upon request, provide all responsible journalists equal access to information which is to be disclosed.

6. A government official should make himself reasonably available to respond to inquiries from journalists.

7. A government official should continuously bear in mind his obligation to account to the public on the discharge of his office and his responsibilities, and should be willing to make full and accurate information available concerning the same at regular and frequent intervals.

8. No agent of the government should impersonate a reporter.

B. SPECIFIC GUIDELINES FOR JOURNALISTS

1. A journalist should report the news impartially and fairly.

2. A journalist should assume full responsibility for the accuracy and truthfulness of any news he reports. He should adequately qualify the reliability of any unidentified news source whenever making public information from such source, to enable the public properly to decide the weight to be given to the information.

3. A journalist should protect the freedom of the press, while giving due consideration to the Constitutional rights of others, including the right of persons accused of crime to due process of law.

4. A journalist should avoid activities which might create a conflict of interest, and should promptly disclose to his employer any actual or potential conflict.

5. A journalist should file with his employer regular reports of outside compensation and financial interests.

6. A journalist should refrain from publicly undisclosed extracurricular activities which might raise questions about his professional objectivity.

* * *

The irreducible issue with which we are concerned is the right and need of the citizenry to be fully, accurately, and continually informed of the action and policies of its public servants. This requirement, which the First Amendment guarantees, imposes on both government and news media the obligations to repair their badly damaged professional relations, to restore mutual respect and collaboration in the faithful release and reporting of public information, and to subordinate their respective institutional interests to the overriding interests of an enlightened and responsible electorate.

Tables

Table 1
ASSOCIATED PRESS "SOURCE BREADTH," SHOWING ORIGIN
BY DATELINE OF AP STORIES FILED FROM VIETNAM IN FEBRUARY-MARCH 1968

Dateline	Number of Stories									
	Feb.1-4	5-11	12-18	19-25	26-Mar.3	4-10	11-17	18-24	25-31	Totals
Saigon	36	74	63	74	67	78	86	74	103	655
Khe Sanh		6	6	12	10	6	8	1	4	53
Hue	4	10	11	17	4	3	1	1	1	51
Da Nang	2	2	1	1		2	2	2	5	17
Delta		5		1	3	2	2			13
Central Highlands	1	1	1	1	1	2	1		1	7
Totals	43	98	81	106	84	93	99	78	114	796

Note to Table 1: This table is based on AP files of stories filed by the Saigon bureau. The preponderance of Saigon datelines distorts somewhat the activity of AP reporters in the hinterland, since their reports were on occasion summarized in the Saigon war wrap-ups without also appearing as separate stories. Our reading of AP dispatches, however, indicates that such incorporations occurred infrequently. The Saigon dateline appeared on successive versions of the same day's war wrap-up and sidebars on the air war, naval action, etc., artificially multiplying the number of "Saigon" datelines by a factor of two on some days. We do see the table as reflecting: (1) AP's preoccupation with a few locales, e.g., Saigon, Khe Sanh, Hue; (2) the fall-off in non-Saigon stories in March; and (3) the absence of any systematic coverage of developments in the Delta and Central Highlands.

Table 2
ASSOCIATED PRESS NIGHT LEADS ORIGINATING IN SAIGON AND SUMMARIZING DAILY WAR DEVELOPMENTS IN FEBRUARY-MARCH 1968

Subject	Locale of Story Action and Number of Mentions in Leads									
	Feb. 1-4	5-11	12-18	19-25	26-Mar. 3	4-10	11-17	18-24	25-31	Totals
Allied ground initiative	HSH 3	HHSH 4		SSHH 4	S 1	XX 2	XX 2	SSX 3	SS 2	21
Allied losses	X 1	X 1		S 1	*K Dmz SSS 5	*KXX 3	X 1	*K 1	*X 1	14
Enemy ground initiative	XHK 3	KKK 3	Dmz S 3	S 1	KKS 3	XK 2	XK 2	SXK 3	XX 2	18
Enemy bombardment only			SS 2	KS 2	SS 2	XX 2	Dmz} X 2		X 1	14
Neither initiative	H 1	H 1	HSH 1		Dmz 1	Dmz 1				6
Enemy attack looming	K 1	K 1	KS 2	SSSS 4	SS 2		D'phu} XK 3	SK 2		15
Enemy losses	XXX 3	X 1		S 1	S 1	XXX 3	Dmz} X 2		S 1	12
Saigon/Tan Son Nhut	1	1	3	2	3	1	1	3	2	17
Khe Sanh	1	3		1	2	1	1	1		11
Hue	2	3	3	2		2				10
DMZ			1		1		1	1		5
Naval action					X 1					1
S.V. or allied troops	HX 2	HKK HSHH 7		SH 2	KK 2	Dmz} K 2			X 1	16
U.S. troops	HXHK 4	XXH 3	SHS 3	KS 2	Dmz K 2					14
Air war		1	1	2	1			2	3	10
Totals	22	29	19	24	27	19	15	16	13	184

H = Hue; K = Khe Sanh; S = Saigon area; Dmz = Demilitarized Zone; X = elsewhere or overall; D'phu = Dienbienphu comparison story; *aircraft loss.

Note to Table 2: This rough analysis was based on examination of file copies of 60 AP night leads out of Saigon in the period designated. For our purposes, the "night lead" consists of the two opening paragraphs of the overall AP war wrap-up written in Saigon for morning newspapers in the United States. As many as three successive night leads, incorporating fresh developments, were transmitted from Saigon on a given day; we picked the latest in the files (see index of AP stories from Vietnam). The night leads were the prime source of Vietnam news for the vast majority of AP's clients--newspapers and radio-TV stations. The first two paragraphs usually governed the newspaper headline and supplied the entire radio or television report, although the complete dispatch might total as much as 1,100 words--far more than any but the larger newspapers had space for.

Our categories were defined broadly:

Allied ground initiative: U.S. Marine counterattacks at Hue, the U.S. Army sweep at My Lai, ARVN counterattacks in Saigon, and the allies' post-March 10 "Resolve to Win" offensive around Saigon.

Allied losses: U.S. and ARVN casualties, cited by number or indicated as "losses"; the downing of a U.S. aircraft (which, however irrelevant to the war's overall course, got into the lead four times).

Enemy ground initiative: Vietcong or North Vietnamese infantry attacks against allied forces (rather than merely bombardments or "attacks by fire"), notably at Khe Sanh, the Demilitarized Zone, or around Saigon.

Enemy bombardment only: "bombardments" ranging from 500 or more rockets and shells dropped on Khe Sanh, to a hit-and-run rocket attack on Tan Son Nhut Airport near Saigon, or simultaneous low-intensity mortar fire against a dozen towns and cities (mid-February). AP and UPI tended to give all such bombardments prominence.

Neither initiative: reports of no-gain by either side, notably in the Hue battle.

Enemy attack looming: explicit statements that the North Vietnamese were expected to attack or about to attack, at Saigon or Khe Sanh. (One lead linked Khe Sanh to the 1954 French disaster at Dienbienphu.)

Enemy losses: official announcements in Saigon of (exaggerated) enemy overall losses and reports of enemy casualties in specific actions, including the 167 body count for My Lai.

Saigon/Tan Son Nhut, Khe Sanh, Hue, DMZ: the primary loci of the action reported on; 38 of the 60 night leads focused on Saigon, Khe Sanh, or Hue.

Naval action: the interception of North Vietnamese blockade runners.

South Vietnamese or allied (U.S. and South Vietnamese) troops: mentioned in 16 AP night leads out of 60, and, as the table indicates, cited as present by the AP (in contrast to TV and others) early during the Khe Sanh siege.

U.S. troops: mentioned alone in 14 leads.

(continued next page)

Note to Table 2: (*continued*)

Air war: covered U.S. air strikes against North Vietnam and accounted for 10 mentions in night leads, although "Air North" was largely tangential to the immediate tactical situation described elsewhere in the war wrap-up.

Our analysis shows that, not unexpectedly, the "negative" statements showing allied forces at a disadvantage (the categories Allied losses, Enemy ground initiative, Enemy bombardment only, Enemy attack looming) outnumbered those showing Hanoi's forces at a disadvantage (Allied ground initiative and Enemy losses) in the early stages of the Tet offensive. Overall, for the entire February-March period, "negative" statements totaled 61, "positive" statements 33. Statements showing neither side at an advantage numbered 6.

What is interesting is that the preponderance of "negative" statements in AP night leads continued during the March 4-March 31 period--a period that began a month after the Vietcong-North Vietnamese forces withdrew from most of the towns and cities attacked, and 10 days after the recapture of Hue by the allies. During that period, the North Vietnamese launched several probes at Khe Sanh, and the allies were far from securing all of the countryside left "insecure" by Tet. But the observable overall military situation was improving sharply, with the announcement of the "Resolve to Win" offensive, the decline in enemy shelling of Khe Sanh, and the slackening of fresh enemy initiatives.

The traditional war wrap-up focus on *specifics*, however insignificant, helps account for this preponderance of "negative" statements in March--three U.S. plane crashes and six enemy bombardments. So does the wire-service penchant for "what's next": Five times in March the AP night lead included speculation on "looming enemy attacks," including a reference to Dienbienphu. Subtract these irrelevancies from the AP night leads, and a closer approximation to the observable *overall* battlefield reality would have emerged. But in March 1968 the AP's "negative" tilt, resulting from wire-service habits and competition for editors' attention, provided the grist for more extended distortions of the reality by other media.

Table 3
NEW YORK *TIMES* AND WASHINGTON *POST* "SOURCE BREADTH," SHOWING
ORIGIN BY DATELINE OF *TIMES* AND *POST* STORIES FILED FROM VIETNAM IN FEBRUARY–MARCH 1968

Dateline		Feb. 1-4	5-11	12-18	19-25	26-Mar. 3	4-10	11-17	18-24	25-31	Totals	Totals All Stories
Saigon	*Times*	*5* 9	*12* 9	*8* 7	*9* 10	*11* 8	*11* 6	*10* 10	*10* 10	*8* 9	*84* 78	162
	Post	*10* 7	*9* 17	*8* 7	*11* 11	*8* 12	*9* 7	*3* 12	*5* 8	*2* 18	*65* 99	164
Khe Sanh	*Times*		1	2	1	*1*	*1*	2		1	*2* 7	9
	Post		2	1	2	1				1	*3* 7	10
Hue	*Times*	*2*	*3* 2	*1* 1	*3* 3	*2* 3			1		*11* 10	21
	Post		*1*	*3* 2	*4* 5	*1* 3				1	*9* 11	20
Da Nang	*Times*	*1*	*1* 1	1	1					2	*2* 5	7
	Post		1	*1*	*1*				*1*	1	*3* 2	5
Delta	*Times*		*1* 1	1		1	*1*	*1*			*1* 3	4
	Post		1			1	1	*6*			*1* 9	10
Central Highlands	*Times*	1	1	1			*1*	1	1	1	*0* 7	7
	Post						*1*		1		*1* 1	2
Elsewhere	*Times*						*1*	1	1	*1* 2	*1* 6	7
	Post					2	2	1	1	2	*0* 1	6
Totals	*Times*	*8* 10	*16* 15	*11* 12	*12* 15	*13* 14	*12* 9	*10* 14	*10* 13	*9* 14	*101* 116	217
	Post	*10* 7	*12* 21	*12* 11	*16* 18	*10* 16	*11* 10	*3* 19	*6* 10	*2* 23	*82* 135	217

Italics indicate page-one stories.

Note to Table 3: This table distorts the origins of published articles, whether from wire services or the papers' own Saigon correspondents, much less than does Table 1, since staff-written stories from the field were seldom incorporated into stories filed from Saigon. The table also indicates which stories got page-one coverage. See the story index for each newspaper for the writer or wire-service authorship of each story, as well as for its location in the paper.

Table 4

NEW YORK *TIMES* STORIES DEALING WITH VIETNAM DEVELOPMENTS BUT ORIGINATING IN WASHINGTON OR ELSEWHERE OUTSIDE SOUTH VIETNAM AND LAOS IN FEBRUARY-MARCH 1968

Subject	Feb. 1-4	5-11	12-18	19-25	26-Mar. 3	4-10	11-17	18-24	25-31	Totals	Totals All Stories
					Number of Stories						
Johnson	3		*3*	*1*	*1* 1	*1*	*2*	*1* 3	*1*	*12* 4	16
Administration, other	2	*1* 1	*1* 1	*2* 2	*1* 2	*1* 5	*2* 2	2	*1* 6	*9* 23	32
Hawks, Congress		*1*	*1*	1		*1*	*1*		*1*	*5* 1	6
Antis, Congress	2	*1* 2	3	*1* 4	*3*	*1*	*2*	*2*	*2* 2	*12* 14	26
Antis, other		3	8	*1* 6	*3* 4	13	6	*4* 7	*1* 3	*10* 50	60
"Nukes"		3	*4*					1		*4* 4	8
Diplomacy		*1* 2	*3* 2	*2* 1	*1*	2	*2* 1	1	1	*6* 10	16
Troops			*1*		*1*	*1*	*2* 1			*8* 2	10
Hanoi, statements	2	*6*	*1*	*1*	3		*1* 1	*1*	*1* 1	*4* 12	16
Polls, Nixon-Romney	*1* 1	3	2			*1* 1	2		1	*2* 8	10
Administration, negative polls	*1* 1		*1* 1	*1*		1	1	2	1	*4* 7	11
Administration, positive polls		*1* 1		4	1	1	1	2	1	*1* 10	11
Vietnam, negative		*1*	*1* 1		*1* 1	*1* 3	1	*2*	2	*4* 9	13
Vietnam, positive		1	3			1	1		1	*0* 7	7
Totals	*7* 5	*6* 21	*14* 21	*10* 22	*12* 12	*6* 26	*10* 17	*10* 19	*6* 18	*81* 161	242

Italics indicate page-one stories.

Table 5

WASHINGTON *POST* STORIES DEALING WITH VIETNAM DEVELOPMENTS BUT ORIGINATING IN
WASHINGTON OR ELSEWHERE OUTSIDE SOUTH VIETNAM AND LAOS IN FEBRUARY-MARCH 1968

Subject					Number of Stories						
	Feb. 1-4	5-11	12-18	19-25	26-Mar. 3	4-10	11-17	18-24	25-31	Totals	Totals All Stories
Johnson	*2*	*1* 4	*4*	2	*4*	2	*2*	*4* 1	4	*22* 3	25
Administration, other	*2* 1	*1* 4	*1* 1	*1*	*1* 3	*1* 1	*2* 1		*1* 2	*10* 13	23
Hawks, Congress		1	1	1	1					*0* 4	4
Antis, Congress	*1*	*1* 3	*1* 1	*1* 2	2	*1* 1	*2* 1	*5* 2	1	*10* 13	23
Antis, other	1	3	1	1		2	5	3	1	*3* 16	19
"Nukes"		1	*1* 1				1			*1* 3	4
Diplomacy	1	*2* 2	*2* 1	*1* 2	1	*2*		3		*5* 9	14
Troops		*1*	*1*	2	1		*1* 2			*6* 3	9
Hanoi, statements	5	*1* 1	*1* 1	1	1					*2* 10	12
Polls, Nixon-Romney	1	3	*1* 3	1	1	*1*	1			*2* 9	11
Administration, negative polls		1	1	*4*	*2*	3	2		*1* 3	*11* 8	19
Administration, positive polls			*1*	*1*	*1*	2				*4* 0	4
Vietnam, negative	*1*	*1* 1	*1*	*1*		*2*			*1*	*4* 3	7
Vietnam, positive			2							*0* 2	2
Totals	*5* 9	*7* 20	*12* 13	*13* 8	*8* 9	*10* 8	*7* 13	*11* 9	*7* 7	*80* 96	176

Italics indicate page-one stories.

Note to Tables 4 and 5: These tables compare *Times* and *Post* treatment of various aspects of domestic Vietnam "debate," diplomatic moves, public opinion polls, and reports from Hanoi or by Washington-based reporters concerning the situation on the ground in Vietnam. No commentary or editorials are included, nor is it reporting *from* Vietnam. We are concerned as much with the "play"--position on or off page one--of stories as with the number in each category. We categorized each story by its dominant subject, as expressed in headline and the first few paragraphs.

The *Times*, not unexpectedly, produced a greater volume of stories than did the *Post,* by a margin of 242 to 176. However, if both newspapers' coverage of non-Congressional doves is excluded from the count, the margin narrows considerably, to 182 to 157. In short, the *Times*'s receptivity to activities and statements of peace groups gave such groups access to that paper which they did not get in the *Post.* One-fourth of the *Times*'s 242 items-- and one-eight of its page-one stories--in this table dealt with non-Congressional protest, much of it in universities, against the Johnson war policy. The *Post,* for its part, was markedly more generous to President Johnson, putting him on page one almost twice as many times as the *Times* did.

All told, if one adds up the total "play" given to the Administration and its critics, there is this picture:

	Times		*Post*	
	Page One	Inside	Page One	Inside
Unfavorable (Antis, Congress; Antis, other; Hanoi statements; Administration, negative polls; Vietnam, negative)	34	92	30	50
Favorable (Johnson; Administration, other; Hawks, Congress; Administration, positive polls; Vietnam, positive)	27	45	36	22

In short, the negative or unfavorable "play" on page one was about the same for both newspapers; both, inside, were heavily unfavorable. There was far greater access to page one in the *Post,* unfavorable page-one staff-written stories on the making page one of that paper a good deal more favorable to the Administration than was the *Times.*

It is worth noting that, both on the *Times* and on the *Post,* unfavorable page-one staff-written stories on the Vietnam military situation, originating in Washington or New York, were more numerous in March (when the situation on the ground was improving) than in February. In many categories, there was little difference between the two papers--the page-one "play" given to the possibility of more troops for Vietnam, the statements of G.O.P. Presidential hopefuls, the rumors and reports of diplomatic endeavor. The *Post,* as always, was more interested in public opinion polls (15 page-one stories) than the *Times* (five). The *Times* gave more prominence than the *Post* to the speculative furor over possible use of nuclear weapons in Vietnam, and more attention to Hanoi's statements.

Few surprises crop up in this table, except for the degree of the *Post*'s sensitivity to Johnson, and the high proportion of its news space which the *Times,* to a greater extent than any other medium at Tet, gave over to non-Congressional doves. (The AP provided a steady flow of such copy to its clients, but none of them appeared to use as much of it as did the *Times*.) The *Times*'s orientation toward the university campuses, where so much of such protest was generated, may have reinforced its receptivity to this news, even as the *Post* management's once-close personal relationship with Johnson may have helped the President's prominence in that newspaper.

Note to Tables 6-13: These tables were prepared from an analysis of Vietnam-related articles in the Sunday and Monday editions of the New York *Times* and the Washington *Post* during the designated period--a sampling that included the bulk of the commentary, but only a small percentage of the stories. The "statements" were those perceived, arranged by subject-matter categories, and rated "positive," "negative," or "neutral" with respect to the Administration side of the Vietnam argument. We do not claim that the ratings are infallible, but we believe they are consistent; the trends over time, and other aspects, interest us more than "ratings" of individual stories.

For the *Times*, our sampling of page-one stories from Vietnam showed that, overall, they contained a higher ratio of negative to positive statements (63-40) than did these allotted space inside the paper (45 to 37). (This trend, however, changed in March when positive statements gained more visibility.) In our sampling of *Times* reporting from Washington and elsewhere, the reverse was true, indicative of the dominance of Administration statements in early February which got on page one, and of the *Times*'s penchant for recording antiwar statements, which mostly landed inside. (Table 4 shows that of all 242 *Times* stories in this domestic category, no fewer than 60 were devoted to the actions and statements of antiwar groups and 26 dealt similarly with Congressional doves; of these 86 "protest" stories, 22 landed on page one.)

For the *Times* sampling overall, the tone was negative even in March, when military recovery was underway in Vietnam. The decline in quantity that month of both reporting and commentary "statements" was marked. But in several of the "military" categories, it can be seen that something akin to balance began to emerge in the reporting from Vietnam in March 1968, reflecting the situation on the ground. During the month, also, an upswing trend occurred in commentary from Vietnam, when negative statements outweighed positive by only 14 to 9. No such trend occurred in commentary written in Washington and elsewhere, however; the negative continued to dominate, 28 to 4, in the period March 4-31, despite the military recovery.

For the *Post*, page-one stories from Vietnam were, as for the *Times*, more negative (52 to 40) than those on inside pages (48 to 49), where there was something like a balance over the two-month period covered in our sampling. To a greater extent than the *Times*, however, the *Post* reporting from Vietnam reflected the upturn in the military situation in March, even as the prominence and quantity of that reporting diminished. In March, positive statements on page one (9) reached rough parity with negative (11), and inside the paper outnumbered the latter (25 to 17).

Post reporting from Washington was more negative than *Post* reporting from Vietnam--64 negative to 39 positive statements in domestic reporting, again partly because of the rebroadcast effect of the debate in Washington over Vietnam policy. But the *Post* was far less negative in this sphere than the *Times*, partly because the former paid little attention to non-Congressional doves and campus protest. The *Post* sharply cut the visibility of the Vietnam battle and its domestic reverberations in March by devoting more page-one space to national politics.

Scanty *Post* commentary from Vietnam was heavily concentrated in February, and negative overall *Post* commentary from Washington and elsewhere was characteristically far more voluminous, and erratic as to tone; it showed no upturn to match *Post* reporting from Vietnam.

If one adds up all the statements across the range of the sample for the *Times* and the *Post*, one finds this pattern:

	Times		*Post*	
	N	P	N	P
Reporting from Vietnam	108	77	100	89
Reporting from Washington, etc.	85	33	64	39
Commentary from Vietnam	52	11	19	2
Commentary from U.S.	89	9	41	21

In short, the *Times* was more negative than the *Post*, especially in its domestic commentary and reporting. Both newspapers, respectively, were far more negative in their domestic commentary than in their Vietnam reporting; commentary from Vietnam in both papers, but particularly in the *Post*, was heavily concentrated in the early February period, and tended to fade out, while the domestic commentary on the Vietnam crisis flowed on indefatigably.

Table 6

"POSITIVE" AND "NEGATIVE" STATEMENTS IN NEW YORK *TIMES* REPORTING FROM SOUTH VIETNAM IN FEBRUARY-MARCH 1968

Statements	Feb. 1-4	5-11	12-18	19-25	26-Mar. 3	4-10	11-17	18-24	25-31	Totals	Totals All Statements
Tet is military victory or defeat for enemy	2P 1N			2P			1N			4P 1P / 1N 1N	7
Tet is psychological victory or defeat for enemy in Vietnam	1P 3N 4N									1P 4N / 3N	8
Tet is psychological victory or defeat for enemy in U.S.	1N	1N				1N				2N	2
War is unwinnable, too costly, etc.; Johnson policy is right or wrong											
U.S. strategy and tactics	3N 4N	3P 2P			2N					3N 4N	7
U.S. troop morale	3P 2P						1P		2P	6P 7P / 1N 2N	15
Khe Sanh, all references except Dienbienphu	1N 4X 3X	1N 1X			2X		1X	2X		2N 8X / 5X 8X	15
Khe Sanh, compared to Dienbienphu						1N			1N	1N	1
Enemy weapons, behavior, tactics, and strategy	2N 6N	2N	5N			1N				10N 6N	16
Enemy has initiative, will or may attack; or U.S./S.V. has initiative, is moving offensively	1P 2N 11N	8N	2N 1N	3P 1N	3P 2P	4N	6P 3P / 2N	3N	2P 6N	13P 7P / 28N 12N	60
U.S. or enemy is responsible for civilian destruction and deaths	2P 2N	3P 1N		2P		2P				2P 7P / 3N	12
S.V. police/military performance	1P 2P / 6N 5N			1P		1P				3P 2P / 6N 5N	16
GVN has or lacks popular support	2N				3P 1P					3P 1P / 2N	6
GVN response to Tet emergency	1P			4P 1N / 2N	1P / 2N	1P	2P 1N		2P	2P 11P / 4N 3N	30
Pacification is temporarily set back, crippled indefinitely, or dead	2P 2N / 2N			3P 1N	1P	1P				6P 1P / 2N 2N	11
U.S. is or is not considering use of nuclear weapons											
U.S. is planning or not, needs or does not, big troop increase, reserve call-up, or more taxes				2N						2N	2
Totals	11P 7P / 32N 24N / 4X 3X	3P 5P / 12N 1N / 1X	7N 1N	11P 4P / 2N 5N / 1N	6P 5P / 2N 2N / 2X	3P 2P / 5N	6P 6P / 4N 1X	2P 3N / 2X	6P 7N	40P 37P / 63N 45N / 5X 8X	198
	47 34	16 6	7 1	13 9	8 9	8 2	6 11	3 5	13	13 (108/90)	

Sunday and Monday editions only.
Italics indicate page-one stories.
P = positive; N = negative; X = neutral.

Table 7

"POSITIVE" AND "NEGATIVE" STATEMENTS IN NEW YORK *TIMES*
REPORTING FROM WASHINGTON AND ELSEWHERE OUTSIDE VIETNAM IN FEBRUARY–MARCH 1968

Statements	Feb. 1-4	5-11	12-18	19-25	26-Mar. 3	4-10	11-17	18-24	25-31	Totals	Totals All Statements
Tet is military victory or defeat for enemy	4P 1N					*1P 1N*				5P 1N *1N*	7
Tet is psychological victory or defeat for enemy in Vietnam	*1P*									*1P*	1
Tet is psychological victory or defeat for enemy in U.S.	2N	2N				*1N*				1N *4N*	5
War is unwinnable, too costly, etc.; Johnson policy is right or wrong	1P 5N	1N	*3P 3N*	*1N 3N*	2P *5N*	*4N*	1P 2P *2N 2N*		2N	7P 2P 15N *16N*	40
U.S. strategy and tactics	3P	1P				*3N*			*1N*	3P 1P *4N*	8
U.S. troop morale											
Khe Sanh, all references except Dienbienphu	2X	1X	2X							4X *1X*	5
Khe Sanh, compared to Dienbienphu		1N	*1N*			*1N*				1N *2N*	3
Enemy weapons, behavior, tactics, and strategy		*2P*					*1N*			2P *1N*	3
Enemy has initiative, will or may attack; or U.S./S.V. has initiative, is moving offensively	*2N*	*3N*							*1N*	*6N*	6
U.S. or enemy is responsible for civilian destruction and deaths	3P *7N*	1P 1N	*1N*							3P *1P* 7N *2N*	13
S.V. police/military performance		2P 2N					*2N*			2P *4N*	6
GVN has or lacks popular support	2N					*1N*				1N *2N*	3
GVN response to Tet emergency	1N	1N		*3N*		*1N*	*1P*			1P *5N*	6
Pacification is temporarily set back, crippled indefinitely, or dead	1N	1N					*1N*			*3N*	3
U.S. is or is not considering use of nuclear weapons		*2N*		3N						5N	5
U.S. is planning or not, needs or does not, big troop increase, reserve call-up, or more taxes	*1P*					1P *3N*	*2P*		1P *1N*	5P *4N*	9
Totals	13P *9N* 13N *2X* / 24	2P *4P* 3N *10N* *1X* / 15	3P *4N* 2X / 9	1N *6N* / 6	2P *5N* / 7	2P *13N* / 15	3P *3P* 2N *10N* / 13		1P *3N* / 6	26P *7P* 40N *45N* 4X *1X* (70) *(53)*	123

Sunday and Monday editions only.
Italics indicate page-one stories.
P = positive; N = negative; X = neutral.

Table 8

"POSITIVE" AND "NEGATIVE" STATEMENTS IN NEW YORK *TIMES* COMMENTARY FROM SOUTH VIETNAM IN FEBRUARY-MARCH 1968

Number of Statements

Statements	Feb. 1-4	5-11	12-18	19-25	26-Mar. 3	4-10	11-17	18-24	25-31	Totals	Totals All Statements
Tet is military victory or defeat for enemy											
Tet is psychological victory or defeat for enemy in Vietnam	3N	1N							1N	5N	5
Tet is psychological victory or defeat for enemy in U.S.	2N									2N	2
War is unwinnable, too costly, etc.; Johnson policy is right or wrong	4N	1N		1N	2N				1N	9N	9
U.S. strategy and tactics			1N 1X	1X	1X			2X		1N 5X	6
U.S. troop morale											
Khe Sanh, all references except Dienbienphu				1N						1N	1
Khe Sanh, compared to Dienbienphu											
Enemy weapons, behavior, tactics, and strategy				1N	1N		1P 1N			1P 3N	4
Enemy has initiative, will or may attack; or U.S./S.V. has initiative, is moving offensively	2N		2N	2N	3N	1N	2P	2P 2N		4P 12N	16
U.S. or enemy is responsible for civilian destruction and deaths						1N				1N	1
S.V. police/military performance	1N	2N 1P				1P	2N		1N	2P 6N	8
GVN has or lacks popular support			1N			1P			1N	1P 2N	3
GVN response to Tet emergency		5N 1P				1P			1N	2P 6N	8
Pacification is temporarily set back, crippled indefinitely, or dead				1N	1N	1P			1N	1P 3N	4
U.S. is or is not considering use of nuclear weapons											
U.S. is planning or not, needs or does not, big troop increase, reserve call-up, or more taxes						1N				1N	1
Totals	12N	2P 9N	4N 1X	6N 1X	7N 1X	4P 3N	3P 3N	2P 2N 2X	6N	11P 52N 5X	(11P)(52N)(5X)
	12	11	5	7	8	7	6	6	6	(68)	68

Sunday and Monday editions only.

P = positive; N = negative; X = neutral.

Table 9
"POSITIVE" AND "NEGATIVE" STATEMENTS IN NEW YORK *TIMES*
COMMENTARY FROM WASHINGTON AND ELSEWHERE OUTSIDE VIETNAM IN FEBRUARY-MARCH 1968

Statements	Feb. 1-4	5-11	12-18	19-25	26-Mar. 3	4-10	11-17	18-24	25-31	Totals	Totals All Statements
					Number of Statements						
Tet is military victory or defeat for enemy	1P					1N		1N		1P 2N	3
Tet is psychological victory or defeat for enemy in Vietnam	1P 1N								1N	1P 2N	3
Tet is psychological victory or defeat for enemy in U.S.	3N	1N					1N	2N		7N	7
War is unwinnable, too costly, etc.; Johnson policy is right or wrong	4N	4N	1N	2N		3N	5N	3N	1N	23N	23
U.S. strategy and tactics	1N	1N						2N	1P	1P 4N	5
U.S. troop morale											
Khe Sanh, all references except Dienbienphu	2P 4X	2X						1X		2P 7X	9
Khe Sanh, compared to Dienbienphu	1P 6N 1X	1X								1P 6N 2X	9
Enemy weapons, behavior, tactics, and strategy	1N	3N			1N		1N			6N	6
Enemy has initiative, will or may attack; or U.S./S.V. has initiative, is moving offensively	6N	2N		1N		1N				10N	10
U.S. or enemy is responsible for civilian destruction and deaths											
S.V. police/military performance	4N				1N			1N		6N	6
GVN has or lacks popular support	1N	1N					1N			3N	3
GVN response to Tet emergency	3N	3N						1P	1N	1P 7N	8
Pacification is temporarily set back, crippled indefinitely, or dead		2N					1N	1N		4N	4
U.S. is or is not considering use of nuclear weapons			1N	1N						2N	2
U.S. is planning or not, needs or does not, big troop increase, reserve call-up, or more taxes	2N				4N			1P 1N	1P	2P 7N	9
Totals	5P 32N 5X	17N 3X	2N	4N	6N	5N	9N	2P 11N 1X	2P 3N	9P 89N 9X	(9P)(89N)(9X)
	42	20	2	4	6	5	9	14	5	(107)	107

Sunday and Monday editions only.
P = positive; N = negative; X = neutral.

Table 10

"POSITIVE" AND "NEGATIVE" STATEMENTS IN WASHINGTON *POST* REPORTING FROM SOUTH VIETNAM IN FEBRUARY-MARCH 1968

Statements	Number of Statements									Totals	Totals All Statements
	Feb. 1-4	5-11	12-18	19-25	26-Mar. 3	4-10	11-17	18-24	25-31		
Tet is military victory or defeat for enemy	1P 2N					1N				1P 3N	4
Tet is psychological victory or defeat for enemy in Vietnam	*1P 1N*		2P				2P 1N			*1P 1N* 4P 1N	7
Tet is psychological victory or defeat for enemy in U.S.							1N			1N	1
War is unwinnable, too costly, etc.; Johnson policy is right or wrong				*2N*	*2P*					*1P 2N*	3
U.S. strategy and tactics	1P 2P / 4N 2N	1P 5N / 2P				1N	1P 2N		1P 2N	4P 5P / 6N 12N	27
U.S. troop morale	3P	2P		2P 2N				*1P 1N*		1P 9P / 1N 2N	13
Khe Sanh, all references except Dienbienphu	3X	1P 1X / *2X*			*2X*		*1X*			1P 1X / 8X *1X*	10
Khe Sanh, compared to Dienbienphu		1P								1P	1
Enemy weapons, behavior, tactics, and strategy	2P 3P / 3N 4N	*1P*		*1N*				*2P 3N*		7P 3P / 5N 4N	19
Enemy has initiative, will or may attack; or U.S./S.V. has initiative, is moving offensively	8P 1P / 12N 2N	*4N 3N*	*3N*	1P 1N / *1N*	*1N*	2N	2P / *2N*	1N	3P	9P 7P / 23N 8N	47
U.S. or enemy is responsible for civilian destruction and deaths	2P 3N	*1P*		*1P*	*1P*	1N	1N	*1N*	*1P*	3P 3N / 4N	10
S.V. police/military performance	3P 2P / 2N 1N	1P 1N / *1N*		*1P*		5P 4N	1N		*1P*	4P 9P / 3N 6N	22
GVN has or lacks popular support	2N / *1N*						*2N*	*1N*		*1P 1P* / 2N 2N	7
GVN response to Tet emergency	3P 2N			*1P*		1N 4P	*1P* 2P / *1N*		*3P*	8P 6P / 3N 2N	19
Pacification is temporarily set back, crippled indefinitely, or dead	*1N*			3P				1P		*1P 3P / 1N*	5
U.S. is or is not considering use of nuclear weapons											
U.S. is planning or not, needs or does not, big troop increase, reserve call-up, or more taxes				3N						3N	3
Totals	22P 11P / 29N 16N / 3X — 54 *27*	1P 6P / 4N 9N / 2X 1X — 16 *7*	2P 2P / 3N — 5 *2*	4P 5P / 4N 5N / 2X — 8 *11*	2P 1N 2X — 5	10P 10N — 20	2P 7P / 6N 5N / 1X — 9 *12*	4P 2P / 5N — 9 *2*	6P 2N / 3P — *3*	40P 49P / 52N 48N / 8X 1X — 8(100)(98)	(89P) (100N) (9X) — 198

Sunday and Monday editions only.
Italics indicate page-one stories.
P = positive; N = negative; X = neutral.

Table 11
"POSITIVE" AND "NEGATIVE" STATEMENTS IN WASHINGTON *POST*
REPORTING FROM WASHINGTON AND ELSEWHERE OUTSIDE VIETNAM IN FEBRUARY-MARCH 1968

Number of Statements

Statements	Feb. 1-4	5-11	12-18	19-25	26-Mar. 3	4-10	11-17	18-24	25-31	Totals	Totals All Statements
Tet is military victory or defeat for enemy	*3P* 6P								*1P*	*4P* 6P	10
Tet is psychological victory or defeat for enemy in Vietnam	*2N*						1P			*1P* 1P / *2N* 1N	5
Tet is psychological victory or defeat for enemy in U.S.	*1N*						2N		2N	*5N*	5
War is unwinnable, too costly, etc.; Johnson policy is right or wrong	*1P* 2P / *7N*	*1N*			*3P* 1N		*4P* 1N / 2N		*1N*	*10P* 2P / *4N* 11N	27
U.S. strategy and tactics	*2P*		*2P*	*2N*					*1N*	*2P* 1N / *4N*	7
U.S. troop morale			*1N*								
Khe Sanh, all references except Dienbienphu	*1X*								*1P* 1X	*1P* / *2X*	3
Khe Sanh compared to Dienbienphu	*2N*									*2N*	2
Enemy weapons, behavior, tactics, and strategy	*1N* 5N					*1P*				*1P* / *2N* 5N	8
Enemy has initiative, will or may attack; or U.S./S.V. has initiative, is moving offensively	*2P* 3N / *4N*					*1N*	*1N*		*1P*	*3P* / *4N* 5N	12
U.S. or enemy is responsible for civilian destruction and deaths						*1P*	*2N* 1N			*2N* 1N	3
S.V. police/military performance	*1N*						*1P*			*1P* 1N	2
GVN has or lacks popular support	*3N*									*1N* 3N	4
GVN response to Tet emergency	*1P*					*1N* 2N	*1N*			*1P* 1N / *4N*	6
Pacification is temporarily set back, crippled indefinitely, or dead											
U.S. is or is not considering use of nuclear weapons											
U.S. is planning or not, needs or does not, big troop increase, reserve call-up, or more taxes	*2N*					*2P* 2P / *1N* 1N	*2P* 2P / *1P* 1N		*1P*	*5P* 1P / *4N* 1N	11
Totals	*6P* 12P / *12N* 21N / *1X*	*1N*	*2P* 1N	*2N*	*3P* 1N	*2P* 6N / *2P* 3N	*2P* 7P / *1N* 10N		*4P* 3N / *1X*	*24P* 15P / *34N* 30N / *2X*	(36P) (64N) (2X)
	19 33	1	2	2	4	8 3	17 6		8 1	*60)* (45)	105

Sunday and Monday editions only.
Italics indicate page-one stories.
P = positive; N = negative; X = neutral.

Table 12
"POSITIVE" AND "NEGATIVE" STATEMENTS IN WASHINGTON *POST* COMMENTARY FROM SOUTH VIETNAM IN FEBRUARY-MARCH 1968

Statements	Feb. 1-4	5-11	12-18	19-25	26-Mar. 3	4-10	11-17	18-24	25-31	Totals	Totals All Statements
Tet is military victory or defeat for enemy											
Tet is psychological victory or defeat for enemy in Vietnam	2N		2N							4N	4
Tet is psychological victory or defeat for enemy in U.S.											
War is unwinnable, too costly, etc.; Johnson policy is right or wrong				2N						2N	2
U.S. strategy and tactics	3N			1N						4N	4
U.S. troop morale											
Khe Sanh, all references except Dienbienphu				1P 5N						1P 5N	6
Khe Sanh, compared to Dienbienphu				1X						1X	1
Enemy weapons, behavior, tactics, and strategy	1P									1P	1
Enemy has initiative, will or may attack; or U.S./S.V. has initiative, is moving offensively				1N						1N	1
U.S. or enemy is responsible for civilian destruction and deaths	1N									1N	1
S.V. police/military performance											
GVN has or lacks popular support			1N							1N	1
GVN response to Tet emergency			1N							1N	1
Pacification is temporarily set back, crippled indefinitely, or dead											
U.S. is or is not considering use of nuclear weapons											
U.S. is planning or not, needs or does not, big troop increase, reserve call-up, or more taxes											
Totals	1P 6N		4N	1P 9N 1X						2P 19N 1X	(2P) (19N) (1X)
	7		4	11						(22)	22

Number of Statements

Sunday and Monday editions only.
P = positive; N = negative; X = neutral.

Table 13

"POSITIVE" AND "NEGATIVE" STATEMENTS IN WASHINGTON *POST*
COMMENTARY FROM WASHINGTON AND ELSEWHERE OUTSIDE VIETNAM IN FEBRUARY-MARCH 1968

Statements	Number of Statements									Totals	Totals All Statements
	Feb. 1-4	5-11	12-18	19-25	26-Mar. 3	4-10	11-17	18-24	25-31		
Tet is military victory or defeat for enemy	2P			2P			1N		1P	5P 1N	6
Tet is psychological victory or defeat for enemy in Vietnam	1P 1N			1P			1N			2P 2N	4
Tet is psychological victory or defeat for enemy in U.S.									2N	2N	2
War is unwinnable, too costly, etc.; Johnson policy is right or wrong	1P 3N	1N		1P 1N	1P		2N	2N		3P 9N	12
U.S. strategy and tactics	1N	1N		1P				1P 3N	1N	2P 6N	8
U.S. troop morale											5
Khe Sanh, all references except Dienbienphu	1X			1X			1X		1P 1X	1P 4X	5
Khe Sanh, compared to Dienbienphu							1X			1X	1
Enemy weapons, behavior, tactics, and strategy	2P			3P 1N			3N			5P 4N	9
Enemy has initiative, will or may attack; or U.S./S.V. has initiative, is moving offensively	2N			1P			1N		1P	2P 3N	5
U.S. or enemy is responsible for civilian destruction and deaths					1N			2N		3N	3
S.V. police/military performance											
GVN has or lacks popular support											
GVN response to Tet emergency	2N	2N						2N		6N	6
Pacification is temporarily set back, crippled indefinitely, or dead	2N						1N			3N	3
U.S. is or is not considering use of nuclear weapons											
U.S. is planning or not, needs or does not, big troop increase, reserve call-up, or more taxes	1N				1N				1P	1P 2N	3
Totals	6P 12N 1X	4N		9P 2N 1X	1P 2N		9N 2X	1P 9N	4P 3N 1X	21P 41N 5X	67
	19	4		12	3		11	10	8	(67)	

Sunday and Monday editions only.

P = positive; N = negative; X = neutral.

Table 14
SUBJECT MATTER OF NETWORK FILM REPORTS
FROM VIETNAM, JANUARY 29-MARCH 22, 1968[a]

	Film Stories		Statements[b]	
Subject	No.	%	No.	%
Combat				
Saigon	21	16	85	19
Hue	16	12	62	13
Khe Sanh[c]	31	24	114	25
Other places	18	13	122	26
All Other Stories	47	35	78	17
Totals	133	100%	461	100%

Table 14-a
SUBJECT MATTER OF "NONCOMBAT" NETWORK FILM REPORTS
FROM VIETNAM, JANUARY 29-MARCH 22, 1968[a]

Subject	Film Stories	
	No.	%
Combat aftermath	11	23
GVN—civilians	3	6
War victims—civilians[d]	4	9
Pacification	7	15
All other noncombat stories[e]	22	47
Totals	47	100%

[a] On ABC, CBS, NBC weekday evening news shows. Data for this table were drawn from an analysis by Professors Lawrence W. Lichty and Thomas W. Hoffer.

[b] Includes any mention of the subject by anchormen or correspondents.

[c] There were five explicit comparisons of Khe Sanh to Dienbienphu by TV network correspondents on the scene; anchormen or other network newsmen in the United States offered the comparison six times.

[d] Civilian war victims and war damage were also prominent in the "Combat" and "Combat aftermath" categories, especially in Hue and Saigon.

[e] Includes, for example, captured Vietcong film, French TV interviews with U.S. POWs in Hanoi, and U.S. troop arrivals in Vietnam.

Table 15
TELEVISION NETWORK HANDLING OF THE QUESTION:
"WHO HAS THE MILITARY INITIATIVE IN VIETNAM?" JANUARY 29-MARCH 22, 1968[a]

	Number of Comments				
	Jan. 29-Feb. 9	12-23	Feb. 26-Mar. 8	11-22	Totals
Hanoi has the initiative, will attack again					
TV reporter in Vietnam	2	6	1		9
U.S. official in Vietnam	(1)				(1)
TV reporter in U.S.	2	7	1	1	11
U.S. official in U.S.		(1)			(1)
Totals	(1) 4	(1) 13	2	1	(2) 20
Allies have the initiative, are attacking					
TV reporter in Vietnam		2			2
U.S. official in Vietnam	(1)				(1)
TV reporter in U.S.				2	2
U.S. official in U.S.			(1)		(1)
Totals	(1)	2	(1)	2	(2) 4

[a]On ABC, CBS, NBC weekday evening news shows. Data for this table were drawn from an analysis by Professors Lawrence W. Lichty and Thomas W. Hoffer.

Note to Table 15: Figures are for explicit comments covering the generalized question of the "initiative"; predictions of enemy assaults against Khe Sanh and other particular points continued well into March. What is particularly noteworthy is the lack of generalized comment about who held the initiative militarily after the allied recapture of Hue on February 24 and the announcement of the allied "Resolve to Win" offensive on March 15.

Table 16
TELEVISION NETWORK "SOURCE BREADTH," SHOWING LOCALES OF FILM
REPORTS OF VIETNAM COMBAT OR ITS AFTERMATH, JANUARY 29-MARCH 22, 1968[a]

		Number of Reports			
Locale	Jan. 29-Feb. 9	12-23	26-Mar. 8	11-22	Total
Combat					
Saigon	16	5	-	-	21
Hue	6	8	2	-	16
Khe Sanh	3	7	12	9	31
Other	7	1	4	6	18
Totals, combat	32	21	18	15	86
Combat aftermath					
U.S. bases[b]	1	4	1	-	6
Hue	-	-	1	-	1
Da Nang	1	-	1	-	2
Other	2	-	-	-	2
Totals, aftermath	4	4	3	0	11

[a]On weekday evening network (ABC, CBS, NBC) news programs. Data for
this table were drawn from an analysis by Professors Lawrence W. Lichty
and Thomas W. Hoffer.

[b]E.g., Tan Son Nhut Airfield after mortar attack.

Table 17
TELEVISION FILM REPORTS SHOWING U.S.,
SOUTH VIETNAMESE, OR COMBINED COMBAT FORCES,
JANUARY 29-MARCH 22, 1968[a]

	Number of Reports
U.S. forces only	61
U.S. and South Vietnamese forces	8
South Vietnamese forces only	18[b]

[a]On weekday evening news programs. Data for this table
were drawn from an analysis by Professors Lawrence W.
Lichty and Thomas W. Hoffer.

[b]Twelve of these 18 reports covered the Saigon fighting
in the early January 29-February 9 period; one showed
ARVN forces at Hue; the ARVN at Khe Sanh were "almost
never mentioned."

Note to Tables 18-20: These tables stem from an analysis of verbal content of weekday evening television news shows in the designated period by ABC, CBS, and NBC, including, as well as reports from Vietnam, statements by officials, TV anchormen in New York, and reporters in the United States. The analysis was made from Vietnam news reports contained in the Pentagon television archives (which are incomplete, but believed by Professors Lichty and Hoffer to include virtually all network film reports from Vietnam).

In general, for each category, I rated those televised "statements"--explicit or implicit, and regardless of factual accuracy--as "positive" which tended to depict the allied side in a favorable light, and as "negative" those which depicted the other side favorably or the allies unfavorably. The ratings are certainly open to challenge. But, here again, we would suggest that the positive-negative trends, over the duration of the Tet offensive and in given categories, are significant. They reflect in part wire-service tendencies--which show up in anchorman reports--to focus on specific mishaps, triumphs, and losses, and in part television's special quest for the dramatic. In terms of the latter, bad news is more dramatic than good news and the specter of possible disaster more exciting than disaster averted.

We would also suggest that the **relative frequency of statements in certain categories is significant.** Some categories (South Vietnamese military/police performance, Pacification) were neglected, some (Khe Sanh) emphasized. CBS focused far more heavily on Khe Sanh in its film reports (as noted in the text) than did ABC and NBC, and it is small wonder that it made more statements about that siege (38) than did its rivals (18 for NBC and 27 for ABC). CBS was also relatively more negative about Khe Sanh than its rivals, possibly to justify its emphasis on the story, and remained more negative well into March. CBS compared the Marines' situation at the outpost to that of the French at Dienbienphu 10 times versus twice for NBC and once for ABC, by my count. The gloomy CBS emphasis on Khe Sanh helped give that network's total statements an unusually negative edge after March 4, even as CBS statements about allied or enemy initiatives, for example, or South Vietnamese government performance began to include some positive notes.

With respect to all three networks, it is worth noting again that a heavy flow of negative statements after the initial attacks on the cities was not counterbalanced by a heavy flow of positive statements in relevant categories as allied recovery began in March. Film coverage, except at Khe Sanh, slackened. In some categories, silence or relative silence descended. Reflecting the "technical" biases of AP night leads, TV anchormen's scripts--buttressed even more strongly by film reports from Vietnam--still tended to depict the allies in worse overall military shape than was really the case. Even more than the other media, television left the inevitably distorted initial impressions of the Tet offensive unmodified by subsequent "catch-up" reporting.

Table 18
"POSITIVE" AND "NEGATIVE" STATEMENTS CONCERNING THE 1968 TET OFFENSIVE
IN ABC TELEVISION DOMESTIC AND FOREIGN REPORTS IN FEBRUARY-MARCH 1968

Statements	Feb. 1-4	5-11	12-18	19-25	26-Mar. 3	4-10	11-17	18-24	25-31	Totals	Totals All Statements
						Number of Statements					
Tet is military victory or defeat for enemy	2P						1N			2P 1N	3
Tet is psychological victory or defeat for enemy in Vietnam		1N		1N						2N	2
Tet is psychological victory or defeat for enemy in U.S.		2N	1P	1N	2P 4N	1N	1P 1N	1P 3N	1P	4P 11N	15
War is unwinnable, too costly, etc.; Johnson policy is right or wrong	1N		1P	1N		1N		1P 3N	1P	2P 3N	5
U.S. strategy and tactics	2P	4P 1N	1P	2P 3N	3P 1N		1N 2P	2N 3P 2N	2P 3N 1P	17P 8N	25
U.S. troop morale		4P 1N	1P	6N	1P 2N			2N 3P 2N	8N	10P 16N 1X	27
Khe Sanh, all references except Dienbienphu	1P 2N 1X	1P	2P 6N	1P 2N	1P 2N				10P 16N 1X	27
Khe Sanh, compared to Dienbienphu							1N		1N	1N	1
Enemy weapons, behavior, tactics, and strategy	2N	1N	6N	3N	1N	3N		1P	1P 1N	2P 14N	16
Enemy has initiative, will or may attack; or U.S./S.V. has initiative, is moving offensively	1P 3N	9N	1P	1P 3N	2P 5N		1P 3N	1P 3N	3P 4N	10P 33N	43
U.S. or enemy is responsible for civilian destruction and deaths	2P 2N	4P	3P 2N	5N	1N	1P	1P	4P	1N	9P 10N	19
S.V. police/military performance	1P 2N	2P 1N	1N 1P	3N	1P 3N	1P			1N	10P 11N	21
GVN has or lacks popular support	1N	2P 2P	1N 1P	1N	1P 1N	5P 3N	1P	3P 2N	3P	3P 3N	6
GVN response to Tet emergency		1N	1N	1N	1P 1N	5P 3N	1P	7P 2N	7P 9N	7P 9N	16
Pacification is temporarily set back, crippled indefinitely, or dead								1P	1N	1P	1
U.S. is or is not considering use of nuclear weapons		1P 1N	1P 1N							2P 2N	4
U.S. is planning or not, needs or does not, big troop increase, reserve call-up, or more taxes	1P 1N		1N	1P 1N	2N		1N			2P 6N	8
Totals	9P 12N (21)	14P 19N 1X (34)	9P 12N (21)	6P 26N (32)	10P 20N (30)	7P 9N (16)	6P 10N (16)	12P 12N (24)	8P 10N (18)	81P 130N	(81P) (130N) (1X) 212

P = positive; N = negative; X = neutral.

Table 19

"POSITIVE" AND "NEGATIVE" STATEMENTS CONCERNING THE 1968 TET OFFENSIVE
IN CBS TELEVISION DOMESTIC AND FOREIGN REPORTS IN FEBRUARY-MARCH 1968

Statements	Feb. 1-4	5-11	12-18	19-25	26-Mar. 3	4-10	11-17	18-24	25-31	Totals	Totals All Statements
						Number of Statements					
Tet is military victory or defeat for enemy	1P									4P 1N	5
Tet is psychological victory or defeat for enemy in Vietnam	2N		1N					1N		1P 4N	5
Tet is psychological victory or defeat for enemy in U.S.											
War is unwinnable, too costly, etc.; Johnson policy is right or wrong		2N		1P 4N	2N	1N	1N	1P 1N	1N	2P 12N	14
U.S. strategy and tactics	1N	2N	1P 3N		1N		1N	2N	1P 1N	2P 11N	13
U.S. troop morale	1P	5P 1N	1P 3N		2P 8N		4N	4P 5N		20P 11N	31
Khe Sanh, all references except Dienbienphu		1P 1X	1P 3N	3N		1P 3N			2N	9P 28N 1X	38
Khe Sanh, compared to Dienbienphu		1P 1N	3N		1N		1P 2N	1N		2P 8N	10
Enemy weapons, behavior, tactics, and strategy		2P 4N	5N	1P 2N	1N	2P 2N		1N	1P 3N	6P 17N	23
Enemy has initiative, will or may attack; or U.S./S.V. has initiative, is moving offensively	4N	10N	1P 5N	1P 2N	6N	1P 4N	2P	3P 1N	3P 3N	11P 35N	46
U.S. or enemy is responsible for civilian destruction and deaths	3N	5N	1P 2N	1P 2N	1N	1N	1P		1N	2P 15N	17
S.V. police/military performance	3P 1N	2P 2N	2P 1N	1N 1P	1P 2N		1P	1P	1P 1N	11P 8N	19
GVN has or lacks popular support	1N	2N		1N 1P						1P 4N	5
GVN response to Tet emergency		3N		2N	1P	2N	2P 1N	2P	1N	5P 9N	14
Pacification is temporarily set back, crippled indefinitely, or dead			1N	1N	3P 3N	1N			1N	3P 7N	10
U.S. is or is not considering use of nuclear weapons		1P 1N								1P 1N	2
U.S. is planning or not; needs or does not; big troop increase, reserve call-up, or more taxes	1N	2P 1N	2N	1N	2N	1P				3P 7N	10
Totals	5P 13N	15P 34N 1X	10P 30N	7P 24N	13P 27N	5P 14N	6P 9N	12P 12N	10P 15N	83P 178N 1X	262
	18	50	40	31	40	19	15	24	25	(262)	

P = positive; N = negative; X = neutral.

Table 20

"POSITIVE" AND "NEGATIVE" STATEMENTS CONCERNING THE 1968 TET OFFENSIVE IN NBC TELEVISION DOMESTIC AND FOREIGN REPORTS IN FEBRUARY-MARCH 1968

Statements	Feb. 1-4	5-11	12-18	19-25	26-Mar. 3	4-10	11-17	18-24	25-31	Totals	Totals All Statements
Tet is military victory or defeat for enemy	1P 1N						1N			2P 2N	4
Tet is psychological victory or defeat for enemy in Vietnam		2N				1N				6N	6
Tet is psychological victory or defeat for enemy in U.S.				3N						3P 10N	13
War is unwinnable, too costly, etc.; Johnson policy is right or wrong		2N	1P 2N	1N		1P	1N	2P	1P	4P 6N	10
U.S. strategy and tactics		2N	1P	1P 4N	4P 2N	3P	1P 2N		1P 2N	13P 10N	23
U.S. troop morale	1N							1P	1P 2N	7P 11N	18
Khe Sanh, all references except Dienbienphu		1P 1N	1N	2P 2N	1N	2P 1N		1P	1P 2N	7P 11N	18
Khe Sanh, compared to Dienbienphu				1N	1N	1P	3N			1P 1N	2
Enemy weapons, behavior, tactics, and strategy	3N		1P 2N	4N	4N	1N	1N	2N		4P 22N	26
Enemy has initiative, will or may attack; or U.S./S.V. has initiative, is moving offensively	1N	7N	2P 2N	2P 9N	7N	1P 5N	2P 1N	2P	2P 1N	11P 33N	44
U.S. or enemy is responsible for civilian destruction and deaths	2P 1N	1P 3N	1P 1N	7N	2P 1N	1P		2P		4P 13N	17
S.V. police/military performance	1P 3N	2P 1N	1P 1N	2P	1N		6N			11P 6N	17
GVN has or lacks popular support	1N	1N		1P 4N	1N					2P 5N	7
GVN response to Tet emergency	1N	1N		2N	1P	1N	1P	1P		1P 6N	7
Pacification is temporarily set back, crippled indefinitely, or dead	1N	1N	1P			3N				1P 4N	5
U.S. is or is not considering use of nuclear weapons			1P							1P	1
U.S. is planning or not, needs or does not, big troop increase, reserve call-up, or more taxes	1N	1N	1N		2N		1N			6N	6
Totals	4P 13N	6P 25N	8P 12N	10P 41N	7P 18N	9P 15N	4P 10N	12P 3N	5P 5N	65P 142N	(65P) (142N)
	17	31	20	51	25	24	14	15	10	(207)	207

P = positive; N = negative; X = neutral.

Note to Tables 21 and 22: It should be emphasized that both *Time* and *Newsweek* were devoted to "analysis" and "explanation" of news in relatively restricted space, and hence tended toward more generalized "statements" than did other media in a given volume of words. Included in the analysis were all Vietnam-related stories and commentary for the designated periods in the two magazines.

In terms of space allotment, both weeklies came closest to television in their heavy focus on Vietnam at the onset of the Tet offensive, and their sharp decline in reporting from Vietnam in March. Total *Time* text devoted to all foreign and domestic Vietnam-related items was approximately 537 column inches in February and 287 inches in March, for a Tet period total of 824 inches. The corresponding *Newsweek* space allocation was 604 inches in February and 342 inches in March, for a total of 946 inches. *Newsweek*'s Vietnam-related material included much explicit, signed "commentary" (by Walter Lippman, Kenneth Crawford, Emmet John Hughes); if this were excluded from the count, the allocation of space to Vietnam would more closely approximate that of *Time*. Despite the overall March decline, both magazines assigned sizable space to partial reappraisals of the Tet offensive's effects at home and abroad after the first week of that month (see Story Index for *Time*, March 15 issue, and *Newsweek*, March 18 issue). In the March 15 issue, *Time* devoted some 140 inches to Vietnam, while *Newsweek* packaged half its March total, 178, around the March 18 Vietnam cover story, "The Agony of Khe Sanh." By the following week, *Time* was down to 49 inches (by our reckoning) on all phases--foreign and domestic--of the Vietnam story, and in the March 29 issue to 21 inches. *Newsweek* went to 82 inches in its March 25 issue, and then to 45 in that of April 1. Both issues of both magazines included heavy focus on domestic political repercussions.

Overall, *Newsweek* was consistently more negative in all subject categories than was *Time*; the latter was more prone to qualify its assertions and to be less apocalyptic in tone. The overall count:

	Positive	Negative
Time	97	169
Newsweek	49	276

In no other medium was the question of a military victory for Hanoi (category one) discussed so extensively, but even so, it was not a dominant theme. In *Time*, statements assigning a military defeat to Hanoi outnumbered those saying the opposite, 8 to 4. In *Newsweek*, Tet was seen as a military gain for Hanoi, 10 to zero, through the March 18 issue; then the subject was dropped.

In several key *military* subject categories (Khe Sanh, Enemy weapons and tactics, South Vietnamese performance), there was a pronounced difference between *Newsweek* and *Time* in March, as allied military recovery began. Taking into account the magazines' practice of advance dating their issues, this is the breakdown:

	Time		*Newsweek*	
	N	P	N	P
Enemy weapons/tactics	3	3	3	2
Who has the initiative?	7	10	8	2
South Vietnamese performance	2	2	4	
	12	12	15	4

The differences were also sharp in the magazines' respective reappraisals of the Tet offensive in March (*Newsweek*'s "Agony of Khe Sanh," *Time*'s even-handed, March 15 "After Tet: Measuring and Repairing the Damage," among other Vietnam-related stories). *Time*'s overall output in the March 15 issue was negative. *Newsweek*'s March 18 "package," stemming from an explicit judgment by the New York editors that Tet showed Administration Vietnam policy to be bankrupt, included articles and headlines on the battlefield and on the South Vietnamese designed to buttress that judgment: At no other point during Tet, after the first week, was *Newsweek* so lavish with space or so negative in content--57 negative statements and 6 positive. Of these, statements giving the "military initiative" to Hanoi accounted for 8 negatives, and unrelievedly adverse comment on the South Vietnamese accounted for 19 (South Vietnamese performance, GVN support, GVN response). The negative dominated *Newsweek*'s reduced coverage of Vietnam through March, although the "military initiative" was quietly awarded to the allies in the March 25 issue ("Into the Pea Patch") after *official announcement* in Saigon of the "Resolve to Win" offensive on March 15.

In sum, both magazines, as did other media, devoted heavy attention to the negative events of February, adding a heavy dose of speculation and analysis. Then editors in both magazines began to focus on other, more dramatic matters, cutting Vietnam coverage after the first week of March. *Time*, after its March 15 issue, began to strike a rough balance in negative and positive statements; *Newsweek* remained heavily negative throughout the two-month Tet period.

Table 21

"POSITIVE" AND "NEGATIVE" STATEMENTS IN *TIME* CONCERNING THE 1968 TET OFFENSIVE AND ITS REPERCUSSIONS, FEBRUARY 9–APRIL 5, 1968

Statements	Number of Statements										
	Feb. 9	16	23	Mar. 1	8	15	22	29	Apr. 5	Totals	Totals All Statements
Tet is military victory or defeat for enemy	2P	3P 1N		1P 3N					2P	8P 4N	12
Tet is psychological victory or defeat for enemy in Vietnam	1P 1N	1P 3N		4N						2P 8N	10
Tet is psychological victory or defeat for enemy in U.S.	2N	1N			1N	1P 1N	1N		1N	1P 7N	8
War is unwinnable, too costly, etc.; Johnson policy is right or wrong	2N	2P 5N	1P 3N	3P 3N	3P	7N	1P 4N	3P 1N	2N	13P 27N	40
U.S. strategy and tactics	1P	4P 3N	2P 2N	3N		2N		1P 4N	2N	8P 16N	24
U.S. troop morale	1P	2P	1N	1P		1P		1P		6P 1N	7
Khe Sanh, all references except Dienbienphu	1P 3X	3P 1N 5X	1N 1X	1N 2X	2N	1X			3P	9P 6N 14X	29
Khe Sanh, compared to Dienbienphu	1P 1X		1N 1X				1X			1P 1N 2X	4
Enemy weapons, behavior, tactics, and strategy	1P 7N	2P 2N	1P 1N	1P 2N		3N				5P 15N	20
Enemy has initiative, will or may attack; or U.S./S.V. has initiative is moving offensively	2N	2P 7N	9N	12N	5N	4P 2N	3P	•	2P 4N	12P 42N	54
U.S. or enemy is responsible for civilian destruction and deaths	1P 1N	1P 2N	1N			1N	1P	1N	1P	5P 5N	10
S.V. police/military performance		2P	1N	1N	2N 4P					4P 4N	8
GVN has or lacks popular support		2P		2N 1P 2N	2N 4P	2P 1N				2P 4N	6
GVN response to Tet emergency	1P	3P 4N				2P 1N	3P 2N	1P	14P 9N	14P 9N	23
Pacification is temporarily set back; crippled indefinitely; or dead	1P	1P 1N	1P 1N	5N		2P 1N				4P 7N	11
U.S. is or is not considering use of nuclear weapons			1P 1N							1P 1N	2
U.S. is planning or not; needs or does not; big troop increase, reserve call-up, or more taxes		2P	3N	2N	2N	4N	1P 1N		1P	2P 12N	14
Totals	10P 15N 4X	30P 30N 5X	6P 25N 3X	7P 40N 2X	7P 12N	10P 23N 1X	9P 8N 1X	6P 7N	12P 9N	97P 169N 16X (282)	282

P = positive; N = negative; X = neutral.

Table 22

"POSITIVE" AND "NEGATIVE" STATEMENTS IN *NEWSWEEK* CONCERNING THE 1968 TET OFFENSIVE AND ITS REPERCUSSIONS, FEBRUARY 12–APRIL 8, 1968

Statements	Feb. 12	19	26	Mar. 4	11	18	25	Apr. 1	8	Totals	Totals All Statements
Tet is military victory or defeat for enemy	2N	1N		3N	2N	2N				10N	10
Tet is psychological victory or defeat for enemy in Vietnam	1P 4N	1P 4N	1P 1N		1N	1N			1N	3P 12N	15
Tet is psychological victory or defeat for enemy in U.S.	2P 2N	1N	3N	1N		1N	2P 3N		1N	4P 12N	16
War is unwinnable, too costly, etc.; Johnson policy is right or wrong	6N	6N	1P 4N	5N	1P 4N	1P 10N	1P 9N	1P 4N		5P 48N	53
U.S. strategy and tactics	8N	1P 10N	1P	3N	1P 1N	5N	3N	3N	1N	2P 33N	35
U.S. troop morale	2P 1N	1P 1N	1N			3P 1N	3N		1N	6P 7N	13
Khe Sanh, all references except Dienbienphu	1N 5X	1X		2N 2X	3N	4N 1X	1N		1P	2P 12N 9X	23
Khe Sanh, compared to Dienbienphu	1X					1P 1X	1N			1P 1N 1X	3
Enemy weapons, behavior, tactics, and strategy	9N	3N	2P 1N	6N	1N	2N	2P		1N	4P 23N	27
Enemy has initiative, will or may attack; or U.S./S.V. has initiative is moving offensively	2N	1P 4N	4N	13N	5N	1P 8N	2P			4P 36N	40
U.S. or enemy is responsible for civilian destruction and deaths	1P 1N	1P 2N	1N	1N	1P 3N					3P 8N	11
S.V. police/military performance	2P 5N	2N	1N			3N		1N		2P 12N	14
GVN has or lacks popular support	2N	5N	1N	3N	1N	4N		1N		14N	14
GVN response to Tet emergency	7N	1P	2P 2N	1N	2P 1N	12N	5N			5P 29N	34
Pacification is temporarily set back, crippled indefinitely, or dead	3N	2N	1N		1P 1N	1N				1P 8N	9
U.S. is or is not considering use of nuclear weapons		1P 1N	1P			1N				2P 1N	3
U.S. is planning or not, needs or does not, big troop increase, reserve call-up, or more taxes	1P		2P	3N	2N	2N	2P 2N	1N	2P	5P 10N	15
Totals	9P 53N 6X	7P 42N 1X	8P 19N	42N 2X	6P 24N	6P 57N 1X	9P 26N	1P 8N	3P 5N	(49P 276N 10X)	335
	68	50	27	44	30	64	35	9	8	(335)	

P = positive; N = negative; X = neutral.

Table 23
CATEGORICAL BREAKDOWN OF VIETNAM-RELATED STILL PHOTOGRAPHS PUBLISHED
IN THE NEW YORK *TIMES*, THE WASHINGTON *POST*, *TIME*, *NEWSWEEK*, AND *LIFE*, FEBRUARY-MARCH 1968

Photographs	*Times* No.	%	*Post* No.	%	*Time* No.	%	*Newsweek* No.	%	*Life* No.	%	Totals No.	%
Subject												
Refugees/civilian casualties	20	.128	26	.154	5	.080	4	.048	7	.146	62	.119
U.S. troops—wounded/dead	15	.094	8	.048	8	.129	13	.157	12	.25	56	.108
U.S. troops—weary/ducking fire	9	.056	3	.018	0	0	6	.072	0	0	18	.035
U.S. troops—combat (no wounded)	14	.088	23	.136	4	.064	7	.084	8	.167	56	.108
U.S. troops—noncombat	12	.075	18	.107	2	.032	5	.060	4	.083	41	.079
S.V. police/troops—wounded/dead	0	0	3	.018	0	0	3	.036	0	0	6	.012
S.V. troops—weary/ducking fire	0	0	0	0	0	0	1	.012	0	0	1	.002
S.V. troops—combat (no wounded)	4	.025	8	.048	1	.016	1	.012	0	0	14	.027
S.V. troops—noncombat	3	.019	1	.006	0	0	1	.012	0	0	5	.010
Air action (air strikes, cargo)	10	.063	7	.042	1	.016	2	.024	3	.063	23	.044
Enemy-inflicted damage/incoming fire	8	.050	6	.036	5	.080	4	.060	6	.125	29	.056
Vietcong/NVA—prisoners/dead	8	.050	7	.042	5	.080	4	.048	2	.042	26	.050
Urban destruction	9	.056	15	.089	6	.096	3	.036	2	.042	35	.067
Allied atrocities	5	.031	5	.030	1	.016	2	.024	0	0	13	.025
Vietcong/NVA atrocities	1	.006	3	.018	3	.048	0	0	0	0	7	.013
Vietcong/NVA troops/civilians	3	.019	6	.036	2	.032	3	.036	4	.083	18	.035
U.S. nonmilitary	2	.013	1	.006	1	.016	0	0	0	0	4	.008
President Johnson	4	.025	1	.006	2	.032	3	.036	0	0	10	.019
Headshots/portraits of others	17	.107	12	.071	12	.194	11	.132	0	0	52	.100
Other	15	.094	15	.089	4	.064	9	.108	0	0	43	.083
Totals[a]	159	.999	168	1.00	62	.995	82	.997	48	1.00	519	1.00
Locale												
Saigon	36	.23	41	.24	22	.35	15	.25	8	.17	122	.24
Hue	37	.23	46	.28	8	.13	12	.20	18	.37	122	.24
Khe Sanh	29	.18	30	.18	4	.07	29	.48	20	.42	112	.21
Other	57	.36	50	.30	28	.45	26	.07	2	.04	163	.31
Totals	159	1.00	168	1.00	62	1.00	82	1.00	48	1.00	519	1.00

[a]Variations from 100% due to rounding.

Note to Table 23: This table was compiled from an examination of all Vietnam-related photographs published by the indicated media during the Tet period. Categorizations of individual photographs were, of course, arbitrary, and some photographs clearly could be assigned to any one of several categories.

In terms of space (or numbers of photographs), the trend reflected that in the printed word--heavy emphasis on Vietnam in February, a sharp decline in March. It was yet another measure of "media attention span." This is shown by the following analysis (in which magazine photographs are dated according to the magazine's closing, not publication, date):

	No. of Photos	
	Feb. 1-Mar. 3	Mar. 4-31
Times	124	35
Post	128	40
Time	50	12
Newsweek	51	31
Life	48	0

In terms of content, the photographs, with the exception of *Time*'s, exaggerated the same tendency toward the "negative" which was apparent in headlines and stories, even after the beginning of the military upturn in March. For example, the New York *Times* published no photographs in the category of "U.S. troops--combat" after March 10, when the allied "Resolve to Win" offensive began. Khe Sanh, the only place in Vietnam where U.S. troops were still under (easing) pressure, accounted for 11 out of 24 *Times* pictures in *all* categories in the middle two full weeks of March, with the *Post* emphasis on Khe Sanh even stronger. Moreover, the loci of most events portrayed photographically reflected the preoccupation in text and headlines with Saigon, Hue, and, later, Khe Sanh. *Newsweek*'s heavy editorial focus on Khe Sanh was more than matched by its pictorial focus: 29 of its 59 action photos (exclusive of its portraits and other miscellaneous pictures) dealt with that battle, and 18 of the 29 showed Americans or South Vietnamese troops either wounded or dead or huddled under fire. None showed allied troops at Khe Sanh firing back.

U.S. journalism's ethnocentricity was even more marked in still photographs than in television or text. South Vietnamese security forces were almost invisible, and U.S. troops were thus portrayed as "doing all the fighting." *Life* led in this regard, publishing no pictures at all of South Vietnamese troops in action, but 24 pictures of U.S. troops in action (and four color pictures of North Vietnamese troops).

At Tet, as in most complicated crises, the published photographic coverage--although it consumed up to 20 percent of the total Vietnam space allocation--dealt with only a narrow range of subjects. Pacification, enemy strategy and tactics, the *scale* of urban destruction, the response of the South Vietnamese Administration to the crisis, the countrywide "situation"--none of these matters lent themselves to traditional U.S. journalistic photography. Photographs were a haphazard series of "little pictures," selected by busy editors for the purpose, in large measure, of adding emotional impact or symbolic illustration to text or, more prosaically, of "brightening up the page." To these ends, the best photographs are those showing grief, shock, destruction, fire, flood, smoke, death, injury, distress. It was small wonder that refugee pictures outnumbered those in any other category in the newspapers. Photographs showing U.S. troops "weary or ducking fire" or "wounded or dead" were more numerous than those showing aggressive "U.S. troops--combat," with the New York *Times* and *Newsweek* prominent in this regard. Over a two-month period, the net result, pictorially, was a mosaic of Vietnam in flames and despair, showing the Vietnamese as victims but seldom as fighters, and American troops under pressure (even after that pressure had eased) from a largely unseen enemy striking heavy blows. This pattern was far stronger in still photos than in television film reports, which, whatever the tone of their accompanying narrative, portrayed allied forces in a greater variety of "postures."

There was no easily available record of which photographs the UPI and AP bureaus in Saigon sent to New York, and which in turn were selected for distribution to the wire services' newspaper and other clients. Interviews with photographers suggested to this writer that, overall, there was no major difference between what was distributed and what was published, except in terms of quantity. In short, the AP and UPI were supplying the kinds of photographs known to have found favor with clients.

One contrast should be noted: *Life*'s February portfolio of Khe Sanh photographs by David Douglas Duncan. Duncan's work gave a far broader notion of the Marines' existence at the embattled base than television did, or than *Newsweek* with its own mini-album of March 18 did. Duncan captured the broad gamut of activity at Khe Sanh, as well as the topography and scale of the area, supplying information as well as drama.

Story Indexes

STORY INDEX: VIETNAM-RELATED STORIES, NEW YORK *TIMES,* JANUARY 31 - MARCH 31, 1968

Vietnam Dateline	Page[#]	Non-Vietnam Dateline	Page[#]	Vietnam Commentary/ Editorial	Page[#]
January 31					

*Foe Invades U.S. Saigon Embassy; Raiders Wiped Out After Six Hours; Vietcong Widen Attack on Cities; Ambassador Safe; Guerrillas Also Strike Presidential Palace and Many Bases
  Tom Buckley (S)
	1	Johnson Receives Flow of Reports; He Meets with Advisors on Saigon Raid, Viewed as New Step-up in Vietnam War
		  Special to *Times* (W)
			1	Washington: The Law of Compensation in Korea and Vietnam
				  James Reston (W)
					40

U.S. Aide in Embassy Villa Kills Guerrilla with Pistol
  Charles Mohr (S)
	1	Writers and Editors to Defy Tax in War Protest, 448 Say They Will Not Pay Any Rise Tied to Conflict, Assail Vietnam Policy
		  C. Gerald Fraser (N.Y.)
			2		

February 1					

Vietcong Press Guerrilla Raids; Martial Law Declared by Thieu; Hue Is Embattled; Other Cities Besieged; Allies Bomb Foe in Cholon Area
  Charles Mohr (S)
	1	President Studies New Call of Reserves and Seoul Aid
		  Roy Reed (W)
			1	Public Opinion in U.S. and South VN Is Viewed as Main Target of New Offensive by VC
				  Hanson W. Baldwin (N.Y.)
					12

Village Endures Night of Terror; Ap Ba, near Da Nang, Counts Its Dead After Battle
  Gene Roberts (D)
	1	Kosygin Ends Talks with Indian Leader
		  Special to *Times* (New Delhi)
			11	Bloody Path to Peace (editorial)	36

		Enemy "Revolutionary Council" Is Reported Formed in Saigon Reuters (Tokyo)	14		
		Appeal by Vietcong Reuters (Singapore)	14		

* denotes lead position.
\# Page numbers for stories which appeared in early editions but were dropped from later ones are indicated by X.

D = Da Nang; H.K. = Hong Kong; K = Khe Sanh; S = Saigon;
W = Washington, D.C.

Vietnam Dateline	Page[#]	Non-Vietnam Dateline	Page[#]	Vietnam Commentary/ Editorial	Page[#]
Text of Thieu Statement on Martial Law AP (S)	14	Two Fly to Hanoi to Return Three Pilots Due to Be Freed (N.Y.)	14		
Embassy Attack: A Fight to Death; Marine Guard Declares He Knew "We Were In for It" AP (S)	14				
Agents Reported Active AP (S)	14				
February 2					
Street Clashes Go On in Vietnam; Foe Still Holds Parts of Cities; Enemy Toll Soars; Offensive Is Running "Out of Steam," Says Westmoreland Charles Mohr (S)	1	Arabs Express Admiration for Struggle of VC Special to *Times* (Beirut)	13	More Than a Diversion (editorial)	34
Offensive Is Said to Pinpoint Enemy's Strengths; Despite U.S. Stress on Toll, VC Gains Are Seen in Morale and Prestige Tom Buckley (S)	12	Excerpts from McNamara's Report to Congress Special to *Times* (W)	16	Washington: North Vietnam's Strategy of Terror James Reston (W)	34
Gains Stressed in Hanoi Agence France Presse (Hanoi)	12	Hanoi Says Aim of Raids Is to Oust Saigon Regime Special to *Times* (H.K.)	1		
U.S. Stresses Foe's Setbacks AP (S)	12	Vietcong's Attacks Shock Washington Tom Wicker (W)	1		
Kontum Is Evacuated Agence France Presse (Kontum)	12	A Resolute Stand; President Won't Halt Bombing--Predicts Khe Sanh Victory Max Frankel (W)	1		
		Peking Charges U.S. Bombed Ships, Says Two Freighters Were Attacked in N. VN (H.K.)	11		
		U.S. Investigates Charges Special to *Times*(W)	11		

Vietnam Dateline	Page[#]	Non-Vietnam Dateline	Page[#]	Vietnam Commentary/ Editorial	Page[#]
U.S. Civilians in Saigon Stalk Snipers near Homes AP (S)	13	Foe Claims Resort City Reuters (H.K.)	12		
Foe Is Said to Execute Two GIs Before Crowd Special to *Times* (S)	13	McNamara Wary on Trend of War, Re-counts "Uneven Progress" in VN in Last Report Hedrick Smith (W)	13		
		Pentagon Lists Servicemen Killed in VN War AP (W)	13		
February 3					
Enemy Hold Out, Street Fighting Rages Within Mile of the Capital's Center Tom Buckley (S)	1	Warning Is Given President Terms U.S. Ready for a Push by Enemy at Khe Sanh Max Frankel (W)	1	Many at U.N. View U.S. as a Con-fused Goliath Drew Middleton (U.N.)	9
Enemy Maintains Tight Grip on Hue Gene Roberts (Hue)	1	Six U.S. Missionaries Killed by Vietcong	1	U.S. Man-power Needs for War Hanson W. Baldwin (N.Y.)	10
Thieu Asks Action to Penalize North Agence France Presse (S)	1	Two Airlines to Lend Planes to Pentagon	3		
Guerrilla Motiva-tion Stressed; "The VC Are Not Afraid to Die" Charles Mohr (S)	9	Transcript of Presi-dent's News Conference on Foreign and Domestic Matters Special to *Times* (W)	8	Vietnam's Korean Front (editorial)	28
Decisive Turn Ex-pected AP (S)	9	A.C.L.U. Shunning Spock Case in Effort to Avoid Suit over Legality of War John Leo	8		
Break in Saigon Curfew Agence France Presse (S)	9	U.S. Ships Sunk, Foe Says AP (Tokyo)	9		
U.S. Wives Calm As Saigon Erupts AP (S)	10	Brown Appeals to Gromyko Reuters (Birmingham, England)	9		
Food Supplies Run Low Special to *Times* (S)	10	VN War Casualties Listed by Pentagon AP (W)	10		

Vietnam Dateline	Page[#]	Non-Vietnam Dateline	Page[#]	Vietnam Commentary/ Editorial	Page[#]
February 4					
*Vietcong Holding Position on Edge of Saigon Airport Tom Buckley (S)	1	Clerics Accuse U.S. of War Crimes Edward B. Fiske	1	The VC Launch Their Revolution (N.Y.)	1E
By Bus, by Truck, on Foot, Foe Built Forces in Saigon AP (S)	1	Cambodians Charge Allies Killed Guard Reuters (Phnom Penh)	3	And the Debate over VN Deepens (N.Y.)	1E
U.S. Marines Seize a 3D Block of Hue Gene Roberts (Hue)	1	Saigon Penicillin Appeal	3	Washington Stunned by One-Two Blow (N.Y.)	2E
		Foe Now Said to Hold Nurse Who Fled Raid	4		
Capture of General Reported Agence France Presse (S)	2	McCarthy Derides Johnson on War Majorie Hunter (W)	11	A Kennedy on Saigon Corruption John W. Finney (W)	2E
Two French Newsmen in Hue Detained Briefly by Enemy Agence France Presse (S)	3	Peking-Inspired Thai Rebellion Believed Blunted Sydney Gruson (Bangkok)	1	The Question in VN (editorial)	12E
Stop at Khe Sanh; A Perilous Rescue Thomas A. Johnson (D)	4	Red Cross Inspects Prisons in Vietnam Special to *Times* (Geneva)	14	Washington: A Strange and Troubled Silence James Reston (W)	12E
War Crisscrosses Suburb of Saigon Charles Mohr (S)	5	The Call to Revolution (Text of Revolution Appeal in S. VN)	13E	The Last Act in VN Richard J. Barnet, *New York Times Magazine*	26
				In the Nation, to Go or Not to Go Tom Wicker (New Haven, Conn.)	13E
February 5					
*Enemy Artillery and Ground Force Assault Khe Sanh Tom Buckley (S)	1	Rusk Says Enemy Rules Out Talks Peter Grose (W)	1		

Vietnam Dateline	Page[#]	Non-Vietnam Dateline	Page[#]	Vietnam Commentary/ Editorial	Page[#]
Two Vietnamese at Embassy Said to Have Aided Attack Charles Mohr (S)	1	Thais Vent Anger over U.S. Buildup Sydney Gruson (Bangkok)	2		
Attacks on Hue Fail to Rout Foe Gene Roberts (Hue)	1	Ban Urged in U.S. on War Research Special to *Times* (Paris)	4		
Thirty-Four Rescued by GIs at Mission in Da Lat AP (S)	1	Johnson Said to Get Pledge on Khe Sanh	14		
U.S. Captain Sentenced in Murder of Vietnamese AP (S)	9	Londoners Give Blood Reuters (London)	14		
Thirty-Eight Americans Rescued UPI (S)	13	Outrage and Horror in Europe Tempered by Some U.S. Sympathy Anthony Lewis (London)	16		
U.S. Cautioning Saigon on Captives' Treatment Agence France Presse (S)	14	VC Say War Is in New Stage Special to *Times* (H.K.)	16		
Clouds Curtail Bombing Agence France Presse (S)	14	Excerpts from Remarks Made by Rusk and McNamara in TV Interview (W)	15		
Saigon Appeals for Refugee Aid Reuters (S)	16				
Twenty Thousand Refugees in Saigon AP (S)	16				
Nonmilitary Aims Reported Agence France Presse (Hanoi)	16				
February 6					
*Streets of Saigon Shelled in Drive to Rout Vietcong Charles Mohr (S)	1	U.S. Identifies Servicemen Killed in Action in VN UPI (W)	9		

Vietnam Dateline	Page[#]	Non-Vietnam Dateline	Page[#]	Vietnam Commentary/ Editorial	Page[#]
U.S. Marines in Hue Drive Wedge into Enemy Units Gene Roberts (Hue)	1	Two Mennonite Volunteers Missing After Attack in Hue UPI (Lancaster, Pa.)	9		
Ky Says Regime Will Arm Public Tom Buckley (S)	1	Thant Will Leave for Moscow Talks Special to *Times* (U.N.)	14		
Civilian Toll High in Mekong Delta AP (Can Tho)	14	Hanoi Says It Downed Plane Reuters (H.K.)	14		
Enemy Attack Described Francois Mazure, Agence France Presse (Hue)	14	Wheeler Deplores Execution AP (W)	14		
		War Critics Lose Arlington Plea Edward B. Fiske (W)	15		
Hanoi Indicates It No Longer Expects Washington to Accept Offer to Negotiate Agence France Presse (Hanoi)	15	Javits and Edward Kennedy Ask War Compromise John W. Finney (W)	15		
		Russell Sees Tragedy AP (Atlanta, Ga.)	15		
Front Warns Against Trials Agence France Presse (Hanoi)	14	Washington Blames Hanoi Special to *Times* (W)	15		
		Kosygin and Hanoi Envoy Meet Reuters (Moscow)	15		
		Nixon Criticizes Curb on Bombing Robert B. Semple, Jr. (Green Bay, Wis.)	17		
		Most in Poll Favor Johnson's Election	26		
February 7					
*Foe, Using Tanks First Time, Mauls Outpost near DMZ, Five of Nine Soviet-Built Vehicles Reported Destroyed in Raid on Camp near Khe Sanh; Base May be Overrun; Allied Defenders, Put at 500, Call for		Control Commission to Act in Cambodia Special to *Times* (New Delhi)	1	Washington: The Flies That Capture the Flypaper James Reston (W)	40
		Vietcong Aide Links *Pueblo* and Vietnam Special to *Times* (Tokyo)	11		

Vietnam Dateline	Page[#]	Non-Vietnam Dateline	Page[#]	Vietnam/ Commentary/ Editorial	Page[#]

A New Phase in Vietcong Push Is Seen by Observers in Hanoi
  Agence France
  Presse (Hanoi)
	15				

Westmoreland Warns of Raids AP (S)	15				

Civilian Wounded Jam Hospital; Boy Scouts Carrying Stretchers
  Thomas A. John-
  son, Special to
  Times (D)
	16				

Guns and Planes Blasting Saigon; Siege in Second Week; Enemy Bat-talions in Action as a Unit near Race Track; In-filtration Goes On; Food Costs Are Rising Tom Buckley (S)	X				
February 8					

*Allied Post Falls to Tank Assault near Buffer Zone; North Vietnamese Overrun Lang Vei Camp--Khe Sanh Outpost Is At-tacked; Saigon Fighting Slows; Search for Enemy Holdouts Goes On in Cholon Sector and Center of Hue
  Charles Mohr (S)
	1	Latest Soviet Tanks Used by Enemy near Khe Sanh
		  William Beecher (W)
			1	After the Tet Offensive (editorial)	42

		Senators to Prod Johnson on Rusk; Com-mittee to Ask Presi-dent to Arrange for Testimony
		  John W. Finney (W)
			13	Observer: The Corner That Turns and Turns
				  Russell Baker (W)
					42

Hanoi Asserts U.S. Suffered Big Loss
  Agence France
  Presse (Hanoi)
	9	Pentagon Lists War Dead from Metropolitan Area
		  AP (W)
			14		

		Hospital Ship Quits Da Nang UPI (Bonn)	14		

Vietnam Dateline	Page[#]	Non-Vietnam Dateline	Page[#]	Vietnam Commentary/ Editorial	Page[#]
A Civilian Aid Plan Started in Vietnam AP (S)	13	U.S. and Hanoi Envoys Met, U.N. Aides Report AP (U.N.)	15		
Survivors Hunt Dead of Ben Tre, Turned to Rubble in Allied Raids Bernard Weinraub (Ben Tre)	14	U.S. Group to Shift VN Missioners (N.Y.) Thant Arrives in Geneva Reuters (Geneva)	15 15		
Foe in Saigon Says He Will Re-conquer Capital and Nation Agence France Presse (S)	14				
Major Describes Move AP (Ben Tre)	14				
Marine Squad Rides to Battle on Motorcycles; Enemy Driven Out of a 70-Block Area in Battle for Hue Gene Roberts (Hue)	14				
Seventy-Six Said to Escape AP (S)	14				
General Cites Foe's Losses Special to *Times* (S)	14				
Two South Koreans Missing in Saigon Area Held by Foe Reuters (S. VN)	14				
People of Da Nang Emerge for Food; Hundreds, Most Since Attack by Vietcong, Go to Market Thomas A. John-son (D)	X				

Vietnam Dateline	Page[#]	Non-Vietnam Dateline	Page[#]	Vietnam Commentary/ Editorial	Page[#]
February 9					
Fifty-Six Marines Die in Battles in Tense Northern Sector; 21 Americans Killed in Assault on Hill at Khe Sanh; Enemy's Toll Is 124; Officers Firm on Holding Base Bernard Weinraub (S)	1	Hanoi Indicates It Is Still Ready to Discuss Peace; U.S. Interest Is Stirred by Official's Rephrasing of Conditions of Talks Agence France Presse (H.K.)	1		
War-Ending Victory Seen as Aim of Enemy's Drive Charles Mohr (S)	1	Kennedy Asserts U.S. Cannot Win; In Broad Indictment of War, He Calls Johnson Claims of Progress "Illusory" Tom Wicker (W)	1		
Khe Sanh Bars Nearly 200 Lang Vei Survivors AP (K)	16	Humphrey Got War Petition from Peace Corps Members Special to *Times* (W)	3		
Six, Including Two Koreans, Executed by Vietcong Agence France Presse (S)	11	Excerpts from Text of Kennedy Speech Special to *Times* (W)	12		
		Tass Reports Speech AP (Moscow)	12		
Two Newsmen Hurt in Saigon AP (S)	12	Casualty Figures Defended AP (Honolulu)	12		
Thieu, in Tears, Orders Stepped-Up Mobilization UPI (S)	16	Goldberg Assails Soviet Role Special to *Times* (U.N.)	16		
Transcript of Interview with Trinh Bernard-Joseph Cabanes, Agence France Presse (Hanoi)	16	Thant and Hanoi Aide Meet AP (New Delhi)	16		
Intelligence Motive Seen (S)	16	Casualties of Vietnam War Are Identified by Pentagon AP (W)	16		
Seizure of Lang Vei Hailed Agence France Presse (Hanoi)	16	New Interest Is Stirred Hedrick Smith (W)	16		

Vietnam Dateline	Page#	Non-Vietnam Dateline	Page#	Vietnam Commentary/ Editorial	Page#
Enemy's Soviet-Designed Rifle Slows Marines' Drive in Hue; AK-47 Makes Sniper a "Machine-Gunner" Who "Can Tie Up an Enemy Company"; Cannons Used to Root Out Foe Gene Roberts (Hue)	17				
Half Saigon Army on Leave for Tet AP (S)	17				
Four Hundred Sixteen Americans Killed in Deadliest War Week Agence France Presse (S)	17				
Rockets and Ground Attack Reuters (S)	16				
Explanation Offered AP (S)	16				
February 10					
GIs Enter Saigon to Help Eliminate Enemy Holdouts; Move Seen as Sign of U.S. Dissatisfaction at Pace of Government Effort; Air Raid Near Haiphong; Bombing Appears to Signal End of Month-Long Curb on Attacks in North Charles Mohr (S)	1	Wilson Sees Hope of Reconciling Stands of Washington and Hanoi Special to *Times* (W)	1	Topics: "Things Fall Apart; the Center Cannot Hold" Robert Kennedy	32
Marines Gain in Hue AP (S)	10	U.S. Girding at Khe Sanh to Avoid a Dienbienphu; Washington Mood Tense Hedrick Smith (W)	1		
		Johnson Holds Reins Max Frankel (W)	1		
		U.S. Reminds Bonn of Risk on Berlin, Stresses Concern in View of Involvement in Asia David Bender (Bonn)	2		

Vietnam Dateline	Page[#]	Non-Vietnam Dateline	Page[#]	Vietnam Commentary/ Editorial	Page[#]
Thieu Outlines His Steps to Mobilize 65,000 More Vietnamese; He Indicates Need for Higher Taxes; President Asks Authority to Rule by Decree on Economic Matters Joseph Treaster (S)	11	Kennedy Is Accused by Saigon Official AP (U.N.)	4		
Khe Sanh Crash Kills Five Reuters (D)	11	Britain to Aid Civilians Special to *Times* (London)	4		
U.S. Physician Hid From Enemy Eight Days UPI (S)	11	Javits Bids Soviet Ask Bombing Halt, Asserts U.S. Is at a Military Stalemate in Vietnam Martin Arnold (N.Y.)	8		
Lang Vei Survivors at Khe Sanh Base Evacuated by Air AP (S)	11	More Soviet Aid Pledged Reuters (Moscow)	10		
U.S. Marine Foiled in Attempt to Hijack Airliner AP (D)	12	Moscow Calls for Talks UPI (Moscow)	10		
South Vietnamese Order French Newsman's Ouster AP (S)	12	Thant Holds Talks in India Reuters (New Delhi)	10		
Rate of U.S. Dollars Soars on Saigon's Black Market Reuters (S)	12	Gallup Calls Public Disillusioned and Cynical; Director of Poll Cites Feeling of Inadequate Leadership in International Relations AP (Princeton, N.J.)	12		
		White House Disputes McCarthy on Atom Arms AP (W)	13		
		Query by Fulbright UPI (W)	13		
		Red Cross Assails Executions in War Special to *Times* (Geneva)	14		
		Romney Challenges Nixon and Kennedy to Disclose Peace Plans Special to *Times* (Kenosha, Wis.)	15		

Vietnam Dateline	Page[#]	Non-Vietnam Dateline	Page[#]	Vietnam Commentary/ Editorial	Page[#]
February 11					
Jet Bombers Seen at Base in North During U.S. Raids; Soviet-Built IL-28s Could Hit Khe Sanh, but Attempt Is Viewed Un-likley; Airfield Struck Anew; A Vietcong Force Assaults Delta Provincial Capi-tal and Burns 1,000 Homes		Kennedy Attacked on VN Speech Special to *Times* (U.N.)	2	Civilian Heroes of War; No Word Is Sent Back from Vietnam on Some Who Did Not Have to Serve Howard A. Rusk,M.D.(N.Y.)	2
Tom Buckley (S)	1	Hanoi's Aide Asked Meeting with Thant Special to *Times* (New Delhi)	2	Asian Pres-sures: Cruel Dilemma for Johnson	
Hue to Da Nang: A Perilous Boat Ride		Rusk Says Climactic Period in VN May Be Nearing		(N.Y.)	1E
Gene Roberts (D)	1	UPI (Atlantic City, N.J.)	2	Illusions and Deceptions Tom Wicker	
Saigon Put on Alert		Russian Says U.S. Bars Talks		(W)	13E
Agence France Presse (S)	2	Reuters (Moscow)	3	Heavy Set-back for Saigon and More Trouble Ahead	
Delta City At-tacked		Flights to Saigon Resume AP (H.K.)	4	(N.Y.)	1E
Reuters (S)	2	Defector in Laos Gives Battle Plan; North Vietnam Called Ready to Attack Saravane		VN Peace Talks (editorial)	12E
Damage in Saigon Is Limited So Far; Fighting Has Leveled Some Relatively Small Areas		Special to *Times* (Vientiane)	5	Some of the Coffins in Vietnam Con-tained Guns (N.Y.)	1E
Charles Mohr, Special to *Times* (S)	3	Clark Kerr Takes Key Role in Urging Peace Talks, Helps Draft a Statement for Negoti-ation Now Group to Seek Initiative by U.S.			
Saigon's Authority Be-lieved to Be in Critical Stage		Lawrence E. Davies (El Cerrito, Calif.)	6		
Bernard Weinraub (S)	3	Asian Church Group Denounces the War Special to *Times* (Bangkok)	6		
Bomb Squad Kept on Run in Saigon; GI Specialists Answering Calls Around the Clock		Romney Assails Saigon's Rulers; In Nebraska, He Says U.S. Should Press for Change			
Joseph Treaster (S)	3	Special to *Times* (Omaha, Nebr.)	42		

Vietnam Dateline	Page#	Non-Vietnam Dateline	Page#	Vietnam Commentary/ Editorial	Page#
Hanoi Warns U.S. of "Dienbienphu" at Khe Sanh Agence France Presse (Hanoi)	3	Rumors on Use of Atomic Arms Stirred by Expert's Asian Trips Walter Sullivan (N.Y.)	70		
U.S. Aircraft Loss at 3,282 Agence France Presse (S)	5				
February 12					
Saigon's Soldiers Battle Big Force Close to Capital; U.S. Copter Gunships Join Sharp Clash Along River--Most of City Is Quiet; Casualty Totals Given--2,119 South Vietnamese and 973 Americans Are Listed as Dead in 12-Day Period Bernard Weinraub (S)	1	Westmoreland Criticized for Deluding Congress AP (Boston)	3	Commander at Khe Sanh-- David Edward Lownds (Man in the News) (N.Y.)	4
		Wilson Cautions on A-Arms in War, Sees "Lunacy" in Any Use of Tactical Atomic Weapons Hedrick Smith (W)	4	War Doubts in Senate; Misgivings over Administration Policy Said to Spread As Offensive Continues John W. Finney (W)	6
Search of a Hamlet near Saigon Shows Nothing--at First Joseph Treaster (S)	1	Mansfield Warns on War Realities; He Says in Maine No Part of South Vn Is Safe Special to *Times* (Orono, Maine)	8		
		Assessments Differ UPI (W)	8		
Hue's Mayor Says Foe Executed 300, Asserts Civilians Were Put in One Grave near City-- Marines Enter Citadel Thomas A. Johnson (Hue)	1	War Foe Sees U.S. as Pro-Diem in '53, Cites Evidence of Interest Year Before French Loss Special to *Times* (Newport, N.H.)	9		
		Thant in Moscow, Expected to Discuss Vietnam Raymond H. Anderson (Moscow)	10		
Two Prisoners Die in Blaze Agence France Presse (Hue)	2	Chinese Assail Thant Talks Reuters (H.K.)	8		

Vietnam Dateline	Page[#]	Non-Vietnam Dateline	Page[#]	Vietnam Commentary/ Editorial	Page[#]
Vietcong Attack Reported UPI (S)	2				
Buddhist Aide Charges U.S. Falsely Accused His Sect Agence France Presse (S)	3				
Step-up Mobiliza-tion Is Begun by South Vietnam AP (S)	17				

February 13

Vietnam Dateline	Page[#]	Non-Vietnam Dateline	Page[#]	Vietnam Commentary/ Editorial	Page[#]
GIs and Vietcong Fight Two Battles; MIG Is Shot Down; 95 of Enemy Re-ported Killed in Clashes; Rockets Hit U.S. Base at Bien Hoa; Foe's Goals Restudied; No Major Ground Attacks Initiated by Enemy, but More Are Expected Charles Mohr (S)	1	President Honors Lincoln and Likens Their War Ordeals Max Frankel (W)	1	In the Nation: When the Going Is Roughest Tom Wicker (W)	42
		Anonymous Call Set Off Rumors of Nuclear Arms for Vietnam John W. Finney (W)	1	Observer: The Fiery Savior Russell Baker (W)	42
		Johnson Sent a For-eign Envoy to Query Hanoi in Raid Letup Hedrick Smith (W)	1		
At Khe Sanh: Life on the Bull's-eye; 5,000 Sandbags Seem Thin to Marines Crouching at Center of Foe's Target AP (K)	1	Defoliation Study Casts Doubt on Long-Term Damage in Viet-nam Walter Sullivan (N.Y.)	4		
U.S. Marines Add to Forces in Hue; Strength Now About 800--Foe Still Entrenched Thomas A. John-son (Hue)	3	Thant Ends Talks with Soviet Chiefs on Vietnam; U.N. Chief Flies to London; *Pravda* Bids U.S. Agree to Peace Negotiations Henry Kamm (Moscow)	5		
GIs Go In Shoot-ing to Clear Ham-let near Saigon Joseph Treaster (S)	3	Poll Finds Rise in War Support from 61 Percent to 74 Percent in Two Months (N.Y.)	5		
		Johnson Talks with Students AP (W)	5		

Vietnam Dateline	Page[#]	Non-Vietnam Dateline	Page[#]	Vietnam Commentary/ Editorial	Page[#]
Saigon Resumes Garbage Pickups After Two Weeks; Health Threat Results from Pileup of Litter During Foe's Attacks in City Bernard Weinraub (S)	3	Difference on Nationality UPI (W)	5		
		Pentagon Identifies Vietnam War Dead AP (W)	6		
U.S. Aide Assesses Strategy of Giap, Says That General May Be Trying to Win by Spring Special to *Times* (S)	4	Westmoreland Is Defended Against Critic in Congress UPI (W)	28		
		Democratic Meeting Will Test Vietnam Sentiment (W)	32		
Foe's Strength at Year End at Ebb, U.S. Booklet Says Reuters (S)	5	War Becomes the Main Issue in Special Campaign in Brooklyn for House Seat Clayton Knowles (N.Y.)	33		
POWs in the South Identify Their Unit as North Vietnam's 33rd Regiment Dispatch of the *Times* of London (Ban Me Thuot)	6	Nixon Sees Vietnam as "Cork in Bottle" Special to *Times* (Dover, N.H.)	33		
Vietnam Troop Need Discussed by Thieu AP (My Tho)	15	Gavin Discloses '54 Invasion Plan, Says Joint Chiefs Favored Landing in North Vietnam (N.Y.)	6		
February 14					
Thirteen Americans Die in Saigon Clashes; Marine Drive Gains in Hue--Pacification Program Almost at a Standstill Bernard Weinraub (S)	1	U.S. Rushes 10,500 to Meet Threat of Vietnam Foe; Call-up Weighed; Proposal Is Reported to Involve a Division of National Guard Max Frankel (W)	1	Washington: Mr. Lincoln and Mr. Johnson James Reston (W)	46
Army Honors 27 Killed As Foe Opened Saigon Attack Special to *Times* (S)	2	Thant Sees Results If Bombing Is Halted Anthony Lewis (London)	1	Another Emergency Escalation (editorial)	46
		Vietnam Parcel Jam Ended AP (W)	2		

Vietnam Dateline	Page#	Non-Vietnam Dateline	Page#	Vietnam Commentary/ Editorial	Page#
Marines at Khe Sanh Clean Rifles and Dig Deeper, Find They "Gotta Keep Busy" to Counteract the Tension and Tedium of Waiting Gene Roberts (S)	2	Johnson's Rating on Vietnam Drops, Gallup Poll Finds Decline to 35 Percent in Public Approval Special to *Times* (Princeton, N.J.)	4		
Censorship Back in Saigon AP (S)	2	Disclosures of U.S. Peace Mission to Hanoi Is Attributed to Rusk Special to *Times* (W)	4		
Marines Gain in Hue Thomas A. Johnson (Hue)	3	Thousands March in Paris to Protest U.S. Role in War Special to *Times* (Paris)	18		
Pacification Program Is Almost at Standstill in South Vietnam Charles Mohr (S)	4	Nixon Developing a Vietnam Stand, Asks Successful End of War and Preventative Diplomacy Robert B. Semple, Jr. (Manchester, N.H.)	29		
Enemy General Killed, Saigon Says Special to *Times* (S)	4	New Peace Party Rejects McCarthy; Coast Group Says Senator Concedes War's Legality Gladwin Hill (Los Angeles)	26		
Pope Aids Vietnam Victims Agence France Presse (S)	4				
February 15					
U.S. Jets Attack Close to Hanoi Bridge and Two Airfields Are Targets of Biggest Raids on North in Six Weeks AP (S)	1	Rusk Says Hanoi Spurns U.S. Terms for Negotiation, Declares "All Explorations to Date" Prove Rejection of Johnson's Position; Two New Contacts Cited; Washington Given Reports After Thant and Fanfani Meet North Vietnamese Hedrick Smith (W)	1	The Strategic Reserve: Serious Depletion Feared as a Result of Decision to Bolster Vietnam Force Neil Sheehan (W)	4
Hanoi Assays Visits Agence France Presse (Hanoi)	2				
Jets Hammer at Hue Citadel Gene Roberts (S)	3	Wheeler Doubts Khe Sanh Will Need Atom Weapons John W. Finney (W)	1		

Vietnam Dateline	Page[#]	Non-Vietnam Dateline	Page[#]	Vietnam Commentary/ Editorial	Page[#]
Vietcong Claim Wide Gains Agence France Presse (Hanoi)	3	Text of the Statement by Rusk on Hanoi Special to *Times* (W)	2		
Fog Closing Gap at Khe Sanh Dispatch of the *Times* of London (K)	3	Fanfani Saw Two Hanoi Aides Special to *Times* (Rome)	2		
Questioning of Captured VC Yield Picture of a Determined Enemy Bernard Weinraub (S)	4	Thant Confers with Hanoi's Envoy and DeGaulle but the Paris Assessment Is That Prospects for Peace Have Weakened Recently Henry Tanner (Paris)	2		
Ailing General Flown to U.S. AP (D)	4	Bunche Defends Thant in Response to Rostow UPI (U.N.)	2		
		Unarmed Navy Plane Downed by a Chinese Communist MIG UPI (W)	2		
		U.S. Warned by Peking Special to *Times* (H.K.)	2		
		Parents of Dead GI Bid Johnson Be Firm UPI (St. Paul, Minn.)	2		
		Washington Discerns No Gain Reuters (W)	2		
		War Protest Clash in Rome AP (Rome)	5		
		Five Hundred Law Teachers Join War Protest, Urge Legal Men to Oppose Johnson's Vietnam Policy Fred P. Graham (W)	25		
		Romney Urges Peace Offensive; Scores Nixon for Lack of Stand Jerry M. Flint (Manchester, N.H.)	26		

Vietnam Dateline	Page[#]	Non-Vietnam Dateline	Page[#]	Vietnam Commentary/ Editorial	Page[#]
		One Hundred Seventy-Six in VISTA Urge Johnson End War; Letter Asks Diverting Funds to Antipoverty Campaign Edith Evans Asbury (N.Y.)	26		

February 16

Vietnam Dateline	Page[#]	Non-Vietnam Dateline	Page[#]	Vietnam Commentary/ Editorial	Page[#]

*U.S. Marines Gain 200 Yards in Day at Hue's Citadel; Advance Is Slow in Spite of a Two-day Bombardment and Close Air Support; An Enemy Unit Routed; Allied Aircraft also Attack Foe near Saigon and at Besieged Khe Sanh Base
  Thomas A. Johnson (Hue)
	1	Goldberg Briefed by Thant on His Efforts for Peace
		  Drew Middleton (U.N.)
			1	A Weary President: He Appears Tense and Aware of U.S. Frustrations
				  Max Frankel (W)
					18

Officials Seek to "Reprime the Pump" of Pacification
  Joseph Treaster (D)
	2	Fulbright Query Attacked by Rusk, but Senator Rejects Charge That Atomic Arms Debate Is Disservice to Nation
		  John W. Finney (W)
			1	Washington: The Budget Deficit and the Moral Deficit
				  James Reston (W)
					36

Wide Allied Air Offensive
  Special to *Times* (S)
	3	Pentagon Steps Up Fight on Drug Use in Vietnam; Sharp Rise Noted in Inquiries into Marijuana Cases for GIs in Last Two Years
		  Special to *Times* (W)
			3	Foreign Affairs: A New Lansdowne Letter
				  C. L. Sulzberger (London)
					36

U.S. Dead in Week 400
  AP (S)
	3	American Pacifist Says Hanoi Will Free Three Today
		  (W)
			3		

Ambush Toll Is 12 Dead
  Agence France Presse (S)
	3	Young Asks Ouster of Westmoreland
		  UPI (W)
			4		

Tunnel Hunt at Khe Sanh
  Agence France Presse (K)
	3	Harvard Students End Fast to Protest the VN War
		  Special to *Times* (Cambridge, Mass.)
			4		

		Romney Terms War in Vietnam His Key Issue in New Hampshire Jerry M. Flint (Manchester, N.H.)	18		

Vietnam Dateline	Page[#]	Non-Vietnam Dateline	Page[#]	Vietnam Commentary/ Editorial	Page[#]
Forty-Two Killed near Saigon in B-52 Bombing Error AP (S)	4				
Saigon Papers Censor Johnson's Peace Offer AP (S)	4				
February 17					
Foe Still Clings to Hue Positions, Again Defies Bombardment and Tear Gas--Enemy's Tanks Seen at Con Thien Gene Roberts (S)	1	President Declares Hanoi Doesn't Want to Negotiate Max Frankel (W)	1	A Bombing Pause--Now (editorial)	29
Refugees Find Hue Provides No Haven Thomas A. Johnson (Hue)	1	Johnson Denies Atom Use in Vietnam Is Considered John W. Finney (W)	1		
Three Dead Enemy Soldiers Reported Chained to Gun; Allied Officers in Hue Assert the Bodies Were Discovered When School Was Taken Reuters (Hue)	3	Hanoi Releases Three U.S. Fliers; They Arrive in Thailand--Are Due Home Today Hedrick Smith (W)	1		
Quang Tri Attack "Imminent" Joseph Treaster (Camp Evans, S. VN)	3	Washington Feels VC Offensive Failed to Gain Maximum Objectives Hanson W. Baldwin (W)	2		
		Casualties of Vietnam War Are Identified by Pentagon AP (W)	2		
		Special Warplane Sent to VN; It Can Locate Foe Despite Fog, Darkness, or Jungle William Beecher (W)	3		
		Three Hundred Fifty Thousand New Refugees Special to *Times* (W)	3		
		Army Study Said to Ask Readiness, Finds Need to Be Prepared for Global Intervention E. W. Kenworthy (W)	4		

Vietnam Dateline	Page[#]	Non-Vietnam Dateline	Page[#]	Vietnam Commentary/ Editorial	Page[#]
		New Strategy Is Urged for Peace (N.Y.)	4		
		Brezhnev Assails U.S. Policies as "Brigand-age," Denounces Moves in Korea, Vietnam, and Mideast--Aid to Hanoi Pledged Henry Kamm (Moscow)	6		
		Transcript of the President's News Conference on Foreign and Domestic Matters Special to *Times* (W)	8		
		Kennedys Decline to Debate Vietnam War with Three in UN Reuters (U.N.)	9		
		Two Hundred Fifty Princeton Students Staging an Antiwar Fast AP (Princeton, N.J.)	10		
		McCarthy, Here, Of-fers War View, Says Americans Ask "Hard Questions" on Implications Steven V. Roberts (N.Y.)	12		
		Airlines Cite Rise in Military Needs; Defense Requests Growing for Com-mercial Planes (N.Y.)	57		
February 18					
Foe's Shells Hit 37 Vietnam Cities and Saigon Field; U.S. Headquarters Is Among Targets at Tan Son Nhut--Barrages Destroy Planes; Blasts Shake Capital; Ground Assaults Reported, but		President Visits Men Going to War, Flies to Carolina Base and Later to California to See Combat Re-inforcements Max Frankel (El Toro Marine Air Station, Calif.)	1	Vietnam: Confrontation at Khe Sanh (N.Y.) U.S. Pes-simistic on Talks (N.Y.)	1E 1E

Vietnam Dateline	Page[#]	Non-Vietnam Dateline	Page[#]	Vietnam Commentary/ Editorial	Page[#]
They Are Less Intense Than in Recent Wave Gene Roberts (S)	1	Johnson's Rating Declines in Poll; Gallup Notes Seven-Point Drop Since Vietcong Offensive After a Three-Month Rise Special to *Times* (Princeton, N.J.)	1		
Assault in Hue Hampered As Foe Sinks Supply Ship Special to *Times* (S)	1				
Hanoi Paper Derides U.S. for Sending More Troops Agence France Presse (Hanoi)	3	Three Freed Airmen Are Back in U.S. in Washington, One Reports Hanoi May Release Others AP (W)	3		
		Thant Again Says Peace Talks Could Follow End of Bombing Sam Pope Brewer (U.N.)	3		
		Vatican Aide's Trip Disclosed AP (Rome)	3		
		Scientists Study Defoliated Areas, Report Concludes Rocklike Laterite Could Result Walter Sullivan	5		
		Four Hundred Enroll in a Harvard Course on "Law and the Lawyer" in the Vietnam War Special to *Times* (Cambridge, Mass.)	7		
		Gore Urges U.S. Quit War Morass, Calls for Negotiations and a Neutralized Vietnam Special to *Times* (Moscow, Idaho)	8		
		Switches by Press on War Reported; Seven Papers More Critical of U.S.--Four More Hawkish Special to *Times* (Boston)	9		

Vietnam Dateline	Page[#]	Non-Vietnam Dateline	Page[#]	Vietnam Commentary/ Editorial	Page[#]
		Meany Accused of Demagoguery; Auto Union Official Asserts War View Was Maligned Special to *Times* (W)	35		
		Romney Grabbing the Peace Issue; Advisors Say Strategy May Win Victory in Primary Jerry M. Flint (Peterborough, N.H.)	37		
February 19					
*Airport Terminal at Saigon Struck in Rocket Attack; A U.S. Serviceman, Waiting to Return Home, Killed by Enemy Missile—21 Hurt, Foe Continues Assault, Vietcong Invade Provincial Capital and Open Prison—47 Places Assaulted Bernard Weinraub (S)	1	Johnson Confers with Eisenhower; Briefs Him on War; Three-Hour Talk in West Caps President's Cross-Country Tour of Military Bases Max Frankel (Palm Desert, Calif.)	1	Communication Failure; Senate's Foreign Relations Committee and Rusk Come Close to Severing Ties John W. Finney (W)	2
Allied Command Divided on Foe's Aim in New Raids Gene Roberts (S)	1	Hanoi Troops Set to Attack in Laos; Threat to Saravane Linked to Khe Sanh—Similarity to Giap's Plan in '54 Seen Sydney Gruson (Vientiane)	1		
Paris-Hanoi Cooperation in Medicine Considered Agence France Presse (Hanoi)	2	10,000 Assail U.S. in West Berlin Rally Philip Shabecoff (Berlin)	1		
Truce Unit's Team Has Abandoned Hue AP (Hue)	4	U.S. Is Accused on Pilots' Return; Two Pacifists See Future Hanoi Releases Imperiled Barnard L. Collier	2		
Politicians in Saigon Form an Anti-Communist Front AP (S)	5	U.S. Aides Report Setbacks for Foe; They Assert Recent Fighting Exacted Heavy Toll Special to *Times* (Palm Desert, Calif.)	3		

Vietnam Dateline	Page#	Non-Vietnam Dateline	Page#	Vietnam Commentary/ Editorial	Page#
Hanoi Paper Scores Johnson's Formula Agence France Presse (Hanoi)	6	Bunker Sees Gains Special to *Times* (W)	3		
		Russian Warns U.S. on A-Arms in War Reuters (Paris)	5		
The Execution of a Vietcong Suspect Marks a Day of Violence in Saigon AP (S)	14	Rome Marchers Driven Off Special to *Times* (Rome)	8		
		Silent March in London Special to *Times* (London)	8		
		Group Gives Plan for World Peace, Urges That All Resources Center on Global Safety	14		
		Harper's and *Atlantic* Put Out "Vietnam Issues"; Monthlies Break Century-Old Tradition to Devote a Full Magazine to the War Henry Raymont (N.Y.)	14		
February 20					
*Foe Hurled Back from Key Village near Saigon Base; Point Within Mortar Range of Field Retaken in Eight Hours--Allies Stalled in Hue; Hanoi Reports Big Gain, Says Drive Brought Mastery over Much of Countryside, but U.S. Disputes Claim Gene Roberts (S)	1	Pacifists' Charges in Return of Pilots Disputed by U.S. Special to *Times* (W)	3	In the Nation: Firepower vs. South Vietnam Tom Wicker (W)	46
		Fulbright Opens Seminar with a Vietnam Twist John W. Finney (W)	4		
		Vietnam War Dead Listed by Pentagon AP (W)	4		
		Humphrey Assesses Offensives Special to *Times* (Bal Harbor, Fla.)	4		

Vietnam Dateline	Page[#]	Non-Vietnam Dateline	Page[#]	Vietnam Commentary/ Editorial	Page[#]
Marine Advance Against Citadel in Hue Stalled; U.S. Troops Raise a Flag, but Enemy Blocks Drive; Tank Repulsed by Rockets--Two Journalists Wounded Charles Mohr (Hue)	2	British Sympathy for U.S. Role in War Rising; Public Criticism of Position in Vietnam Is Tempered by Praise for the GIs Anthony Lewis (London)	4		
A Chaplain Chooses to Stay at the Front and Dies; Marines Recall a "Friendly Guy," Who Was with Them in the Battle for Hue Thomas A. Johnson (Hue)	2	Seoul Aide Says VN Peace Would Set Off War in Thailand UPI (W)	14		
		Mission to Saigon Never Got There Special to *Times* (W)	14		
Vietcong Report Goals of Assault; Front Also Calls for Unity of the Vietnamese Population Agence France Presse (Hanoi)	4	Eastland Offers a Security Bill, It Would Make Aid to Hanoi Punishable as Treason AP (W)	15		
U.S.-Backed Volunteer Unit Must Curb Activity; Security in the Rural Areas Is Reason for Reduction by Major Services Agency Bernard Weinraub (S)	4	Romney Scores Vietnam War in Wisconsin Campaign Speech Special to *Times* (Milwaukee, Wis.)	28		
		Connally Contends Kennedy Criticism of War Hurts U.S. AP (Atlanta, Ga.)	31		
Fund Drive for Vietnamese AP (S)	4				
February 21					
*Enemy Attempts to Put Artillery on Edge of Saigon; Antiaircraft Guns Observed by Pilots Near Airport-- Bombs Thwart Move;		McNamara Tells of Secret Data on Tonkin Attack; He Says Intelligence Source Confirmed Navy Reports--Radio		Foreign Affairs: Delayed Action C. L. Sulzberger (London)	46

Vietnam Dateline	Page[#]	Non-Vietnam Dateline	Page[#]	Vietnam Commentary/ Editorial	Page[#]

Heavy Clash in Suburb; U.S. Troops Report Killing 123 Vietcong--Allies Step Up Patrols in Capital
  Gene Roberts (S)
	1	Monitor Hinted
		  John W. Finney (W)
			1	TV: Disturbing View of Vietnam War; CBS Report Shows Obstacles to Victory; Ingenuity of VC Stressed by Films
				  Jack Gould (N.Y.)
					95

A Pacification Drive Set Back in Key Area
  Bernard Weinraub (Qui Nhon)
	1	Pentagon Identifies Men Killed in Vietnam Combat
		  AP (W)
			2		

Hue Chief Issues Execution Order; Mayor Says Some Enemy Agents Face Death--U.S. Unable to Verify Report
  AP (Hue)
	1	Thant Said to Get Hanoi Assurance; He Meets Johnson Today--Terms for Talks at Issue
		  Drew Middleton (U.N.)
			3		

Six Hundred Newsmen in Vietnam
  AP (S)
	2	Cease-Fire Plan Reported
		  Anthony Lewis (London)
			3		

Powerful Raids Forseen
  Agence France Presse (S)
	2	U.S. Silent on Report
		  Special to *Times* (W)
			3		

Wary Hue Civilians Live Around the Battle, in a Lull They Come Outdoors to Look or Sell Candy
  Thomas A. Johnson (Hue)
	3	French Warning to U.S. Before Jan. 29 Reported
		  Reuters (Geneva)
			3		

Ky Is Said to Quit a Major Position; Action Arouses Speculation on Dissension in Regime
  Special to *Times* (S)
	₋7	U.S. Has No Verification
		  Special to *Times* (W)
			4		

		Hanoi Aide in Sweden AP (Stockholm)	7		
		Kissinger Scores Anti-U.S. Feeling, Tells West Germans They Must Back Americans Philip Shabecoff (Bonn)	8		
		Aid for Vietnam Announced AP (Bonn)	8		
		Rivers Demands Reserve Call-up, Says Control of War Should Be Given Military UPI (W)	9		
		Poland Said to Boycott Check of Laotian Town Reuters (Vientiane)	12		

Vietnam Dateline	Page[#]	Non-Vietnam Dateline	Page[#]	Vietnam Commentary/ Editorial	Page[#]
		Excerpts from McNamara's Statement on Tonkin Incidents Special to *Times* (W)	12		
		Pentagon Requests $2.88-Billion Fund AP (W)	32		
		Hanoi Accuses Laotian Reuters (H.K.)	57		
February 22					
Jets Bomb Enemy near Hue Citadel; Marines Advance; Rockets and Napalm Used in First Air Strikes in Five Days--Foe Being Penned In; More Saigon Fighting; Southern Troops on Attack in the Chinese Quarter-- Missiles Fall at Airport Thomas A. Johnson (S)	1	Fulbright Says McNamara Deceives Public on Tonkin, Asserts Secretary Offered One-Sided Accounts of '64 Raids in Gulf--Morse Declares Destroyer Was Spy Ship John W. Finney (W)	1	In the Nation: Rocky, the Strike and the War Tom Wicker (Albany, N.Y.)	30
Marines at Khe Sanh Find Flaws in Their Defenses Gene Roberts (S)	1	Church Council Urges Peace Bid, Calls on U.S. to Adopt New Foreign Policy, Ending Its Reliance on the Military George Dugan (San Diego, Calif.)	1		
Fog Fails to Lift, and a Marine Dies; Copter Grounded Too Long to Save Men on Hill 881 AP (K)	7	A Johnson Rebuff Stops Abram Race, President Rejects Plea for Softer Vietnam Policy Clayton Knowles (N.Y.)	1		
		Two of Freed Pilots Tell of Beatings Special to *Times* (W)	3		
U.S. Embassy Is Disturbed by Sudden Arrests of Three Key Opposition Leaders in South VN Bernard Weinraub (S)	8	Johnson Burned in Effigy Special to *Times* (Paris)	3		
		U.S. Assailed in Stockholm Special to *Times* (Stockholm)	3		

Vietnam Dateline	Page[#]	Non-Vietnam Dateline	Page[#]	Vietnam Commentary/ Editorial	Page[#]
South Vietnam Relief Job Handed Over by Ky to Thieu Reuters (S)	9	U.S. Official Attacked Special to *Times* (London)	3		
Ships Clog Saigon Port AP (S)	9	Saigon Bars French Writer Special to *Times* (Paris)	7		
Airmobile Division Short of Copters and Supplies; Force, Believed to Be Reserve for Khe Sanh, Is Fighting at Hue and at Quang Tri Joseph Treaster (D)	10	Swiss Establish Channel to Hanoi; Envoy to Peking Named as a Link to North Vietnam Thomas J. Hamilton (Geneva)	9		
Vietcong Leader for Hue Predicts Defeat of Allies Agence France Presse (Hanoi)	10	Vietnam War Dead Listed by Pentagon AP (W)	10		
Court Planned in Hue to Try Enemy Agents AP (Hue)	11	Pentagon Defends Locking Up Rifles UPI (W)	10		
Copters Carry Reinforcements UPI (Hue)	11	Army to Return Men Sent to Vietnam Twice UPI (W)	10		
Fresh Troops Sought Special to *Times* (D)	11	Text of Fulbright's Statement and Excerpts from Morse's on Tonkin Incident Special to *Times* (W)	14		
Police Post Attacked Reuters (S)	11	House Unit Charges War Policy Errors UPI (W)	14		
		Thant Reports to the President on His Vietnam Peace Mission Max Frankel (W)	15		
		Romney Accuses Johnson On War, Sees "Web of Delusion to Distract Us from Truth" Anthony Ripley (Amherst, N.H.)	24		
		Saigon Envoy Warns of Fear and Despair Special to *Times* (W)	26		
		McCarthy Defends Dissent on Vietnam UPI (Madison, Wis.)	29		

Vietnam Dateline	Page[#]	Non-Vietnam Dateline	Page[#]	Vietnam Commentary/ Editorial	Page[#]
		Morse Speaks in Senate E. W. Kenworthy (W)	15		
February 23					
*U.S. Marines Gain a Hue Objective, but Foe Fights on; Americans Reach South Wall of Citadel As Enemy Pushes South Vietnamese Back; Third of Area Cleared but a Final Drive on Inner Royal Palace Sector Is Expected to Be Costly Charles Mohr (Hue)	1	Pentagon Studies a Plan to Call Up 40,000 Reserves; Proposal Would Also Include Special Alert to 130,000--Wheeler Is in Vietnam William Beecher (W)	1	Khe Sanh: Why U.S. Is Making a Stand Neil Sheehan (W)	1
U.S. Dead at 543 in Week, a Record Toll in '68 Rises to 2,242--Saigon Toll Not Disclosed--Wheeler Arrives Tom Buckley (S)	1	Swiss Rule Out a Peace Role Now Thomas J. Hamilton (Geneva)	2		
Spotter Plane over Hue Looks into the Muzzles of Foe's Guns Joseph Treaster (Hue)	3	Vietcong Threaten to Kill U.S. Captives in Reprisal Reuters (H.K.)	4		
Gen. Loan Off to Hue to Question Suspects Reuters (S)	3	Mark Clark Declares Bombing and Blockade Will Speed Talks (N.Y.)	6		
Foe Giving Warfare Lessons with Simple Mortar Gene Roberts (S)	5	Prince Says North Vietnam Has 40,000 Men in Laos Reuters (Paris)	6		
Nine More Arrests Reported in Saigon AP (S)	5	Churches Caution on War Prospects; Council Issues a Warning over "Americanization" George Dugan (San Diego, Calif.)	6		
		President Appoints a Top Saigon Aide UPI (Austin, Tex.)	6		
		Activation Predicted UPI (W)	8		

Vietnam Dateline	Page[#]	Non-Vietnam Dateline	Page[#]	Vietnam Commentary/ Editorial	Page[#]
February 24					
*Enemy Battalion and Allied Force Clash at Khe Sanh; Fighting Outside Perimeter Follows Heaviest Gunfire on Outpost to Date; Saigon Air Base Struck; Four U.S. Servicemen Killed and 36 Wounded in Shelling--Foe Set Back at Hue Special to *Times* (S)	1	Forty-Eight Thousand Face April Draft, Highest Total in 18 Months Benjamin Welles (W)	1	Half-Truths About Tonkin (editorial)	28
In North Vietnam Mountain Refuge Visitor Sees Hidden Schools, Factories and Hospitals Bernard-Joseph Cabanes, Agence France Presse (Hanoi)	1	Captain Confirms Attack in Tonkin; Commander of Two Destroyers Denies Any Provocation in the 1964 Incidents UPI (W)	1		
Refugees Jam Saigon Camps; Rice on Hand but Milk Is Scarce Gene Roberts (S)	3	War Policy Scored in *Wall Street Journal* (N.Y.)	2		
Citadel Fighting Heavy AP (S)	3	Pentagon Identifies Vietnam Casualties UPI (W)	3		
Arrests in Saigon Reported Going On AP (S)	3	General Taylor Will Head Foreign Intelligence Board Reuters (Austin, Tex.)	3		
Allies Disagree on Enemy's Aims; U.S. Girding at Khe Sanh--Saigon Looks to Highlands Special to *Times* (S)	5	Quakers' Group Suspends Programs in South Vietnam AP (Philadelphia, Pa.)	3		
Saigon Bans *Newsweek* AP (S)	7	Guerrillas in Laos Seize a 2nd Outpost AP (Vientiane)	3		
		Leaflets Bombard Fort Jackson, GIs Off Post Douglas Robinson (Columbia, S.C.)	6		
		Rusk Is Identified as Critics' Critic, Said in Background Talk, "Whose Side Are You On?" AP (W)	7		
		McCarthy Charges Tonkin Gulf Deceit UPI (Berlin, N.H.)	9		

Vietnam Dateline	Page[#]	Non-Vietnam Dateline	Page[#]	Vietnam Commentary/ Editorial	Page[#]
Saigon Said to Name New Chief for Delta Reuters (S)	8				
Vietnam Conference Set AP (S)	8				

February 25

Vietnam Dateline	Page[#]	Non-Vietnam Dateline	Page[#]	Vietnam Commentary/ Editorial	Page[#]
*South Vietnamese Seize Hue Palace; Enemy Retreats; Troops, After 21-Day Siege, Find Most of Foe Gone--Fight Seems near End; U.S. Bombs Hanoi Piers; They Are Struck First Time --Two Americans Killed in Tan Son Nhut Clash Charles Mohr (Hue)	1	McNamara Says Destroyers in '64 Warned of Enemy, Tells Senators that Two Ships Remained on Patrol Despite Threat of Hostile Action John W. Finney (W)	1	Impact of Vietnam on Europe Grows Henry Tanner (Paris)	1
U.S. Admits Blow to Pacification; High Official in Saigon Says Foe's Attacks Resulted in a Rural "Vacuum" Bernard Weinraub (S)	1	Thant Urges U.S. Assume Hanoi Good Faith in Talks Drew Middleton (U.N.)	1	Asian Crisis: How the President Sees the War (N.Y.)	1E
Westmoreland Bid for Troops Related UPI (S)	21	Complete Failure Charged Reuters (H.K.)	20	The Foreign Relations Committee-- Advice but No Consent (N.Y.)	1E
South Vietnam Is Reported Giving Arms to Civilians Agence France Presse (S)	21	Two Thousand March Here to Protest War, Also Ask Ban of Any Use of Nuclear Arms in Vietnam Val Adams (N.Y.)	21	As the Enemy Changes Tactics, Concern Grows About Two Critical Zones (N.Y.)	1E
U.S. Bombs Wharves of Hanoi for the First Time Tom Buckley (S)	24	Text of Thant's Statement on Talks About Vietnam Special to Times (U.N.)	24	Peter Brook: "Yes, Let's Be Emotional About Vietnam" Nat Hentoff (N.Y.)	17D
		Radiomen Relay Vietnam Calls; Servicemen Talk to Parents via Father-Son Ham Setup Robert D. McFadden (N.Y.)	26	Troops, More Men for a Tougher War (N.Y.)	2E
		Excerpts from McNamara's Testimony on Tonkin Special to Times (W)	28	Prisoners: Three Who Came Back (N.Y.)	2E

Vietnam Dateline	Page#	Non-Vietnam Dateline	Page#	Vietnam Commentary/ Editorial	Page#
Helicopter Crash Kills Eight Agence France Presse (S)	24	Nine Senators Feel U.S. Overreacted on Tonkin; Members of Fulbright Panel Voice Criticism of Decision to Bomb North Vietnam E. W. Kenworthy (W)	29	Science: A Look at a New Victim of the War-- Plantlife Walter Sullivan (N.Y.)	9E
U.S. Pressed Shift of Vietnam General Special to *Times* (S)	25	Pentagon Disputes Morse on Message Special to *Times* (W)	29	Escalation-- to What End? (editorial)	12E
Skirmishes Flare near Tan Son Nhut; Ten Enemy Soldiers Killed in Three Battles Close to Saigon Tom Buckley (S)	X	Giap Sees Battle in Fierce Phase; At Red Reception in Hanoi He Vows "Every Sacrifice" Special to *Times* (Tokyo)	X	In the Na- tion: The Tonkin Gulf Revisited Tom Wicker (W)	12E
February 26					
*U.S. Camp Hard Hit in a Two-Hour Assault by a Force of 500; At Least 20 GIs Killed at Site 42 Miles from Saigon--11 Vehicles Burned; Planes Drove Foe Away; Raiders Abandon 94 Dead-- Wheeler, After Visit, Sees No Quick End of War Gene Roberts (S)	1	Fulbright Urges Congress Inquiry into War Policy, As- sails Handling of Tonkin Incident--Wil- liam Bundy Defends 1964 Decision Peter Grose (W)	1	Waste on the Red River (editorial)	36
Hue Is Confronted by Food Shortage Reuters (Hue)	1	Raid on Hanoi Described Agence France Presse (H.K.)	2		
Outlook Assessed by Westmoreland; He Doubts Hanoi Can Fight Long, but Asserts He Will Probably Need More Men AP (S)	1	Hanoi Calls for Aid AP (Tokyo)	2		
		Hanoi Aide Leaves Sweden UPI (Stockholm)	3		
Rail Yard at Haiphong Bombed AP (S)	2				

Vietnam Dateline	Page[#]	Non-Vietnam Dateline	Page[#]	Vietnam Commentary/ Editorial	Page[#]
Saigon Holds Two More Monks Agence France Presse (S)	3				
Wounded and Dying Civilians Pack Can Tho Hospital Bernard Weinraub (Can Tho)	3				
February 27					
*Marines' Patrol Mauled 800 Yards Outside Khe Sanh; North Vietnamese Ambush U.S. Platoon and Block Rescue Unit's Efforts; Foe Digs Toward Base; Three Enemy Armored Vehicles Attacked by GIs Only 45 Miles from Saigon AP (S)	1	Mansfield Urges Peace Emphasis, Wants Trial Halt in Bombing in Preference to Heeding Call for More Troops Hedrick Smith (W)	1		
South Vietnamese Remove Second Key Commander Tom Buckley (S)	1	U.S. Forces Urged to Dig In UPI (Hamburg)	2		
		Brown Cites Hanoi on Talk AP (London)	2		
U.S. Tightens Curbs on Battle Reports That Would Aid Foe Special to *Times* (S)	2	Pentagon Defines Terms AP (W)	2		
		Fulbright Called Wrong on Tonkin, Admits Error on One Point, but Calls Data Inadequate Peter Grose (W)	9		
U.S. Pacification Chief to Report to Johnson AP (S)	2	Sixteen Hundred Executives Form Group for a National Anti- war Drive Gladwin Hill (Los Angeles)	9		
Enemy Armor Attacked Special to *Times* (S)	2	President's View UPI (Austin, Tex.)	9		
		G.O.P. Urges Pullout AP (Lincoln City, Oreg.)	5		

Vietnam Dateline	Page[#]	Non-Vietnam Dateline	Page[#]	Vietnam Commentary/ Editorial	Page[#]

Vietcong Indicate Giap Heads Offensive in South; In Broadcast, They Praise Hanoi General and Predict a Triumph at Khe Sanh
  Bernard Weinraub
  (S)
	3				

Cold and Dampness Were Foes of Marines at Hue
  Charles Mohr
  (Hue)
	5				

U.S. Aircraft Loss Is 3,360 Agence France Presse (S)	5				

February 28
*U.S. Troops Repel Raid Near Dak To, Killing 50 of Foe; North Vietnamese Battalion and 400 GIs Fight Two Days in the Central Highlands; Bien Hoa Air Base Hit; Rockets Are Said to Kill 14-- Enemy Toll Put at 148 in Battle near Tam Ky
  Tom Buckley (S)
	1	President Urges Firmness on War in First Visit to Dallas Since Assassination; He Sees a Turning Point in Vietnam
		  Roy Reed (Dallas, Tex.)
			1	Foreign Affairs: The Strategy of Error--I
				  C. L. Sulzberger
				  (Paris)
					46

Conduct of Hue Leaders Called Despair of American Officials
  George McArthur, AP (Hue)
	27	Javits Urges End of War in Opening Bid for Third Term
		  Richard L. Madden (Buffalo, N.Y.)
			1	Escalation, U Thant Style (N.Y.)	46

Life and Death in an Ancient Asian City: Scenes in the Long Fight for Hue
  Don McCullin-Magnum (photo story) (Hue)
	26	*Enterprise* Gets Defense Missile; Navy Speeds Use of System Designed to Balk Styx and Other Antiship Rockets
		  William Beecher (W)
			1		

		Men Killed in Vietnam War Identified by the Pentagon AP (W)	2		
		Dick Gregory Will Fast 40 Days in War Protest (N.Y.)	5		

Vietnam Dateline	Page[#]	Non-Vietnam Dateline	Page[#]	Vietnam Commentary/ Editorial	Page[#]
		McCarthy Says War Is Widely Opposed AP (Cambridge, Mass.)	6		
		U.S. Emphasizes Concern on Laos; It Fears Pro-Red Offensive Imperils Geneva Pacts Hedrick Smith (W)	23		
February 29					
Twenty-Two Killed near Khe Sanh As Foe Shoots Down Transport Copter Tom Buckley (S)	1	U.S. Reappraising Its Use of Troops in Vietnam War; Westmoreland Said to Seek 100,000 to 200,000 More--Wheeler Briefs Johnson William Beecher (W)	1	Top Man in Uniform Earle Gilmore Wheeler (Man in the News) (N.Y.)	2
Marines at Camp Carroll Share Khe Sanh Tension As Clouds Impede Bombers; Importance of Artillery Post Grows near Buffer Zone Joseph Treaster (Camp Carroll, S. VN)	4	France Affirms Report by Thant; Paris Again Says Bombing Halt Would Bring Talks Henry Tanner (Paris)	1		
		Opium Smuggling in Saigon Said to Involve High Aides UPI (W)	7		
Bodies of 100 Found in a Grave near Hue UPI (S)	4	Aid Program Hurt by Vietcong Raids; Gaud Says Attacks Upset All Estimates by U.S. Felix Belair, Jr. (W)	8		
Thieu's Nightclub Ban Is Declared Permanent AP (S)	6	U.S. Identifies War Dead UPI (W)	24		
March 1					
Enemy Harasses Area near Saigon; Americans Say Big Attack on Weekend Is Possible--Foe Loses Arms Ships Tom Buckley (S)	1	Top Scientist Cuts All Links to War; Kistiakowsky Refuses to Go On Advising Pentagon Evert Clark (W)	2	An Outspoken Scientist: George Bogdan Kistiakowsky (Man in the News) (N.Y.)	2

Vietnam Dateline	Page[#]	Non-Vietnam Dateline	Page[#]	Vietnam Commentary/ Editorial	Page[#]

Death Holds Hue in a Quiet Agony
  Bernard Weinraub
  (Hue)
	1	Pentagon Identifies Vietnam Casualties
		  UPI (W)
			3	New Look at Vietnam Needed
				  (editorial)
					36

Shift in Command At Khe Sanh Is Due; Changes Could Decentralize Control in Five Provinces
  Charles Mohr (S)
	3	Kennan Attacks Vietnam Policy as Massive, Unparalleled Error
		  Ronald Sullivan
		  (Newark, N.J.)
			25	Foreign Affairs: The Strategy of Error--II
				  C. L. Sulzberger
				  (Paris)
					36

Nine Killed in Delta Mine Blast
  AP (S)
	3	Mills Says Expanded War Could Force Rise in Taxes
		  Eileen Shanahan (W)
			1		

Food Prices in Saigon Drop After Sharp Rise; U.S. Economists Elated by Decline Since Enemy's Offense in the Cities
  Joseph Treaster
  (S)
	3				

Young Saigon Buddhist Burns Himself to Death AP (S)	3				
Loss of Hue Not Reported Agence France Presse (Hanoi)	4				
Hanoi Says Peace Talks Are Now Up to the U.S. Agence France Presse (Hanoi)	6				
March 2					

Clashes Flare near Saigon; City Put on Alert for Attack; South Vietnamese Paratroopers Battle with Foe near Tan Son Nhut Base--B-52s Batter Enemy at Khe Sanh
  Tom Buckley (S)
	1	Enemy's Use of New Soviet and Chinese Weapons Changes the Pattern of War in Vietnam
		  Hanson W. Baldwin
		  (N.Y.)
			3	Topics: Hanoi Isn't Counting on American Dissent
				  David Mozingo/ John W. Lewis
				  (N.Y.)
					28

		Sixteen South Vietnamese in U.S. and Canada Support a Halt AP (W)	4		

Vietnam Dateline	Page#	Non-Vietnam Dateline	Page#	Vietnam Commentary/ Editorial	Page#
Thieu Is Rebuffed by Saigon's House on Rule by Decree; Emergency Power for Year Denied to President by Legislators, 85 to 10; Setback Is a Surprise; Reversal of Action Possible--Measures Are Taken to Bolster Armed Forces Charles Mohr (S)	1	Casualties of Vietnam War Are Identified by Pentagon UPI (W)	4		
		New War Hearings Weighed by Foreign Relations Board AP (W)	8		
		U.S. Court Upholds the Right to Protest in Bus Station Here Edward Ranzal (N.Y.)	1		
Khe Sanh Attack Repulsed AP (S)	2	Johnson Berates Vietnam Critics, Defends Policy and Touches Political Bases in Texas Max Frankel (Beaumont, Tex.)	X		
Saigon Monk Dies by Fire UPI (S)	3				
Three Newsmen Hurt at Khe Sanh Agence France Presse (K)	4				
March 3					
South Vietnamese Kill 35 of Enemy at Saigon Airport; Action Eases near Capital--21 Die in Vietcong Force Ambushed by U.S. Unit; Coast Road Reopened; Allies Find Caches of Food and Arms--B-52s Strike Foe's Khe Sanh Positions Tom Buckley (S)	1	Antiwar Movement Makes Rapid Gains Among Seminarians Edward B. Fiske (N.Y.)	1	Vietnam Issues: A Grim, Military Chess Game Tom Buckley (S)	3E
		Madison, Wis., Puts War on the Ballot Special to Times (Madison, Wis.)	4	The Manpower Cupboard Is Nearly Bare William Beecher (W)	3E
Citizens in 10 Areas of Saigon Organize Groups for Defense Joseph Treaster (S)	1	Lapp Rejects Idea on Atomic Weapons UPI (W)	9	Weapons: The Enemy's Armory Goes Modern Hanson W. Baldwin (N.Y.)	4E
		Sane Bids the U.S. Uphold Atom Ban, Wants President to Assure the Nation on Vietnam Special to Times (Philadelphia, Pa.)	9		

Vietnam Dateline	Page[#]	Non-Vietnam Dateline	Page[#]	Vietnam Commentary/ Editorial	Page[#]
Saigon Bans *Newsweek* AP (S)	4	End of Bombing Asked (N.Y.)	12	Remembering the Alamo (editorial)	12E
Khe Sanh Wounded Treated in Grim Field Hospital Bernard Weinraub (Dong Ha)	6	Miller and Coffin Attack War in New Haven Rally AP (New Haven, Conn.)	78	Honolulu: A View From Pearl Harbor James Reston (Honolulu)	12E
Pacification Teams Returning to Hamlets Abandoned After Vietcong Drive Charles Mohr (S)	7				
March 4					
*Forty-Eight U.S. Soldiers Killed in Ambush on Edge of Saigon; 28 in Unit of 25th Division Wounded near Airport; Enemy Dead Put at 20; Foe's Buildup Goes On; Reported Troop Movement Spurs Fresh Speculation About Assault on Capital Joseph Treaster (S)	1	Saigon Prodded on Land Reform; House Panel Finds Regime Lags in Vital Program Felix Belair, Jr. (W)	1	Vietnam Reassessment (editorial)	36
Three of Embassy Raiders Survived; Saigon Won't Yield Them to U.S. Tom Buckley (S)	1	British Volunteers for Vietnam Rising AP (London)	3		
General Recalls Days at C.C.N.Y.; Head of 4th Division in Vietnam Started as R.O.T.C. Cadet; On Last Visit Here, He Was Picketed by Foes of War Bernard Weinraub (Pleiku)	2	Sorensen Views U.S. as Caught in a Six-Sided Box in VN Irving Spiegel (N.Y.)	4		
		Lindsay Says Candidates Must Make War Views Clear (N.Y.)	13		

Vietnam Dateline	Page#	Non-Vietnam Dateline	Page#	Vietnam Commentary/ Editorial	Page#
Khe Sanh Marines on Guard for Enemy Tunneling AP (K)	3				
One Hundred Fifty-Seven of Foe Reported Killed UPI (S)	5				
March 5					
GIs and Enemy Battle Eight Hours North of Saigon; Foe Loses 10 Men in Attack in Area of Earlier Ambush--Three Americans Killed; Planes Aid U.S. Troops; Government Forces Kill 42 in Turning Back Another Thrust near Capital Joseph Treaster (S)	1	Foe of War in the Air Force Goes on Trial Today; He Refused to Train Pilots for Possible Duty in VN; Captain Noyd Is Charged with Willfully Disobeying Order Douglas E. Kneeland (Clovis, N. Mex.)	2		
Hanoi Says Drive Opened New Phase Bernard Weinraub (S)	1	Eighteen Democrats Are in Favor of Role for Vietcong; They Urge Administration to Allow the Foe Part in Forming Government John W. Finney (W)	2		
New Enemy Road in Jungle Reported in Highlands Area Dispatch of the *Times* of London (Camp Enari, S. VN)	2	Pentagon Identifies Men Killed in War UPI (W)	2		
		Talks in Italy Reported AP (Tokyo)	3		
Kontum Hospital of U.S. Woman Doctor Raided, She Is Reported to Be Safe--Enemy Kills a Patient and Abducts Two Nurses AP (S)	3	Vietnam Murder Conviction Set Aside by Naval Review AP (W)	3		
		Marcos Sees No Major Effects on Philippines in VN Peace, but Says a Shift in Balance of Power Could Bring an Effort for Peking Accommodation Tom Buckley (Manila)	X		
C.B.S. Man Wounded Twice AP (S)	4				

Vietnam Dateline	Page#	Non-Vietnam Dateline	Page#	Vietnam Commentary/ Editorial	Page#
Cam Ranh Base Attacked AP (S)	3				
March 6					

Vietcong Attack City in the Delta; Fighting Is Heavy; Allied Units Retake Hospital After Hours of Bat-tling--Report 250 of Foe Dead, 1,000 Homes Destroyed; North Vietnamese Continue Shelling Khe Sanh Base-- Shipyard near Hanoi Hit
  Joseph Treaster
  (S)
	1	Nixon Vows to End War with a "New Leader-ship"
		  Robert B. Semple, Jr. (Nashua, N.H.)
			1	Washington: The Paradox of America
				James Reston (W)
					46

		Air Force Scored on Order to Pilot; Trial Under Way for Captain Who Opposes War Douglas E. Kneeland (Clovis, N.M.)	2		
		Expert's Report Assails Saigon on Land Reform Felix Belair, Jr. (W)	2		

War Photographer Dies
  UPI (S)
	2	U.S. Planning to Return Three Prisoners to Hanoi
		  Special to *Times* (W)
			2		

U.S. Civilian Toll Raised
  AP (S)
	2	McKeldin Suggests Halt in the Bombing
		  Special to *Times* (New Haven, Conn.)
			2		

U.S. Aide Says Allies Are About to Seize Offen-sive
  AP (Phu Bai)
	3	U.S. Identifies Men Killed in Vietnam
		  UPI (W)
			3		

		U.S. Troops in Viet-nam Are Said to Get Pep Pills; John Steinbeck 4th Alleges Amphetamines Are Issued in Combat Survival Kits Special to *Times* (W)	4		
		Marine Chief Says Foe's Drive Failed (N.Y.)	10		
		Lag in Economic Growth; Stepping Up Pace from 1967's 2.6 Percent Would Face Limits Arising from the War Albert Kraus (N.Y.)	61		

Vietnam Dateline	Page[#]	Non-Vietnam Dateline	Page[#]	Vietnam Commentary/ Editorial	Page[#]
March 7					

U.S. Command Sees Hue, Not Khe Sanh, as Foe's Main Goal; Senior Spokesman, Noting Shift of Opinion, Predicts Heavy Assault on City; Troop Move Reported; North Vietnamese Division Said to Leave DMZ Area for Positions near Coast
  Gene Roberts (S)
	1	U.S. Denies Saigon Balked Inquiry into Embassy Raid
		  AP (W)
			4		

		Bonn to Give Vietnam View Special to *Times* (Berlin)	4		
		American War Casualties Are Identified by Pentagon UPI (W)	5		

U.S. Plane Carrying 49 Downed Near Khe Sanh
  Joseph Treaster (S)
	1	Gruening Pledges New Study of Corruption in Saigon Regime
		  AP (W)
			6		

		U.N. Offers Swiss a Peace Talks Site Special to *Times* (Geneva)	6		

Saigon Curtails Sports Role
  Reuters (S)
	5	Air Force Trail to Bypass Issue
		  Douglas E. Kneeland (Clovis, N. Mex.)
			7		

Enemy Toll Put at 50,000
  AP (S)
	5	Plan to Sabotage Draft Offices Reported Circulating in U.S.
		  Special to *Times* (W)
			8		

Allied Outpost Attacked
  Agence France Presse (D)
	5	Pentagon Explains GIs Get Pep Pills to Diet and Survive
		  Special to *Times* (W)
			16		

March 8					

Khe Sanh and Dienbienphu: A Comparison; Gen. Giap's Book on Defeat of French Reveals Tactics
  Charles Mohr (S)
	1	*Criticism of War Widens in Senate on Buildup Issue; Fulbright Demands Johnson Consult Congress Before Raising Troop Strength; Kennedy Scores Policy Debate, Produces Signs of Setting Off Revolt over Any Further Escalation
		  John W. Finney (W)
			1	The Enemy Strategist: Vo Nguyen Giap (Man in the News) (N.Y.)
				
				Negative Land Reform (editorial)
					2
					
					38

Vietnam Dateline	Page[#]	Non-Vietnam Dateline	Page[#]	Vietnam Commentary/ Editorial	Page[#]
U.S. Dead in War at 542 for Week; Toll is One Below Record--New Command Set Up in Northern Sector Gene Roberts (S)	1	Pentagon Identifies Vietnam Casualties AP (W)	3	Foreign Affairs: Giap's Round on Points C. L. Sulzberger (Paris)	39
New U.S. Command Set Up in Vietnam; Army Gets Wider Role near DMZ, Under Marines Special to *Times* (S)	2	Jurists Say "Brutality" Is Growing in Vietnam AP (Geneva)	5	Washington: The Perils of Personal Government James Reston (W)	39
Battle near Dong Ha UPI (S)	2	Captain's Beliefs Argued at Trial; Issue of Mental Competence Becomes Defense Point Douglas E. Kneeland (Clovis, N. Mex.)	5		
Mekong Delta Still Paralyzed Five Weeks After Foe's Offensive AP (Vinh Long)	4	Excerpts from Debate in Senate over Administration's Policy in Vietnam Special to *Times* (W)	8		
Saigon Senate Bars Thieu's Power Plea AP (S)	5	Navy Is Using a New Plane Against Enemy at Khe Sanh AP (W)	8		
Saigon to Train Students AP (S)	24				
March 9 One Hundred Sixty-Four of Foe Killed near Marine Base; South Vietnamese Account for Most of Enemy Dead-- U.S. Loses 16 Men Joseph Treaster (S)	1	First Combat Duty for F-111s Is Due in Next Few Days William Beecher (W)	1		
U.S. Jets Bomb Airfield Agence France Presse (S)	2	Captain Is Convicted for Refusal to Train Pilot for Vietnam War Douglas E. Kneeland (Clovis, N. Mex.)	1		
		Vietnam Casualties AP (W)	2		

Vietnam Dateline	Page[#]	Non-Vietnam Dateline	Page[#]	Vietnam Commentary/ Editorial	Page[#]
Losses Exceed Korean War's AP (S)	2	Three Thousand in Philippines Protest Use of Troops in Vietnam - Special to *Times* (Manila)	2		
Newsmen Hurt in Khe Sanh Agence France Presse (S)	2	Invasion of North Vietnam Urged by High Thai Official Special to *Times* (Manila)	2		
		Sharp Says U.S. Force Is Ready for Anything AP (Honolulu)	3		
		Nixon's War Policy Asked by Humphrey Special to *Times* (Springfield, Ill.)	16		
		Aussies Plan Probe in Viet Torture Story New York *Times*- Chicago *Tribune* Service (Sidney)	X		
March 10					
Enemy Hammers Seven Sites on the Outskirts of Saigon Tom Buckley (S)	1	*Westmoreland Requests 206,000 More Men, Stirring Debate in Administration; Force Now 510,000; Some in Defense and State Departments Oppose Increase Special to *Times* (W)	1	Vietnam: Fulbright Tries to Hold Out a Helping Hand John W. Finney (W)	3E
Saigon General Says Foe Has Replaced His Losses Gene Roberts (Can Tho)	1	Captain Noyd Sentenced to a Year at Hard Labor Douglas E. Kneeland (Clovis, N. Mex.)	3	Saigon Tries to Recover from the Blows Charles Mohr (S)	3E
Foe Killed 400 Hue Civilians Reuters (S)	2	Gallup Poll Reports 49 Percent Believe Involvement in VN an Error Special to *Times* (Princeton, N.J.)	4	Now It's a New and Much Meaner War Gene Roberts (S)	3E
War Alters Life in Saigon at Last; Night Spots Shut and Siesta Re- duced Since Tet Attack Joseph Treaster (S)	X			Foreign Affairs: Both War and Peace C. L. Sulz- berger (Paris)	14E

Vietnam Dateline	Page#	Non-Vietnam Dateline	Page#	Vietnam Commentary/ Editorial	Page#
				.Vietnam and the Home Front (editorial)	14E
				In the Nation: Agonizing Reappraisal Tom Wicker (W)	15E
				We Have Failed in Vietnam . . . What Now? Edwin O. Reischauer, *New York Times Magazine*	23
March 11					
North Vietnamese Shells Batter Chain of U.S. Posts; Westmoreland Asserts "Very Heavy Fighting" Is Ahead in Two Areas Tom Buckley (S)	1	Rusk Will Confront His Senate Critics on Vietnam Today Peter Grose (W)	1	Gunnar Myrdal: A Man of Two Roles Werner Wiskari (N.Y.)	14
Stockpiles of Ammunition and Fuel Blown Up-- Khe Sanh Hit Anew Special to *Times* (S)	1	Nixon Withholds His Peace Ideas, Says to Tell Details of Plan Would Sap His Bargaining Position If He's Elected Robert B. Semple, Jr. (Nashua, N.H.)	1	Vietnam: America's Dreyfus Case William V. Shannon (N.Y.)	40
Anti-Red Unity Movement Is Inaugurated in Saigon Gene Roberts (S)	12	*Newsweek* Critical of Johnson on War (N.Y)	10	Suicidal Escalation (editorial)	40
U.S. Study Assails Pacification Plan; Two Experts Assert Saigon Fails to Consult Peasants Thomas A. Johnson (S)	13	Myrdal Finds the Outlook for South Asia Is Gloomy Peter Kihss (N.Y.)	1	News (Good) from Asia (editorial)	40
		Reuther Calls Poverty War As Vital As That in VN (N.Y.)	32		
		Asks Plan to End War UPI (London)	34		

Vietnam Dateline	Page[#]	Non-Vietnam Dateline	Page[#]	Vietnam Commentary/ Editorial	Page[#]
Saigon Schools and Shows Shut Six Weeks, Open Today Agence France Presse (S)	24				
Ky Urges Mobilization AP (S)	12				
Explosions Continue 10 Hours UPI (S)	10				
Provincial Capital Shelled Special to *Times* (S)	X				

March 12

Vietnam Dateline	Page[#]	Non-Vietnam Dateline	Page[#]	Vietnam Commentary/ Editorial	Page[#]

Thieu Discharges Seven Province Chiefs; He Is Said to View Move as Big Advance in Saigon's Fight Against Corruption
  Gene Roberts (S)
	1	*Rusk Tells Panel Of "A to Z" Review of Vietnam War, Concedes Serious Setbacks but Says U.S. and Saigon Are Regaining Initiative; Senators Score Policy; Secretary Assailed in First Public Vietnam Questioning by Committee in Two Years
		  John W. Finney (W)
			1	The Big Peace Battle; Senate Hearing a Stand-off, with Rusk and Fulbright As Far Apart As Before
				  James Reston (W)
					17

South Vietnamese Defeat a Battalion, Say They Killed 102
  Thomas A. Johnson (S)
	1	Aid Funds Facing Delay in Senate; Fulbright Tells Rusk Policy in War Must Be Clarified
		  Felix Belair, Jr. (W)
			1	Secretary Rusk Repeats Himself
				  (editorial)
					42

Airdrops Are Khe Sanh's Lifeline
  Joseph Treaster (S)
	1	Vietnam Casualties
		  UPI (W)
			14		

Heart Surgery at Khe Sanh Saves "Dead" Marine Hero Who Refused to Kill
  AP (K)
	14	Sihanouk Repeats Accusation on Reds
		  Special to *Times* (W)
			13		

		Excerpts from Rusk Testimony on Vietnam and Exchanges with Senate Panel Special to *Times* (W)	16		

Vietnam Dateline	Page[#]	Non-Vietnam Dateline	Page[#]	Vietnam Commentary/ Editorial	Page[#]
		Swedish Aide Concedes Split with U.S. on War AP (Stockholm)	17		
		Laos Says Four Posts Fall to Pro-Reds; Major Battle Reported near Key Position in N.E. UPI (Vientiane)	13		
		Yale President's Son Deferred as a Conscientious Object-or William Borders (New Haven, Conn.)	10		
		Antiwar Boycott Set at Columbia; University Vice President to Take Part in Pro-test John Leo (N.Y.)	11		
		Yale to Readmit Protestors Special to *Times* (New Haven, Conn.)	18		
		U.S. Is Losing War in Vietnam, NBC Declares Jack Gould (N.Y.)	X		
March 13 Big Bombs Blast Foe at Khe Sanh; 2,000 Pounders Are Used--Saigon Claims 194 of Foe Gene Roberts (S)	1	President Urges Patience on War; In Presenting Two Medals of Honor, He Asserts Steady Nation Shall Never Fail Max Frankel (W)	1	Washington: The Vietnam Reappraisal in the Cabi-net James Reston (W)	46
AFL-CIO Aid for Vietnam Reuters (S)	6	Twenty-Two in House Ask Congress to Op-pose Troop Increase; Bipartisan Group Acts Hedrick Smith (W)	1	Foreign Affairs: A New Look in Paris C. L. Sulz-berger (Paris)	46
San Diego Police Add to Woes of Khe Sanh UPI (K)	13			Patient and Steady (editorial)	46
Clash at Estuary UPI (S)	15				

Vietnam Dateline	Page#	Non-Vietnam Dateline	Page#	Vietnam Commentary/ Editorial	Page#
Air Strikes near Hanoi Agence France Presse (S)	15	Greater Tax Rise Seen Eileen Shanahan (W)	1		
Hanoi Describes Raid Agence France Presse (Hanoi)	15	Rusk Tells Panel We Will Consult on Any Troop Rise; He Avoids Pledge to Confer in Advance, but Johnson Is Said to Be Ready to; Ful-			
Shantytown in Saigon, Wrecked by War, Rebuilt; Lean-tos and Houses Go Up in Waterfront Area Where Nearly Half Million Lived Thomas A. John- son (S)	16	bright Is Critical, Says Secretary Is Unclear--Vietnam Policy Attacked Again As Hearing Ends John W. Finney (W)	1		
Air Crash at Khe Sanh Killed Photographer, Agency Says Reuters (S)	17	Swedish Opposition Backs Stand on U.S. UPI (Stockholm)	2		
Enemy Repelled near Supply Base; 194 Slain in Heavy Assault near Link to Khe Sanh UPI (S)	X	Excerpts from Rusk Testimony Before Senate Panel and Questions from Members Special to _Times_ (W)	14		
No-Confidence Move Collapses in Saigon Special to _Times_ (S)	X	High Pentagon Aides Urge Call-up of 30,000 Men William Beecher (W)	15		
		Hershey Studies Draft Deferrals, May Endorse Completion of Semesters by Graduates Neil Sheehan (W)	15		
		Rusk Performance Before Senate Unit Praised by Johnson UPI (W)	15		
		Vietnam Casualties AP (W)	15		
		Attacks Reported at Three Places in Laos UPI (Vientiane)	16		
		Sixty-Nine Percent in Poll Back a Pullout in War; Gallup Finds Hawks, Too, Favor Withdrawal Plan Special to _Times_ (Princeton, N.J.)	17		

Vietnam Dateline	Page[#]	Non-Vietnam Dateline	Page[#]	Vietnam Commentary/ Editorial	Page[#]
		Recent Losses by Catholics in Vietnam Termed Serious AP (Rome)	20		
March 14					
Large North Vietnamese Unit Sighted in Delta for First Time Tom Buckley (S)	1	Johnson Seeking Ways to Recover Initiative in War; Any Retreat Is Ruled Out As His Key Advisers Pursue Broad Policy Review Max Frankel (W)	1	Khe Sanh Disturbs Many in Marines; Some Voice Objections to a Static Defense but Doubt a Dien-	
Saigon Says Guerrilla Unit Will Invade North Vietnam AP (S)	2	Days Are Numbered for Khe Sanh, Foe Says UPI (Tokyo)	2	bienphu Parallel Hanson W. Baldwin	
Through Heavy Clouds, Bombs Scar Terrain Around Khe Sanh Joseph Treaster (S)	3	Opening of U.S. Army Hospital in Tokyo Put Off After Protests J. Anthony Lukas (Tokyo)	6	(N.Y.) In the Nation:	1
Komer Returns to Saigon AP (S)	16	Cambodia Revolt Is Said to Expand; Forces Led by Communists Reported in More Areas Hedrick Smith (W)	7	McCarthy and St. Crispin Tom Wicker (Manchester, N.H.)	42
		Laotians Say They Repel North Vietnamese Forces AP (Vientiane)	7	Observer: Let's Keep This Show Off the Road Russell	
		Nixon to Maintain Stand on Vietnam; His Aides Expect No Shift Despite McCarthy Vote Robert B. Semple, Jr. (W)	30	Baker (W) TV: A Hawk Takes to ABC Airwaves; Howard K.	42
		Izvestia Terms Vote Protest Against War Reuters (Moscow)	31	Smith Calls for All-Out Conflict; Vigorous Commentary Gets Brief Spot Jack Gould (N.Y.)	87

Vietnam Dateline	Page[#]	Non-Vietnam Dateline	Page[#]	Vietnam Commentary/ Editorial	Page[#]
March 15					
Casualties of U.S. Top Korea War's; the Total Reflects Fewer Killed and More Wounded 　Gene Roberts (S)	1	Lindsay Is Critical of Nixon on War, But He'd Back Him 　Richard Reeves (N.Y.)	1		
Ky Would Join in Drive 　AP (S)	2	Saigon Cautioned on Invasion Talk; Rusk Aide Cites '66 Pledge Against Move into North 　Hedrick Smith (W)	2		
U.S. Terms Enemy Weaker 　AP (S)	2	Vietnam Casualties 　AP (W)	4		
Saigon Balks U.S. on Political Foes; Regime Still Holds Many in "Protective Custody" 　Bernard Weinraub (S)	3	War Wounds Fatal to an Antiwar Hero 　AP (Miami, Fla.)	8		
		Torture of Vietnamese by Australian Admitted 　AP (Canberra)	11		
Ruined Ben Tre, After 45 Days, Still Awaits Saigon's Aid; Regime Has Offered Nothing in Effort to Rebuild Town 　Peter Arnett, AP (Ben Tre)	3	Nixon Urges Rise in Allied Soldiers, Says Eisenhower Diplomacy Is Needed to End War 　UPI (Marshfield, Wis.)	26		
Hue Civilian Toll Is 3,776 　AP (S)	40	Ribicoff Backs Troop Cut 　UPI (W)	35		
March 16					
Allied Units Open the Biggest Drive of Vietnam War; 50,000 Men Seek to Capture or Destroy Enemy Forces Believed near Saigon 　Gene Roberts (S)	1	Vietnam Casualties 　AP (W)	3	No Place for Bystanders (editorial)	30
		Deserter Returning to U.S. Changed Mind in Sweden 　AP (Stockholm)	3		
Saigon Frees Monk Briefly 　AP (S)	3	Sixty-Three Percent of Protestants in U.S. Disapprove Johnson War Policy 　(N.Y.)	4		

Vietnam Dateline	Page[#]	Non-Vietnam Dateline	Page[#]	Vietnam Commentary/ Editorial	Page[#]
Thieu Orders Drive on Black Markets AP (S)	9	Romney Calls Vote Protest over War AP (Lansing, Mich.)	14		
Paper in Saigon Asserts Many Oppose Role of U.S. Reuters (S)	12	Eisenhower Backs Course of War, Says We're on Right Track, Supports Gold Action Gladwin Hill (Indio, Calif.)	15		
		Pentagon Defends Information Policy UPI (W)	17		
March 17					
GIs, in Pincer Move, Kill 128 in Day-Long Battle Special to *Times* (S)	1	U.S. to Put More Men in Vietnam; Call-up Moderate; 35,000- 50,000 Men May Go-- Reservists Face Active Duty Robert H. Phelps (W)	1	Vietnam Pressures: Johnson Weighs a New Escalation (N.Y.)	2E
Enemy Asserts GI Joined Vietcong Agence France Presse (S)	2	Saigon's Inertia Disappoints U.S.; Some Officials Fear Enemy Has Recovered Faster Hedrick Smith (W)	3	New Test for Military (N.Y.)	2E
One Reform Is Achieved Tom Buckley (S)	3	Sweden Defends Stand on Vietnam John M. Lee (Stockholm)	3	Rusk vs. the Committee-- Again a Stand-off (N.Y.)	2E
Error Kills Americans Reuters (S)	5	Lord Avon Asserts Pacification in Vietnam Must Precede Talks; He Would Urge the Russians to Put Pressure on North Vietnam for Negotiations Drew Middleton (N.Y.)	4	In the Nation: Guns, Butter and Folly Tom Wicker (W)	13E
Highland Troops See Little of Foe; Pattern of Actions Similar to Those of a Year Ago Joseph Treaster (Pleiku)	6			Another Opinion: Views on South Asia Gunnar Myrdal (N.Y.)	13E
Foe Digs Deeper Outside Khe Sanh; Dirt Piles Up As Marines Hear Machinery Whir Reuters (K)	7	War, Negro Demands, Election Are Found Dividing Americans Steven V. Roberts (Chicago)	45		
North Vietnam's Comments Stress New Attacks near Khe Sanh Bernard Weinraub (S)	7	Kennedy Challenges "Illusions" on War Peter Grose (W)	59		

Vietnam Dateline	Page[#]	Non-Vietnam Dateline	Page[#]	Vietnam Commentary/ Editorial	Page[#]
Saigon Censorship Deplored UPI (S)	69	Business Taking a Stand on Vietnam (N.Y.)	1F	Sorensen Says, Of Course the War Will Be a Campaign Issue Theodore C. Sorensen, *New York Times Magazine*	30
March 18					
Foe Hurled Back at Khe Sanh Base; South Vietnamese Halt 600 Believed to Be Testing Defenses at Outpost AP (S)	1	Kennedy Made Johnson Offer to Forgo Race; War Basic Issue; Senator Backed Study Panel but President Rejected the Plan Tom Wicker (W)	1	Draft Reform by Directive (editorial)	44
Marines Kill 83 of Foe Special to *Times* (S)	1	Two Hundred in Britain Held in Antiwar Protest at U.S. Embassy Alvin Shuster (London)	1		
Foe Tries to Breach Defenses Agence France Presse (K)	2	Hanoi Reports U.S. Jet Is Down and Crew Held AP (Tokyo)	2		
South Vietnam's Economy Termed Battered by Enemy Offensive Bernard Weinraub (S)	3	Six F-111s in Thailand for Tests in Air War AP (Bangkok)	3		
		Boat Ordered for Vietnam Said to Be Rotting in U.S. AP (W)	10		
		Text of Kennedy Statement on Talks (W)	50		
		Oregon Democrats Urge Negotiated VN Peace Lawrence E. Davies (Eugene, Oreg.)	51		
		Johnson Backers Ask Bombing Halt Special to *Times* (Reno, Nev.)	51		

Vietnam Dateline	Page[#]	Non-Vietnam Dateline	Page[#]	Vietnam Commentary/ Editorial	Page[#]
March 19					
Fighting Is Heavy near Buffer Zone; 67 Enemy Soldiers and 12 Marines Killed in Five-Hour Clash North of Dong Ha Special to *Times* (S)	1	*President Asks for Austerity to Win the War; Tells Farm Union Delegates in Minnesota It's Time for Total National Effort; A Gibe at Cowardice; Johnson Denounces Critics and Praises Advisors, Affirms Commitments Robert H. Phelps (Minneapolis, Minn.)	1	Gen. Davis, at Clark Base, Reflects on Change in Military Life Thomas A. Johnson (Clark Air Force Base, Philippines)	4
Vietcong Force Routed AP (S)	2			Commission on Vietnam (editorial)	47
Eighty Aid Volunteers Decide to Leave South Vietnam UPI (S)	3	Students Cheer Kennedy in Attack on War Policy John Herbers (Manhattan, Kans.)	1		
Ky Sees a Danger in Aid from Allies Reuters (S)	3	McCarthy Is Cool to Kennedy Move, Calls His Offer to Johnson Offensive to the Senate Foreign Relations Group E. W. Kenworthy (Brunswick, Maine)	1		
U.S. Shifts I Corps Advisor AP (S)	3				
Troops in Big Allied Drive Find Heat Is the Enemy Gene Roberts (Cu Chi)	5	U.S. Undervalued Enemy's Strength Before Offensive; CIA Reports Forces Were Significantly Larger Than Intelligence Estimates Gap Is 50,000 to 100,000; New Assessment of Foe's Manpower Is Awaited-- Losses Are in Dispute Neil Sheehan (W)	1		
		One Hundred Thirty-Nine in House Support Drive for a Review of Policy in VN John W. Finney (W)	32		
		Humphrey Scores Kennedy on War, Says He Switched Stand; Kind Words for McCarthy Roy Reed (W)	35		

Vietnam Dateline	Page[#]	Non-Vietnam Dateline	Page[#]	Vietnam Commentary/ Editorial	Page[#]
		Excerpts from Speech by President Special to *Times* (Minneapolis, Minn.)	35		
		Open U.S. Hospital in Tokyo UPI (Tokyo)	36		
		U.S. Tanker Planes Using Taiwan Base Special to *Times* (Taipei)	37		
March 20					
Arms Cache Found near Saigon Base; South Vietnamese Capture Weapons Hidden Within Range of Tan Son Nhut Bernard Weinraub (S)	1	Mayor Urges Youths to Aid War Resistance Richard Reeves (N.Y.)	1	Transformation of American Politics James Reston (W)	46
Enemy Said to Get B-52 Raid Alerts Special to *Times* (S)	1	Vietnam Casualties AP (W)	3		
Two Vietnam Refugee Projects Are Studies in Success and Failure Joseph Treaster (Pleiku)	2	Poll Finds 27 Percent Favor Atom Arms in Vietnam Special to *Times* (Princeton, N.J.)	3		
		Two Missionaries, Captured a Month Ago, Are Alive (N.Y.)	3		
Allied Estimate on Foe Increases; North Vietnamese in South Said to Number 84,000 Charles Mohr (S)	3	Pentagon Sets a Draft of 44,000 Men in May AP (W)	9		
Movies Reopen in Saigon Reuters (S)	3	Johnson Defiant on Vietnam View, Tells Foes Course Is Set and America Will Prevail Max Frankel (W)	32		
Saigon Police Close Stalls Selling Black Market Goods (S)	3				

Vietnam Dateline	Page[#]	Non-Vietnam Dateline	Page[#]	Vietnam Commentary/ Editorial	Page[#]
March 21					
Saigon Air Base Shelled by Foe; 15 Rounds Do Light Damage in Face of Allied Sweep Joseph Treaster (S)	13	'68 Gain Was Seen by Westmoreland 29 Days Before Tet Attacks; He Defined U.S. Goals, Did Not Expect Offensive Neil Sheehan (W)	1	Johnson's Counterattack: His Speeches on Vietnam Policy Mark Swift Response to Political Challengers Max Frankel (W)	36
Reform of Regime Pledged by Thieu; Three Plans Outlined AP (S)	14	Johnson Warns of "Phony Peace" UPI (W)	5		
Hanoi Radio Is Cool to Race by Kennedy Special to *Times* (S)	36	Shoup, Calling for Talks, Doubts Military Victory John W. Finney (W)	12	In the Nation: The New Politics Tom Wicker (W)	46
		Oklahoma's Senate Backs War, 45 to 0 AP (Oklahoma City, Okla.)	12		
		Paris Gives Refuge to Nine U.S. War Foes UPI (Paris)	12		
		Vietnam Casualties AP (W)	13		
		Hilsman Bids U.S. De-escalate War; Ex-Rusk Aide Also Would "De-Americanize" Conflict Special to *Times* (U.N.)	15		
		The Vietnam Issue (N.Y.)	37		
		A Quemoy Pullout Is Studied by U.S.; Pressure on Chiang Denied; Step Linked to Cut in Aid Special to *Times* (W)	4		
March 22					
U.S. Planes Press Strikes in North, Biggest in Month; Improved Weather Permits Raids near Haiphong and Hanoi and in Panhandle;		Sixty Percent in L.I. War Poll Oppose U.S. Policies Roy R. Silver (Mineola, N.Y.)	1	Foreign Affairs: Giap of Arabia C. L. Sulzberger (Cairo)	46

Vietnam Dateline	Page[#]	Non-Vietnam Dateline	Page[#]	Vietnam Commentary/ Editorial	Page[#]

Foe Shells Allied Base; 336 Americans Are Killed in South in Week, Lowest Toll Since Enemy Drive
  Joseph Treaster
  (S)
	1	Switzerland Denies Plan to Recognize Hanoi Soon
		  Special to *Times*
		  (Geneva)
			3		

U.S. Aides Pleased by Thieu's Speech; President Stresses Action on Corruption and Bigger Role for Saigon's Forces
  Bernard Weinraub
  (S)
	1	U.S. Sees Signs of Unrest
		  Special to *Times* (W)
			3		

		Vietnam Casualties AP (W)	3		
		Shelling of Southern Town Reported by Laotian Officials UPI (Vientiane)	6		

Foes of Regime Warned by Hanoi; Penalties, Including Death, Decreed for Subversion
  Agence France Presse (Hanoi)
	3	Johnson Affirms Vietnam Resolve, Declares Will of U.S. Won't Break Under Frustration
		  Special to *Times* (W)
			7		

Saigon Relents, Frees Unionist; Move Follows Plea by Aide of American Labor Group
  Special to *Times*
  (S)
	6	Meany Gets Report
		  Special to *Times* (W)
			6		

March 23					

U.S. Jets Bomb Rail Yards and Supply Lines in North
  Joseph Treaster
  (S)
	1	Westmoreland to Leave Vietnam, Head the Army; U.S. May Add 30,000 Troops; Shift Due by July; President Announces Change for General Recently Criticized
		  Max Frankel (W)
			1	Westmoreland's Transfer
				  (editorial)
					30

Regrets to Leave
  AP (S)
	12			Topics: The Strategy of the Weak in Vietnam
				  William Pfaff (N.Y.)
					30

Vietcong Defections Down AP (S)	13				

Vietnam Dateline	Page[#]	Non-Vietnam Dateline	Page[#]	Vietnam Commentary/ Editorial	Page[#]
March into North Is Favored by Ky but Saigon Opposes Attack, He Says in Visit to Carrier Bernard Weinraub (aboard the USS *Kitty Hawk*, off N. VN)	13	Five Hundred Sixty-Five Thousand Total Is in View; Strategy Change Weighed William Beecher (W)	1		
		Rift with Pentagon Holds Up Aid Bill Special to *Times* (W)	1		
Hue Lives in Fear of a New Attack; Rebuilding of City Put Off; Defenses Are Bolstered Gene Roberts (Hue)	13	Thai Aide Deplores War Debate in U.S. AP (Bangkok)	2		
		Swiss Reject Move for Ties from Hanoi Special to *Times* (Geneva)	5		
Mobile Guns Imperil Khe Sanh AP (S)	13	Transcript of the President's News Conference on Foreign and Domestic Matters Special to *Times* (W)	12		
Word Reaches Saigon AP (S)	X	Vietnam Casualties AP (W)	13		
		Schlesinger Urges Pullout at Khe Sanh AP (W)	X		
March 24					
Westmoreland Departure Could Spur War Changes Charles Mohr (S)	1	Hanoi Says Resolve of People Is Firm Reuters (H.K.)	6	Within the Administration a Kind of Malaise over Vietnam Neil Sheehan (W)	3E
		Sweden Confirms Contact with Hanoi UPI (Stockholm)	8		
Khe Sanh Shelled Heavily by Enemy; U.S. Describes Casualties as Light--Planes Pound a Chemical Plant in North Joseph Treaster (S)	1	Sorensen Denies Kennedy Overture on War to Johnson AP (Villanova, Pa.)	31	Now It's Operation Slog Joseph Treaster (S)	3E
Bunker's Deputy Arrives AP (S)	3	Havana Radio Is a Major Relay for Propaganda of Asian Reds Jack Gould	44	Washington: Vietnam Reappraisal-- A to Z or A to B? James Reston (W)	16E

Vietnam Dateline	Page[#]	Non-Vietnam Dateline	Page[#]	Vietnam Commentary/ Editorial	Page[#]
Hanoi Says Rifle Got Jet Agence France Presse (Hanoi)	7	Humphrey Stirs Vietnam Debate; Wisconsin Students Heated but Most Support Him Special to *Times* (Stevens Point, Wis.)	54	Needed: A Vietnam Strategy (editorial)	16E
Thieu Expected to Dismiss at Least Six More Provincial Chiefs Bernard Weinraub (S)	7	Clifford Orders Inquiry on Leaks; He Acts After Publication of Secret Military Data Special to *Times* (W)	9	Year of Surprises Tom Wicker (W)	17E
		Way-Out Weapons William Beecher (Aberdeen, Md.)	X	When the Black GI Comes Back from Vietnam Sol Stern *New York Times Magazine*	26

March 25

Vietnam Dateline	Page[#]	Non-Vietnam Dateline	Page[#]	Vietnam Commentary/ Editorial	Page[#]
Work on McNamara Line in Vietnam near Standstill Gene Roberts (Dong Ha)	1	House Panel Divided on Aid Bill Secrecy Felix Belair, Jr. (W)	1	Students Become a Worldwide Force for Change Fred M. Hechinger	1
Foe Keeps Up Fire on Khe Sanh Base; 625 Shells Hit Outpost on Second Day of Heavy Attack; B-52 Jets Retaliate Joseph Treaster (S)	1	Top Marine Opposes War Policy Change AP (W)	2		
U.S. Copter Assault Company Has a Tragic Day Bernard Weinraub (Lai Khe)	2	Spock Bid to Test War Legality Expected to Be Opposed Today; Dept. of Justice Wants Draft Foes' Trial Focused on Conspiracy Charge Fred P. Graham (W)	5		
Marines to Start New Village Plan; Pacification Teams to Move from Hamlet to Hamlet Agence France Presse (Da Nang)	2	Three Thousand London Marchers Denounce Vietnam War Special to *Times* (London)	10		
Hanoi Area Bombed Agence France Presse (Hanoi)	3	Vote Urges De-escalation UPI (Lincoln, Mass.)	16		

Vietnam Dateline	Page[#]	Non-Vietnam Dateline	Page[#]	Vietnam Commentary/ Editorial	Page[#]
March 26					
Allies Kill 243 Vietcong in a Battle near Saigon Special to *Times* (S)	1	General Says U.S. Can Hold Khe Sanh; Marine Chief Is Confident Foe Can't Halt Supplies AP (W)	3		
U.S. Aide in Saigon Quits in Protest; He Charges U.S. Programs in Vietnam Are Failing Bernard Weinraub (S)	1	Vietnam Casualties AP (W) U.S. Brief Denies That War Is Issue in Spock Trial John H. Fenton (Boston)	3 5		
F-111 Flies First Raid Against North Vietnam AP (S)	2	"Basic" War Support Down in Six Weeks to 54 Percent, Poll Finds (N.Y.)	6		
Plague in Tay Ninh Endangers Saigon Dispatch of the *Times* of London (Tay Ninh, S. VN)	6	Tax Free Funds Asked to Aid War; Patman Report Gives Data on Winthrop Rockefeller AP (W)	11		
Seven Killed in Artillery Error AP (S)	23	Report on Vietnam Said to Be Critical UPI (W)	11		
		Lindsay Renews Criticism of War, Tells Columbia Group He Hopes for Rockefeller Race Richard Reeves (N.Y.)	20		
		Coalition Vows Peaceful Protest at Chicago National Convention Donald Janson (Chicago)	20		
		Ball Bids U.S. Seek a New World Power Balance Special to *Times* (W)	4		

Vietnam Dateline	Page[#]	Non-Vietnam Dateline	Page[#]	Vietnam Commentary/ Editorial	Page[#]
March 27					
Foe Penetrates U.S. Perimeter West of Kontum; 135 North Vietnamese Dead in Attack on Artillery Post in the Central Highlands; 19 Americans Killed; Clash Continues on Ridges Outside Camp After GIs Repulse Two Battalions Bernard Weinraub (S)	1	Gen. Abrams in Capital, Sees President and Aides Neil Sheehan (W)	1	Poison Gas Boomerangs (editorial)	46
		Mansfield Opposes Any Troop Buildup John W. Finney (W)	1		
		Eisenhower Hits Peace Candidates, Says He Will Not Support Advocates of Pullout, Charges Near-Treason (N.Y.)	1		
Four More Province Chiefs Are Dismissed by Thieu AP (S)	2	Battleship *New Jersey* Starts Her Pre-Vietnam Trials UPI (Philadephia, Pa.)	1		
Women Join Enemy Assault AP (Trang Bang)	3	Daley's Senate Candidate Voices Concern over Vietnam Policy Donald Janson (Chicago)	1		
Critical Ex-Official Disputed by Komer AP (S)	3	Vietnam Casualties AP (W)	2		
Khe Sanh Battling a New Enemy-- Rats AP (K)	23	Criticism of U.S. Up in Scandinavia; Economics and VN War Main Causes of Concern John M. Lee (Copenhagen)	5		
		Swedish Red Cross Official Returns from Visit to Hanoi AP (Stockholm)	18		
		Ex-Prisoner of VC Seeks Duty in VN AP (Seaside, Calif.)	28		

Vietnam Dateline	Page[#]	Non-Vietnam Dateline	Page[#]	Vietnam Commentary/ Editorial	Page[#]
March 28					
U.S. Jets Pound Rails near China; Vital Yard at Lang Giai Hit-- GIs Battle Entrenched Foe North of Saigon Bernard Weinraub (S)	1	Abrams Leaves for VN After Talks in Capital AP (W)	3	Indonesia's Patient, Tough Leader: Suharto (Man in the News) (N.Y.)	8
		Fulbright Urges Peace Negotiator AP (W)	3	In the Nation: King Lyndon Commands the Waves Tom Wicker (W)	46
U.S. Officers Say Air Power Makes Khe Sanh a Disaster for Foe Gene Roberts (D)	2	Vietnam Casualties AP (W)	2		
		Jersey Bishop Calls VN Policy a Bar to Peace Deirdre Carmody	5		
A Defector Tells of Foe's Hospitals; Surgeon Traces Locations of Five Stations in Cambodia Joseph Treaster (S)	3	B'nai B'rith Group Urges Quick Start for Talks on Peace Special to *Times* (W)	6		
		Shift of Westmoreland Is Hailed by Reischauer UPI (San Francisco)	7		
In Hue, Graves Disclose Executions by the Enemy Stewart Harris, The *Times* of London (Hue)	4	Gen. Shoup Reveals VN Peace Plan Special to *Times* (Putney, Vt.)	13		
South Vietnam Gets a Second New Party Reuters (S)	5	Pentagon Seeking to Curtail Navy's F-111 and to Develop an Alternative Jet Neil Sheehan (W)	23		
		Army Will Not Return Ex-POW to VN AP (W)	26		
		Daley Finds War Review Need; Says President Studies Policy Donald Janson (Chicago)	41		
		McCarthy Says Johnson Focus on Asia Perils Ties to Europe; Senator Warns NATO Allies Now Regard U.S. in Fear Rather than Respect E. W. Kenworthy (Milwaukee, Wis.)	41		

Vietnam Dateline	Page#	Non-Vietnam Dateline	Page#	Vietnam Commentary/ Editorial	Page#
March 29					
First F-111 Jet Lost and North Vietnam Reports Downing It Bernard Weinraub (S)	1	Sharp Sees Pickup in Allied Offensive Special to *Times* (Wellington, New Zealand)	2	Spring Comes to the Potomac James Reston (W)	40
Thieu Recalls Ambassadors for Secret Talks in Saigon Reuters (S)	5	Protestors in Japan Storm U.S. Hospital Reuters (Tokyo)	2		
Hanoi Broadcasts Claim UPI (S)	12	Saigon Official Warns Against Cut in Military Aid Plan Special to *Times* (W)	11		
One of Dong Hoi Raiders Reuters (S)	12	Vietnam Casualties AP (W)	11		
Four in Jail in Saigon Score Police State, Plan Hunger Strike Special to *Times* (S)	15	U.S. Denies Vessel Was Struck AP (W)	12		
A Soviet Rocket Device for Aiming Is Captured AP (S)	19	Senate Unit Bars Navy F-111B Jets; First Loss of the Air Force Model Reported in Asia John W. Finney (W)	13		
U.S. Unites Fight; Entrenched Foe; Battle Fought near Saigon with Vietcong Concealed in Tunnels and Caves Bernard Weinraub (S)	X	Fear in Hamlets Is Still Hampering Pacification; Officials Term Psychological Blows a Greater Setback Than Physical Damage Hedrick Smith (W)	14		
		Twenty-One in House Offer Tonkin Repealer; Would Void War Resolution to Assert a Policy Role AP (W)	15		
		Vietnam Rattles Contentment at Swedish School; Issue of War Intrudes upon Apolitical Uppsala, Where Grievances Are Few Special to *Times* (Uppsala, Sweden)	18		

Vietnam Dateline	Page[#]	Non-Vietnam Dateline	Page[#]	Vietnam Commentary/ Editorial	Page[#]
		Governor Meets with Thant at U.N. Special to *Times* (U.N.)	27		
		Military Aid Queried at Hearing as Pentagon Official Defends It Felix Belair, Jr. (W)	X		
March 30 Bunker Asks Role for Gen. Palmer; Key Post Believed Sought in Revamping of Forces Bernard Weinraub (S)	1	Peking Charges Bombing by U.S. of Mission in Laos AP (Tokyo)	6	Aggressive General: Bruce Palmer, Jr. (Man in the News) (N.Y.)	12
		Vietnam Casualties AP (W)	10	Topics: Thoughts on the Presidency Eugene J. McCarthy	32
Search Continues for F-111 Lost on Vietnam Raid Joseph Treaster (S)	10	U.S. Frees Three Captives After Discussion with Hanoi Hedrick Smith (W)	11		
		Freed Prisoners Accuse U.S. UPI (Vientiane)	11	Two Counts Against Arms Aid (editorial) (N.Y.)	X
		Scheuer Sees Policy Change (N.Y.)	11		
		White House Is Silent Special to *Times* (W)	11		
		Collingwood of CBS Is Admitted to Hanoi	11		
		Johnson Is Called Peace Candidate UPI (W)	18		
		Ignatius Seeks to Allay Fears on Soviet Navy Gains Neil Sheehan (W)	X		
		GIs Learn Tactics of Foe Homer Bigart (Colorado Springs, Colo.)	X		

Vietnam Dateline	Page#	Non-Vietnam Dateline	Page#	Vietnam Commentary/ Editorial	Page#
March 31					
Second F-111 Jet Fighter Down in Southeast Asia Special to *Times* (S)	1	Johnson to Talk to Nation Tonight on Vietnam War; Speech to Deal "Rather Fully" with Buildup of Forces and Additional Costs Max Frankel (W)	1		
Two More in Provinces Removed by Thieu AP (S)	2	Capt. Levy Moved to an Isolated Cell Paul Hofman	1	In the Field, More of the Same Gradualism Hanson W. Baldwin (N.Y.)	4E
U.S. Builds Up Forces in Two Northern Provinces As Enemy Threatens Bases Gene Roberts (Dong Ha)	3	Vietcong Promise to Free Two Women AP (Tokyo) Pentagon to Spur Output of Rifles for Vietnam AP (W)	2 3	In Saigon, More Frustration Bernard Weinraub (S)	4E
General Mobilization Threatened by Thieu AP (S)	3	Vietnamese in U.S. Are Split on War but Dean of Community Sees No Strong Backing for Foe (N.Y.)	5	Muddling Through in Vietnam (editorial)	12E
Foe Announces Truce in April in Four Provinces Reuters (S)	3	U.S. Employees Set an Antiwar Rally to Take VN Protest to White House Today Ben A. Franklin (W)	8		
Pilot Praises F-111 After Raid in North AP (S)	4	Rusk Off to Attend New Zealand Talks AP (W)	9		
		Speech on Vietnam Slated for Tonight Canceled by Nixon Special to *Times* (W)	39		
		Text of White House Statement and Transcript of Johnson's News Conference Special to *Times* (W)	38		

STORY INDEX: VIETNAM-RELATED STORIES, WASHINGTON *POST,*
JANUARY 31 - MARCH 31, 1968

Vietnam Dateline	Page[#]	Non-Vietnam Dateline	Page[#]	Vietnam Commentary/ Editorial	Page[#]
January 31					
*VC Invade U.S. Embassy; Assault Crushed by GIs Lee Lescaze (S)	A1	Writers Vow Tax Revolt over War Staff Writer (N.Y.)	A5	Khe Sanh: Holding the End of the Line Ward Just (W)	A20
Gunfire Ends Da Nang Holiday Peter Braestrup (D)	A1	Reds Said to Marshal Power, Held Capable of Fighting Large Battles Stanley Karnow (H.K.)	A9	Policy-Makers and Generals Worry over Massive	
Security Drop Seen in Areas Wash. *Post* Foreign Service (S)	A1	VC Seen Resorting to Multiple-Shock Offensive Strategy Murrey Marder	A11	Buildup at Khe Sanh Evans/Novak	
		U.S. Keeping Close Tab on Enemy Drive	A11	(W)	A21
February 1					
*Thieu Rules by Decree, Reds Press Offensive, Foe's Toll Estimated at 5,000 Peter Braestrup, Lee Lescaze (S)	A1	U.S. Voices Confidence, Raids Were Expected Ward Just (W)	A1	Thieu's Martial Law Order Poses Threat Murrey Marder (W)	A6
Hanoi's Leader Charges Allies Broke Tet Truce News Dispatches (S)	A1	*Le Monde* Sees End of Last U.S. Myths News Dispatches (Paris)	A6	Rationalizing the VN Rampage (editorial)	A20
Battle at the Palace Ends in Nearby Hotel Los Angeles *Times* (S)	A4	U.S. Refuses to Disclose Aid Given Allies Helping Saigon (W) Two Go to Hanoi for Pilots' Release AP (N.Y.)	A9 A28	Khe Sanh Situation Now Shows Viet Foe Makes Strategy Work	
Newsmen Hail Shot in Saigon UPI (S)	A6			Joseph Kraft (W)	A21

* denotes lead position.
\# Page numbers for stories which appeared in early editions but were dropped from later ones are indicated by X.

D = Da Nang; H.K. = Hong Kong; K = Khe Sanh; S = Saigon;
W = Washington, D.C.

390

Vietnam Dateline	Page#	Non-Vietnam Dateline	Page#	Vietnam Commentary/ Editorial	Page#
February 3					
Allied Attack Stalls in Imperial Capital News Dispatches (S)	A1	*LBJ Calls Uprising Failure; Vietcong Holding On in Hue; Thieu Asks More Bombing; President Sees Repulse of New Drive Carroll Kilpatrick (W)	A1	Terms for a Bombing Halt (editorial)	A12
Thieu Urges Retaliation on North Lee Lescaze (S)	A1			Allied Figures on Casualties Are Thrown into Question Lee Lescaze (S)	A13
Enemy Deaths Put at 12,704 AP (S)	A1	Transcript of News Conf.; LBJ: "We Feel Reasonably Sure of Our Strength (W)	A10	S. Viet People Resent Americans Drew Pearson/Jack Anderson (W)	E21
Allies Pursue Vietcong in Outskirts of Saigon News Dispatches (S)	A6	U.S. Experts Concede Gain by VC Murrey Marder (W)	A1		
Khe Sanh: A Dusty Cow Town Waiting for the Shootout AP (K)	A6	Percy, Romney Ask VC Truth News Dispatches (W)	A2	Khe Sanh: Holding the End of the Line Ward Just (W)	X
Six Missionaries Slain UPI (S)	A6	Seoul Hints at Viet Pullout Unless U.S. Aid Increases R. Halloran (Seoul)	A4		
Bunker Denies U.S. Is Aiding VC Reuters (S)	A7	New Alliance Asks Talks with NLF News Dispatches	A6		
		Soviets Urged to Help Stop War News Dispatches	A7		
		Cambodia Sees New Red Revolt UPI (Phnom Penh)	A15		
February 4					
Enemy Is Able to Hit Anew Lee Lescaze (S)	A1	Top Aides to Go on TV to Allay U.S. Doubts George Lardner, Jr.	A1	Guerrillas Wreck Pacification Plan Ward Just (W)	B1
Vietnam Reds Resist Attacks in Hue Again News Dispatches (S)	A1	Vietcong Mount Political Offensive Stanley Karnow (H.K.)	A8	Deeper, Ever Deeper; Soldiers Now in VN Were Babies When	
How VC Infiltrated Saigon Peter Arnett, AP (S)	A1	Hanoi Says Foundation Is Laid for More Victories News Dispatches (H.K.)	A9		

Vietnam Dateline	Page#	Non-Vietnam Dateline	Page#	Vietnam Commentary/ Editorial	Page#
American Toll Highest of War UPI (S)	A1	McCarthy Raps U.S. Reports on Viet Progress AP	A17	U.S. Involvement Began Drew Pearson (W)	B7
U.S. Attack Traps Civilians; Death in the Saigon Suburbs Wash. *Post* Foreign Service	A5	Religious Leaders Publish Study Accusing U.S. of War Crimes in VN Leroy F. Aarons (N.Y.)	A22		
U.S. Explains How It Makes Viet Body Count AP (S)	A10	Hilsman Sees U.S. on Road to Invasion AP (San Francisco)	A30		
		Cambodia Accuses Allies of Intrusion Reuters (Phnom Penh)	A6		
February 5					
Saigon Is Under Strict Curfew; New Attack Feared Any Time Lee Lescaze (S)	A1	Attacks Dim Prospect of Viet Talks Murrey Marder (W)	A1	McNamara, Rusk: A Mood Contrast L. Stern (W)	A8
Barrage Follows Ground Probes; Bombs Fail to Rout Foe in Hue News Dispatches (S)	A1	VC Renew Call for an Uprising Reuters (H.K.)	A5	Westmoreland Likely to Keep Viet Post Drew Pearson (W)	C7
Marines Dig In at Khe Sanh	A1	Joint Chiefs Endorse Defense of Khe Sanh UPI	A6		
General Sees Foe Set for New Attacks Wash. *Post* Foreign Service (S)	A5	Sen. Moss Criticizes Intelligence on Attacks UPI (Salt Lake City, Ut.)	A6		
No Time for Pause in Watchfulness Reuters (S)	A5	Hilsman "Advice" Scorned by Rusk	A1		
Raids Add 175,000 to Refugee Rolls Wash. *Post* Foreign Service (S)	A6				
Marines Are Digging In at Khe Sanh Peter Braestrup (K)	A10				

Vietnam Dateline	Page[#]	Non-Vietnam Dateline	Page[#]	Vietnam Commentary/ Editorial	Page[#]
February 6					
VC Overrun Police Station in Saigon Raid News Dispatches (S)	A1	Nixon Demands U.S. "Tell Truth" About VC Strength, Raid Curb Called Mistake D. Broder (Green Bay, Wis.)	A2	Saigon Arrival: A Royal Welcome Keyes Beech, Chicago Daily *News* Foreign Service (S)	A14
A Third of My Tho Destroyed in Delta Battle Lee Lescaze (My Tho)	A1	Romney Says People Are Bewildered Ward Just (Albany, N.Y.)	A2	Red Glare of Battle Illuminates Lessons of VN Joseph Kraft (W)	A15
Saigon Bar Girl Carries On Reuters (S)	A5	Ted Kennedy Assails S. Vietnam Corruption Richard Harwood (W)	A8		
S. Vietnam Plans to Arm Civilians Wash. *Post* Foreign Service (S)	A8	Vietcong Warn Against Trials Reuters (H.K.)	A8		
U.S. Embassy Drivers May Have Aided Foe AP (S)	A8	U.S. Bombing Since Jan. Avoided Big Cities in North George C. Wilson (W)	A9		
Curbside Execution Stirs a Viet Debate AP (S)	A8				
Refugees Tax Hospital in Saigon Reuters (S)	X				
February 7					
*U.S. Post Attacked by Tanks; Foe Uses Them First Time in Lang Vei Fight News Dispatches (S)	A1	U.S. Reveals Secret Bids to Hanoi Since August Murrey Marder (W)	A1	On Westmoreland, Generals and War Marquis Childs (W)	A20
Violence Lashes Out at Cholon Residents Lee Lescaze (S)	A11	Romney Blasts "Deceit"; in New Hampshire Ward Just (Manchester, N.H.)	A1	Brooding on Viet Setback Ignores Fearful Cost to Enemy Joseph Alsop (W)	A21
		VC Bars Coalition with Regime in Saigon, Moscow Office Says Wash. *Post* Foreign Service (Moscow)	A11		

Vietnam Dateline	Page[#]	Non-Vietnam Dateline	Page[#]	Vietnam Commentary/ Editorial	Page[#]
		VC Aim Seen to Boost Its Role in Settlement Stanley Karnow (H.K.)	A16		
		Rough Going Seen for Saigon (W)	X		
February 8					
*Special Forces Post at Lang Vei Falls to Reds; Hill Position at Khe Sanh Is Attacked News Dispatches (S)	A1	Have Rusk Testify, Senators Tell LBJ Robert C. Albright (W)	A1	Unexpected Saigon Unity in Crisis Is Gleam of Hope for Viet Future Evans/Novak (W)	A21
Allies Assess Strengths and Failings Peter Braestrup (D)	A1	Viet Policy Attack Mounted by Romney and McCarthy	A2		
Many U.S. Civilians Are Liberated in Hue William Tuohy, Los Angeles *Times* (Hue)	A8	Test of Thieu's Regime Now Is Its Capacity to Restore Order Murrey Marder (W)	A5		
Ben Tre: Only Part of City Was Saved Lee Lescaze (Ben Tre)	A10	Tremendous Blow Struck at Allies, Vietcong Claims Stanley Karnow (H.K.)	A6		
Raids on North Worth the Cost, Bombing Chief Says George Esper, AP (S)	A11	Gronowski Reported Meeting Hanoi Envoy News Dispatches (U.N.)	A5		
February 9					
*Lost Base Gives Reds Key Route News Dispatches (S)	A1	N. Vietnam Modifies Talk Terms Murrey Marder (W)	A1	Hanoi Places Heavy Stakes on Two Throws of the Dice Joseph Alsop (W)	A21
Lang Vei: Green Beret Defenders Lose a Strange Underground War News Dispatches (K)	A1	Kennedy Calls for End to Illusion on VN Ward Just (W)	A1		

Vietnam Dateline	Page[#]	Non-Vietnam Dateline	Page[#]	Vietnam Commentary/ Editorial	Page[#]
Hue: Marines Move from House to House in Grueling and Intimate Fighting William Tuohy, Los Angeles *Times* (Hue)	Al	Wilson Urges Caution on Viet Moves Carroll Kilpatrick (W)	Al		
Saigon Is Returning to Its Normal Pattern Lee Lescaze (S)	A8	Chinese Urge VC to Press Current Offensive Stanley Karnow (H.K.)	A8		
Lang Vei Allies Denied Refuge AP (K)	A10	Soviet Tanks Used in VN Date from '50s (W)	A8		
Pacification Funds Diverted to Recovery AP (S)	A10	Area Man Believed Prisoner (W)	A8		
Allied, Red Tolls Reach Record High News Dispatches (S)	A10	Johnson Reassures Gen. Westmoreland (W)	A8		
S. VN to Increase Mobilization UPI (S)	A11	Mansfield Backs Rusk on Secrecy UPI (W)	A13		
Flier Uses Magic to Win Viet Hearts AP (Can Tho)	X				
February 10					
GI Unit Is Moved to Saigon; U.S. Resumes Bombing Raids near Haiphong News Dispatches (S)	Al	Nothing New, Says U.S. of Hanoi Talk Murrey Marder (W)	Al	Nixon Talks Hint Shift from His Hard Line on Vn D. Broder (W)	A2
S. Vietnam to Speed Up Mobilization Lee Lescaze (S)	Al	No A-Arms Requested for VN, U.S. Says George C. Wilson (W)	Al		
		Romney Says Nixon Has No Peace Plan AP (Kenosha, Wis.)	A2	Gen. Westmoreland Ouster Is Urged Drew Pearson (W)	B11
The Analogy of Dienbienphu AP (S)	A6	Pacifists Due in Hanoi (Vientiane)	A6		
		VC Order Quotes Ho's Call for Attack News Dispatches	A6		

Vietnam Dateline	Page[#]	Non-Vietnam Dateline	Page[#]	Vietnam Commentary/ Editorial	Page[#]
February 12					

*Jets Hit at Hanoi Defenses, Radio Complex Raided by U.S. for First Time
  News Dispatches (S)
	A1	War Support Spurts After Tet Attacks--Harris Survey
		  Louis Harris (W)
			A1	RFK Is Unwise in Accepting Peace at Any Price Counsel
				  Joseph Alsop (W)
					A15

Weather and Thin Ranks Slow Marines' Tough Fight in Hue
  Peter Braestrup (Hue)
	A1	A-Arm Use Called Lunacy by Wilson
		  Warren Unna (W)
			A1	Red Gains in Viet Cities like Last Nazi Spasm at the Bulge
				  William S. White (W)
					A15

Saigon Plans to Call Up 65,000 More
  Wash. *Post* Foreign Service (S)
	A10	Helms Pessimistic on War
		  Post Scripts (W)
			A2		

Reds Said to Execute 300 in Hue
  AP (Hue)
	A11	U.S. Mistakes in VN War Listed by Nixon
		  UPI (Concord, N.H.)
			A5		

Saigon Accuses Clique of VC Contact
  Lee Lescaze (S)
	A13	Rep. Heckler Raps Delusion by Westy
		  AP (Boston)
			A6		

U.S. Official Hints Shifts to Protect Viet Cities
  Stanley Karnow (S)
	A13	Hanoi Lists U.S. Raids' Casualties
		  UPI (Moscow)
			A11		

		Mansfield Cites Saigon Shakiness News Dispatches (Orono, Maine)	A17		
February 13					

*Citadel of Hue Bombed; U.S. Marines Join Drive to Clear Fortress
  News Dispatches (S)
	A1	Data on Tonkin Action Pondered by Senators
		  Richard Harwood (W)
			A1		

VCs Uncertain of Objectives, First Data on POWs Suggest
  Stanley Karnow (S)
	A1	Johnson Says U.S. Must Fight On
		  Carroll Kilpatrick (W)
			A1		

		Trip to Hanoi Made by U.S. Emissary UPI (W)	A1		

Vietnam Dateline	Page[#]	Non-Vietnam Dateline	Page[#]	Vietnam Commentary/ Editorial	Page[#]
Street Fighting in Some Cities Obscures a Success at Da Nang Peter Braestrup (D)	A1	Nixon Says U.S. Can't Afford Defeat Ward Just (Dover, N.H.)	A2		
Viet Army Morale Seen Aim of Offensive Lee Lescaze (S)	A10	Gen. Westmoreland Defended Against "Delusion" Charge UPI (W)	A8		
Thieu Says More U.S. Troops Are Needed to End War Faster AP (My Tho)	A14	Gavin Tells of '54 Talk of Invading N. Vietnam	A9		
		Pearson on A-Arms Special to *Post* (Ottawa)	A11		
Marine Saw Reds Kill Two Civilians UPI (S)	A14				
February 14					
Allies Attack Reds in Saigon Suburb News Dispatches (S)	A1	Ten Thousand Five Hundred More GIs Going to VN in Buildup Rush John Maffre (W)	A1	Why Not Missiles? (editorial)	A22
Schools Are Havens for Viet Refugees Lee Lescaze (S)	A10	Thant Sees Wilson; Next Stop Is Paris News Dispatches	A1	A Proposal-- Give Hanoi Specific Choices Roger Fisher (Cambridge, Mass.)	A22
		Ted Kennedy Tests War Sentiment at Home Ward Just (Lynn, Mass.)	A2	Raided Towns Look to Saigon Stanley Karnow (S)	A16
		VC Offensive Cuts LBJ Support--Gallup Poll George Gallup (Princeton, N.J.)	A7	Vets of Dienbienphu Appraise Khe Sanh Edward Mortimer, London Sunday *Times* (Paris)	A18
		Hints of Viet "Break" Discounted in U.S. Murrey Marder (W)	A24	VN at Annapolis (editorial)	A22

Vietnam Dateline	Page#	Non-Vietnam Dateline	Page#	Vietnam Commentary/ Editorial	Page#
				Disparity of Views: Media, Officials Marquis Childs (W)	A22
				Romney's Criticism of Saigon Viewed as Windfall for Nixon William S. White (W)	A23
February 15					
Allies Press Attack on Hue Citadel News Dispatches (S)	A1	U.S. Seeks to Counter Pressure Murrey Marder (W)	A1	Unsung Americans (editorial)	A24
		U.N. Leader Sees Hanoi's Paris Envoy Ronald Koven, *International Herald Tribune* (Paris)	A1	Short-Term Swings of Opinion Blind LBJ to Basic U.S. Mood Joseph Kraft (W)	A25
		Red Chinese Shoot Down Navy Plane George C. Wilson (W)	A1		
		N.Y. Democrats Back Johnson but Not His Vietnam Policies UPI (Buffalo, N.Y.)	A2		
		Hill Experts Put Vietnam Spending at $32 Billion Eric Wentworth (W)	A4		
		Red Guns at Khe Sanh Are Mobile AP (H.K.)	A19		
		Text of Rusk on Talks: "Not Interested in Propaganda" (W)	A20		
		U.S. to Keep Viet Force at 525,000 (W)	D2		

Vietnam Dateline	Page#	Non-Vietnam Dateline	Page#	Vietnam Commentary/ Editorial	Page#
February 16					
GI Deaths Hit 400 for Week, Vietnam Toll Nearly Equals War's Record News Dispatches (S)	A1	Fulbright and Rusk Clash on Atom Talk Robert C. Albright (W)	A1	U.S. Warily Eyes Hanoi Strategy Murrey Marder (W)	A14
Hue: Fires Pinpoint the Foe Lee Lescaze (Hue)	A1	Romney Accuses Nixon of "Me-Too" Viet Policy D. Broder (Concord, N.H.)	A1	Rumor About Attack Persists in Saigon's Credibility Gap	
Pacification Future in Doubt Stanley Karnow (S)	A15	Nixon Warns on Tactical A-Weapons AP (Boston)	A2	Flora Lewis (S)	A21
		Pacification Gets Help of Computer George C. Wilson (W)	A15	U.S. Had to Scrap 1968 War Plan Even Before Assault on Viet Cities Evans/Novak (W)	A21
		Thant Tells Goldberg of Peace Effort R. Estabrook, Wash. *Post* Foreign Service (U.N.)	A14		
		Swiss Said Offering to Mediate in VN AP (Bern)	A14		
		Hanoi's Overture Detailed by Italians Leo J. Wollemborg, Special to *Post* (Rome)	A16		
		Some Viet-Bound Again AP (W)	A16		
		Ninety-Seven at Va. Law School Oppose Viet Policy (W)	B6		
February 17					
Truck Route Said to Help Foe in Hue Bruce Pigott, Reuters (Hue)	A1	Johnson Doubts Hanoi Wants to Talk, Backs Gen. Westmoreland Carroll Kilpatrick (W)	A1	Fiction and Guile of Hanoi's Non-Peace Offensive Is Clear Roscoe Drummond (S)	A13
Security Is a Bunker for Khe Sanh Platoon Peter Braestrup (K)	A10	McCarthy Asks Probe of A-Arms AP (N.Y.)	A2		

Vietnam Dateline	Page[#]	Non-Vietnam Dateline	Page[#]	Vietnam Commentary/ Editorial	Page[#]
Viet Raids Kill 3,799 Civilians Reuters (S)	A10	Johnson: Gen. Westmoreland Has My Full Support; Transcript of WH News Conference (W)	A6	A-Weapons Must Be Limited If Used in South Vietnam J. Lederberg (W)	A13
		Diplomats Doubt Thant Will Tell White House Anything New R. Estabrook, Wash. *Post* Foreign Servie (U.N.)	A6		
		Graduate Students Draftable J. W. Anderson (W)	A1		
		Strategy Is Defended by General Johnson George C. Wilson (W)	A10		
		Hanoi Sees Saigon Collapse UPI (Tokyo)	A10		
		N. VN Frees Three American Pilots News Dispatches	A1		
		Hunt Given Up for Pilot Shot Down by Chinese AP (W)	A15		
		U.S. World Role Study Kept Secret by Pentagon AP (W)	A11		
		GIs Combat Conviction Reversed William Shumann (W)	A7		
February 18 Enemy Shells Saigon Airfield, 30 Other Bases; Red Assaults on Ground Are Few Peter Braestrup (S)	A1	Reforms Halted U.S. Aid Misuse in Laos, Stabilized Currency John T. Wheeler, AP (Vientiane)	E1	Are There Peace Signs in the Rubble? P. Geyelin (W)	B1
Thieu Lost Prestige in VC Thrusts Stanley Karnow (S)	A1	Johnson Drops In on Troop Take-offs George Lardner, Jr. (Ft. Bragg, Calif.)	A1	Hue--A Symbol to All Vietnamese Warren Unna (W)	B6
		Draft Call of Oldest Laid to President Morton Mintz (W)	A1		

Vietnam Dateline	Page[#]	Non-Vietnam Dateline	Page[#]	Vietnam Commentary/ Editorial	Page[#]
Estimates of Guerrillas Left in Saigon Vary Wash. *Post* Foreign Service (S)	A10	Romney Renews Viet Criticism D. Broder (Swanzey, N.H.)	A2	Any Guerrillas Live Here? Jared Stout (W)	B3
Reds Order Hue Civilian March Don Oberdorfer, Chicago *Daily News* (Hue)	A27	Shell-Spewing AF Gunships Going to War AP (W)	A20		
		Malik Sees Saigon Victory UPI (Djakarta)	A27		
Shelling by Reds Subsides; Some Ground Action Follows Foe's Barrages AP (S)	X	Kosygin Joins Brezhnev in Appealing for U.S. Bomb Halts Wash. *Post* Foreign Service (Moscow)	A28		
		U Thant "Convinced" Hanoi Would Talk Reuters (U.N.)	A28		
		Vatican Aide Reportedly Meets N. Vietnamese AP (Vatican City)	X		
February 19					
Saigon's Airport Shelled; Red Barrages Through South Appear to Ebb News Dispatches (S)	A1	VC Drive Held Aid to Allies; LBJ Tells Ike Saigon May Be Stronger Now George Lardner, Jr. (Palm Desert, Calif.)	A1	Allies Seen Putting Stress on Military Stanley Karnow (S)	A1
Shortage of Men, Air Support Slow Marine Drive in Hue Lee Lescaze (Hue)	A1	Soviet Marshal Warns on Use of Atom Bombs Reuters (Paris)	A17	Major Failure in City Battles Was Enemy's, Not the Allies' Joseph Alsop (W)	A21
Anti-Red Front Forms in Saigon Barry Kramer, AP (S)	A1				
A Drink of Water . . . Then Death AP (Binh Loi Bridge, S. VN)	A1				

Vietnam Dateline	Page[#]	Non-Vietnam Dateline	Page[#]	Vietnam Commentary/ Editorial	Page[#]

Khe Sanh Waits and Probes Strategy
  Peter Braestrup
  (K)
	A19				

February 20					

*Reds Ease Attacks on Viet Cities
  Peter Braestrup
  (S)
	A1	U.S. Worried by Strides in Soviet Strategic Arms
		  George C. Wilson (W)
			A1	War Signs Suggest Johnson Is Sold on Iron-Will Myth
				  Joseph Kraft
				  (W)
					A17

Hue Marines: Bitter As They Are Brave
  Lee Lescaze
  (Hue)
	A1	Eastland Offers Bill Making It Treason to Aid N. Vietnam
		  AP (W)
			A4	McCarthy and Romney Shape Primaries into a VN Poll
				  D. Broder
				  (W)
					A17

Eighteen Days Under the Bed, He Eludes Foe in Hue Wash. *Post* Foreign Service
  (Hue)
	A14	Pacifying Did Stop, Says HHH
		  F. Porter (Bal Harbour, Fla.)
			A1		

North Vietnam Claims Complete Tet Victory
  UPI (S)
	A15	Sen. Fulbright Derides Rostow
		  UPI (W)
			A6		

Saigon Police Detain Two Politicians
  (S)
	X	Thant Seeks New Peace Plan
		  R. Estabrook (U.N.)
			A7		

		UNICEF Sends Aid to S. VN Reuters (Paris)	A15		
		Some Viet-Bound GIs Are Returnees UPI (W)	A15		

		Sweden to Recognize Hanoi
		  Wilfrid Fleisher, Special to *Post*
		  (Stockholm)
			A17		

		Debate on VN Snarls Md. Senate R. Homan (Annapolis, Md.)	C6		
		Freed Pilots "Chose" Use of AF Plane (W)	A15		

		Bunche Optimistic on VN Talks
		  Los Angeles *Times*
		  (Fullerton, Calif.)
			A6		

Vietnam Dateline	Page#	Non-Vietnam Dateline	Page#	Vietnam Commentary/ Editorial	Page#
		Hanoi, VC See Peace After LBJ Re-election (N.Y.)	A7		

February 21

Vietnam Dateline	Page#	Non-Vietnam Dateline	Page#	Vietnam Commentary/ Editorial	Page#
Allies Fight VC Battalion on Western Edge of Saigon Peter Braestrup (S)	A1	Ky, Thang Quit Recovery Unit; U.S. Officials Disappointed Murrey Marder (W)	A36	War, Inflation and Taxes (editorial)	A20
Marine Leader Sees Weeks of Hue Battle News Dispatches (D)	A1	N. Vietnam Envoy's Sweden Visit Is Now Seen as "Peace"Mission Special to *Post* (Stockholm)	A36		
Saigon Police Arrest Monk Tri Quang AP (S)	A36	Tonkin Critics Rebuffed; McNamara Denies Attack Was Provoked Warren Unna (W)	A1		
Commission Leaves Hue AP (Hue)	F6	Marines Use Seven Tons of Bomb Per Kill (W)	A3		
A Vietcong Sees Fight to the End Mark Frankland, London *Observer* (S)	F7	Canadian Diplomat Sees No Give in Hanoi's Position on Peace Talks R. Estabrook, Wash. *Post* Foreign Service (U.N.)	A21		
Executions Planned for Hue Communists News Dispatches (Hue)	X	President to Receive Thant's Report Today (W)	A25		
		All-Out War Urged by Rep. Rivers UPI (W)	A26		
		McNamara on Tonkin: Attacks Were Not Provoked (Partial Text of McN. Statement to For. Rel. Comm.) (W)	A33		
		Accts. of VC Violence Recall Country's Fierce History Dennis Bloodworth (Singapore)	F1		

Vietnam Dateline	Page[#]	Non-Vietnam Dateline	Page[#]	Vietnam Commentary/ Editorial	Page[#]
		Pueblo Crew Again Threatened Los Angeles *Times* (Moscow)	A30		
		Missile Bases at Sea Proposed George C. Wilson (W)	C20		
February 22 U.S. Relieves Unit Hard Hit at Hue Lee Lescaze (Hue)	A1	Johnson Reiterates Peace Talk Terms Murrey Marder (W)	A1	McNamara and Tonkin (editorial)	A12
Viet Political Arrests Disturb U.S. Embassy Peter Braestrup (S)	A10	McCarthy Blames LBJ for GI Deaths in War UPI (Madison, Wis.)	A2	Thant's Call on Johnson Shows Logic of Peacemaker's Moves Joseph Kraft (W)	A13
Ky Resigns as Head of Committee on Relief Reuters (S)	A10	War Stirs Conflict on Priorities George C. Wilson (W)	A10		
		VC Claims 70 Sites Hit in Second Drive Reuters (H.K.)	A14		
Hamlet Safety Is Post-Tet Problem Peter Braestrup (Nhi Binh)	X	Seminary Group Condemns War UPI (St. Meinrad, Ind.)	A14		
		Anti-Viet Marches in Lisbon and Paris Reuters (Lisbon)	A15		
		Hawk Challenge Is Met Head-on by Sen. Fulbright Harry Kelly, AP (Little Rock, Ark.)	E12		
		Radio Hanoi Claims GI Defects to Vietcong News Dispatches	X		
		McNamara Is Rebuked by Fulbright Warren Unna (W)	A1		
		Australia Recognizes Cambodian Borders Reuters (Canberra)	A10		
		Swedes Feel Hanoi Bars Talks Now Wilfrid Fleisher, Special to *Post* (Stockholm)	X		

Vietnam Dateline	Page#	Non-Vietnam Dateline	Page#	Vietnam Commentary/ Editorial	Page#
February 23					
*GI Losses for Week Set Record News Dispatches (S)	A1	Morse Releases Secret Material Richard Harwood (W)	A1	Saigon Governmental Reform Is Key to How War Will End Flora Lewis (S)	A17
A Somber View of the Foe Peter Braestrup (S)	A1	Log of Events Before Bombing of VN by U.S. in 1964 Walter Pincus (W)	A1		
Saigon Arrests Continue amid a Drive for Unity Lee Lescaze (S)	A1	Dissent Disturbs Ft. Jackson N. von Hoffman (Ft. Jackson, S.C.)	A1	Talks Seen upon Word of Raids' Halt Victor Zorza, *Manchester*	
U.S. Marines Capture Strategic Corner of Hue's Citadel News Dispatches (Hue)	A9	More Reserve Calls, Bigger Draft Seen UPI (W)	A2	*Guardian* (London)	A12
		Churchmen Urge Viet Negotiations Los Angeles *Times* (San Diego, Calif.)	A7		
Foe Tightens Ring Around Khe Sanh John T. Wheeler, AP (K)	A10	Judge at Capt. Levy's Trial Becomes Critic of War (W)	A8		
The Soldiers Available Wash. *Post* Foreign Service (S)	A12	Morse and McNamara Contentions on Tonkin Gulf Events Chalmers M. Roberts (W)	A14		
		Eight Doctors to Leave for Saigon Today UPI (Chicago)	A18		
February 24					
Hue Allies Storm VC Fortress News Dispatches (S)	A1	U.S. Plans April Draft of 48,000 George C. Wilson (W)	A1	Critics of Gen. Westmoreland Aren't Aware of Viet Realities Roscoe Drummond (S)	A11
More Political Leaders Are Arrested in Saigon News Dispatches (S)	A1	U.S. Tonkin Role Faulted by Senators Richard Harwood (W)	A1		
		Provocation Is Denied by U.S. Skipper Donald H. May, UPI (W)	A1	Reds Attack Throughout S.E. Asia Jack Anderson (H.K.)	E13
Big Barrage Hits Khe Sanh News Dispatches (S)	A1	Romney Warns of War Disaster Special to *Post* (Portland, Oreg.)	A2		

Vietnam Dateline	Page[#]	Non-Vietnam Dateline	Page[#]	Vietnam Commentary/ Editorial	Page[#]
Hue Marines Keep Determined Vigil over a Dead Comrade Lee Lescaze (Hue)	A8	McNamara's Policies Hit by Nixon AP (Portsmouth, N.H.)	A2		
Saigon Shifts Key Command News Dispatches (S)	A8	U.N. Role Urged in VN News Dispatches (Bloomington, Ind.)	A8		
Foe Shells Air-field, Killing 15 News Dispatches (S)	X	Seven Viet Allies Schedule Meeting of Ministers UPI (W)	A8		
Captured VC Gives Version of Red Plan AP (S)	X	Next Move Up to U.S., Thant Feels Wash. *Post* Foreign Service (U.N.)	A8		
		Men Under Fire Denied Arms, AF Sergeant Says UPI (W)	A8		
		VC Says U.S. Using Poison Gas Reuters (H.K.)	A8		
		Gen. Giap Foresees Fierce Phase of War AP (Tokyo)	A8		
		VN Plague Feared Spreading Thomas O'Toole (W)	A11		
		Pathet Lao Overrun Garrison News Dispatches (Vientiane)	A14		
		Cambodia Lays Kill-ings to Allies News Dispatches (Phnom Penh)	A14		
		Nixon Hits Handling of Ship Loss UPI (Superior, Wis.)	X		
		Rusk Sees Progress on *Pueblo* UPI (Phoenix, Ariz.)	X		
February 25					
Allies Clear Enemy from Hue's Palace Fred Emery, London Sunday *Times* (Hue)	A1	Tonkin Records Reveal Conflicts in U.S. '64 Stand; McNamara Dis-puted on Viet Foray Richard Harwood (W)	A1	Illusions Dog Us in War Stanley Karnow (S)	D1

Vietnam Dateline	Page[#]	Non-Vietnam Dateline	Page[#]	Vietnam Commentary/ Editorial	Page[#]
Westmoreland Said to Want 50,000 GIs UPI (S)	Al	U Thant Renews Viet Plea, Predicts Talks in "Few Days" If Raids Stop R. Estabrook (U.N.)	Al	Khe Sanh Is Quite Takeable David Leitch, London Sunday *Times* (K)	Dl
Vacuum Remains in S. Vietnam's Rural Areas Reuters (S)	Al0	Humphrey, at AU, Derides Protesters, Given Ovation As 40 Walk Out D. Robinson (W)	Al	Giap Offensive Aims at War's End by Midyear Douglas Pike, USIA (W)	D3
Hanoi Port Is Bombed AP (S)	Al0	Tonkin Transcript (W)	Al		
Three Wounded Marines Make the Perilous Journey Out of Hue Lee Lescaze (Hue)	Al2	Viet Position Hurts Stevenson Chances UPI (Chicago)	A2	The Tonkin Legacy (editorial)	D8
		Probe Due in Case of Tonkin Witness UPI (W)	Al2		
Charlie Company Has a Rough Time with Two Snipers in a Bamboo Thicket Jack Foisie, Los Angeles *Times* (North of Hue)	Al3	Protesters Told to Form NLF in U.S. UPI (N.Y.)	E4	New VN Escalation Would Revive Tax Proposal Hobart Rowen (W)	Hl
		"Greatest Battle Ever Fought" (VC material to be read to VC troops before Tet) (W)	D3		
U.S. Official Admits "Setback" in Pacification UPI (S)	X	Pacification a Failure, North Vietnam Claims (H.K.)	X		
		Laos Reds Overrun Royal Army Outpost AP (Vientiane)	X		
		Souvanna Says Hanoi Has 40,000 in Laos Reuters (Paris)	X		
		Laos Troops Retake Post Seized by Reds News Dispatches (Vientiane)	X		
February 26					
*Hue Ruin Inspected by Thieu; Civilian Toll Is Put at 5,400 Killed or Hurt News Dispatches (Hue)	Al	Reds' Offensive Leaves U.S. with Maze of Uncertainties Murrey Marder and Chalmers M. Roberts (W)	Al	Pike's VC Attack Postmortem Refutes Senate Doves' Views Joseph Alsop (W)	Al3

Vietnam Dateline	Page#	Non-Vietnam Dateline	Page#	Vietnam Commentary/ Editorial	Page#
Troop Increase "Probably" Needed, Westmoreland Says AP (S)	A1	Fulbright Asks Policy Review Warren Unna (W)	A1	Fulbright Inquiry Called Jab at U.S., Whitewash of Hanoi William S. White (W)	A13
Viet Civilian Life Valued at $17 to $34 Reuters (S)	A10	Law Students Study Viet War Post Scripts (W)	A2		
		Freed Pilots' Story Viewed Warily Post Scripts (W)	A2	President Grows More Aggressive, Sounds like a Commander-in-Chief Evans/Novak (W)	A13
U.S. Base Hard Hit by VC Force News Dispatches (S)	A10	Two Defoliation Probers Quit; One Cites Terrific Pressure Thomas O'Toole	A10		
		Wheeler Says Foe Has Reserve UPI (Bangkok)	A10	Red Drive Casts Harsh Light on Military, Political Failings Lee Lescaze (S)	A14
		Force Pentagon to Build New A-Ships, Hill Urged George C. Wilson (W)	A1		
February 27					
Khe Sanh Unit Badly Mauled in Red Trap News Dispatches (K)	A1	Tonkin Gulf Attack Justified Bombing of North, U.S. Says Warren Unna (W)	A1	McNamara's Departure Means Failure in Managerial Faith Joseph Kraft (W)	A17
U.S. to Limit Reports on Casualties Lee Lescaze (S)	A1	Concord Favors Staying in War AP (Concord, Mass.)	A6		
Viet Corps Chiefs Replaced AP (S)	A15	War Censoring Rejected Here John Maffre (W)	A14	Corruption Is Saigon's Major Foe Jack Anderson (S)	B9
U.S. Stepping Up Raids on North, Officials Say UPI (S)	A15	War Passes Through Hue's Gates (W)	A15		
		Reds Intensify Attacks in Laos AP (Pak Sane, Laos)	A14		
		U.S. and Taiwan to Hold War Games Next Month R. Halloran, Wash. *Post* Foreign Service (Tokyo)	A14		

Vietnam Dateline	Page[#]	Non-Vietnam Dateline	Page[#]	Vietnam Commentary/ Editorial	Page[#]
		War Fears Grip Lao Royal Capital (Luang Prabang)	X		
February 28					
VC Shell Field; 14 Are Killed News Dispatches (S)	A1	LBJ Meets Today on Viet Future, May Ask Funds, Higher Tax Rise Carroll Kilpatrick (W)	A1	VN Casualty Reports (editorial)	A14
War-Stricken City of Hue Digs Out to Face Host of Problems Peter Braestrup (Hue)	A6	Uneasy Truce Descends on Tonkin Gulf Dispute Walter Pincus (W)	A1	Intelligence Fails on VC Offensive Marquis Childs (W)	A14
Fifty Politicians in Saigon Jails Bruce Pigott, Reuters (S)	A6	Johnson Urges War Unity Eve Edstrom (Dallas, Tex.)	A1	The President Should Approve More GIs and Call Reserves	
Allies Weigh Armor Threat News Dispatches (S)	X	A New Kind of War, an Old Tactic (W)	A6	Joseph Alsop (W)	A15
		Sen. Fulbright Hints of Committee Retaliation Warren Unna (W)	A6	Thieu Criticized for Lag on Reforms Jack Anderson (S)	D17
		Hanoi Held Set to Reply to Raid Halt *International Herald Tribune* (Paris)	A6		
		U.S. Bombers Said to Aid Laos News Dispatches	A7		
February 29					
Saigon Shifts Key Posts Reuters (S)	X	LBJ Sees Top Aides on War; No Decision Reported on Troop Increase Carroll Kilpatrick (W)	A1	New Strategy, Redeployment Seen U.S. Need, Not More Men Joseph Kraft (W)	A25
Thieu Shuts S. Vietnam Night Spots Permanently AP (S)	A26	A Vietcong Pincer Strategy Is Unfolding Murrey Marder (W)	A23	Debasing the Debate (editorial)	A24
Question in Assessing Casualties Is Effect on Enemy Capability Lee Lescaze (S)	A20	Russell Criticizes Westmoreland Tactics AP (Atlanta, Ga.)	X		

Vietnam Dateline	Page[#]	Non-Vietnam Dateline	Page[#]	Vietnam Commentary/ Editorial	Page[#]

Capture of Hue Citadel Was a Must for S. Viet Unit
  Peter Braestrup
  (Hue)
	A22	LBJ Praise Moves McNamara
		  (W)
			A1	Fog Blocks Khe Sanh Supply Planes
				  Jack Anderson (D)
					C15

Reinforcements in Vietnam
  News Dispatches
  (S)
	A21	Secret Tonkin Cables Cited in Morse Attack
		  Warren Unna (W)
			A1	Johnson's Decision on Men, Money Could Add Third to Viet War Budget
				  Evans/Novak
				  (W)
					A25

		Gaud Says Foreign Aid Helps War Effort R. Lyons (W)	A22		
		Officer Who Talked on Tonkin Restored AP (W)	A5		
March 1					

GIs Suffer Second Highest Weekly Toll
  News Dispatches
  (S)
	A1	Tonkin Data Disclosed by Sen. Morse
		  Walter Pincus (W)
			A1	Robert McNamara After Seven Years
				  Marquis Childs (W)
					A20

Immolation in Saigon
  AP (S)
	A17	Science Adviser Cuts Military Ties in Viet Dispute
		  Thomas O'Toole (W)
			A5	Mood of Pessimism Prevails in Mekong Capital of Can Tho
				  Flora Lewis
				  (Can Tho)
					A21

B-52s Help Crush Thrust at Khe Sanh
  AP (S)
	X	Johnson Reported Studying Long-Haul, Not Quickie, Troop Increase
		  Chalmers M. Roberts
		  (W)
			A13	Despite Mistakes, McNamara Seen as the Nation's Greatest
				  Joseph Alsop
				  (W)
					A21

		Snafus Bedevil McNamara Farewell
		  John Maffre (W)
			A1	A Night at the Pleiku Command Post
				  Jack Anderson (Pleiku)
					B11

				Safer Skies (editorial)	A20

Vietnam Dateline	Page[#]	Non-Vietnam Dateline	Page[#]	Vietnam Commentary/ Editorial	Page[#]
March 2					
Three Battles Break Out near Vietnam DMZ AP (S)	A1	Theft Not Confined to Saigon, LBJ Says (Beaumont, Tex.)	A4	Demands of Vietnam Hobble Our Steps to Outer World J. Lederberg (W)	A13
Thieu Signs Reform but Gets Rebuff Lee Lescaze (S)	A1	Hanoi Lauds Four Senators for Asking Halt in Bombing Chalmers M. Roberts (W)	A10		
House Bars New Powers for Thieu William Tuohy, Los Angeles *Times* (S)	X	Hill Group Weighs Spur to Peace Talk Murrey Marder (W)	A15	A S. Vietnam Warlord Is Interviewed Jack Anderson (Pleiku)	D15
Viet Official Differs with U.S. on Enemy Aims Raymond R. Coffey, Chicago *Daily News* (S)	A10	Clifford Joins the Cabinet as Defense Chief Elizabeth Shelton (W)	A4		
South Viets Prove Fighters in Hue Peter Braestrup (Hue)	A11				
Saigon Army Missing 10 Percent Since Tet Wash. *Post* Foreign Service (S)	A10				
March 3					
Vietcong Caught in Two Traps; Ambushes Rout Enemy Units near Airfields UPI (S)	A1	Johnson Hails U.S. Strength; Might Is Called Shield Against Aggression Carroll Kilpatrick (Marietta, Ga.)	A1	Plight of Khe Sanh Called Not So Dire Brig. Gen. S.L.A. Marshall (Ret.) Los Angeles *Times*	A20
Khe Sanh: A U.S. Obsession? Lee Lescaze (S)	A1	War, Cities Are Issues in Rocky-Nixon Race Leroy F. Aarons (N.Y.)	A2	Is There a Choice on More Troops? Chalmers M. Roberts (W)	B6
Saigon Paper Asks Invasion of the North AP (S)	A17	McCarthy Appeals to Romney Voters AP (Nashua, N.H.)	A2		

Vietnam Dateline	Page[#]	Non-Vietnam Dateline	Page[#]	Vietnam Commentary/ Editorial	Page[#]
Marine Leaders Criticized as Unimaginative William Tuohy, Los Angeles *Times* (S)	A18	For Weary Vietnam Veterans Sydney Successful as Haven Gordon Tait, AP (Sydney) Gen. Navarre Doubts VC Will Win UPI (Vence, France)	A5 A22		
March 4 *GI Patrol Trapped, 48 Killed, Allied Bases Hit in Series of Shellings News Dispatches (S) Khe Sanh Marines Use Divining Rods AP (K) Quang Tri Pushes Ahead Again Peter Braestrup (Quang Tri city)	A1 A1 A9	Vietcong Program Held Better; House Report Censures AID and Saigon on Land Reform Warren Unna (W) Large Units Scarce for Vietnam Buildup John Maffre (W) D.C. Democratic Chief Won't Be Delegate, Dudley Splits with Party on Viet Issue Robert L. Asher (W) Shows in VN Put Off Post Scripts (W) Sorensen Pessimistic on War UPI (N.Y.) Britons Volunteering for VN War Duty AP (London)	A1 A1 A1 A2 A9 A10	Envoy Bunker Keeps Cool Under Fire Jack Anderson (S)	C7
March 5 Reds Hit Cam Ranh Base for First Time News Dispatches (S) Saigon Police Seek to Link Buddhists, VC Lee Lescaze (S) Decree Power Request Opposed in Viet Senate UPI (S)	A1 A1 A9	Clash on War Policy; Chairman Ousted by D.C. Democrats E. Carper (W) Eighteen Hill Democrats Offer Vietnam Plan UPI (W)	A1 A9		

Vietnam Dateline	Page[#]	Non-Vietnam Dateline	Page[#]	Vietnam Commentary/ Editorial	Page[#]
Newspaper in Saigon Suspended for Three Days AP (S)	A9				
Copters Run Constant Risks to Supply Khe Sanh Outposts Peter Braestrup (Quang Tri base)	A10				
March 6					
Delta City Hit After Foe's Assault Fails News Dispatches (S)	A1	Nixon Says He'd End War, Contends LBJ Has Not Used Power Wisely AP (Hampton, N.H.)	A1	Thailand Has No Faint Hearts in War on Red Aggression Roscoe Drummond (Bangkok)	A23
New Drive Seen but Not at Khe Sanh Reuters (Phu Bai)	A1	Johnson Presses War Study Carroll Kilpatrick (W)	A7	Rocky Hawkish in '64--What About '68? Chalmers M.	
U.S. Civilian Losses Are Given as 57 AP (S)	A20	Bundy Says VC Dealt Sharp Blow (W)	A11	Roberts (W)	A6
		Strong Indications Link Driver to VC (W)	A20	Maoists Hope for a Long Viet War Stanley	
U.S. Trying to Return Three to Hanoi as Goodwill Act UPI (S)	A20	De Gaulle Said to See Viet A-Peril Reuters (Paris)	A16	Karnow (H.K.)	A18
				Vietnam Mission--A Return to First Principles (editorial)	A22
				Gen. Wheeler's War Report Asks Painful and Crucial Action Joseph Alsop (W)	A23

Vietnam Dateline	Page[#]	Non-Vietnam Dateline	Page[#]	Vietnam Commentary/ Editorial	Page[#]
				LBJ Demand for War Support Oath Behind Adlai Stevenson Rejection Evans/Novak (W)	A23
				GIs Battle Viets in Rice Paddies Jack Anderson (Can Tho)	B11
March 7					
Foe Seen Aiming at Hue, U.S. Says Reds Deploy Forces Close to City Peter Braestrup (S)	A1	VC Watching Ad Irks McCarthy Ward Just (Manchester, N.H.)	A1		
		Viet View Clarified by Illinois Candidate *Chicago Sun Times*	A2		
Forty-Nine Feared Lost As Reds Down Plane News Dispatches (S)	A1	Swiss Announce Talks with N. Vietnam David Egil, Special to *Post* (Geneva)	A11		
Mine Explosion Kills Cameraman in S. Vietnam UPI (S)	A2	Hue Cited by Nasser to Officers News Dispatches	A14		
Westmoreland Praises Marines in Vietnam AP (S)	A10	Senate Report Says Saigon Corruption Prolongs the War UPI (W)	X		
March 8					
Viet Senate Rejects Thieu Decree Power Peter Braestrup (S)	A1	*Senators Ask Voice in Any GI Buildup; Fulbright Warns of New Request; Mansfield, RFK State Misgivings D. Broder (W)	A1	Cruel Irony of the Enclave Theory Murrey Marder (W)	A20
Week's GI Toll Climbs to 542 News Dispatches (S)	A18	Week's GI Toll Climbs to 542 (W)	A1	Surveillance Ships Worth an Effort Marquis Childs (W)	A20

Vietnam Dateline	Page#	Non-Vietnam Dateline	Page#	Vietnam Commentary/ Editorial	Page#
		"Reds-Are-Watching" Ad Drive in N.H. Widened Walter Pincus (W)	A2		
		Allies Schedule Meeting Reuters (Wellington, New Zealand)	A12		
March 10 *Red Unit Is Mauled by GIs; Jets, Artillery Help Kill 129 near Da Nang AP (S)	A1	Rusk to Confront War Critics in Public Murrey Marder (W)	A10		
Four Hundred Slayings Laid to Enemy (S)	A18	War Looms as Key Issue in Wisconsin on April 2 Richard Harwood (Milwaukee, Wis.)	A1		
Ky Praises His Troops' Valor Peter Braestrup (S)	A26	VC Offensive Hit 1,000 U.S. Aircraft (W)	A1		
Allies Trying to Seize Offensive in the Delta Lee Lescaze (Can Tho)	A27	Forty-Nine Percent in U.S. Think Viet War Was Mistake--Gallup Poll (W)	A18		
		Vietnam Intellectual Backs Cease-Fire, New Elections Chalmers M. Roberts (W)	G1		
		How I Escaped from the Vietcong Pvt. Roger D. Anderson (*Parade* Mag.) (Dayton, Tex.)	8		
		Two Hundred Six Thousand Draft Call Hinted Murrey Marder (W)	A1		
March 11 U.S. Sites in DMZ Area Hit, New Command Is Activated in Northern Zone News Dispatches (S)	A1	War Is Undergoing Searching Scrutiny Chalmers M. Roberts (W)	A1	Why Sen. Clark's Non-Facts Don't Lessen Viet Troop Need Joseph Alsop (W)	A13
		Antiwar Lieutenant Pickets White House (W)	A3		

Vietnam Dateline	Page#	Non-Vietnam Dateline	Page#	Vietnam Commentary/ Editorial	Page#
Vital Saigon-Delta Route Attacked, Enemy Seen Trying to Cut Flow of Food George C. Wilson (Dong Tam)	A10	GI Buildup in Vietnam Is Opposed by Bundy Special to *Post* (Cambridge, Mass.)	A10	Thieu's Dilemma: Troop Operations Outside Towns Vital to Success Evans/Novak (W)	A13
Reds in Saigon Area Believed Hurt Peter Braestrup (Bien Hoa)	A10	Troop Call Seen Helping McCarthy Thomas O'Toole (W)	A4		
Asia Study Stresses Self-Help Special to *Post* (S)	A11				
March 12					
Eight Province Chiefs Replaced by Thieu Nguyen Ngoc Rao, Special to *Post* (S)	A1	*Critics Press Rusk at Six-Hour Hearing; Troop Issue Skirted; Meet Again Today Murrey Marder (W)	A1	Absence of McNamara Opens VN Policy to All Leaders Joseph Kraft (W)	A17
S. Viet Troops Kill 102 Reds near DMZ News Dispatches (S)	A1	A Long Day of Contention Chalmers M. Roberts (W)	A1		
Saigon Plan in Buildup Questioned Peter Braestrup (S)	A9	LBJ Warns on Dissension Within Nation Carroll Kilpatrick (W)	A5		
		Viet Compromises Urged by *Newsweek* UPI (N.Y.)	A9		
		Troop Call-up Need Is Urgent, Stennis Says (W)	A9		
		Rusk at Hearing: . . "Not Just a Problem of S. VN"; Fulbright: "Can We Afford Disillusionment of Our Youth?" (Partial Transcript) (W)	A10-A11		

Vietnam Dateline	Page[#]	Non-Vietnam Dateline	Page[#]	Vietnam Commentary/ Editorial	Page[#]
		Rusk Testimony Sends Stock Averages Higher Philip Greer (N.Y.)	D6		
		War Contingencies Could Force Income Tax Increase, Mills Says UPI (W)	D6		
March 13			.		
Allies Drive to Clear Vital Delta Route George C. Wilson (Dong Tam)	A18	Rusk Shuns Pledge on Troops Murrey Marder (W)	A1	VN Doubts, Misgivings Persist Chalmers M. Roberts (W)	A11
Allies Report Killing 288 Reds in Three Clashes South of DMZ News Dispatches (S)	A18	LBJ Urges U.S. Firmness Carroll Kilpatrick (W)	A1	Contribution of the Hearings (editorial)	A20
Plan for Viet Confidence Vote Killed News Dispatches (S)	A22	Fulbright: The Idea Is to Influence You into a Wiser Policy (Partial Transcript of Rusk Testimony Before the Senate For. Rel. Comm.) (W)	A10	U.S. Promises to Free World Challenged by Attack on Policy William S. White (W)	A21
		Pacifists Return to Work (W)	A11	Cool Rusk Disperses Smog over Senate's Vietnam Role Roscoe Drummond (W)	A21
		U.S. Presses Allies for Viet Troops UPI (W)	A11		
		Sweden Says It Stands by Viet Criticism Wilfrid Fleisher, Special to *Post* (Stockholm)	A16	Guerrilla Tactics Used Against Hanoi Jack Anderson (S)	D15
		Phase Out of Viet War Is Favored by Majority Gallup Poll George Gallup (Princeton, N.J.)	A21		
		War Needs Curb Domestic Air Service C. Koprowski (W)	D7		
		GI Defector Quits Sweden, Gives Up News Dispatches (Frankfurt)	A1		

Vietnam Dateline	Page#	Non-Vietnam Dateline	Page#	Vietnam Commentary/ Editorial	Page#
March 14					
Road Is Vietcong Goal in Fighting in Delta George C. Wilson (Dong Tam)	A1	Nixon Saves Viet Plan Until He Is Nominated Relman Morin, AP (N.Y.)	A2	Rising Policy Control by Military Cited Drew Pearson (W)	F7
Militant Buddhist Freed by Saigon Government AP (S)	A20	India Is Told U.S. Has Paid a Family for Raid Death in Hanoi Reuters (New Delhi)	A13		
Saigon Unit Forms to Go North AP (S)	A22	Clifford Declines to Testify Before Fulbright Committee Despite Rusk's Promise (W)	A20		
U.S. Convoy Is Rescued from Trap (S)	A22	Nine Hundred U.S. Employees Sign Viet-Peace Plea (W)	A20		
"Search-Destroy" Term Is Dropped Wash. *Post* Foreign Service (My Tho)	A22	A-Expert to Advise on Viet Pacification AP (W)	A20		
Planes Strike Close to Hanoi, Haiphong News Dispatches (S)	X	Iowa Governor Calls for Bombing Halt UPI (Des Moines, Iowa)	A20		
		Navy Warns of Improved Russian Subs D. Hoffman (W)	A8		
		Laotian Reds' Threat to River Town Eased AP (Vientiane)	X		
March 15					
GIs' Toll Hits 500 Again; Deaths High Despite Lack of Major Fight News Dispatches (S)	A1	U.S. Warns Ky Against Invading North Warren Unna (W)	A8	No Halfway House Between Victory, Defeat in VN Joseph Alsop (W)	A17
Vietnam Seen Facing Jump in Inflation George C. Wilson (S)	A8	Danes' China Envoy Visiting Hanoi Soon Special to *Post* (Copenhagen)	A8	Disturbing Parallels Noted in Saigon Jack Anderson (S)	B15
		U.S. Aides Plan Anti-war Vigil UPI (W)	A8		
		U.S. Policy on Vietnam Scored by Rep. Mathias (W)	C11		

Vietnam Dateline	Page[#]	Non-Vietnam Dateline	Page[#]	Vietnam Commentary/ Editorial	Page[#]

Island Begins New Life Under VC Rule
  Lee Lescaze
  (Vinh Long)
	A9			Submarine Strength Letter to the Ed., Samuel S. Stratton (W)	A17

Weekly Casualty Report for Vietnam Combatants
  News Dispatches
  (S)
	A9				

March 16					

Viet Allies Launch Biggest Offensive
  AP (S)
	A1	Marchers Protest War Taxes
		  N. von Hoffman (W)
			A3	Politics and Economics of War Are Backdrop for Reappraisal Chalmers M. Roberts (W)	A13

A Delta City's Puzzle: Can the Pieces Be Put Together? VC Attack Shook Old Ideas and Loyalties
  Lee Lescaze
  (Vinh Long)
	A10	Viet Pull-out Vote Scheduled in Madison
		  AP (Madison, Wis.)
		Protestants Criticize LBJ
		  AP (N.Y.)
			A7
			
			A10		

Thieu Orders Crackdown on S. Vietnam's Black Market
  Nguyen Ngoc Rao, Special to *Post*
  (S)
	A10	Hanoi Said to Shun Troops from China
		  Reuters (H.K.)
			A10		

S. Viet Civilians Given Arms
  Peter Braestrup
  (S)
	A10				

Allies Prepare Release of Three UPI (S)	A10				
March 17					

Thieu's Rule Unshaken by Tet
  Nguyen Ngoc Rao, Special to *Post*
  (S)
	A16	*LBJ Seeks Austerity, Victory; Troops Will Be Boosted
		  William Chapman (W)
			A1	Kennedy Candidacy Brings New Challenge to War Policy Murrey Marder (W)	A8

Vietnam Dateline	Page#	Non-Vietnam Dateline	Page#	Vietnam Commentary/ Editorial	Page#
		London Routs Anti-U.S. Mob Alfred Friendly/ Peter Osnos, Wash. *Post* Foreign Service (London)	A1		
March 19					
Marines Hit Enemy near DMZ, Kill 67 News Dispatches (S)	A1	*Full Effort in War Asked by Johnson; Tells Nation to Join in Austerity Carroll Kilpatrick (Minn.)	A1	A Vietnam Commission (editorial)	A8
War-Weary Hue's Animosities Grow Lee Lescaze (Hue)	A11	Only "Difficult Compromise" Can End War, Kennedy Says Richard Harwood (N.Y.)	A1	*Cercle Sportif* Hasn't Changed Lee Lescaze (S)	A8
IVS Losing Half of Staff in VN UPI (S)	A11	HUAC Eyes U.S. Worker War Protest AP (W)	A2	Viet Commission Affair Shows War Debasement of Public Life Joseph Kraft (W)	A9
		Ted Kennedy Book Hits Asia Policy AP (W)	A7		
		War Foes Win at Chicago Museum D.J.R. Bruckner, Los Angeles *Times* (Chicago)	A9		
		Sihanouk Offers to Play Host for Peace Talks	A10		
		Review of Vietnam War Policies Is Urged by 140 House Members UPI (W)	A11		
		Soviets Plan 20 Percent Rise in Shipments to Reds AP (Moscow)	A11		
March 20					
Defectors Claim Reds Tipped on B-52 Raids News Dispatches (S)	A14	Conscience of a Deserter, Hatred of War Drives GI into Exile J. Hoagland (W)	A1	U.S. Will Ask Chiang to Quit Isles Jack Anderson (Taipei)	B7

Vietnam Dateline	Page#	Non-Vietnam Dateline	Page#	Vietnam Commentary/ Editorial	Page#
B-52s Continue Raids at Khe Sanh News Dispatches (S)	A14	Rocky Shifts, Favors Viet "Accommodation" P. Geyelin (W)	A1		
Black Market Raided AP (S)	A14	LBJ: Foe's Target Is U.S. Will Carroll Kilpatrick (W)	A1		
Militia Unit Presses VC Hard Peter Braestrup (Phu Cuong)	A23	Adlai's Backing of War Not Relevant, Son Says UPI (South Bend, Ind.)	A2		
		Hanoi Envoy Sees Swiss; Mediation Move Denied Reuters (Bern)	A14		
		May Draft Call Is for 44,000, All to Army UPI (W)	A24		
		A-Arms in Vietnam Seen Barred by Pact Murrey Marder (W)	A24		
		Anti-LBJ Forces Join Here; RFK-McCarthy Groups Merge for Primary Robert L. Asher (W)	A1		
March 21					
Foe Leaving Saigon Area, U.S. Reports News Dispatches (S)	A1	Brandt's Party Wants Viet Bombing Stopped Dan Morgan, Wash. *Post* Foreign Service (Nuremberg)	A1	Kennedy's Plan Recalls Seward's J. R. Wiggins (W)	A20
Press Censorship Is Eased by Saigon Reuters (S)	A10	McCarthy Offers Eight-Point Plan on How to End Vietnam War Chalmers M. Roberts (W)	A2		
Doctors Leave Hue Despite Direct Order Lee Lescaze (Hue)	A22	Viet Policy Is Assailed by Lindsay UPI (N.Y.)	A3		
GIs Say Three-Day Pass Given for Killing Foe Ronald Laramy, Reuters (Ben Cat)	A23	Treaties Cited as a Curb in Asia on Any President Warren Unna (W)	A6		

Vietnam Dateline	Page[#]	Non-Vietnam Dateline	Page[#]	Vietnam Commentary/ Editorial	Page[#]
		Shoup Urges Wide Latitude for Hanoi on Peace Talks John Maffre (W)	A7		
		Premier: Sweden Is Firm on Vietnam Wilfrid Fleisher, Special to *Post* (Stockholm)	A22		
		State Dept. Silent on Taipei Story AP (W)	A7		
March 22					
Thieu Warns on "Abuses," Tells Nation of 135,000-Man Boost in Army Lee Lescaze (S)	A1	RFK Says Johnson Divides the Nation Richard Harwood (Nashville, Tenn.)	A1		
American Deaths in Vietnam Surpass 20,000 News Dispatches (S)	A19	LBJ Hails Courage of S. Vietnamese Carroll Kilpatrick (W)	A1		
Weekly Battle Casualties News Dispatches (S)	A19	IRS Acts to Counter Antiwar Tax Protest UPI (W)	A19		
Viets Set Sweeping Reforms; Thieu Plans 135,000-Man Boost in Army William Tuohy, Los Angeles *Times* (S)	X				
March 23					
B-52s Strike Enemy Bases near Saigon News Dispatches (S)	A1	*Westmoreland Named Army's Chief of Staff Carroll Kilpatrick (W)	A1	LBJ Opens Options to Maneuver Murrey Marder (W)	A10
		Peace Talk in Switzerland; Hanoi Envoy Affirms Negotiation Terms News Dispatches (Bern)	A14	S. Vietnam's War (editorial)	A12

Vietnam Dateline	Page[#]	Non-Vietnam Dateline	Page[#]	Vietnam Commentary/ Editorial	Page[#]
Invasion of the North Advisable, Ky Asserts Lee Lescaze (aboard the USS *Kitty Hawk*)	A14	Ho Warns Internal Foes of Hanoi (W)	A14	Westmoreland Leaving Successor with Some Big Tactical Questions George C. Wilson (S)	A13
Information Chief Chosen Wash. *Post* Foreign Service (S)	A14	Hanoi Culture Minister Is in Paris for Rally *International Herald Tribune* (Paris)	A14		
		Nitze Also Declines to Testify Warren Unna (W)	A4		
		Shock Waves in Pentagon; Navy May Lose Hawaii Post John Maffre (W)	A10		
March 24					
Busy Spotter Pilot Helps Clear Road to Khe Sanh Peter Braestrup (D)	A1	House Debate on War Goes On AP (W)	A13	The Candidates on War Chalmers M. Roberts (W)	B1
U.S. Bombs Chemical Plant for First Time News Dispatches (S)	A21	House Trims Claws of Bill on Viet War Wash. *Post* Special Writer (Annapolis, Md.)	A16	The Little Marine and His New Boots John Randolph, Los Angeles *Times* (K)	B1
Generals Facing Viet Challenge George C. Wilson (S)	A22	Sweden Reveals Its Role as a Contact Between U.S. and Hanoi Wilfrid Fleisher, Special to *Post* (Stockholm)	A19	Is the Dog of War off His Leash? Abram Chayes (W)	B3
		Fighting More Intense, Souvanna Warns Laos Reuters (Vientiane)	A21	The Shift in Saigon (editorial)	B6
		Westmoreland Failed, Tass Writer Says AP (Moscow)	A22	Gold, Dollar Threats Affecting War Policy Hobart Rowen (W)	F1
		Wilson Says Military Victory "Ain't" to Be Won in Vietnam (Ayr, Scotland)	A22		
		Viet Children Arrive for Medical Care (W)	A32		

Vietnam Dateline	Page#	Non-Vietnam Dateline	Page#	Vietnam Commentary/ Editorial	Page#
March 25					
Higher U.S. Losses Seen in Vietnam George C. Wilson (S)	All	Support for War Slips to 54 Percent (W)	A1	Johnson Faces Big Vietnam Decisions Peter Braestrup (S)	A10
U.S. Troops Kill 44 in Push near Saigon News Dispatches (S)	All	Viet Commission Once Live Topic Post Scripts (W)	A2		
		War Called Threat to U.S. Influence UPI (Milwaukee, Wis.)	A4	Westmoreland's Replacement Hints Wavering LBJ Support	
B-52s Bomb Around Khe Sanh After Another Heavy Barrage AP (S)	X	Australian Labor Chief Urges Bombing Pause Reuters (Brisbane)	All	Joseph Alsop (S)	A15
		The Harris Survey: Viet War Support Declines to 54 Percent Louis Harris (W)	A16	Younger Military Critics of Viet Policy Emerging into Positions of Power	
		Machen Fully Supports U.S. Policy in Vietnam (W)	A2	Ted Sell, Los Angeles *Times* (W)	A15
		Two Hundred Fifty U.S. Employees at Protest Leon Dash, Wash. *Post* Special Writer (W)	B2	Nerve Gas on the Loose (editorial)	A14
		China Units Reported Inside Laos Chicago *Daily News* (Sam Thong, Laos)	C1		
March 26					
Two Hundred Forty-Three Reds Reported Slain in Saigon-Area Battle News Dispatches (S)	A14	*War Held Periling Economy; Treasury Aide Says Choice Is Guns or Butter Warren Unna (W)	A1		
Vietnam's "River Rats" Run Enemy Gantlet Peter Braestrup (Cua Viet)	A15	Johnson Ties War to Freedom in U.S. Frank C. Porter (W)	A1		
		Justice Defends Legality of U.S. Role in Vietnam (W)	A3		

Vietnam Dateline	Page#	Non-Vietnam Dateline	Page#	Vietnam Commentary/ Editorial	Page#
		Congressmen Asked to Attend Protest Against VN War (W)	D6		
March 28					
CIA's Role Disputed in Pacification AP (S)	A14	The President and the General End War Survey Carroll Kilpatrick (W)	A1	Kennedy Disappoints Young Radicals by Softened Attack on War and LBJ Evans/Novak (Los Angeles)	A21
Last-Gasp Red Drive Seen John N. Fallon, UPI (S)	A26	Daley Seen Testing State Antiwar Views Special to *Post* (Chicago)	A6		
Ninety-Nine Vietcong Killed near Cambodia AP (S)	A27	Premier: Sweden Acts as Link for Viet Foes Wilfrid Fleisher (Stockholm)	A28	Few U.S. Officers Back Ideas for a New War Strategy Peter Braestrup (D)	A25
Thieu's Supporters Form New Party Nguyen Ngoc Rao, Special to *Post* (S)	A27	Peacemaker Post Is Urged by Fulbright Robert C. Albright (W)	A31	Shriver Still Wanted the Paris Post Drew Pearson/Jack Anderson (W)	F7
Seven Hundred Eight Cases of Plague Found in S. Vietnam AP (S)	A27	Johns Hopkins Group Opposes Vietnam Policy (W)	A27		
		Lao Forces Seen Hard Hit by Communists' Rice Raids Jack Foisie, Los Angeles *Times* (Vientiane)	A26		
March 29					
Allies Report 194 of Foe Killed News Dispatches (S)	A14	Nixon Asks New U.S. Role, Sets Transition from Current Involvement Chalmers M. Roberts (Milwaukee, Wis.)	A1	Don't Overlook Possibility of Talks Before Nov. Joseph Alsop (S)	A21
Bien Hoa Is "Running Scared" Lee Lescaze (Bien Hoa)	A14	Adm. Sharp Says Bombing Is Necessary Reuters (Wellington, New Zealand)	A14		
New Neurosis Found in GIs UPI (S)	A14	Twenty-One Offer Tonkin Repealer UPI (W)	A14		

Vietnam Dateline	Page[#]	Non-Vietnam Dateline	Page[#]	Vietnam Commentary/ Editorial	Page[#]
Saigon Hotel Bill Blitzes Neutrals Reuters (S)	A14	Malaysia Premier Warns of Doom If U.S. Gives Up the Vietnam War Reuters (Kuala Lumpur)	A14		
U.S. Strategy Failing, S. Viet Minister Says Raymond R. Coffey, Chicago *Daily News* Service (S)	A16	AID Rules Employees Can't Sign Protests (W)	A18		
American Deaths Increase Slightly AP (S)	A16	Hospital Protest (Tokyo)	A22		
Four Vietnamese Vow Hunger Strike in Jail Wash. *Post* Foreign Service (S)	A16	Hill Unit Blocks Navy Jet; Funds Denied; AF Version of F-111 Crashes John Maffre (W)	A1		
March 30 Lost F-111 Could Be Technological Gold Mine for Reds George C. Wilson (S)	A14	Three North Vietnamese Released by U.S. News Dispatches (W)	A1	Political Calendar Crowding Johnson on His War Options Murrey Marder (W)	A11
VC Document Gives Failures of Tet Drive AP (S)	A14	Dudley Quizzes Party on War Robert L. Asher (W)	A8	U.S. War Intelligence Called Faulty Jack Anderson (W)	E13
Reds Shell U.S. Airfield, Hit Copters AP (S)	A14			Think Tank Put on the Defensive John Maffre (W)	A10
Komer Calls Aide Charge "Grotesque" UPI (S)	A14				
Vietnam Truce Body Reducing Its Staff Los Angeles *Times* (S)	D17			Congress Should Examine Biological Warfare Tests J. Lederberg (W)	A11

Vietnam Dateline	Page[#]	Non-Vietnam Dateline	Page[#]	Vietnam Commentary/ Editorial	Page[#]
March 31					
One Hundred Fifteen Enemy Killed by Khe Sanh Patrol News Dispatches (S)	A1	Johnson to Speak Tonight, Hints at Major Decisions on Vietnam War Carroll Kilpatrick (W)	A1	Stage Set for New Viet Move Murrey Marder (W)	A1
Second F-111-A Crashes; Crew Saved AP (S)	A1	LBJ Ratings Hit New Lows (W)	A1	A Case for Withdrawal from VN David Felix (Cambridge, Mass.)	B6
Allied Army Shift at DMZ Is Set Back George C. Wilson (Hue)	A18	Johnson's War and Job Ratings Sink--Gallup Poll George Gallup (Princeton, N.J.)	A2		
Two Province Chiefs Fired by Thieu UPI (S)	A18	Rifle Output Stepped Up for Saigon Troops Ward Just (W)	A18		
Control Commission Announces Cutback UPI (S)	A19	Diem Brother Replaced as Archbishop of Hue UPI (Vatican City)	A18		
Thieu Vows Full Call-up in Autumn News Dispatches (S)	A1	Vietcong to Free Two U.S. Women Captured During Battle of Hue News Dispatches (Tokyo)	A19		
Marines Kill 130 at Khe Sanh News Dispatches (S)	X	CBS Newsman Admitted by Hanoi AP (N.Y.)	A22		

Dateline		Story
February 1		
S	Vigilantes-029-532A	U.S. civilian defends his home against VC in Saigon; details. (Peter Arnett)
Ban Me Thuot	Battle Town-021-246P	Description of battle at mountain town of Ban Me Thuot; details. (Lewis Simons)
S	Viet Execution-063-907A	Brigadier General Loan, Chief of S. VNese national police, executes captured VC officer and is photographed doing the deed.
S	Note to Managing Editors-047-519P	Account of how AP newsmen and photographers cover VN developments; details.
S	War Map Summary-058 627P	Sharpest action at northernmost crisis point, Quang Tri city; action at Hue, Kontum, Qui Nhon, Ban Me Thuot, Saigon, Ben Tri, etc.
S	4 nt ld Vietnam-120 1137P	U.S. Marines and RSVN battle communists in Hue, on fourth day of coordinated nationwide assaults; statistics, details (5) (Edwin White)
S	Westmoreland-051-936P	Westmoreland predicts enemy will follow up present campaign against key S. VNese cities with drive in northern end of country; quotes, details, statistics. (George Esper)
D	Hue-101	U.S. Marines and SVN battle 1,000 VC in Hue.
S	Vietnam Echoes Spotlight-480-1045P Adv. Sun. AMs Feb 4	Similarities and dissimilarities of Khe Sanh-Dienbienphu. (William Ryan)
February 2		
S	Coffins-008-233A	Business brisk at Saigon's coffin-maker shops--the only open in Saigon; reports on Saigon fighting; details. (Peter Arnett)

NOTE: This compilation is from AP files, but may be incomplete. In some cases, due to difficulties in reproduction from the files, identifying headings, time indicators, or file numbers are incomplete or lacking.

D = Da Nang; K = Khe Sanh; S = Saigon; nt ld = night lead.

Dateline	Story	
S	Battle-018-346A	Group of VC eating in Saigon restaurant when RSVN found them; report on Saigon battle. (Edward Adams)
S	War Map Summary-033-315P	Action in Hue, Ban Me Thuot, Da Lat, Phu Cuong, Saigon, Moc Hoa, etc.
S	Note to Managing Editors-013-398A	Account of how AP newsmen and photographers are covering VN War; details.
Hue	044-708A	Four battalions of communist troops control most of Hue's streets; details. (John Lengel)
S	81-1002A	Description of American house-wife's life in Saigon during present offensive; details. (C. Simons)
Hue	Hue Description-106-1225P	Description of ancient imperial capital of Hue now under enemy attack; details.
K	Khe Sanh-004-125P	Description of Khe Sanh; details; statistics (3). (George McArthur)
S	Photographer-097-939P	UPI photographer shot five times in street fighting and is in serious condition.
S	2 nt ld Vietnam-091-1022P	Widespread fighting in fifth day of offensive in key S. VNese cities: Hue, Saigon, Da Nang; report from Radio Hanoi; quotes from President Ky; details (7). (Edwin White)
S	109-1116P	S. VNese government drops leaf-lets over Saigon and suburbs saying VC have mixed in with population.
February 3		
S	099-143A	"With eight days left for the legislature to accept or reject President Nguyn Van Thieu's declaration of martial law, the S. VNese House of Representatives is to meet Sunday."
Dau Tieng	War Vignette-077-857A	Story of Army doctor Eli Wayne Straight, right out of medical school into VN War; quotes. (George McArthur)

Dateline	Story	
S	083-929A	Sixteen-year old VN girl firing machine gun at U.S. jeeps, captured.
S	Viet Comment-093-1030A	U.S. officer says communists suffered "substantial military defeat" in Tet offensive, but have capacity for second wave of attacks; quotes.
S	Saigon Instructions 096-1040A	Saigon's residents being told, among other things, to put sleeping pills in food of VC if forced to feed them; told in leaflets.
D	1231P	Two French correspondents reported they were held captive for three hours by NVN during street fighting in Hue.
S	Golf Course-016-154P	VC fighting near Saigon's only golf course; details. (Peter Arnett)
D	Northern Vietnam-020-219P	Description of heavy fighting throughout northern S. VN; details, statistics. (George McArthur)
S	War Map Summary-044-506P	Action in Khe Sanh, Hue, Da Lat, Phan Thiet, Xuan Loc, Saigon, Ban Tre, Vinh Long.
S	Casualty Report-078-852P	U.S. command announces 14,997 enemy killed last week, more than 13 times allied killed; statistics on "bloodiest week of the war for both sides".
S	2 nt 1d Viet-Casualties-83-908P	Article explains how allied command reach casualty figures; statistics.
S	2 nt 1d Vietnam-083-919P	Allies fight house-to-house in Hue and other S. VNese cities; communists cleared from Saigon; action on northern border; details (7). (Edwin White)
S	Viet Atrocities-003-1213P	National police chief "draws his pistol and executes a VC prisoner on a Saigon street"; bitterness toward fighting reveals itself in war atrocities. (Robert Ohman)
Hue	Hue Fighting-097-1225A	Description of fighting at Hue; details. (John Lengel)

Dateline		Story
Hue	65-4	U.S. civilian Don Bradley tells of hiding in his apartment for three days while enemy fought allies outside his front door; quotes.
Hue	Hue Marines-078	Description of Marine patrol fighting in streets of Hue; details. (John Lengel)
S	Flower Truck	Description of undercover infiltration of Saigon by VC for Tet attacks. (Peter Arnett)

February 4

S	Viet Intelligence-120P	U.S. Intelligence reports that communists used 60,000 men in Tet offensive and, despite heavy casualties, have enough men to mount another attack of same size; details. (Robert Tuckman)
Hue	Hue Battle-012-158P	"S. VNese Skyraiders bombed the ancient walls of Hue's Citadel Sunday in an unsuccessful attempt to open a breach for assaulting infantrymen." (John Lengel)
S	Viet-Saigon Mood-015-228P	Describes mood in Saigon on Sunday afternoon. (Lewis Simons)
S	Missionary Rescue-032-327P	Thirty-four missionaries rescued from hilltop mission in Da Lat by U.S. shortly before it was overrun by VC, say U.S. officials; details. (Barry Kramer)
S	Civilians-40-436P	Report on how civilians suffered in recent attack reveals that people are taking brunt of war; details. (Barry Kramer)
S	Viet War Map Summary-047-528P	Action in Gio Dinh, Gio Linh, Hue, Pleiku, Da Lat, Lai Khe, Saigon, My Tho; details.
Hue	Vietnam-Marines-035-355P	Describes makeup of U.S. Marines fighting in Hue; details.
S	Viet-Prisoners-161-616P	Six execution stakes at Saigon's central market removed, leading to speculation that U.S. urged S. VNese government to be less harsh on captured VC.
S	3 nt 1d Vietnam-086-919P	N. VN launched heavy attack against Khe Sanh beginning what may be long-expected offensive in northern VN; details (9). (Edwin White).

Dateline	Story	
February 5		
S	Realities of War-022-416A	Six days of fighting make Saigon face realities of war; description. (Peter Arnett)
S	Drivers-039-538A	U.S. Mission investigating reports that two VN chauffeurs employed by U.S. Embassy, helped VC in attack against embassy.
S	Shooting Reaction-31-548A	U.S. Army officers discuss VN police chief murdering VC in Saigon street while picture is taken; quotes.
K	Personality in the News-034-634A	Feature on Colonel Lownds and his Marines at Khe Sanh, a man with "the caution of a banker and the zest of a hardened combat man."
S	048-848A	Dana Stone, UPI photographer, wounded in Hue street battle.
S	Hue Fighting-080-1046A	"Street-fighting U.S. Marines seemed to find their city legs today, smoothly maneuvering through hallways, leaping hedges, and firing all the way against an enemy that shows no sign of leaving this rubble-strewn city"; details. (John Lengel)
S	3 nt ld Vietnam-118-111P	Second week of heavy fighting all over S. VN and RSVN Army claims to have recaptured all but one Citadel of Hue; details (7). (Edwin White)
Can Tho	Mekong-003-111P	Enemy attacked 11 of Mekong Delta's 16 province capitals and 1,250 civilians killed, 3,000 wounded, 80,000-120,000 homeless; description of situation in Delta. (Barry Kramer)
K	nt ld Khe Sanh Battle-008-250P	Speculation on whether Marines will be able to hold fortress of Khe Sanh; statistics, details. (John Wheeler)
S	Vietnam War Map Summary-028-335P	Action at Khe Sanh, Hue, Saigon, My Tho, Ben Tre, Can Tho; details.
S	Viet-Refugees-080-746P	Forty-six thousand seven hundred VN civilians homeless in Saigon because of continued street fighting, a canvass of 33 refugee centers shows.

Dateline		Story
S	119-1116P	Vice President Ky warns of possibility of new VC attack on Saigon and says government plans "to arm the people to provide them the means of their own defense."
February 6		
S	Vietnam-2-EUA	"The communists pushed their biggest offensive of the war into its second week today in Saigon and Hue, defying superior allied firepower to slug it out in the devastated streets"; details, statistics; also air war.
S	033-3A	Westmoreland says "allied forces have blunted the communist offensive and 'turned the tables,' but still warned of a possible second attack wave"; quotes.
S	Cemetery-300-517A	U.S. search for VC snipers in Saigon cemetery and RSVN colonel and family slain by VC; details. (Robert Ohman)
S	Vietnam-City by City-9-544A	Details on action in various S. VNese cities.
S	Refugees-022-346A	"Tens of thousands of refugees" flee homes for safe Saigon; description of Saigon scene. (Peter Arnett)
Hue	57-741A	AP photographer Rick Merron wounded while covering Hue battle.
Hue	Battle-3-840A	U.S. Marines recapture Thua Thien province headquarters building from enemy and hoist U.S. flag; details on fighting in Hue. (John Lengel)
S	Suu-103-1112A	Antigovernmental politician Suu put into "protective custody" by Saigon police.
S	Vietnam-Recruits-104-1120A	French businessman says VC enlisted young men and women in Saigon suburb of Binh Tay and led them into battle against government troops.
S	Viet Analysis-081-242P	News analysis of allied military reaction to enemy Tet-spring offensive; details. (Peter Arnett)
S	War Map Summary-076-726P	Action in Saigon, Khe Sanh, Da Nang, Hue, Kontum, Pleiku, Ban Me Thuot, Delta, Vinh Long.

Dateline		Story
S	132-1134P	S. Korean Embassy official and Korean newspaper representative kidnaped by VC.
S	Precede Manila Plane-135-1148P	Wreckage of Navy patrol plane lost off S. VN found at sea and bodies of two of 12 crewmen recovered, say Navy headquarters.
S	3 nt ld Vietnam-136-1201A	N. VNese infantrymen with tanks and flamethrowers attack Lang Vei camp of Green Berets; details, statistics.

February 7

S	Bombing-002-125A	General Momyer, USAF, defends bombing of N. VN in interview; quotes. (George Esper)
S	Vietnam-2-837A	N. VN sends first Russian tanks into war against RSVN and U.S. at Lang Vei camp; details.
Hue	Hue Refugees-068-922A	"Amid the battle for Hue . . . thousands of homeless and hopeless civilians huddle in fear and apprehension"; description of refugee situation in Hue. (George McArthur)
S	Bombing-35-1114A	General Momyer looking back on three years of bombing against N. VN concludes losses worthwhile and effects on enemy widespread; quotes; statistics.
S	Viet-Recovery-92-224P	"With U.S. help, S. VN has launched 'Operation Recovery,' a multimillion-dollar effort to take care of the civilian victims of fighting in the cities"; statistics.
S	nt ld Vietnam Recovery-047-527P	U.S. and S. VNese join in "Operation Recovery" to care for civilian victims of VC; details.
S	Bulletin-Viet-186-726P	"Communist troops overran the Lang Vei Special Forces camp Wednesday night, with 316 allied defenders killed, wounded, or missing," reports ARVN headquarters.
S	Vietnam-Casualties-190-748P	U.S. command says 24,662 communists killed in last nine days of fighting; 2,043 allies killed, including 703 U.S.; statistics.

Dateline		Story
S	5 nt 1d Vietnam-137-1145P	Lang Vei Special Forces camp fell after siege by N. VNese with Soviet-built tanks, say U.S. officials; details on fighting in Saigon, Hue, air war in N. VN. (Edwin White)
Ben Tre	Destroyed-110-323P	"It became necessary to destroy the town to save it"; details. (Peter Arnett)
February 8		
S	Tet Leaves-041-551A	Approximately half of S. VNese Army was on Tet leave during enemy offensive, say sources; details. (Robert Tuckman)
S	Summary-749A	Brigadier General Sidle reports five major "trouble spots" where fighting still underway after 10 days: Hue, Dak To, Da Lat, Saigon, Cao Lanh.
S	Vietnam-3-841A	Long-awaited enemy offensive may have begun in northern provinces, with NVN attacking Khe Sanh and Lang Vei; details.
Hue	Hue Communists-093-946A	Intelligence sources say communists that attacked Hue came with complete dossiers of enemies to be executed or arrested; details. (George McArthur)
S	Saigon Scene-109-1150A	Scene in Saigon nine days after beginning of VC attack; battle continues. (Robert Ohman)
S	Executions-025-1005A	Vo Thanh Son, VN free-lance cameraman says while captive, VC attempted to execute him three times; quotes. (Barry Kramer)
D	War Vignettes-132-1233P	Description of helicopter mission to Khe Sanh. (George McArthur)
S	Recovery-006-129P	S. VN government allotting $6.08 million for national recovery of damages from Tet offensive, disrupting pacification effort; details. (Barry Kramer)
K	Lang Vei Survivors-032-348P	How Khe Sanh and S. VN. dealing with survivors of Lang Vei attack by enemy; details. (John Wheeler)
S	nt 1d Correspondents-051-535P	Dang Van Phuoc, AP photographer, and Howard Tuckner, NBC correspondent wounded while covering street battle in Saigon's Chinese quarter.

Dateline	Story	
Vinh Long	Mekong Delta-052-450P	Description of destruction wrought on Mekong Delta by Tet offensive; details, statistics. (Edward Adams)
S	Vietnam Document-059-614P	U.S. captures document used to indoctrinate VC; quotes.
S	068-646P	"For six days and nights, a pert blonde British Embassy employee hid under beds with 17 VN who were protecting her from communist troops."
S	War Map Summary-073-705P	Action in Saigon, Khe Sanh, Hue, Da Nang, Dak To, Da Lat, Cao Lanh; details.
S	Vietnam Coverage-314-900P	Description of hectic life of correspondent covering VN War. (Peter Arnett)
Hue	Viet Civilians-105-1059P	U.S. Marines free seven U.S. civilians who had been in communist-controlled area of Hue since city overrun.

February 9

S	Vietnam Tet-38-YA	VC "Order of the Day" captured by U.S. troops quotes Ho Chi Minh as calling for all-out attack for Tet.
K	Khe Sanh-Dienbienphu-023-353A	Comparison between battle of Dienbienphu and that at Khe Sanh; details.
S	037-537A	S. VNese government commands French reporter Francois Mazur to leave country for being "pro-VC," and "spreading false rumors and false news."
S	057-812A	U.S. revises figures showing 19 American civilians killed in city fighting beginning January 30, and another 12 or 13 are missing.
S	Vietnam-3-842A	"Helicopters landed U.S. troops on Saigon's racetrack today to help rout out die-hard VC forces as the N. VNese increased pressure against Da Nang and more communist tanks were reported sighted near Khe Sanh"; details (3).
S	Thieu-059-823A	In retaliation to heavy enemy attacks Thieu puts freeze on military discharges, recalls veterans, drafts 18- and 19-year olds ahead of schedule.

Dateline		Story
D	Urgent-051-904A	U.S. Marine private attempts to hijack jet with servicemen on leave; details.
K	Morale-51-1138A	Though casualties are high at Khe Sanh, so are spirits of the soldiers. (John Wheeler)
S	City Scene-088-138P	Scene in Saigon; contrast between dangerous suburbs and peaceful downtown. (Peter Arnett)
S	Vietnam Damage-84-857P	RSVN government official statistics of result of communist offensive: 22,000 homes destroyed, 350,000 refugees, 3,071 civilians killed, 2,295 allied military deaths, 26,621 enemy deaths.
S	3 nt ld Vietnam-097-930P	U.S. Navy jets attack airfield near Haiphong, signaling end of month-long U.S. restraint on bombing around N. VNese key cities; details, statistics on fighting, Thieu's speech, etc. (6). (Edwin White)
S	2 nt ld Refugee-126-1152P	U.S. Marines help airlift 5,000 or 6,000 refugees from Khe Sanh combat base, but many natives "went back into the hills"; details. (George Esper)
S	107-1145P	Courtney Niles, NBC electronic engineer, was killed during Hue street fighting, his company reports.
Hue	Lang Vei-015	Description of fight at Lang Vei, lost by allies due to N. VNese using Russian-made tanks. (John Wheeler)
February 10		
Hue	Americans-029-515A	At least five Americans known to have been executed by communist forces in Hue.
S	Red Bombers-031-524A	American pilots sight two, possibly three, Soviet-made bombers on N. VNese airfield, says U.S. military spokesman.
S	Vietnam-3-842A	U.S. warplanes raided Haiphong area Friday for first time in month, ending bombing restriction ordered by Johnson while U.S. looked into peace proposals; details (3).

Dateline	Story	
Dau Tieng	War Vignettes-076-1013A	Story about servicemen wounded in VN whom no one would believe. (George McArthur)
S	Viet Civilians-082-1042A	U.S. estimates of civilian losses in recent fighting trailing those of Saigon government; statistics.
S	Saigon Air View-75-1059A	Description of Saigon from the air. (John Nance)
K	Khe Sanh-007-1228P	"The Marines are digging in for the big one" at Khe Sanh; details, statistics, quotes. (Lewis Simons)
Hue	Hue Description-010-1243P	"In the rubbled wake of roaring street fighting between communist and U.S. Marines in Hue, the chief impression is that things cannot be the same again"; details. (John Lengel)
S	War Map Summary-058-445P	Action in Khe Sanh, Saigon, Hue, Da Nang, Pleiku, Tan An; details.
S	2 nt ld Vietnam-108-914P	U.S. and S. VNese troops reported killing 212 enemy in battle north of Saigon; fighting in Hue, air war, other action; details (4). (Edwin White)
February 11		
Hue	Viet-Executions-009-1220P	Communists in Hue executed 300 civilians and buried them in a mass grave south of the city, province chief says. (George McArthur)
S	Viet-Refugees-015-1251P	Informants report VC guerrillas infiltrating refugee camps filled with S. VNese who fled their homes during two weeks of Tet offensive; statistics; details. (Barry Kramer)
S	Viet-Mobilization-050-351P	S. VN begins mobilization with 65,000 new troops.
S.	Vietnam-104-915P	U.S. Marines move up Perfume River to attack N. VNese in Hue; details on fighting in Saigon, air war, (5). (George Esper)
S	125-11P	Bodies of two South Koreans executed by VC in Saigon recovered by police.

Dateline		Story
February 12		
S	Viet-Buddhists-044-715A	Militant Buddhist faction accused U.S. of slandering Buddhist church and taking advantage of the recent VC attacks in Saigon to retaliate against it.
S	Vietnam-2-837A	"Fresh U.S. Marines moved Sunday night into Hue's Citadel, where the enemy has held out nearly two weeks against S. VNese forces, and other Americans battled communist holdouts near the Saigon race track."
S	Vietnam-9-912A	"Vietnamese warplanes bombed and strafed communist forces holding out in Hue's Citadel today after U.S. Marine reinforcements were sent into the walled fortress for the first time in the two-week battle"; statistics, details of other fighting.
My Tho	Vietnam-Troops-24-1004A	President Thieu says more U.S. troops are needed to hasten victory in VN War; quotes.
Hue	Vietnam-Hue-29-1023A	"Vietnamese warplanes strafed and bombed communist forces inside the Citadel today for the first time in 10 days as the cloud cover lifted to about 4,000 feet."
K	Life in the V Ring-002-108P	Description of U.S. troops under fire; quotes. (John Wheeler)
Hue	nt ld Vietnam-Hue-031-427P	"The shadowy political arm of Vietnam's dissident Buddhist minority helped the communists when they almost overran Hue," said S. VNese officials; details, statistics. (George McArthur)
My Tho	nt ld Vietnam-Theiu-023-527P	President Thieu toured four Mekong Delta cities hit by VC offensive and said more U.S. troops needed if VN War to end soon; details, quotes. (Barry Kramer)
S	MIG-Viet-084-845P	USAF jet shot Russian-designed MIG-21 out of skies over N. VN, says military spokesman.
S	Vietnam-015-245P	News analysis of enemy strategic intentions. (Peter Arnett)

Dateline	Story	
February 13		
K	Lang Vei-015-305A	When N. VNese overran Lang Vei Special Forces camp, the garrison undoubtedly included communist agents and traitors, say military sources.
Hue	How Hue Looks-023-419A	Description of how Hue looks after weeks of constant fighting. (George McArthur)
S	031-454A	S. VNese government reimposed censorship on local newspapers, as they began publishing after two-week shutdown.
S	Vietnam-2-836A	"U.S. and South Vietnamese Marines launched a ground assault against strong enemy forces inside the walled Citadel of Hue today, but heavy small-arms, machine-gun, and rocket fire drove them back"; details (3), and other war action.
S	Boy Photographer-065-837A	Story about 12-year-old boy photographer working in Saigon with his VNese photographer father; Lo Manh Hung. (John Nance)
S	073-910A	Mass burials in Saigon.
S	Vietnam General-1006A	National police say Major General Do, high-ranking N. VNese military official, killed in Saigon.
S	Vietnam-51-1155A	"Raiding closer to Saigon than ever before, U.S. B-52 Strato-fortresses dumped tons of bombs today on suspected communist troop concentrations seven miles north-northeast of the capital."
S	Vietnam-90-215P	"Allied forces fought communist holdouts at Saigon and Hue Wednesday and braced for a new Red offensive with the prospect of swift reinforcement by 10,500 fresh U.S. Army and Marine combat troops."
K	Atheists-097-1142P	Marine chaplain finds athiests in foxholes. (John Wheeler)
S	2 nt ld Vietnam-095-10P	Allies battle enemy in Hue and Saigon and prepared for expected new offensive along DMZ, with prospect of new U.S. Army and Marine troops; details (3). (Edwin White)

Dateline		Story
February 14		
S	Casualties-033-754A	Twenty thousand civilians killed or wounded in 12 days of Tet offensive, say U.S. officials.
S	Vietnam-2-836A	"U.S. fighter-bombers shot down two MIG-17 jets today, blasting three N. VNese airfields and lent a hand to U.S. Marines trying to drive diehard communist holdouts from the walled Citadel of Hue"; details (3).
Hue	War Vignette-080-935A	Story about Marines fighting in Hue; details. (George McArthur)
S	Freighter-20-1002A	U.S. merchant ship unloading military supplies near Saigon hit by communist mortars and rifles, says U.S. command.
S	Viet-Rescue-78-1142A	Army rescues eight Roman Catholic nuns and 200 S. VNese girls.
D	Viet-Air War-024-303P	"History's most concentrated aerial bombing campaign is underway around the U.S. Marine base at Khe Sanh in an effort to break the communist siege ring, a qualified USAF source said Wednesday"; details. (John Wheeler)
S	120-1058P	Two French missionary priests killed in Hue.
S	129-1244A	Australian Embassy says Australian Keith Hyland, the "duckfeather king of S. VN," thought captured by VC in Saigon.
S	3 nt 1d Vietnam-130-1252A	"U.S. jets blasted Hue's historic Citadel for the second day Thursday after other American warplanes hit the Hanoi area with the heaviest strikes in six weeks"; details (3). (Edwin White)
February 15		
S	Casualties-024-445A	American casualties in VN War drop slightly from record total of previous week; statistics.
S	LBJ Censored-041-631A	S. VN censors Johnson's remarks on his willingness to meet with N. VN on peace talks. (Barry Kramer)

Dateline	Story	
S	Vietnam-3-847A	"Heavy fighting continued inside the historic walled Citadel at Hue today, the number of U.S. combat planes lost in the air war against N. VN reached 800, the U.S. command reported another battle just outside Hue, and enemy mortar fire around Khe Sanh killed 14 U.S. Marines and wounded 135."
Hue	Hue Bridge-068-914A	S. VNese soldiers removed pontoon bridge which was the only remaining connection across the Perfume River which divides Hue.
S	Vietnam-27-1014A	"U.S. Marine jets bombed the massive brownstone walls of Hue's Citadel for the first time today and American destroyers kept up an off-shore bombardment of pockets in the ancient city where N. VNese remnants held out for a sixteenth day"' details (3).
S	nt ld Mistake Bombing-044-113P	Forty persons killed when U.S. planes mistakenly dropped 50 tons of bombs outside a target zone near Saigon; details. (Peter Arnett)
K	Khe Sanh-041-425P	U.S. Marines at Khe Sanh were advised that N. VNese in area could possibly be supported by aircraft in expected battle; statistics. (John Lengel)
K	Why Khe Sanh-073-658P	Reasons why Khe Sanh is so militarily and psychologically important in VN War.
S	Vietnam Tape-083-1004A	U.S. Mission releases translation of recorded tape which VC planned to play over government radio station in a propaganda phase of Tet offensive; quotes.
S	Viet Aid-130-1050P	At least seven nations sending supplies to S. VN following appeal by Foreign Office for aid to civilian victims, says U.S. Mission.
S	2 nt ld Vietnam-126-1131P	"U.S. and Vietnamese Marines--after edging 200 yards Thursday through rubble of a land, sea, and air bombardment--sought Friday to tighten the noose around 800 N. VNese holding part of Hue's once-majestic Citadel for the seventeenth day"; details on action in Saigon, Khe Sanh, statistics on casualties, etc.

Dateline		Story
February 16		
S	038-603A	Twenty-five U.S. civilians killed in Tet offensive, said U.S. Consulate.
S	Vietnam Delta-070-925A	U.S. command said U.S. Infantrymen are in action 82 miles south of Saigon, their deepest penetration of Mekong Delta in the war.
Hue	Refugees-072-935A	Description of refugees in Hue--in their pitiful state; quotes. (Lewis Simons)
S	Citadel-079-1013A	Past battles of Hue's Citadel--history.
K	Khe Sanh-006-125P	Quotes from and description of Khe Sanh battle camp; quotes. (John Lengel)
S	2 nt ld Vietnam-102-914P	For second time, enemy tanks spotted near S. VN northern frontier; communist forces for eighteenth day hold Hue's Citadel; details (3), statistics, action in Quang Tri. (Edwin White)
February 17		
S	Vietnam-3-845A	U.S. planes aim 1.5 million pounds of explosives at enemy threatening Khe Sanh, says U.S. command.
S	064-902A	U.S. officials say some cases of bubonic plague found in cities hit during Tet offensive.
Hue	Hue Fighting-067-917A	Enemy force of 500 in Hue's Citadel beaten back another 200 yards; details. (George McArthur)
S	Attack-61-1227P	"A series of explosions rocked Saigon early Sunday and U.S. military officers said Tan Son Nhut Air Base in the city's outskirts 'apparently is under attack'"; details.
Hue	Buried Marine-078-651P	Story about Marine buried under street rubble for six hours in Hue.
Hue	Hue Press-51-935P	Newsmen from all over the world begin pouring into Hue.

Dateline		Story
S	Tan Son Nhut-112-1036P	One U.S. airman killed, 60 wounded in rocket and mortar attack on Saigon's Tan Son Nhut Air Base.
S	Tabulation-115-1103P	City-by-city run-down on second wave of communist attacks; details, statistics.
S	5 nt 1d Vietnam-111-1110P	"Communist shells hit Saigon and 30 other S. VNese cities Sunday in coordinated second-wave attack predicted to follow Tet offensive; details, statistics. (Edwin White)

February 18

Hue	Firepower-010-1237P	U.S. command decides to use all necessary firepower to rout enemy from S. VNese cities and take bad publicity for property destruction as an unavoidable by-product.
Binh Loi Bridge	Vietnam-Prisoner-033-322P	"With the death toll mounting daily, human life is being snuffed out as casually as candlelight"; description of fighting in Saigon; details, quotes. (Peter Arnett)
S	War Map-056-533P	Run-down of action in towns and military installations hit during second enemy offensive: Khe Sanh, Hue, Phan Thiet, Kontum, Saigon, Cat Lai, Bien Hoa Air Base, Ben Tre.
Hue	ICC-Viet-080-728P	ICC field team is casualty of communist attack on Hue.
S	2 1d Vietnam Roundup-105-1030P	Communist rocket hit Saigon airport terminal filled with U.S. servicemen, killing one, wounding 21; details; action in Saigon, Khe Sanh, Hue, etc. (George Esper)
S	Vietnam-Political-015	More than 200 S. VNese politicians --many strongly opposed to present government--met to form anticommunist front.
S	Evaluation-058-556P	Pike analysis of VC intentions and objectives at Tet.

February 19

S	Airport-036-550A	Description of scene of Tan Son Nhut airport when it was hit by enemy fire. (Barry Kramer)

Dateline		Story
S	Vietnam-2-836A	"Battle-weary U.S. Marines moving behind a protective umbrella of artillery pushed 400 yards through the rubbled ruins of Hue's Citadel today to the brink of one of the last communist strongholds in VN's old capital"; details (3); fighting in Saigon.
S	Viet-Surrender-075-938A	VC who surrendered during Tet offensive said they had been sent into battle with assurances that S. VNese people and government troops would help them "liberate the country from the American imperialists."
S	Viet-Appeal-46-1137A	Westmoreland appeals for contributions to relief funds for VN victims of enemy offensive.
S	097-1142A	Alvin Webb, AP correspondent, wounded in Hue.
Quang Ngai	Gas-098-1148A	Riot-control gas used by allied forces in S. VN can cause deaths, but rarely does. (John Lengel)
Hue	Citadel-006-133P	History and description of Hue's Citadel. (Lewis Simons)
S	2 nt ld Vietnam-099-943P	"Fighting that stemmed from the first two punches of the communists' winter-spring offensive was fading Tuesday and allied commanders, trying to anticipate a possible third blow, turned their attention to the encircled U.S. Marine base at Khe Sanh": description of heavy war action throughout Saigon in second enemy offensive; details. (Edwin White)
Hue	Hue Battle-138-1217A	Description of Hue on night of Tet offensive. (George McArthur)
February 20		
S	Civilian Casualties-20-1023A	VN officials say number of civilian casualties in offensive approach 14,000.
Hue	Hue Patrols-099-1104A	S. VNese military chief of Hue ordered looters shot on sight and announced public executions of arrested enemy agents; details. (George McArthur)

Dateline	Story	
S	Mobilization-006-118P	S. VNese in face of intensified enemy action, plans to increase forces by 65,000 men; details. (Barry Kramer)
S	2 nt ld Vietnam-101-542P	U.S. kill 123 VC in Saigon's suburbs; action in Mekong Delta, Hue, across S. VN. Details (5). (Edwin White)
Hue	nt ld Chaplain-085-727P	Story about U.S. Army chaplain serving in Hue; details. (George McArthur)
S	nt ld Viet Political-041-922P	S. VN's government's reaction to Tet offensive shows divisive politics. (George Esper)
S	Viet-Air War-112-934P	USAF bombed near Red China's border to bomb N. VNese railroad.
S	Pershing Precede New York-098-10P	Grandson of late General Pershing killed in action while leading his platoon in search for missing soldier, Army discloses.
D	Citadel-1035P	Commander of Marines in VN, Lieutenant General Cushman, Jr., says fighting to capture Hue's Citadel could go on for weeks.
Hue	142-1238A	"Remember the Citadel" is new battle cry of U.S. soldiers in S. VN.
February 21		
S	Vietnam-3-841A	U.S. Marines bomb Hue for first time in five days.
S	Vietnam-8-954A	"U.S. Marine jets returned to the battle of Hue for the first time in five days today, raining bombs, rockets, and napalm into communist troops dug in among a row of shanties just outside the fortressed Citadel's south wall"; details.
Hue	Hue Trials-1008A	Lieutenant General Lam orders military court to try communist agents captured in Hue.
K	Viet-Flag-080-1103A	Each day Marines raise U.S. flag on Hill 881, in middle of war-torn Khe Sanh; details. (John Wheeler)
S	Vietnam Political-022-229P	U.S. seeking explanation from Thieu administration for arrest of three prominent antigovernment politicians; details. (Barry Kramer)

Dateline		Story
K	Viet-Wounded-027-304P	Description of rescue of wounded Marine; details. (John Wheeler)
S	2 nt ld Vietnam-096-610P	Battles in Saigon suburbs as U.S. troops clash with VC believed to be gathering for another attack; fighting in Hue, Khe Sanh; details (5).
S	117-954P	U.S. command lists Rev. McDonigal, Army chaplain, as missing in action, not dead.
S	War Spotlights-395-1152P	Sum-up report of scope of Tet offensive; details, statistics. (Peter Arnett)
S	118-1249P	Strict curfew and lack of storage space in warehouses causing major backup of ships in Saigon's commercial port.
February 22		
S	Bulletin-021-415A	U.S. command reports U.S. planes attacked Hanoi Radio's transmitter for first time in war.
S	010-753A	Aircraft carrier *Enterprise* returns to S. VN after being diverted to Korean waters because of *Pueblo* crisis.
S	Vietnam-Political-064-812A	At least nine more persons arrested in S. VNese government's current political crackdown making number of opponents seized to 12; details. (Barry Kramer)
Hue	Fighting-007-915A	"Taking casualties nearly every foot of the way, U.S. Marines stormed their way to a portion of the south wall of Hue's Citadel today after winding out the last pockets of resistance in their sector"; details, quotes. (John Lengel)
Hue	079-925A	One of biggest communist political figures taken was captured in Hue.
S	Economy-110-1213P	Retail food prices fell more than 30 percent in Saigon indicating that food is flowing more freely into the capital.

Dateline	Story	
S	nt 1d Vietnam-Roundup-006-138P	U.S. Marines take south wall of Citadel "against crumbling enemy resistance," while outside city U.S. Marines cut supply routes; action in Saigon, Khe Sanh, Cu Chi, Lai Khe; statistics, details (5). (Edwin White)
K	nt 1d Khe Sanh-017-224P	Report on tactics used at Khe Sanh, and military leader's reactions to them; details. (John Wheeler)
S	War Map Summary-086-8P	Action in Khe Sanh, Saigon, Mekong Delta.
S	Casualties-025-905P	Number of U.S. killed in VN War climbed to all-time high of 548 last week, and 2,347 wounded, says U.S. command; statistics.
S	Wheeler-108-1005P	General Wheeler arrives for visit in S. VN to convey to Westmoreland "the great confidence" placed in him by Johnson.
S	Threat-033	U.S. sources say elements of two enemy divisions still are menacing Saigon and some forces are within six miles of capital.

February 23

S	65-827A	S. VNese government banned *Newsweek* magazine for second straight week because of an article critical of the government.
S	Vietnam-3-839A	"N. VN threw a new battalion of troops at Hue's Citadel Thursday, and on another front sent their heaviest artillery barrage in two weeks thundering down on the U.S. Marine combat base at Khe Sanh; details (4).
S	Vietnam-78-1248P	U.S. command announced a detach-ment of U.S. air cavalrymen moved into Hue to help Marines and S. VNese troops routing out enemy.
S	Battle Plan-83-105P	Captured enemy officer gives S. VN what he says is outline of Hanoi's master plan in current offensive.

Dateline		Story
S	4 ld Airport Shelling- 071-1020P	VC rockets crashed into Saigon's Tan Son Nhut Air Base killing four U.S. servicemen, wounding 31, destroying nearby houses; details (4).
S	Air War-115-1026P	"American bombers swarmed over the Vinh area of N. VN Friday and pounded the city's airfield and two railroad bridges."
S	4 nt ld Vietnam-123- 1059P	U.S. command reports S. VNese troops take Hue's Citadel; details, fighting in Saigon, Khe Sanh, etc. (Edwin White)
Hue	Hue-005-1116P	"After 24 days of savage fighting, which still continues. . . , the population of Hue is slowly awakening like a sick man still in mortal peril."
Hue	Flag-127-1127P	S. VNese soldiers raise Saigon flag over Hue's Citadel.
S	Viet-Politics-084	A former Presidential candidate, labor leaders, and militant Buddhist monks arrested by S. VNese government in its crack- down on political opposition.
February 24		
S	Refugees-016-246A	Seven-ten percent of S. VNese people homeless, so government faces staggering refugee problem; statistics, details. (William Ryan)
S	Tan Son Nhut-041-552A	Description of air base Tan Son Nhut under fire; quotes. (Barry Kramer)
S	Wheeler-044-688A	General Wheeler flew to Da Nang to confer with commanders directing operations at Khe Sanh and elsewhere in north.
S	Vietnam-3-840A	S. VNese forces recaptured palace grounds of Hue after 25 days, but fighting continues in other parts of Citadel; details (3).
Hue	Hue Palace-079-945A	Description of damage done on Citadel in Hue. (George McArthur)
K	Khe Sanh-044-1217P	"North Vietnamese gunners chipped away at Khe Sanh's combat base and it's 5,000 U.S. Marine defenders again Saturday, not overwhelming them, not destroying them--just

Dateline		Story
		chipping away"; description of Khe Sanh scene, quotes. (Lewis Simons)
S	Viet-Hue-049-426P	Reason why it is taking so long for allied forces to drive enemy out of Hue's Citadel. (George Esper)
S	Vietnam Pacification-050-435P	U.S. official conceded pacification program has suffered a "con- siderable setback" from Tet of- fensive; statistics, details. (William Ryan)
S	2 nt ld Vietnam-096-926P	U.S. command says U.S. airplanes attacked Hanoi's river port for first time in war, as one of several strikes around N. VNese capital; details (4), action at Hue, Khe Sanh, Saigon. (Edwin White)
February 25		
S	Vietnam-Wheeler-023-232P	General Wheeler left for Washington with recommendation to Johnson for increase in U.S. troops.
Hue	Hue-024-241P	"S. VNese troops cooked their rice meals in peace Sunday on the steps of the old imperial throne room in Hue's Citadel, but U.S. Marines fought stiff skirmishes with N. VNese along an in- filtration route south of the city"; details, statistics. (John Lengel)
S	Viet-Bombers-077-830P	U.S. bombers attack major N. VNese railroad yard near Haiphong, U.S. command reports; details.
S	Vietnam-019-845P	U.S. battles 500 VC in Mekong Delta who tried to overrun U.S. patrol base, seize heavy artillery, and block rice line from Mekong Delta to Saigon; details, air war, Khe Sanh, etc. (3). (George Esper)
S	Westmoreland-003-123P	Westmoreland interview. (Wes Gallagher)
February 26		
S	Westmoreland-003-129A	Westmoreland says more U.S. troops needed in VN; quotes, details (5). (Robert Tuckman) (Incomplete)

Dateline	Story	
S	With Westmoreland-031-453A	Recent visitor to Hanoi says N. VNese are convinced of their victories in Tet offensive. (Barry Kramer)
S	Vietnam-2-835A	N. VNese troops ambushed U.S. platoon near Khe Sanh; details (3).
S	Clampdown-14-947A	Westmoreland's headquarters beginning new policy to withhold more information from press.
S	Viet-Komer-080-1036A	Komer, head of pacification program, is going to Washington for personal report to Johnson.
S	Vietnam-95-156P	N. VNese troops "mauled a U.S. Marine patrol and blocked a rescue platoon 800 yards outside the combat base at Khe Sanh today."
Hue	Hue-015-210P	Description of civilian victims returning to destroyed homes in Hue. (John Lengel)
S	Viet-Korean-050-516P	Detonator from mine exploded near entrance to S. Korean Embassy in Saigon.
S	Viet-Indemnification-055-533P	S. VNese government will pay indemnification for civilian casualties, ranging from $8.40 for a wounded child to $33.60 for dead adult.
S	nt ld Viet-Withhold-058-720P	U.S. command restricting military information to be available to press; details.
S	Airfield-176-741P	VC shell Saigon's Tan Son Nhut Air Base.
S	2 nt ld Vietnam-094-925P	U.S. Green Berets destroy one of three communist armored vehicles near Saigon; action in Saigon, Khe Sanh; details (7). (Edwin White)
S	Shakeup-106-955P	Two of S. VN's four Corps commanders replaced in the highest level shakeup in S. VNese army in two years, says official spokesman; details. (Barry Kramer)
February 27		
S	022-405A	Thieu and other top officials have narrow escape as four-engine plane has engine failure.

Dateline	Story	
S	Vietnam Today I-065-818A	What is outlook a month after Tet attacks? Peter Arnett and William Ryan write first of three-part analysis, cite Saigon's "atmosphere of fear and foreboding."
K	Waiting-070-854A	Getting out of Khe Sanh almost as hard as staying. Feature on airlift. (Lewis Simons)
S	Viet-Information-073-907A	General Sidle says new policy of withholding information applies only to enemy attacks on fixed U.S. bases.
Hue	Hue-074-913A	Communist gunners blow up U.S. ammunition boat in only action around retaken city. Sixty percent of Hue's buildings reported damaged, say U.S. officials. (Robert Ohman)
S	Vietnam Today II-075-923A	Second Arnett-Ryan situationer says "Communists still press the initiative. . . . Thousands of U.S. troops are bogged down in the stalemate of the Khe Sanh and [DMZ] sectors. Bloody battles are expected. . . . The Red offensive has forced the allies to the defensive. . . . ARVN performance [has been] uneven at best. . . . [Pacification] set back least 18 months."
K	Khe Sanh Ambush-080-954A	Over-eager Marine lieutenant leads platoon patrol into communist ambush. (John Wheeler)
S	Vietnam Today III-083-1037A	Third Arnett-Ryan situationer says Tet attacks brought "fresh threat" to economy. Corruption still bad. "There is little safety anywhere in Vietnam."
Hue	Hue-005-118P	When N. VNese forces overran Hue, the city's administrative structure vanished "like a punctured soap bubble," complicating recovery. (George McArthur)
S	Vietnam 2 nt 1d-092-927P	Shelling of Bien Hoa airport and Tan Son Nhut "lent support to fears of another Red drive" on Saigon. Lengthy war wrap-up. (Edwin White)

Dateline		Story
February 28		
S	Vietnam Roundup-020-332A	"Fear of a second big VC drive into Saigon grew today as communist gunners shelled the nearby Bien Hoa air base and other military targets around the S. VNese capital"; action Dak To, Kam Ty, N. VN air; details. (George Esper)
S	Vietnam Roundup-034-525A	"Four thousand U.S. paratroopers from the 82nd Airborne Division have arrived in VN to bolster allied defenses," says U.S. command.
Chu Lai	056-731A	82nd leaves U.S. quickly and are rushed to VN.
S	Vietnam-3-839A	"Guided by radar, U.S. air force fighter-bombers flew through overcast skies today to attack targets in the Hanoi area for the second day in a row"; details (3).
S	Vietnam-Thieu-101-1103A	S. VNese President Thieu places permanent ban on VN nightclubs and dance halls.
S	With Viet-French-098-845P	S. VN's Foreign Minister Do says N. VN would have to say how it planned to de-escalate war before bombing could be stopped.
S	3 nt ld Vietnam-113-857P	N. VN shot down U.S. helicopter near Khe Sanh: 22 U.S. servicemen were killed and one wounded; other skirmishes; details (5). (Robert Tuckman)
S	1120P	Col. Felix "Doc" Blanchard, an Army football great, logged six missions over N. VN since reporting February 13.
S	Vietnam Outlook-041-405P	Allies being kept jittery, but there is also the possibility that VC are suffering severe manpower problem; details. (William Ryan)
February 29		
S	Vietnam Roundup-020-348A	"South Vietnamese Army troops uncovered a mass grave containing about 100 bodies on eastern outskirts of Hue today"; details on other war action. (George Esper)

Dateline		Story
K	Bombing-014-351A	Description of "calm before battle" at Khe Sanh. (John Wheeler)
S	Casualties-025-425A	U.S. command reports American casualties last week second highest in VN War, with 470 killed and 2,675 wounded; statistics (3).
S	Vietnam Roundup-023-521A	"Radio-guided American bombers attacked three vital targets near Hanoi and Haiphong Wednesday, including a N. VNese Army barracks hit for the first time in the war, the U.S. command announced today: details of action in air, statistics on casualties, Thu Duc, etc. (3). (George Esper)
S	La Note-53-820A	Sixty-five American civilians dead, captured, or unaccounted for since Tet; statistics.
Hue	War Vignettes-092-1045A	Medic performs amputation with hacksaw; story about Dr. Stephen Bernie operating in Hue during battle.
S	Arrests-097-1106A	Arrest of 20 Saigon government opponents had approval of Cabinet, say informed sources. (Barry Kramer)
S	nt ld Casualties-011-125P	More U.S. servicemen have been killed in action during last four weeks than during all first five years of U.S. involvement in VN War; statistics. (Robert Tuckman)
S	Shelling-142-441P	Tan Son Nhut Air Base near Saigon shelled again.
S	2 nt ld Vietnam-091-909P	U.S. Navy battles with N. VNese trawlers attempting to land munitions on S. VNese coast; details (4); statistics on casualties, Khe Sanh, etc. (Lewis Simons)
S	Immolation-101-940P	Buddhist layman burned himself to death as gesture of prayer for VN's suffering people, say police.
S	Plague-006	Sixty cases of bubonic plague reported in Tay Ninh province northwest of Saigon; three have died.
S	Giap Strategy-069-642P	(William Ryan)

Dateline		Story

March 1

S	Vietnam Roundup-018-339A	"U.S. and S. VNese naval forces racked up their biggest score of the war today with the destruction of three 100-foot enemy trawlers which the U.S. command said were loaded with guns and ammunition"; quotes; action in Saigon, Central Highlands, Mekong Delta. (George Esper)
K	Vietnam Roundup-036-530A	"More than 500 N. VNese soldiers attacked the Khe Sanh combat base through the fog before dawn today"; details, statistics, action with trawlers, in air war. (Peter Arnett)
S	068-815A	Lieutenant General Rosson named deputy commander of U.S. forces fighting in S. VNese northern provinces.
S	Vietnam Political-080-935A	S. VNese House of Representatives reject President Thieu's bid to promulgate decrees on economic and financial affairs for one year.
K	Newsmen-092-1031A	Russ Bensley, CBS producer, and John Smith, cameraman, injured while filming at Khe Sanh.
S	nt ld Vietnam Political-003-112P	Effect of martial law on S. VN: question raised in light of President Thieu's bid to impose it for a year, which was defeated in S. VN's House of Representatives; details. (William Ryan)
K	Khe Sanh Hills-011-157P	Description of life at Khe Sanh, "under increasing pressure of raids and bombardments and [where] the cruelest punishment of all is being taken by U.S. Marines surrounding the main base" in hillside protective outposts; details. (John Wheeler)
S	3 nt ld Vietnam-085-837P	"Heavy fighting developed at opposite ends of the Demilitarized Zone Friday, with U.S. Marines and S. VNese units battling communist troops near the South China Sea coast and government soldiers repelling an assault on the Marine base at Khe Sanh"; details (5), statistics. (Lewis Simons)

Dateline	Story	
S	Air War-093-930P	Navy jets strike several targets in and around Hanoi and Haiphong.

March 2

S	Vietnam Roundup-019-349A	"Allied forces fought heavy battles at both ends of S. VN's northern frontier Friday and reported killing 330 enemy soldiers, many of them with a sheet of machine-gun fire from armored vehicles"; air war, details, statistics. (George Esper)
S	047-648A	Saigon newspaper called for an invasion of N. VN.
S	Trawlers-049-701A	Salvage crews recover weapons, munitions, and 14 dead from three enemy trawlers destroyed along S. VN's coast; details.
S	051-712A	Two millions pounds of food and supplies arrive in Hue after a month of fighting.
S	058-762A	*Newsweek* magazine says S. VN banned it for third straight week for publishing articles critical of government.
S	Viet-Allies-75-935A	Australian, New Zealand and S. Korean forces have killed more than 1,000 enemy in three separate operations since mid-January, say allied announcements; statistics.
S	Communist Weapons-083-1020A	Tet offensive shows good enemy weapons in abundance; report of enemy arsonal; statistics. (George McArthur)
S	Vietnam-ARVN-006-1219P	U.S. military sources say it is now necessary to begin preparing S. VNese army to fight its own war; present state of ARVN. (William Ryan)
S	nt ld Vietnam-010-1237P	"Fighter bombers from the U.S. Air Force, Navy, and Marine Corps joined massive B-52 Stratofortresses Saturday in pounding N. VNese concentrations ringing the Marine combat base at Khe Sanh"; details, radio broadcasts, action in Hue, Saigon. (Lewis Simons)

Dateline		Story
S	Black Market-019-145P	Tet offensive put crimp in Saigon's black market because of martial law and curfews.
S	2 nt ld Vietnam-079-857P	"U.S. B-52 bombers hit at N. VNese positions only six-tenths of a mile from Khe Sanh," and Marine, Navy, Army action to help Marines at Khe Sanh; details (3). (Lewis Simons)
March 3		
K	Viet-Tunnels-1259P	U.S. Marines at Khe Sanh using divining rods to detect enemy tunnels; details, quotes. (Peter Arnett)
S	4-427P	Navy destroyer USS *Hull* under attack from N. VNese shore batteries four times in last 10 days.
S	2 nt ld Vietnam-079-857P	"U.S. B-52 bombers hit at N. VNese positions only six-tenths of mile from Khe Sanh combat base." (Lewis Simons)
S	Vietnam-087-1134P	"A 200-man communist force killed 48 U.S. troops and wounded 28 in an ambush along a key highway nine miles north of Saigon, says U.S. command; action at Khe Sanh, Da Nang, air war, Mekong Delta; details (5). (George Esper)
S	5 nt ld Vietnam-121	"The VC made their first attack of the war on the big U.S. Air Base at Cam Ranh Bay late Monday night." (Lewis Simons)
March 4		
S	Vietnam Roundup-024-400A	"U.S. Marines and air cavalrymen smashed into communist troops Sunday in a series of battles in the northern sector of S. VN and reported killing nearly 300 of the enemy"; action at Da Nang, Khe Sanh, Duc Duc, Saigon, Ban Me Thuot; statistics, details. (George Esper).
S	Embassy-031-451A	American security officials trying to learn if any VC still on U.S. Embassy payroll, are being thwarted by S. VNese police. (Barry Kramer)

Dateline	Story	
S	Vietnam Roundup-041-552A	"U.S. Marines and air cavalrymen smashed into communist troops Sunday in a series of battles in northern sector"; action in Kontum, air war. (George Esper)
S	061-803A	CBS television producer Russ Bensley wounded at Khe Sanh, wounded again when his hospital at Da Nang was hit by enemy rockets.
S	062-806A	Rate of enemy defections to S. VN is continuing low, say government figures.
S	Vietnam Roundup-075-952A	"Communist forces sent hundreds of rockets and mortars slamming into allied air bases, command posts, and other installations today, and seized a hospital run by an American woman doctor"; details; statistics. (George Esper)
S	Tan Son Nhut-079-1025A	Description of Saigon's Tan Son Nhut Airport.
Landing Zone Gator	Airborne-096-1131A	508th Airborne Infantry, 3rd Brigade, 82nd Division complaining because of unprecedented second tour of duty in VN; quotes. (John Lengel)
S	Viet-Buddhists-090-1133A	S. VNese national police produced tape recording and text of communist broadcast in attempt to link militant Buddhist Thich Tri Quang with VC.
S	Vietnam-94-210P	"Planes and guns roared around the edges of Saigon early Tuesday after communist forces mounted their heaviest coordinated attacks in two weeks throughout the country."
Cu Chi	Ambush-015-214P	Description of ambush on Charley Company on March 2; quotes, details, statistics. (Albert Chang)
Kontum	nt ld Vietnam-Hospital-026-329P	Description of VC takeover of hospital run by U.S. woman doctor; quotes, details.
S	Australian-092-947P	American-born wife of Australian businessman, Keith Hyland, appeals to VC to free him.

Dateline		Story
S	096-957P	S. VNese militia on operation near Hue uncovers one ton TNT with mark "Made in Poland," say military sources.
S	2 nt ld Vietnam-008-1022P	"Communist forces shelled more allied military bases and airfields Wednesday for the third day in a row"; fighting in Tuy Hoa, Lai Thieu. (Lewis Simons)
D	110-1115P	Nineteen S. VNese civilians killed, 88 wounded by VN in northern 1st Corps military area Monday, military sources report; statistics.

March 5

S	Vietnam Roundup-013-324A	"The VC fired some of their biggest rockets Monday night into the Cam Ranh Bay base, once considered the safest spot in S. VN, and then continued widespread shelling of provincial capitals and military bases for the second day today"; details, fighting at Tuy Hoa, Saigon, Lai Khe, Khe Sanh. (George Esper)
S	Vietnam Roundup-030-521A	VC invaded provincial capital and shelled 40 other towns and military installations in second day of widespread coordinated mortar and rocket attacks; fighting at Cam Ranh Bay, Ca Mau, Saigon; details. (George Esper) (Incomplete)
S	054-716A	U.S. Mission says 57 American civilians killed, captured, or missing as result of Tet offensive; statistics.
S	2 ld Vietnam Roundup-063-828A	"Three hundred N. VNese troops invaded a provincial capital at the southern end of VN today and seized the hospital, but government troops drove them out of the city after a day-long fight"; details, statistics. (George Esper)
S	Cam Ranh Bay-078-954A	Description of VC attack on Cam Ranh Bay, thought to be invulnerable. (Lewis Simons)

Dateline	Story	
K	Khe Sanh Special Report-089-1047A	Description of typical day at Khe Sanh; description, details, quotes. (Peter Arnett)
S	231P	"The Reds Monday mounted their heaviest coordinated attacks across VN in two weeks"; details. (Lewis Simons)
Phu Bai	Vietnam Outlook-156-640P	Battle for Khe Sanh and other allied positions south of DMZ will end in enemy defeat, says senior U.S. military source.
Kontum	Hospital-085-1028P	Description of battle where VC took Dr. Patricia Smith's hospital; quotes. (Barry Kramer)

March 6

S	Vietnam Roundup-017-304A	VC shelled 10 allied bases and airfields, but U.S. command said damage and casualties light; action at Loc Ninh, Ca Mau, Da Nang, Con Thien, Khe Sanh, Dong Ha; details.
S	029-415A	Hiromichi Mine, Japanese photographer for UPI, killed, 11th in VN War.
S	038-540A	U.S. releasing three N. VNese sailors, says U.S. Mission, in exchange for the three U.S. airmen freed by N. VN last month.
S	Target-043-615A	Senior U.S. officer says he believes Hue and not Khe Sanh is next enemy objective; quotes. (Robert Tuckman)
S	Command Change-44-640A	Westmoreland says upset that accounts of his command change in northern S. VN interpreted his actions as reflecting disappointment with U.S. Marines there; quotes.
S	Vietnam Roundup-056-717A	"U.S. forces killed 110 enemy soldiers in three sharp clashes in the past 24 hours," U.S. spokesmen reported today; details on war; statistics. (George Esper)
S	Award-77-955A	Col. William Moncrief, Jr., received National Order 5th Class, highest S. VN award ever given to foreigner, for his contributions to civilian health program.

Dateline		Story
S	Communist Weapons-083-1020A	Description of fine arsenal of VN communists; details. (George Esper)
S	Tet Losses-089-1022A	U.S. officers say N. VN and VN lost 50,000 dead from Tet offensive; statistics. (Robert Tuckman)
S	2 ld Vietnam Roundup-090-1029A	"Communist gunners besieging Khe Sanh shot down a U.S. Air Force C-123 transport"; statistics. (George Esper)
S	Vietnam-86-219P	Helicopters hunt for 49 Americans from C-123 transport shot down by enemy near Khe Sanh.
Hue	Hue Aftermath-35-355P	Description of Hue after battle, "a city bled to death," quotes, details (3). (William Ryan)
S	2 nt ld Vietnam-072-810P	USAF transport with 49 aboard shot down by N. VN near Khe Sanh; all aboard presumed killed; action at Da Nang, Ban Me Thuot, etc., details (95). (Lewis Simons)
VN	AP News Digest-011	Chief of U.S. advisory team says in private reports to foreign aid agency that U.S. should intervene to stamp out corruption in Saigon government.

March 7

Vinh Long	Delta-001-112A	Description after tour of Mekong Delta and three major cities; details. (George McArthur)
VN	AP News Digest-011-227A	Five weeks after Tet offensive, Mekong Delta is only beginning to recover; other war action.
S	Vietnam-Political-020-339A	Some members of S. VNese House of Assembly are trying to line up support for motion of no confidence in government.
S	Vietnam Roundup-023-358A	Near-record 542 Americans killed in S. VN last week; statistics; air war, action at Con Thien, Khe Sanh, politics in Saigon; details (5). (George Esper)
S	Vietnam-Political-033-511A	President Thieu's request for additional special powers in face of communist offensive, turned down by S. VNese Senate. (Barry Kramer)

Dateline	Story	
S	Vietnam-Korea Casualties-083-1030A	Number of American combat casualties in VN almost equal to U.S. losses in Korean War; statistics.
K	Khe Sanh Special Report-089-1047A	Typical day in Khe Sanh; quotes, details. (Peter Arnett)
S	nt ld Vietnam Political-023-238P	Rebuff by Senate and petition circulating among representatives indicate growing political trouble for President Thieu. (Barry Kramer)
K	Hoodlum Priest-037-420P	Story about Rev. Walter Driscoll, the "Hoodlum Priest" of Khe Sanh; details. (Peter Arnett)
S	Command-094-908P	Westmoreland announces setting up new headquarters leaving U.S. Marines in command of S. VN's northern provinces, but Army general installed to direct operations at Khe Sanh and Hue, describes unique command change.
S	2 nt ld Vietnam-104-1051P	Tet offensive make U.S. casualties for first nine weeks of 1968 three times that of 1967; action near Dong Ha, Tuy Hoa, Khe Sanh, air war; statistics. (George Esper)

March 8

Vinh Long	Delta-112A	Effect of Tet offensive on towns and countryside of Mekong Delta; details. (George McArthur)
S	Corruption-008-209A	Group of politicians says it will propose publicly that program be launched to combat corruption in VNese government; details on corruption. (William Ryan)
S	Vietnam Roundup-015-314A	Lt. Gen. William Rosson in charge of defense of northernmost sector of S. VN, including Khe Sanh; action at Dong Ha, air war, Bunker on pacification; details. (George Esper)
S	Vietnam Roundup-032-643A	U.S. command reports savage fighting below DMZ and announced appointment of Lieutenant General Rosson as commander of northern frontier; details, action at Khe Sanh, Dong Ha. (George Esper)

Dateline		Story
S	Political-063-844A	"A motion to discuss whether to vote on a motion of no confidence against government will be placed on the agenda of South Vietnam's House of Representatives." (Barry Kramer)
S	Personality in the News-060-648P	Biography of William Rosson, new commander of northern section of S. VN and an Army Lieutenant General; details. (C. Doe)
S	070-725P	Twenty-three countries and international organizations have answered S. VN's call for emergency aid following Tet offensive.
S	nt ld Vietnam-007-957P	"South Vietnamese Rangers starred again Friday in defense of the U.S. Marine base at Khe Sanh"; action at Dong Ha, Cua Viet River Valley, Hue, air war, details, statistics. (Lewis Simons)
S	Dienbienphu Special Report-A103-1211P-Adv. Wed. PMs Mar. 13	Dienbienphu anniversary. (William Ryan)

March 9

S	Rosson-014-317A	Explains significance of making Army Lieutenant General Rosson head of critical area which before was considered Marine Corps domain; details. (Robert Tuckman)
S	Vietnam Roundup-018-409A	VN ground war scattered small clashes but U.S. bombers pounded suspected enemy positions near Khe Sanh and Hue, "now considered likely targets for a major enemy assault"; details. (George Esper)
S	Vietnam Roundup-5A	"Pouring out of a sheet of machine-gun fire from advancing armored personnel carriers, U.S. infantrymen tore into communist troops along the coastal lowlands below Da Nang today." (George Esper)
S	Wirephoto-029-524A	Robert Ellison, news photographer, listed as missing after his plane was shot down near Khe Sanh.

Dateline		Story
S	042-632A	U.S. Mission says 139 VN civilians were killed last week in VC terror incidents to bring toll since Tet to 5,831; statistics.
S	050-711A	Navy says VC had been taxing boats passing on Bassac River in Mekong Delta.
S	40-716A	Catholic Relief Services, overseas aid agency of American Catholics, says three American sister-nurses being sent to Kontum to help re-establish Agency-supported hospital overrun by VC.
Can Tho	Thang-054-736A	S. VN's 4th Corps head, Major General Thang, says communists already have refilled their ranks with new recruits, but they are young and untrained; quotes. (Barry Kramer)
S	Escorts-47-827A	"Since Air Force transport planes are prime targets for N. VNese gunners around Khe Sanh, the U.S. Navy is providing fighter escorts for the larger, slower craft"; details.
S	2 ld Vietnam Roundup-077-1037A	Communist troops "broke contact" with U.S. infantrymen after day-long battle near Da Nang. (George Esper)
S	Vietnam-098-904P	Westmoreland activated new military command and gave it the task of blocking five enemy divisions about to attack S. VN's northernmost provinces; details. (Robert Tuckman)
S	2 nt ld Vietnam-101-1008P	U.S. infantrymen killed 129 enemy without suffering a single fatality in the coastal lowlands, say U.S. command; details. (Lewis Simons)
Hue	Hue-003	Bodies of 20 VNese killed in Hue battle still lie at former communist command post awaiting identification. President Thieu visits Hue. (Ki Sam Kim)

Dateline		Story
March 10		
S	Viet-Front-019-153P	"Calling for an end to 'rampant corruption' in S. VN, the militantly anticommunist National Salvation Front held its first convention in Saigon;" details. (Barry Kramer)
S	Ky-Mobilization-109-114P	Vice President Ky says general mobilization in VN needed to speed up end to war; quotes. (Barry Kramer)
S	Vietnam-009-1128P	Press conferences with Ky and Westmoreland; action at Saigon, Cao Lanh, Khe Sanh, air war; details. (Incomplete)
D	Cushman-113-1135P	Lieutenant General Cushman, U.S. Marine commander, says new corps command created in S. VN's northernmost provinces because of enemy buildup below DMZ; quotes. (George McArthur)
March 11		
S	Vietnam Roundup-023-436A	"South Vietnamese infantrymen reported killing 102 enemy troops in a northern frontier battle Sunday, but enemy gunners blew up tons of ammunition at a U.S. Navy base just below the eastern end of the Demilitarized Zone"; action at Thua Thien and Quang Tri, air war, Saigon-- political action, statistics; details (4). (Robert Tuckman)
S	717A	New curfew hours in Saigon.
S	Protest-065-859A	S. VN's Mission to International Control Commission complains against military aid to N. VN from U.S.S.R. and Poland.
S	Vietnam Provinces-074-956A	"In the biggest house cleaning since the communist Lunar New Year offensive, the S. VNese government fired six of the nation's 44 province chiefs today." (Barry Kramer)
S	nt ld Province Chiefs-023-315P	"The S. VNese government began a long-promised attack on corruption and incompetence among the nation's 44 province chiefs Monday by firing six of them;" details. (Barry Kramer)

Dateline	Story	
K	nt 1d Viet-Objector-017-545P	Story of Marine Johnathan Spicer, who hated war, was jeered by his fellows, but became a hero; details. (John Wheeler)

March 12

Phu Cat	Sgt. Wolfe-014-307A	Air Force Sgt. John Wolfe is serving in VN despite fact that he has six motherless children.
S	Vietnam Roundup-019-345A	U.S. kill 78 enemy in 7-1/2 hour coastal battle while N. VNese inflict "moderate" casualties on S. VNese troops below DMZ; action at Tam Ky, Dong Ha, air war. (Robert Ohman)
S	Vietnam Roundup-037-532A	U.S. warplanes make 76 missions against N. VN including attack on radio communications station near Hanoi.
S	048-706A	Move to force S. VNese House of Representatives to consider no confidence vote against government has failed.
K	Flag-063-858A	Story about how Marines at Khe Sanh had to lower their Canadian flag for safety; quotes. (Peter Arnett)
S	Vietnam Mobilization-072-956A	Saigon *Daily News* reports S. VNese Defense officer says plans for general mobilization have been drawn up, but there have been no moves to put it into effect.
S	094-1107A	Saigon city government bans all private construction on new structures for one year.
D	McNamara Wall-013-234P	McNamara Wall is being built in the eastern lowlands of DMZ, but it is under secrecy.
S	2 nt 1d Vietnam-120-906P	Fresh fighting in Bien Hoa, Khe Sanh, Tam Ky; details, statistics (4). (Edwin White)

March 13

S	Vietnam Roundup-025-438A	Allied troops reported killing 300 enemy soldiers in battles at Dong Ha, Quang Tri, Quang Ngai city, Hoi An; politics, air war; details, statistics. (Robert Ohman)

Dateline		Story
S	122-1215P	House of Representatives sent $800 million national budget to Senate after cutting from budget asked by President Thieu.
S	nt ld March to North-017-411P	Saigon government says VN volunteers are forming guerrilla "liberation army" under retired generals to invade N. VN, and U.S. is surprised; quotes, details. (Barry Kramer)
S	053-553P	S. VNese army officer sentenced to die for embezzling $17,200 from his battalion, official VN press says.
S	2 nt ld Vietnam-103-1002P	VC forces ambush U.S. military envoy in Central Highlands, but were hit by S. VNese armored units, says U.S. command; action in Mekong Delta, Hoi An, Khe Sanh, air war; details (4). (Edwin White)
S	Hue Casualties-112-1101P	More than four percent of Hue's population killed or wounded during attack, show Saigon's official figures; statistics.
S	Vietnam Napalm-128	N. VNese troops around Khe Sanh wear cloth capes to protect them from the flames of napalm, says wounded government officer.
March 14		
S	Vietnam Roundup-019-312A	Enemy troops hit Army supply convoy, but they were attacked by American tanks and helicopters; details, action at Khe Sanh, Dong, Ha, air war; statistics. (Robert Ohman)
S	Casualties-035-433A	U.S. death toll in VN tops 500 for third time in weeks, says U.S. command; statistics.
Vinh Long	War Vignettes-073-818A	Story about helicopter hero Capt. Robin Miller, who is always in the right spot at the right time; quotes. (George McArthur)
S	Casualties-089-938A	American combat deaths through seven years of war pass 20,000 mark; statistics.

Dateline	Story	
S	Vietnam-Khe Sanh-105-1045A	Radio Hanoi says morale of U.S. Marines at Khe Sanh is low; quotes.
Ben Tre	Ben Tre Revisited-005-125P	Story about Ben Tre, a town the allies had to destroy in order to save; details. (Peter Arnett)
S	447A	Vice President Ky called on VN people to liberate N. VN from communism and reunify the country.
S	nt 1d Invasion-016-246P	Vice President Ky says he will accompany a projected invasion army to Hanoi and N. VN; quotes. (Barry Kramer)
S	2 nt 1d Vietnam-105-922P	VC hit seven U.S. and S. VNese military bases and an airfield, say allied spokesmen; details on attacks Quang Tri, Dong Ha, Cua Viet, Pleiku, My Tho, Saigon; air war; statistics (5). (Edwin White)
March 15		
S	March to the North-010-213A	Describes efforts being made to organize volunteer army to invade N. VN and reactions of S. VN government and U.S. advisors. (Barry Kramer)
S	Vietnam Roundup-017-317A	U.S. Navy pilots bomb railroad-highway bridge and power plant near Haiphong port in N. VN; action at Khe Sanh, Dong Ha, on Cua Viet River; details. (Robert Ohman) (Incomplete)
S	Vietnam Roundup-028-440A	Fifty thousand U.S. and S. VN troops sweeping between Saigon and Cambodian borders in biggest operation of VN War, says U.S. command; details (4), statistics. (Robert Ohman)
S	053-555A	Leader of militant antigovernment Buddhist faction, Thich Tri Quang, arrested by Saigon police.
Vinh Long	War Vignettes-073-818A	Story about Robin Miller, helicopter hero; quotes. (George McArthur)
S	Air Losses-3/4 7/8-839A	U.S. command announced that 2,007 airplanes and 1,480 helicopters have been lost in VN War to enemy fire, accidents, other causes; statistics.

Dateline		Story
S	Black Market-070-853A	President Thieu ordered for nationwide crackdown on black market activities, bars, night-clubs, brothels that opened despite government ban. (Barry Kramer)
S	nt 1d Vietnam Economy-075-733P	Economists say Tet offensive set situation for inflation in VN; statistics, quotes. (Barry Kramer)
S	2 nt 1d Vietnam-094	S. VNese Rangers and U.S. forces claim victory in swamplands near Saigon as enemy deaths reach near 600; details. (Robert Tuckman) (Incomplete)

March 16

S	Vietnam Roundup-016-314A	Allied forces around Saigon conduct "biggest hunt-and-kill operation" and report killing 81 VC; details, air war, inflation in VN. (Robert Ohman)
S	032-618A	U.S. infantrymen "in a hide-and-seek fight" along S. VN's central coast killed 128 VC, says U.S. command.
S	058-817A	This week's issue of _Newsweek_ banned from newsstands by S. VNese government.
S	Vietnam-Agency Cuts-025-203P	U.S. will reduce size of 3,000-member force of civilians working in S. VN, in line with Johnson's plans to stem flow of dollars overseas. (Barry Kramer)
S	084-830P	Seven American soldiers killed, 29 wounded in mistaken bombing by U.S. Marine plane, says U.S. military headquarters.

March 17

USS _Ticonderoga_	Tonkin Spotlight-517-1115P	Story about T. Bruce Denmark, catapult officer aboard USS _Ticonderoga_. (Joseph Holloway, Jr.)
K	Rangers-218P	Waiting for an attack that may never come is eroding the morale of S. VNese Ranger battalion guarding near Khe Sanh.
S	Awards-15-510P	Describes how two Navy fliers won the Navy Cross for bombing Hanoi; quotes.

Dateline	Story	
S	2 1d Vietnam-141-1131P	S. VNese Rangers repel attacking N. VNese infantrymen from Khe Sanh; action near Saigon, air war; details. (Robert Ohman)

March 18

S	Vietnam Roundup-022-422A	S. VNese Rangers fight off another attack on Khe Sanh, and allied troops around Saigon claim enemy death toll exceeding 800 in first week of their big drive; action at Tram Lak, Gio Linh, air war; details. (Robert Ohman)
S	Bombing-51-700A	U.S. Navy jets from carrier *Bon Homme Richard* "pounded N. VNese troops and mortar positions threatening Khe Sanh."
S	058-755A	Veteran Foreign Service officer, Charles Cross, appointed to top American civilian advisory post in S. VN's northern 1st Corps.
S	War Vignettes-068-925A	Graffiti in VN, used by soldiers as form of expression. (George McArthur)
S	80-1034A	U.S. officials say 6,000 VNese civilians killed in VC terrorist incidents in this year; statistics.
S	Viet Forces-011-149P	S. VNese government will increase its armed forces by 123,000 men this year which U.S. will equip, say informed sources.
S	2 nt 1d Vietnam Roundup-090-855P	"Charging through a hail of rocket fire, a company of U.S. Marines overran N. VNese trenches below the Demilitarized Zone Monday and killed 67 of the enemy, the U.S. command reported"; air war, action in Saigon, details. (John Lengel)
K	Khe Sanh-095-940P	Two Marines who were at shelling of Con Thien last fall say it was worse than now at Khe Sanh; quotes.
Laos	Laos Spotlight-541-1014P	Laos may provide the key to approaching settlement in VN; details.

Dateline		Story
March 19		
S	Vietnam Roundup-020-357A	U.S. Marines overran band of N. VNese and reported killing 67 in new fighting below eastern end of DMZ; fighting at Dong Ha, Khe Sanh, Saigon, air war; details. (Robert Ohman)
S	023-426A	Six N. VNese defectors say that Hanoi's intelligence sources provide as much as 24 hours advance notice and location of U.S. B-52 bombing raids in S. VN. (Barry Kramer)
S	Morale-028-509A	Morale amazingly good among U.S. forces in VN. (George McArthur)
K	Wirephoto-043-634A	The two wives of a Bru Montagnard tribesman are last two women to leave Khe Sanh.
S	Graft-061-806A	Premier Loc orders investigation of reported corruption in Hue.
S	nt ld Vietnam Roundup-007-924P	U.S. and S. VNese drive to root enemy from Saigon turned up big arms cache possibly intended for attacks on Tan Son Nhut Air Base; statistics on casualties; action at Kien Hoa, coastal plains, air war; details. (John Lengel)
S	Viet-Black Market-112-1029P	Police close Saigon's black market.
S	Tribute-125-1149P	Memorial service held at Tan Son Nhut Air Base to honor four soldiers who defended it during January 31 attack.
March 20		
S	Vietnam Roundup-011-245A	Intelligence reports indicate that the 13,000 VC menacing Saigon have withdrawn toward Cambodian border; air war, action in Saigon, black market raid. (Robert Ohman)
S	Vietnam Roundup-029-413A	"Some 13,000 hard-core VC have faded into their jungle hideaways near the Cambodian border, easing the threat of a second invasion of Saigon, senior American officials said today." (Robert Ohman)

Dateline	Story	
D	Spotter Plane-079-1006A	Story about Charles Rushforth who flies a "spotter plane" which checks on enemy troops around Khe Sanh; quotes, details. (Edwin White)
S	2 ld Vietnam Roundup-093-1056A	"Troops of the U.S. Americal Division reported they killed 111 N. VNese regulars in a battle today on the northern coast at a cost of three American wounded." (Robert Ohman)
S	2 nt ld Vietnam Round-up-106-1019P	VC shelled Tan Son Nhut Air Base with little effect and allies killed 142 enemy in nearby battle; details (6), air war. (John Lengel)
S	129-1217A	President Thieu promised to increase S. VNese armed forces by 35,000, crack down on corruption, and improve government machinery; quotes.
S	3 ld Vietnam Roundup-113-1230P	"Troops of the U.S. Americal Division reported they killed 111 N. VNese regulars today in a series of skirmishes on or near the north coast." (Robert Ohman)
March 21		
S	Vietnam Roundup-031-457A	Allies kill 167 VC close to Saigon and 15 enemy shells land at Tan Son Nhut airport; details, statistics; action at Khe Sanh, Dong Ha, Cua Viet, Phu Bai. (George Esper)
S	Thieu-038-532A	President Thieu says S. VN's allies are increasing their military and economic commitment to S. VN, and so he has ordered 135,000 additional troops; details. (Barry Kramer)
S	Casualties-057-735A	Allied headquarters announced American, S. VNese, enemy casualties decreased last week; statistics.
S	Vietnam Roundup-098-1055A	Ten thousand American troops launch five new drives to regain initiative after Tet offensive; details, statistics. (George Esper)

Dateline		Story
S	nt ld Thieu-046-526P	"President Nguyen Van Thieu will try to follow up his pledge Thursday to crack down on corruption by clipping the wings of the nation's four warlord corps commanders, informed sources said"; details. (Barry Kramer)
S	Red Strategy-048-537P	Analysis of communist strategy in VN, particularly on northern provinces; details. (John Wheeler)
S	3 nt ld Vietnam-104-958P	"Allied forces are sweeping hills, planes and jungles in six operations designed to wrest the initiative from the enemy, the U.S. command disclosed Thursday"; details. (John Lengel)
S	Khe Sanh-091	Top U.S. military spokesman Brigadier General Sidle says enemy threat to Khe Sanh has neither lessened nor increased.
March 22		
Aboard Carrier *Kitty Hawk*	Ky-047-703A	Vice President Ky says that he has asked U.S. to supply S. VNese Air Force with fighter-bombers so it could join U.S. in air raids against N. VN.
S	Vietnam-6-910A	"American fighter-bombers smashed 165 N. VNese trucks carrying military supplies to the communists' troops along the DMZ in the last two days," says U.S. command.
S	077-10A	Number of VC defectors continues to run well below 1967 pace, says American spokesman.
S	Amphibious-89-1027A	Navy spokesman say U.S. amphibious force is suffering danger on its routine supply missions in VN.
S	Westmoreland-134-1019P	Westmoreland says he was told of his impending transfer to Washington in telephone call from General Wheeler, and that he regrets his departure before victory is won; details.
S	2 nt ld Vietnam Round-up-109-450P	"Radar-guided U.S. Air Force jets darted through heavy clouds to within 18 miles of Red China Friday and attacked a key N. VNese railyard, the U.S. command

Dateline	Story
	reported"; details; action at Khe Sanh, Mekong Delta, Camp Carroll. (John Lengel)

March 23

Dateline	Story	
S	Westmoreland Reaction-049-007A	"American GIs and officers mostly agree today that Gen. William C. Westmoreland did a good job as U.S. commander in VN"; quotes.
Aboard Carrier *Kitty Hawk*	Ky-047-703A	Vice President Ky says he has asked U.S. to supply S. VNese Air Force with modern jet bombers so it could join U.S. in air raids against N. VN; quotes. (Barry Kramer)
S	Vietnam-15-942A	Westmoreland says he regrets leaving VN before "the battle is over."
S	4-722A	Author and veteran politician Tran Van An confirmed report that he will head newly created Ministry of Information in S. VNese government.
S	2 nt ld Vietnam-078-727P	"The VC shelled Pleiku in the Central Highlands early Sunday and sent a suicide squad into the city to attack a government radio station"; action in air war over N. VN, Khe Sanh, details, quotes. (John Lengel)
S	nt ld Westmoreland-006-1227P	Analysis of Westmoreland and his contributions to U.S. strategy in VN; details. (Peter Arnett)
Qui Nhon	Translator-50-838P	Tran Thi Phuong, a VN translator, will attend U.S. university on gifts of grateful Americans; quotes. (Joseph Holloway, Jr.)
S	097-1115P	Ambassador Samuel D. Berger arrives in Saigon to assume new post as deputy to U.S. Ambassador Ellsworth Bunker.

March 24

Dateline	Story	
S	2 ld Vietnam-0125-1134P	"Fire from enemy gunners surrounding Khe Sanh brought down one U.S. Marine helicopter and damaged another Sunday"; action in air war in N. VN, near DMZ, naval action. (George Esper)

Dateline		Story
S	Viet-Sergeant Major-8-445P	Story about Sgt. Maj. Donald Hord, who is getting his third commander in two weeks; quotes. (Albert Chang)
D	124-1130P	Army doctor successfully removes live grenade that was embedded in leg of 19-year-old soldier.

March 25

S	Vietnam Roundup-016-308A	"North Vietnamese gunners shot down two U.S. Marine helicopters near Khe Sanh Sunday, but eased up in their shelling of the northwest frontier fortress after two days of heavy bombardment"; action at Saigon, Kontum, Mekong Delta; details. (George Esper)
S	Vietnam Roundup-040-610A	"American helicopter gunships and fighter-bombers have smashed 245 sampans carrying weapons and food to VC troops in the Mekong Delta in the last three days, the U.S. command said today"; action at Khe Sanh, Camp Carroll, Saigon; details, statistics. (George Esper)
S	Vietnam-at-a-Glance-048-705A	Saigon--U.S. destroys 245 sampans in Mekong Delta; Khe Sanh--N. VNese down two Marine helicopters; Washington--shortage of skilled Saigon government personnel and corruption obstacles to success of pacification program; Marine Corps commandant Chapman says N. VN "can't force us out"; N.Y.--Senator Morton says Tonkin Gulf incident "may have been the result of deliberate provocation."
D	Operation-73-959A	Story about U.S. Army doctor who removed live grenade from leg of soldier; quotes. (John Lengel)
D	War Vignettes-085-1121A	Story about Rogerlio Salcido, an Air Force policeman at Da Nang, who picked up rocket that exploded but left him alive. (George McArthur)

Dateline	Story	
S	2 nt ld War-086-823P	"American and S. VNese infantrymen, pushing the biggest allied of-fensive of the war around Saigon, killed 243 VC troops in fighting still raging Tuesday morning, the U.S. command announced"; air war, action near Hue, Khe Sanh, on VC sampans in Mekong Delta, statistics, details (6).
S	F-111-099-925P	F-111 flies first combat mission over N. VN; quotes, details.
S	Komer-Roche-013	Ambassador Komer, head of U.S. pacification program, says, "The guy [who said program supervised by CIA] must be making it up." (Barry Kramer) (Incomplete)

March 26

S	Vietnam Roundup-022-343A	"Allied forces pushed through rice paddies and hedgerows today pursuing a battered VC force that broke off a sharp 24-hour battle near Saigon shortly before dawn"; details on air war, action at Trang Bang, statistics. (George Esper)
S	Resignation-026-416A	Sidney Roche, who spent more than four years in military and civilian posts in S. VN, quitting because, despite enemy successes, U.S. is following "the same old policies"; quotes. (Robert Tuckman)
S	Vietnam Roundup-037-504A	"Nearly 1,000 N. VNese troops, armed with flamethrowers and rocket-propelled grenades, at-tacked an American artillery base in the Central Highlands of S. VN today"; action near Saigon, air war, Khe Sanh; details. (George Esper)
D	Cushman-038-510A	U.S. commander of northern S. VN Cushman says N. VN abandoned protracted war to go all-out to win northern sector; quotes.
S	060-753A	VC terrorists killed 209 civilians, wounded 364, abducted 634 in last two weeks, say U.S. officials; statistics.

Dateline		Story
Trang Bang	Trang Bang-069-838A	At least six women took part in VC assault on American armored column "rushing" to reinforce troops in Trang Bang, say military officials; details, quotes. (Albert Chang)
S	920A	Story about Danile Wadiaeff who came to VN to fix military women's hair; quotes. (Jurate Kazickas)
S	Thieu-081-950A	President Thieu removes four more province chiefs, bringing number to 12 those replaced in last two weeks because of inefficiency. (Barry Kramer)
K	Khe Sanh-014-224P	Marines at Khe Sanh battling rats; details. (John Wheeler)
S	2 nt ld Vietnam-100-956P	"One thousand N. VNese threw themselves in waves at an American artillery base in the Central Highlands before dawn Tuesday and were repelled with heavy losses"; action in air; details. (George Esper)
S	108-1104P	AP photographer Al Chang slightly wounded while covering U.S. 25th Infantry Division troops.
S	nt ld Resignation-110-1125P	Robert Komer, head of U.S. pacification program, dismisses as ridiculous statements by Sidney Roche, retired Army lieutenant colonel who quit, that U.S. is failing in VN; quotes.
S	Tet Spotlight-602/604-1038P	GVN post-Tet performance. (Barry Kramer)
March 27		
S	Vietnam Roundup-016-336A	"American infantrymen led by an armored column battled their way into a Vietcong-held hamlet 28 miles northwest of Saigon today against stiff defensive fire from a network of trenches and sniper positions"; action at Khe Sanh, Soc Trang, Saigon; details. (George Esper)
S	Komer-Roche-022-425A	U.S. CIA provides "a fairly substantial part" of necessities for S. VN's pacification program, says informed source responding to accusation by ex-employee Roche. (Barry Kramer)

Dateline	Story	
S	Vietnam Roundup-041-642A	American troops battle VC for control of tiny hamlet near Saigon in fourth day of heavy fighting; details, statistics.
Ap Long Muc	Battle Eyewitness-056-815A	Story about U.S. forces fighting with VC in hamlet of Ap Long Muc near Saigon; quotes, details. (Albert Chang)
S	Cameraman-68-818A	Uno Hews, cameraman for CBS, wounded during combat operation near Saigon.
S	058-820A	S. VN's ambassador to U.S., Diem, called home by Thieu for consultations, says Foreign Minister Do.
S	069-933A	Three S. VNese generals, recently removed from high command, given new important positions; U.S. officials consider them ineffective.
S	Ground Rules-080-1018A	U.S. military command reaffirms its long-standing "ground rules" covering withholding of information about VN War from newsmen.
S	092-1103A	U.S. officials say 708 suspected cases of bubonic plague in S. VN in first 11 weeks of 1968, less than half of last year.
S	2 nt ld Vietnam Roundup-117-998P	"U.S. troops called in artillery and air strikes of napalm only 50 yards from their positions Wednesday in a battle for a hamlet northwest of Saigon near Cambodia's border"; action near Khe Sanh, air war, details. (Edwin White)
Hue	Hue-053	Description of Hue "striving to bring itself back from the ravages of the Lunar New Year fighting; details. (Richard Merron)
S	Abrams-Vietnam-080-727P	General Abrams returns to VN after Washington talks with Johnson.

March 28

| S | Casualties-027-425A | Statistics on numbers killed in VN War. |

Dateline		Story
S	Vietnam Roundup-038-620A	U.S. B-52s hit N. VNese supply depots and command centers in A Shau Valley west of Hue; action at Khe Sanh, Saigon, details. (George Esper)
D	Marine Choppers-020-225P	Marines suffering from "chopper gap"--Army has more helicopters for operations than Marines; details. (John Wheeler, John Lengel)
S	7-226P	Sgt. Richard McCoy captures first Soviet rocket-aiming device of VN War, report Army officials.
S	Vietnam Roundup-022-349A	U.S. command reports 2,000 VC killed in Quyet Thang offensive in Saigon, the largest allied operation of the war; action in Trang Bang, Ap Long Muc, Khe Sanh, air war; details. (George Esper)
S	2 nt ld Vietnam Roundup-107-904P	Air Force looses new F-111A jets on combat mission, reports U.S. command; details, action at Hue, Ap Long Muc; statistics (6). (Edwin White)

March 29

S	Vietnam Roundup-023-320A	N. VN claims to have shot down F-111A; action at Khe Sanh, near Saigon, statistics, Mekong Delta; details (4). (George Esper)
S	F-111 Pilot-024-338A	U.S. Air Force senior pilot Arnet says F-111 performance over N. VN is outstanding; quotes. (George Esper) (Incomplete)
S	Vietnam Roundup-018-338A	Monsoon weather which has been protecting N. VN from air attacks, breaks, leaving way for increased American action unless Johnson orders pause; air war, Khe Sanh. (George Esper)
S	Prisoners-033-428A	U.S. officials announce release of three N. VNese POW seamen by Army; details.
S	Vietnam Roundup-036-630A	S. VNese civilian irregular forces kill 40 guerrillas in two ambushes in central S. VN, says U.S. command.

Dateline		Story
S	046-720A	President Thieu removed two more province chiefs, bringing month's total to 14.
S	048-736A	ICC says shortage of funds is forcing it to cut its staff and withdraw all five field inspection teams in S. VN.
S	Destroyer-074-828A	U.S. 7th Fleet says N. VNese shore batteries fired on destroyer *Epperson*, but there were no damages nor casualties.
K	058-838A	Khe Sanh is question of strategy; controversy rages among both U.S. and enemy; details. (John Wheeler)
S	Air War-089-816P	U.S. Air Force jets dueled with Soviet-made MIG interceptors over N. VN; details.
S	2 nt ld Vietnam Roundup-097-908P	VC shell U.S. helicopter field and five allied infantry bases, say military spokesmen; action at Camp Holloway, Song Be, New Life, air war. (Edwin White)
S	Caches-108-1023P	VC defector leads Navy force to big arms caches, weapons repair shop, munitions factory in Mekong Delta village near Saigon.
S	2 nt ld ICC-121-1158P	ICC announces severe staff cutback because of lack of funds.
S	Vietcong-072-818A	VC high command told all communist guerrilla units two days after start of Tet that they had won an important victory. (Michael Goldsmith)
March 30		
S	046-726A	President Thieu removed two more S. VNese province chiefs, making 14 replaced this month.
S	073-1028A	U.S. air base at Bien Hoa claims to be busiest airport in the world, with takeoff or landing every 37 seconds.
S	4 nt ld Vietnam-112-908P	Air Force reported crash of second of the six F-111As that entered VN War less than a week ago; the two crew members were rescued; action at Khe Sanh, Saigon politics, details (6). (Robert Tuckman)

Dateline		Story
S	Mobilization-119-1015P	S. VN will order general mobilization this fall if VC continue their attacks, said President Thieu; details.
S	Tet Spotlight-602-1030P	Analysis of reaction of Saigon government to Tet offensive; quotes, details. (Barry Kramer)
March 31		
S	Vietnam-Government-029-217P	President Thieu reported Sunday to be planning top-level overhaul of his government, including dismissal of Premier Loc and Brigadier General Loan; details.
S	F-111-Rescue-014-242P	U.S. Air Force released names of two fliers rescued after crash of second F-111 in northern Thailand; details.
S	Vietnam-Kill Ratio-032-257P	Allies killing average of six enemy for every man they lose in overall combat, say military officials; statistics.
S	Viet-Fatigue-2-418P	American GIs afflicted by new kind of combat fatigue because of nature of VN War. (Michael Goldsmith)
S	13-529P	Truck convoys in N. VN's southern Panhandle hit by U.S. fliers from fleet carrier _Ticonderoga_, Navy sources report; details.
S	2 1d Vietnam-129-905P	U.S. command halted air and sea blows against N. VN except for southern end of country; air war, Saigon politics. F-111, Thu Doc, Hue, A Shau, details (7). (George Esper)
S	5 nt 1d Vietnam Roundup-125-1038P	American warplanes bomb supply target near N. VN's Demilitarized Zone, but bombing curtailment by Johnson will allow raids at least that far north; details. (Edwin White)
S	Tet Spotlight-604-1045P	(First page of Tet Spotlight missing)
S	Johnson-GI Reaction-123-1138P	Reactions of GIs to Johnson's decision not to run for re-election; quotes.

Dateline	Story	
February 1		
W	McNamara-Vietnam-077-1026A	McNamara's report on VN; statistics, quotes, details (6). (F. Hoffman)
W	Johnson-Asia-091-1135A	Senator Stennis says "expansion of the war" would probably require additional forces above allocated 525,000; quotes from Stennis, Mansfield, Young; details (4). (J. Bell)
Prague	North Vietnam-094-1146A	"N. VN was bracing today for U.S. bombings in retaliation for heavy communist attacks in S. VN, a Czechoslovak news agency dispatch from Hanoi reported;" quotes.
Beverly Hills, Calif.	Krulack-061-338P	Lt. Gen. Krulak, commander of Marines in VN and Pacific, calls VC suicide raids in Saigon "acts of desperation"; quotes. (C. McFadden)
W	Johnson-Bombing-034-347P	Johnson says bombing of N. VN will continue until enemy gives better sign that halt would not mean more terrorism and aggression; quotes. (F. Lewin)
Tokyo	Asian-Vietnam-037-418P	Thailand, Philippines, Japan, Nationalist China react with shock to communist attacks in VN; details. (K. Tateishi)
W	nt ld McNamara-031-431P	McNamara reports to Congress that N. VN is expected to increase armed strength in S. VN in next few months; details, quotes, statistics (5). (B. Horton)
Tokyo	nt ld Red China Charge-045-505P	Communist China charges U.S. planes on bombing missions over N. VNese ports hit Chinese freighters in N. VNese ports January 20 and 27 in "deliberate provocations" against Chinese; details.

Note: This compilation is from AP files, but may be incomplete. In some cases, due to difficulties in reproduction from the files, identifying headings, time indicators, or file numbers are incomplete or lacking.

H. K. = Hong Kong; W = Washington, D.C.; nt ld = night lead.

Dateline		Story
W	Intermediaries-085-802P	State Department gives acknowledgment to Professor Zinn and Rev. C. Berrigan, who are going to Hanoi as intermediaries in release of three U.S. fliers by N. VN.
W	Bartlett-104-931P	Governor Bartlett of Oklahoma rescued from traffic jam by Johnson and receives personal briefing on VN.
W	Ridgway-105-932P	Johnson called in retired Army General Ridgway for discussions on VN and Korea.
Tokyo	Hanoi-Vietcong-121-1145P	VC representative in Hanoi quoted as saying "simultaneous" repeated attacks underway in more than 40 S. VNese towns and villages; details. (J. Roderick)
N.Y.	ACLU-119	ACLU refuses to defend persons refusing to register for military if they do so as protest against draft or VN War.
February 2		
San Francisco	Hilsman-134-116A	Former Assistant Secretary of State for Far Eastern Affairs says, "If we keep our present objective," invasion of N. VN by U.S. "seems inevitable."
Tokyo	060-805A	Red China says attack on Saigon and U.S. Embassy demonstrates that days U.S. "can hang on in S. VN are numbered"; quotes.
Phnom Penh	068-845A	Prince Sihanouk denounces communist activity among Cambodian tribe near Laos and S. VN border.
Moscow	083-1015A	*Izvestia* describes atmosphere in Washington as "panicky" because recent VC successes occurred in Presidential election year; quotes.
Vientiane	Airmen-95-1103A	Two Americans on their way to Hanoi to collect three captured U.S. pilots being freed by N. VN, delayed in Vientiane by VN war crisis.
W	US-Asia-113-1242P	Johnson reports military phases of communist offensive failed in VN, but avoids saying if war is being won; details of news conference.

Dateline		Story
W	Johnson-049-537P	Johnson portrayed "general uprising of VN communist" failure and no increase in combat troops at this time; details, quotes (6). (D. Cornell)
Tokyo	Chou-VC-063-642P	Premier Chou of Communist China congratulates VC on "exceedingly brilliant victories."
N.Y.	Missionaries-081-752P	Six American missionaries slain by VC in Ban Me Thuot; details.
New Haven, Conn.	104-956P	Yale chaplain Coffin says he will lead VN protest march to Arlington Cemetery.
Tokyo	Hanoi-Vietnam-106-1139P	VC reported that U.S. naval craft sunk in five-day communist offensive in VN; details (3).

February 3

Tokyo	Hanoi-Vietnam-048-638A	N. VN hints that communist offensive in S. VN prelude of more to come on larger scale; quotes.
San Francisco	057-722A	Roger Hilsman, former Assistant Secretary of State for Far Eastern Affairs, says if U.S. continues on present policy, it is "inevitable" that it will invade N. VN; quotes.
Phnom Penh	082-923A	Cambodia accuses U.S. and S. VN of firing on Cambodian border post, killing three, wounding one.
Kuala Lumpur	Missionaries-75-1022A	Son of U.S. missionary parents slain by VC in Ban Me Thuot says he was sure his father expected to die in VN War; quotes. (M. Belkind)
London	Vietnam-Analysis-023-114P	W. European military experts believe N. VN intends offensive in S. VN to expose U.S. as "paper tiger" before calling for peace talks to end war; details. (L. Nevin)
N.Y.	13-155P	Interdenominational organization, Clergy and Laymen Concerned About VN, issues report accusing U.S. of "war crime" in VN; details.

Dateline		Story
W	Tonkin Gulf-018-211P	McNamara will go before Senate Foreign Relations Committee to defend Johnson's actions in Gulf of Tonkin incident; review of controversy. (R. Gray)
W	Clergymen-Demonstra-tion-052-353P	Army Secretary Resor rejects bid by churchmen's organization to hold memorial service at Arlington Cemetery, in protest of VN War; quotes.
Tokyo	043-455P	Premier Chou En Lai of Red China told VC in Peking that final communist victory in VN is "coming even nearer," says New China News Agency.
W	US-Vietnam-051-546P	Senator McCarthy says events in VN prove Administration's reports of action in VN are "products of their own self-deception"; quotes.
W	Congress-Asia-60-637P	Senator Morton accuses Administration of "hoodwinking" American people about gravity of VC offensive; quotes.
N.Y.	nt ld Missionaries-059-754P	Missionary nurse Betty Olsen believed prisoner of VC.
Kansas City, Kans.	2 nt ld Hatfield-GOP-1131-1101P	Senator Hatfield says VN War fought from Washington not by generals and admirals; quotes. (L. Hall)
W	Clergymen-Arlington Cemetery-17	National Committee of Clergy and Laymen appeals to McNamara to allow them to hold memorial service in Arlington Cemetery for servicemen who died in VN.
February 4		
Miami, Fla.	Missionary-035-344P	Missionary nurse Mildred Ade will return to work with lepers in VN despite VC killing six of her friends; quotes. (B. Gassay)
W	Rusk-Vietnam-042-455P	Rusk says U.S. recently "exercised some restraint" in bombing N. VN while exploring possibility of peace talks with Hanoi; details (4).
Atlanta, Ga.	Russell-Vietnam-11-511P	Senator Russell says U.S. was not obligated to become involved in VN War; quotes.

Dateline		Story
W	Dirksen-052-550P	Senator Dirksen says VC attacks in S. VN mean they are "desperate"; quotes.
Warsaw	Poland-054-556P	Poland says it rejects suggestions on strengthening policing role of ICC because action would violate Cambodia's sovereign rights.
London	Westmoreland-037-652P	British newspapers say there are strong demands in Washington for firing Westmoreland; quotes. (G. Watts)
Milan	Drug-072-713P	International pharmaceuticals dealer Gubbay denies charge that he sold S. VN plain sea water for which U.S. paid $24,000.
London	Blood-33-821P	Three hundred pints of blood being sent to VC and N. VN from British donors.
St. Paul, Minn.	46-958P	At the same time Macalaster College citing David Gitelson for distinguished civilian service, he was killed by VC in VN.
N.Y.	Viet-Magazine-091-1035P	According to *Time* magazine, each member of Joint Chiefs of Staff has signed paper saying he believes Khe Sanh can be defended, at Johnson's request.
Baltimore, Md.	Sheerin-50-1131P	Rev. Sheerin, editor-in-chief of *Catholic World*, asks at peace convocation if fighting in VN is fighting against God.

February 5		
Little Rock, Ark.	Fulbright-001-106A	Political problems created for Fulbright as a result of his dove stance toward VN War; quotes, details. (H. Kelley)
W	Vietnam-Korea-011-248A	Rusk says N. VN helped VC on Tet attack knowing U.S. bombing of N. VN lightened while peace moves were under exploration; details (4); quotes. (B. Horton)
Atlanta, Ga.	Russell-30-335A	Senator Russell says U.S. involvement in VN is "one of the greatest tragedies of our history"; quotes.
Vientiane	Laos-51-727A	Speculation on whether Laos is destined to become second front in VN War. (J. Wheeler)

Dateline		Story
W	Senate-Vietnam-120-1P	Senator Kennedy says VC won political victory through city attacks and Senator Mansfield says "time for serious talks" with Saigon government; quotes from Senate.
Charleston, S.C.	1-110P	Representative Rivers urges U.S. use greater firepower in VN War; quotes.
Moscow	Viet-Ho-049-529P	N. VNese President Ho tells VC their recent attacks "have created a favorable situation to resist the U.S. aggression and unite the VN people on an all-nation basis," Tass reports.
Frankfurt	71-705P	Demonstrators attack U.S. trade center in opposition to VN War.
Moscow	Viet-Tass-079-744P	Tass reports VC claim to have taken prisoner U.S. colonel, platoon, heads of Hue city administration, during Hue fighting.
Miami, Fla.	136-1147P	Senator Morse says U.S. eventually will be driven out of Asia; quotes.
W	Washington Roundup-086	McNamara will appear before Senate Foreign Relations Committee in closed session February 2 to review 1964 Tonkin Gulf incident.
W	nt ld Clergy-145-1207A	Two thousand clergymen rebuffed when District Court refuses to allow them to hold memorial service for VN War dead at Arlington Cemetery.

February 6

Dateline		Story
W	US-Vietnam-322A	Senator Edward Kennedy says massive VC attacks on S. VNese population centers reveal "deadly apathy" of S. VNese government; quotes.
Stockholm	Deserters-64-819A	"Sweden granted asylum today to six more American deserters, raising the number of those allowed to stay to 13."
Bangkok	Viet-Housewife-127-101P	U.S. housewife Laurie Magee tape-recorded battle of Saigon; quotes. (P. O'Loughlin)

Dateline	Story	
Bangkok	Viet-Congressmen-80-133P	Representatives Clark, Clausen, Cleveland, Cramer during four-hour visit to Saigon were informed of wholesale massacre of Methodist missionaries by VC in Ban Me Thuot.
W	US-Vietnam-124-412P	State Department reports one U.S. AID officer killed, five injured, one missing as result of VC offensive against S. VNese cities.
W	Wheeler-Khe Sanh-41-516P	Wheeler says psychological as well as military reasons are basis for Joint Chiefs of Staff recommendation to Johnson that Khe Sanh be defended; quotes.
W	Clergymen-065-642P	"A clergymen-led organization dedicated to an end to the U.S. part in the VN War closed out a two-day mobilization meeting Tuesday on a note of solidarity with the combined civil rights-peace movement led by Dr. M. L. King, Jr." (W. Mobley)
Brunswick, Maine	Plane-720P	Navy spokesman says massive search underway off S. VNese coast for missing patrol plane with 12 aboard.
W	Fulbright-TV-802P	Senator Fulbright complains that high-level Administration officials discuss U.S. foreign policy on TV while refusing to go before Senate Foreign Relations Committee.
W	Atrocities-083-804P	General Wheeler deplores publicized execution of VC by RSVN police chief, but suggests it occurred "more in a flash of outrage" than in cold blood.
London	Vietnam-British-093-828P	Prime Minister Wilson says enemy offensive makes peacemaking in VN much more difficult. (A. Gavshon)
Tokyo	Vietnam-Japanese-117-1015P	Two Japanese diplomats caught in battle in Hue say they had impression populace sympathetic to VC.
Olean, N.Y.	Henry-122-1115P	Navy Corpsman Daniel B. Henry who helped remove live shell from soldier's leg last August was killed in VN, says his mother.

Dateline		Story
Tokyo	Viet-Vietcong-127-1116P	VC military command claims current enemy offensive in six days "wiped out 10,000 plus U.S. and 40,000 allied troops"; quotes, statistics.
N.Y.	133-1137P	Christian and Missionary Alliance announces evacuation of all U.S. and Canadian women and children from staff in S. VN because of "worsening war conditions."

February 7

New Delhi	057-803A	U.S.S.R. declares U.S. "continuing aggression" in VN threatens world peace and hampers world trade and economic progress.
Albany, N.Y.	Schlesinger-Sorensen-78-812A	Two men closely linked to JFK speak out on war: Schlesinger anti-U.S. policy, Sorensen pro.
Phnom Penh	072-938A	Cambodia protests against U.S. for attack by "American-S. VNese" on frontier village of Phnom Penh.
W	Medal of Honor-74-117P	Army Sgt. Donald R. Long receives Medal of Honor posthumously for fighting in VN.
Odessa, Del.	Bishop-Vietnam-120-135P	Bishop Lord of St. Paul's Methodist Church criticizes past bishop for siding with Clergy and Laymen Concerned About VN.
London	Vietnam-Analyst-91-219P	Victor Zorza, British expert on communist affairs, says communists in VN failed to achieve even minimum objective of their offensive, and heavy casualties make renewal of campaign doubtful; quotes.
Moscow	025-320P	N. VNese Ambassador Chan had "friendly and cordial" meeting with Foreign Minister Gromyko, says Tass.
W	Gavin-029-343P	General Gavin says if U.S. had adopted his strategy of using U.S. troops to hold fortified positions in S. VN, last week's VC assaults would have been stopped cold.
W	Rusk-Vietnam-030-354P	Rusk refuses to say if there are any peace probes with N. VN; quotes.

Dateline		Story
Vatican City	Vietnam-Vatican-166-622P	Vatican publication suggests VN War being fought over heads of VN people.
U.N.	Gronowski-179-659P	U.S. Ambassador Gronowski had secret meeting January 26 with N. VNese emissary in Warsaw, U.N. diplomats say.
W	Rusk-Viet-183-719P	Senate Foreign Relations Committee votes to ask Johnson to direct Rusk to appear in public to discuss VN and other work issues.
St. Louis, Mo.	World Service Note-124-1027P	Japanese ambassador to U.S. Shimoda says Japanese government seeks early peace in VN.
W	Tanks-Vietnam-130-1149P	Marine Headquarters say Soviet-built tanks N. VN used in capturing Lang Vei were PT-76s rather than T-34s initially reported by U.S. command.
W	Rusk-McNamara-118	NBC Bureau Chief Monroe says network initiated appearances of Secretary Rusk and McNamara on last Sunday's "Meet the Press."

February 8

Dateline		Story
Syracuse, N.Y.	Black Sergeant-008-8A	Melvin Murrel, "Black Sergeant of Tuy Hoa," wanted by VC, now wanted by U.S. organizations to speak on VN; quotes. (H. Pelkey)
Tokyo	078-839A	Pathet Lao claims it killed three U.S. advisors in northern Laos January 23.
Chicago	Kennedy-Vietnam-112-1114A	Robert Kennedy charges Johnson's VN policies based on illusion; quotes.
W	104-1223P	"Lieutenant General Gavin says communist attacks on 35 S. VNese population centers substantiate and reinforce his enclave theory."
W	Viet Victims-010-148P	State Department says five Americans connected with U.S. Mission killed and one missing in communist offensive.
Tokyo	Vietnam-Hanoi-027-308P	N. VNese Foreign Minister Trinh says peace talks "will begin as soon as the U.S. proved it stopped bombing and all other acts of war" against N. VN, reports Hanoi Radio.

Dateline		Story
Honolulu	With Kennedy-065-339P	Marine Corp's Pacific Commander Krulak defends U.S. official estimates of number of enemy killed in VN cities.
Cleveland, Ohio	52-349P	U.S. Coast Guard tells how Chief Boatswain's Mate Roger Syria made VN fishermen smile by providing with photos.
W	nt ld US-Vietnam-036-413P	State Department studying statement by N. VNese Foreign Minister Trinh that N. VN may wish to keep peace exchanges operating with U.S. alongside communist military offensive; details. (J. Hightower)
Chicago	nt ld Kennedy-Vietnam-048-420P	Robert Kennedy says that U.S. military effort to resolve VN War is "like sending a lion to halt an epidemic of jungle rot"; quotes.
Paris	050-528P	Retired Soviet Chief of Staff Sokolovsky says U.S. has lost VN War.
Moscow	With Chicago-067-647P	Tass reports on Senator R. Kennedy's speech criticizing Johnson's handling of VN War.
New Delhi	nt ld Thant-046-743P	U.N. Secretary General Thant discusses VN War with N. VNese Consul General Hoa.
W	Percy-Mortars-091-830P	Senator Percy says VC mortars assault on his party in December endangered neither his wife nor helicopter rescuers; quotes.
February 9		
Tokyo	Viet Peace-024-408A	N. VN makes peace bid to U.S. for "as soon as the U.S. has proved that it has really stopped unconditionally the bombings and all other acts of war"; quotes.
N.Y.	82-1027A	Senator Javits says U.S. must acknowledge a stalemate in VN and make clear to U.S.S.R. that "accordingly we seek a political and diplomatic compromise."

Dateline		Story
W	US Vietnam-23-1042A	A source close to Robert Kennedy says his new attack on U.S. VN policies does not mark the start of a "systematic" assault on Johnson's war strategy.
Vientiane	Fliers-93-1121A	Two-man American peace delegation leaves Laos to receive three U.S. fliers promised freedom by N. VN.
Geneva	Red Cross-105-1208P	International Red Cross Committee says both belligerents in VN War to observe "elementary and universally recognized rules of humane treatment"; quotes.
Ottowa	113-1229P	Prime Minister Pearson says VN War "should be brought to an end and peace negotiations begun."
W	Military Thaw-102	Defense Department ends four-month freeze on military construction projects unrelated to VN War.
Beeville, Tex.	nt ld Plane Hero-1P	Mother of hero of attempted airplane hijacking in VN says her son is a "man who is hard to shake up."
London	Vietnam-Wilson-009-143P	"Behind Prime Minister Wilson's plea for American restraint in VN is his belief that Russian leaders are reappraising President Johnson's approach to peace talks"; details. (A. Gavshon)
W	Civilian Casualties-98-205P	State Department released names of five U.S. civilian officers killed during fighting in Hue.
W	Vietnam-AID-033-351P	Official concedes that some American commodities sent to VN are being diverted into communist-held areas and there is no way to halt this completely; details. (S. Davis)
W	Denial-149-552P	Defense Department denies China's claim that U.S. warplanes bombed their ships in N. VNese ports.
W	Nuclear Weapons-050-549P	White House and Pentagon describe as false and ridiculous speculation that military plans to use nuclear weapons in VN and is stockpiling them there.
U.N.	Kennedy-Vietnam-059-634P	S. VNese U.N. observer charges Robert Kennedy with making "unfair and unfounded criticism" against people and government of S. VN.

Dateline	Story	
N.Y.	Missionaries-71-858P	Three of six missionaries slain by VC were shot in a trench, and a fourth as he raced across open ground, their headquarters say. (G. Cornell)
W	Vietnam-096-923P	U.S. officials say communists may launch second attack wave on S. VNese cities, but it is likely to be weaker than the first.
Tokyo	Hanoi-Khe Sanh-120-1122P	N. VN says Khe Sanh will be another Dienbienphu, on radio broadcast.
Syracuse, N.Y.	Kennedy Lead-122-1131P	Robert Kennedy criticizes S. VNese government for not taking enough interest in VN War; quotes.

February 10

W	US-Vietnam-001-109A	U.S. officials expect communists to launch second attack against S. VNese cities, but predicts second offensive weaker than first details. (J. Hightower)
W	North Vietnam-Nuclear-003-121A	Senator Fulbright wrote Rusk asking for report on rumors that U.S. will use nuclear weapons if U.S. meets military reverses in VN, as Senator McCarthy alleges. (J. Bell)
W	Vietnam-Travel-004-126A	Pentagon urges congressmen to postpone trips to S. VN.
Montgomery, Ala.	8-305A	Newspaper editor Eugene Patterson says U.S. cannot win VN War militarily, but may win by waiting for settlement of what is essentially a political war.
El Cerrito, Calif.	28-513A	Former University of California President Clark Kerr joins NEGOTIATIONS NOW, moderates seeking end to VN War.
Phnom Penh	0320530A	Prince Sihanouk thanks N. VNese Premier Long for gift of pistol captured from downed American pilot.
W	Vietnam-AID-040-623A	Top official of AID says communists receive some commodities sent to VN.
Columbus, Ohio	ONA-Canham-40-638A	Editor of *Christian Science Monitor* Canham says U.S. does not have "the makings of victory" in VN.

Dateline	Story	
Moscow	Vietnam-Brezhnev-042-639A	Brezhnev tells VC's man in Moscow that VNese people can "count on the brotherly aid and support of the Soviet people."
W	Conscientious Objectors-061-711A	Though two organizations spend more than $200,000 a year to counsel conscientious objectors, Selective Service notes no increase in proportion of men with the exemption; details, statistics. (D. Barnes)
Vientiane	060-756A	ICC plane returns from Hanoi without three captured U.S. airmen held by N. VN.
Laos	Laos-Attack-069-9A	N. VNese Army troops preparing attack on S. Laotian town of Saravane, says communist defector.
Dallas, Tex.	Gov. Connally-3-1157A	Governor Connally says "We are going to win the war in VN"; quotes. (K. Siner)
U.N.	Vietnam-UN-64-101P	S. VN's U.N. Ambassador Chi accuses Senator R. Kennedy of "irresponsible ignorance of the true nature" of VN War.
Independence, Kans.	Curtis-73-159P	Senator Curtis criticizes foreign policies of both Johnson and Kennedy Administrations; quotes.
W	US-Vietnam-75-208P	Senator Mansfield says Johnson repeatedly expresses confidence in Westmoreland's ability to cope with threatened communist offensive at Khe Sanh; details (3).
Moscow	Thant-Vietnam-030-229P	U.N. Secretary Thant flying to Moscow; informed sources doubt U.S.S.R. and Britain will call another Geneva conference. (H. Bradsher)
London	Vietnam-Europe-041-318P	AP press survey of reaction to U.S. in VN shows "many Western European friends have turned on the U.S."; details, quotes. (L. Nevin)
W	Viet Intelligence-047-404P	Twelve days after Tet offensive, U.S. concedes gaps in intelligence, but cites many more mistakes by enemy. (L. Gulick)
W	nt ld US-Vietnam-023-405P	Senator Mansfield says Johnson has repeatedly expressed full confidence in Westmoreland's ability to come with enemy threat at Khe Sanh; quotes. (J. Bell)

Dateline	Story	
Ft. Gordon, Calif.	nt ld Soldier-36-414P	Decision expected on whether soldier protesting U.S. in VN and refusing to wear uniform will be jailed and fined.
New Delhi	Vietnam Casualties-053-427P	N. VNese Consul-General Hoa in New Delhi declared that communists killed 10,000 U.S. and 40,000 S. VNese in week of fighting up to February 5.
Gastonia, N.C.	Wife in Vietnam-057-451P	Dr. Charlie Glenn awaits his wife serving in VN as volunteer civilian doctor.
Cincinnati, Ohio	Antiwar Demonstrations-49-515P	One hundred fifty persons protest U.S. in VN in Cincinnati. (B. Beard)
London	With Moscow Thant-Viet-56-546P	London *Observer* carries story saying U.S.S.R. wants quick negotiations between U.S. and N. VN to settle war.
Louisville, Ky.	72-713P	Representative Laird joined Senator Morton in criticizing Johnson's handling of VN War; quotes.
Dallas, Tex.	Humphrey-100-845P	Hubert Humphrey branded recent VC offensive as act of infamy and failure, and said VC might be trying for position of strength for bargaining; quotes. (J. Bodnar)
Atlantic City, N.J.	Rusk-085-1205A	Rusk says VN War now in climatic period, and "there will be no question about the outcome" if U.S. troops are backed on home front; quotes.
Moscow	Vietnam-Tass-116-1240A	Tass says U.S. will be dealt "an even stronger rebuff" if it escalates VN War in retaliation for "recent VC victories."
February 11		
Newport, N.H.	42-1207P	"Sanford Gottlieb, executive director of the Committee For a Sane Nuclear Policy, said Sunday night that American officials were interested in putting the late Ngo Dinh Diem in power more than a year before the French were defeated at Dienbienphu in 1954."

Dateline	Story	
Canberra	Viet-Aussies-011-122P	Army Department says five more Australians killed, five wounded in VN, bringing total Australian casualties to 168 killed and 662 wounded.
W	Wilson-024-310P	Prime Minister Wilson said San Antonio formula for bombing halt is "the road to peace" in VN, and he has carried U.S. peace proposal to Soviet Premier Kosygin; quotes.
Moscow	Viet-Thant-042-317P	U.N. Secretary-General Thant arrived from India and informants said he discussed with Premier Kosygin prospects on VN peace. (H. Bradsher)
Tokyo	Vietnam-Vietcong-344P	- Hanoi Radio says VC announced plans to strengthen its "solidarity with an alliance of national, democratic, and peace forces" in S. VN.
W	Southeast Asia-4-441P	Former Ambassador to Thailand Martin says S.E. Asia's chances for making its own way in the world "look very good."
Tokyo	065-510P	Communist China's news agency described Soviet Premier Kosygin, Prime Minister Wilson, Yugoslav Tito as American "lackeys who are whipping up a new peace talks campaign" over VN.
Paris	Vietcong Strategy-075-558P	"The main aim of the VC offensive in S. VN is to eliminate or discredit the existing administrative machinery and keep the Saigon government from eventual negotiations, according to a well-studied assessment here." (D. Mason)
W	Reischauer-Galbraith-083-641P	Reischauer and Galbraith, both former ambassadors, criticize VN War and urge negotiations; quotes.
N.Y.	Gavin-087-717P	Former Lieutenant General Gavin recommends that U.S. end war in VN by halting bombing of N. VN, undertaking his "enclave" strategy, and begin negotiations for peace; details.
Boston	090-728P	Representative Heckler says Westmoreland "is engaged in vain art of self-delusion" and "is certainly deluding members of Congress"; quotes.

Dateline		Story
W	Asia-Congress-99-824P	Senator Mansfield proposes that U.S. take negotiations action to stop VN War and gain *Pueblo* crew; quotes from interview; details.
Orono, Maine	With Congress-Asia-1108P	Mansfield calls for two-thirds reduction of U.S. military strength in Europe and sharp curtailment of bombing of N. VN; quotes.
Topeka, Kans.	Landon Lead-41-1205A	Alf Landon said he agrees that use of strategic nuclear weapons in VN would be lunacy; quotes.

February 12

Moscow	2 ld Vietnam Peace-078-508A	Soviet Union publicly urged on VNese communists to new victories while discussing secret peace prospects with U.N. Secretary Thant; details. (A. Collings)
W	House-Westmoreland-076-743P	Representative Mahon criticizes efforts to discredit Westmoreland.
London	nt ld Vietnam Peace-029-415P	U.N. Secretary-General Thant comes to London after U.S.S.R. seeking Britain's help to stop escalation of VN War and get peace talks started. (A. Gavshon)
W	Harris Poll-057-525P	U.S. support for war effort jumped from 61 percent in December to 74 percent in February, says Harris poll; statistics.
N.Y.	55-629P	USO assistant director Jan Moorhead describes her time during Saigon attack; quotes. (E. Smith)
W	Johnson-065-650P	Johnson says that despite communist offensive in VN, his San Antonio Formula for peace talks still stands; quotes.
U.N.	UN-South Viet-078-754P	In a U.N. newsletter, S. VNese Ambassador Chi says U.S. critics of S. VN were "nervous" and sounding like colonial administrators.
Charlotte, N.C.	085-847P	Soldier, relieving his brother in VN, finds out he died.
W	Body Count-100-100P	Description of method U.S. command in Saigon arrives at figures for number of enemy dead; quotes.

Dateline	Story	
Chicago	Pucinski-109-11P	Representative Pucinski says Presidential emissary was in Hanoi to discuss terms for bombing halt and negotiations to end VN War, when enemy attacked U.S. Saigon Embassy
N.Y.	Vietnam-GOP-111-1140P	Hatfield and Javits say that Johnson believed he has taken as much action as is possible to end VN War.
Phila-delphia, Pa.	123-1245A	Senator Hickenlooper says U.S. should not slacken its bombing raids in VN.
H.K.	Note-48-1255A	"The yacht *Phoenix* and its crew of American pacifists were a week overdue Monday in returning to Hong Kong from N. VN, but a spokesman for the Quaker action group said the boat probably has not left Haiphong."
February 13		
W	Desertions-005-140A	Navy and Marine Corps post five- and six-year highs in desertion convictions; statistics. (B. Horton)
W	US-Vietnam-9-916A	Johnson says despite Tet offensive he will halt bombing of N. VN, begin peace talks, and let enemy "write the agenda" if N. VN doesn't "try a doublecross."
W	Harassment-12-930A	Widows and mothers whose husbands and sons were killed in VN are being subjected to harassment.
	North Vietnam Survival-077-942A	AP correspondent answers questions by readers on how N. VN manages to survive after three years of U.S. bombing; details; statistics. (W. Ryan)
Dover, N.H.	Nixon-23-1011A	Nixon is engaged in dispute with Governor Romney where Nixon takes harder line on the war.
Manila	Medics-39-1112A	While 15 Filipino medics treated S. VNese soldiers and civilians in Saigon, other soldiers looted their quarters, the *Daily Mirror* reported.
W	Press Criticism-095-1128A	High Administration official meeting privately with newsmen is critical of coverage of VN War.
Bangkok	Pilots-47-1142A	Three U.S. pilots whom N. VN promised to release are expected in Vientiane Friday, says U.S. Embassy in Laos.

Dateline		Story
W	US-VN-64-1239P	U.S. sending 10,500 additional Army and Marine ground combat troops to S. VN, says Defense Department; details (4).
W	Precede Pucinski-Hanoi-1257P	Administration sources say U.S. diplomatic approaches to N. VN made through third party, but denied that American went to Hanoi as Presidential emissary, as said Pucinski.
W	nt ld US-Vietnam-022-311P	U.S. sending additional 10,500 Army and Marines to S. VN as insurance against second enemy city offensive and assault on Khe Sanh; details; statistics. (F. Hoffman)
W	Vietnam Mail-110-324P	Post Office says backlog of 350 tons of packages for servicemen in VN expected to be cleared up this week.
W	029-344P	Army reportedly collecting $70.21 from VN veteran who lost his rifle in combat.
London	nt ld Viet-Thant-031-359P	U.N. Secretary-General Thant met with Wilson on war in VN.
Paris	074-823P	Estimated 10,000 communist-led demonstrators protesting against U.S. in VN parade in Paris.
Moscow	Viet-Defections-077-832P	Tass said many RSVN troops in S. VN northern provinces have defected to VC.
N.Y.	Viet-Airlines-082-906P	Many of nation's airlines asked to commit more planes to VN airlift of men and supplies.
Conway, Ark.	Fulbright-098-920P	Senator Fulbright says "real alternative" to VN War is to give up idea that enemy will unconditionally surrender.
H.K.	Viet-Phoenix-099-1020P	Pacifist yacht *Phoenix* returns to Hong Kong from Hanoi, where it delivered $7,500 worth of medical supplies to N. VN Red Cross.
Columbia, S.C.	109-1141P	Scheduled "pray-in" by Ft. Jackson soldiers fails to come off.

Dateline		Story
W	137	"Reports in at least three U.S. newspapers that four U.S. nuclear scientists are in Vietnam on a Pentagon mission have caused the "Women Strike for Peace" group to drop everything and plan a trip to several embassies Thursday."
W	13	Pentagon says Westmoreland has not asked for increase over 525,000-man level now authorized in VN.

February 14

Melbourne	033-457A	Arthur Caldwell, former leader of Australia's Labor Party, says Johnson should be impeached "because he said the war in VN could be won when it is now being lost."
Alpena, Mich.	33-531A	Representative Riegle says war in VN is "an endless Asian grinder" and that Johnson is refusing to make either of the two decisions that would end the conflict.
Paris	Thant-9-927A	U.N. Secretary-General Thant made trip to Paris to possibly receive message from Hanoi.
Tokyo	Vietnam-Hanoi-12-936A	Radio Hanoi says U.S. jets attacked populated area of Hanoi, first raid of the year.
W	US-Vietnam-1001A	Senator Morton questions necessity of U.S. stand at Khe Sanh.
H.K.	089-1019A	Communist newspaper reports that N. VNese fire on U.S. Marines at Khe Sanh, then pull their artillery through tunnels to new positions.
H.K.	Vietnam-China-27-1025A	Hong Kong *Star* says Red China has promised N. VN more workers and nuclear weapons, "if needed."
Bangkok	Pilots-1142A	Three U.S. pilots N. VN promised to free expected in Vientiane Friday night, says U.S. embassy.
U.N.	Vietnam-Kennedy-98-121P	S. VNese Ambassador Chi at U.N. charges that Senator Edward Kennedy has joined his brother Senator Robert Kennedy in making unjustified attacks on S. VNese war efforts.

Dateline		Story
W	Lawyers-Vietnam-020-224P	Four thousand five hundred law teachers and students sign statement opposing U.S. policy in VN.
W	Byrd-Vietnam-107-250P	Senator Byrd calls on Administration to reappraise VN policies and "develop a sense of urgency" toward ending war.
Rome	Vietnam-Italy-027-318P	Foreign Minister Fanfani held meetings with N. VNese representatives on possibility of beginning peace talks, says Ministry.
W	Air Guard-129-407P	Air National Guard and Air Force Reserve units will help transport the 10,500 new U.S. troops to VN, says Senator Stennis.
Paris	Thant-134-430P	U.N. Secretary-General Thant conferred with N. VNese diplomat and is convinced that peace in VN is as far away as ever; details (3).
Ottawa	Canada-Viet-070-650P	Foreign Secretary Martin said he received report from Canadian diplomat who spent time in Hanoi, but refused to reveal contents.
Ottawa	045-449P	Canadian child psychologist and mother sent cablegram to Pope Paul VI asking him to become hostage in Hanoi to stop "barbarous American bombardment."
W	Rusk-Vietnam-047-457P	Rusk says N. VN thus far rejected Johnson's San Antonio formula for peace in VN; text of statement issued by Rusk on possibility of peace settlement on VN; details.
W	Vietnam Call-Up-003-536	New call-up of 10,500 combat troops cuts into reserve of full-time soldiers; details. (F. Hoffman)
N.Y.	Gallup Poll-063-618P	Half of adult Americans polled since Tet offensive disapprove of way Johnson is handling war, while only one-third approve, shows latest Gallup poll; statistics.
Strouds-burg, Pa.	Marine-075-719P	Mother of a dead Marine killed in VN refuses military funeral for her son.

Dateline	Story	
W	Lost Rifle-078-739P	Army says discharged VN veteran Ernest Wagner is being billed $71.20 for losing rifle because investigating officer found him negligent; quotes. (F. Hoffman)
W	Wheeler-082-754P	General Wheeler says he does not believe nuclear weapons necessary in defending Khe Sanh.
New Delhi	Viet-Civilians-088-817P	S. VNese Foreign Minister Do says S. VNese civilians paid a "very high price" at enemy hands during Tet offensive.
Moscow	Viet-Victory Claim-090-830P	VC representative praised "big and unselfish assistance of the Soviet Union" which will lead to "new major victories."
Philadelphia, Pa.	Haiphong Talk-97-957P	William Mimms, most recent American to return from N. VN says he saw enough evidence in Haiphong to convince him that U.S. cannot win VN War.
N.Y.	124-1156P	One hundred seventy-seven Vista Volunteers urge Johnson to end U.S. involvement in VN and concentrate on eradicating poverty in America.

February 15

W	Vietnam-Peace-005-143A	Although latest round of peace probings between U.S. and N. VN has not been promising, Rusk says U.S. remains interested in peace; details, quotes. (J. Hightower)
Boston	055-757A	Harvard Professor Galbraith says collapse of S. VNese government and Army are imminent.
W	US Air Losses-8-920A	U.S. has already lost 800 aircraft in N. VN and Pentagon scientist Foster warns higher loss rates perhaps ahead.
W	US-Vietnam-12-935A	Rusk indirectly accuses Senator Fulbright of "a disservice to the country" for questioning whether U.S. nuclear weapons will be used in VN.

Dateline	Story	
W	Medal of Honor-53-1149A	28th Medal of Honor awarded to soldier who killed eight enemy in December 1966, says Pentagon.
Burlington, Wis.	115-1223P	Representative Schadeberg is asking Army Secretary Reasor to investigate VN soldier's assertion that U.S. battalion had all its rifles and sidearms locked up when it came under fire February 8.
W	Westmoreland-73-1240P	Johnson has every justification to relieve Westmoreland from VN command, says Senator Young.
W	AID-Investigation-75-128P	State Department investigators reported to Senate Foreign Relations Committee on irregularities and laxity in U.S. assistance programs in 30 countries, including VN.
Boston	Nixon-96-142P	Nixon says use of nuclear weapons to protect Khe Sanh "would be neither necessary nor desirable."
W	US-Vietnam-003-230P	Senator Mansfield says he expects Johnson to seek increase in defense budget and that he thinks Westmoreland is doing excellent job; details, quotes (3). (J. Bell)
Bern	Viet-Peace-026-303P	Switzerland, acting on its own initiative, has dispatched diplomat to Hanoi to mediate peace.
W	Rusk-Nuclear-123-311P	"U.S. Secretary of State Dean Rusk has quoted Presidential Press Secretary George Christian in reply to J. W. Fulbright, Democrat-Ark., about sending atomic weapons to S. VN."
W	Paratroopers-Vietnam-038-405P	Pentagon says nearly half of paratroopers in an Army brigade going to S. VN have seen duty there before; statistics. (F. Hoffman)
Jacksonville, Oreg.	Family-143-431P	Parents of Douglas Rowden, whose two older brothers have been killed in VN, will fight to keep him from being drafted.

Dateline		Story
Milwaukee, Wis.	060-405P	Representative Davis says Westmoreland says Johnson will dismiss Westmoreland from head of U.S. in VN "before Easter."
London	2 nt ld Vietnam-Thant-049-504P	N. VN's top diplomats in Asia and Europe told U.N. Secretary-General Thant N. VN rejects Johnson's terms for peace talks; details. (A. Gavshon)
Havana	052-517P	Prime Minister Castro reaffirms his willingness to send Cuban volunteers to VN to help communists.
W	nt ld US-Vietnam-070-542P	Pentagon official Dr. Foster and Representative Riegle estimate growing enemy strength in VN; details.
Lancaster, Pa.	nt ld Chief-057-543P	Former Lancaster police chief volunteering as civilian in VN in protest to antiwar demonstrators killed by sniper.
W	Rusk-Fulbright-078-718P	Senator Fulbright says it would be a national disaster if U.S. troops in VN are placed in such danger "as to require nuclear weapons to prevent their destruction"; quotes.
U.N.	nt ld Vietnam-Thant-085-741P	U.N. Secretary-General Thant told U.S. Ambassador Goldberg about his recent talks overseas on VN and Goldberg said information was "very useful."
W	Vietnam Rifle-100-852P	Representative Schadeberg is receiving donations to pay for rifle lost by soldier in VN.
February 16		
Bakersfield, Calif.	With Washington Prisoners-139-110A	Mrs. Sol Mathneyhear informed her son freed with two other U.S. pilots by N. VN.
W	US Air Losses-001-114A	U.S. has already lost 800 aircraft in N. VN and Pentagon's Dr. Foster warns higher losses perhaps ahead; details, statistics. (B. Horton)
W	Khe Sanh-005-150A	Some U.S. military analysts predict N. VN may use bombardment instead of infantry to attack Khe Sanh; details. (F. Hoffman)

Dateline	Story	
W	Viet-Prisoners-42-1128A	State Department said they believed N. VN was releasing three captured U.S. officers but lacked confirmation that release has already occurred.
W	Viet-Prisoners-49-1151A	State Department received word from Vientiane that three U.S. pilots freed by N. VN have arrived in Laos; details (3).
W	Rusk-Marines-55-1208P	Rusk awarded Heroic Service Citation to Marine guards who protected U.S.'s Saigon Embassy during Tet offensive.
W	US-Vietnam-63-1238P	Johnson will meet with U.N. Secretary-General Thant next Wednesday, says Washington.
Atlanta, Ga.	Court-Martial-87-143P	Army court-martial returns verdict of innocent in case of Negro veteran of VN accused of calling white officer a "white bastard."
W	Army-Korea-Vietnam-89-151P	Secretary of Army Reasor predicts talks on Korea, Vietnam; details.
W	Guard Flights-034-411P	Pentagon triples number of flights assigned to Air National Guard to move shipment of 10,500 combat troops to VN.
Oscoda, Mich.	Overly-With-Flyers-058-552P	Mrs. Ruth Overly talks to freed pilot husband.
W	nt 1d US-Vietnam-042-619P	U.N. Secretary Thant will talk to Johnson about peace-finding trip; details. (L. Gulick)
Leningrad	Brezhnev-075-708P	U.S.S.R. party chief Brezhnev called on U.S. government to "heed the voice of reason and consider realistically" N. VNese terms for peace talks.
Clark Air Force Base	Precede Vientiane Fliers-004-742P	Three U.S. freed pilots arrive in Philippines and say they are happy to be going home; details (5).
W	Quick Kill-160-926P	VN War has developed new technique of "quick kill . . . of fast, unaimed, instinct shooting" says General Johnson, Army Chief of Staff, to Senate Armed Services Committee.
Laredo, Tex.	Prisoner Texas-121-935P	Mrs. Black, wife of freed U.S. pilot, talks to husband.

Dateline		Story
Princeton, N.J.	118-1011P	Two hundred fifty Princeton University students pledge participation in weekend fast protesting VN War.
Johnson City, Tenn.	Airmen-reaction-109-1139A	Mother of John Black, one of freed U.S. pilots is overjoyed at son's release; quotes.
Milwaukee, Wis.	711	Major General Stone said he locked up rifles and sidearms prior to enemy attack in VN because "the camp is heavily defended" and because of the incidence of accidental gunshot wounds.
W	Washington Roundup-100	State Department says put number of refugees in VN resulting from Tet offensive as 350,000.

February 17

Vatican City	Vietnam-Pope-062-856A	Vatican disclosed Pope Paul VI's top diplomat made secret trip to Paris last month to confer with N. VNese there.
Clark Air Force Base	Airmen-6-913A	First released U.S. pilots to be freed by N. VN talked with their wives, and are fine.
U.N.	Vietnam-UN Lead-108-1049P	Diplomatic sources said N. VN has told Thant that it is willing to make military de-escalation an item on agenda of any opening peace talks; details.
W	Airmen-127-1249A	The three released U.S. pilots arrive in Washington and said they understood there was a possibility that more pilots would be released. (J. Adam)
Vientiane	Laos-Thai-74-135P	Laotian and Thai forces are on full alert for any communist probes in their countries following new enemy offensive in S. VN.
W	Vietnam-Critics-030-242P	Administration is wanting to limit debate over VN War, but does not know how, and so in sharpening disagreement--news analysis. (J. Hightower)

Dateline		Story
Moscow, Idaho	Gore-Vietnam-37- 312P	Senator Gore says neutralization of S. VN is key to honorable disengagement; quotes.
San Antonio, Tex.	nt ld Capt. Black-51- 345P	Mrs. Black left her home for reunion with her AF husband re- leased by N. VN.
Laken- heath, England	40-345P	All Americans ordered out of sight when peace demonstrators marched into housing area of this USAF base protesting VN War.
Pope Air Force Base, N.C.	Johnson-114-438P	Johnson arrives on secret flight to visit units of 82nd Airborne waiting to leave for VN; details (3).
El Toro Marine Air Station, Calif.	4 ld Johnson-126-510P	Johnson visits leaving troops in El Toro Marine Air Station in California and Pope Air Force Base in North Carolina; details, quotes. (D. Cornell)
W	Gunship-055-512P	C-130 cargo planes refitted as fighters are being assigned to VN War.
London	57-515P	London *Observer* says Hanoi does not appear to be seriously interested in any form of peace negotiations for ending VN War.
Spring- field, Ill.	70-519P	General Taylor says VC "has been forced to change his strategy."
Los Angeles	97-625P	Three hundred California state and county officials send Johnson a telegram saying his VN policies hurt California Democratic Party.
Moscow	Vietnam-Kosygin-077- 645P	Premier Kosygin told Communist Party meeting it is "untrue" that N. VN is not ready for peace talks with U.S.
Boston	Editorial Survey-12- 647P	Boston *Globe* says seven metro- politan newspapers switched from editorial endorsement of Ad- ministration's VN policies to criticism; statistics, details on editorial survey.
Holly, Mich.	29-809P	Mrs. Phelps, hearing that her son is heading back for VN combat, says "They're going to kill him this time."

Dateline	Story	
Berlin	nt ld Viet Congress-101-833P	Two U.S. burned draft cards during leftist-sponsored VN congress.
U.N.	Vietnam-UN-108-1049P	U.N. proceedings on VN.

February 18

Berlin	Vietnam-March-037-338P	VC flags held in march by thousands of youths protesting U.S. engagement in VN; details. (H. Erb)
El Toro Marine Air Station, Calif.	Johnson-Troops-042-414P	Description of response of leaving U.S. troops for VN to visit by Johnson and Johnson's reaction to troops. (F. Cormier)
N.Y.	Pilots-053-523P	Rev. Berrigan and Professor Zinn, U.S. pacifists who collected freed U.S. pilots from N. VN, said U.S. handling of affair was "inept and cold blooded."
Grand Island, Nebr.	30-628P	National Commander of American Legion says, "If it takes an all-out war effort to achieve a military victory in VN, then we must support our fighting men."
Los Angeles	62-710P	Report that recent fighting in VN killed 18 out of 51 orphans whom a southern California group has tried to bring from VN to U.S. is called false.
N.Y.	078-722P	Recent Tet offensive has resulted in sharp decline in number of people who approve Johnson's performance, says Gallup poll; statistics.
Tokyo	Vietnam-Committee-066-633P	N. VN broadcast says People's Revolutionary Committee calls for overthrow of S. VNese government administrative organs in Hue and surrounding Thua Thien province.
Palm Desert, Calif.	2 ld Johnson-084-751P	Johnson calls on Ike after "telling American fighting men the enemy in VN will fail to break the will and hopes of the United States"; details, quotes. (D. Cornell)

Dateline		Story
Le Havre	091-822P	"More than 2,000 communist-led demonstrators Sunday greeted a Soviet ship that will carry 600 tons of food, clothing, and medical supplies to N. VN."
Dayton, Ohio	Overly-54-927P	Lt. Col. Norris Overly, one of freed U.S. pilots, is home for son's 10th birthday.
Cumber-land, Md.	Mother-63-1024P	Army and U.S. Red Cross launch search for mother of serviceman seriously wounded in VN who has been asking for her, said youth's grandmother.
February 19		
Berlin	Viet-March-034-536A	West Germany's New Left climaxed weekend of demonstration against U.S. VN involvement with adoption of program to help communist war effort by undermining U.S. forces in Europe. (O. Doelling)
W	Johnson-12-939A	Johnson, after transcontinental tour, meeting with Eisenhower, says more troops will be sent if needed in VN.
Boston	Kennedy-Draft-36-1113A	Senator Edward Kennedy says he will file legislation for revision of draft law.
Evans-ville, Ind.	Hartke-77-120P	Senator Hartke says current VC offensive is aided by "corruption, built-in inefficiency, and organized profiteering" in S. VNese government and Army.
W	6-221P	Representative Bray says U.S. reserve dangerously weakened by recent transfer of 10,500 combat troops to VN.
W	Airman-017-241P	State Department did not deny report that three released U.S. airmen had been ordered to fly back to U.S. on military aircraft, a charge made by two pacifists; details.
North Easton, Mass.	18-302P	Senator E. Kennedy proposed that U.S. change its VN strategy from search-and-destroy missions to clear-and-hold policy.

Dateline		Story
W	Civilian Casualties-107-311P	Eight U.S. civilian officials killed in enemy offensive, says State Department.
Tokyo	Vietcong-035-437P	VC says "the struggle ahead will be very fierce and arduous" in S. VN despite "great victories."
W	Fulbright-Vietnam-40-437P	Senator Fulbright says latest White House appraisal of VN situation is wholly irrational.
Moscow	037-448P	Ambassador of N. VN to U.S.S.R. Cham has been issued visa to visit Sweden, says Swedish Embassy.
East Point, Ga.	Precede Saigon Day-060-619P	Teenager receives marriage proposal over telephone from boyfriend in VN; quotes.
Atlanta, Ga.	Connally-061-626P	Governor Connally of Texas says Senator Robert Kennedy's position on VN damaged U.S. conduct of foreign affairs.
Clio, Mich.	Precede IVS-Viet-64-627P	Woman teaching high school in Hue is prisoner of VC, say her parents.
W	nt ld Senate-Vietnam-76-712P	White House appraisal of recent events in VN drew criticism from Fulbright and Senator Pearson.
Marlboro, Mass.	074-725P	Father makes public letter from soldier son in VN making assertion that his company was mortared and they were without weapons; quotes.
N.Y.	087-820P	Second Lt. R. Pershing, grandson of late Gen. J. Pershing, killed in action in VN.
Tokyo	Vietcong-Viet-103-1023P	VC claims many S. VNese soldiers defected to communists in Hue and established an organization to help enemy.
February 20		
W	US-Asia-15-1008A	McNamara to appear before closed session of Senate Foreign Relations Committee to testify on 1964 Gulf of Tonkin incident.
	Servicmen-Johnson-10-1012A	Reactions of U.S. servicemen Johnson visited in surprise sendoff of new U.S. troops for VN.

Dateline		Story
W	US-Asia-93-213P	"Senators participating in a closed-door review of the 1964 Tonkin Gulf incident disagreed today on whether Defense Secretary Robert S. McNamara was shedding any more light on the events."
W	US-Asia-98-233P	McNamara said U.S. has intelligence reports of "highly classified and unimpeachable nature" which establish N. VNese naval attacks on U.S. destroyers in August 1964; details (3).
Fredericktown, Ohio	McMahon-093-806P	Sgt. William McMahon killed during attack on Tan Son Nhut Airport Terminal.
U.N.	Human Rights-UN-113-937P	Soviet Ambassador Morozov charged that U.S. trampling human rights in VN.
February 21		
Bern	Vietnam-Swiss-070-012A	Swiss ambassador in Peking Rossetti completes four days of talks in Hanoi.
W	Military Manpower-005-146A	Pentagon intends to maintain one-year VN duty tour regardless of other action to raise U.S. manpower in S.E. Asia; details. (F. Hoffman)
W	Tonkin Gulf-13-1015A	Senator Fulbright says McNamara has not satisfactorily explained Gulf of Tonkin incident, despite 7-1/2 hour session with Senate committee.
W	Vietnam-Diem-16-1028A	S. VNese Ambassador Diem says unconditional halt to bombing of N. VN would be used by Hanoi to put more pressure on allied forces and "sew division and discord among us."
Medford, Oreg.	015-1053A	Jackson County Draft Board gave one-year deferment to Douglas Rowden, brother of two men who died in VN.
W	US-Vietnam-22-1055A	Administration expresses little optimism that Thant-Johnson talks will produce any new U.S. peace move.
W	LBJ-Thant-41-1151A	Johnson welcomes Thant for talks about VN peace.

Dateline	Story
Stockholm	Viet-Sweden-112-1226P — N. VNese Ambassador to Moscow Chan emerged from two days of talks with Swedish government to restate Hanoi's terms for peace talks.
W	Air Force-Vietnam-010-132P — Air Force leaders ask Congress for $29 billion to continue bombing in N. VN and S. VN.
W	Tonkin-104-250P — Senator Fulbright challenges McNamara's statement that government has unimpeachable evidence of second N. VNese attack on U.S. destroyers in 1964 Tonkin Gulf incident.
W	nt ld US-Vietnam-052-520P — Johnson and Thant talked about VN without any evident progress toward negotiations to end war; details. (L. Gulick)
W	Gardiner-033-526P — AID official tells how Army medic helped him when he was wounded in Saigon; quotes. (M. Cole)
Ithaca, N.Y.	058-717P — Rev. Daniel Berrigan, who helped in rescue of released U.S. pilots from N. VN, said men told him they had memorized names of fellow captives.
Berlin	nt ld Rally Roundup-088-741P — West Berliners turned out in John F. Kennedy Square for massive rally in support of U.S. policy, while protests held in Paris, West Berlin, Stockholm.
W	nt ld Tonkin-079-824P — Senator Fulbright charged McNamara with misleading Congress on 1964 Tonkin Gulf incident at time it happened and now; details (3). (R. Gray)
W	Vietnam-House-04-848P — House Armed Services subcommittee says U.S. should launch an offensive in VN; quotes.
Brighton, England	With Berlin-115-946P — Students demonstrating against VN War throw paint over U.S. Embassy official Beers and daughter.
U.N.	Thant Return-121-1014P — Secretary General Thant returned from talks.

Dateline		Story
February 22		
Grand Island, Nebr.	004-1218P	Parents of wounded soldier in VN speak to him after being told he was dead.
	Executions-107-1205P	Radio Hanoi says communists will carry out "appropriate action" if S. VN holds public executions of captured communists in Hue.
Austin, Tex.	Johnson-Ford-002-208P	Texas White House says selection of new deputy ambassador to S. VN is Samuel D. Berger, and labeled as "rumor" speculation that Henry Ford II may receive major federal job; details.
W	nt ld Tonkin-091-327P	Defense security censors pronounce testimony by McNamara on 1964 Gulf of Tonkin incident ready for public disclosure; details, quotes. (B. Horton)
N.Y.	Ch Note-60-647P	Retired General Clark, commander of UN during Korean War, says U.S. should step up bombing of N. VN, but does not advocate use of nuclear weapons.
San Diego, Calif.	nt ld Churches-80-518P	"Increased military activity by either side will hamper, rather than promote, an early settlement of the VN War, the general board of the National Council of Churches said Thursday"; quotes.
Las Cruces, N.M.	115-907P	Former New Mexico governor Mechem's son killed in VN.
W	Mobilization-118-1148P	Joint Chiefs of Staff propose call-up of 50,000 Army National Guardsmen and Marine reservists to bolster U.S. forces in U.S. depleted by VN War; details. (F. Hoffman)
February 23		
Manila	053-635A	Philippine House of Representatives approves resolution calling for U.N. intervention in VN.
North Bergen, N.J.	With Hue Battle-089-1031A	New Jersey Marine unfurls U.S. flag over Hue's Citadel; quotes from parents.
W	Gardiner-Vietnam-23-1051A	Former Director of AID in Saigon, Gardiner, says U.S. "creating more VC than we are destroying."

Dateline		Story
Phila- delphia, Pa.	100-1120A	American Friends Service Committee is temporarily suspending its programs in VN because of danger.
Moscow	Soviet Military-47- 1124A	Communist Party leader Brezhnev declares U.S. main cause of war in world and calls VN a "criminal, dirty war."
W	Draft-51-1131A	Pentagon orders 48,000 men drafted in April, the highest monthly call in 2-1/2 years; statistics.
London	Tucson Asked-101- 1231P	London *Times* reports "President Johnson is now determined to fight the war to the finish."
W	Tonkin-Skippers-128- 136P	Officer in charge of the two U.S. destroyers involved in Gulf of Tonkin incident, Captain Herrick, says his ships were on routine patrol; quotes, details.
N.Y.	008-142P	*Wall Street Journal*, which has supported Administration in VN, says, "The American people should be getting ready to accept, if they haven't already, the prospect that the whole VN effort may be doomed"; quotes.
W	Viet Allies-96-2P	U.S. officials say there will be meeting of countries who have troops in VN: U.S., S. VN, Thailand, S. Korea, Philippines, Australia, New Zealand--to be held in New Zealand.
W	US-Vietnam-003-406P	Fifty Thousand National Guardsmen and Marines reservists would be called up in tentative plan by Joint Chiefs of Saff to fill in for those missing because of VN War; details, statistics.
U.N.	Thant-Vietnam- 418P	U Thant determined to put before world--especially American people--full account of his latest efforts to bring about negotiations for VN peace.
Blooming- ton, Ind.	Mansfield-31-436P	Senator Mansfield said suspension of bombing in N. VN probably would bring Hanoi to conference table; quotes.
Phoenix, Ariz.	063-438P	Rusk says that VN attacks on S. VNese cities means that "issues are drawing to a head" in war; quotes.

Dateline		Story
W	Tonkin Gulf-54-625P	Senator Gruening says McNamara did not tell whole truth about Tonkin Gulf incident when it happened or at Senate Committee review last week.
W	Rusk-075-729P	Rusk is the Administration official who told a group of newsmen that criticism of the handling of VN War sometimes gets to the point "when the question is, whose side are you on"; quotes.
Paris	1053P	National Council of the Peace Movement announces three days of demonstrations against VN War beginning March 15.
Tokyo	Giap-125	General Giap, N. VNese mastermind of enemy offensive, quoted as saying battle in S. VN is entering "a fierce phase," in which there will be continual attacks.

February 24

Dateline		Story
Stockholm	Defectors-057-7A	American deserts in Sweden set their goal at 2,000 defectors; details.
W	Gruening-Vietnam-5-255A	Senator Gruening says he will propose plan for "getting the U.S. out of this ridiculous war in VN"; quotes. (B. Meyer)
W	US-Vietnam-10-908A	Administration expresses hope that Rusk's appearance before Senate Foreign Relations Committee in March will defuse feud between Rusk and Senator Fulbright.
U.N.	Thant-Vietnam-16-933A	Thant has prepared comprehensive statement of how he thinks peace can be brought about in VN.
W	North Vietnam AID-022-156P	U.S.S.R. is apparently N. VN's largest supplier of weapons and economic aid, and its assistance may rise if war escalates; details, statistics. (L. Gulick)
W	World Court-Findley-23-224P	Representative Findley says U.S. should turn over its international disputes--including VN War--to International Court of Justice for settlement.

Dateline	Story	
W	Tonkin Highlights-29-349P	Highlights from transcript of Senate Foreign Relations Committee hearings where McNamara testified on Tonkin Gulf incident; details, quotes (6).
W	Military Manpower-044-353P	Pentagon officials say decision on whether to call up reservists is waiting until General Wheeler returns from VN; statistics. (F. Hoffman)
W	Tonkin-032-401P	Analysis of McNamara's report to Senate Foreign Relations Committee on Gulf of Tonkin incident in 1964; quotes, details (9). (R. Gray, W. Mears)
Philadelphia, Pa.	052-447P	Woman doctor missing in Hue, believed captive, says American Friends Service Committee.
W	Three Naval Incidents-056-505P	Reasons why U.S. reacted so differently in three similar naval incidents involving the *Maddox* and *C. Turner Joy*, *Liberty* and *Pueblo* explained by McNamara; quotes. (H. Rosenthal)
W	Tonkin-545P	The transcript of Senate Foreign Relations Committee's questioning of McNamara is 110 pages long; approval of Tonkin Gulf resolution, in 1964, resulted from hearings which are 36 pages long.
N.Y.	Wirephoto NY-59-551P	Crowd estimated at 2,000 demonstrated in front of U.S. Mission to U.N. to protest possible use of nuclear weapons in VN.
Atlanta, Ga.	nt ld Democrat-62-605P	Ambassador-at-Large Harriman says U.S. cannot stop bombing N. VN to entice peace talks unless N. VN understands it cannot use opportunity to strike S. VN; quotes.
U.N.	2 nt ld Thant-Vietnam-089-857P	Secretary-General Thant says peace talks will begin as soon as U.S. stops bombing N. VN; details (5), text of Thant's address. (M. Harrelson)
W	Tonkin-937P	Continuing confusion over Gulf of Tonkin incident despite McNamara's 7-1/2 hour testimony; details, quotes (3).

Dateline		Story
W	Personality in the News-095-1034P	Biography of John J. Herrick, commander of ships involved in 1964 Tonkin Gulf incident. (M. Barr)
Ft. Bragg, N.C.	Prisoner-090-1049A	Comments from ex-POW St. James Jackson; quotes. (F. Girard)
W	127-1158P	Mexican-Americans from California died in VN War last year more than twice their ratio in the general population, says Representative Brown: statistics.
February 25		
N.Y.	022-223P	Biography of reporter (Wes Gallagher) who held interview with Westmoreland.
Stockholm	Defectors-032-326P	Description of meeting of U.S. defectors organizing in Stockholm; quotes. (W. Grimsley)
Cleveland, Ohio	With Vietnam-Wheeler-2-414P	Senator Young said Johnson will call up active Army reservists and part of National Guard in a week or so.
W	Vietnam-Peace Talks-037-415P	U.N. Secretary-General Thant's call for halt in bombing of N. VN spurred by S. VNese President Thieu and Undersecretary of State Bundy; quotes.
Moscow	5-429P	Tass says Dr. Spock, expert on child care who advises young people to avoid draft, has written to leading Soviet scientists thanking them for their supporting anti-VN efforts in U.S.
W	Vietnam-Tonkin-041-448P	Senator Fulbright says even if Administration version of Tonkin Gulf incident is accepted, the first U.S. air strikes against N. VN were unjustified; quotes.
Lincoln City, Oreg.	33-630P	"Strong sentiment for withdrawal of American troops from Vietnam has developed among Oregon Republicans, especially the younger ones." (P. Harvey)
Oxford, Ohio	Taylor-41-650P	General Taylor says N. VN tactics of striking cities is "dismal failure" in terms of long-range objectives; quotes.

Dateline	Story	
Framing- ham, Mass.	Legion and McCarthy- 46-729P	American Legion "demands that all political restrictions be lifted from the military as to the nature and scope of targets to be destroyed in N. VN"; quotes.
Tokyo	North Viet-Aid Call- 092-1035P	N. VN calls on communist countries and nations to condemn U.S. war actions in S. VN and urged them to help communists in war effort.
Sydney	R & R Spotlight-392- 1140P	Description of U.S. servicemen on R & R in Australia. (G. Tait)

February 26

Miami Beach, Fla.	152-103A	Senator E. Kennedy says if U.S. cannot get VC to conference table, U.S. should reduce fighting.
London	Brown-Vietnam-084- 1026A	Foreign Secretary Brown says Hanoi, not U.S. is holding back peace talks.
Phila- delphia, Pa.	091-1106A	Student leaders from Harvard, Yale, Columbia, Brown, Dartmouth sign statement condemning U.S. participation in VN War as "wrong, unjustified, and not in the national interest."
W	US-Vietnam-013-154P	Senator Mansfield calls for trial suspension in bombing of N. VN as possible peace alternative to escalating the war; details on U.S. feelings towards peace prospects; continuing debate between Fulbright and McNamara, etc., details (4).
Pak Sane, Laos	nt ld Laotian-026- 451P	Force of N. VN and Laotian communists seize Laotian military outpost on border of Laos and Thailand; details, statistics.
Vientiane	Reds-Laos-049-513P	Laos troops claim killing 186 N. VN soldiers and recapturing southern Laos town overrun by communists.
W	nt ld Congress-Viet- nam-48-519P	Senate debate over VN: Johnson wishes to meet with members of Senate Foreign Relations Committee, says Senator Mansfield.
W	War Pictures-072- 703P	Representative Taylor questions use of photographs in U.S. papers of VC being executed by S. VN military.

Dateline		Story
Honolulu	Wheeler-113-726P	General Wheeler says U.S. forces were not taken by surprise by VN Tet offensive, and reports of gaps in U.S. intelligence were "erroneous and derogatory."
Los Angeles	143-852P	Police Chief Reddin says many of the leaders and participants in antiwar demonstration last June 23 have been identified as communists.
February 27		
W	Moss-Censorship-003-119A	Chairman of House Government Information subcommittee, Moss, investigating new U.S. restrictions on release of VN War news, says reports on war's progress must not be censored; details. (W. Moran)
W	Congress-Vietnam-123-135A	Senator Symington proposes that U.S. move troops from Europe to VN; quotes from other senators on VN War.
W	Gardiner-Vietnam-010-225A	Gardiner, former head of AID in VN, says U.S. is "creating more VC than we are destroying"; details.
Miami Beach, Fla.	051-753A	Senator E. Kennedy says recent fighting in Hue is best "example of our miscalculations" in war.
W	Congress-Vietnam-1005A	Senator Russell expresses uneasiness about U.S. military position at Khe Sanh.
London	Vietnam-Wilson-095-1055A	Prime Minister Wilson says next peace move is up to Hanoi.
Denver, Colo.	111-1126A	Distinguished Service Cross awarded to Army Sp4c. Stanley E. Greene, who was wounded and partially blinded saving his comrades from a VC hand grenade.
Dallas, Tex.	nt ld Johnson-023-257P	Johnson uses trip to Dallas to talk on VN War; quotes.
Detroit, Mich.	Ford-Bombing-14-306P	Representative Ford said U.S. has stopped bombing N. VN for up to 20 days within last month without any effect.
W	Laos-023-307P	For second day, State Department shows concern over possibly developing communist drive into Laos.

Dateline		Story
Austin, Tex.	Johnson-Wheeler-066-532P	General Wheeler will report to Johnson Wednesday on trip to VN.
Tokyo	Viet-Hanoi-059-558P	Hanoi broadcast claims communist forces killed, wounded, or captured 90,000+ allied troops in less than a month of Tet offensive; statistics.
Raleigh, N.C.	071-656P	Marine who walked 400 miles to attract support for U.S. in VN has been killed there.
W	McNamara-038-716P	Continuing investigations into Tonkin Gulf incident reveals scientist who had charge of National Security Agency at time, may be called to testify to Senate Foreign Relations Committee.
W	Rifle-089-816P	Representative Schadeberg says Army abandoned its attempt to collect $70.21 from VN veteran who lost his rifle.
Oberlin, Ohio	Recruiters-8-1116P	One hundred thirty Oberlin College faculty vote to temporarily ban military recruiters from campus.
W	Navy Officer-117-1234P	McNamara confirmed that psychiatric examination was given to Navy officer who discussed 1964 Tonkin Gulf incident with Senator Fulbright.
February 28		
W	US-Vietnam-001-109A	U.S. officials disappointed by S. VN's failure to launch fast attacks on enemy forces weakened by severe losses from Tet offensive; details, analysis. (J. Hightower)
College-ville, Pa.	With Wirephoto-077-932A	Interview with one of Marines who defended Saigon U.S. Embassy during Tet offensive; quotes.
Vientiane	085-952A	N. VNese fight Laotian Army near Attopeu in southeast Laos.
W	Vietnam-Taxes-21-1012A	Any war escalation in VN will mean tax hike.
W	Gruening-Vietnam-19-1045A	Senator Gruening says he has proof that "the highest S. VNese government officials" have been involved in smuggling gold and opium into the country; details, quotes (5).

Dateline		Story
W	Tonkin-24-1107A	Senate Foreign Relations Committee plans no further hearings on Gulf of Tonkin incident, instead emphasize its power over military commitments.
W	Congress-Vietnam-116-1206P	Senator Hatfield offers resolution calling on Johnson to consult Congress before any expansion of ground war beyond VN; quotes.
London	118-1214P	Bishop of Wollwich, Rev. Robinson, quit Labor Party in protest of British government's posture on VN and immigration.
W	Doctor Draft-126-1P	Pentagon says smallest draft in three years for armed forces medical people.
Paris	nt ld Viet-French-003-110P	France has information "explicitly" stating that unconditional halt of U.S. bombing of N. VN would open peace talks; details. (H. Hudson)
Boston	Romney-6-146P	Governor Romney says call-up of reserves will be another example of the "Vietnam tail wagging the global dog and our domestic dog."
W	Reischauer-Asia-112-248P	Harvard Professor Reischauer told Congress U.S. should withdraw military commitments in Asia but retain commitments with Japan, S. Korea, Taiwan, Philippines.
W	Johnson-Wheeler-045-418P	General Wheeler gave Johnson and other officials war report that could lead to more troops in VN; details. (B. Horton)
Rome	Vietnam-Italian-047-426P	Foreign Minister Fanfani told Parliament he had suggested to Hanoi possible ways to settle VN War.
Philadelphia, Pa.	Humphrey-107-952P	VP Hubert Humphrey says U.S. must continue to fight aggression in VN even if it means more troops; quotes. (L. Lindner)
W	nt ld Tonkin-114-1037P	Navy says it restored to full duty commander who was given psychiatric examination after volunteering information to Senate Foreign Relations Committee on Gulf of Tonkin; details (3). (H. Rosenthal)

Dateline		Story
Atlanta, Ga.	Russell-129-1152P	Senator Russell criticizes Westmoreland for sticking to "outmoded World War II tactics" in fighting VC, says the Atlanta *Constitution*.

February 29

W	Tonkin-17-458A	"Reprisal action is feared by the Navy commander who took information on the Gulf of Tonkin incident to the Senate Foreign Relations Committee, says Chairman J. W. Fulbright"; details.
W	Wyman-Vietnam-18-505A	Representative Wyman believes God is on the side of U.S. in VN.
W	Vietnam-Taxes-21-1012A	Any escalation of U.S. troops in VN may generate tax hike.
W	Reischauer-Vietnam-150-517P	Former U.S. Ambassador to Japan Reischauer tells Congress that if Saigon regime collapsed, the U.S. would have to negotiate a withdrawal from VN; quotes.
W	Kistiakowsky-131-1159P	Dr. Kistiakowsky, who developed explosive trigger for atomic bomb, severs all ties with Pentagon because of VN War.
Tokyo	Viet-Hanoi-122	Hanoi says that next move toward VN peace talks must be halt to U.S. bombing of N. VN, but it promised "the talks will begin as soon as this unconditional stop has been proved."

March 1

W	Tonkin-72-946A	Senator Morris questions whether first shots in Tonkin Gulf incident were intended as warnings to N. VNese torpedo boats, meaning there was U.S. provocation.
Moscow	947A	Soviet Trade Union Congress urges workers of world to "hamper the transportation" of U.S. troops and military cargo to VN.
Tallahassee, Fla.	Humphrey-037-458P	Hubert Humphrey says no responsible U.S. official is advocating use of nuclear weapons in VN.

Dateline		Story
U.N.	nt ld Thant-Vietnam-060-633P	U.N. Secretary-General Thant says both public and private responses to his latest statement on how to bring peace to VN are "very encouraging."
Tokyo	105-1047P	VC's political organization in Saigon says that if "patriots" held by S. VN are executed it will take reprisals against U.S. prisoners.
Beaumont, Tex.	3 nt ld Johnson-119-1107P	"President Johnson slipped out of the White House for the third straight weekend Friday, made a morale-boosting trip to America's space nerve center, then told a group of fellow Texans that America will continue to fight aggression in VN"; details (6), quotes. (H. Kelley)
Honolulu	115-1118P	General Beach, Army's Commander-in-Chief in Pacific, says communists in VN are "fighting skillfully and determinedly."
March 2		
Boston	039	Dr. Benjamin Spock files motion challenging constitutionality of U.S. draft laws.
Boston	116-1234A	John Kenneth Galbraith says Administration's policy of continued escalation in VN "is an indication that all we have been doing all these years is relying on bad advice and reinforcing failure."
March 3		
London	045-40-P	U.S. Embassy spokesmen say several hundred Britons volunteering each week for service in VN since Tet.
W	Vietnam-Land-057-537P	House Government Operations Committee says meaningful land reform in S. VN unlikely without pressure from U.S. on Saigon regime; quotes.
N.Y.	38-709P	Theodore C. Sorensen, former John Kennedy aide, says he was "bleakly pessimistic" about VN War.

Dateline		Story
Oxford, Ohio	Debate-62-1026P	Harrison Salisbury, Pulitzer Prize winning journalist, debates VN issue at University of Miami.

March 4

W	Vietnam-Land-020-333A	House Committee says VC gaining loyalties of rural S. VNese by bringing about land reforms which S. VNese government unwilling to institute.
W	Scotus-Vietnam-088-1124A	Supreme Court reviews whether school children have right to wear black arm bands in protest of VN War--ruling affirmed.
W	Peace Plan-98-122P	Eighteen House Democrats offer plan for negotiated settlement to VN War, based on free elections in S. VN with full participation; quotes.
North-ampton, Mass.	066-652P	Smith College students begin fast in protest of VN War.
St. Paul, Minn.	Freeman-Vietnam-41-459P	Secretary of Agriculture Freeman declares Johnson head of "doves" not "hawks" in controversy over U.S. participation in VN War; quotes.
Tokyo	098-1005P	N. VN reported it has had official talks with Italy on war settlement.

March 5

Susan-ville, Calif.	027-312A	H. L. Hummell, who mailed antiwar propaganda to VN widow, said it was his intent "to expose the unjust slaughter of innocent people . . . and to stop the conflict and perhaps save the life of other parents' sons."
W	D.C. Democrats-064-831A	D.C. Democratic Committee removed Dudley as Chairman because of his opposition to Johnson's war policies.
Savannah, Ga.	Rivers-79-954A	Representative Rivers says he is displeased with DMZ in VN and will do something about it.
Milwaukee, Wis.	Dirksen-094-1003A	Senator Dirksen says one reason he defended Johnson's war policies was to avoid providing propaganda to VC; quotes.

Dateline	Story	
Stockholm	98-1134A	Swedish Aliens Commission grants asylum for humanitarian reasons to seven U.S. Army deserters.
Seattle, Wash.	Vietnam Doctors-030-1225P	Four Seattle doctors who served in S. VN say medical misinformation about VN is being spread by anti-war groups "as a propaganda tool to whitewash the VC"; details, quotes.
W	Vietnam-Censorship-113-1236P	Senator Byrd told Senate it makes sense for U.S. command to withhold information on damage inflicted by enemy on targets in VN; quotes.
W	Johnson-Wheeler-83-138P	Johnson continuing to meet with advisors and discuss General Wheeler's report from VN, but he has made no decisions, says White House.
W	Russell-Vietnam-90-204P	Senator Russell advocates blockading of entire N. VN coast and incessant bombing of rail lines from China to cut off supplies; quotes.
W	Bundy-Bombing-121-409P	Assistant Secretary of State Bundy says bombing of N. VN not considered by U.S. until after 1964 Presidential election.
Los Angeles	Hayden-152-626P	Son of actor Sterling Hayden burns his induction papers and refuses to be drafted.
Paris	A French Look at Khe Sanh-039-755P	French general whose army was defeated at Dienbienphu discusses tactics at Khe Sanh; quotes, details. (B. LaVallee)
W	Attack Probe-102-938P	State Department says S. VNese government has cooperated fully in U.S. inquiry into VC attack on U.S. Embassy in Saigon on January 30.
W	Vietnam Tours-087-939P	Representatives Shriver and Gurney offer resolution specifying that VN veterans may not be reassigned there until after one year in U.S.
New Haven, Conn.	41-1017P	Former Governor McKeldin of Maryland says U.S. should withdraw from VN "without indecent haste, but equally without hesitation;" quotes.

Dateline	Story	

March 6

W	Corruption-002-113A	Top U.S. civilian advisor says U.S. must take initiative to root out corruption in Saigon government because there aren't enough honest VNese officials to do the job; quotes, details. (D. Barnes)
Bern	Swiss-Vietnam-073-908A	Swiss government announces N. VNese Foreign Minister will visit Switzerland soon.
N.Y.	Gavin-83-1016A	Retired Lieutenant General Gavin, critic of Johnson's policies, mentioned as possible Republican Presidential or VP candidate, and is open to political office.
W	Drugs-Vietnam-151P	Defense Department says stimulant drugs are included in Air Force and Special Forces kits in VN, but use of stimulant is not widespread.
W	nt ld Corruption-023-243P	New investigation of S. VN's government corruption promised by Senator Gruening after U.S. advisor says corruption very widespread; details, quotes. (D. Barnes)
W	Dogs Vietnam-050-541P	Army Institute of Research working to find ways to use dogs in VN War. (M. Cole)
Littleton, N.H.	Nixon-130-542P	Nixon says when war in VN is over, U.S. should end military draft and turn into all-volunteer army.
San Francisco	160-836P	Folk singer Joan Baez will open draft resistance tour.
N.Y.	Antiwar-103-1024P	Robert Bly, winner of National Book Award for poetry, turned over prize to antiwar group.

March 7

W	Corruption-004-137A	Frustration of U.S. contending with corruption in S. VNese government told in reports from advisors; quotes, details. (D. Barnes)
W	Vietnam Air Workhorse-015-307A	A Navy plane, A-7A Corsair, being used to help Marines at Khe Sanh; statistics on plane. (B. Horton)
W	Congress-Troops-16-950A	Senate investigators begin study of U.S. troop levels in Korea and at home to see if VN War has drained reserve strength below safe levels.

Dateline		Story
Tokyo	Vietnam Peace-079-1018A	N. VN, through contacts with Switzerland, Sweden, and Italy, seem to suggest it is ready to begin peace actions. (J. Roderick)
London	Vietnam Support-88-1051A	Extraordinary responses by British citizens to Tet offensive. (A. Gavshon)
Phnom Penh	Apology-43-1135A	U.S. apologizes for two violations of Cambodian territory by U.S. troops in S. VN, says official Cambodian news agency.
Seoul	Korea-46-1147A	S. Korea is "sounding out" VN War allies on idea of forming new Asian-Pacific military alliance to defend area against communists, says Donghwa News Agency.
W	nt ld Corruption-033-355P	Secret military maneuver to seize all contraband in S. VN and dump it was recommended by U.S. civilian advisor as one way to end VN corruption; quotes, details on reports. (D. Barnes)
London	Dog-047-525P	Britain's Kennel Club says U.S. should use existing type of dog for VN War instead of trying to produce new breed; quotes.
W	nt ld Senate-Vietnam-807P	Senate debate over Johnson VN policies; quotes. (R. Gray)
Honolulu	Sharp-125	Admiral Sharp, Pacific Military commander, says U.S. forces in VN are well deployed to take care of anything enemy might try.

March 8		
W	Vietnam-Casualties-002-117A	U.S. battle deaths in VN escalating at such a rate that they may surpass those of Korean War by Presidential elections; statistics. (F. Hoffman)
Melbourne	Accusation-075-956A	John Sorell, correspondent of Melbourne *Herald*, wrote of use of water torture by Australian troops in VN in effort to extract information from suspected VC; quotes.
W	US-Vietnam-20-1008A	Senators R. Kennedy and Fulbright demand that Congress be given a say before any major buildup in VN by U.S.

Dateline		Story
W	US-Vietnam-090-1164A	Clifford says Johnson is keeping an open mind on question of more troops for VN; details of informal press conference.
St. Paul, Minn.	Soldier-0060-1235P	Sgt. John Weber killed in VN less than three months after he fought for eight hours with enemy bullet in his chest.
W	Marine Corporal-77-103P	Navy Appellate officials recommended that Marine Cpl. Stanley Luczko, whose court martial conviction for murder of S. VNese woman was set aside, be found guilty of lesser charge of unpremeditated murder.
Oxford, England	Fast-11-245P	Ten U.S. students end five-day fast to protest VN War.
W	US-Cambodia-110-355P	U.S. regrets for any Cambodian casualties that may have occurred in recent frontier incident, but denies that U.S. forces caused them.
Ottawa	Vietnam-Peace-053-610P	Hanoi rejected more peace offers than Washington has, says Prime Minister Pearson.
Havana	Cuba-Viet-054-613P	Cuba announces sister-cities program with VN, including symbolic link between Bay of Pigs and Dienbienphu.
Stockholm	Ambassador-157-7P	Recall of U.S. Ambassador William Heath from Sweden as result of decline in relations from VN War.
Chicago	nt ld Hartke-112-1027P	Senator Hartke urged U.S. to halt bombing N. VN unconditionally and de-emphasize ground action during trial period to stimulate peace talks.
W	Vietnam-Clark-118-1058P	S. VN should be required to initiate efforts leading to compromise with NLF as condition for further U.S. help, says Senator Clark.

March 9

Dateline		Story
Fayette-ville, Ark.	Mansfield-Foreign Policy-035-146A	Senator Mansfield says U.S. foreign policies "may well be taking too much out of this nation"; quotes.
Munich	65-1108A	Dr. Walter Marseille, psychoanalyst, says he is giving up his naturalized U.S. citizenship in protest of U.S. in VN War.

Dateline		Story
Clovis, N.M.	Noyd Trial-24-101A	Air Force Captain Noyde convicted at court-martial for refusing to help train student pilot to fight in VN War.
W	TFX-Vietnam-002-1211P	Air Force TFX preparing for first VN combat mission.
W	Rusk-Senate-028-256P	Confrontation between Secretary of State Rusk and Senator Fulbright; details. (L. Gulick)
Clovis, N.M.	Noyde Trial-103-405P	Noyde sentenced to one year hard labor and is dismissed from Air Force without pay for refusing on religious grounds to help train student pilot for duty in VN War.
March 10		
Princeton, N.J.	Gallup-038-316P	Gallup poll indicates that more Americans now than ever before feel the U.S. was wrong to get involved with VN militarily; statistics.
London	Antiwar-068-627P	Describes multitude of antiwar organizations in Europe; details. (L. Heinzerling)
W	US-Vietnam-082-718P	Policy-making State Department official says U.S. and S. VN at critical period during months ahead; details on policy questions. (S. Davis)
W	Soldier-Sign-025-720P	Second Lt. Dennis Morrisseau, who picketed White House in protest against VN War, was turned over to military authorities.
Baltimore, Md.	43-1053P	Nhat Hanh, Buddhist Monk, says the people of S. VN feel "they are being destroyed" by U.S.
March 11		
Dallas, Tex.	85-1053A	Senator Tower says N. VN should be quarantined before U.S. sends sizable numbers of additional troops to S. VN; quotes.
W	Text-39-414P	Partial texts of prepared opening statements by Rusk and Fulbright at hearing of Senate Foreign Relations Committee which dealt with U.S. policy in VN; quotes (4).

Dateline	Story	
W	VFW-Dissent-59-630P	Joseph Scerra, Commander in Chief of VFW, urged Congress to "take action to silence irresponsible dissent" against VN War; quotes.
W	2 nt ld US-Viet-084-743P	Senator Fulbright insists that Administration define role of Congress in future VN War planning before Congress considers any new foreign-aid legislation; details (3); quotes. (J. Mohbat)

March 12

W	US-Vietnam-20-1020A	Dispute flared between Secretary of State Rusk and Senator Fulbright over whether Congress should have voice in deciding on any major increase in U.S. fighting force in VN; quotes.
W	US-Vietnam-29-1103A	Despite pressure from Senator Fulbright, Rusk balked at pledging consultation with Congress prior to Presidential decision of whether to send more troops into S. VN; details, quotes (8).
W	US-Vietnam-100-249P	Rusk and Senate Foreign Relations Committee end wide-range, public review of VN policy without agreement on question of giving Congress voice in sending more troops to VN; quotes, details (6).
W	Rusk 1 Nato-105-313P	Rusk rejected suggestion that U.S. should withdraw troops from Europe if reinforcements are needed in VN; quotes.
Des Moines, Iowa	28-429P	Johnson acted on misinformation in escalating VN War, says Governor Harold Hughes.
W	nt ld Medal of Honor-037-441P	Johnson says, "If we are patient, if we do not become the willing victims of our own despair," U.S. will never fail--said at ceremony for Medals of Honor to two Marines serving in VN. (F. Cormier)
Vatican City	043-513P	Vatican says Roman Catholic Church has suffered serious losses in S. VN during past few weeks.

Dateline		Story
Stockholm	Viet-Swedes-048-540P	Swedish leftists demonstrate against U.S. policy in VN, while Parliament's Foreign Affairs Committee meets to discuss deterioration of U.S.-Swedish relations.
W	Viet-Russell-050-608P	Senator Russell says it is confession of moral weakness by this country not to "take the steps necessary to diminish the fighting power of our enemies in VN"; quotes.
W	Johnson-Rusk-136-1050P	Johnson praises Rusk's defense of U.S. policy in VN before Senate Foreign Relations Committee and says there would be no retreat from America's world responsibilities.
Vientiane	120-1249P	Laotian Royal Army sources reported battle with government forces near American base in Thailand.
March 13		
W	Kahn-104-119A	Thermonuclear war strategist Herman Kahn is going to VN to advise U.S. military on pacification program, says Pentagon.
W	Vietnam Troop Levels-00-127A	Explains ramifications of fight between Senate and Johnson over decision-making power of Congress concerning increasing troop levels in VN; details. (J. Hightower)
Vientiane	Laotian-038-607A	Laotian government troops pushed back N. VNese who had driven to within six miles of Thakhek, across Mekong River from a U.S. air base in Thailand, says Laotian military.
Vatican City	129-1248P	*L'Osservatore Romano* says that VC killed hundreds of Roman Catholics at Hue and forced student priests to study Marxism during the Tet offensive.
Tokyo	Hospital-81-123P	U.S. Army says it has postponed opening of Tokyo hospital because demonstrators say hospital will help draw Japan into VN War.
Des Moines, Iowa	2-206P	Governor Harold Hughes says U.S. should unconditionally halt bombing of N. VN in hopes of drawing communists to peace tables.

Dateline	Story	
W	Fulbright-House-006-127P	Senator Fulbright told by Representative Hays that House of Representatives is an equal part of the legislative process.
W	US-Vietnam-98-217P	State Department inquiring into reports from Saigon that volunteer guerrilla army is being formed to operate inside N. VN.
W	Vietnam-POWs-045-521P	American Red Cross authorities have been meeting with representatives of VN in Czechoslovakia in so-far failing effort to get food packages and mail to U.S. POWs; details. (F. Hoffman)
Princeton, N.J.	069-723P	Majority of Americans surveyed favor gradual withdrawal of U.S. from S. VN, says Gallup poll; statistics.
Tokyo	092-853P	N. VN denounces U.S. and Japan for using Okinawa for U.S. bombers, claiming they go on missions to "slaughter the S. VNese people."
Phila-delphia, Pa.	Viet Vet Jobs-104-945P	Viet vets get job training for careers in Post Office; quotes. (L. Linder)

March 14

Bonn	Bundestag-069-750A	Chancellor Kiesinger's chief spokesmen say his Christian Democratic Party has not forgotten communists are the aggressors in VN; quotes.
Canberra	921A	Army Minister Lynch tells Australian House of Representatives that one of his Army's interrogating officers used water treatment while questioning a suspected VC.
W	US-Vietnam-011-208P	U.S. foreign aid agency agrees to conduct advanced screening of commercial transactions it finances; details, on Congress, Rusk, Clifford, quotes. (R. Gray)
Miami, Fla.	Gentle Hero-019-308P	Pvt. Jonathan Spicer, the Marine hero who hated war, dies in Japanese hospital at age of 19; quotes from father. (S. Douthat)

Dateline		Story
Des Moines, Iowa	29-323P	Dr. Arthur Larson, consultant to Johnson, says U.S. should "accept the fact of a divided world" and end VN War by trading Russia a partitioned Germany for a partitioned VN; quotes.
Vienna	042-515P	Foreign Minister Waldheim told Parliament that N. VN's ambassador to Hungary told him his government was ready for negotiations "as soon as the other side stopped bombing and all acts of fighting."
Kansas City, Kans.	072-8P	Pfc. James Carter calls his home after they are told he is dead; quotes.
W	Clifford-082-809P	Secretary of Defense Clifford declines invitation to appear before Senate Foreign Relations Committee.
N.Y.	Viet-ABC-121-1030P	ABC says the U.S. lost 1,000 planes and helicopters during Tet offensive, not the 500 the Pentagon says.
W	Washington Roundup-085	State Department says U.S. remains opposed to invasion of N. VN.
Grosse Pointe, Mich.	141-1211A	Dr. M. L. King says he opposes U.S. involvement in VN War because "injustice anywhere is a threat to justice everywhere."
W	Second Wave-062	S. VNese Ambassador Diem says he received information that VC and N. VN are planning a second wave attack on Saigon Friday night.
March 15		
Tokyo	106-1132A	Radio Moscow says U.S. is using earth satellites in VN War.
W	Businessmen-Vietnam-6-225P	Head of businessmen's group, Business Executives Move for Vietnam Peace, announces nationwide direct mailing campaign against VN War.
Indio, Calif.	010-542P	Eisenhower says one of the problems of trying to end VN War is "I don't think the American people really feel inspired to do anything."

Dateline		Story
W	US-Vietnam-44-545P	Foreign Aid Director William Gaud says U.S. is doing all it can in S. VN "to get the government to face up to the problems of corruption."
W	Aircraft Losses-67-731P	Pentagon refuses to say how many U.S. aircraft have been destroyed or damaged in S. VN since Tet offensive.
N.Y.	Poll-079-810P	Sixty-three percent of U.S. Protestants disapprove of way Johnson is handling war, a poll among members of nine major denominations indicated; statistics. (G. Cornell)
N.Y.	082-821P	Senator Percy says U.S. should agree to direct negotiations with VC as well as with N. VN.
W	Vietnam Volunteers-094-915P	Defense Department says more than 176,000 Army and Navy men have volunteered for duty in VN since 1963; statistics.

Dateline		Story
March 16		
Brussels	Vietnam-Gold-1/8-326A	European concern about VN War affecting gold market; details. (C. Hartman)
Tokyo	026-435A	N. VN is donating 50,000 tons of rice and 100 tons of medical supplies to those in S. VN made homeless by war.
W	Clausen-Viet-49-442P	Representative Clausen urges Johnson to call summit conference of Far East nations and form Free Asian Security Force to replace U.S. ground forces in VN.
Tokyo	97-1250P	N. VN says U.S. A-6 Intruder warplane shot down over N. VN and crewmen captured.
W	Hosmer-46-428P	Intensified air strikes in N. VN favored by nearly three-fourths of those responding to a poll conducted by Representative Hosmer in his California district.
Baltimore, Md.	60-541P	Former U.S. Senator Paul Douglas says if U.S. loses VN, it will lose all of Asia.

Dateline		Story
The Hague	Demonstrations-065-735P	Big demonstration supporting U.S. held in The Hague.
French Lick, Ind.	Humphrey-083-1017P	Humphrey says within past few days "an intensive review has been undertaken within our government to find some better or more effective way to peace"; quotes. (I. Miller)
Bangkok	F-111	U.S. Air Force introduces F-111 into air war over VN; details, description

March 17		
Tokyo	Viet-Captured-014-1243P	N. VN says U.S. A-6 Intruder shot down near Hanoi and crewmen captured.
Bangkok	Vietnam F-111-021-143P	U.S. Air Force introduces F-111 fighter-bomber into air war over N. VN; details. (P. O'Loughlin)
W	nt ld Johnson-Jobs-036-306P	Johnson says U.S. will win in VN if Hanoi refuses to negotiate; details. (J. Beckler)
W	Vietnam Reinforce-ments-045-404P	Authoritative source says there will be "moderate increase" in U.S. troops in S. VN; details.
W	Barbed Tape-5-418P	Army creates new razor barbed steel spring to replace wire barriers now on battlefield. (B. Horton)
London	Vietnam-British-032-504P	Biggest anti-American demonstration in London draws 10,000 to American Embassy; details. (D. Lancashire)
Tokyo	099-740P	French Communist Party leader assures N. VN his party will increase support for VN communists, reports VN News Agency.
San Antonio, Tex.	Christian-55-752P	U.S. officials still believe massive attack "is intended" in Khe Sanh area of VN, says Presidential Press Secretary Christian.
W	Prison Firm-54-845P	Firm comprised of convicts in federal penitentiaries is manufacturing items for use in VN War.
N.Y.	Peace Hoax-127-1015P	Janos Radvanyi, former Hungarian charge d'affaires in Washington, says that a "peace hoax" perpetrated by Hungarian Foreign Minister Janos Peter led to U.S. 37-day halt in bombing of N. VN in 1965-66.

Dateline		Story
Tokyo	Defector-82-1134P	N. VN reported U.S. soldier defected to VC and issued appeal to all other Negro soldiers to oppose U.S. war in VN.
Chicago	Museum Demonstrators-87-1158P	Group of antiwar demonstrators "captured" U.S. Army exhibit at Chicago Museum of Science and Industry.
W	Rusk-Fulbright-128-1219A	Senate war critics fight with Administration officials over VN War; details. (R. Gray)

March 18

W	US-Vietnam-006-153A	Johnson is expected to increase U.S. troop strength in VN by at least one more division--35,000; details (3). (J. Hightower)
W	Vietnam-Air Losses-017-340A	U.S. loss of planes and helicopters in VN exceeds those in Korea; statistics. (F. Hoffman)
St. Louis, Mo.	055-749A	Danish Ambassador Ronne to U.S. says Danish official went to Hanoi at request of N. VN.
Manhattan, Kans.	Kennedy-10-937A	Senator R. Kennedy launches his Presidential campaign with denunciation of Johnson's VN War strategy.
Minneapolis, Minn.	Johnson-39-1131A	Johnson calls on American people for "a program of national austerity" and an all-out effort to win VN War; quotes.
Minneapolis, Minn.	Johnson-74-126P	Johnson appealed to all Americans to unite behind government in "a program of national austerity" until peace is achieved in VN.
W	Vietnam-Prisoners-014-213P	State Department spokesman says arrangements being made to return to Hanoi three N. VNese sailors who are allies' POWs.
Moscow	015-219P	Official says Soviet ships will carry 20 percent more cargoes to N. VN port of Haiphong this year than last.
W	Kennedy Book-107-320P	In E. Kennedy's first book _Decisions for a Decade_, he says destruction caused by U.S. military in S. VN is only causing more problems for future; quotes.

Dateline	Story	
W	Marine Corporal-22-341P	Case of Marine Cpl. Stanley Luczko, convicted of killing S. VN woman, is being returned from VN for possible new trial.
W	nt ld-Vietnam-039-510P	One-third of House membership urged approval of proposal calling for immediate congressional review of U.S. VN policy; details, quotes.
Baltimore, Md.	Professor-96-940P	Rev. Richard McSorley, Georgetown University Law professor, says "America is schizophrenic on the subject of the VN War."
W	Napalm-024-1/8P	All about napalm and its uses in VN. (B. Horton)
Chicago	Captured-39	Exhibit of equipment used by U.S. Army in VN captured by antiwar demonstrators in Chicago.

March 19		
Bellingham, Wash.	Canadian-Viet-54-530A	U.S. attracting many Canadians to fight in VN War, both men and women.
Bern	Swiss-Vietnam-071-909A	Mai Van Bo, N. VNese representative in France, arrives for talks with Swiss government.
Ottawa	074-916A	Foreign Minister Paul Martin says Canadian government still believes a halt to U.S. bombing of N. VN "is first priority," but both sides seem unlikely to make peace move now.
Ta Khli, Thailand	Vietnam-F-111-087-1029A	U.S. Air Force put its new F-111 fighter-bomber through precombat flight tests. (P. O'Loughlin)
N.Y.	Business Mirror-1101A	Businessmen becoming more antiwar, even forming group, Business Executives Move for Vietnam Peace; details, quotes on business community negative reaction to VN War. (J. Cuniff)
W	Kennedy-Asia-47-1202P	Senator E. Kennedy challenges U.S. containment policies toward China, U.S. military tactics in VN, and rationale for massive U.S. presence in Asia in his first book, *Decisions for a Decade*; quotes.

Dateline		Story
N.Y.	110-1231P	Two American missionaries captured by VC are alive and well, according to word received.
W	Draft Call-103-307P	Pentagon calls for drafting of 44,000 men in May.
W	Johnson-Vietnam-109-344P	White House says Johnson consults various people on S.E. Asian policy, but no serious consideration is being made to create commission to examine this policy.
W	Pilots-190-532P	West Germany supports U.S. war effort in VN with pilots, technical experts, money, says commentary published in N. VN.
W	Senate-Vietnam-159-647P	Gen. David Shoup, retired commandant of Marine Corps, will testify on VN War before Senate Foreign Relations Committee.
W	Vietnam-Troops-071-711P	White House decision to commit 33,000 more troops to VN is almost final, say Congressional sources.
Honolulu	116-1115P	Lt. Gen. Victor Krulak, commander of Marine Corps in Pacific, says U.S. people need patience in understanding VN War; quotes.
W	US-Vietnam-037	House Committee on Un-American Activities is investigating organization of federal employees who oppose U.S. in VN War, Federal Employees Against the War.
Traverse City, Mich.	Vietnamese Girl-060	Traverse City raising money to help VN girl who saved many American lives.
March 20		
Manila	059-806A	Philippine's 2,000-man noncombat group in VN begin returning home.
W	Johnson-Vietnam-15-1000A	Johnson evokes FDR's pre-World War II call for containment of aggression in new plea for home-front support of his VN policies.
Paris	Defectors-French-067-1020A	Five U.S. Army deserters and four draft dodgers who say they are "working against the war in VN" apply for French residence permits; (4) details, quotes. (R. Angove)

Dateline		Story
W	Senate-Vietnam-1153A	Former Marine commandant, David Shoup, in testimony before Senate Foreign Relations Committee, says U.S. military victory in VN "cannot come to pass"; quotes. (R. Gray)
Elyria, Ohio	With Defectors-97-1257P	One of four draft dodgers who applied for French residence permits saying they are "working against the war in VN" was active in antiwar protests while attending Mount Union College. (Larry Cox)
Ann Arbor, Mich.	Coffin-12-247P	Yale University chaplain, Rev. William S. Coffin, says his opposition to VN War is "a lover's quarrel" with U.S.
W	Reischauer-044-508P	Former Ambassador Edwin O. Reischauer, war critic, denies White House statement that Johnson consults with him on matters of S.E. Asia policy; quotes. (J. Heller)
Nürnberg	Vietnam-German-062-624P	Social Democratic Party convention asked U.S. to stop bombing N. VN.
N.Y.	Hilsman-110-1015P	Former Assistant Secretary of State Roger Hilsman calls for de-escalation of VN War, de-Americanizing of it, and broadening of VN government; quotes.
W	nt ld Senate-Vietnam-014-449P	Former Marine Corps commandant, David Shoup, tells Senate Foreign Relations Committee military victory is impossible, and submits his own peace plan; details, quotes.
Syracuse, N.Y.	39	Sixteen-year-old youth critically burned himself in apparent protest against VN War.
March 21		
W	US-Vietnam-005-945A	Congressional sources say Administration will ask for $3.3 billion more for VN War, which will cause another round of war policy debates on Capitol Hill; details, quotes. (C. Leubsdorf)

Dateline		Story
Bern	087-1005A	N. VN continues to reject idea of peace talks while U.S. is bombing their country, diplomatic sources say.
N.Y.	047-1201P	New York *Times* reveals classified year-end report by Westmoreland predicting great allied headway during 1968, both militarily and with pacification program; details.
N.Y.	Business Mirror-11-1220P	Second article revealing business community's reaction (antiwar) to VN War; this one on organization, Business Executives Move for Vietnam Peace; details. (J. Cuniff)
W	Wall Eye-037-438P	Pentagon has accelerated production of television-guided glide bomb to help minimize aircraft losses as U.S. prepares for intensified bombing of N. VN. (B. Horton)
W	nt ld Johnson Viet-038-447P	Johnson says that America's will will not "break in frustration" in VN, and peace with honor will be won.
Tokyo	078-758P	N. VN issued new decree to deal with espionage, treason, and other counterrevolutionary activity.
W	Kennedy-Vietnam-105-1233A	Senator E. Kennedy says destruction caused by American military is only making future more difficult for S. VN, in his book *Decisions for a Decade*; quotes. (G. Thelen, Jr.)

March 22

Pittsburgh, Pa.	US-Vietnam-5-907A	Hubert Humphrey says Johnson has undertaken in recent days "an intensive review" to find "some better or more effective way to peace" in VN.
Tokyo	North Vietnam-071-927A	Hanoi Radio says "reactionary elements" are operating inside N. VN.
Bern	064-221P	N. VNese government officially informed Swiss government that it is "seriously prepared" to enter into peace talks with U.S. following unconditional halt to bombing N. VN; details.

Dateline		Story
W	US-Vietnam-019-234P	Hubert Humphrey aroused widespread speculation that Johnson is planning new peace offensive--but associate says Humphrey didn't mean quite that; details. (J. Hightower)
W	Johnson-069-704P	Westmoreland is returning home to become Army Chief of Staff, Johnson announces appointment; details (7). (D. Cornell)
Honolulu	Sharp-129-908P	Adm. U.S. Grant Sharp, commander in chief of Pacific, declines comment on Johnson's announcement that he will ask Sharp to remain on in order to have smooth transition in military shifts.
Paris	Resisters-017-939P	Group of U.S. military deserters and "draft resisters" defy police and hold rally against VN War; details. (R. Angove)
Tokyo	120-1118P	VC claimed that in 45 days of attacks it wiped out more than 40 percent of U.S. and allied military strength in VN; quotes.
Kiamesha Lake, N.Y.	131-1215A	Rabbi Eli Bohnen suggests chaplains of all faiths cease to be part of the military establishment so they can counsel servicemen according to conscience, not military rules.
March 23		
W	US-Vietnam-045-543A	Undersecretary of State Rostow says critics of Administration's war policies have not defined alternative to it; quotes.
Stockholm	051-706A	Swedish foreign office has helped to serve as communication link between Washington and Hanoi for last 18 months, says foreign office spokesman.
Tokyo	061-825A	N. VNese newspaper says VC Tet offensive broke U.S. war strategy and "tipped the balance of forces definitely in favor of the revolution."
W	Westmoreland-4-858A	Speculation as to meaning and implications of Johnson's decision to remove Westmoreland as head of VN operations; details (6).

Dateline	Story	
Moscow	Westmoreland-078-10A	Soviet journalist calls Westmoreland "unlucky wretch" returning to Washington in failure.
	Johnson-at-a-Glance-35-1053A	Highlights of Johnson's Friday news conference; Westmoreland becomes Army Chief of Staff, Shriver Ambassador to France, etc.
W	Foreign Aid-56-1159A	Senate Foreign Relations Committee demands that Clifford testify in public on U.S. military aid instead of sending Pentagon substitutes, and demand could delay Congressional action on Administration's Foreign Aid Bill.
W	Viet Protest-22-241P	*Foreign Service Journal*, magazine published by an association of career diplomats, says it refused to accept advertisement by group of federal employees opposing Johnson VN policy.
W	nt ld Westmoreland-30-334P	Senior military officers predict General Abrams will succeed Westmoreland as commander in VN.
W	House-Vietnam-031-341P	Bipartisan House group desires to change floor rules in order to carry out a full floor debate on U.S. war policies; details. (T. Seppy)
W	Clifford-Leaks-97-431P	Secretary of Defense Clifford moves to discourage leaks of secret information to newsmen.
Moscow	Defector-045-507P	Moscow television broadcast statement of American soldier who said he defected from U.S. Air Force after becoming convinced VN is a "criminal war"; details.
Tokyo	537P	Communist China's official news agency describes Westmoreland as "another scapegoat for defeat" in VN War.
Rome	064-618P	Thousands of left-wing students hanged effigy of Johnson and then marched on U.S. Embassy in Rome.
Philadelphia, Pa.	542P	Arthur M. Schlesinger, Jr., former Kennedy aide, says Westmoreland's promotion amounts to recall.
Springfield, Mo.	Bolling-087-726P	Representative Bolling says, "We have got to have a truce in VN or escalate the war into nuclear weapons."

Dateline		Story
Phila- delphia, Pa.	Asian Conference-66- 825P	Philip Habib, representative of State Department, says if U.S. withdraws from VN, Asian nations would need American-supplied nuclear weapons to resist communist ag- gression; quotes.
Chicago	Bishop Dougherty-85- 952P	Bishop Dougherty, President of Seton Hall University, calls for discussion of question of ending VN War by negotiations.

March 24

London	Vietnam-Templer-014- 116P	Field Marshal Sir Gerald Templer, who beat communist guerrillas in Malaya after World War II, says, "If the Americans pull out of Vietnam, the communists will take over the whole of Southeast Asia --and Burma, India, right up to the Caspian Sea would go"; quotes, details. (G. Watts)
London	051-510P	Hundreds of antiwar demonstrators try surging into Downing Street to present petitions to Prime Minister Wilson.
Grand Rapids, Mich.	Marathon-Viet-052-516P	Americans from 44 states responded with more than $50,000 in pledges in telephone marathon supporting U.S. fighting men in VN; details.
Henderson, N.C.	29-839P	U.S. Senator Ervin says federal employees have the right to protest U.S. policy in VN.
New Orleans, La.	Defector's Wife-112- 857P	Wife of man appearing on Moscow television saying he defected because of VN War says she does not understand her husband's actions; quotes. (B. Thomas)
Chicago	Antiwar-43-923P	Chicago *Sun-Times* says group of national antiwar and civil rights leaders approved plans to demonstrate at Democratic National Convention.

March 25

W	Chapman-001-108A	Gen. Leonard Chapman Jr., new Marine Corps commandant, says com- munists "can't force us out" of Khe Sanh; quotes, details. (F. Hoffman)

Dateline		Story
W	US-Vietnam-026-428A	U.S. AID officials cite corruption and lack of skilled S. VNese government personnel as major obstacles to progress in pacification and redevelopment programs in VN; details. (L. Gulick)
N.Y.	028-425A	Senator Morton says Tonkin Gulf incident may "have been the result of deliberate provocation"; article in *Saturday Evening Post*; quotes.
New Orleans, La.	042-618A	Mrs. J. W. Wright says she is puzzled by Moscow television broadcast where man identified as her husband said he defected because he opposed VN War; quotes.
W	Chapman-006-1216P	Commander of Marines Chapman opposes any change in basic U.S. military strategy in VN, saying U.S. can win "if we just persevere"; quotes, details (3). (F. Hoffman)
Buckholts, Tex.	Soldier-40-320P	Parents of soldier, who had live grenade removed from his leg in VN, react to operation.
Philadelphia, Pa.	nt ld Battleship-022-329P	USS *New Jersey*, in reserve fleet for more than 10 years, leaves for sea trials to prepare it to fight in VN.
Boston	Spock-075-715P	Government asserts that courts have no authority to consider legality of VN War in case of baby doctor Spock, Yale chaplain William Coffin, Jr., and others; details (3).
W	nt ld Johnson-017-907P	Johnson says he will fight off election-year political attacks while standing firm in VN; quotes from speeches. (N. Gilbride)
Hayes, Kans.	Landon-114-905P	Alf Landon says wild dollar speculation and military power by Johnson has led to worldwide distrust of Johnson's financial understanding, his military judgment, his political decisions; quotes.
W	Barr-122-1207A	Undersecretary of Treasury Joseph Barr says any supplemental appropriations for VN War must be balanced by reductions elsewhere in federal budget or U.S. will face deficits threatening "severe erosion of the dollar."

Dateline		Story
March 26		
H.K.	059-750A	"Red Chinese hospitals in the border province of Kwangsi are so packed with wounded N. VNese soldiers they are refusing to accept Chinese patients," a Hong Kong Chinese just back from Kwangsi said today.
W	Aid-Vietnam-18-1019A	Congress was told by AID that damages suffered in Tet offensive amounted to $120 million--without including losses in Hue or northern IV corps area.
W	Mansfield-Vietnam-43-1146A	Senator Mansfield says he opposes any increase of U.S. troop strength in VN; quotes.
Canberra	Viet-Aussie-114-1226P	Australian government believes bombing of N. VN serves important military objectives, says Foreign Minister Paul Hasluck.
Des Moines, Iowa	016-213P	"Methodist bishops in eight states called Tuesday for a unilateral cease-fire in VN by the United States and South Vietnam"; quotes.
W	nt ld Vietnam-Finance-019-302P	White House gives cool response--but not firm denial--to view that U.S. cannot meet war and domestic needs without reducing its standard of living; quotes, details. (J. Baluch)
Seaside, Calif.	Johnson-085-518P	Army Sgt. Edward R. Johnson, who has survived 3-1/2 years of VC imprisonment, asks for return duty in VN; quotes.
W	nt ld Abrams-067-623P	Army General Abrams confers with Johnson in secrecy; details, quotes. (F. Hoffman)
N.Y.	Eisenhower-074-712P	Eisenhower writes in *Reader's Digest* that he would not support any candidate for office "who advocates capitulation" in VN; quotes.
W	Clark Draft-162-740P	Attorney-General Ramsey Clark says he favors a form of national service for young people--as an alternative to the draft, but substitute should not "stand as a moral justification for an individual refusing to serve in armed forces."

Dateline		Story
Stockholm	088-824P	Olof Stroh, first Red Cross of- ficial from the West invited to N. VN, returns after week in Hanoi.
W	Viet-Finance Round- up-024	"A top Treasury official has told Congress the nation can't afford both guns and butter."
March 27		
N.Y.	Vietnam-Nuclear-119- 1003A	Special consultant to Johnson, John Roche, says use of nuclear weapons in VN War "is inconceivable under the present Administration."
W	Abrams-Vietnam-43- 1206P	Pentagon says General Abrams may end his Washington trip shortly and return to VN--"regarded as the man who will succeed" Westmoreland.
W	Hopkins Letter-112- 1242P	Three-fourths of students and faculty of Johns Hopkins School of Advanced International Studies sign letter to Johnson urging "disengagement" policy in VN.
Tokyo	Hospital-69-116P	Despite protests from residents of Oji, U.S. will open hospital in Japan.
N.Y.	Eisenhower-024-210P	Eisenhower accuses VN War dissenters of giving "aid and comfort to the enemy," and says in *Reader's Digest* article that their behavior is probably "making honorable negotiations impossible"; quotes.
Phila- delphia, Pa.	nt ld Jersey-045-458P	USS *New Jersey*, world's only active battleship, sails in trials to prepare it for active duty off VN.
W	Fulbright-Vietnam- 140-540P	Senator Fulbright offers Senate resolution calling for appointment of independent, Cabinet-level negotiator for peace in VN.
Chicago	Clark-Vietnam-143- 554P	Mayor Daley says VN "situation has to be reviewed time and time again and President Johnson must be reviewing it"; said in response to statement by William Clark, Attorney-General of Illinois, who expressed concern.
W	Military Spending-152- 618P	Treasury reports military spending for February dropped by 10.6 percent; statistics.

Dateline		Story
N.Y.	086-737P	ACLU charges that Congressional investigation of government employees who have protested VN War amounts to intimidation.
W	2 nt ld Abrams Vietnam-087-804P	Army General Abrams leaves for VN saying enemy "has the capability to conduct offensive operations whenever he feels the time is right"; quotes. (D. Cornell)
W	937P	Army Sgt. Edward R. Johnson who spent 3-1/2 years as VC captive will not return to S. VN as he requested because its against Army policy.
March 28		
W	US-Vietnam-01-110A	General Abrams leaves Washington for VN without leaving a clue to future U.S. troop plans or to his own military future; quotes. (R. Gray)
W	Komer-Vietnam-018-312A	Ambassador Robert Komer says VC dealt pacification program in VN real setback with Tet offensive; details. (L. Gulick)
Bangkok	Asian Special Report-097-1149A	"Leaders in a number of areas of noncommunist Asia say they detect growing uncertainty, doubts, and fears about the U.S. and about their own countries' futures"; details. (W. Ryan)
W	Mother-181-713P	Senator Margaret Smith reads to Senate letter from woman whose son was killed in VN which said that "last night I wept for my country."
W	F-111-104-1212	Defense Department announced that one of Air Force's new F-111 fighter-bombers missing on mission over S.E. Asia; details. (B. Horton)
Canberra	108-1229P	Defense Minister Allen Fairhall tells Parliament that Australia could have no faith in integrity of arrangements made with N. VNese, whose pledge means so little.

Dateline		Story
W	Epperson-106-229P	Pentagon denies Hanoi Radio report that destroyer *Epperson* had been hit and set ablaze off N. VN.
W	Congress-Vietnam-039-404P	Repeal of Tonkin Gulf resolution urged by 21 House members; quotes.
W	nt 1d Vietnam Casualties-040-414P	Enemy losses in VN reported by Defense Department to reach 320,129 killed through March 16; statistics. (G. Bridge)
Tokyo	US Protest-189-806P	Four hundred radical students storm new U.S. Army hospital for VN War casualties at Oji, Japan.
March 29		
Tokyo	142A	N. VN says it shot down F-111A fighter over Ha Tinh province Thursday.
W	F-111A Loss-025-339A	Effect of loss of F-111; details. (F. Hoffman)
Baton Rouge, La.	Taylor-42-740A	Maxwell Taylor, former U.S. ambassador to S. VN, describes U.S. response to current shift in enemy strategy and key question in conduct of VN War.
Hiroshima	Reynolds-44-817A	Dr. Earle Reynolds, American peace worker who took cargo of medical supplies to N. VN, says passport, revoked by U.S. government, is again valid.
Phila-delphia, Pa.	122-147P	Three copies of film of voyage of Quaker *Phoenix* yacht to N. VN have been held up by Treasury Department and will be returned to their Canadian maker, a Quaker Action Group.
W	Prisoners-88-204P	State Department says return of three N. VNese sailors to Hanoi was result of direct contact between U.S. Ambassador and a ranking N. VNese diplomat in neutral Laos.
Jackson, Mich.	24-359P	Jackson *Citizen-Patriot* published letter from Pvt. Ralph D. Denman, deserter, which says he was a member of "this military circus" and left "to work against the war in VN"; quotes.
W	Woman Marine-135-520P	Woman Marine corporal Mary Elizabeth Burnes asks for discharge because she disagrees with U.S. policy in VN; court-martial ordered.

Dateline		Story
N.Y.	062-607P	Young college correspondent Dee Dembart says marijuana is purchased openly and used widely by U.S. soldiers in VN; details.
W	Bomb Lull?-066-621P	Report that Johnson was considering N. VN bombing pause met with non-committal response at White House.
Montana	092-636P	U.S. Senator Mansfield calls for confrontation in U.N. Security Council of all powers directly involved in VN conflict. (M. Liblen)

March 30

Dateline		Story
Tokyo	129-134A	N. VN claims to have shot down second F-111 over N. VN Saturday; details. (Incomplete)
N.Y.	016-311A	CBS News says correspondent Charles Collingwood admitted to N. VN for indefinite stay and is now in Hanoi preparing radio and television reports.
Tokyo	031-534A	VC says between battles in Khe Sanh its troops compose poems-- example.
Vatican City	067-946A	Pope Paul VI deprived Archbishop Thuc, broth of slain VNese Presi-dent, of all authority over Archdiocese of Hue, the Vatican announces.
W	F-111-77-123P	New F-111 crashes in Thailand, says Pentagon.
Clio, Mich.	With Tokyo-041-309P	Paul Johnson hears news that his daughter and another woman, held captive since attack on Hue, to be freed by VC.
W	nt ld Johnson-048-405P	Johnson says he intends to tell nation Sunday night of increase in troops and spending for VN War--but not on huge scale; details, quotes (4). (D. Cornell)
Paris	036-5P	Twelve hundred youths demonstrate in support for U.S. and S. VN, in Paris demonstration.
W	Vietnam-Military-034-539P	Johnson's report to nation Sunday night is expected to disclose end results of more than month of high-level discussions of VN military problems; details. (F. Hoffman)

Dateline		Story
Tokyo	nt ld Women POWs -701P	VC will free before Monday two American women captured during Tet offensive; details.
Tokyo	730P	N. VN describes as "rumors" reports that U.S. and N.VN representatives established contacts in Laos in connection with release of POWs.
W	Rifles-020-924P	Pentagon announces plans to step up production of M-16 rifles to speed modernization of S. VNese army; details.
W	With F-111-52-1057P	Senator Mundt says Senate Investigations Subcommittee should reopen its probe of controversial F-111 unless Pentagon halts its use in VN.
Honolulu	96-1135P	Secretary of State Rusk in Honolulu en route to New Zealand for talks with VN allies.

March 31

W	Vietnam News-042-334P	Rostow and Taylor, two of Johnson's advisors, portray enemy's Tet offensive in S. VN as partial victory for U.S., reviving Administration claim that has drawn sharp criticism; quotes.
Boston	28-649A	Asian scholar Dr. Owen Lattimore says U.S. policy in S.E. Asia is contributing to spread of communism rather than stopping it; quotes.
Ft. Bragg, N.C.	446P	Four hundred U.S. paratroopers sent to VN in February returned to Ft. Bragg because they had been home less than six months before their second combat tour began.
W	Negotiation-061-521P	George Ball talks about a "deal" with N. VN rather than "negotiations."
W	Viet Protest-064-528P	Several federal employees opposed to VN War delivered to White House statement outlining their stand.
Dallas, Tex.	Mood of Texas-076-533P	Dallas *Morning News* reports statewide interviews indicate mood of Texas on VN War shifted from hawk to moderate dove.
Temple, Tex.	85-733P	Texas publisher Frank W. Mayborn analyzes VN War and comes up with feeling that U.S. is winning. (F. Mayborn)

Dateline	Story	
Welling- ton, New Zealand	093-820P	Military advisors of SEATO call for sustained and increased military effectiveness in VN.
Hamburg	Ky-Stern-103-916P	Vice President Ky of S. VN quoted by *Stern* magazine as saying that main American motive in VN is self-interest, that his government is useless and corrupt and that "we need a revolution"; details.
W	5 ld Johnson-113- 930P	Johnson stunned nation by declaring "I shall not seek--and will not accept--the nomination of my party for another term as your President"; details (9).
W	Johnson Reaction-144- 1154P	Reaction to Johnson's decision not to run from various politicians; quotes.
H.K.	Reaction-Johnson-61- 1225A	Americans, British, Europeans, Chinese in Hong Kong at first refused to believe Johnson's decision not to accept second bid for Presidency.

STORY INDEX: STORIES FROM VIETNAM, UNITED PRESS INTERNATIONAL,
FEBRUARY 1 - MARCH 31, 1968

Dateline		Story
February 1		
Phu Bai	Hue-439B-1214P	VC forces in Hue repulse U.S. and RSVN Marines for second day; details. (Richard Oliver)
S	Mop-up-041B-1109A	RSVN recapture Tan Son Nhut Air Base from VC.
S	Hospital-432B-1032A	U.S. Army's 3rd Field Hospital's patients guard building during attack. (Thomas Corpora)
S	Assessment-036B-1045A	Westmoreland's assessment of battle areas in I Corps; details.
S	Westy-020B-735A	Westmoreland says communists had policy of "go for broke" in offensive against northern provinces in S. VN. (Kate Webb)
February 2-4	none	
February 5		
S	Policeman-510B-216P	Saigon police chief, Colonel Luan, reports policeman killed by disguised VC.
S	Food-044B-1055A	U.S. Mission reports mounting shortage of available food.
S	Food-202B-144P	U.S. Mission reports rising food prices in Saigon and distribution problems for refugees.
S	Suu-421B-905	Tran Duc Suu, ABC cameraman, wounded by shrapnel in Saigon.
S	Ky-511B-219P	VC sent letter to a S. VNese general a week before Tet offensive asking him to defect, says Ky.
February 6		
S	Sun-538B-913P	S. VNese police take former Chief of State and Presidential candidate Suu into protective custody.

NOTE: No files were available for United Press International Vietnam-related stories from outside Vietnam. This compilation is from UPI files, but may be incomplete. In some cases, due to difficulties in reproduction from the files, identifying headings, time indicators, or file numbers are incomplete or lacking.

D = Da Nang; K = Khe Sanh; S = Saigon; nt ld = night lead.

Dateline		Story
S	Khe Sanh-030B-858A	U.S. Marines wait for enemy at Khe Sanh fort. (Thomas Corpora)
S	Viet-6-911A	VC, U.S. fighting in Saigon and Hue; details, statistics.
S	add Viet-40-1051A	In air war U.S. and enemy each lose plane near Hanoi; U.S. bombs various other troops in South; statistics.
S	Viet Defenses-8-918A	Despite U.S. warnings, VC attacks on S. VNese cities caught SVN troops' defenses "relaxed in Pearl Harbor style," says U.S. official.
February 7		
S	Viet-6-905A	First enemy tank attack of war overruns Green Beret camp near N. VNese border.
S	Rosson-528B-623P	Major General Rosson says VC Tet offensive spent and allies have "a unique opportunity to shorten the war"; statistics, details.
S	Ben Tre-533B-736P	War has "pretty well chewed" Mekong Delta city of Ben Tre; statistics. (Daniel Southerland)
S	Viet-122-324P	Green Berets recapture their Lang Vei camp from N. VN in first Red armored assault of war.
S	Americans-52-1115A	VC killed 17 U.S. civilians in Saigon during two weeks of Tet offensive, U.S. officials report.
S	Viet-117-733P	U.S. Major General Rosson says because of Tet offensive allies have "a unique opportunity to shorten the war."
February 8		
S	Viet-126-307P	Heavy fighting in S. VN's three northern provinces as N. VNese troops use Russian tanks in Green Berets' Lang Vei area.
S	Tives-032B-938A	May take two weeks to dislodge "well organized" VC in Saigon, U.S. advisors say; details. (Thomas Corpora)

Dateline		Story
S	Air-021B-749A	Navy bombers attack Hai Duong rail yard in N. VN; details.
S	Newsmen-025B-835A	Newsman Howard Tuckner of NBC and Dang Van Phuoc of AP wounded in Saigon street fighting; photo.
S	Viet Casualties-7-855A	Record 416 U.S. died last week in VN and U.S. troop strength passed half-million mark, say military officials; statistics.
S	Viet-8-902A	N. VN hit Khe Sanh with record barrage and occupies camp where eight U.S. fight their way out of bunkers; details.
February 9		
S	Viet-110-209P	Enemy moves supplies across Laotian border for battle at Khe Sanh as U.S. attempts stoppage "with fearsome artillery and air attacks"; details.
D	Plane-22-941A	U.S. Marine fails to hijack commercial airliner in S. VN.
S	Mobilization-8-854A	President Thieu decrees draft of students, civil servants, and vets; urges continued bombings of N.VN and "increased punishment of the communist aggressors" in speech before S. VNese National Assembly.
S	Viet-6-848A	U.S. spokesman says that "Marine jets smashed a communist tank column with bombs, rockets, and flaming napalm" near U.S. fort, Khe Sanh; details.
S	Quotes-16B-645A	President Thieu: "If we stop the bombing we will take more casualties." Capt. Robert Ritz, veteran of jungle fighting, says of Saigon street fighting: "The snipers are everywhere. I saw more action than all the time I've been in VN."
S	Pratt-441B-1125A	U.S. AID worker Dr. Lawrence Pratt says he hid for eight days in house in Cholon to keep from being killed by VC; details.

Dateline		Story
February 10		
S	Battle-72-402P	"Explosions at a burning ammunition dump rocked the city" as U.S.'s 25th Division and S. VNese battle 1,000 VC in Saigon outskirts; details.
S	Viet-61-215P	U.S. command discloses presence of three N. VNese Russian-make jet bombers near Khe Sanh which may be used in battle; details.
S	2 ld Viet-206A-114P	U.S. officials say "twin jet Soviet bombers are poised on N. VNese airfields only minutes away from Khe Sanh"; statistics. (Eugene Risher)
S	Viet-6-846A	Same as above; details.
S	Viet-22-1024A	S. VNese Defense Department officials say no plans yet to implement Thieu's "speeded-up mobilization announcement." VC kill at least 19 U.S. civilians in 11 days of Tet offensive and 12 reported missing.
S	nt ld Plane-203B-1256P	Description of plush military charter flight into Saigon--"a heck of a way to go to war"; details. (Robert Ibrahim)
S	Toll-224B-553P	VC killed 28 U.S. civilians, wounded five, since January 29, U.S. Embassy reports; details.
S	nt ld Cemetery-248B-9P	Neighborhood watch Saigon cemetery battle between SVN and VC; details. (Nathan Gibson)
S	Thieu-401B-516A	S. VNese Defense Department has no plans to implement President Thieu's "speed up mobilization" announcement.
February 11		
	none	
February 12		
S	Viet-6-846A	Five hundred U.S. Marines begin drive to retake Hue; details.

Dateline		Story
February 13		
Hue	Hue-109-224P	"American Marines doggedly fought their way inch-by-inch up the streets of the northern half of Hue Tuesday toward the communist-held Citadel"; details. (Richard Oliver)
Hue	nt ld Hue-204B-202P	Same as above. (Richard Oliver)
S	Air-427B-1026A	U.S. warplanes down 108th N. VNese MIG of war over N. VN; details.
S	Air-035B-1037A	U.S. Navy jets knock out another enemy tank near Khe Sanh, says U.S. spokesman.
S	Viet-7-850A	Police official says Major General Do, Deputy Commander of N. VNese Army, killed in Saigon street fighting; details.
S	Viet-6-846A	Allies kill 133 VC in Saigon's outskirts and bomb to prevent second invasion; details.
February 14		
S	Viet-6-852A	U.S. Marines withdraw as bombers hit Hue Citadel with bombs, rockets, and napalm; details.
S	1 add Viet-42-1033A	Radio Hanoi says six U.S. planes shot down in N. VN.
February 15		
S	Air-029B-1A	U.S. bombers take advantage of break in monsoon weather and bomb every major N. VNese airfield except Hanoi's commercial airport; details. (Kate Webb)
S	nt ld Casualties-206B-243P	Four hundred U.S. troops killed, bringing two-week total to 816, "bloodiest of the war"; statistics.
S	Viet-6-852A	Allies try to dislodge "communist suicide battalion" in Hue's fortress and general fighting in Saigon; details.
S	Viet Casualties-7-856A	Four hundred U.S. troops killed; same as nt ld Casualties 206B-243P.

Dateline		Story
S	add Viet-63-1155A	N. VNese reinforcements headed to help foe in Hue.
Hue	nt ld Corpsman-221A-313P	Story about wounded corpsman and friend in Hue; details. (Richard Oliver)
S	2 ld Viet-11A-1133A	Same as add Viet-63-1155A. (Eugene Risher)
S	Bombs-123-314P	U.S. Air Force jets kill 44 and wound 57 when they miss target area near Saigon; details.
February 16		
S	Viet-83-1239P	Enemy holds in Hue fortress as U.S. Marines try to rout them out.
Hue	Hue-100A-1A	Description of battle at Hue; details. (Alvin Webb, Jr.)
S	Viet-848A	"A Marine charge drove communist troops in Hue back up against the towering walls of the Imperial Citadel today and Marine tanks shelled guerrillas trying to flee their last urban stronghold in S. VN"; details.
February 17		
S	Viet-68-140P	Enemy forces launch new full-scale offensive drive in S. VN; details.
S	1 add Viet-70-155P	Explosion at Tan Son Nhut Air Base and fighting throughout Saigon.
Hue	nt ld Citadel-224A	Description of Hue Citadel battle; details. (Alvin Webb, Jr.)
S	Viet-5-842A	U.S. Marines attempt to retake Hue's fortress; details.
S	Viet-66-132P	Enemy forces attack Tan Son Nhut Air Base and U.S. military headquarters in Saigon as part of larger "offensive"' details.
S	1 nt ld Viet-117-127P	Seventy-plus Marines killed and 600 wounded in Hue battle.
S	2 nt ld Viet-215A-110P	Enemy attack Saigon's air base in U.S. military headquarters. (Eugene Risher)
S	3 nt ld Viet-234A-326P	N. VN and VC opened "second offensive with attacks throughout three-fourths of S. VN; details.

Dateline		Story
S	1 add 3 nt 1d Viet-235A-330P	Seventy U.S. troops, 3,000 enemy killed in Hue, and Tan Son Nhut airfield and U.S. military headquarters attacked; details.
S	2 add 3 nt 1d Viet-236-333P	First reports on fighting in Highlands and Delta sketchy.
S	3 add 3 nt 1d Viet-238A-349P	Details on above.
S	Explosion-58-1258P	Explosion at Saigon's Tan Son Nhut Air Base.
February 18		
S	Viet-016D-730A	Allied forces say they were ready for second VC wave of attacks; details.
S	Boxcars-218B-749P	Enemy attacks on Saigon air base damages six U.S. cargo planes.
S	Smith-500B-517P	Story on Maj. Desmal Smith's confrontation with VC squad; details. (Kate Webb)
S	Chaplain-203B-440P	Wounded Air Force chaplain tells of attack on Tan Son Nhut Air Base; details. (W. Reilly)
S	Chaplain-204B-444P	Details on above.
S	Ship-525B-926P	USS *Hanner*, destroyer, leaves VN after 20 days of support fire in battle of Hue; quotes.
S	Rescue-521B-910P	Lt. Ronald Lewis describes how he used helicopter to save four crewmen whose helicopter crashed into sea off N. VN; details.
S	Westy-522B-912P	Westmoreland working late at headquarters when it was bombed by VC.
February 19		
S	Viet-6-905A	VC blast Westmoreland's headquarters, GIs at air base, cut rail lines in this "second battle of Saigon"; details.
S	add Viet-26-1003A	VC attack Tan Son Nhut Air Base in Saigon again.
S	add Viet-33-1017A	N. VNese radio said that two-day-old Tet offensive brought communists closer to "complete" victory.

Dateline		Story
S	add Viet-89-1255P	Details on Viet-6-905A.
S	Prisoners-238A-450P	Captured VC report months of training before Tet offensive; details. (Kate Webb)
S	1 add nt 1d Prisoners-241A-601P	Details on above.
S	Radio-437-1020A	Radio Hanoi says Tet offensive has brought enemy closer to "complete" victory in VN War; quotes.
S	Sampans-441B-1111A	U.S. Army sinks 20 enemy sampans loaded with weapons near Saigon.
S	Hanoi-528B-622P	Same as Radio-437-1020A.
S	Front-261B-1144P	Members of 25 diverse VN organizations agree to support S. VNese government. (Daniel Southerland)
February 20		
S	Viet-98-1249P	S. VNese troops battle VC near Saigon as spokesmen warn of possible new invasion of Saigon; details.
S	add Viet-45-1039A	Mayor of Hue says captured VC executed.
S	Viet-6-909A	General fighting in S. VN at Saigon, DMZ, etc.; details; statistics.
S	Air-434B-1022A	U.S. Air Force sinks enemy gunboat and 19 sampans in a Mekong Delta canal; details.
S	nt 1d Viet-221B-250P	S. VNese police place two anti-government political leaders in "protective custody" amid rumors of new enemy assault on Saigon; details.
February 21		
S	Hue-6-852A	"UPI correspondent Richard V. Oliver reported the Leathernecks hacked their way through suicidal communist defenders" in Hue's imperial fortress.
D	Suspects-257B-1208A	Gen. Hoang Lan said VC suspects in Hue would be tried by military courts but not executed in public; snipers shot on sight; details, quotes.

Dateline	Story	
S	Bombers-435B-1123A	U.S. added 50 percent more B-52 bombers and used them at Khe Sanh battle.
Hue	nt 1d Hue-226B-509P	Description of fighting in Hue; details. (Richard Oliver)
S	Viet-7-914A	U.S. Marines launch predawn ground assault against VC in Hue; details.
S	add Viet-22C-1008A	Fighting in Mekong Delta provincial capitals and various other places in S. VN.
S	Bombers-61-1139A	Same as Bombers-435B-1123A.
February 22		
S	nt 1d Air-203A-133P	U.S. jets bomb Hanoi's main radio transmitter, but propaganda broadcasts continue uninterrupted; details.
S	Air-438B	Description of U.S. air action in VN.
S	Wheeler-549B-1123P	General Wheeler in Saigon says Westmoreland has full backing of Johnson, Secretary of Defense, and Joint Chiefs of Staff.
S	Posture-515B-420P	U.S. military spokesman says VC around Saigon have not "gone into a withdrawal posture."
S	3 1d Viet-079A-941A	"U.S. Marines fighting foot by bloodsoaked foot today captured a Vietcong watchtower on the southeastern corner of Hue's old Imperial City"; details. (Eugene Risher)
S	4 1d Viet-102A-1157A	"U.S. Marines attacking behind a wall of flaming napalm today virtually sealed off the suicidal band of Vietcong who have held the Imperial City fortress in Hue 23 days"; details. (Eugene Risher)
S	1 add 4 1d Viet-105A-1206P	Other major developments of VN War.
S	Viet Casualties-5-848A	In costliest week of war, U.S. lost 543; details; statistics.

Dateline	Story	
February 23		
S	Wheeler-858A	General Wheeler in Saigon says Westmoreland has full backing of Johnson, Defense Secretary, and Joint Chiefs of Staff.
Hue	1 ld Hue-294A-1145P	S. VNese forces attack VC stronghold in Hue. (Robert Ibrahim)
S	1 add 3 ld Viet-290A-1130P	VC attack Saigon's Tan Son Nhut Air Base hitting U.S. military barracks and S. VNese civilian homes; details.
S	2 add 3 ld Viet-292A-1138P	Details on allied attack on Hue Citadel.
S	3 ld Viet-239A-1120P	Same as above. (Thomas Cheatham)
Hue	Hue-275A-947P	Detailed report on battle at Hue. (Richard Oliver)
S	2 ld Viet-273A-832	Same as 1 add 3 ld Viet-290A-1130P. (Thomas Cheatham)
S	Hue-50-1120A	U.S. Marines wait for political decision on what tactics to use in retaking Hue from enemy; details.
Hue	Flag-538B-1129A	Marines place flag in Imperial City wall in Hue.
February 24		
S	nt ld Viet-206A-1258P	Enemy launches rocket attack against U.S. Marine and Air Force base at Da Nang; details of war action in all VN. (Thomas Cheatham)
S	Troops-6-845A	U.S. commanders in VN ask for another 50,000 to 100,000 troops to regain initiative in war.
S	Pacify-060A-750A	Pacification program suffers "considerable setback" from enemy attack on cities and towns, says U.S. official; details.
S	Air-250-630P	U.S. unleashes one of heaviest air bombardments of war against enemy troops threatening Khe Sanh; details.
S	Troops-214A-158P	Westmoreland wants between 50,000 and 100,000 more troops to mount allied offensive in VN.
S	Pacification-224A-312P	U.S. Army official concedes that communist offensive has dealt pacification program in S. VN "a considerable setback"; details. (Daniel Southerland)

Dateline		Story
S	Diplomats-510B-310P	Members of diplomatic corps sending dependents to other countries for safety in anticipation of renewed enemy attacks; details. (Kate Webb)
S	day 1d Viet-013A-252A	S. VNese troops pull down enemy flag hanging from tower of Hue's Imperial Citadel; details. (Eugene Risher)
S	Air Base-020A-343A	Army sergeant's description of scene when VC attacked Army 3rd field hospital. (Nathan Gibson)
S	Change-305A-1232A	Major General Ewell assumes command of U.S. 9th Infantry Division.
February 25		
S	nt 1d Saigon-207A-228P	General Saigon scene; details. (R. Miller)
S	nt 1d Viet-201A	RSVN troops aid U.S. in defense of Tan Son Nhut Air Base, Saigon against VC attacks; details. (John Walsh)
S	The Other War in VN-255A	Can Pacification Succeed? Report on pacification program in VN; details and analysis. (Daniel Southerland)
S	nt 1d Saigon-021A-1121A	Same as nt 1d Saigon-207A-228P. (R. Miller)
S	Viet-258A-850P	U.S. Navy jets bomb Haiphong railroad yard in N. VN. (John Walsh)
S	1 add 1 1d Viet-259A-9P	Repeat of above; details.
S	Komer-213B-647P	Chief of U.S. pacification program in VN will fly to Washington to give Johnson personal rundown on effects of communist city offensive on program.
S	Air-504B-530P	U.S. warplanes fly over N. VN's capital to attack port facilities for first time in war and to hit Hanoi radio station and army barracks; details.

Dateline	Story	
February 26		
Hue	Hue-281A	U.S. Marines leave Hue; details. (Robert Kaylor, Jr.)
S	nt ld Security-280A-456P	U.S. command decrees censorship on details of enemy attacks to "deny the enemy information of intelligence value"; details.
S	Bombings-5-854A	U.S. will accelerate bombing N. VN in next two months; details.
S	Viet-80-1213P	ARVN paratroopers route VC battalion into path of U.S. tanks near Tan Son Nhut Air Base.
S	Troops-7-901A	General Wheeler returns to Washington with requests for 50,000 to 100,000 more troops for VN.
S	Viet-6-858A	Allied troops route VC battalion shelling Saigon's Tan Son Nhut Air Base; details.
S	Security-53A-17A	Same as nt ld Security-280A-456P.
February 27		
S	Generals-078A-912A	Two ARVN corps commanders fired by Saigon government as urged by U.S. military who "sought more aggressive VN Army leaders"; details. (John Walsh)
S	Censor-271A-719P	U.S. military officially says no more detailed on-the-scene news reporting on VC shelling of U.S. bases; details.
S	Viet-144-303P	U.S. planes bombing neutral Laos to support Laotian Army fighting N. VNese troops; details.
S	Laos-8-917A	Same as above.
S	Viet-5-909A	Green Berets "smashed" first enemy tank probe of Saigon area and allies fight enemy in Saigon suburbs; details.
S	3 ld Viet-125A-236P	Same as above. (Eugene Risher)
Hoc Mon	Hicks-019B-653A	Feature report on battle in Hoc Mon; details, quotes. (Nathan Gibson)
S	2 ld Viet-058A-724A	Same as Viet-5-909A. (Eugene Risher)

Dateline		Story
S	1 add 2 ld Viet-060A-740A	Details on above.
Cu Chi	Linville-415B-820A	Feature on frequently wounded U.S. Sergeant Linville in VN; details. (Nathan Gibson)
S	nt ld Viet-217A-218P	Same as Viet-144-303P. (John Walsh)
S	1 add nt ld Viet-220A-237P	Details on above; statistics.
S	Civilians-244B-754P	RSVN government says hundreds more civilians than soldiers killed during VC Tet offensive; statistics.

February 28

S	2 ld Viet-093A-1041A	N. VNese dig trenches at Khe Sanh where 16,000 N. VNese surround 6,000 U.S. Marines.
S	1 add 2 ld Viet-094A-1046A	U.S. will raise number of U.S. troops in S. VN to 499,000; details.
S	Viet-6-913A	VC attack five allied bases around Saigon and N. VNese troops in Central Highlands; details.
S	1 ld Viet-280A-842P	RSVN found bodies of 100 soldiers and civilians in grave in Hue.
S	1 add 1 ld Viet-281A-844P	Details on above.
S	2 add 2 ld Viet-296A-100P	U.S. in Hue killed 37 enemy, captured 7; five U.S. killed, 11 wounded in mop-up; details.
S	2 ld Viet-294A-955	Enemy surrounding Khe Sanh shot down U.S. helicopter killing 22 Marines. (John Walsh)
S	Thieu-312A-1145P	President Thieu decides to close all bars "in view of the present critical situation."
S	Censor-017A-318A	U.S. censorship rule on newsmen permits no more detailed on-the-scene reporting of VC shelling of U.S. bases; details. (Thomas Cheatham)
S	day ld Viet-014A	Same as Viet-6-913A; details. (Eugene Risher)
S	nt ld Viet-203S	Description of battle at Khe Sanh; details. (John Walsh)

Dateline		Story
S	nt ld Airborne-219A-304P	Four-thousand-man brigade of 82nd Airborne arrives in S. VN as reinforcements; details. (Thomas Cheatham)
S	Air-434B-1110A	U.S. Navy jets bomb again Haiphong rail yards in N. VN; details.
S	Viet-903A	U.S. spokesmen say U.S. bombers hitting N. VNese air base being built up possibly to launch first enemy air attacks against S. VN; details.
S	Viet Casualties-7	Communists killed passes 300,000; statistics on all casualties.
K	Flight-096A-1034A	Description of flight to Khe Sanh. (Robert Ibrahim)
February 29		
S	Viet Casualties-7-907A	Number of communists killed in VN War exceeds 300,000, say U.S. officials; statistics.
S	Viet-6-903A	U.S. bombers hitting N. VNese base possibly being built to launch first air war against S. VN; details.
K	Flight-096A-1034	Feature story about battle at Khe Sanh; details. (Robert Ibrahim)
S	Security-053A-817A	U.S. military command announces tightening restrictions on disclosure of specific details of enemy attacks.
S	1 ld Viet-273A-817P	Allied patrol boats intercept four trawlers running ammunition and guns to VC in S. VN; destroyed three. (John Walsh)
S	1 add 1 ld Viet-275A-833P	Details on above.
S	2 ld Viet-280-915A	Same as 1 ld Viet-273A-817P. (John Walsh)
S	1 ld Viet-038A-554A	U.S. bombers hitting N. VNese base possibly being built to launch first air war against S. VN; details on other war action. (Eugene Risher)

Dateline	Story	
S	1 add 1 ld Viet-039A-558A	Details on above.
S	2 add 1 ld Viet-041A-635A	Details on above.
S	2 ld Viet-063A-806A	Number of communists killed in VN War exceeds 300,000, say U.S. officials. (Eugene Risher)
S	1 add 2 ld Viet-066A-820	Other war action.
S	3 ld Viet-083A	Same as above.
S	day ld Viet-015A-243A	U.S. bombers strike N. VNese troops who shot down troop-carrying Marine helicopter near Khe Sanh; details on other war action.
S	nt ld Casualties-206A-144P	Four hundred seventy U.S. troops killed in combat last week; statistics.
S	1 add nt ld Casualties-211A-217P	Other war action; details.
S	Bar girls-422B-829A	Twenty thousand Saigon bar girls looking for work since President Thieu closed all bars and night clubs "in view of the present critical situation."
S	Air-042B	U.S. Air Force and Navy planes bomb key radio base and Haiphong rail yards near Hanoi.
March 1		
S	Rescue-076A-1041A	Air force para-rescue man describes typical pilot rescue; details. (Robert Kaylor, Jr.)
S	nt ld Viet-212A-215P	Allies repulse first major ground attack by N. VN against surrounded U.S. Marine base at Khe Sanh; details.
S	Kitty-065A-938A	After 61 days of launching air strikes against N. VN, U.S. aircraft carrier *Kitty Hawk* replaced by USS *Ticonderoga*.
S	1 add nt ld Viet-215A-236P	Other details on VN War.
S	day ld Viet-009A	U.S. Navy and Coast Guard patrols smashed largest communist attempt to run supply ships through allied blockade of S. VNese coast; details. (Eugene Risher)

Dateline		Story
S	Stewart-049D-1020A	Lt. Charles S. Stewart escapes death four times.
Anderson Base	Cockatoos-414B-730A	Cockatoos cause trouble for Australian task force; details.
K	Khe Sanh	"The Fort That Holds Its Breath"; description of U.S. Marine force at Khe Sanh; details. (Robert Ibrahim)
S	1 ld Viet-022A-501A	"U.S. forces destroyed five communist supply ships and captured a sixth today in what military officials called the 'most important' naval battle of the VN War." (Eugene Risher)
S	1 add 1 ld Viet-023A-506A	Details on above.
S	nt ld Thieu-203A-126P	President Thieu says that corruption in S. VN is a national shame and he is determined to stop it; quotes. (Daniel Southerland)
Cam Ranh Bay	Trawler-1053A	Enemy trawler bearing war supplies for VC in S. VN permitted by U.S. vessels to escape.
S	2 ld Viet	U.S. and RSVN forces beat back series of enemy attacks along DMZ; details.
S	Viet-6-9A	U.S. forces destroy five enemy supply ships and capture six in "most important" naval battle of VN War; details.
Cam Ranh Bay	Viet Trawler-55-102P	Same as Trawler-1053A; details.
Nui Dat	Vietcong-111-240P	VC appeal to U.S. and Australian troops to throw down guns in leaflet.
S	Khe Sanh-86-105P	N. VN in first major attack at Khe Sanh repelled by ARVN.
K	C-123-052A-845A	C-123 transport plane shot down by enemy in attempted take-off from Khe Sanh.
S	Burning-254B-1152P	Buddhist monk burns himself to death leaving note saying, "I died to pray for peace for the people" in Saigon.

Dateline		Story
March 2		
K	Company-031B-840A	Story about Marines fighting at Khe Sanh.
S	nt ld Thieu-219A-213P	President Thieu signs executive order designed to combat corruption and inefficiency in government and excesses by military; details. (Daniel Southerland)
S	nt ld-129P	U.S. paratroops ambush enemy company near Bien Hoa; fighting at Khe Sanh; U.S. recovers ammunition from attacked trawlers; air action over both S. VN and N. VN; details. (John Walsh)
K	nt ld Battle-203A-1240P	Description of N. VNese attack of Khe Sanh; details; quotes. (Robert Ibrahim)
S	Air-098A	U.S. Navy pilots bomb Hanoi, Haiphong, and railroad yard in N. VN.
S	Viet-036A-502	U.S. and RSVN attacked VC guerrillas threatening two largest allied air bases in S. VN; details.
S	Reform-052A-635A	President Thieu signs order to cut down on warlord tactics and government corruption. (Daniel Southerland)
S	Wounded-046A-547A	Two CBS newsmen wounded while covering action at Khe Sanh.
S	day ld Viet-016A-229A	"Allied troops laid down murderous fire across the barbed-wire perimeter of Khe Sanh today and repulsed one of several N. VNese thrusts against U.S. strongpoints below the DMZ. U.S. spokesmen said today; details on air action over N. VN; DMZ fighting. (Eugene Risher)
S	nt ld Viet-280A-835P	U.S. bombed near Khe Sanh "to help hold back thousands of N. VNese closing in on the Marines' fort on S. VN's northern frontier, military spokesmen said." (John Walsh)

Dateline		Story
S	Trawlers-237A-401P	U.S. Navy recovered weapons from sunken enemy trawlers but were unable to discover origins of boats; details.
S	Tien-3A-440P	U.S. authorities giving close attention to VC threat implying they may set up communist government in S. VN.
March 3		
S	nt ld Massacre-211A-242P	Ninety-five S. VNese civilians found in mass graves in Hue, killed by VC for refusing to fire at U.S. planes during battle of Hue last month.
Can Tho	Can Tho-009A-649A	"The Mekong Delta: VN Food Basket and Vital Battlefield"; description of effects of Tet offensive on town of Can Tho and farmland in Mekong Delta; details. (A. Dibble)
S	nt ld Viet-210A-233P	VC killed 48 U.S., wounded 28, in ambush of 100-man patrol near Saigon; details of fighting in Saigon, Hue, N. VN air; arrival of 3,500 Marine regiment in VN. (John Walsh)
S	Viet-021D-620A	U.S. troops in Saigon's outskirts ambushed by VC.
S	nt ld Troops-218A-329P	Thirty-five hundred more U.S. troops arrive and S. VNese government will furnish 125,000 additional men for war; details. (Daniel Southerland)
March 4		
S	Air-038B	Navy jets flew against targets in N. VN; details.
S	Hospital-230B-1147P	Charity hospital operated by U.S. woman doctor overrun by VC troops and converted into mortar launching site.
S	nt ld Viet-207A-153P	U.S. command describes new enemy rocket and artillery attacks on allied bases and villages as "harassment tactics"; air war; details. (John Walsh)

Dateline		Story
S	day 1d Viet-011A-212A	Communist rocket and mortar attacks in S. VN struck two major U.S. air bases, an army headquarters camp, a navy hospital, an oil storage complex near Saigon. (Eugene Risher)
S	Rebut-523B-525P	U.S. command issued statement disputing communist claims of "unprecedented successes" in 1968 offensive.
S	Newspaper-518B-427P	S. VNese government shuts down Chinh Luan newspaper for misquoting Premier Loc.
S	Thieu-079A-1030A	President Thieu's appeal for special economic and financial power to cope with economic problems caused by Tet offensive resisted by S. VNese senate.
S	Viet-226A-838P	Communist rocketeers attacked U.S. air base at Cam Ranh Bay for first time. (John Walsh)
S	Viet-6-857A	Communist forces attacked 12 U.S. bases and four provincial capitals in third coordinated nationwide attack in 33 days; details.
D	Newsmen-64-1138	Russ Bensley, CBS TV producer, wounded second time at Khe Sanh.

March 5

S	Mine-202A-124P	UPI photographer Hiromichi Mine seriously wounded near Vgu Tai.
S	1 1d Viet-543A	VC invaded Quan Long and shelled seven other provincial capitals; details. (Eugene Risher)
S	2 1d Viet-094A-1057A	ARVN kill 195 VC who invade Quan Long; details. (Eugene Risher)
S	nt 1d Prisoners-204A-135P	U.S. trying to return three N. VNese POWs as good-will gesture for release last month of three U.S. pilots by N. VN.
S	nt 1d Viet-207A-156P	VC battalion invaded S. VN's southernmost provincial capital Tuesday, occupied civilian hospital for 11 hours, battled government troops in streets; fighting in Saigon; details. (John Walsh)

Dateline		Story
S	day ld Viet-016A- 350A	"Communist guerrillas today shelled seven provincial capitals and three U.S. posts, including the only base in S. VN judged secure enough for a visit by President Johnson; details. (Eugene Risher)
S	Return-5A-239A	U.S. is attempting to return three captured N. VNese seamen to Hanoi as good-will gesture. (Thomas Cheatham)

March 6

S	Viet-6-907A	U.S. commanders feel next major communist offensive in S. VN will be at Hue instead of Khe Sanh; details; allies retake Quan Long.
S	Westy-083A-855A	Westmoreland reaffirms his faith in U.S. Marines holding northern provinces of S. VN against 60,000-70,000 N. VNese, in formal statement; details. (Thomas Cheatham)
Quan Long	Mission-091A-926A	Description of unsuccessful attack of VC on Quan Long; details. (Robert Kaylor, Jr.)
S	Plane-49-923A	"Communist ground fire shot down a C-123 transport at Khe Sanh today killing all 47 persons aboard."
S	Marines-44-1105A	Same as Westy-083A-855A.
S	3 ld Viet-94A-947A	Communists shot down C-123 transport at Khe Sanh, and at Quan Long S. VNese troops killed 275 VC; drove them out of city; details. (Eugene Risher)
S	2 ld Viet-304A	U.S. troops defending sections of S. VN's borders killed 132 communist troops. (John Walsh)
S	nt ld Mine-264A-752P	UPI combat photographer Hiromichi Mine died from burns received when U.S. armored personnel carrier hit communist mine near Hue and burst into flames.
S	Mine-021A-313A	Same as above.
S	nt ld Viet-205A	In a day of heavy fighting all over VN, N. VN down U.S. C-123 plane approaching Khe Sanh, killing 47 Americans; details. (John Walsh)

Dateline		Story
S	4 ld Viet-114A-1115A	Communist ground fire shot down U.S. AF C-123 plane flying reinforcements into Khe Sanh, killing all 47 persons aboard. (Eugene Risher)
S	1 ld Viet-039A-513A	Allied forces recapture Quan Long and kill 275 VC.
March 7		
S	Viet-6-858A	"U.S. suffered 542 troops killed in combat last week, most from S. VN's northern provinces where "heavy fighting raged today"; statistics.
March 8		
S	Viet Command-7-9A	Lt. Gen. William B. ("Battling Bill") Rosson takes command of "Marines and Army troops facing the threat of a massive N. VN invasion," in the provisional corps covering S. VN's northern provinces.
S	nt ld Bunker-240B-742P	U.S. Ambassador Bunker says S. VNese government "moved quickly and vigorously" in recovery program to counter recent VC offensive; quotes. (Daniel Southerland)
S	Viet-6-852A	U.S. casualties in VN War surpass total of U.S. killed and wounded in Korean War, show official reports; statistics; details on fighting northeast of Dong Ha, Lang Vei, Khe Sanh, air missions.
S	Viet-107-230P	U.S. and ARVN "took some of the initiative away" from enemy south of DMZ, with fiercest combat to date around Khe Sanh.
S	nt ld Rosson-267A-819P	Biography of Lt. Gen. William B. ("Battling Bill") Rosson, just appointed commander of provisional corps covering S. VN's two northern provinces; (Richard Oliver)
D	Shakeup-188-830P	USAF announces it is taking from Marines control of U.S. air support in S. VN's northern quarter.

Dateline		Story
March 9		
S	3 ld Viet-204A-1125A	U.S. kill 129 communists below Da Nang in battle still raging, and at Khe Sanh barrage exploded U.S. tear gas canisters among U.S. Marines; details. (Eugene Risher)
Hue	City-203A-1117A	Description of Hue and effects of VC attack. (Richard Oliver)
Dak To	Roads-093A-1011A	Communists building high-speed roads used for hauling heavy supplies from Cambodia into S. VN.
K	Khe Sanh-021B-701A	Description of fighting at Khe Sanh of Charley Battery, part of Marine artillery. (Nathan Gibson)
Dak To	nt ld Roads-220A-3P	Communist work gangs built network of heavy-duty supply roads into S. VN from Cambodia; details. (Perry Young)
S	Air-043B	Targets in air war, including offshore water traffic, Thai Binh Transshipment point, N. VN, Khe Sanh, S. VN, hit by U.S. planes.
S	Viet-51-1206P	Same as 3 ld Viet-204A-1125A.
S	Ky-507B-2117P	Vice President Ky predicts next communist attack in Saigon area.
March 10		
	none	
March 11		
S	nt ld Viet-206A-215P	Battlefront reports say communists with loudspeakers had tunneled to within 100 yards of Khe Sanh and were urging ARVN to abandon Americans at fortress and surrender; details. (John Walsh)
D	Cushman-017A-241A	Marine Lieutenant General Cushman says battle for Khe Sanh is "titanic firepower struggle" which he is convinced the allies can win; quotes; details. (R. Miller)

Dateline		Story
S	Road-033A-518A	Communist guerrillas putting finishing touches on high-speed road across S. VN's northern quarter to supply impending N. VNese offensive from Laos, say U.S. military. (Thomas Cheatham)
S	day 1d Viet-015A-217A	Military spokesmen say continual mortar, rocket, artillery fire against U.S. Marine base at Khe Sanh; details. (Eugene Risher)
S	2 1d Viet-084A	Communist guerrillas planted loudspeakers at Khe Sanh through which they urged S. VNese to defect; S. VNese Rangers replied with mortar fire. (Eugene Risher)
S	1 1d Viet-036A-539A	N. VN lost 107 men attacking allies on S. VN's northern frontier and fired artillery, rocket, mortar rounds into three Marine bases near border, says U.S. spokesmen.
S	Air-423B	U.S. bombers bomb key bridges in Haiphong-Hanoi area, power plant, airfield, railroad yards, radar sites, missile sites in N. VN.
S	1 1d Viet-260A-848P	Two month-long search-and-destroy missions in Saigon area have killed 5,970 communists, say U.S. officials.
S	Shakeup-101P	President Thieu replaced eight of 44 province chiefs in biggest shakeup of local VNese government to date, say government sources.
S	2 1d Viet-272A-1011P	U.S. command announces end of two search-and-destroy missions in Saigon area and reported 5,970 enemy killed in months-long fighting. (John Walsh)

<u>March 12</u>

S	nt 1d Viet-210A	U.S. Marines and ARVN Rangers went on special alert at Khe Sanh and U.S. bombers struck enemies surrounding Marine base with new delayed fuse bomb. (John Walsh)
K	Bunkers-025B-705A	Feature of life at Khe Sanh for Marines. (Nathan Gibson)
S	day 1d Viet-013A-234A	U.S. troops killed 5,970 communists in two antiguerrilla operations in Saigon area, say U.S. spokesmen; statistical details. (Eugene Risher)

Dateline	Story	
S	Shakeup-028A-524A	Colonel and seven lieutenant colonels take command of eight S. VN's 44 provinces in President Thieu's biggest local government shake-up to date, say government sources. (Daniel Southerland)
S	1 ld Viet-027A-518A	U.S. Air Force bombers "pounded N. VNese ringing the Marine fort of Khe Sanh" with bombs "capable of smashing communist attack tunnels." (Eugene Risher)
K	Wanted-028B-753A	Marine at Khe Sanh wanted for jaywalking by San Diego police.
S	1 ld Viet-259A-804P	Allies kill 194 N. VNese troops in fighting near U.S. Marine supply base at Cua Viet, say government spokesmen.
S	Battle-234A-513P	Comparison of French war in VN to U.S. war in VN; statistics; details. (Richard Oliver)
S	Morale	Describes high morale of American troops in VN; details; analysis. (Eugene Risher)
March 13		
S	1 ld Viet-026A-450A	U.S. jets bombed for first time secret communist jungle highway supplying N. VNese Army, say U.S. spokesmen. (Eugene Risher)
S	3 ld Viet-096A-1206P	U.S. bombers hit communists surrounding Khe Sanh and newly discovered communist supply road toward Khe Sanh; new threat to Saigon; details. (Eugene Risher)
S	2 ld Viet-058A-908A	U.S. bombs new communist supply road leading toward Khe Sanh and at Khe Sanh border area 519 communists killed in battle that began last Sunday; details. (Eugene Risher)
S	Saigon-063B-1148A	U.S. intelligence says more N. VNese troops filtered into area around Saigon during past 10 days to join comrades hiding since Tet offensive.
S	day ld Viet-010A	Sudden silence at Khe Sanh, but elsewhere allied border troops say 229 enemy killed; details. (Eugene Risher)

Dateline		Story
S	nt ld Viet-208A	"Stratofortresses dumped tons of blockbusters" on newly discovered jungle road in S. VN being used by N. VN to channel supplies and men to Khe Sanh and other U.S. outposts; details. (John Walsh)
S	Khe Sanh-14-949	UPI correspondent Nat Gibson describes as "eerie" a sudden silence on Khe Sanh today, 14th anniversary of Dienbienphu.
S	Viet-12-941A	B-52s bombed high-speed communist supply road heading toward Khe Sanh and front reports from border areas say 519 N. VNese killed in heavy battles that began last Sunday.
March 14		
S	1 ld Viet-294A-929P	Communist forces threatening U.S. bases south of DMZ hit U.S. Marine installations around Cua Viet and Dong Ha with rocket and artillery fire and sank U.S. assault boat on Cua Viet River, say U.S. military; details; statistics. (Thomas Cheatham)
S	2 ld Viet-117A-1217P	Five-hundred nine U.S. forces killed and 2,766 wounded last week, U.S. command announces; total highest casualty figure of war, while communist losses lowest in six weeks; statistics. (John Walsh)
S	Khe Sanh-070A-854A	"Hanoi said the allied base of Khe Sanh is the 'Valley of Death' for 6,000 U.S. Marines and S. VNese troops"; quotes.
S	Inflation-039A-600A	S. VN appears heading for inflation because of Tet offensive, say economic sources.
S	nt ld Viet-206A-152P	Five-hundred nine U.S. killed, 2,766 wounded in costliest week of VN War; relative calm in S. VN Thursday, fighting at Khe Sanh; statistics; bombings in N. VN; quotes. (Thomas Cheatham)
S	1 ld Viet-026A-502A	U.S. jets strike N. VN the heaviest "blow in more than a month," bombing 20 major targets in Hanoi-Haiphong area alone, say U.S. officials; details. (John Walsh)

Dateline		Story
S	day 1d Viet-009A-215A	U.S. bombers twice bombed enemies ringing Khe Sanh, but Hanoi claimed Marines are doomed; fighting at Dong Ha, N. VNese bomb truck convoy in Central Highlands, bombing of area around N. VN's Haiphong; details. (John Walsh)
S	Viet Casualties-14-940A	U.S. spokesmen said 509 U.S. troops killed in VN combat, making total Americans killed in war 20,000 plus; statistics.

March 15

S	Viet-150-258P	"A huge assault force of Americans and South Vietnamese pressing the biggest allied offensive of the war into its sixth day Saturday morning reported killing 233 communists in the five provinces ringing Saigon."
S	2 1d Viet-088A	Parts of three divisions under personal command of Westmoreland began largest campaign of war to seek-and-destroy communist forces in and around Saigon, it was announced today. (John Walsh)
S	1 1d Viet-031A-506A	U.S. announces start of VN War's largest campaign named "Operation Certain Victory," aimed at destroying enemy forces in and around Saigon; details. (John Walsh)
S	Viet-15-920	U.S. officials announced start of "Operation Certain Victory"; the 30,000-man drive already has killed at least 215 communists.
S	Viet-13-937A	U.S. jets struck N. VN in heaviest bombing in more than a month, say U.S. spokesmen; in S. VN enemy ambushed two U.S. army truck convoys, propaganda against Khe Sanh; details.
S	Viet Casualties-14-940A	U.S. spokesmen say 509 U.S. died in VN combat last week, making total of Americans killed during war over 20,000.

Dateline		Story
S	Viet Prisoners-92-1256P	Allies completing plans for return of three N. VNese seamen to Hanoi as good-will gesture for communists' release of three U.S. pilots last month.
S	day ld Viet-009A-154A	Communist troops shelled U.S. bases and blew up U.S. assault boat on S. VN's northern frontier. (John Walsh)
S	1 ld Viet-277A-930P	U.S. backfired VC ambush attempt on outskirts of Saigon, killing 81 enemy troops without losing a man, say U.S. spokesmen; details.
D	nt ld Trenches-221A-330P	U.S. military sources report finding three trenches built by N. VNese troops at eastern end of Khe Sanh fortress airstrip; quotes.
S	Viet-209A-159P	Assault force of U.S. and RSVN pressing biggest allied offensive of war into sixth day report killing 233 enemy troops in five provinces ringing Saigon; details. (Thomas Cheatham)
S	3 day ld Viet-204A-131P	Elements of five U.S. and S. VNese divisions under Westmoreland's personal command launch biggest operation of war to seek-and-destroy communists in five provinces around Saigon; statistics; details. (John Walsh)
S	nt ld Prisoners-206A-148P	Allies made final plan for release of three N. VNese POWs reciprocating Hanoi's release of three U.S. bomber pilots.
S	Viet Draft-154-412	RSVN drafting 19-year-olds, say government officials.

March 16

S	nt ld Viet-212A-147P	U.S. assault team traps VC and kills 128 north of Saigon [in My Lai]; statistics, details. (Thomas Cheatham)
S	nt ld-605P	Vice President Ky wants 300,000 more RSVN troops because reliance on American allies could force country under "the slavery of foreigners"; statistics, quotes, details. (Daniel Southerland)

Dateline		Story
S	Ky-438B-1124A	Vice President Ky says RSVN should increase armed forces by 300,000 so as not to rely wholly on U.S. military aid; quotes.
S	nt ld Press-513B-203P	Four Saigon newspaper publishers ask S. VNese government to abolish unconstitutional press censorship.
S	Air-023B	Navy jets bomb another key communications center in N. VN.
S	2 ld Viet-053A-807A	"U.S. troops clearing communists from the Saigon area today pushed to 323 the number of guerrillas slain in the allies 'Operation Resolve to Win', military spokesmen said." (John Walsh)
S	Planes-055A-812A	Air Force summons 16 C-130 Hercules transport planes from U.S. to bolster supply effort in S. VN's northern provinces.
S	3 ld Viet-063A-852A	U.S. kill 128 VC at My Lai, "Pink Village," on beach of South China Sea. (John Walsh)
K	Guns-075A	Battle of Khe Sanh; description of death by mortar shell. (Nathan Gibson)
S	1 ld Viet-024A-505A	"U.S. infantrymen tangled with communist forces threatening the northern city of Quang Ngai today and U.S. spokesmen reported 128 guerrillas slain in the bitter fighting." (John Walsh)
Cau Mau	Delta-296A	Description of Cau Mau, "either a major part of the defense against the communists or the end of the line." (Robert Kaylor, Jr.)

March 17

D	Rescue-031A-1126A	"Jolly Green Giants," large U.S. helicopters, rescue U.S. troops especially airplane crews downed in N. VNese water. (R. Miller)
S	1 nt ld Viet-286A-933P	Communists attack Kontum, but U.S. and ARVN "smashed" VC attempt to seize prison housing VC captives; details. (Thomas Cheatham)

Dateline		Story
S	2 nt ld Viet-945P	Four hundred N. VNese charged out of trenches to drive against U.S. Marines at Khe Sanh. (Thomas Cheatham)
S	Haiphong-213B-1135P	Two Navy pilots say they have bombing accuracy enough to hit N. VN's Haiphong docks without damaging international shipping.
S	Air-221B	U.S. pilots bombing Haiphong-Hanoi area report knocking two spans out of Haiphong's Kien An Highway Bridge less than two miles from city's center.
S	F-111-245D	U.S. Air Force announced arrival of F-111A supersonic fighter-bomber in VN--"a major effort to bolster America's air punch over N. VN."
S	nt ld Viet-224A-341P	Enemy hit Central Highland bastion at Kontum in night rocket and mortar assault; other fighting south of DMZ and around Saigon; air war--communists report shooting down another U.S. flier; details. (Thomas Cheatham)
K	Tunnels-246D-510A	U.S. seismologists instruct Marines in using electronics gear to detect communist tunnels under Khe Sanh.
S	Viet-252D-640P	U.S. most sophisticated jet fighter-bomber, AF F-111A, arrived in S. VN Sunday.
S	Viet-003D	Enemy launched rocket and mortar attacks on airfield and military headquarters in Kontum.
K	Bird Dog-0348	Ride in plane "Bird Dog" over N. VN in a bombing mission. (Richard Oliver)
March 18		
S	1 ld Viet-270A-912P	U.S. Marines killed 67 enemy in battle near U.S. base at Dong Ha; details. (Thomas Cheatham)
S	2 ld Viet-1202P	U.S. planes and artillery battle communist village threatening Dong Ha outpost, the supply head for entire DMZ, and S. VNese Rangers "hurl back" attack on Khe Sanh. (John Walsh)

Dateline		Story
S	IVS-080A-956A	Half the staff of International Voluntary Services decide to leave VN because of poor security in provinces since communist Tet offensive, says IVS spokesman.
S	1 ld Viet-028A-521A	"Dienbienphu tactics failed the communists today at Khe Sanh." (John Walsh)
S	Nolan-032B-959A	Radio Hanoi said U.S. Army corporal, McKinley Nolan, defected to VC.
S	nt ld Viet-205A-152P	Communist troops in Dong Ha village "near Khe Sanh" trap U.S. Marine troops; details. (Thomas Cheatham)
March 19		
S	Bombings-911A	Former VC officer says that communist intelligence network tips off guerrillas in VN 24 hours ahead of raids by U.S. bombers, giving approximate time and place.
S	Migs-7-913A	N. VNese building fleet of MIG jet interceptors to meet U.S. raids expected when monsoon weather lifts from Hanoi-Haiphong area, says U.S. source.
S	Viet-8-918A	"B-52s struck the N. VNese troops surrounding Khe Sanh five times today."
March 20		
Vinh Long	City-089A	"This Mekong Delta city is a city of fear and bitterness"; details on description of Vinh Long. (Daniel Southerland)
S	nt ld Viet-217A-931P	U.S. intelligence offices report "fantastically high" N. VNese casualties; enemy troops to withdraw from the Khe Sanh area, preventing enemy capture of fort; details. (Thomas Cheatham)
S	Sensors-041B-759P	U.S. "seeding" Ho Chi Minh Trail in Laos with detectors that report enemy troop movements toward S. VN, say military sources. (Thomas Cheatham)

Dateline		Story
S	1 ld Viet-276A-828P	VC shell U.S. air base at Tan Son Nhut in first time in two weeks.
S	Air-041B-1050A	U.S. planes attacked enemy forces and supply lines threatening Khe Sanh, says U.S. command; details.
S	nt ld Market-205A-135P	Saigon police seized U.S. post exchange products worth millions of dollars in raid hitting 2,000 plus stalls on Saigon's black market; details. (Daniel Souther-land)
S	2 ld Viet-110A	U.S. military and intelligence sources say communist siege of Khe Sanh failed because of high enemy casualties and end of mon-soon rains that hampered U.S. airpower; details. (John Walsh)
S	3 ld Viet	Same as above.
S	Market-082A-858A	Saigon police raid more than 2,000 vending stalls on black market and seize thousands of dollars worth of U.S. PX goods.
S	1 ld Viet-031A-522A	USAF B-52s bomb N. VNese tank near Khe Sanh.
S	Stars-096A	Airmen at Tan Son Nhut Air Base pay tribute to defenders who died defending base during Tet offen-sive.
K	Tunnels-075A-830A	U.S. Marines using sophisticated equipment to seek out communist tunnels at Khe Sanh; details. (Raymond Wilkinson)
S	Censorship	Government spokesman says press censorship in VN after Tet attacks to be lifted.
S	Recruit-070A	U.S. officers say Tet offensive brought increase in VC recruiting in Saigon area.
S	day ld Viet-011C-230A	USAF B-52 struck six times enemy positions, four near Khe Sanh, say U.S. officers; details on other developments. (John Walsh)

Dateline		Story
March 21		
S	2 ld Viet-288A-919A	U.S. killed 112 enemy along S. VN's northern coast and did not lose a man, say U.S. spokesmen. (Thomas Cheatham)
S	1 ld Viet-275A-806P	VC forces attack three allied military bases around Saigon, say government spokesmen. (Thomas Cheatham)
S	nt ld Casualties-202A-119P	U.S. command reports 336 U.S. killed in VN combat last week, increasing total in six years of war to 20,096; statistics.
S	nt ld Viet-204A	U.S. spokesmen announce five new operations in "counterpunch" against enemy and said 799 VC killed and U.S. planes hit N. VN with heavy air raids. (Thomas Cheatham)
S	Thieu-033A-532A	President Thieu says S. VN will draft 135,000 more men by end of year; statistics. (Perry Young)
S	1 ld Viet-034A-536A	U.S. battle deaths in VN War pass 20,000 mark, say U.S. spokesmen. (John Walsh)
S	2 ld Viet-034A-707A	U.S. battle deaths in VN War pass 20,000 mark and President Thieu announces S. VNese government will draft 135,000 more men. (John Walsh)
S	day ld Viet-011A-235A	Allies kill at least 142 VC west of Saigon and guerrillas shell Tan Son Nhut Air Base; details. (John Walsh)
S	Prices-045B-1151A	Saigon prices, inflated during Tet offensive, keep falling as economy approaches normal, say U.S. economic officials.
S	Viet-8-920A	Heavy ground fighting in two areas of S. VN, and in N. VN U.S. planes strike their heaviest blows in months.

Dateline		Story
March 22		
S	Viet-8-857A	U.S. tanks and troops rescue ambushed patrol and killed 122 enemy on S. VN's north coast without losing any U.S. troops.
S	2 ld Viet-106A-1140A	B-52s strike "Iron Triangle," enemy stronghold believed sheltering many of VC driven out of Saigon area; statistics, details. (John Walsh)
S	1 ld Viet-273A-848P	U.S. helicopters sink 30 sampans running guns in Mekong Delta canals. (Thomas Cheatham)
S	1 ld Viet-047A-512A	U.S. tanks and troops rescue ambushed patrol and killed 112 enemy on S. VN's north coast Thursday without loss of U.S. life, say military spokesmen. (John Walsh)
S	day ld Viet-008A-204A	VC shelled allied bases near Saigon, doing little damage, and on northern coast of S. VN U.S. troops kill 223 enemy in two days fighting; details. (John Walsh)
S	nt ld Viet-202A	U.S. B-52 dropped estimated 200,000 pounds of bombs on "Iron Triangle" north of Saigon, "blitzing" jungle stronghold of VC who escaped U.S. troops during Tet offensive.
March 23		
S	Statements-256P	"Progress of VN War as charted in statements of" Westmoreland; quotes, details; by date.
S	Statement-011A-115A	Westmoreland says he is honored to be appointed Chief of Staff of Army but sorry to leave VN before end of war.
S	day ld Viet-242A	U.S. helicopters sink 30 sampans carrying enemy war goods through canals near Cambodian border, say U.S. spokesmen; other details. (John Walsh)
S	1 ld Viet-029A-434A	N. VNese gunners attack Khe Sanh in heaviest action in month. (John Walsh)

Dateline		Story
S	1 ld Viet-261A-830P	VC raiders fail in attempt to blow up government radio station at Pleiku. (Thomas Cheatham)
S	Air-033B-9A	U.S. Navy planes bombed chemical plant between Hanoi and Haiphong for first time in war; details.
March 24		
S	Viet-550A	RSVN kill 20 VC in Mekong Delta near Saigon; other developments; details.
S	nt ld Viet-213A	Six B-52 missions on N. VN lifted pressure on Khe Sanh Marines, and ARVN troops killed 20 VC in Mekong Delta. (Thomas Cheatham)
S	1 ld Viet-271A-922P	U.S. troops "tore into" communists near Saigon with artillery, machine guns, air pressure, killing 44 enemy; after B-52 raids, enemy shell Khe Sanh; details; statistics.
D	Spookies-002A	"Spookies"--old DC-3s are making the nights rough for the VC; details. (R. Miller)
D	War Reporting-003A	Reporter describes reporting VN War as "the most bizarre conflict ever covered by the press"; details.
March 25		
S	Red Tanks-16-942A	N. VNese troops in tanks attack U.S. air cavalrymen near Hue; details.
S	Viet-7-906	U.S. troops killed 114 VC in Saigon's suburbs; U.S. helicopters destroy VC fleet of 165 sampans attempting to run supplies to VC at Saigon; details.
S	Hairdresser-097A-1135A	Monsieur Daniel, Lynda Bird Johnson Robb's hairdresser, ends week's tour cutting 350 nurses, Wacs, Waves in VN.
D	Grenade-025A-417A	Maj. Kenneth Cass plucked live grenade from leg of U.S. soldier, says U.S. army.
S	1 ld Viet-033A-459A	U.S. troops kill 114 guerrillas in Saigon's suburbs and U.S. helicopters destroy VC fleet of 165 sampans running supplies to enemy in Saigon; details. (John Walsh)

Dateline		Story
S	2 ld Viet-266A-1015P	Allied kill 243 VC in battle near Saigon, and over N. VN F-111 fighter-bomber made first combat debut; details. (Thomas Cheatham)
S	1 ld Viet-262A-915P	Allies report killing 243 VC in heavy fighting near Saigon, say U.S. spokesmen.
S	F-111-270A-11P	Controversial F-111A completes first combat mission over N. VN, say U.S. spokesmen.
S	2 ld Viet-266A-1015P	Allies report killing 243 VC in battle near Saigon and U.S. spokesmen say F-111 fighter-bomber makes first mission over N. VN. (Thomas Cheatham)
S	nt ld Viet-204A-134P	N. VN protecting vital infiltration tunnel ambush company of 200 American air cavalrymen near Khe Sanh; details. (Thomas Cheatham)
March 26		
S	Viet-7-910A	One thousand to 1,500 N. VNese overran part of U.S. Army position in Central Highlands; battle still underway; details.
S	Viet-25-1007A	Force of 300 U.S. killed 135 enemy in onslaught by 1,000-1,500 enemy troops, with GIs losing 19 dead and 51 wounded.
S	F-111-9-919A	Pilots say F-111 surprised communists in combat mission over N. VN.
Kontum	Highlands-105A-1223P	Life at Kontum, scene of large battle seven weeks ago; details. (Perry Young)
S	Roche-089A-1110A	Sidney Roche, U.S. pacification official, has resigned post to protest "losing policy" in VN, says almost every aspect of U.S. involvement here has failed.
D	Cushman-082A-1026A	Marine Lieutenant General Cushman, commander of S. VNese I Corps, says 30,000 enemy have been killed in fighting there this year; quotes. (Richard Oliver)

Dateline	Story	
S	1 ld Viet-030A-456A	One thousand to 1,500 N. VNese overran part of U.S. army position in Central Highlands. (John Walsh)
S	2 ld Viet-063A-914A	Three hundred U.S. threw back 1,000-1,500 enemy in four-hour battle in Central Highlands; details. (John Walsh)
S	nt ld Roche-246A-540P	Sidney J. Roche, US AID Mission official who resigned post to protest "losing policy" in VN, blames VNese corruption and U.S. inefficiency for failure of U.S. in VN; quotes; details. (Richard Oliver)
S	1 ld Viet-278A-942P	U.S. troops outnumbered five to one, killed 153 enemy in one of two battles near Cambodian border. (Thomas Cheatham)
Quang Tri	Burns-001B-503A	"His friends call Capt. Tom Burns, 27, magnet because he attracts communist gunfire wherever he goes"; shot-down helicopter pilot escapes.
D	Grenade-029B-840A	Pfc. Hillman saved by Army medicine when live grenade becomes embedded in his leg.
S	nt ld Viet-211A-206P	"Outnumbered American infantrymen Tuesday hurled back an assault by a flamethrowing force of up to 1,500 N. VNese soldiers after the communists had partly overrun a U.S. artillery base menacing their high-speed supply road from Cambodia; details. (Thomas Cheatham)
S	F-111-034A-519A	F-111 fighter-bomber, amid controversy, went to war for first time and blasted communist targets in N. VN, says U.S. command. (Thomas Cheatham)
S	day ld Viet-137A	"Allied troops today fought the Vietcong near Saigon in what may be the biggest battle of the biggest antiguerrilla campaign of the VN War"; details. (John Walsh)

Dateline		Story
March 27		
S	Air War-80-1230P	U.S. pilots returning from missions over N. VN say enemy interceptors avoiding dogfights, saving their efforts for massive U.S. raids expected when monsoon rains end.
S	Viet-7-920A	Allied troops report killing 421 enemy in battles throughout S. VN; statistics.
S	Red Offensive	S. VNese President Thieu predicts last-gasp enemy offensive within two or three months designed to give enemy substantial victory and bargaining position in this U.S. Presidential election year.
S	Plague-058A-858A	Outbreak of bubonic plague killed six persons in provinces around Saigon, says World Health Organization.
S	Viet Pacification-198-720P	Sidney Roche, resigned U.S. official, charged black market profits and money from prostitution filling pockets of some S. VNese Army generals; quotes.
S	Letter-5559B-1120P	VNese press reports father of U.S. soldier killed in VN wrote President Thieu saying loss of son has not shaken his support of war effort.
S	1 ld Viet-034A-538A	Allied troops report killing 421 enemy in battles throughout S. VN. (John Walsh)
S	Thieu-025A-355A	President Thieu predicts last-gasp enemy offensive within "two or three months" designed to give enemy victory and bargaining position in this U.S. Presidential election year; quotes. (John Fallon)
S	day ld Viet-013A-2A	Allied troops kill 323 enemy in battles all over S. VN; details. (John Walsh)
S	2 ld Viet-1202P	U.S. pilots returning from missions over N. VN say N. VNese avoiding dogfights, waiting for expected U.S. raids after monsoon rains end. (John Walsh)

Dateline		Story
S	nt ld Viet-210A-215P	Enemy MIGs avoiding dogfights over N. VN to "preserve a deadly counterpunch" for use against expected U.S. raids when monsoon rains end; other action at Trang Bang battle; details. (Thomas Cheatham)
S	nt ld Thieu-212A	President Thieu predicted enemy would lanuch last-gasp offensive to secure victory and bargaining position; quotes. (John Fallon)
S	1 ld Viet-272A-843P	U.S. soldiers attack N. VNese hiding in rubber plantation near Saigon, killing 99, say U.S. spokesmen; (Thomas Cheatham)
D	Wilson-505B-215P	U.S. Marine Corporal Wilson relieved of action when he was permanently blinded in VN fighting.

March 28

S	Combat Fatigue-28-1022A	U.S. Army mental health specialists report discovery of combat fatigue peculiar to VN War.
S	Viet-6-910A	Allies attacked and routed N. VNese attempted to infiltrate near Hue and killed 131 enemy, say military spokesmen.
S	Viet Casualties-9-916A	Weekly casualty report of 349 U.S. dead increase of 13 over previous week, say U.S. spokesmen.
S	day ld Viet-004A-149A	U.S. infantrymen kill 99 N. VNese in 30-hour battle in French 'ubber plantation near Saigon, say U.S. spokesmen. (John Walsh)
S	Letter-401B-515P	Father of U.S. soldier killed in VN wrote President Thieu that his son's death has not shaken his support of war effort, reports VNese press.
S	1 nt ld Viet-84A-1058P	New F-111A fighter-bomber reported lost over N. VN; details. (John Walsh)
S	nt ld Fatigue-261A-856P	U.S. fighting in VN suffering from new form of combat fatigue which becomes severe near end of 12-month tours of duty, say two U.S. Army mental health experts; details. (Richard Oliver)

Dateline		Story
S	Intruder-027B-906A	Description of A-6 Intruder, a small plane with radar which is "America's answer to the blanket of monsoon cloud now covering lucrative targets in N. VN"; details. (Thomas Cheatham)
S	Air-029B-953A	U.S. command says enemy shot down F-4 plane over VN, the 814th U.S. plane lost over N. VN.
S	Casualties-030B-957A	Allied killed 2,223 enemy last week, fewest since before Tet offensive, say U.S. spokesmen; statistics.
S	nt ld Viet-217A-310P	U.S. B-52s blast jungle highway leading to Hue area and allied commanders reported killing 194 enemy moving along coastal flats near Hue; details. (Thomas Cheatham)
S	Volunteer-422B-915A	Description of rescue by U.S. Army Lt. Robert D. Cozart of seven wounded RSVN.
S	2 day ld Plane-131A-110P	F-111A fighter-bomber overdue on mission just three days after it flew its first mission over N. VN.
S	Viet-928A	U.S. and S. VNese killed 131 N. VNese in jungles south of Hue, said military spokesmen.
S	Fatigue-032A-454A	Two U.S. Army mental health specialists reported discovery of new kind of combat fatigue peculiar to VN War called "combat neurosis"; details; quotes. (Richard Oliver)
S	1 ld Viet-035A-509A	U.S. planes and government Rangers attacked and routed N. VNese trying to infiltrate near Hue, and killed 131 of them, say military. (John Walsh)
March 29		
S	Viet-114-158P	U.S. command maintained secrecy in search for missing F-111 fighter-bomber suspected in enemy hands, which would be major intelligence gain for communists.
S	Viet Talks-78-1209P	U.S. returns three captured N. VNese seamen to Hanoi as result of secret negotiations between U.S. Embassy officials and N. VNese government representatives, the second in war.

Dateline		Story
S	Viet Corruption-69-1144A	Chief of U.S. pacification efforts in VN, Robert Komer, dismissed as "grotesque" charge that half of $450 million per year of U.S. aid is stolen by corrupt VNese officials.
S	Viet Talks-9-905A	U.S. Embassy officials met secretly with N. VNese government representatives in first known negotiations of war, say diplomatic sources.
S	Viet-10-910A	AF F-111As went back to air war despite first loss of them that N. VN claims to have shot down; details of other war action.
S	Meeting-029A-404A	Same as Viet Talks-9-905A. (Thomas Cheatham)
K	Plague-037A-450A	Bubonic plague may be spreading among N. VNese troops surrounding Khe Sanh fort, say U.S. spokesmen, so all Marines inoculated. (Raymond Wilkinson)
S	1 ld Meeting	U.S. returned three captured N. VNese seamen to Hanoi as result of secret negotiations between U.S. Embassy and N. VNese negotiators. (Thomas Cheatham)
S	1 ld Viet-047A-559A	AF F-111A jets went back to war despite loss of one of them. (John Walsh)
S	Corruption-116A-1116A	Same as Viet Corruption-69-1144A
S	2 day ld Viet-204A-137P	Same as Viet-114-158P. (John Walsh)
S	nt ld Viet-224A-3P	USAF F-111A bombers based in Thailand hit N. VN for fifth successive day, despite increasing fears one of secret jets fallen into enemy hands; details. (Thomas Cheatham)
S	1 nt ld Viet-278A-854P	USAF battling N. VNese MIGs for first time in six weeks may have shot down at least one, U.S. spokesmen said. (John Walsh)
S	Loc-434B-1119A	S. VNese Senate called Premier Loc and two other ministers to account for their unpreparedness for communists' Tet offensive, says Senate spokesman.

Dateline   Story

S	Aussies-028B-841A	Westmoreland praised "know-how and determination" of Australian forces fighting VC south of Saigon.

March 30

S	2 ld Viet-089A-1046A	U.S. Marines, patrolling perimeter at Khe Sanh, ran into N. VNese battalion of 350-400 men and killed 40; details. (John Walsh)
S	ICC-016A-241A	International Control Commission (ICC) is cutting down operations for lack of money, it said; details. (Kate Webb)
S	day ld Viet-012A-224A	U.S. and enemy jets battled over N. VN for first time in six weeks; details. (John Walsh)
S	1 ld Viet-040A-603A	Anticommunist rebellions broke out in guerrilla-controlled sections of S. VN's northern provinces, say U.S. intelligence officers. (John Walsh)
S	nt ld Viet-213A-110P	Outnumbered U.S. Marine patrol ran into N. VNese battalion near Khe Sanh, killing 40 enemy before pulling back with "moderate" losses; details. (Thomas Cheatham)
S	1 nt ld Viet-3P	"Outnumbered U.S. Marines, pushing out of their encircled Khe Sanh bastion, fought a bitter hours-long battle with N. VNese troops Saturday, as Saigon headquarters announced the loss of a second F-111A bomber in the skies over N. VN"; details. (Thomas Cheatham)
S	3 nt ld Viet-291A-836P	U.S. Marines kill 115 N. VNese Saturday in battle around Khe Sanh and 47 enemy elsewhere along DMZ, and another U.S. F-111A bomber lost. (John Walsh)
S	4 nt ld Viet-299A-907P	Same as above.
S	Thieu-318A-1150P	President Thieu threatened to order general mobilization putting all S. VNese men and women between 18 and 40 in armed forces.

Dateline		Story
S	nt ld Revolts-206A-1250P	Peasants have revolted against N. VNese and VC troops in at least three villages in S. VN's north, say U.S. intelligence sources; details. (R. Miller)
S	Reform-067A-811A	President Thieu fired two more province chiefs as part of his anticorruption drive.
March 31		
S	Bunker-308A-106A	U.S. Ambassador Bunker refused to comment on how Johnson's decision not to seek re-election might effect course of VN War.
S	Vietnamese-306A	President Thieu refuses to comment on Johnson's decision not to seek re-election.
S	nt ld Commission-215B-345P	Nearly defunct International Control Commission said it was cutting back its operations even further because of lack of funds; details; quotes. (Kate Webb)
S	1 ld Viet-255A-903P	S. VNese warplanes bomb suspected VC strongholds in Saigon's outskirts and snipers all over Saigon; USAF grounded new F-111A fighter-bombers after two crashes in three days. (John Walsh)
S	1 nt ld Viet-61-1001A	"RSVN warplanes bombed and strafed communist positions on the outskirts of Saigon Sunday night." (Eugene Risher)
S	Viet-612A	U.S. Marines launched their first major assault since siege of Khe Sanh began and killed 130 N. VNese in two battles near base, say military spokesmen.
S	nt ld Viet-204A-214P	S. VNese planes strafed suspected VC strongholds on Saigon's outskirts and communist snipers in streets all over the city; details (1). (Thomas Cheatham)
S	Thieu-237A-635P	President Thieu threatened to decree general mobilization Sunday and vowed S. VN would continue fighting communists even if U.S. withdrew its support; quotes. (Daniel Southerland)

STORY INDEX: VIETNAM-RELATED STORIES, CBS-TV WEEKDAY EVENING NEWS,
JANUARY 31 - MARCH 29, 1968

Anchorman	Film Report	Commentary/Special
January 31	From Vietnam	
"The tide apparently is turning in the Vietcong's stunning series of coordinated attacks"; war wrap-up; declaration of martial law. (Walter Cronkite)	Embassy fight; Americans still don't know if VC "drove or walked to embassy grounds"; bloody scene, dead bodies strewn in garden. (Donald Webster)	"Saigon Under Fire"
Ho Chi Minh described attacks as answer to Johnson's statement that Americans are winning, expressed happiness over what he called VC victories. (Cronkite)		
Captured communist documents outline winter-spring offensive aimed at strengthening enemy's position for peace talks; U.S. command expects Khe Sanh "to bear the brunt of that offensive." (Cronkite)	A bad week at Khe Sanh; Marines interviewed. (Jeff Gralnick)	
	From Outside Vietnam	
State Department spokesman Robert McCloskey said that in spite of VC raids the U.S. is continuing efforts to see if N.VN wants peace talks. (Cronkite)		
Johnson conferred with Congressional leaders and Cabinet members about events in VN and Korea; White House said U.S. command in Saigon knew in advance about VC raids but could do little to prevent them because Saigon is an open city. (Cronkite)		

NOTE: This index was compiled on the basis of CBS transcripts, which include more CBS stories than do the Defense Department archives used elsewhere in this study for comparative statistical purposes.

Anchorman	Film Report	Commentary/Special
February 1	**From Vietnam**	
Offensive in "fourth day," bitter fighting continues; VC claimed they have seized initiative and that S.VNese troops have defected by the hundreds; Westmoreland said VC drive has been blunted, still expects big push below DMZ at any time; war wrap-up. (Cronkite)		
Bold VC attack on embassy captured the headlines, but there was a lot of action elsewhere in the heart of the capital. (Cronkite)	Battle at radio station; battle at apartment building across from Presidential Palace; "apparent object" of attack is home of Korean ambassador; fighting "reminiscent of World War II"; Bunker interviewed. (Webster)	
VC hitting scores of towns and villages. (Cronkite)	VC took over Nam O last night, hoisted flag; 5,000 villagers fled in terror from bombing; ARVN halted by sniper; Marines and Rangers finally entered village; CBS cameraman Alex Brauer hit. (George Syvertsen)	
Brauer only superficially wounded. (Cronkite)		
	From Outside Vietnam	
Senator Frank Moss, critic on VN, at Da Nang when communists attacked, conceded that the experience has changed his thinking on the war. (Cronkite)		
Johnson considering further mobilization of reserves; Senator Stennis said new communist offensive may require more troops in VN; in public appearances, Johnson left no doubt VN is dominating his thoughts. (Cronkite)	Johnson statement: "We are fighting...to prevent any further expansion of totalitarian coercion"; McNamara statement on meaning of offensive; Wheeler statement: enemy effort not successful; Fulbright statement: "It's more like a stalemate"; Johnson on bombing. (Dan Rather)	

Anchorman	Film Report	Commentary/Special
McNamara told Congress one of main problems of the war is S.VNese themselves. (Cronkite)		

February 2	From Vietnam	
"Saigon, despite all the official statements, re-mains under siege"; VC control large sections of sprawling slums; food sit-uation chaotic; continuous sniper fire; columns of smoke over capital; war wrap-up. (Cronkite)		
Despite continuing allied attacks, large parts of Hue still fly the commu-nist flag. (Cronkite)	Battle of Hue, aerial view; house-to-house fighting filmed by cam-eraman John Schneider, first newsman into em-battled city; Marines and Rangers trying to root out at least a battalion of VC; VC proved they could take and hold al-most any area they chose. (Gralnick)	
Saigon sources told CBS News the job of recap-turing Hue may be given to Abrams. (Cronkite)		
Heaviest fighting in Sai-gon at militant Buddhist pagoda that government claims was VC command post. (Cronkite)	An Quang Pagoda has al-ways been "a thorn in the side of the government"; symbol of opposition; anyone who happens to live near or be near is suspect; last night there were lots of VC here; ready to storm pagoda; dozens of women and chil-dren cowering inside--"a few of them may even be Vietcong"; the government hasn't won any friends here today. (Webster)	
One of tragic aspects of Saigon battle is that many of its victims fled to the capital thinking it safe from war. (Cronkite)	Air strike in downtown Saigon; thousands of refugees; not quite clear why there had to be an air strike; elsewhere the city looks "like one the Americans seem to have invaded and taken over." (Webster)	

Anchorman	Film Report	Commentary/Special
U.S. casualty figures; six American missionaries massacred. (Cronkite)		

From Outside Vietnam

Anchorman	Film Report	Commentary/Special
Johnson called in reporters to give assessment of VN situation. (Cronkite)	Johnson statement: knew that communists planned massive winter-spring offensive, and "the stated purposes of the general uprising, a military victory or a psychological victory, have failed"; President "was straining to appear candid," admitted that "I may have made some mistakes." (Rather)	
President's confidence not shared on Capitol Hill; Percy declared VC "won a tremendous psychological victory"; Mansfield said enemy "achieved an objective of sorts" in causing suspension of constitutional government; VNese expressed admiration for VC courage; political and psychological factors not yet fully assessed, but initial indicators are that VC "apparently have substantial support in the major cities." (Cronkite)		
Red China hailed VC offensive as brilliant victory that made Johnson "the laughingstock of the world." (Cronkite)		
Pentagon and Saigon officials denied earlier report that Abrams is taking over the post in I Corps. (Cronkite)		

Anchorman	Film Report	Commentary/Special

February 5	From Vietnam	
Heavy new fighting in Saigon; enemy still controlled most of Hue; parts of Cholon in flames, "apparently set off by government air and artillery strikes"; full impact of offensive "just now becoming apparent." (Cronkite)	"For Americans in VN, the world turned upside down"; Brigadier General Davidson interviewed on possible second wave; Komer interviewed on reassessment of situation; scope and quality of attacks' impact on S. VNese "isn't clear yet, but it's there"; GVN performed poorly, "has never enjoyed any broad base of popular support. . . . Our troubles in VN may be just beginning." (Robert Schakne)	
Fighting in Delta; My Tho hardest hit, 25 percent destroyed, mostly "caused by allied air and artillery strikes." (Cronkite)		
VC at their most tenacious in Hue. (Cronkite)	Lieutenant Colonel Cheatham interviewed on his objective, type of fighting, civilians; "The assault, but only one Marine runs forward . . . two other Marines, one of whom is killed, get beyond the wall. . . . It is inch by shattered inch in the five-day battle for Hue." (John Laurence)	
Casualty report. (Cronkite)		
S. VNese drawing considerable criticism for unpreparedness; Ky said offensive demonstrates S. VN Army of 600,000 is not large enough to protect all population centers, plans defense force of civilian militiamen. (Cronkite)		

Anchorman	Film Report	Commentary/Special
S. VNese House of Representatives adopted resolution asking U.S. and other allies to strengthen assistance. (Cronkite)		
	From Outside Vietnam	
Khe Sanh fell silent again; U.S. generals assured Johnson Khe Sanh will not be "another Dienbienphu"; military unified in that view. (Cronkite)	Wheeler statement that "Khe Sanh can be and should be defended"; "We do not plan to sustain a Dienbienphu." (Neil Strauser)	
Senator Edward Kennedy commented on U.S. involvement and VN events. (Cronkite)	Kennedy statement: "No place in VN that is secure"; VC and "their allies from the North achieved an outstanding political victory."	
U Thant may be about to try VN peace initiative, plans talks with Kosygin and Wilson. (Cronkite)		
February 6	From Vietnam	
Large sections of Saigon being contested; "for the time being, at least, the Vietcong appear to be gaining in strength in the capital." (Cronkite)	Fighting in Saigon slum area; VC difficult to dislodge, "obviously knew the section well"; thousands of terror-stricken civilians fleeing; curfew keeps them from making a living, food prices have tripled; VC "trying to create as much misery as possible for the government and for the people." (Syvertsen)	
Marines recaptured provincial headquarters in Hue, pulled down communist flag, hoisted American flag instead of S. VNese flag; fighting at Khe Sanh; 12,000 American troops shifted to positions below the DMZ. (Cronkite)		

Anchorman		Commentary/Special
Westmoreland congratu-lates troops, said com-munist defeat so great "it may measurably shorten the war." (Cronkite)		
	From Outside Vietnam	
Head of VC delegation to Moscow said attacks will gain in intensity, ob-jective "is to overthrow the Saigon puppets." (Cronkite)		Mexican reaction to Tet offensive and *Pueblo* incident. (Eric Sevareid)
Kosygin had 50-minute meeting with Ambassador Llewellyn Thompson; speculation that VN was main topic. (Cronkite)		
Clergy and laymen opposed to the war conducted silent demonstration in Arlington National Cemetery. (Cronkite)	Three thousand war opponents led by Martin Luther King in 10 minutes of silent meditation; King statement. (Daniel Schorr)	
Antiwar protest in West Germany. (Cronkite)		
February 7	From Vietnam	
In "what could be the prelude to a mass N. VNese invasion of S. VN," NVA troops overran Lang Vei and occupied it for sever-al hours. (Cronkite)	Lang Vei commander Lieutenant Colonel Schungel interviewed (during preceding summer). (Webster)	
Not certain if Schungel was still at Lang Vei, but camp commander, "who-ever he was, was among those listed as survivors." (Cronkite)		
Battle for Hue in tenth day; communists still con-trol a good part of the city. (Cronkite)	Marines advancing "bloody inch by inch"; VC flag pulled down, American flag raised; prisoners taken, sometimes give valuable information, but "there are so many pris-oners, there's really nothing left to be learned"; Marines in their element. (Webster)	

Anchorman	Film Report	Commentary/Special
Flag lowered because rule prohibits flying U.S. flag over GVN installations. (Cronkite) More heavy fighting near Da Nang, in Da Lat, Vinh Long, and Cholon. (Cronkite) CBS VNese cameraman captured by VC; efforts under way to gain his release. (Cronkite)		
	From Outside Vietnam	
New phase of warfare in S. VN has killed or wounded "at least 11,000 civilians and produced 300,000 new refugees," only part of the tragic story. (Cronkite) Wilson flying to U.S.; presumably will brief Johnson on his "apparently unproductive meetings with Soviet leaders on Vietnam." (Cronkite) Fulbright to write Johnson and demand Rusk appearance before Senate Foreign Relations Committee. (Cronkite)		"The casualty list . . . includes more than bodies. It includes truth, the meaning of language, and human reason"; credibility gap; civilian victims; Ben Tre major. (Sevareid)
February 8	From Vietnam	
Fighting below DMZ at Gio Linh, Dong Ha, Camp Carroll, and Khe Sanh; Lang Vei has been captured; "there is a hint here of the same tactics employed by Giap in taking Dienbienphu." (Cronkite) No welcome at Khe Sanh for surviving Montagnard and VNese defenders of Lang Vei. (Cronkite)	Two Green Berets who escaped from Lang Vei interviewed; events at the camp; some played dead to escape being shot. (Murray Fromson)	

Anchorman	Film Report	Commentary/Special
Enemy troops captured village near Da Nang; more fighting in Saigon and Hue. (Cronkite)		
Fighting continues in Saigon; only three of capital's nine districts are secure. (Cronkite)	Fighting in Cholon; GIs interviewed; Saigon Hospital; until now, death or wounding of innocent civilians mainly in country; "now the VC have carried the war into the cities and there seems to be no place to hide from the bombs and the bullets." (Syvertsen)	
Five thousand more U.S. soldiers committed to the war last week; one GI for every 30 S. VNese. (Cronkite)		
VC assault on S. VN's cities produced record casualties last week. (Cronkite)		
CBS cameraman Vo Thanh Son escaped from VC captors "thanks to an American helicopter"; he was about to be executed as a government spy when the copter arrived. (Cronkite)		
	From Outside Vietnam	
Johnson has lifted recent restrictions on attacking military targets in Hanoi-Haiphong areas; Rusk had announced earlier that peace probes failed to bring positive response. (Cronkite)		
Senator Robert Kennedy asserted that recent events have "finally shattered the mask of official illusion" about the war. (Cronkite)	Kennedy statement.	

Anchorman	Film Report	Commentary/Special
		Analysis of Kennedy speech; "American dilemma is a profound one. . . . So great significance rides with the developing battle at Khe Sanh." (Sevareid)
Kennedy's office said speech "in no way changes his often-stated position that he expects to support President Johnson for re-election." (Cronkite) Cronkite leaving for VN "for a personal look at the situation there." (Cronkite)		
February 9	From Vietnam	
Abrams taking personal charge in threatened I Corps, underlining seriousness of situation there; more NVA troops and tanks spotted moving from Laos into positions around Khe Sanh; other NVA troops massing south of Da Nang; continued fighting in Hue and Da Lat. (Harry Reasoner)		
U.S. and ARVN forces trying to drive VC units out of Cholon. (Reasoner)	Pitched, running battle continuing; VC prisoner interviewed; advisor to 35th Ranger Battalion interviewed; General Loan arrives for inspection, last week shot and killed a prisoner in cold blood. (Laurence)	
U.S. officials hope communist attacks will prompt GVN to take more determined action; Thieu announced speed-up of mobilization plans. (Reasoner)		

Anchorman	Film Report	Commentary/Special
One Italian and three French journalists captured by VC; during brief detainment were well treated, given Pepsis and U.S. cigarettes. (Reasoner)	Alessandro Casella, who was captured by VC, interviewed. (Syvertsen)	
Marine tried to hijack airliner at Da Nang. (Reasoner)		
"In terms of pure destruction, no area suffered more than the Mekong Delta." (Reasoner)	Damage from fighting in Vinh Long is massive; Lieutenant Colonel Roberge and a GI interviewed; people bitter, seem to blame government troops as much as communists; 20-30 percent of all buildings destroyed; people's "loyalties may be in the balance." (Schakne)	
Officials reversed themselves today and Lang Vei survivors and refugees were flown to Da Nang. (Reasoner)		
	From Outside Vietnam	
U.S.S.R. prepared to match U.S. in any escalation of the war; Tass said offensive shows that allied military victory "is out of the question." (Reasoner)		
White House denied that next U.S. military step in VN might involve tactical nuclear weapons; Pentagon denied that stockpiles are already in S. VN, "but the denials still did not wipe out the basis for the concern." (Reasoner)	Two reports "touched off all of the anguish"; a small team of nuclear weapons experts left for S. VN last weekend; another report is that such weapons are already there; Foreign Relations Committee members fear pressure on White House if Khe Sanh were seriously threatened. (Marvin Kalb)	

Anchorman	Film Report	Commentary/Special
February 12	From Vietnam	
Thieu said more American troops will be needed for early end to the war. (Reasoner)		
Saigon quiet except for few clashes on outskirts; most of fighting concentrated in Cholon. (Reasoner)	Burning square block of Cholon; residents try to save what they can; soldier interviewed; Loan ordered troops to clear VC out this weekend, "a job many consider impossible"; "people caught in the middle suffering the most." (Gralnick)	
S. VNese planes attacked Citadel; 500 Marines have joined ARVN drive at Hue; more shelling at Khe Sanh, U.S. commanders still looking for major ground assault by N. VNese regulars. (Reasoner)		
We have received first report from Walter Cronkite. (Reasoner)	"One's first impression here is not of the great concern and alarm that we felt back home." Airport fairly normal; Presidential Palace "remarkably unguarded"; no tanks, no machine-gun nests; war watchers on roof; killing "terribly unreal." (Cronkite)	
	From Outside Vietnam	
U Thant discusses peace proposals with Moscow. (Reasoner)		
Sevareid comments on VN developments abroad and at home. (Reasoner)		Sharp rise in popular support for Johnson; sharp rise in criticism "among those who react intellectually more than emotionally, including congressmen and the press"; Pike VC analysis; "who in command is listening to whose advice?" (Sevareid)

Anchorman	Film Report	Commentary/Special
February 13	From Vietnam	
VC repulsed another U.S./ S. VN attack in Hue; GVN spokesman said substantial part of historical and art treasures already destroyed. (Reasoner)		
Fighting in Saigon suburbs; B-52s attacked only seven miles from capital. (Reasoner)		
S. VNese officials claim communists have lost 32,000 men killed, several thousand captured. (Reasoner)	VC prisoners interviewed; they want to go home, say "the wish of any bird . . . to fly to his own nest." (Syvertsen)	
Deputy commander of communist troops in S. VN, Maj. Gen. Tran Do, killed in Saigon fighting, body identified. (Reasoner)		
One thousand persons killed in Saigon fighting buried in three mass graves. (Reasoner)	Thousands of wounded civilians in Saigon Hospital; Mme. Thieu and Mme. Ky visit; Mme. Ky interviewed; whom do victims blame?--"these are the people without the guns." (Peter Kalischer)	
U.S. Navy pilot Lt. Com. John McCain shot down last October; communists permitted French TV producer to interview him. (Reasoner)	McCain interview: family, treatment by N. VNese, how shot down, message to wife. (Francois Chalis)	
	From Outside Vietnam	
Ten thousand five hundred more troops being flown to VN; represents speed-up in timetable for raising U.S. troop strength. Dan Rather reports Johnson considering call-up of Army/Marine reserves to fill vacuum. (Reasoner)		
Rusk told 200 congressmen last week that non-American emissary representing Washington went to Hanoi on peace mission. (Reasoner)		

Anchorman	Film Report	Commentary/Special
U Thant postponed return from Moscow; plans Paris meeting with N. VNese and VC officials. (Reasoner)		
News of troop increase "may have upset Wall Street"; stocks down. (Reasoner)		
Mansfield said anonymous phone call started recent speculation on nuclear weapons, is concerned that such unsubstantial specu- lation "can get such wide- spread circulation." (Reasoner)		
McCarthy campaigning in New Hampshire. (Reasoner)	"Before sunrise, with the temperature near zero, is no time to discuss VN and Senator McCarthy doesn't try." (Rather)	
February 14	**From Vietnam**	
American pilots reported shooting down two MIG-17s over N. VN; N. VN claimed U.S. jets attacked popula- tion centers in Hanoi; al- lied troops withdrew from Citadel to permit dive- bombing, enemy inflicted heavy casualties on Marine battalion. (Reasoner)		
Fighting at Khe Sanh. (Reasoner)	Closest thing to trench warfare in VN; Lieutenant Colonel Alderman talking with operations officer; GVN troops retreating during enemy attack "will be shot on sight by the Marines"; Lownds inter- viewed: dug-in well enough; "one place where the Americans cannot claim they have the ini- tiative." (Fromson)	
Impact of recent offensive against S. VN's population centers. (Reasoner)	"Life on the surface has returned to normal. But what's below the sur- face?" VC suffered	

Anchorman	Film Report	Commentary/Special
	military defeat; ARVN reacted better than expected; credibility gap widened; pacification "may have been set back by years." (Cronkite)	
Contact with guerrilla force northwest of Saigon; B-52s in same sector yesterday missed target area, may have caused casualties among friendly VNese. (Reasoner)		
	From Outside Vietnam	
For a while VN peace talks seemed a distinct possibility; U Thant sudden trip to Paris; Hanoi representatives conferred with Foreign Minister Fanfani; Rusk said situation unchanged. (Reasoner)	"A feeling has grown . . . that peace talks are nearing. Rusk wanted to demolish that feeling tonight. His statement was tough, almost belligerent." (M. Kalb)	
China said two Navy planes violated its air space, one shot down. (Reasoner)		
Offensive in VN "demonstrated not only that the enemy can strike almost at will, but also that he is well armed for the job." (Reasoner)	Harold Johnson of Army's Foreign Science and Technology Center interviewed on enemy's weapons; "far cry from the bows and arrows and the punji sticks that the VC started out with." (Strauser)	
February 15	From Vietnam	
Marines advance 200 yards inside Citadel, take stone tower; made little progress prior to introduction of massive firepower. (Reasoner)	Nastiest kind of street fighting; Charlie still in there; "nothing functions in Hue any more, as things should function in a city"; no place in VN "symbolic of so many things. . . . Nowhere did the communists score so great a success . . . and they are still here." (Schakne)	

Anchorman	Film Report	Commentary/Special
Regiment of N. VN troops reported heading toward Hue. (Reasoner)		
U.S. casualty report; B-52s mistakenly bombed area near Saigon, many casualties, presumably civilians. (Reasoner)		
More shelling at Khe Sanh; some observers still convinced communists hope to "turn Khe Sanh into a small-scale Dienbienphu." (Reasoner)	Marines interviewed on their "impression of the place"; U.S. commanders say Khe Sanh is no Dien- bienphu, "but for the Marines here it's just as badly situated." (Kalischer)	
GVN censors deleted from local newspapers Johnson's remarks that peace talk offer still stands. (Reasoner)		
	From Outside Vietnam	
Republican Congressman Glenn Davis predicted Johnson will replace Westmoreland; Senator Young said Westmoreland ought to be replaced, "has been outwitted and out-generaled by the com- munists"; McNamara praised Westmoreland. (Reasoner)	McNamara statement: "No general of U.S. forces in this century who has led his men more bril- liantly, whose forces have a higher morale, or who has accomplished more militarily."	
Nixon said use of nuclear weapons at Khe Sanh neither necessary nor desirable. (Reasoner)		
February 16	From Vietnam	
N. VN Premier Pham Van Dong quoted as saying N. VN will talk peace if U.S. unconditionally halts bombing. (Reasoner)		
Battle for Hue in eighteenth day; Marine of- ficer said enemy appeared "determined to fight to the last man"; communists getting supplies and		

Anchorman	Film Report	Commentary/Special
ammunition from outside. (Reasoner)		
More shelling at Khe Sanh. (Reasoner)	"Showdown is approaching"; feeling that sizable communist force would be difficult to stop; Marines live "like moles"; situation tense. (Fromson)	
N. VN released three American pilots, humanitarian gesture; they "had shown repentance" for bombing the North. (Reasoner)		
7th Fleet denied permission to rescue pilot shot down off Hainan. (Reasoner)		
	From Outside Vietnam	
Johnson held impromptu news conference. (Reasoner)	Johnson statement: on nuclear weapons, Westmoreland, troop levels, possible peace negotiations. (Rather)	
Johnson will discuss VN situation with U Thant. (Reasoner)		
Robert Jensen dropped out of college and joined Marines; killed in VN; parent's don't want military funeral. (Reasoner)	Jensens interviewed: "He was not a killer." (Ron Miller)	Jensen tragedy represents very heart of moral dilemma of the war. (Sevareid)
Romney got hostile reception from workers in New Hampshire. (Reasoner)	Romney hitting harder at Nixon and VN; Romney statement on war: "Look, they're winning. We're not winning. We're losing, thus far." (Richard Plante)	
February 19	From Vietnam	
Allied advance in Hue "still is being measured in yards"; casualties heavy. (Reasoner)	"One nasty little fire fight right after another"; Marine interviewed; "as the fight for Hue moves into the	

Anchorman	Film Report	Commentary/Special
	third week, the city anything but secure." (Gralnick) Fighting a little like the battle of Bastogne; Hue cut off, no air support or supply. (Cronkite)	
S. VNese police reported indications of N. VNese withdrawal from Hue. (Reasoner)		
VC destroyed bridge connecting Tan Son Nhut with U.S. installation at Bien Hoa; airport shelled. (Reasoner)	Wounded soldiers at airport interviewed; shelling hasn't stopped planes. (Kalischer)	
Revised casualty figures on attack against air terminal. (Reasoner)		
	From Outside Vietnam	
Demonstrations in Europe against U.S. policies in Southeast Asia. (Reasoner)		
February 20	From Vietnam	
Fighting on edge of Saigon, U.S. officers said another large-scale ground attack "may be imminent"; VNese troops still held positions in "rock piles that once were the walls and buildings of the Citadel of Hue." (Reasoner)	Lieutenant General Cushman interviewed: enemy may be able to hold out a few days; civilians incensed and fearful, about 150 killed. (Laurence)	"Vietcong" (Bernard Kalb)
Most of fighting in Hue in and around the Citadel. (Reasoner)	Background report on Citadel; destruction of "an architectural and artistic treasure." (Richard Hottelet)	
Six hundred seventeen thousand new refugees since offensive began; one of more extreme cases at Ben Tre; Ben Tre major quoted. (Reasoner)	Forty percent of Ben Tre destroyed or damaged; one out of every three families became refugees; William Janssen, agricultural advisor, interviewed, sees no military solution. (Kalischer)	

Anchorman	Film Report	Commentary/Special
Favorite pastimes at Khe Sanh. (Reasoner)	Surviving in the V-Ring; Marines interviewed; play antiwar song, "Where Have All the Flowers Gone." (Laurence)	
February 21	**From Vietnam**	
Jets dropped napalm, bombs, rockets over Citadel as clouds lifted; Marines 50 yards closer than yesterday. (Reasoner)	"American flag flies on the Citadel wall, but there is no breeze to blow it"; longest, bloodiest battle of war; human casualties staggering; kill ratio three to one; Marines interviewed; "have had enough of the Citadel"; command sending in replacements. (Laurence)	
Cushman said reason battalion being replaced is "it has run out of steam." (Reasoner)		
S. VNese officials announced military tribunal to try suspected communist agents captured in Hue; no executions without proper trial. (Reasoner)		
One hundred twenty-three VC reported killed north of Tan Son Nhut; four helicopters shot down on outskirts of Saigon; Tri Quang, militant Buddhist leader, in protective custody; two other GVN opponents arrested. (Reasoner)		
	From Outside Vietnam	
U Thant met with Johnson; if his objective was to convince Johnson on unconditional bombing halt, "then he failed." (Reasoner)		

Anchorman	Film Report	Commentary/Special
Fulbright dissatisfied with McNamara seven-hour explanation of Tonkin Gulf incidents. (Reasoner)	Foreign Relations Committee hearings; Professor James Thomson, China expert, thinks Rusk is "tired and ought to be replaced"; Fulbright statement attacking McNamara, classified information. (M. Kalb)	Two levels to VN debate: validity of military/pacification strategies; assumption of U.S. foreign policy. (Sevareid)
February 22	**From Vietnam**	
U.S. suffered heaviest casualties last week; raised U.S. toll to 18,239. (Reasoner)	N. VNese tightening ring around Khe Sanh; full-scale assault expected; as enemy moves closer, U.S. bombs closer to own positions; encirclement "so tight," major withdrawal or reinforcement impossible without heavy casualties. (Film: John Schneider, voice-over: Reasoner)	
Marines stormed south wall of Citadel; 200-300 N. VNese believed occupying Hue Palace, cut off by U.S./S.VN troops. (Reasoner)	Cameraman Vinh Dan captured by N. VNese in Citadel said he worked for French TV, was allowed to take film of communists; shows youth of soldiers, modern weaponry; "no inclination to withdraw." (Fromson)	
Two enemy divisions threatening Saigon, some forces within six miles of capital. (Reasoner)		
U.S. planes bombed Radio Hanoi transmitter, failed to silence radio. (Reasoner)		
Twelve arrested in S. VN political crackdown. (Reasoner)		
	From Outside Vietnam	
Communist troops overran Laotian outpost Tha Thom; Souvanna Phouma said in *Le Monde* interview there are 40,000 N. VNese troops in Laos. (Reasoner)		

Anchorman	Film Report	Commentary/Special
Congressman R. Leggett predicted 100,000 troop request; Senator J. Pearson sees indications of higher draft calls, activation of more reserve units. (Reasoner) Antiwar demonstrations in Europe. (Reasoner)		
February 23	From Vietnam	
Tan Son Nhut Air Base shelled again; no casualties or damage to airstrip; 11 civilians near base killed. (Reasoner) Twenty-fourth day of battle for Hue; Marines within three blocks of Imperial Palace; delayed final assault pending decision on air/artillery support; until now, allies avoided shelling palace "because of its cultural and historical importance." (Reasoner) Heaviest barrage at Khe Sanh in two weeks; casualty report. (Reasoner)		
	From Outside Vietnam	
Huge draft call for April; plan to call up some reserves; reflects "VN's drain on military manpower"; decision awaits Wheeler's return from VN. (Reasoner) Optimistic assertions on war disputed by CIA. (Reasoner)	CIA VN reports much bleaker than Administration's public assessments; running feud between some CIA men and Walt Rostow, one of original architects of VN policy. (Rather)	

Anchorman	Film Report	Commentary/Special
Wall Street Journal warns that U.S. VN effort "may be doomed"; its information shows U.S. "may well face a disaster." (Reasoner)		
Major defender of Johnson VN policies will testify before Senate Foreign Relations Committee. (Reasoner)	Fulbright, "who is leading a personal war against the war, announced a diplomatic triumph"; Rusk will testify; Fulbright statement; Warneke statement on the *Maddox*; each side feels it has "monopoly on the truth." (M. Kalb)	
Brezhnev denounced U.S. for VN War. (Reasoner)		

February 26	From Vietnam	
Marine patrol ambushed 800 yards outside Khe Sanh, heavy casualties; new censorship regulations: no details on number of enemy shells, casualties, damage. (Reasoner)	Khe Sanh under siege since January 21; exposed position; resembles "giant dart board"; Marine humor (sign says "Welcome, Red Hordes") even though living "like moles"; extremely dangerous, extremely dirty; base awaits "another night of shelling." (Film: Schneider, voice-over: Reasoner)	
Westmoreland still expects large-scale ground attack at Khe Sanh; Wheeler doubts it. (Reasoner)		
Wheeler returning to Washington; some reports said he'll request 50,000 to 100,000 more troops. (Reasoner)		

	From Outside Vietnam	
Fulbright said time has come for full-scale Congressional review of present U.S. VN policies; Rusk queried on Fulbright suggestion. (Reasoner)	Rusk statement at news conference.	

Anchorman	Film Report	Commentary/Special
Johnson satisfied Congress had all the facts for Gulf of Tonkin resolution; convinced N. VNese attacks were unprovoked. (Reasoner)		
U.S. command placed new restrictions on reporting, as noted earlier. (Reasoner)		Censorship at the source; credibility-gap feud between government and press. (Sevareid)
February 27	From Vietnam	
"Here is a vignette . . . [filmed in Hue] that illustrates the nature of the bitter fight for the cities, the VC Tet offensive, and the nature of the American fighting men who thwarted it." (Cronkite)	Lieutenant Colonel Gravel interviewed on what happened at Hue, destruction. (Cronkite)	
		"Who, What, When, Where, Why" (Cronkite)
	From Outside Vietnam	
State Department concerned over communist offensive in Laos; M. Kalb learned that concern "has been translated into direct American air support of Laotian troops"; speculation communists seek to expand bases for infiltration into S. VN. (Cronkite)		
Senator Symington proposed U.S. fill VN manpower needs with troops from Europe. (Cronkite)		
Graduate schools call for drafting by random lottery. (Cronkite)		
Johnson's first Dallas visit since John F. Kennedy's assassination. (Cronkite)	Secret Servicemen visibly nervous as Johnson spoke at length on VN; Johnson statement: "America's word is America's bond."	

Anchorman	Film Report	Commentary/Special
	Six antiwar pickets, no incidents. (Rather)	
February 28	From Vietnam	
Heavy fighting for second day around Kontum; light casualties at Khe Sanh when more than 100 rocket/ mortar rounds were fired into Marine positions. (Cronkite)		
U.S. command got part of 10,500 fresh troops as 4,000 men airlifted to Chu Lai; another 4,000 reported enroute. (Cronkite)		
Any victory will have to be measured in "the success of the so-called pacification program"; Komer's computers pumped out success story for two years; now, because of Tet offensive, "his program is shambles." (Cronkite)	Pacification "the biggest casualty" of offensive; at a complete stop in most of country; Deputy Pacification Advisor for Tuy Phuoc interviewed, admits discouragement. (Schakne)	
Komer concerned RD teams not getting back to countryside fast enough, "but no matter how fast they get back to their posts now, much of the damage has been done." (Cronkite)		
Thieu said S. VN has entered critical period; "quite an understatement"; nightclubs and dance halls closed as part of austerity program. (Cronkite)		
	From Outside Vietnam	
France said it has information that unconditional bombing halt enough to open negotiations; State Department aware of French views, sees situation unchanged. (Cronkite)		

Anchorman	Film Report	Commentary/Special
Johnson briefed by Wheeler and Komer. (Cronkite)	Principal advisors hear "grim VN briefing"; believed centered on recommendations for 50-100,000 more troops; Johnson gives McNamara Medal of Freedom, "lavished him with praise"; Johnson/ McNamara statements. (Rather)	
Komer one of key figures at earlier meeting; in his area of responsibility that allied effort "in a way, stands or falls." (Cronkite)		
Senator Gruening says top S. VNese officials involved in opium and gold smuggling ring in Saigon. (Cronkite)		
Senator Edward Kennedy introduced draft reform legislation. (Cronkite)		
February 29	From Vietnam	
Casualty figures show more Americans killed in four-week Tet offensive than in first five years of U.S. involvement. (Cronkite)		
Tan Son Nhut shelled again; N. VN claimed U.S. planes attacked Hanoi suburbs today; U.S. command said jets hit targets in Hanoi area yesterday; rare good weather permitted B-52s to make saturation raids around Khe Sanh, napalm dropped into enemy trenches. (Cronkite)		

Anchorman	Film Report	Commentary/Special
Khe Sanh seems "a microcosm of the whole war . . . not very much that is rational about it. It isn't even of any major strategic value at the moment." (Cronkite)	"The question is, will the attack come, and if so, can Khe Sanh hold?" Giap tactics; he must see the similarities with Dienbienphu; "but there are as many differences." Lieutenant Colonel Humphreys interviewed on air support. (Laurence)	
"The confidence (Col. Humphrey's) is admirable but the evidence is less encouraging." (Cronkite)		
Marines at Khe Sanh getting artillery help from Camp Carroll. (Cronkite)	"The 175 mm. gunners want you to know they are Army gunners, surrounded by Marines, who are surrounded by N. VNese; Major Reedell interviewed about terrain; Lieutenant Kelly interviewed on patrols; may never be an attack, but "nobody ever stops digging." (Kalischer)	
Khe Sanh "mostly a symbol. But of what? Pride? Morale? Bravery? Or administrative intransigence and military miscalculation?" (Cronkite)		
	From Outside Vietnam	
Sihanouk accused China again of directing guerrilla warfare in western Cambodia; if this not halted, he will resign as chief of state. (Cronkite)		
March 1	From Vietnam	
Five hundred N. VNese troops in first major ground assault at Khe Sanh; at least 70 enemy killed by air strikes and Rangers. (Cronkite)	N. VNese so bold "one soldier has actually penetrated . . . actually entered the Marine base . . . didn't get very far, gunned down just a few feet inside the perimeter." U.S. advisor to Rangers	

Anchorman	Film Report	Commentary/Special
	interviewed on infiltrator; N. VNese digging trenches; "already one communist soldier has gotten through. What the Marines are waiting for is for 10- or 20,000 of them to try." (Webster)	
Three CBS staffers wounded or injured at Khe Sanh during the day. (Cronkite)		
VN House of Representatives rejected Thieu request for special economic powers; "vote represents, in a somewhat primitive way, a lack of confidence" in present GVN. (Cronkite)	Thieu interviewed on martial law, censorship, corruption; Nguyen Xuan Oanh interviewed on what government must do to win people's confidence. (Cronkite)	VN lacks leadership material; several VN intellectuals suggesting U.S. take over completely; might alleviate need for more military escalation. (Cronkite)
	From Outside Vietnam	
Clifford sworn in as Secretary of Defense; praised by Johnson. (Cronkite)		
Some thoughts on the war in VN and the war in America's streets. (Cronkite)		Yesterday the U.S. "found itself fighting two revolutionary wars." (Sevareid)
March 4	From Vietnam	
Rocket/mortar attacks against 12 allied bases, dozens of villages, several hospitals; harassment tactics, not prelude to new offensive. (Cronkite)		
U.S. Navy hospital in Da Nang among today's targets; CBS Producer Russ Bensley hit second time since Friday. (Cronkite)	Khe Sanh runway; burning C-123; Bensley interviewed: VN "is probably the worst place on earth to try to make moral or political judgments about	

Anchorman	Film Report	Commentary/Special
Another hospital attacked in Kontum; operated for Montagnard tribespeople by Dr. Patricia Smith; she escaped. (Cronkite)	the war. . . . You're just too close to it." New war in VN, "no place is safe." (Webster) (1966 films)	Causes of Hanoi's change in strategy; Ky statement on reasons for offensive. (Cronkite)
	From Outside Vietnam	
Johnson said long copper strike "is affecting the nation's VN effort." (Cronkite)		
March 5	From Vietnam	
Communists shelled 18 cities and towns, 21 U.S. and S. VN military installations; Cam Ranh Bay base hit for first time, considered safest base in VN, Johnson visited there; heaviest fighting in Ca Mau, important center of pacification program; GVN units in full control tonight. (Cronkite)		
Enemy has bigger and better weapons, more ambitious methods to supply themselves. (Cronkite)	Old concept of VC guerrilla doesn't hold true anymore; 122 mm. rockets hitting Tan Son Nhut; infiltration on vast inland waterway system; VC dressed as civilian, blue nylon underwear gave him away. (Webster)	
High U.S. military source predicted big enemy assault below DMZ within next six weeks and that they'll be defeated: "they have presented themselves on a silver platter to allied forces." (Cronkite)		

Anchorman	Film Report	Commentary/Special
U.S. reported attempting to return three captured N. VNese sailors to Hanoi; no indication Hanoi would accept the men. (Cronkite)		
	From Outside Vietnam	
Sweden granted asylum to seven more American deserters; makes 20 U.S. defectors given refuge there. (Cronkite)		
Rusk will go before Senate Foreign Relations Committee next week. (Cronkite)	"An increasingly anguished" Fulbright wrote Rusk on *Pueblo*; urged not to allow dispute with Rusk to become personal, he said: "Our differences are much deeper. The country is on a disastrous course in VN and Rusk is one of those responsible." (M. Kalb)	
Nixon reminded voters he was on Eisenhower team which ended Korean War. (Cronkite)	Nixon statement in New Hampshire: failure in VN is "failure of our leadership in Washington, D.C." New leadership can end the war.	
		VN War as campaign issue. (Sevareid)
March 6	From Vietnam	
USAF transport plane with 44 Marines/five crewmen shot down approaching Khe Sanh; no sign of survivors; planes and helicopters only lifeline and "the lifeline is constantly in jeopardy." (Cronkite)	Getting in and out of Khe Sanh more dangerous than being there; runway littered with wreckage; Captain Crowell interviewed: flying into Khe Sanh most dangerous mission in VN. (Webster)	
Was to have been 45th Marine on downed plane but at last minute he decided to mail package to his mother. (Cronkite)		

Anchorman	Film Report	Commentary/Special
Three hundred thirty-five communists reported killed in Central Highlands and Ca Mau; scores of civilians killed, 1,000 houses destroyed in Ca Mau battle. (Cronkite) U.S. Saigon command estimated 50,000 communists, about 2,000 Americans, and 4,000 S. VNese troops killed since beginning of offensive. (Cronkite) Senior American officer believes enemy hurt badly, lacks capacity for major action, but will continue to spoil the countryside, try recapture Hue. (Cronkite)		
	From Outside Vietnam	
Senator Gruening plans new investigation of GVN corruption after reports by a U.S. advisor who doubts "there ever will be any reasonable degree of honesty in VNese officialdom." (Cronkite)		
Renewed criticism of U.S. VN policies came from George F. Kennan. (Cronkite)	Kennan interviewed; sees present course leading to war involving China, possibly Russia, or national humiliation. (Josh Darsa)	
Nixon said U.S. should abolish draft, create volunteer army when VN War ends. (Cronkite)		
McCarthy's anti-VN candidacy against Johnson picking up momentum; he took issue with Democratic tactics beings used against him. (Cronkite)	Johnson campaign ad; McCarthy statement: "Rusk and others would like to keep us from even free discussion by suggesting that even free discussion is an aid and comfort and encourages the Asian communists."	

Anchorman	Film Report	Commentary/Special
Paul Newman supporting McCarthy. (Cronkite)	Newman interviewed.	
McCarthy gets top spot on California primary ballot. (Cronkite)		
March 7	**From Vietnam**	
Three thousand two hundred fifty-four Americans killed in first nine weeks of 1968, three times more than same 1967 period; U.S., S.VNese, and enemy casualties in last week's action. (Cronkite)		
B-52s bombed enemy positions around Khe Sanh but communist gunners knocked out another USAF transport plane. (Cronkite)		
Though concentrated on cities, Tet offensive had devastating effects in outlying provinces; "enemy still roams at will" in the Delta. (Cronkite)	Highway 12 "can truly be called a highway of death"; VC again demonstrating they control most of countryside; Major Anderson jubilant about battle's outcome; Ca Mau in ruins, most of shells "fired by so-called friendly forces." (Bert Quint)	
S. VN Senate rejected Thieu's request for emergency economic powers; petition in House calls for no-confidence vote. (Cronkite)		
	From Outside Vietnam	
Frustrations and divisions over VN triggered one of angriest Senate debates in years. (Cronkite)	Robert Kennedy asked, "Is it right to see S. VNese troops looting in Hue, and yet the President . . . says, 'We have stealing in Beaumont?'" Statement on escalation, credibility gap; shouting-match between hawks and doves; Hatfield interviewed. (Roger Mudd)	.

Anchorman	Film Report	Commentary/Special
Robert Kennedy under new pressure to oppose Johnson. (Cronkite)	Robert Kennedy and advisors considering Rockefeller-type candidacy; growing concern over VN escalation; new life in McCarthy campaign seen by Kennedys as barometer of antiwar, anti-Johnson feeling. (Paul Hart)	McCarthy analyzed. (Sevareid)
March 8	From Vietnam	
Two hundred seventy enemy troops reported killed below DMZ, 30 by Rangers at Khe Sanh; S. VNese lieutenant, wounded and cut off from his patrol, killed himself to keep his men "from risking their lives to save him." (Cronkite)		
Defense Department released films showing intensity of enemy fire at Khe Sanh's airstrip. (Cronkite)	C-130 hit by ground fire; N. VNese gunners getting more and more accurate; film taken late February. (Film: Marine Corps, voice-over: Steve Rowan)	
Lieutenant General Rosson put in charge of operations at Khe Sanh and from Hue north; Cushman still in overall command of northern provinces; Rosson considered counter-guerrilla warfare expert. (Cronkite)		
	From Outside Vietnam	
Clifford said troop increase still under review; Senate doves yesterday demanded Congress be consulted before any new escalation; today McGee "ripped into the doves" for attacking President while enemy is on offensive. (Cronkite)	McGee statement: attacks "very badly timed"; was a planned outburst; might have been "a very honorable and balanced exchange of views."	

Anchorman	Film Report	Commentary/Special
U.S. Ambassador to Sweden returning to Washington for consultations; U.S.-Swedish relations strained since Sweden began granting asylum to U.S. deserters; Ambassador Heath target of anti-American demonstrations. (Cronkite)		
Sihanouk said unless China stops directing guerrillas in Cambodia's northern provinces, he'll side with U.S. and see that VC lose sanctuaries there. (Cronkite)		
Write-in campaign in Johnson's behalf being waged in New Hampshire. (Cronkite)	Johnson campaign headquarters; campaign effort intense; tape-recorded ad with statement on VN; "hawkish" Senator McIntyre standing in for Johnson; McIntyre interviewed on what primary means to President politically and psychologically. (Mort Dean)	
Humphrey challenges Nixon to tell nation how he would end the war. (Cronkite)		
March 11	From Vietnam	
Five hundred forty rounds of mortar, artillery, and rockets fired at Khe Sanh; casualties, damage reported light; enemy loudspeakers urged Rangers to surrender, they responded with mortar barrage; other GVN units reported killing 102 N. VNese below DMZ. (Cronkite)		
GVN took major step in long-promised campaign against corruption and incompetence; fired six province chiefs, including Colonel Pham Van Khoa, who		

Anchorman	Film Report	Commentary/Special
was accused of lagging in restoring civil order in Hue. (Cronkite)		
	From Outside Vietnam	
Rusk and Foreign Relations Committee in first public confrontation in more than two years on VN; Rusk defended Johnson VN policies; Fulbright said they were "nothing short of disastrous." (Cronkite)	Excerpts of Mansfield-Gore-Rusk exchange on bombing, infiltration rate, negotiations, escalation, Wheeler report; "entire situation is under consideration from A to Z."	Senate confrontation on "America's agony"; context and climate of the debate changed. (Sevareid)
Rusk to appear again tomorrow. (Cronkite)		
Johnson had something to say about dissension, "obviously had his VN critics in mind." (Cronkite)	Johnson statement at White House ceremony: "Great deal of our weaknesses are caused by pitting our strength against each other and chewing on ourselves."	
Yale University said students who go to prison rather than be drafted will be allowed back in school. (Cronkite)		
March 12	From Vietnam	
Khe Sanh Marines on special alert; "the reason: exactly 14 years ago, N. VN's General Giap began the siege of Dienbienphu . . . and the question is whether Khe Sanh can become another Dienbienphu." (Cronkite)	Battle of Dienbienphu "as seen in film from both sides on *The Twentieth Century*." (Voice-over: Cronkite)	
"Then what of Khe Sanh and those 5,500 Marines surrounded . . . by the same General Giap?" Disturbingly familiar scenes; Khe Sanh and Dienbienphu compared by newsman who covered both. (Cronkite)	Francois Sully interviewed: "I thought to myself, oh, my God, Dienbienphu all over again . . . first mistake is to be there." Lieutenant General Rosson interviewed on differences: U.S. has much greater air power. (Webster)	

Anchorman	Film Report	Commentary/Special
	From Outside Vietnam	
No change of mind or policies on either side in Senate hearings; Fulbright failed to get pledge that Congress would be consulted before any decision to escalate the war. (Cronkite)	Fulbright-Rusk exchange on consulting Congress, escalation, credibility gap.	Case of Fulbright vs. Rusk; Congressional feeling against the war. (Severeid)
One-fourth of House members favor resolution calling for immediate review of U.S. Southeast Asia policies; strong bipartisan feeling Administration should consult Congress before new escalation. (Cronkite)		
Johnson determined to see the war through to a successful conclusion. (Cronkite)	Dual Medal of Honor ceremony gave Johnson platform to tell Americans "his view of their VN responsibilities"; Johnson statement: cannot "become the willing victims of our own despair." (Rather)	
Three deserters go back to units in West Germany. (Cronkite)		
Partial returns in New Hampshire voting; with 12 percent of vote in, Johnson has 52 percent, McCarthy 41 percent. (Cronkite)		
March 13	From Vietnam	
Khe Sanh on special alert, 14th anniversary of start "of the epic Dienbienphu siege"; no enemy attack, only "eerie silence"; B-52s bombed newly discovered jungle road from Laos. (Cronkite)		

Anchorman	Film Report	Commentary/Special
GVN spokesman said volunteers are forming "liberation army" to invade N. VN; U.S. has long barred invasion of North; State Department says it knows nothing about guerrilla army. (Cronkite)		
	From Outside Vietnam	
Robert Kennedy all but declared his Presidential candidacy in wake of McCarthy's remarkable showing in New Hampshire; actively reconsidering his support for Johnson. (Cronkite)	Robert Kennedy interviewed on possible candidacy, political situation, divisions in country, VN: primary results "indicated this great concern within the Democratic Party, this uneasiness, this restlessness about the future of the country"; some policies in VN "can lead to a catastrophic ending." (Cronkite)	
Results of New Hampshire primary. (Cronkite)		
Robert Kennedy met privately with McCarthy, no advisors present; said they merely restated their public positions. (Cronkite)		
McCarthy expects to win in Wisconsin; Johnson Wisconsin campaign chief conceded President could be underdog, even though his name will be on ballot. (Cronkite)		
Defense Department intelligence team going to VN to try to find out how many enemy troops killed during offensive; correspondents on scene usually scoff at official figures "as far too high." (Cronkite)		

Anchorman	Film Report	Commentary/Special
New Hampshire primary and "today's aftermath have completely changed" '68 Presidential picture. (Cronkite)		How primary results have changed campaign; "anything can happen." (Sevareid)
March 14	From Vietnam	
U.S. troops killed in VN since January 1961 "almost certainly passed the 20,000 mark" this week. (Cronkite)		
Heavy raids against Hanoi-Haiphong area for first time in six weeks; major sweep-and-destroy operation south of Saigon; U.S. officials claim allies have "regained the offensive." (Cronkite)		
Khe Sanh still awaits all-out enemy attack; small probe beaten back; B-52s pound N. VNese positions; in bluntest threat, Hanoi Radio said the "days of Khe Sanh's defenders are limited." (Cronkite)	"Stomach-turning anxiety" of flight to Khe Sanh, wondering if C-123 is "fated to join the graveyard of twisted wrecks" along runway; one C-123 hit, another downed with 44 aboard; two in one day is "a pretty good bag" for enemy gunners; will take even more courage to fly in. (Syvertsen)	
	From Outside Vietnam	
McCarthy will run in South Dakota and Indiana primaries. (Cronkite)	McCarthy statement on Robert Kennedy.	
Robert Kennedy thinking of running for President; McCarthy supporters urge Kennedy not to run. (Cronkite)		
Jonathan Spicer, private in Medical Corps who refused to kill, died of his wounds in Japanese hospital. (Cronkite)		

Anchorman	Film Report	Commentary/Special
March 15	From Vietnam	
War wrap-up: 50,000 U.S./ S.VN troops launched Operation Resolved to Win aimed at throwing off balance estimated 20,000 enemy troops still threatening Saigon; at least a fourth of Khe Sanh airstrip unusable, almost all supplies being parachuted in; C-123 landed today, first plane to make it in three days but airstrip was shut down for several hours for repairs. (Cronkite)		
Thieu once again ordered strict crackdown on black market, bars, brothels. (Cronkite)		
	From Outside Vietnam	
Robert Kennedy plans to run to win, "not merely to dissent from President Johnson's policies." (Cronkite)		
March 18	From Vietnam	
U.S. officials announced 767 enemy troops killed in week-old allied offensive around Saigon. (Reasoner)		
U.S. planes and artillery "completely leveled a thatched-roofed village" near Dong Ha after N. VNese troops holed up there cut down U.S. Marine patrol. (Reasoner)		
Rangers turned back charge of 400 communist troops against Khe Sanh. (Reasoner)	Routine of existence has developed at Khe Sanh; supply almost solely by helicopter; big cargo planes can't land any more; Marines keep digging, barbed wire all over the base and waiting	

Anchorman	Film Report	Commentary/Special
	to be unrolled; Marines hope enemy will hit soon to "end the agony of waiting." (Gralnick)	
GVN will reportedly increase armed forces by 125,000 men this year; U.S. has agreed to equip them; will require general mobilization. (Reasoner)		
	From Outside Vietnam	
Johnson and Robert Kennedy dramatized width of disagreement between them, voiced "unyielding stands on the major issue dividing them, Vietnam." (Reasoner)	Johnson Minneapolis visit "a microcosm of what his whole campaign . . . likely will be"; Johnson statement to National Farmers' Union: seek triumph of justice; Kennedy/McCarthy claims that war can't be won "weaken this country's moral fiber and help the enemy." (Rather)	
Robert Kennedy campaign begins in Kansas. (Reasoner)		
Preparations for Wisconsin primary begin. (Reasoner)	McCarthy statement on Robert Kennedy.	
Antiwar demonstration took place in London. (Reasoner)		
March 19	**From Vietnam**	
Two VC defectors claimed N. VN spy network was giving enemy 24 hours' warning on time and targets of B-52 bombers; U.S. official called story "baloney"; CBS correspondent Steve Rowan learned that, until a few months ago, it was true; the source: S. VNese province chiefs who got advance warnings from U.S. (Reasoner)		

Anchorman	Film Report	Commentary/Special
Eight hundred twenty-one enemy killed in allied sweeping operation around Saigon, but contact still not made with "major enemy units"; key allied position is Fire Support Base Buffalo, "which doesn't say much about the Godforsaken place." (Reasoner)	Fire Support Base Buffalo might well win award for "dustiest place in Vietnam"; units pulled in from Cambodian border to try to stop infiltration near capital; unusual situation, with American tanks/troops getting aerial support from VN Air Force; head of artillery interviewed. (Webster)	
	From Outside Vietnam	
McCarthy would support Robert Kennedy or even a Republican with an anti-VN record if he is unable to win nomination himself. (Reasoner)	McCarthy statement at Howard University, thinks he could end the war, "any President could." (Richard McLaughlin)	
Rockefeller gives impression he'll announce his candidacy soon. (Reasoner)	Rockefeller statement; refused to label himself a hawk or dove; decried oversimplification of VN issue, "an apparent slap at . . . Nixon's campaign pledge to end the war." (Dean)	
		Status of Presidential campaign; changing one's mind on VN doesn't necessarily mean personal inconsistency: situation changed and/or some men learned some new things. (Sevareid)
Pentagon called for 44,000 men to be drafted in May. (Reasoner)		
Eight more U.S. deserters granted asylum in Sweden; 28 have it so far; 24 more have applied. (Reasoner)		

Anchorman	Film Report	Commentary/Special
Johnson made another "hard-hitting defense" of his VN policy; declared the offensive "is aimed at the citizens of America. It's designed to crack America's will," but America will stand firm. (Reasoner) White House said Johnson has no plans for special commission to reexamine VN policy; Robert Kennedy reportedly offered to stay out of primaries if such a commission were appointed. (Reasoner)		

March 20	**From Vietnam**	
U.S. military/intelligence sources claimed siege of Khe Sanh has failed due to "fantastically high" enemy casualties from U.S. air strikes; N. VNese reinforcing and may attack other U.S. bases below DMZ; Marines steadily improving their defenses. (Reasoner) Enemy units have eluded allied operation around Saigon, retreating to Cambodian border; but enemy still close enough--30 to 50 miles away--to continue to threaten the capital. (Reasoner)	Marines preparing for possibility enemy will use tanks at Khe Sanh; practicing with antitank weapon; constant shelling is taking its toll, regular stream of casualties; N. VNese shooting at almost every helicopter; airstrip "all but closed." (Film: Schneider, voice-over: Gralnick)	

	From Outside Vietnam	
"Outspoken critic of U.S. VN policy," General Shoup, testified before Fulbright's Foreign Relations Committee. (Reasoner)	Shoup proved "Fulbright's kind of military man"; Shoup testimony: military victory not possible if present course followed; U.S. commanders not mistaken in holding Khe Sanh,	

Anchorman	Film Report	Commentary/Special
	doesn't think it can be taken. (Rowan)	
Five U.S. deserters and four draft dodgers were granted residence and work permits by French government; about 100 other draft dodgers and deserters in France. (Reasoner)		
Truman supports Johnson on the war. (Reasoner)	Truman interviewed.	
March 21	From Vietnam	
U.S. command reported 10,000 American troops have launched five new operations from Saigon to Central Highlands; aim in part "is to regain the initiative . . . lost to the communists during their Tet offensive." (Reasoner)		
Allied and enemy casualties down sharply last week. (Reasoner)		
Thieu said S. VN's armed forces will be increased by 135,000, including 18- and 19-year olds; again pledged crackdown on corruption. (Reasoner)		
Retail prices in Saigon fell again last week; now only eight percent above levels prior to Tet offensive. (Reasoner)		
	From Outside Vietnam	
Johnson emphasized determination to persist in his VN policies. (Reasoner)	Johnson statement to 17 civilians going to VN to help in pacification program: "Our determination won't crack. We will win peace with honor." Praised S. VNese determination to be free. (Rather)	

Anchorman	Film Report	Commentary/Special
Swedish government de- nounced U.S. policies in VN, said Johnson Ad- ministration bears heavy responsibility for refusing to halt bombing; no mention made of the communists. (Reasoner)		
March 22	From Vietnam	
U.S. command reported allied forces have made significant contact with enemy troops in all corps areas; no immediate word on overall casualties. (Reasoner)		
B-52s bombed Iron Triangle north of Saigon, "old Vietcong stronghold" believed sheltering many of estimated 13,000 enemy troops who have avoided major contact with Operation Resolved to Win. (Reasoner)		
Khe Sanh "may be in greater danger than ever" because of highly mobile 37 mm. antiaircraft guns now encircling it; crucial factor in defense is air support; the guns represent serious threat to supply planes and jets; communists "used the same guns to knock down French planes trying to supply the men of Dienbienphu." (Reasoner)		
	From Outside Vietnam	
"There were some dramatic developments at the White House." (Reasoner)	Johnson announced West- moreland is to be new Army Chief of Staff; Abrams under considera- tion as commander in VN; Wheeler to stay another year as Chief of JCS; Westmoreland promotion won't change tactics or strategy, Johnson said. (Rather)	

Anchorman	Film Report	Commentary/Special
Patrick Nugent getting cool reception from his National Guard unit; he had expressed his desire to be sent to VN, a wish not shared by the other men. (Reasoner)		
March 25	From Vietnam	
UPI reported a company of U.S. 1st Air Cavalry Division was ambushed by N. VNese troops 20 miles west of Hue; moderate American losses. (Reasoner)		
U.S. pilots reported destroying 245 VC sampans south of Saigon, "presumably . . . carrying supplies and food to enemy troops in the Mekong Delta." (Reasoner)		
	From Outside Vietnam	
In fighting campaign speech, Johnson vigorously defended his VN policy; "clearly aimed his attack at Democratic as well as Republican political rivals." (Reasoner)	At AFL-CIO Building Trades Legislative Conference, Johnson found strong anti-Kennedy sentiment; tone set by Meany; Meany statement endorsing Johnson on VN; Johnson statement: our will being tested, must help get justice "for all people of the world." (Rather)	
Republican Congressman Richard Schweiker charged Pentagon classified report on pacification program because of its critical conclusions; he read report earlier, said it concluded VNese people will never support GVN until it permits and encourages "broadly based political organizations." (Reasoner)		

Anchorman	Film Report	Commentary/Special
March 26	From Vietnam	

Anchorman	Film Report	Commentary/Special
One thousand N. VNese regulars with machine guns and flamethrowers tried to overrun U.S. artillery post in Central Highlands; 300 defenders beat off attack with aid of helicopter gunships and jet fighters; 135 communists, 19 Americans killed. (Cronkite)		
Allied troops claimed killing 284 VC in district town 28 miles northwest of Saigon; 10 Americans reported killed; part of major search-and-destroy operation around Saigon; "not all phases of it have been productive." (Cronkite)	"There is supposed to be a major offensive going on now. . . . These men are part of it, but they never heard of it"; doing the same thing all along; very tough going; only enemy today is 90-degree heat; Long Truong village peasants work land by day, VC own it at night; Captain Shaw interviewed on how to distinguish friend from foe; mission over "and the war apparently no closer to an end than it was this morning." (Quint)	
Swing-wing F-111As made combat debut in raids against N. VN's southern Panhandle. (Cronkite)		
One of top U.S. pacification officials quit his job "in protest over what he calls a losing policy in the war." (Cronkite)	Sidney Roche interviewed: ARVN getting worse, not better; World War II equipment, leadership "extremely poor," poor performance in field; RF and PF blunted VC attacks against the cities; widespread corruption, half USAID aid "disappears or is dissipated"; no 100 percent military solution; Komer interviewed, rebuts Roche charges. (Webster)	

Anchorman	Film Report	Commentary/Special
Thieu fired four more province chiefs in his crackdown on incompetence and corruption. (Cronkite)		
	From Outside Vietnam	
Abrams in Washington for conferences on the war; met with Johnson; there has been speculation he will take over U.S. command in VN. (Cronkite)		
Eisenhower doubts allies could have won World War II if there had been dissent then like there is now over VN, some of which "verges on treason." (Cronkite)		
Senator Mansfield opposed to any additional troop buildup in S. VN; Johnson reportedly may commit up to 35,000 more troops; Mansfield argued further escalation can only hurt chances for peace talks. (Cronkite)		
USS *New Jersey* taken out of mothballs "so her massive armament . . . could be aimed at targets in VN" in fall. (Cronkite)		
Sato has demanded U.S. Army hospital for VN war wounded be moved out of Tokyo; hospital has been target of leftist protests and complaints from residents fearing tropical diseases. (Cronkite)		
White House reacted coolly to Undersecretary of Treasury Barr's testimony at Senate hearing that nation cannot maintain guns-and-butter economy. (Cronkite)		
Nixon reportedly would seek summit conference with Russia as first step in ending war if he's elected. (Cronkite)		

Anchorman	Film Report	Commentary/Special
McCarthy campaigned for Republican votes in Wisconsin; Johnson supporters have called him the underdog. (Cronkite)	Johnson headquarters; TV ads by Johnson and Humphrey; Johnson VN policies under attack; widespread feeling of mistrust among voters. (Noel Benti)	Presidential campaign and VN; Tet, not McCarthy, produced serious review of policy/ strategy. (Sevareid)
March 27	**From Vietnam**	
U.S., S. VNese, and enemy casualties in Operation Resolved to Win; one major objective is to remove threat of another major communist attack on Saigon. (Cronkite)	"It's almost like cowboys and Indians"; enemy fire pouring in, in spite of heavy U.S. air strikes; some American casualties from own air support; medics' toughness of spirit and sacrifice "hard to imagine"; CBS cameraman Ude Nesch "got a scratch, piece of shrapnel in his hand," angry he can't work any more today. (Quint)	
Final sequence filmed by NBC cameraman Vo Win. (Cronkite)		
Thieu predicted another major communist offensive in May or June; criticized VN policy critics in U.S. for hindering war effort. (Cronkite)		
Three S. VNese generals recently removed from high commands have been given important new positions; American field officers regarded all three as "incompetent or ineffective." (Cronkite)		
U.S. Embassy spokesman said bubonic plague killed 56 persons in S. VN this year. (Cronkite)		

Anchorman	Film Report	Commentary/Special
	From Outside Vietnam	
Number-two U.S. officer in VN, "some believe he soon will be number one," had long meeting at White House today. (Cronkite)	Abrams meeting with Johnson, National Security Council, discussed modernizing, enlarging, and making ARVN more effective; obviously leading candidate for Westmoreland's job. (Rather)	
March 28	From Vietnam	
Double trouble for F-111 today; an F-111A has been lost. (Cronkite)		
Radio Hanoi reports women of N. VN militia hit U.S. destroyer *Epperson* yesterday, set her afire; Navy says its "absolutely untrue." (Cronkite)		
B-52s smashed enemy positions in A Shau Valley for second day; trying to blunt communist buildup again threatening Hue. (Cronkite)		
Less than 100 artillery rounds hit Khe Sanh, far below daily average. (Cronkite)	Short-range duel, N. VNese only 200 yards or less away; trying to knock out N. VNese machine-gunner; only measure of success is whether planes get in without being shot; tomorrow "the duel will go on." (Gralnick)	
U.S., S. VNese, and enemy weekly casualties. (Cronkite)		
	From Outside Vietnam	
Senate Armed Services Committee voted to scrap Navy version of F-111; CBS News in Washington learned that the one shot down today never reached target in N. VN. (Cronkite)		

Anchorman	Film Report	Commentary/Special
Militant leftist students and other Japanese fought bloody battle with Tokyo police in protest over planned opening of U.S. Army hospital for VN's wounded. (Cronkite)		
Humphrey addressed enthusiastic labor group. (Cronkite)	Humphrey statement: "If we'll stand by our commitments . . . we can have peace for our children and . . . for ourselves."	
Fulbright says Johnson "runs an extremely grave risk of being dumped by the Democrats unless he modifies VN policy." (Cronkite)		
VN is key factor in Wisconsin race. (Cronkite)	Referendum in Madison on immediate cease-fire/withdrawal; campaigning. (Plante)	
March 29	From Vietnam	
F-111A back in action today, striking targets in N. VN's southern Panhandle; same area where one believed to have gone down yesterday. (Cronkite)		
Communists shot down U.S. helicopter three miles from Khe Sanh; base hit by some 200 rounds, casualties reported light. (Cronkite)	Khe Sanh "a target range" for N. VNese who've "flattened virtually every building, blown away every tent with a constant rain of rockets and mortars. . . . No rhyme or reason, apparently just a reminder that they are out there." Seabees asked if they're scared; "no end in sight." (Gralnick)	

Anchorman	Film Report	Commentary/Special
	From Outside Vietnam	
Johnson told Young Democrats that "just wishing for peace won't bring it." (Cronkite)		
In Vientiane, U.S. officials released three captured N. VNese sailors in response to Hanoi's release of three U.S. pilots last month; direct U.S.-N.VN talks preceded today's actions. (Cronkite)		
Court martial ordered for woman Marine who wants out because she's opposed to U.S. policy in VN. (Cronkite)		

NOTE TO *TIME* AND *NEWSWEEK* STORY INDEXES: The articles listed are those concerned wholly or in part with Tet and its side effects in the United States and elsewhere. As previously pointed out, it should be remembered that--for example--the *Time* issue dealing with the events of the week ending Saturday, February 3, went to press Sunday, February 4; appeared on newsstands on Monday, February 5, in the eastern United States; and was advance-dated February 9. *Newsweek*'s production-distribution-sales cycle followed roughly the same pattern, but the issue dealing with the events of that same week was advance-dated to February 12, or eight days after the magazine "closed." Thus, the editorial use of the phrase "last week," particularly in *Newsweek*, required special mental adjustments on the part of the reader.

STORY INDEX: VIETNAM-RELATED STORIES, *TIME*, FEBRUARY 9–APRIL 5, 1968

STORY INDEX: VIETNAM-RELATED STORIES, *NEWSWEEK,* FEBRUARY 12-APRIL 8, 1968

Picture Indexes

PICTURE INDEX: VIETNAM-RELATED PICTURES, NEW YORK *TIMES,*
FEBRUARY 1–MARCH 31, 1968

Caption	Column Width	Page
February 1		
As the Fighting Raged: Military policemen seek protection behind a wall outside the consular section of U.S. Embassy in Saigon. Bodies of two American soldiers, slain by guerrillas who raided the compound, lie nearby. (AP)	4	1
In Saigon: Firemen extinguishing fire at the government's radio station after Vietcong terrorists were driven from the building. The bodies of the guerrillas lie on the sidewalk. They had set fire to the station before being routed. (AP	4	14
Taking Out the Dead: With the bodies of American soldiers in the back, a U.S. armored personnel carrier moves cautiously through the outskirts of Saigon, near Tan Son Nhut. The soldiers were killed by Vietcong. (UPI)	4	14
February 2		
Guerrilla Dies: Brig. Gen. Nguyen Ngoc Loan, national police chief, executes a man identified as a Vietcong terrorist in Saigon. Man wore civilian dress and had a pistol. A picture sequence of the execution is on page 12.	4	1
His Family Slain by Vietcong: A South Vietnamese officer carries the body of one of his children from his home. Terrorists overran the base of his unit in Saigon, beheaded an officer, and killed women and children. (AP)	2	1
[1] Prisoner: Man in checked shirt, who had been identified as a Vietcong officer, is guarded by a Marine after being captured near the An Quang Pagoda in Saigon. He was carrying a pistol when captured.	2+	12
[2] Execution: Brig. Gen. Nguyen Ngoc Loan, South Vietnam's national police chief, kills prisoner with a single round from his revolver. [Loan's gun to prisoner's head.] The prisoner's face shows the impact of the bullet. He had been turned over to General Loan after his capture.	3	12
[3] Death: The body of the prisoner sprawls in the street as General Loan holsters his revolver. The General said: "They killed many Americans and many of our people." [The three] pictures were taken by Eddie Adams, Associated Press photographer.	2+	12

NOTE: On days for which there are no entries, no pertinent contemporary pictures appeared in the paper. Where no picture credit is shown, none was given.

Caption	Column Width	Page
U.S. Armor on the Move: U.S. troops in armored vehicles moving through the center of Saigon yesterday on their way to Cholon, Chinese section, where street fighting broke out between Vietcong and government forces. (AP)	4	12
Searching for Snipers: Household effects made a pile of debris over railroad tracks in the Cholon section of Saigon yesterday as South Vietnamese soldiers continued to comb the area in a hunt for Vietcong snipers. (UPI)	4	13
Tears for the Dying: Vietnamese women weep as another woman, foreground, lies dying after being wounded during the fighting around the An Quang Pagoda in Saigon. [Vietnamese women squat over bloody body, one holding a child in her arms.] Vietcong terrorists had taken positions near the pagoda, but were killed or captured. (AP)	3	13
Ron Fleming, left, and Richard Taylor watching for snipers from the balcony of Taylor's house in the Chilang area. (AP)	2	13

February 3

Rescue Under Fire: Members of the U.S. Marine Corps dragging a wounded comrade back across a bridge at Hue after an unsuccessful attempt to dislodge North Vietnamese and Vietcong troops from positions in the city. (AP)	4	1
In Northern Suburb of Saigon: South Vietnamese soldiers in armored vehicle move past burned buildings to retake area from Vietcong.	5	9
Wounded: Marine, with bandage on leg, waits for assistance in leaving bridge at Hue [propped up on elbow, holding rifle with other hand]. (AP)	3	9
Wounded Boy Clings to Mother: Child hit in Da Nang struggles as medics try to carry him to aid station [boy's head bandaged, grabbing mother's shirt but held down by medic]. (UPI)	4	10

February 4

Hue: Gunners of U.S. Marine Corps guard post against Vietcong and North Vietnamese. (AP)	3	1
Da Nang: Woman passes body of man killed in Vietcong ambush of South Vietnamese jeep. (UPI)	3	1
South Vietnamese infantrymen, one firing a bazooka, fight Vietcong, who occupy house in the southwestern part of Saigon. Fighting in the capital subsided into skirmishes. (AP)	3	2
Under Fire: American Marines crouching near a tank after snipers opened up on them from rear on Thursday in Hue. (UPI)	4	3
Cities Under Siege of Terror: A Vietnamese town dweller running for cover with his child, while soldiers man their	4+	1E

Caption	Column Width	Page

sandbag defenses, symbolizes the ordeal into which South Vietnam's cities were plunged last week by the Vietcong's nationwide urban offensive. Beaten back in most places, the Vietcong may nevertheless have scored psychological gains. (AP)

February 5

Caption	Column Width	Page
After the Battle Subsided: A young Vietnamese girl sits beside a portable stove in the ruins near Saigon's An Quang Pagoda, an area heavily damaged in the fighting. (AP)	3	1
Fire cover was provided by a U.S. Marine, left, as his comrades dragged a wounded buddy to safety in Hue, where fighting continued. An American general said that the enemy had been fighting at a rate far below maximum effort. (UPI)	4	14
Crying: Vietcong suspect, his hand tied to another prisoner, at a POW collection point in Saigon yesterday. (AP_	2	14
Fighting in the streets of Hue, South Vietnam, for fifth straight day yesterday, Marines took up positions by side of a road. A dead comrade and his helmet lie in front of them. (AP)	3	15
A Vietcong guerrilla 16 years old being hustled through Da Nang streets. He was caught carrying explosives. (AP)	2	15
Homeless civilians in Hue crouching under guard after being driven from their homes by heavy fighting Saturday [women and children, hands over head]. Small pockets of enemy resistance continue to hold out. (UPI)	3	15
Searching for snipers, a U.S. Marine kicking in a front door during house-to-house fighting in Hue Saturday. Guerrillas have set up committees to rule in areas taken. (UPI)	3	15
In Saigon, U.S. Army tanks rumbled through the streets. New attacks were reported yesterday in the Cholon district and a strict curfew was imposed on American civilians. (UPI)	3	15
In Paris, demonstrators showed their opposition to U.S. involvement in Vietnam by burning an American flag. (AP)	2	15
Flight of a Family: In a small village north of Da Nang, a woman covers her ears as she flees a spot where South Vietnamese troops have taken up positions. A small boy gestures for his brother, at left, to hurry. (UPI)	4	16

February 6

Caption	Column Width	Page
Fighting in the streets of Hue: An American Marine raises his M-16 above a wall to fire at North Vietnamese and Vietcong in the ancient Vietnamese capital. (UPI)	2	1
War Refugees: A Vietnamese woman and children fleeing downtown Saigon after fire broke out during heavy fighting yesterday. Fighting was heaviest near central market.	3	14

Caption	Column Width	Page
War Casualty: A U.S. Marine carrying a seriously wounded Vietnamese girl through the shattered wall of her home in Hue during heavy street fighting in the city on Sunday. (AP)	3	14

February 7

Fire Fighters: Children in Cholon district of Saigon forming a bucket brigade yesterday to put out fire in what remains in father's machine shop, leveled by air strikes. (UPI)	3	1
Street Scene in Hue During Recent Heavy Fighting: Two Vietnamese lie dead near a hand-drawn cart [looks like two children], and a third, upper right, lies in road behind jeep as tank looks for foe. (UPI)	3	14
Destruction in Saigon: A view of Cholon, the Chinese section in the southern part of Saigon, after fires, bombing, and street fighting between the Vietcong guerrillas and the allied forces destroy a whole block in the area. (AP)	4	14
Civil casualties lie in hallway of a hospital in My Tho, South Vietnam. A quarter of the city's buildings was said to be destroyed. Official position reported 1,500 civilians in this hospital and an antibiotic shortage. (UPI)	2	15

February 8

U.S. Marine, loaded with gear, wheeling to battle in Hue on requisitioned motorbike. (AP)	3	14
Saigon: South Vietnamese troops firing at Vietcong barricade yesterday as the battle for Cholon section continued. (AP)	4	14

February 9

Arrive at Khe Sanh: South Vietnamese irregular soldiers reaching the U.S. Marine base after fleeing from Lang Vei. Nearly 200 of the survivors were stripped of their weapons and turned out into the enemy-controlled countryside. (AP)	4	16

February 10

Americans Go to Cholon: Members of the 199th Light Infantry Brigade at the race track in southern Saigon, after arrival in copters to aid South Vietnamese troops. (AP)	3	1
Mission of Mercy: Wounded girl and mother ride cycle to hospital from Cholon section of Saigon. Man at left is carrying a white flag. They are passing a South Vietnamese policeman on duty in the troubled city. (UPI)	4	11

Caption	Column Width	Page

Caption	Column Width	Page
Gen. William C. Westmoreland and Ambassador Ellsworth Bunker, rear, at the service [kneeling before helmets of soldiers; lead was: "Army Honors 27 Killed"]. (UPI)	3	2
U.S. Marines charging across a bridge in the ancient capital [Hue]. Allies have been reluctant to shell Citadel's buildings. (UPI)	4	3
Maj. Gen. Tran Do. (AP)	1	4

February 15

Caption	Column Width	Page
A U.S. Marine spotter, right, crouches behind a heavily sandbagged bunker as a North Vietnamese shell explodes.	4	1
A reinforced post office at the Marine outpost was built underground to replace one destroyed by enemy shells.	4	1
A-1 Skyraider, a U.S. Navy dive bomber of the type shot down yesterday by a Chinese MIG jet. Plane was attacked into Chinese air space over Gulf of Tonkin. (UPI)	3	2
Combat-ready Marines being loaded on a transport plane at El Toro, California, yesterday for 11-hour trip to Vietnam.	2	3
In Hue, Marines and South Vietnamese troops at the gate of the Citadel, where the enemy continued to hold out. (AP)	2	3
A wounded Vietcong watches a South Vietnamese medical team render aid to a wounded man. Action occurred during a recent battle in Cholon, the Chinese section of Saigon. (UPI)	3	4

February 16

Caption	Column Width	Page
Washday at Hue: South Vietnamese women look up from their washing as a U.S. helicopter lands on the grounds at the University of Hue. Hundreds of Vietnamese have taken refuge on the campus during the fighting in their city. (UPI)	4	3

February 17

Caption	Column Width	Page
Supplying Khe Sanh by Parachute: Parachutes on cargo containers billow in the barbed-wire defense around the Marine outpost. Supplies were dropped yesterday because poor visibility prevented cargo planes from landing. (AP)	4	2
U.S. Marine jet bomber drops napalm canister over a part of the walled stronghold of the ancient imperial capital [Hue] where enemy troops are believed to be. Area is residential. (AP)	3	3
Exploding napalm sends black smoke over the city. The troops in the area were backed by land and naval artillery. (AP)	2	3

Caption	Column Width	Page
Three American fliers, first to be freed by Hanoi, leave for U.S.: Maj. Norris M. Overly, Capt. Jon D. Black, Ens. David P. Matheny [three head shots]. (AP)	1 each	7

February 18

Helping Hands: Two U.S. Marines help a third, wounded in the fighting to regain control of Hue, down the steps from the wall in the ancient imperial capital of Vietnam [building, trees in ruins]. (UPI)	3	1

February 19

A military policeman patrolling below Tan Son Nhut airport control tower in Saigon yesterday. The tower was hit but not disabled by Vietcong shells. (AP)	3	1
[1] A seriously wounded Vietcong suspect guerrilla in jail, Ngo Van Tranh, being offered water yesterday morning by a South Vietnamese Marine in Saigon. The suspect, wounded after the start of a new Vietcong assault on Saigon, said he had been taken from his home in Thu Duc, northeast of Saigon, night before by Vietcong and forced to carry ammunition.	2	14
[2] The suspect is then questioned and threatened by another South Vietnamese Marine. A third Vietnamese Marine first knifed prisoner, then killed him with a rifle-burst. (Both, AP)	3 each	14
Tank Ambulance in Hue: Wounded U.S. Marines being carried to an evacuation point [transported by tank]. Only tanks could travel city's ruined streets. (AP)	5	14
Chapel Ruins: Father Joseph Long, left, Vietnamese chaplain, walking with U.S. chaplain, Maj. Lewie H. Miller, through U.S. Air Force chapel destroyed at Tan Son Nhut airport. (AP)	3	14
Flight: A South Vietnamese soldier helping a woman and child escape from fighting in northeast Saigon yesterday. (AP)	4	14
Airport Hit: Tan Son Nhut airport in Saigon after Vietcong troops shelled it yesterday. (AP)	3	14

February 20

A Vietcong rocket crew firing an antitank rocket at an American tank during the recent fighting in Hue.	4	1
Vietcong soldiers setting up a machine-gun position in Hue. Photographs and captions were released by Hanoi yesterday. (UPI)	4	1

Caption	Column Width	Page
South Vietnamese police, using pistol and automatic rifle, firing into burning building in northeast Saigon yesterday. (AP)	4	3
Lt. Richard W. Pershing (grandson of General Pershing) killed in Vietnam [head shot]. (AP.)	1	5

February 21

A Pause in the Fighting: U.S. Marines resting in the rubble of one of the towers of the Citadel in Hue. They were waiting for artillery strikes before attempting to advance. (AP)	3	1
U.S. Marines placing the flag atop the battered eastern wall of the Citadel in Hue. (AP)	3	3

February 22

Determined: Col. David E. Lownds, camp commander at Khe Sanh, said camp would be held despite concern voiced about defenses. (David Douglas Duncan--*Life*/ABC)	1	10

February 23

Khe Sanh's lifeline is its landing strip, favorite target for the enemy. It is under such constant shell fire that planes do not come to a full stop while unloading [chopper approaching landing]. (David Douglas Duncan--*Life*/ABC)	3	1
Dug In . . . And Still Digging: Marines are not always visible at ground level in Khe Sanh. Sandbag bunkers--such as this one next to the runway--offer them protection from the daily mortar barrages. Intensive enemy fire prevents the Marines from building stronger fortifications. (David Douglas Duncan--*Life*/ABC)	5	2
War's Deadly Debris: Unexploded shells--scorched in an attack on Khe Sanh's ammunition dump--line a road in the beleaguered garrison. Marines will bury them. (David Douglas Duncan--*Life*/ABC)	3	2
In Hue, a U.S. Navy landing craft flies her flag amid the fire and smoke from a burning ship near the north bank of Huong River. The Citadel, where Marines surmounted the south wall yesterday, burns in the background. (AP)	4	3

February 24

Strengthening Defense at Khe Sanh: Marines use a bulldozer at the base in South Vietnam. In the background smoke rises from bombs dropped by American planes or enemy troops that have moved close to the perimeter. (AP)	4	1
Sky Rations for Khe Sanh: Packages of food are lowered by parachutes to Marines. (UPI)	3	3

Caption	Column Width	Page
Military Chief in Saigon: Gen. Earle G. Wheeler, center, Chairman of the Joint Chiefs of Staff, is met by Gen. William C. Westmoreland, at left, the commander of U.S. forces, and Ambassador Ellsworth Bunker. His visit is expected to last several days [head shots]. (AP)	3	4

February 25

Plan Rebuilding in Saigon: Nguyen Van Loc, at center in dark tunic, Premier of South Vietnam, confers with aides amid devastation of Cholon. Bulldozers have cleared Chinese section, which was a stronghold of the Vietcong. (AP)	4	1
U Thant arriving for his news conference yesterday. (Not from VN) (UPI)	1	24
Involved in Gulf of Tonkin: The *Turner Joy*, one of the two U.S. destroyers that were attacked by North Vietnamese craft on August 4, 1964, while on intelligence patrol. (AP)	3	29
After Incidents: The *Maddox*, the other destroyer involved, at San Diego, California, on her return from Vietnam. (AP)	2	29
Vessel's Commander: Capt. John J. Herrick, who was aboard the *Maddox* at time of the encounter, sent message before attack suggesting North Vietnam considered ships as enemies [head shot]. (AP)	1	29
Clash over Vietnam: President Johnson and Senator Fulbright chat in happier times--in 1966, before their relations were embittered by the Senator's leading role in Congressional dissent against the President's Vietnam policies. The dissent grew harsher last week [head shots]. (Not from VN) (UPI)	4	1E
Hard Battle: U.S. Marines press assault to clear stubborn foe from Hue's ancient imperial Citadel. (AP)	5+	2E

February 27

Casualty Evacuated at Khe Sanh: U.S. Marines running with a stretcher to a helicopter at Khe Sanh. North Vietnamese prevented a rescue platoon from reaching a patrol that was ambushed yesterday 800 yards outside base. (AP)	4	1

February 28

A Marine Corps infantryman aiming hand grenade at enemy guerrillas in bunker close by. (Don McCullin--Magnum)	5	26
No Time for Ceremony: Marines dragging comrade away after he was hit by sniper fire [holding his arms, his feet dragging; under the head: "Life and Death in an Ancient Asian City: Scenes in the Long Fight for Hue"]. (McCullin)	3	26

Caption	Column Width	Page
Just big enough to toddle through a combat area, this girl [bloody face and head bandage] was found and aided by Marines. (McCullin)	3	26
This was a North Vietnamese soldier [dead]. Scattered near him are snapshots and cartridges. (McCullin)	3	26
The wounded girl in the photo at left, responding to first aid by the men who found her, was carried to a place away from the fighting [by an American soldier, while Vietnamese follow]. (McCullin)	5	26
Grenade fragment struck man and daughter as they hid in bunker [man holding head, standing, blood streaming from him and small child]. (McCullin)	2+	26
Unable to walk, aged woman is carried through ruined street [soldier lifting her, face forward, through rubble]. (McCullin)	2+	26
Caption in the middle of all pictures on page 26: Battle for Hue, the ancient capital of Vietnam, was fought from house to house, catching up the people of the city in the unrelenting conflict. No one was too old or too young to be involved. These pictures were taken by a young English photographer who was in the midst of the bitter fighting for 11 days.		

February 29

| High-level Briefing: Gen. Earle G. Wheeler, Chairman of the Joint Chiefs of Staff, reports to President Johnson and Cabinet members on his recent trip to South Vietnam. (AP) | 3 | 2 |

March 1

| [Left photo:] (NY 15--March 21) Requiem and Thanksgiving --American soldiers kneel and bow as they pray for their dead and give thanks that they are alive, as they attend Protestant field service in War Zone C after one of the most furious battles of the Vietnam War. These are men of the 3rd Brigade, 4th U.S. Infantry Division, which mauled a Red regiment yesterday, killing 423 communists at a cost of 30 dead, 109 wounded, and three missing. (AP wirephoto by radio from Saigon) (gww30945stf) 1967 | 2+ | 3 |
| [Right photo, same picture:] (41) Hsinhua Radiophoto, Peking, March 24, 1967--U.S. aggressors have recently received sound beatings from South Vietnam Liberation Army in C area. Photo shows demoralized U.S. soldiers of the 3rd Brigade of the 4th Infantry Division, who survived the attack. | 2+ | 3 |

Caption	Column Width	Page

Caption in box under the two pictures: Deception: The *AP Log*, An Associated Press weekly newsletter analyzing the news agency's news and photo coverage, reported yesterday that it had caught Hsinhua, the Chinese Communist press agency, at photo fakery. The Associated Press caption, left, describes American soldiers praying. Hsinhua apparently intercepted the signals forming the picture, and redistributed it with a caption purporting to show the soldiers demoralized after being beaten. Over the years, various Chinese Communist press agencies have been exposed by Western newspapers and agencies for faking stories, documents, and whole newspapers as well as photographs. Photos ostensibly showing activities of the North Vietnam Army and Vietcong soldiers in South Vietnam "need extensive research to determine authenticity," the Associated Press declared.

March 2

Eight-column headline: Enemy's Use of New Soviet and Chinese Weapons Changes the Pattern of War in Vietnam.

	Column Width	Page
Foe's basic weapon is the AK-47, a gas-operated, automatic assault rifle. It uses 7.62 mm. cartridges in 30-round magazines, effective range is 440 yards. It is heavier but more reliable than the U.S. M-16 which uses an 18- or 20-round magazine [picture of the AK-47].	3	3
Simple but deadly is this tube that launches 140 mm. rockets at a distance of 9,850 yards. It is built in the Soviet Union in cluster of 8, 16, and 17. The Vietcong-- who prefer mobile weapons--use the individual tubes mounted on wooden planks. In this form the tubes were first used in attacks on the U.S. base at Da Nang in February 1967 [picture of the tube and a rocket]. (AP)	3	3
One-man weapons are the RPG-2 antitank grenade launcher, left, the AK-47 rifle and the SKS carbine. The RPG-2 fires four to six 82 mm. rounds a minute, its effective range is 165 yards. The SKS uses 7.62 mm. ammunition in 10-round clips, its effective range is 440 yards [picture of a GI holding a RPG-2 and a SKS carbine in each of his hands, the AK-47 leans against his chest]. (UPI)	2	3
Recent innovation is the RPG-7 grenade launcher, an improved, more powerful version of the RPG-2. Weapon has two pistol grips instead of one, and telescopic, not blade, sight. Its projectile has a rocket assist that extends range to 550 yards, 50 shorter than that of the U.S. 106 mm. recoilless rifle. The RPG-7 is, however, more mobile [picture of the RPG-7].	3	3
Used recently in attacks on Saigon's Tan Son Nhut airport are the 107 mm. rocket, left, and the 122 mm. rocket. The 122 mm. shells are over six feet long, weight about 100 pounds, have a range of 12,000 yards. The U.S. has no exact comparable weapon. The 107 mm. rocket--fired from	1+	3

Caption	Column Width	Page
recoilless gun--was first used two weeks ago [picture of a GI standing beside a 122 mm. rocket, next to it is the 107 mm. rocket]. (AP)		
Most widely used mortars are the 82 mm. (top) and 60 mm. pieces shown. The 82 mm. mortar can fire 25 rounds a minute, a distance of 3,300 yards. The 60 mm. weapon--a copy of the U.S. M-2--has maximum rate of fire of 35 r.p.m. Only 42 pounds, it can be carried by one man [two pictures, one of the 82 mm. mortar, the other the 62 mm. mortar]. (DOD)	1+	3

March 3

Knocking Out an Enemy Gun at Khe Sanh: A U.S. Skyraider shows dark against the hills at left as it streaks away after bombing a newly installed North Vietnamese gun close to the perimeter of U.S. Marine Corps base. (UPI)	4	1

March 4

Maj. Gen. Charles P. Stone. (N.Y. *Times*)	1	2
Not Standard Equipment: Lt. Marshall R. Wells, commander of a Marine company at Khe Sanh, with brass divining rods. Rods are supposed to dip over enemy tunnels. (AP)	3	3

March 5

Escapes Vietcong: Dr. Patricia M. Smith of Seattle examining a Vietnamese girl in her hospital in Kontum. Dr. Smith escaped when the hospital was overrun by Vietcong. (AP)	3	3

March 6

At Khe Sanh: An American jet fires rockets into North Vietnamese positions that surround the Marine outpost. (UPI)	4	1
On the Double: At the U.S. Marine Corps base at Khe Sanh, which is encircled by North Vietnamese troops, boarding a plane is a desperate and swift action because of the peril of artillery attack. These men went on leave [Marines running toward plane]. (AP)	4	3

March 7

Returning to Normal: Against the background of the bridge destroyed in recent fighting at Hue, Vietnamese women wash laundry in the Huong River. South Vietnamese MP stands on girder and directs returning refugees. (AP)	4	1

Caption	Column Width	Page

March 8

Marines take cover as a helicopter prepares to land at the Khe Sanh garrison. North Vietnamese gunners open fire whenever a plane or helicopter approaches U.S. outpost. (UPI) — **3** — **1**

Trying for another Dienbienphu? [head shot of Giap] (Black Star) — **1** — **2**

U.S. Marines man the perimeter of the Khe Sanh garrison, searching for signs of enemy activity. At least 20,000 North Vietnamese troops surround 6,000 Marines based there. (UPI) — **3** — **3**

Maj. Gen. Nguyen Duc Thang is the new chief of the IV Corps area in the Delta [head shot; under headline: "Mekong Delta Still Paralyzed Five Weeks After Foe's Offensive"]. (AP) — **1** — **4**

March 10

Natural Defense in North Vietnam: One of the many caves in the country being used as cover against U.S. bombing raids. This one, photographed by a Japanese newsman, shelters small factory. Sign expresses determination. (Nippon Dempa News via AP) — **4** — **1**

Low-Level Mission: A U.S. cargo plane flies over Khe Sanh while dropping supplies to the besieged Americans. Some of the pallets loaded with supplies accidentally fell on the bunkers, killing one Marine, wounding another. (*Stars and Stripes* via AP) — **4** — **3**

Airborne Relief: Because the outpost at Khe Sanh is surrounded by enemy forces and the airstrip comes under constant heavy artillery fire, supplies for the U.S. Marines there are dropped by parachute. (UPI) — **3** — **3E**

March 12

Transport plane rises after supply drop at Khe Sanh. (AP) — **2** — **1**

Jonathan M. Spicer [head shot; under headline: "Heart Surgery at Khe Sanh Saves 'Dead' Marine Hero Who Refused to Kill"]. (AP) — **1** — **14**

March 13

Marines Honored: President Johnson congratulating Lt. John J. McGinty, 3rd, left, and Maj. Robert J. Modrzejewski in ceremonies at White House yesterday. Both men won the Medal of Honor for valor during Operation Hastings in Vietnam, July 1966. (AP) — **3** — **1**

Caption	Column Width	Page
Listening for the Enemy: Theodore Rutkowski, U.S. Navy medical corpsman, uses a stethoscope to determine if North Vietnamese troops are undermining the outpost at Khe Sanh. Julian Kalama, a Marine, guards and watches. (AP)	4	15

March 14

Caption	Column Width	Page
Khe Sanh: Aerial view of the Marine outpost 15 miles south of the Demilitarized Zone. U.S. bombers and fighter-bombers yesterday hammered enemy positions surrounding the beleaguered camp. At top right is rocket pod on plane from which photograph was taken. (UPI)	3	1
Bombs dropped by U.S. planes form a curtain of flying debris 200 feet from South Vietnamese positions in Khe Sanh. (AP)	4	3

March 15

Caption	Column Width	Page
Merchants transact business outside the tangled ruins of the market hall in Ben Tre, destroyed more than a month ago [some structure still remaining]. (AP)	4	3

March 16

Caption	Column Width	Page
Key Point at Khe Sanh: Ambulances park outside main medical aid station at U.S. Marine outpost near the DMZ. The tin-roof building is the reception station; the medical facilities are below ground, the entrance protected by sandbags. (AP)	4	3

March 17

Caption	Column Width	Page
Under Attack: Members of U.S. 1st Cavalry Division (Airmobile) hitting the ground as an enemy rocket struck a runway at Camp Evans, north of Phu Bai, on Friday. Men were reinforcements who had just arrived at camp. (UPI)	4	3

March 19

Caption	Column Width	Page
New Combat Plane for Vietnam: U.S. Air Force F-111s in formation. The fighter-bomber landed in Thailand on Sunday and will be tested over North Vietnam. The jets, capable of 1,500 miles an hour, cost $3 million each. (UPI)	4	1

March 20

Caption	Column Width	Page
Air Rescue: A helicopter lifting four members of U.S. 1st Cavalry Division. They cabled from a position near Hue last week [long cables extended from chopper to four men]. The technique has become standard procedure for recovering troops from areas without landing zones. (UPI)	2	3

Caption	Column Width	Page

March 23

General Westmoreland [head shot, with story on his leaving Vietnam to become Army Chief of Staff]. (UPI) — 1 — 12

March 24

Back from Philippines: Gen. William C. Westmoreland, after visit to family, is greeted in Vietnam by deputy, Gen. Creighton W. Abrams, left, who may succeed him. (AP) — 3 — 1

War-Weary: Tired U.S. soldiers rest after a battle. Sign on wall in left background says, "There is no grudge between Vietnamese and American people. Why killing each other? Let's hand-in-hand build up our friendship." (UPI) — 5 — 3E

March 25

Drawn in the Dust: Pointing to a crude sketch in dirt outside his home, an elderly South Vietnamese answers questions of a 25th Infantry Division intelligence officer, left, through an interpreter. Vietcong had been spotted by a U.S. helicopter in area earlier. The incident occurred in a village 15 miles to the northwest of Saigon. (AP) — 4 — 1

Enrolled in U.S. College: Tran Thi Phuong, secretary-translator to commander in Qui Nhon. The 20-year-old South Vietnamese has been entered for next fall in North-western Michigan College by the Grand Traverse Council of Churches. Council will pay expenses. She was recommended in a letter by Capt. Richard Defer, a pilot at Qui Nhon, in a letter to aunt in Traverse City, Michigan. (AP) — 2 — 3

March 26

An Honorary Ranger: Ta Thai Manh, 13 years old, as he was given a medal and the right to wear the uniform of the South Vietnamese Rangers. He was cited for service in his native village near Saigon. Captured by the Vietcong, he escaped and led Rangers to seize seven of his captors. (AP) — 2 — 3

March 27

Wounded in Ambush: Members of the 7th Regiment of the U.S. 1st Cavalry Division (Airmobile) make their way to helicopter landing zone for removal to medical aid station. Unit was set upon Monday by North Vietnamese tanks 25 miles west of Hue. (UPI) — 3 — 3

Caption	Column Width	Page
March 28 Comrades of wounded man [bandage around head], center, lead him from the field of battle at Trangbang, South Vietnam. Men of 25th Infantry Division were engaged in one of sharpest battles in recent weeks. Al Chang of the Associated Press was wounded after taking picture. (AP)	3	1
March 30 Aggressive General, Bruce Palmer, Jr., sixth in the class of '36. (AP)	1	12
March 31 Brief Rest for the Weary: Battle-worn soldiers of the 1st Cavalry Division seize a chance to rest in area west of Hue, despite noisy chopper landing with supplies. (UPI)	3	3
Marines leaving El Toro, California, for Vietnam. The enemy's Tet offensive has led another escalation in the war, adding $3 billion or more to the cost [story in "Business and Finance" section on wrong forecasts for new year]. (AP)	2	1 (Business and Finance section)

Caption	Column Width	Page
February 1		
Bodies of Red attackers lie before firemen fighting Saigon radio station blaze.	3	A1
U.S. military police, positioned alongside slain comrades, fight it out with communists at embassy compound in Saigon. (AP)	4	A1
Ho Chi Minh: "very happy" [hailing communist victory; head shot]. (AP)	1	A6
Vietcong, who breached U.S. Embassy wall with recoilless rifle, were subdued by troops brought in by copter [showing aerial view and areas of action]. (UPI)	4	A7
February 2		
Execution: South Vietnamese police chief, Brig. Gen. Nguyen Ngoc Loan, executes a Vietcong officer on Saigon street. The officer, in civilian garb and carrying a pistol, had been captured by South Vietnamese Marines. Explaining the summary execution, Loan said, "They killed many Americans and many of my people." Communists had staged several executions since fighting broke out in the capital, and the relatives of government officers had been among their victims. Picture was taken yesterday by AP photographer Eddie Adams at the instant Loan fired.	5	A1
An army truck, its driver lying dead behind it, burns as Rangers dash past in Saigon. Body of dead policeman lies in the foreground. (AP)	5	A4
Ron Fleming and a neighbor man post M.O. (AP)	2	A4
Troops search Saigon building for Vietcong guerrillas. (UPI)	2	A4
Vietnamese major carries body of daughter, killed with rest of family by Reds. (AP)	3	A5
Frightened girl blocks out sound of fighting in Saigon. (AP)	2	A6
Holding his ears against the din of gunfire, a terrified youngster runs past a dead civilian during the street fighting in Da Nang. (AP)	5	A7

NOTE: On days for which there are no entries, no pertinent contemporary pictures appeared in the paper. Where no picture credit is shown, none was given.

Caption	Column Width	Page

February 3

U.S. Marines pull wounded comrades back off the bridge across the Perfume River in Hue Wednesday. The Americans were falling back under heavy fire from enemy troops holed up in the city's old imperial Citadel. The Marines eventually succeeded in crossing the bridge. Saturday morning the enemy still held parts of Hue. (AP)   —   4   —   A1

Vietcong Victim: The Vietcong reportedly killed six American missionaries, three of them women, in an attack on the Central Highlands town of Ban Me Thuot. Robert Zeimer, 49, was among those slain   [head shot]. (AP)   —   1   —   A1

Trying to get Vietcong sniper to reveal his position in a building near Saigon, South Vietnamese soldier uses helmet-on-pole trick. (UPI)   —   5   —   A6

Saigon fighting has taken a heavy civilian toll. From left: A woman wounded by shrapnel is led away by her husband; a cyclist in Chinese quarter inspects a body; a woman dies near An Quang Pagoda. (AP)   —   2+, -3, -3   —   A7

Saigon Battle Scene: South Vietnamese troops fire bazookas at holed-up Vietcong [with transcript of Johnson's news conference: "Feel sure of our strength"]. (AP)   —   4   —   A10

February 4

Vietcong killed in the battle for the Central Highlands town of Pleiku are placed in field. (AP)   —   4   —   A1

Marines take cover behind a tank in Hue when Vietcong snipers open fire. One man lies along the vehicle's superstructure. (UPI)   —   5   —   A1

Saigon Battle Scenes: From left, government soldier uses tombstone as shield; Huynh Ngoc Huong, 16, is captured after she fired machine gun at U.S. jeeps in Cholon; father carries child as gas station burns at rear. (UPI)   —   4+, 1+, 2+   —   A4

Cautious Approach: A Vietnamese soldier on the western section of Saigon advances slowly toward a burning building believed to house Vietcong guerrillas. (UPI)   —   2+   —   A5

Wounded Marines arrive at an aid station in the American military advisory compound during Hue fighting. (AP)   —   4   —   A6

Shell Collector: Keeping a wary eye out for gunfire, a Saigon child collects .50 caliber shell casings. (UPI)   —   2   —   A10

February 5

Marines battle entrenched communists from second-story balcony overlooking U.S. military compound at Hue. (UPI)   —   4   —   A1

Caption	Column Width	Page
Residents of Hue, driven from their homes in fighting [hands on head], are put under guard prior to search for communist suspects. (UPI)	4	A1
Marine machine-gun post overlooks part of Hue, two-thirds controlled by Reds. (UPI)	3	A5
February 6		
A corpsman, sheltered by bullet-pocked wall, calls for aid for wounded Marine during fighting in Hue last week [with another soldier who appears dead]. (UPI)	4	A1
Vietnamese woman carriers her laundry from river at My Tho, a major Mekong Delta town shattered in fighting [with story: "A Third of My Tho Destroyed"]. (AP)	4	A1
U.S. Marine carries seriously wounded Vietnamese girl through wall of Hue home. (AP)	3	A9
February 8		
Hue: Residents find their homes reduced to rubble [view from above, with Lang Vei headlines; story head: "Allies Assess Strengths and Failings]. (UPI)	2	A1
Saigon: South Vietnamese troops fire weapons into Cholon area, blockaded by Vietcong guerrillas. (AP)	4	A1
Saigon fighting victim, a boy of 5, suffered leg burns, head bruises. (AP)	1	A4
Marine at Khe Sanh waits out North Vietnamese shelling [with story head: "Tremendous Blow Struck at Allies, Vietcong Claims"]. (UPI)	2	A6
Refugees huddle for protection under truck during street fighting in Saigon between Vietcong and allied troops. (AP)	4	A8
February 9		
Wounded Lang Vei defender is helped to evacuation helicopter at Khe Sanh. (AP)	3	A1
Soviet tanks used in Vietnam date from '50s. (AP)	5	A8
Flag-Raising: Marines hoist U.S. flag over the provincial headquarters in Hue, taken from communists. South Vietnam flag later replaced U.S.'s. (AP)	2	A8
U.S. Marines run across a clearing on their way to the communist-held Citadel in embattled city of Hue. (UPI)	4	A10

Caption	Column Width	Page
February 10		
General Abrams . . . moving north. (The Washington *Post*)	1	A1
American Army troops, one with mortar tube on his shoulder, move toward positions at Saigon race track. (AP)	4	A1
Entrenched U.S. Marines, preparing fortifications for expected enemy attack, fill up sandbags at Khe Sanh [with story about Khe Sanh-Dienbienphu]. (UPI)	4	A6
Bodies of some of the seven people executed by Vietcong lie in the streets of Saigon 2-1/2 days after the deed. (AP)	4	A7
February 11		
This Soviet-built Ilyushin-28 attack-bomber is the same type as three planes U.S. pilots have spotted on a North Vietnamese airfield. The planes--which first appeared in Moscow in 1950--have a top speed of 580 m.p.h., less than the speed of sound. Large numbers of them have been made and they are used by many Soviet allies. (AP)	4	A1
Keeping their heads down, Vietnamese Rangers help wounded comrade in Saigon. (AP)	3	A9
Saigon government faces a big rebuilding job in cities like My Tho, heavily damaged in Vietcong offensive [aerial view of damaged homes]. (UPI)	4	A16
Giap: Snow-covered volcano.	1+	C4
February 12		
This residential area in Cholon, Saigon's Chinese quarter, lay in ruins after days of fighting against Reds. (AP)	4	A1
Marines pinned down in fighting near Hue Citadel radio for support. (UPI)	2+	A1
Marines fire mortar across Hue's Perfume River to communist positions. (UPI)	2+	A1
February 13		
With Cholon burning behind them, refugees stream toward the center of Saigon, away from the recent fighting. (AP)	4	A1
A Vietnamese refugee brings her wounded baby to a medical aid station in Hue. (UPI)	3	A1
These children crowded into Saigon's Central Hospital are victims of the fighting last week between allied and communist forces. The total number of civilian casualties is unknown, but estimates run into the thousands. (AP)	4	A10

Caption	Column Width	Page
A South Vietnamese soldier holds out his lacerated arms as he arrives at a Saigon hospital in a bicycle taxi. The soldier was wounded by a rocket explosion last week during fighting to clear the Vietcong from the capital.	-4	A1

February 14

Caption	Column Width	Page
Gen. William C. Westmoreland and U.S. Ambassador to Saigon Ellsworth Bunker kneel in prayer at rites for 27 U.S. military policemen killed defending embassy and other installations. Each helmet represents a slain man and carries his unit insignia and the initials MP for military police or SG for security guard, an MP branch. (UPI)	4	A1
Vietnamese boy who lost both of his legs in Saigon street fighting sits on carton in hospital for support. (AP)	2	A1
A sobbing girl walks down a rubble-strewn street in Hue after being treated for multiple wounds. (UPI)	1	A10
As houses burn behind them, South Vietnamese Rangers move through former Vietcong stronghold in Cholon, Saigon. (AP)	4	A16
Bodies of three Vietnamese civilians, including woman in foreground, were found bound and blindfolded in section of Saigon where South Vietnamese Rangers annihilated Vietcong unit. Civilians were believed to be Reds' victims. (AP)	4	A18

February 15

Caption	Column Width	Page
U.S. Marines and government troops enter one of the gates of the Hue Citadel. (UPI)	-3	A19
Apprehension: A wounded Vietcong prisoner reacts guardedly as medical team dresses his wounds following fighting in Saigon's Cholon district. (UPI)	3	A20

February 16

Caption	Column Width	Page
An old woman of Hue in a refugee assembly center. (AP)	2	A14
Using a makeshift litter hung from bicycle tires, South Vietnamese carry wounded man to Hue aid station. (UPI)	4	A15

February 17

Caption	Column Width	Page
As enemy mortar shell explodes at Khe Sanh, one Marine crouches in bunker and another looks for enemy guns. (UPI)	4	A10
Couple in Hue beg U.S. Marines for release of their son, held as a Vietcong suspect. (AP)	3	A10

Caption	Column Width	Page
[Three photographs:] Capt. Jon D. Black, Maj. Norris M. Overly, Lt. David P. Matheny . . . released American fliers reach Udorn. (UPI)	1/2 each	A14

February 18

President bids farewell to men of the 82nd Airborne, El Toro, California.	2	A1
For six hours, U.S. Marine Pfc. Thomas F. Zwetow was buried under a collapsed wall during the battle for the Citadel in Hue. Then some nearby Marines discovered him and, in left picture, begin digging him out. One rescuer holds Zwetow's hand (arrow) while clawing at the rubble. In center, the Wisconsin Marine is halfway out, and at right he is finally free and offered a canteen. Zwetow was only slightly injured. (AP, UPI)	2+ 2+ 2+	A10
Three captured American pilots leave Vientiane, Laos, after their release by North Vietnam. Ambassador William Sullivan (dark suit) accompanied the three--from left: Capt. Jon Black, Lt. (jg.) David Matheny, and Maj. Norris Overly. The three flew to Washington and were to enter military hospitals for medical checkups. (AP)	4	A16
A boat links parts of bridge over Perfume River in Hue destroyed by communists. (UPI)	3	A27
Soldiers of the 1st Cavalry Division carry a wounded buddy under heavy shelling. (UPI)	4	B3
Vo Nguyen Giap . . . last week the Washington *Post* published a picture of Pham Van Dong, Prime Minister of North Vietnam, in its "Outlook" section and incorrectly identified him as General Giap, Hanoi's Minister of Defense and the "Tiger of Dienbienphu." The man above is Giap [head shot]. (AP)	1+	B4
Black market flourishes in Saigon, not in Vientiane.	2	E1

February 19

U.S. Marine fires into communist stronghold from battered wall of Hue Citadel. (UPI)	3	A1
Two pictures, no captions: (1) Vietnamese Marines give wounded man who aided Vietcong drink of water; (2) another group shot him. (AP) Short AP story, with head, "A Drink of Water . . . Then Death"; explanation of shooting wounded VC.	5 (2+) (2+)	A1

Caption	Column Width	Page
These residents of Hue, carrying away what belongings they can, are among the 67,000 refugees created by the heavy fighting of past three weeks in the city. (UPI)	3	A15
Jet fighters lay down a line of defensive fire in support of C-130 transport leaving Khe Sanh. (USAF)	4	A19

February 20

Marines give aid to wounded comrade amid rubble of Hue, where intense fighting has raged for three weeks. (UPI)	4	A1
Marines gather in section of Hue outside Citadel laid waste in fighting. (UPI)	2+	A1
As the bodies of two Vietcong lie nearby, two Marines survey wreckage of house destroyed as suspected Red hideout. (UPI)	4	A14
Machine gun atop tank is fired into burning buildings in section of Saigon where communists held several blocks. (AP)	4	A15

February 21

Stars and Stripes, mounted on tree branch supported by chair, are flown above wall of Hue Citadel by U.S. Marines. Properly, only Saigon flag should fly over city. Lt. Gen. Robert Cushman, Jr., commander of U.S. Marines in Vietnam, said today that the battle for the Citadel may last as long as several weeks. A fresh unit is going in. (AP)	3	A1
Navy photo of USS *Turner Joy* which figured with USS *Maddox* in Tonkin attack. (USN)	3	A33
Marines atop a battered watchtower in Hue look for signs of the entrenched enemy. (AP)	3	A36
Vietcong cross a South Vietnamese river in photo from an official communist source. (UPI)	3	F1
Photo captured at a Vietcong base camp near Saigon shows girls posing with rifles at a political meeting. (UPI)	-4	F1
This teen-aged guerrilla, shoeless but with French grenades on his belt, was captured a few weeks after being photographed. (AP)	1	F6

February 22

U.S. Marine snipers fire across the Perfume River at North Vietnamese holed-up in the Citadel of Hue. (AP)	4	A10

Caption	Column Width	Page
February 23		
A squad of Marines test-fire their rifles before advancing down a contested street in the battle for Hue. (UPI)	4	A9
A hidden Marine trains his rifle down a canal in Hue. (UPI)	2	A9
Using a piece of plywood as a washboard, a U.S. Marine does his laundry in a trench at Khe Sanh combat base. (AP)	4	A10
February 24		
With smoke rising from American bomb strikes beyond their perimeter, U.S. Marines work at the beleaguered combat base of Khe Sanh in northern South Vietnam. (AP)	6	A1
Delta commander Maj. Gen. Nguyen Duc Thang, who formerly headed South Vietnam's pacification program, has been assigned to the Mekong Delta command.	1	A1
[Three photographs:] Lance Cpl. James Avella hoists American flag atop telephone pole after Marines captured southeast corner of Hue Citadel Thursday. (AP, UPI)	2+ 1+ 1+	A8
Vietnam Visitor: Gen. Earle G. Wheeler, center, Chairman of the Joint Chiefs of Staff, is met by Gen. William C. Westmoreland, commander of U.S. forces in Vietnam, and Ambassador Ellsworth Bunker, on his arrival in Saigon. (AP)	3	A8
February 25		
U.S. Marines rush through hole in a wall during the battle for Hue last week. (UPI)	3	A10
Army private displays 6-foot, 4-inch, 122 mm. rocket, the type used in enemy shelling of Tan Son Nhut Air Base. At left is enemy's new, more mobile 107 mm. rocket. (AP)	-1	A10
Waiting for Charlie at Khe Sanh—and ready to duck his calling cards. (UPI)	-4	D1
The engines are kept running while Marines rush their wounded to the plane at the Khe Sanh airstrip. (AP)	-4	D2
February 26		
Troops of the U.S. 1st Cavalry Division (Airmobile) guard Vietcong suspects on a road just north of Hue. (UPI)	4	A1
War comes to the urban centers: U.S. tanks rumbling through Saigon early this month. (UPI)	2+	A8
A Vietnamese boy, his legs injured by an artillery blast, is carried to a helicopter by troops of the U.S. 1st Cavalry Division (Airmobile). The boy was wounded in heavy fighting for a village just north of the City of Hue. (UPI)	4	A10

Caption	Column Width	Page

February 27

President Nguyen Van Thieu of South Vietnam, touring war-scarred Hue, presents towel to an elderly refugee. (UPI)

4 — A1

Two pictures, no captions: (1) ruin of gateway--from 70 percent destroyed--with wounded soldier walking, with head: "War Passes Through Hue's Gates" (UPI); (2) picture taken in 1961 showing patrols filing through another gate, showing difference (National Geographic Society).

2 — A15

4

February 28

A U.S. Marine on patrol in Hue wears an expression oddly similar to that of a Vietnamese warrior's statue. (AP)

2 — A1

Three pictures, no captions: (1) GIs squeezed in dugout at Hue (UPI); (2) World War I photo of trenches dug by French near Verdun (Yale University Press); (3) trenches dug by Union troops (Wide World Photo); all with headline: "A New Kind of War, an Old Tactic."

1+ — A6
3+
-2

Marine gunner at Khe Sanh throws aside shell casing after returning enemy fire. (AP)

3 — A6

February 29

As houseboats glide down Perfume River toward Hue, now in allied hands, clouds rise from napalm strike on village of Tudinh west of city.   South Vietnamese commander ordered strike because of suspected enemy concentration. (AP)

-4 — A21

North Vietnam's Defense Minister, Gen. Vo Nguyen Giap, checks one of Hanoi's many antiaircraft units. (AP)

2 — A23

March 1

Shopkeepers and their families move through rubble [houses ruined] in one of Hue's main streets, damaged in recent fighting. (AP)

4 — A1

Enemy mortar round explodes as it hits Khe Sanh runway, just missing U.S. plane that had parachuted supplies. (AP)

4 — A14

March 2

Khe Sanh supplies are dropped by parachute because enemy shelling has made use of the airstrip hazardous. (AP)

2 — A1

Last month's fighting in Cholon, the Chinese quarter of Saigon, left broad areas of ruin. A shortage of trucks hampers the cleanup. (UPI)

5 — A10

Caption	Column Width	Page
South Vietnamese soldier looks at ruined houses destroyed in month's fighting inside Hue Citadel. (AP)	4	A11
March 3		
Vietnamese Ranger stands guard as his buddy looks for enemy weapons at Khe Sanh. (UPI)	3	A1
Skyraider, silhouetted at left, bombs enemy position outside base at Khe Sanh. (UPI)	3	A18
American Marine catches a nap in the shelter of a sandbag wall near the Khe Sanh airstrip. He is waiting to catch a plane for rest and recuperation leave. (AP)	2	A20
March 4		
Lt. Marshall R. Wells searches for enemy tunnels [with divining rods] dug under the Marine combat base at Khe Sanh, South Vietnam. (AP)	4	A1
March 5		
A Vietnamese family returns to badly damaged home in Hue, recently recaptured. (AP)	3	A9
March 6		
Air-drops like this one at Khe Sanh keep the isolated Marine combat base functioning. Supplies are parachuted when enemy shellings and weather keep cargo planes away. (UPI)	6	A1
March 8		
Khe Sanh Marines duck as a landing helicopter runs the gauntlet of enemy fire. (UPI)	-3	A16
A U.S. Crusader jet makes a rocket attack against North Vietnamese position near the American base at Khe Sanh. (AP)	4	A18
March 9		
Vietcong prisoner [bandaged around mouth, head shot] glares at South Koreans who captured him near coastal Qui Nhon. (AP)	3	A1

Caption	Column Width	Page
Two Scenes in North: Two captured American pilots, Air Force 1st Lt. Robert A. Abbott and Navy Lt. Cmdr. Hugh A. Stafford, meet with a North Vietnamese official in Hanoi, according to the caption supplied by the Japanese news agency Nippon Dempa News. Letters on table are said to be from their families. Second picture shows damage in the port city of Haiphong presumably caused by American bombing. Workers at bottom of picture remove rubble near a stone slab which carries an inscription expressing hatred of the U.S. raids, according to the Japanese news agency. (AP)	5 (2+) (2+)	A12
Medical corpsmen at Khe Sanh give a transfusion to a wounded U.S. Marine. (AP)	3	A12
Gen. William B. Rosson . . . moves north [head shot]. (UPI)	1	A12

March 10

Caption	Column Width	Page
U.S. Marine guides blindfolded Vietcong suspect to inter-rogation in Hue. Suspects hold each other's clothing. (AP)	4	A1
U.S. Marine stands watch with a machine gun at a bunker on Khe Sanh perimeter. (UPI)	3	A18
Young Victims of War: Two Vietnamese children (above) play at refugee camp on the grounds of Hue University, where they were taken after the communist offensive last month. The picture was one of the last taken by UPI photographer Hiromichi Mine, who was killed in a battle last Wednesday. At left, a little girl, whose father and two sisters were killed, eats grapefruit at another camp in Saigon. (Bill Snead--UPI)	-2 -2	A25

March 11

Caption	Column Width	Page
White phosphorous bomb streamers create fire and smoke sceeen to help make the landing of supply planes at the besieged U.S. Marine outpost at Khe Sanh. Enemy ground fire has destroyed a number of airplanes at the base. (AP)	4	A10

March 12

Caption	Column Width	Page
Why Personnel Carriers Are Armored: A Vietcong grenade explodes against a machine-gun shield as U.S. Americal Division makes sweep near Tam Ky, about 25 miles south of Da Nang. No one was seriously wounded. (AP)	4	A9
Marine test-fires carbine he had cut down at Khe Sanh for close-quarter fighting. (AP)	3	A14

Caption	Column Width	Page
March 13		
A Navy hospital corpsman uses his stethoscope to try to detect enemy tunneling inside Khe Sanh's barbed wire. (AP)	4	A18
March 15		
Damaged C-123 transport standing on Khe Sanh's runway is finished off by enemy mortar and rocket barrage. (AP)	4	A8
Salvage Detail: Supplies that missed the drop zone at Khe Sanh are retrieved by Marines, who bring all that can be saved back to main part of the base. (UPI)	2	A9
Threatened: Khe Sanh is a "valley of death" for the 6,000 U.S. Marines and South Vietnamese troops stationed there, an official North Vietnamese news agency dispatch said yesterday. In unusual threat, Hanoi said Khe Sanh would be "a real burial ground for the U.S. puppets." Photo emphasizes base's airstrip, its link with the world. (UPI)	4	A12
March 16		
A couple of U.S. Marines race back from the patrol outside the perimeter of Khe Sanh. Other Marines in sandbagged positions inside the perimeter cover their comrades. (AP)	6	A10
War Victim: Vietnamese boy arrives at Copenhagen's Kastrup Airport. The Danish branch of an international welfare group brought 22 wounded Vietnamese children, aged 3 to 12, to Denmark for medical treatment. (UPI)	2	A10
March 17		
U.S. troops duck for cover as an enemy rocket hits the runway at Camp Evans, just north of the base at Phu Bai. (UPI)	4	A16
A U.S. helicopter gunner views traffic along Route 4, a key link between Saigon and the rich Mekong Delta. (AP)	4	A18
March 19		
An Air Force C-123 transport skims over a helicopter shot down inside besieged U.S. Marine base at Khe Sanh. (AP)	4	A11
March 20		
Dud bomb lies in Haiphong street, beside sign warning that other unexploded U.S. bombs are nearby and the area is off limits, according to Japanese agency, Nippon Dempa News, whose photographer made this picture. (UPI)	2	A14

Caption	Column Width	Page
Chopper Pickup: Four U.S. 1st Cavalry Division soldiers, clinging to extra-long cables, were lifted from a "hot spot" near Hue recently. It's a common Vietnam practice when helicopters can't land. (UPI)	2	A23
March 23		
With bayonet in one hand and hank of hair in the other, South Vietnamese noncom questions suspected Vietcong. (AP)	2	A14
March 24		
An Air Force spotter plane checks damage in Vietnam. (DOD)	2	A18
March 25		
Ready for Sea: Three of the nine 16-inch guns on the reactivated battleship USS *New Jersey* point skyward during practice before the ship goes out for sea trials. She'll be used to shell coast in Vietnam War. (AP)	2	A10
A village elder maps the location of Vietcong group for an allied force. (AP)	-3	A11
March 26		
American soldiers await the results of an air strike before moving into a communist-held village south of Da Nang. (AP)	4	A14
March 27		
Big Guns: The reactivated USS *New Jersey* went out to sea from the Philadelphia Navy Yard yesterday boasting enormous guns for eventual service off Vietnam. It has three turrets of three 16-inch guns each and 10 turrets of two 5-inch guns each. (Steve Szabo--Washington *Post*)	3	A1
Reactivated USS *New Jersey*, world's only battleship in service, glides down the Delaware River. Her skipper is Capt. J. Edward Snyder, Jr. (Steve Szabo--Washington *Post*)	6	A10
March 28		
Troops of the U.S. 1st Cavalry Division guide in heli-copters on a search-and-destroy mission in I Corps. (AP)	4	A25
March 29		
Marines en route to Hue prepare to return any sniper fire [guns level on side of boat]. The boat carries ammunition to old Vietnamese capital. (DOD)	4	A14

Caption	Column Width	Page
Tran Van Do . . . peace but how? [head shot]. (AP)	1	A16
A version of U.S. F-111A fighter-bomber reported overdue on Asia mission. (UPI)	3	A17
March 30		
Marines flatten against sandbags as communist shells hit Khe Sanh during daily barrage at the base. (AP)	4	A14

Caption	Page
February 9	
A guerrilla is taken alive during the embassy battle.	cover
An American MP, followed by an embassy employee, races for cover during the battle at the embassy.	22
Helicopter carrying troops of the 101st Airborne Division eases down for landing on embassy roof.	23
Wounded Vietnamese civilian shot in his car when he failed to stop at a U.S. roadblock is carried to an ambulance by MP.	22
Two comrades aid a GI wounded near the embassy during the six-hour battle.	22
Beside bodies of slain GIs, soldiers crouch at the consulate entrance and try to spot snipers in compound.	23
Flattened behind a tree, two U.S. soldiers lay down covering fire across the street from the embassy.	23
In Saigon, South Vietnamese soldiers drag away a guerrilla killed during assault on government billet.	24
In Da Nang, a boy holding his ears against the sound of battle runs past the body of a slain civilian.	25
A father carries his frightened child on a Da Nang street.	25
Khe Sanh: 6,000 Marines Dug In for Battle. Morning sun burns off the drifting fog at Khe Sanh and Marines rise from their bunkers (above) to peer into the enemy-infested hills just beyond. To survive the daily bombardment of mortar, rocket, and heavy howitzer fire, the 6,000-man garrison has carved out and equipped bunkers (far left) large enough to live in. At near left rescuers struggle to free the pilot from a spotter plane that crashed after being hit by enemy fire. They got him out alive. Below, a Navy chaplain, Lt. Ray Stubbe of Milwaukee (standing), conducts Sunday service for Marines, who kneel helmetless but wearing flak-jackets, at their sandbagged position on the Khe Sanh perimeter. (Dick Swanson--*Life*)	26-27
A Sprawling Arsenal That Was Delivered by Air (Khe Sanh overview). (Dick Swanson--*Life*)	28-29
February 16	
North Vietnamese soldiers with Chinese AK-47 automatic rifles guard captured strongpoint in Hue.	cover

NOTE: For weeks for which there are no entries, no pertinent contemporary pictures appeared in the magazine. (*Life* published a number of historical Vietnam pictures in its March 22, 1968, issue dealing with Ho Chi Minh and prior peace feelers.)

Caption	Page
A tense interlude with the enemy in Hue. In the garden of a captured villa in Hue, a North Vietnamese officer (left foreground) and his men allow Cathy Leroy to photograph them as they await a counterattack by U.S. Marines. (Catherine Leroy)	22-23
Caught in an enemy-held part of Hue, Cathy took shelter in a church crowded with hostile refugees (left). Nearby a mother lay with her baby (above). (Catherine Leroy)	24
The frowning North Vietnamese above balked at being photographed. But Cathy got this picture of him--with his captured U.S. military radio. (Catherine Leroy)	25
Behind the garden wall, two North Vietnamese pose with their Soviet-made weapons: a carbine (left) and grenade launcher (above). Below, the North Vietnamese pretend to fire into a captured U.S. M-41 tank, while Cathy reaches for a camera. Picture was taken by her colleague, Francois Mazure. (Catherine Leroy; Francois Mazure)	25 24-25
House-to-House Struggle to Regain the Imperial City: The former imperial capital of Vietnam, Hue, is strategically located astride Highway No. 1 just 50 miles south of the DMZ. When the communist offensive began, 2,000 Vietcong and North Vietnamese regulars seized the entire city except for a few isolated military posts. From these bastions U.S. Marines and South Vietnamese infantry slowly fought back through the city. For days their progress could be measured only in city blocks retaken. At left, U.S. tanks inch down a tree-lined street, providing cover for Marines, two of whom lie dead on the sidewalk. Below, Marines lob mortar shells over a house into an enemy concentration. U.S. warships shelled the city and South Vietnamese planes bombed the walled enclave, once the home of emperors, where 700 North Vietnamese had holed up. After a week of heavy fighting, over half the enemy invaders were dead and most of the city was retaken--but at a great cost in civilian and military lives. At lower left a Viet- namese woman huddles in terror and grief next to the blanketed body of her child, killed along the road to Hue. (Catherine Leroy)	26-27 27 26-27
For Civilians Between the Guns, No Place to Hide: Driven from their homes in Hue, frightened refugees approach U.S. Marines under a truce flag. The communist attacks on more than 30 of South Vietnam's major cities took a huge civilian toll, leaving several thousand dead and 300,000 homeless. U.S. officials warned that the enemy, despite having suffered losses estimated at 25,000, the heaviest of the war, still was capable of a new wave of strikes against the cities.	28-29

February 23

In the mist hanging low over this remote bombarded valley, Marines await the next move of the enemy surrounding them. (David Douglas Duncan)	20-21

Caption	Page

[Five pictures:] This cheerless slab of metal is Khe Sanh's heart, and when movement across it is stopped by artillery fire or fog, Khe Sanh begins to die. North Vietnamese gunners, controlled by mountaintop observers, rarely miss hitting something or someone with every salvo--on the airstrip itself or the narrow perimeter where Marines live like prairie dogs in and out of a vast colony of bunkers. On a tough night five or six rockets crash in every minute. (David Douglas Duncan) — 22-23 (page and a half)

Enemy Fire Zeroing In--Planes Hit--Runway Blocked--Blaze Fought: Enemy sharpshooters rocket every plane attempting to land. Few medevac choppers make [it] without being perforated by machine-gun bullets and often return with wounded--even dead--crewmen. Workhorse C-130s come in treetop high, unload without coming to a full stop, then thunder off fast as possible into the relative safety of the misty sky. Even so they get hit. The one at right survived rocketing during unloading (expecting an explosion, the wounded are hurried away) to be repaired and flown off days later. But another C-130, machine-gunned during its final seconds in the air, skidded the length of the runway in a fireball of aviation fuel and blew up (below), killing most of the crew and the five Marine passengers. Struggling to save their lives--and to keep the runway clear--the rescue team fought the holocaust with foam. They pull bodies (right center) from the still-hot wreckage which blocked the airstrip nearly all day. Finally the rescue team chief, who had never found time to put on his gas mask, stood exhausted by the hulk (bottom right) and helpless tears marked his face. (David Douglas Duncan)

- 24-25
- 24-25
- 24-25
- 25
- 25

Beyond the Wire and Far Off in the Ridges, a Target: The snipers of Khe Sanh work in three-man teams. When they drop an enemy, each man of the team is credited with a kill. Here Lance Cpl. Albert Miranda, 19, of El Paso, Texas, squeezes off a shot at a North Vietnamese soldier so far away as to be invisible without the help of glasses or exceptionally keen sight. His fellow sniper, Lance Cpl. David Burdwell, 20, of Wichita Falls, Texas (center), calls the shot together with their platoon lieutenant, Alec Bodenwiser, of Portland, Oregon, the third member of the team. For hours they sit motionless, stalking with their telescopic sights a quarry who, at the fatal moment, may feel alone--and safe. (David Douglas Duncan) — 26-27

Tender Precision, Bombs Slammed In Close to the Trenches: The only words that matter after a while are "Incoming!" and "Outgoing!" One day an incoming rocket ignited the aviation fuel hoses, turning them into sputtering fuses (above) leading straight to the main gasoline dump. A single wild spark might have sent the whole tank farm sky-high, but a handful of men doused the flames. Farther around the perimeter other Marines (above right) passed scorched but unexploded artillery shells--a deadly debris from direct hits on the main ammo dump--with tender precision into a hole for burial. By

- 28
- 29

Caption	Page

Caption	Column Width	Page
February 9		
Hanoi's General Giap: "Days of Death in Vietnam"		cover
U.S. Reinforcements Beside Dead GIs at Saigon Embassy: A very dear price for the temporary encouragement. (AP)	2	15
Vietcong Dead in Da Nang: Sending the Monkey on its malign way [rows of bodies, one charred]. (Don Sider)	1	22
U.S. Ambassador Ellsworth Bunker inspects bodies of Vietcong on embassy grounds [with several others and MPs with flaks, two VC sprawled, bloody]. (color) (Dick Swanson--*Life*)	3	22a
In aftermath of other Cong raids in Saigon, U.S. dead are loaded onto armored vehicle [thrown one on top of another, slightly black-charred faces and hands]. (color)(John Stewart)	3	22a
In recapture of the embassy, U.S. military police take cover near slain guerrilla. (color) (Dick Swanson--*Life*)	3+	22b
With antitank rocket, attackers blasted gaping hole in embassy's concrete wall [soldiers with guns and civilians stand looking at dead VC, who aren't too visible in pictures]. (color) (Dick Swanson--*Life*)	3	22b
With brusque urgency of men under fire, GIs drag body of fallen comrade out of range of Vietcong attack in Saigon's airport area. (color) (John Stewart)	3	22c
[Two pictures:] Wounded, and armed only with a pistol, GI glares at the enemy; second later (below), he collapses as buddy comes to his aid [Negro with MP badge, no helmet, with flak and bloody bandage around eyes; second picture, white soldier with helmet at his side]. (color) (John Stewart)	2 2+	22d
The Battle of Bunker's Bunker [aerial with explanation of each building]. (AP)	2	23
In Hue a medical corpsman summons help for wounded U.S. Marines [soldiers lying all over wall in background]. (UPI)	2+	24
A picture that will go into the history books shows the execution of a Vietcong officer (right), who was captured by ARVN Marines in Saigon. He was taken to Brig. Gen. Nguyen Ngoc Loan, chief of South Vietnam's police, who shot him through the head, saying later: "They killed many Americans and many of our people." (AP)	1-1/2	24-25
In Da Nang, South Vietnamese civilians carrying children flee the battle [and dead man or boy in street]. (UPI)	2+	25

Caption	Column Width	Page
South Vietnamese youngsters and their belongings are packed into a motorcycle cab, getting away from the fighting in Saigon. (AP)	2+	32-33
Bleeding heavily, a Vietcong suspect is seized by South Vietnamese soldiers in embattled Da Nang [blood coming from mouth, looks young]. (Don Sider)	1-1/2	32
A U.S. civilian, slumped in his Volkswagen, was shot dead by a jittery ARVN soldier in Saigon when he refused orders to stop [blood all over shirt]. (Wally Terry)	1-3/4	32
Carrying his dead child, an officer finds that his family has been killed in a Saigon army compound. (AP)	1+	33
Right, the bodies of the camp commander, wife, and six children, all machine-gunned by the raiders.	1-1/2	33
A Da Nang mother cradling her child rushes past an immobilized truck to escape the shooting. (Don Sider)	1-3/4	33
A U.S. soldier pulls a wounded Saigon civilian to safety after the attack on the U.S. Embassy. (UPI)	1-1/3	33

February 16

John Kenneth Galbraith: The All-purpose Critic		cover
Westmoreland at Green Beret Camp in Vietnam: History's judgment might depend on one battle [Khe Sanh]. (Co Rentmeester--*Life*)	1+	19
General Abrams: Familiar hot spot [setting up forward command post at Phu Bai]. (Paul Conklin)	1	20
Forlorn amid the rubble of their former homes, destroyed in a savage battle between ARVN troops and communists, these Saigonese suddenly find themselves refugees in their own city. (John Cantwell)	2+	32-33
Children form a futile bucket brigade to save their father's machine shop in the Cholon section of Saigon, seized by the Reds and bombed by the allies [rubble, smoke]. (UPI)	1-3/4	33
Devastated by fire and shell, the buildings of Qui Nhon, a coastal city of 111,000, mutely recall the recent Vietcong assault. (Wally Terry)	3	33
Ruins of Ben Tre's Market Place: Lesson for city dwellers in what the peasants have long recognized. (Le Minh)	2	34
Khe Sanh: Ready to Fight [story head]. Another "incoming" has just hit a tent, seriously wounding three Marines. Corpsmen struggle to get out the wounded. (Don Sider)	2+	38-39

Caption	Column Width	Page
Howard K. and Jack Smith in Vietnam: Facts to face in the dispiriting sixties [disillusioned with journalism, thinks one-sided VN stories anti-U.S., refers to Loan shooting]. (ABC)	1	42

March 8

Flares and Artillery Flashes on Saigon's Outskirts: Fear and foreboding beneath the veneer. (John Gordon--Empire)	2	28
The Road Ahead: How Vietnamese Leaders See It [headline]. Nguyen Cao Ky, H. T. Ky et al.	1/2	29
GIs at Grave of Thompsons and Woltong: Leon Graswold (missionary); Robert Ziemer (minister); Ruth Woltong (nurse); Carolyn Graswold (daughter).	4 head shots 1/2	29

March 15

Carrying Out Wounded on Tank During Battle of Hue: Profound skepticism whether any more would do any good [faces bandaged, one getting transfusion]. (John Olson--*Stars and Stripes*)	2+	13
Holding High the Bayonets in North Vietnam: Also, a new and sophisticated array of weapons. (Sovfoto)	1+	14
Marines Leaving Camp Pendleton for Vietnam: Stretched to their Leathernecked limit [lined up getting into plane]. (Larry Le--P.I.)	2+	15
Captured Russian-Made 122-MM. Rocket Launcher in Saigon: Sophistication along with an unnerving whoosh-crack. (John Cantwell)	2+	21
After "Tet": Measuring and Repairing the Damage [story head]. Armed allied convoys on highway in Bien Hoa. (Glenn Troelstrup)	2	22
Struggling back toward normal in Hue [on bikes, dirt road, rubble]. (Le Minh)	2+	23
Vo Huynh Under Fire Outside Saigon: Nothing soft anywhere any more [Huynh holding camera, story on cameraman's hard job in VN, and TV crews in general]. (Le Cung)	1	48

March 22

Bomb damage in Haiphong but no anniversary fireworks [city street; 14th anniversary of Dienbienphu]. (UPI)	1+	25
North Vietnamese Prisoners on Display in Laos: The flanks may need protection.	2+	26

Caption	Column Width	Page
March 29 Abrams and Westmoreland in Saigon: Speculation about other changes as well. (AP)	1+	21

PICTURE INDEX: VIETNAM-RELATED PICTURES, *NEWSWEEK,* FEBRUARY 5 - MARCH 25, 1968

Caption	Column Width	Page
February 5		
The Battle of Khe Sanh: Wounded Marine during lull in the bombardment. (AP)	2	39
February 12		
GIs Routing Vietcong from Saigon Embassy: MPs with guns on grass. (From NBC's "Huntley-Brinkley Report")		cover
[Head:] Hanoi Attacks and Scores a Major Psychological Blow; [in smaller caps:] Slain Vietcong at U.S. Embassy. (John Donnelly--*Newsweek*)	1 (page deep)	23
[Head:] The VC's Week of Terror. [Caption:] The Embassy Battle: U.S. military police led by security officer Leo Crampsey pour bullets into the first floor of Mission co-ordinator George Jacobson's house, where a Vietcong is holed up. A tear-gas grenade is thrown up to Jacobson, trapped in his second-story bedroom. Soon afterward he used a pistol, also tossed up to him, to kill the last enemy intruder--whose comrades' bodies (next page) already littered embassy area. (color) (From NBC's "Huntley-Brinkley Report")	3 (-2) (1-1/2)	25
(VC lying near tree--bloody--with MP near pillars.) (color) (Ray Cranbourne--Empire-Black Star)	whole page	26
(Aerial view of American Embassy and chronological explanation.) (*Newsweek*)	2	27
(Ground view of American Embassy.) (*Newsweek*)	1	27
Panic: Clutching her ID papers, this girl seeks her parents in Saigon [small girl crying]. (AP)	2	28
Instant Justice: General Loan executes a Vietcong terrorist in the street. (AP)	2+	29
Wounded Khe Sanh Marine: Above ground, two is a crowd [whole face bandaged]. (UPI)	2	31
Everett G. Martin [head shot]. [In box:] In January, after months of indirect harassment, the South Vietnamese government effectively expelled *Newsweek*'s Saigon bureau chief, Everett Martin. Though no formal reason was given for the expulsion, the evident cause for it was official anger at *Newsweek* articles dealing with corruption and ineptitude in the South Vietnamese government and army. Below, Martin, who is now in N.Y. pending reassignment to Hong Kong, reflects on the current Vietcong offensive in the light of his two years in Vietnam.	1/2	32

Caption	Column Width	Page
Thang: No hope [Maj. Gen. Nguyen Duc Thang, deputy chief of staff of RVNAF].	1	33
Vietcong suspect is led to police chief Loan, who fires a bullet into his brain. (AP)	1/2	66
Tuckner: A Battle on Tape [bending over with mike in hand]. (NBC's Tuckner went through the embassy gate with the MPs; too dark to film, he "talked" story onto tape.) (NBC)	1	66
Adams: His camera was there [photograph of Loan, picture of him in fatigues].	1	67

February 19

Caption	Column Width	Page
Westmoreland. (James Pickerell--Black Star)		cover
Saigon Battlefield: South Vietnamese Rangers firing at Vietcong. (AP)	2+	33
The Toll: A GI carries a wounded Vietnamese; a boy walks in rubble. (AP, UPI)	1 1+	33 33
Westmoreland: Too many tasks. (Francois Sully--*Newsweek*)	1	34
Abrams: Next in line? (AP)	1	34
House by House: Stubborn Vietcong attackers still held large parts of Hue, and U.S. Marines had to dig them out in some of the hardest fighting of the war. American snipers crouch on a rooftop (above) as one of their number dashes to safety. Struck in the head by mortar fragments (below), a Marine is treated where he fell. Then, because no other exit is safe, his buddies lower him in a sling to the waiting arms of the medics below. (color) (Paul Stephanus--Empire-Black Star).	3 (page)	25
Night Light: Flares dropped by U.S. planes cast a weird glow over Da Nang's waterfront. (color) (Catherine Leroy--Black Star)	3 (1 page +)	36
Two Made It: But a third Marine (far right) is cut down crossing a Hue street. (Kyoichi Sawada--UPI)	3-3/4	36
Toll: Vietcong killed while attacking Da Nang are displayed for a formal body count [lined up on ground]. (Paul Stephanus--Empire-Black Star)	2-1/4	37
Bewilderment: New refugees huddle in Hue, arms raised in surrender to U.S. Marines. (Kyoichi Sawada--UPI)	2-1/2	37
Casualty: Wounded South Vietnamese soldier waits for evacuation [face shot, bandaged forehead and chin]. (Dana Stone--UPI)	1+	37

Caption	Column Width	Page
A Day at Khe Sanh: Marine mortarmen (left) watch as a C-130 rolls down the runway (1) under the guns of the North Vietnamese infesting the misty hills beyond. With a shout of "Incoming!" other (2) Marines scramble to cover at the start of a bombardment. The legend scrawled on the helmet of Lance Cpl. James G. Jones [head shot] of Pensacola attests to Leatherneck humor in the face of a dangerous mission [it reads, "I'm not a tourist, I live here"]. (color) (Paul Stephanus--Empire-Black Star)	2+ -3 1	38
Giap: Familiar gambit? [head shot] (Charles Bonnay-- Black Star)	1	39
Encounter in Hue: A Vietcong suspect is questioned at knife-point. (UPI)	2	40
[Head:] How the U.S. Lost Lang Vei. [Caption:] Survivor: Lang Vei defender reaches Khe Sanh [man with gun and bandaged head]. (AP)	1+	42

February 26

Vietnamese students. (Dan McCoy--Black Star)		cover
[Head:] The Second Wave? Westmoreland and Ambassador Bunker honor soldiers slain in Tet offensive. (UPI)	2	33
General Do: No body [head shot; top communist commander killed in Cholon]. (AP)	1	33
Assault on Hue Citadel: U.S. Marines advance through the rubble. (UPI)	2	34

March 4

Wheeler in Vietnam: Taking stock. (AP)	1	19
[Head:] Waiting for the Second Wave. [Caption:] Yard by Yard: U.S. Marines blast away at the VC, rush forward to plant the flag--and occasionally rest in the rubble--they inch through the Citadel of Hue [three pictures: from behind half-destroyed wall; flags; resting in ruins]. (UPI, AP, AP)	1 2+ 1+	28 28 29
[Head:] In Weapons: Getting Better. [Caption:] Arsenal: VC soldier with AK-47. (Catherine Leroy--Black Star)	1	30
Communist B-40 "tank-buster." (AP)	1	30
140-mm. launcher and rocket. (AP)	1	30

March 11

Inside Khe Sanh: A wounded Marine is evacuated from the besieged outpost. (AP)	2	58
[Head:] Waiting: Khe Sanh and Saigon. [Caption:] Khe Sanh Marines under enemy fire. (AP)	1	58

Caption	Column Width	Page
Incoming and Outgoing: Marine shields a wounded comrade from enemy mortar barrage. The vast sea of shell casings (below) testifies to the volume of artillery fire hurled back at enemy. (Robert Ellison--Empire-Black Star)	3 3	35 35
Lifeline: Parachutes drop critically needed food and weapons to sandbag-protected base. (color) Mercy Mission: A South Vietnamese soldier carried wounded buddy back from patrol. (color) Evacuation: Stretcher-bearers rush a wounded Marine toward a waiting helicopter. (color) (Robert Ellison--Empire-Black Star)	-2 1+ -3	36 36 36
Ky, Thieu, and Bunker: Stuck with a sacred cow. (Manh Chuan--*Newsweek*)	-2	37
Black Market: Business as usual. (AP)	1	38
ARVN Troops: How aggressive? (UPI)	1	38

March 25

"Delta Med" in Action: Khe Sanh victims receive critical first aid [inside hospital]. (Robert Stokes)	2	41

CREDITS AND ACKNOWLEDGMENTS

We are grateful to the following for their kind permission to re-
print copyrighted material, not only that specified below, but--
in the case of the news media--the numerous shorter quotations of
50 words or more which appear throughout the book. We list here
only those texts, or excerpts from texts, amounting to at least
250 words:

© American Broadcasting Companies, Inc. 1977. Reprinted by per-
mission: 248-49, 386: "ABC Evening News," Feb. 6, 1968; 397-98:
"ABC Evening News," Feb. 5, 1968; 469-70: "ABC Evening News,"
Feb. 29, 1968.

Reprinted by permission of Associated Press: (Vol. I:) 33-34:
"Continuing Story: Report of Foreign News Committee" (APME *Red
Book*); 127-28: Al35WX, Washington, RZ1056PES, President Johnson,
Jan. 30, 1968; 194-95: AP, AO15, Vietnam News Analysis, Feb. 12,
1968, Peter Arnett; 239-40: AP, 40, Civilians, Feb. 4, 1968,
Barry Kramer; 251-52: AP, AOO3, Feb. 5, 1968, Barry Kramer;
254-55: AP, Al10-111, Destroyed, Feb. 7, 1968, Peter Arnett;
268-69: AP, AO1O, Hue Descriptive, Feb. 10, 1968, John Lengel;
271-72: AP, AO15, Feb. 26, 1968, John Lengel; 297-99: AP, AO44,
Feb. 2, 1968, John Lengel; 363-65: "Reds Bombed at Khe Sanh, Foe
Still Shells Marine Base Despite Record Air Assault" (in Washington *Evening Star*); 367-68: AP, AOO4, Khe Sanh, Feb. 2, 1968,
George McArthur; 460-61: "Pictures at an Execution" (*AP Log*);
509-10: AP, OO5, Hue Officials, Feb. 27, 1968, George McArthur;
511-13: AP, A602 and A604, Mar. 26, 1968, Barry Kramer; 632-34:
AP, AOO3WX, North Vietnam Nuclear, Feb. 10, 1968, Jack Bell.
(Vol. II:) 142-45: "Life in the V Ring," John T. Wheeler; 155-66:
Gen. William C. Westmoreland, interview by Wes Gallagher.

© G. A. Bailey and L. W. Lichty 1971; copyright 1972, *Journalism
Quarterly*, University of Minnesota 55455: (Vol. II:) 266-81:
"Rough Justice on a Saigon Street," G. A. Bailey and L. W. Lichty,
Journalism Quarterly, 49, no. 2 (Summer 1972), 221-29, 238.

Reprinted by permission of *Broadcasting*: (Vol. I:) 38-39: "The
21-Inch View of Vietnam: Big Enough Picture?" Leonard Zeidenberg
(*Television* magazine).

© 1977 CBS Inc.: (Vol. I:) 175, 466: "CBS Evening News," Feb.
12, 1968; 303-05: "CBS Evening News," Feb. 7, 1968; 306-07, 386-
87: "CBS Evening News," Feb. 15, 1968; 388-89: "CBS Evening News,"
Feb. 29, 1968; 393-95: "CBS Evening News," Mar. 29, 1968; 402-03:
"CBS Evening News," Mar. 12, 1968; 563-64: "Dimension" (radio),
Feb. 28, 1968. (Vol. II:) 180-89: "Who, What, When, Where, Why:
Report from Vietnam by Walter Cronkite."

right Time Inc.:   (Vol. I:) 164-65, 246, 275-76, 427-28, 555:   "The
War: The General's Gamble"; 183-84:   "South Vietnam: Saigon Under
Siege," William Rademaekers; 321-22:   "Battle of Hue," David Green-
way; 324-25:   "Fight for a Citadel"; 429-30, 526, 659-60:   "The
War: The General's Biggest Battle"; 430-31:   "Fall of Lang Vei";
435-37:   "Waiting for the Thrust"; 527, 664:   "The War: Critical
Season"; 528-29:   "A Sense of Urgency"; 660-62:   "The Great Mogul";
662-63:   "The War: Thin Green Line."   (Vol. II:) 149-51:   "Khe
Sanh: Ready to Fight," Don Sider; 222-25:   "After Tet: Measuring
and Repairing the Damage."

Copyright, 1968, Los Angeles *Times*.   Reprinted by permission:
(Vol. II:) 146-48: "Landing at Khe Sanh an Agonizing Ordeal,"
William Tuohy.

©1968 by The New York Times Company.   Reprinted by permission:
(Vol. I:) 69-70:   "Footnotes on the Vietnam Dispatches," Bernard
Weinraub (*The New York Times Magazine*); 110-13:   "Foe Invades U.S.
Saigon Embassy," Thomas Buckley; 114-17:   "U.S. Aide in Embassy
Villa Kills Guerrilla with Pistol," Charles Mohr; 128-29:   "John-
son Receives Flow of Reports"; 209-10:   "North Vietnam's Strategy
of Terror," James Reston; 211-12:   "Topics: Hanoi Isn't Counting
on American Dissent," John W. Lewis and David Mozingo; 213-15:
"Guerrilla Motivation Stressed: 'The VC Are Not Afraid to Die,'"
Charles Mohr; 309-10:   "Attacks on Hue Fail to Rout Foe," Gene
Roberts; 310-12:   "Hue to Da Nang: A Perilous Boat Ride," Gene
Roberts; 333-34:   "GIs in Pincer Move, Kill 128 in Daylong
Battle"; 416-17:   "Jet Bombers Seen at Base in North During U.S.
Raids," Thomas Buckley; 552-53:   "A Pacification Drive Setback in
Key Area," Bernard Weinraub; 583-84:   "U.S. Manpower Needs for
War, Foe's Drives Focus Attention on Troop Ceiling at 525,000,"
Hanson Baldwin; 589-90:   "The Manpower Cupboard Is Nearly Bare,"
William Beecher; 600-08:   "Westmoreland Requests 206,000 More
Men," Neil Sheehan and Hedrick Smith; 629-30:   "War Doubts in
Senate; Misgivings over Administration Policy Said to Spread As
Offensive Continues," John Finney.   (Vol. II:) 120-22:   "Sur-
vivors Hunt Dead of Ben Tre, Turned to Rubble in Allied Raids,"
Bernard Weinraub; 177-79:   "U.S. Admits Blow to Pacification,"
Bernard Weinraub; 190-92:   "Pacification Teams Returning to Ham-
lets Abandoned After Vietcong Drive," Charles Mohr; 237-40:   "U.S.
Officers Say Air Power Makes Khe Sanh a Disaster for Foe," Gene
Roberts.

Printed with the permission of United Press International: (Vol.
I:) 257-58:   533B, Ben Tre, Feb. 7, 1968, Dan Southerland; 261:
009A, Mar. 3, 1968, Arnold Dibble; 300-01:   224A, Citadel NL, Feb.
17, 1968, Alvin Webb, Jr.; 357-58:   017A, Cushman NX, Mar. 11,
1968, Robert C. Miller.

© 1968 by *Variety*:   (Vol. I:) 654-56:   "NBC-TV Busts Out with Down-
beat on Vietnam via Frank McGee & Co.," Bill Greeley.

PICTURE CREDITS

© 1968 by The Washington *Post*, reprinted by permission--1, 4.
© 1968 by The New York *Times* Company.   Reprinted by permission--2,
3.   Reprinted by permission from TIME, The Weekly News Magazine;
copyright Time Inc., 1968--5.   Robert Ellison, Black Star--6.
Stan Stearns, United Press International--7.   Kamoto; Courtesy of
the Lyndon B. Johnson Library--8.   Larry Lichty--9, 10, 107, 108,
109, 110, 111.   Wide World--11, 12, 13, 14, 15, 18, 19, 20, 23,
27, 28, 29, 37, 48, 49, 50, 52, 53, 55, 56, 57, 68.   U.S. Air
Force--16, 26, 42.   Co Rentmeester, Time-Life Picture Agency,
© Time Inc.--17.   Department of Defense (Marine Corps)--22, 40, 41,
44, 45, 46, 47, 70, 106.   Department of Defense (U.S. Army)--24,
25, 30, 32, 33, 36, 38, 43.   Larry Burrows, Time-Life Picture
Agency, © Time Inc.--31.   Dick Swanson, Time-Life Picture Agency,
© Time Inc.--34, 35.   Kyoichi Sawada, United Press International--
39.   Barbara Gluck Treaster--51, 54, 58, 60, 72, 73, 74, 75, 76,
77, 101.   Eugene V. Risher--59.   Nik Wheeler, United Press Inter-
national--61.   *Editor and Publisher*--62, 80.   Becky Lescaze--64,
83.   Courtesy of the Washington *Post*--65, 66, 67, 69.   James
Pickerell, Time-Life Picture Agency, © Time Inc.--78.   Courtesy
of the New York *Times*--79, 81, 85, 87, 90.   Jill Krementz--82.
Courtesy of the Philadelphia *Inquirer*--84.   Joseph Treaster--86.
Ben Martin, *Time* Magazine, © Time Inc.--88, 99.   Courtesy of the
Boston *Globe*--89.   Philip Perkis--91.   David Gahr, *Time* Magazine,
© Time Inc.--92, 95.   Dirck Halstead, *Time* Magazine, © Time Inc.--
93.   Harold Ellithorpe, *Time* Magazine, © Time Inc.--94.   William
Marmon, *Time* Magazine, © Time Inc.--96.   *Time* Magazine, © Time
Inc.--97.   Eddie Adams, *Time* Magazine, © Time Inc.--98.   Courtesy
of *Newsweek* Magazine--100.   NBC News--102.   ABC News--103.   CBS
News--104, 105.

About those who participated in this project:

PETER BRAESTRUP was born June 8, 1929, the son of the Danish-born physicist, Carl Bjorn Braestrup, in New York City. He grew up in Scarsdale, New York, attended Riverdale Country School, and secured his first newspaper job as a summer stringer for the New Haven (Connecticut) *Register*. At Yale (B.A. 1951), he worked on the Yale *Daily News*, went to the 1948 Presidential conventions as a *Life* messenger boy, and with three classmates ran a summer weekly, *The Connecticut Shore* (circ. 1200), in 1949. In 1951-53, he served in the Marine Corps as a 2nd Lieutenant, went to Korea, was wounded in the defense of Outpost Reno (1952), and later released to inactive duty. In 1953, *Time* hired him as a staff writer, then sent him to Chicago to cover labor, politics, and civil rights in the Midwest and South (1955-57). He joined the New York *Herald Tribune* in 1957 as an investigative reporter; he spent a month in Tunisia and Algeria with the Algerian FLN guerrillas; the *Tribune* nominated him for a Pulitzer Prize in 1958. Awarded a Nieman Fellowship at Harvard in 1959-60, he was recruited for the New York *Times* Washington bureau by James B. Reston; he covered the New Frontier as general assignment reporter. The *Times* sent him abroad, first to newly independent Algeria (1962-65), then to Paris (1965), then to Bangkok (1966-68), where he began to cover the Indo-China war. In January 1968, just before Tet, he joined the Washington *Post* as Saigon bureau chief, returning to the home office in 1969 as a staff writer. In 1972, he returned to Vietnam to help cover Hanoi's Easter offensive. In 1973, he became a Fellow at the Woodrow Wilson International Center for Scholars at the Smithsonian, on leave from the *Post*. In 1975, he joined the Center staff as editor of publications, including the new *Wilson Quarterly*. He has written numerous magazine articles, published in *Harper's*, the *Atlantic*, the *New Leader*, *Army*, and the *Marine Corps Gazette*, among others. He is married to the former Angelica Hollins; they have three children, Angelica, Elizabeth Kate, and Carl Peter.

BURNS W. ROPER, chairman of the board of the Roper Organization, Inc., has been engaged in marketing and opinion research since 1946. He has directed corporate marketing and public affairs studies; political surveys for candidates of both major parties and the Public Broadcasting System; legal-evidence studies for leading law firms and their clients; and sociological studies for various universities, foundations, and government agencies. He writes a weekly syndicated newspaper column, "The Roper Poll." He has also authored a number of articles, both for research and other journals, and has made frequent appearances on both radio and television. In addition, he has served as an expert witness in legal cases involving consumer research and public opinion. He is past president of the Market Research Council and the chairman of the board of the Roper Public Opinion Research Center at Williams College. Mr. Roper attended Yale University and served as bomber pilot in the Eighth Air Force during World War II.

LEONARD R. SUSSMAN, director of this study, has been since January 1967 executive director of Freedom House. The national nongovernmental organization engages in foreign and domestic policy-formulation, research, and publication for the purpose of strengthening free institutions: channels of communication, higher education, and government processes. Mr. Sussman edits *Freedom at Issue*, a bimonthly that frequently examines free-press questions. He has written extensively on this subject for general and journalism publications in the United States, Australia, and Europe, and contributed the chapter on "Scholars and the Press" in *The Idea of a Modern University*, edited by Sidney Hook. He has arranged conferences on press-government relations and foreign-policy issues. After receiving his Master's degree from the Graduate School of Journalism of Columbia University, he served as foreign-news editor of a daily newspaper, wire-service reporter, and press secretary to the governor of Puerto Rico. He was an organizer and is a trustee of the International Council on the Future of the University. He served in the U.S. Army for two and one-half years during World War II and received the Legion of Merit for organizing public information services.

PATRICIA A. MCCORMACK, who edited the two volumes, is assistant to the director of Freedom House. She has worked as editor and researcher on many publications, including textbooks on the Soviet Union, Eastern Europe, and Communist China; as a senior editor for the Catholic Youth Encyclopedia; and as associate editor of social studies books at Scholastic Publications. She attended Barnard College and Columbia University, where she earned the Master's degree in Latin literature.